The Colditz Myth

The
Colditz Myth

British and Commonwealth Prisoners of
War in Nazi Germany

S. P. MACKENZIE

OXFORD
UNIVERSITY PRESS

OXFORD

UNIVERSITY PRESS

Great Clarendon Street, Oxford OX2 6DP

Oxford University Press is a department of the University of Oxford.
It furthers the University's objective of excellence in research, scholarship, and
education by publishing worldwide in

Oxford New York

Auckland Bangkok Buenos Aires Cape Town Chennai
Dar es Salaam Delhi Hong Kong Istanbul Karachi Kolkata
Kuala Lumpur Madrid Melbourne Mexico City Mumbai Nairobi
São Paulo Shanghai Taipei Tokyo Toronto

Oxford is a registered trade mark of Oxford University Press
in the UK and in certain other countries

Published in the United States
by Oxford University Press Inc., New York

British Library Cataloguing in Publication Data
Data available

Library of Congress Cataloging in Publication Data
Data available

ISBN 0-19-926210-1

1 3 5 7 9 10 8 6 4 2

Typeset by Kolam Information Services Pvt. Ltd, Pondicherry, India
Printed in Great Britain on acid-free paper by
Biddles Ltd,
Kings Lynn, Norfolk

Preface and Acknowledgements

As its title and subtitle suggest, the purpose of this book is essentially twofold. The first aim is to explore the nature and development of the popular perceptions associated with Colditz. How did this most famous of prisoner-of-war camps come to assume such mythical proportions in the British public imagination? The second goal is to explore the extent to which the reality differed from the image in connection with the British prisoner-of-war-experience in general and within the walls of Colditz itself. Was life behind the wire really akin to a Greyfriars version of a public school?

The introductory chapter examines the development of what has sometimes been dubbed the Colditz industry. There follow two chapters dealing with initial elements of the POW experience, beginning with surrender on the battlefield and ending with arrival in the permanent camps inside the Third Reich. The next chapters compare and contrast the camps themselves and those who ran them. (Here and subsequently the true situation at Colditz is examined after the state of affairs elsewhere has been explored in order to ensure a comparative perspective.) A number of the most significant factors impinging on both bodily and mental health and well-being inside German camps—from food and clothing to religion and politics—form the subject matter of Chapter 5. Chapter 6 chronicles the kinds of work other-rank prisoners were obliged to undertake at the behest of the enemy, along with the recreational pursuits of both officers and men held captive. The way in which prisoners could suffer or, more rarely, benefit from spontaneous actions in addition to the policy decisions of their captors forms the subject-matter of Chapter 7. Chapter 8 looks at British attitudes toward various other national contingents, as well as how ordinary Germans and neutral visitors were perceived. The nature and extent of efforts to continue the war behind the wire, along with their opposite, outright collaboration, are the focus of the next chapter. Escaping is of course central to the mythology surrounding British prisoners of war in Nazi Germany, and, with the groundwork having been laid through discussion of less prominent but sometimes more vital aspects of POW life, discussion of this high-profile but oft-misunderstood activity is examined at length in Chapter 10. The final two chapters chronicle the period leading up to and following final liberation. The Conclusion seeks to sum up the ways in which the Colditz Myth needs to be placed in context.

A book of this kind would not have been possible without assistance from staff members at a variety of libraries and archives. I would therefore like to thank, collectively, the staff of the BBC Written Archive; the Contemporary Medical Archives Centre; the Guildhall Library; the House of Lords Record Office; the Imperial War Museum (the departments of documents, printed books, and the sound archive); the National Archives (a.k.a. the Public Record Office); the National Sound Archive; the Norfolk Record Office; the Second World War Experience Centre developed by Dr Peter Liddle; Research and Information Services at the RAF Museum; the Thomas Cooper Library (especially the inter-library loan staff) at the University of South Carolina; and the University of New Brunswick Archives and Special Collections. I would also like to thank Bart Brodowski for translation of Polish-language material.

I would like to acknowledge and thank the following persons and organizations for permission to quote extracts from collections to which they hold the copyright: The Colditz Society for the Colditz Society Video Archive; Mr Eric Laker for his wartime diary; Mrs G. V. Barnard for the diary of John Mansel; Dr M. B. Booth for the war diaries of his father, E. Booth; Miss Diana Campbell for the papers of her father, C. N. S. Campbell; Celia Rambaut for the papers of Paddy Denton; David Evans for the memoirs of his father, R. P. Evans; Miss Peggy King for the POW diary of C. G. King; Sandra Luckett for the papers of D. W. Luckett; Caroline Manners for the war diary of G. R. Manners; H. L. Martin for his memoir, 'Lasting Impressions'; Alan Masters for the memoirs of his father, S. C. Masters; Ms Lisa Munby for the diaries of her father, A. N. L. Munby; the family and the Airey Neave Trust for the papers of Airey Neave; Sidney T. Payne for the papers of his brother-in-law, W. Kite; Mrs Dorothy Smith for the memoirs of her late husband, Geoffrey W. Smith; Douglas Swift for his narrative 'On a Bright Day in May'; Mrs Maureen E. Tateson for the narrative account by Tom Tateson; Mr Julian Walker for the papers of D. H. Walker; Ms Sonya

West for the papers of Victor West; Mr G. Willatt for his papers; J. H. Witte for his narrative account of his life as a Kriegie; and Gill Foster for the diaries of her father, Geoff Wright. Efforts have been made to contact all other copyright-holders, and any omissions are entirely unintentional.

Finally I would also like to express my gratitude to Ruth Parr, commissioning editor for the history list at Oxford University Press, and the various anonymous readers she persuaded to read greater or lesser portions of the original manuscript. Their collective comments proved to be of considerable value in shaping the final product. Responsibility for remaining problems rests, of course, entirely with the author.

Contents

List of Illustrations

List of Abbreviations

ABC	American Broadcasting Corporation
BBC	British Broadcasting Corporation (Written Archives Centre)
BEF	British Expeditionary Force
BFI	British Film Institute Library, London
BL	British Library, London
BQSM	Battery Quartermaster Sergeant
BRC	British Red Cross
CMAC	Contemporary Medical Archives Centre
CRU	Civil Resettlement Unit
CSVA	Colditz Society Video Archive
GL	Guildhall Library
GOC	General Officer Commanding
HLRO	House of Lords Record Office
ICRC	International Committee of the Red Cross
IOR	India Office Records (British Library)
IWM	Imperial War Museum (Department of Documents)
IWM (Books)	Imperial War Museum (Department of Books)
IWM (Rolf)	Imperial War Museum (Department of Documents: David Rolf collection)
IWMSA	Imperial War Museum (Department of Sound)
LC	Peter Liddle Collection, University of Leeds
MO	Medical Officer
NARS	National Archives and Record Service
NRO	Norfolk Record Office
NSA	National Sound Archive
OKW	Oberkommando der Wehrmacht

POW	Prisoner of War
OCTU	Officer Candidate Training Unit
PBS	Public Broadcasting System
PP	Protecting Power
PRO	Public Record Office [The National Archives]
PWX	Ex-Prisoner of War Organization SHAEF
QMS	Quartermaster-Sergeant
QVR	Queen Victoria's Rifles
RAAF	Royal Australian Air Force
RAF	Royal Air Force
RAFM	RAF Museum
RAFVR	Royal Air Force Volunteer Reserve
RAMC	Royal Army Medical Corps
RAMP	Recovered Allied Military Personnel
RASC	Royal Army Service Corps
RAOC	Royal Army Ordinance Corps
RC	Red Cross
RCAF	Royal Canadian Air Force
RN	Royal Navy
RNVR	Royal Navy Volunteer Reserve
RSM	Regimental Sergeant Major
SAO	Senior American Officer
SAS	Special Air Service
SBO	Senior British Officer
SBNCO	Senior British Non-Commissioned Officer
SBS	Special Boat Section
SHAEF	Supreme Headquarters Allied Expeditionary Forces
SOE	Special Operations Executive
SPM	author interview
SWWEC	Second World War Experience Centre
UNB	University of New Brunswick
UNWCC	United Nations War Crimes Commission
USAAF	United States Army Air Forces.
WO	Warrant Officer
YMCA	Young Men's Christian Association

Main British Prisoner
of War Camps
Mentioned in Text

N O R T H

S E A

SWEDEN
• Copenhagen

DENMARK

Kiel Canal

• Sassnitz

Lübeck

Barth, I

• Swinemüde

Sandbostel, XB
• Hamburg

Stettin

Marlag und
Milag Nord

Elbe

Stargard, IID

NETHERLANDS

Weser

Fallingbostel, XIB/357

Altengrabow,
XIA

• Berlin

Brunswick, 79

Steglitz, IIID

Oder

G E R M A N Y

Luckenwalde, IIIA

Kirchhain, IIIE

Sagan, III

BELGIUM

Rhine

Warburg, VIB

Spangenberg, IXA/H

Leipzig

Sagan, VIIIC

Mühlberg, IVB

Rotenburg, IXA

Coldiz,
IVC

Görlitz, VIIIA

Bad Sulza, IXC

Dresden

Hadamar, XIIB

Hartmannsdorf, IVF

Limburg,
XIIA

Oberursel
(Dulag Luft)

Trier

Mainz

Frankfurt
a-M

Hammelburg, XIIIC

Prague •

• Luxembourg

BOHEMIA

Saarbrücken

Nuremberg

LORRAINE

Nuremberg, XIIID

Hohenfels, 383

Eichstätt, VIIB

Strasbourg

Ulm

Danube

Moosburg, VIIA

ALSACE

Munich

Basle

Biberach, VB

Tittmoning, VIID

Laufen, VIIC

LIECHTENSTEIN

Berne

AUSTRIA

SWITZERLAND

Wolfsberg, XVIIIA

Geneva

I T A L Y

Source: Based on Foot and Langley, *MI9: The British Secret Service that
Fostered Escape and Evasion 1939–1945* (Bodley Head: London, 1979) p.99.

BALTIC
SEA

Heydekrug, VI ○

REICHSKOMMISSARIAT

OSTLAND

EAST
PRUSSIA

● Danzig

○ Gross
Tychow, IV

□ Marienburg, XXB

● Bialystok

Thorn, XXA □

□◆ Schubin, XXIB

Vistula

□ Posen, XXID

● Warsaw

REICHSKOMMISSARIAT

UKRAINE

GENERAL

GOVERNMENT

Bankau,
VII ○

Lamsdorf,
VIIIB/344 □

OF POLAND

● Lemberg

◆ Mährisch Trübau, VIIIF

MORAVIA

SLOVAKIA

● Tri Duby

● Vienna

RUMANIA

● Budapest

HUNGARY

Danube

○ Airmen's Camps Stalag Luft system
◆ Officers' Camps Oflags
□ Other Ranks' Camps Stalags
—·—·— Boundary of Germany, 1937
— — — Other 1937 boundaries
———— Boundary of 'Greater Germany', 1942
– – – Other 1942 boundaries

0   100   200 miles
0   100   200   300 km

CROATIA

Introduction
The Colditz Phenomenon

Sir, Is there no escape from Colditz?

(letter to *The Times*, 1974)[1]

There is a picture of Colditz in people's minds. Whatever you or I think about it is irrelevant...

(letter from one former prisoner of Oflag IVC to another, 1981)[2]

Surely not *another* book on Colditz! After all, over the past fifty years the story has been told many times, in a variety of ways, and from a number of perspectives. Far more has been written about Colditz than about any other camp, relative to the size of the population, in which British prisoners were held during the Second World War. As long ago as the mid-1980s the 'full story' could be purchased, while at the dawn of the twenty-first century the 'definitive history' appeared on bookshelves. Surely there is nothing much left to write about?[3]

In fact in a rather paradoxical fashion there is. For the very success and scale of what one observer dubbed the 'Colditz industry'—a number of best-sellers, a popular feature film, a hugely successful television drama series, several TV documentaries, plus assorted games and toys—has helped create what is arguably a rather distorted view of what life was like both inside Colditz (officially Oflag IVC) and in Nazi Germany in general for British and Commonwealth prisoners of war.

Aided and abetted by books and films celebrating episodes such as the Great Escape and the Wooden Horse that occurred elsewhere, the Colditz Story was central in creating an enduring set of popular assumptions in which life behind the wire was interpreted, both figuratively and sometimes literally, in sporting terms. Escape was the name of the game, with the team from Oflag IVC topping the league tables in terms of home runs. The popular image of what went on at Colditz castle, and by extension what happened at more anonymous camps elsewhere in the Greater Reich in more diluted form, became and remained one in which prisoners bore the burden of captivity with a light heart while helping one another with schemes to outwit and ultimately evade their captors. Like many enduring images this is based on a solid core of historical fact. But it is a core around which audiences, and those who have successfully catered for them, have unconsciously woven layers of generalized meaning based on selective evidence that serve their own needs rather better than the cause of a full and balanced understanding of the past. It remains, as a critic observed a quarter-of-a-century ago, 'another of those stories so peculiarly attractive to the British of moral victory wrested from defeat, laced throughout with understated heroism and that absurd sense of humour which is the pride and inverted swank of Englishmen'.[4]

The problem with the Colditz Myth is that it drastically oversimplifies and distorts the general experience in Germany and even that of prisoners held inside the *Schloss* itself. The emphasis on escapes, which in any case were less pervasive than is commonly assumed, has meant less exciting aspects of the POW experience have been underplayed or ignored. Though conditions were better than what men captured on the Eastern Front or Allied troops who fell into Japanese hands were forced to undergo, life for servicemen treated as *Engländer* by the Third Reich—Commonwealth and Empire men as well as those from the United Kingdom—was rarely the stuff of *Boy's Own*. Privation, boredom, uncertainty, occasional danger, and much else besides made POW life for most men resemble an endurance test rather than a light-hearted game. Much of what is assumed, furthermore, is based on tales of escapes by officers—not least from Oflag IVC—thereby obscuring the sometimes quite different experience of the majority of POWs without commissions who were put to work in the Third Reich. What is more, what was true for one set of prisoners in one location at one particular time—be it at Colditz or elsewhere—might not be true for another. The experience of being in enemy hands varied a good deal. Though the myth continues to appeal to many people, a more comprehensive examination of the prisoner-of-war experience can perhaps give us a truer idea of the multifaceted nature of life behind the wire. It might also yield a less escape-fixated appreciation of the hurdles that these men faced so long ago. Colditz, in short, needs to be placed in context.[5]

In order to do this, however, it is first necessary to chronicle how Colditz came to establish itself and remain firmly in the British popular consciousness. Why did this small camp, only one among several dozen (hundreds, if working camps are included) in which British prisoners

Falcon Press in early 1946. Though containing much of historical interest, and beautifully produced, *Detour* was a volume of reminiscence rather than a tale of escapes per se. While copies made their way into libraries in some unexpected places, it was not widely reviewed and never reissued.[9]

Meanwhile another, more fictionalized account of life in Colditz was attracting a certain amount of notice in literary circles. Micky Burn, the former *Times* man, had been captured fighting with the commandos at St-Nazaire. Eventually sent to Oflag IVC, he had, among other things, begun work on a novel about life in the castle. Though the characters were ostensibly fictional, the author suggested that only 'a few small liberties' were taken with other matters (for example, changing the name but not the location of the castle), and reviewers took the book to be largely autobiographical. Finished by the end of 1945, *Yes, Farewell* was published by Jonathan Cape in March 1946. An overtly political work—the farewell in the title is for liberalism in the face of the onward historical march of communism—it was also an unflinching look at human nature in captivity. Charles Marriott, writing for the *Manchester Guardian*, found it 'absorbing', while the *Times Literary Supplement* reviewer labelled it an 'extremely intelligent' if 'disturbing and resolutely frank' story of men living 'in an atmosphere that is fatigued and febrile, pervaded by boredom and a morose negativeness of spirit'. This sort of approach, however, did not suggest a future of mass sales. 'Mr. Burn, as a novelist', the *TLS* critic concluded, 'substitutes a subjective mood for action, ideas for character, and a political philosophy for imaginative sympathy.' Marriott also thought that what episodes of drama and action there were in the book, when placed next to the 'overpoweringly real' atmospheric stuff, 'suffer by comparison.' Though it went through several impressions and was reprinted twice, the book's tone was too stark, and by the dawn of the Cold War its politics too hard left, to appeal to a mass audience in the late 1940s and early 1950s.[10]

Moreover, attempts at breaking out were peripheral to the plot, and within a few years it became very obvious that what the public really wanted in the way of reminiscences by former POWs were tales of ingenious and ultimately successful escapes. *The Wooden Horse*, an account of the three-man tunnel dug from under a vaulting horse at Sagan written by one of the participants, Eric Williams, first appeared in February 1949 under the Collins imprint, and was an immediate success. Several million copies would eventually be sold, and within seventeen months of publication the story had been turned into a feature film that, in turn, became a major box-office success in Britain. In 1950 Faber put out *The Great Escape*, the story of the Stalag Luft III tunnel break as written up by the Australian journalist Paul Brickhill (who had been at Sagan but had not taken part in the break), which also went through multiple editions. *The Great Escape* launched Brickhill on a career of writing best-selling accounts of British wartime exploits, and so successful was *The Wooden Horse* that Williams wrote a 'prequel' describing an earlier, albeit less spectacular, escape attempt, entitled *The Tunnel*. This book was put out by Collins in 1951 and was itself reissued more than half-a-dozen times in subsequent years.[11]

If adventure was what the public wanted, the many and varied break-out schemes that had been mounted at Colditz offered an obvious means of catering to demand. Pat Reid, who had served as escape officer in the castle before orchestrating his own successful home-run attempt, was undoubtedly conscious of this. Though an engineer by training and latterly a diplomat, Reid had both good raw material to work with and certain models to draw on in writing up his account. As a youth he had read avidly the popular first-person prisoner-of-war narratives—some of them with illustrations—that had appeared between the world wars, including *The Escaping Club* by A. J. Evans, *Within Four Walls* by M. C. C. Harrison and H. A. Cartwright, and *The Road to En-Dor* by E. H. Jones. These had all concentrated on the business of escaping, and at times presented captivity and attempts to evade it almost as a school-boy adventure. Pat Reid consciously adopted a similarly light-hearted tone, later explaining that he wanted to avoid a narrative that could be read as 'one great damn moan about the sufferings we went through'. Instead he stressed the uniqueness of Colditz, the near-constant escape plotting, various humorous episodes, and in general the high spirits of all concerned, when describing the camp from his arrival up to the point nearly two years later when he successfully escaped to Switzerland.

While sifting through *Detour*, contacting over a dozen fellow ex-captives to buttress his own memory, and getting permission from the *Illustrated London News* to reproduce some of the John Watton drawings, Reid set to work outlining the escapes mounted from, and escapades undertaken within, 'the bad boys' camp'. After he finished Reid quoted Evans's words about the need for 'one of the men who was there' to tell 'the whole story of Colditz' as justification for the enterprise. 'This book is the story of Colditz', he explained in the prologue. 'I was one of the men who was imprisoned there.' In a manner typical of the book's boyishly enthusiastic style, the opening of the final paragraph of this prologue read as follows: 'If you feel in a mood to launch into the feverish underground activity of a camp full of diehards, read on.'[12]

Published in the summer of 1952 by Hodder & Stoughton, *The Colditz Story* was received in generally favourable terms by the critics. The writing was praised for its 'pace and humour' (*Times Literary Supplement*), its 'attractive simplicity' (*Observer*), and the 'disarming modesty' of its author (*Sunday Times*), and the subject-matter was declared of great interest. What went on at Colditz in the way of breakout attempts 'challenges comparison with any of the escape stories of World War II' (*Daily Telegraph*). Yet there were also occasional notes of cynicism or asperity concerning secondary matters of substance or major aspects of style. Terence Prittie, himself a former officer POW who had already written up his escape experiences, suggested in the *Manchester Guardian* that the Germans were not as wrong-headed about security matters as Reid portrayed them to be at Colditz, and left it unclear as to whether he thought the author had consciously tried—or, if he had, had succeeded in—writing a best-seller. Guy Ramsey, writing for the *Daily Telegraph*, thought the book smacked too much of the atmosphere of 'the *Gem*, the *Magnet*, and the *Boy's Own Paper*', indeed almost to the point of parody.[13]

However, it was precisely that aspect of *The Colditz Story*, along with the exciting subject-matter—i.e. escapes—that made the book so attractive to the general public. It was an adventure tale of high-spirited and gallant young men risking their lives to outwit the enemy against all the odds, full of incident and humour as well as containing plenty of illustrations. 'I think you can take it for granted', Hodder & Stoughton explained in a letter to the author six months after publication, 'that we have sold at least 25,000 copies—a very remarkable scale for a 15/- book, and one that can have few competitors, if any, in this year of grace.' Within fourteen months over 32,000 copies had been sold, and sales continued to be brisk: for example, 1,830 copies were bought between October 1953 and March of the following year, and a paperback edition put out by Pan Books at 2 shillings appeared in January 1954. 'There are not many authors who can boast such sales as these', the publisher reminded Reid that June.[14]

As *The Colditz Story* was taking off, another former inhabitant of the castle was about to enter the publishing fray. Airey Neave, then a barrister, and a man Pat Reid did not mention in his acknowledgements as being among the ex-prisoners of the castle he had talked to, decided to write up a personal account of his POW experiences, culminating in an escape that gave him the distinction of being the first British officer to make it home from Colditz. Having stood unsuccessfully as a Conservative candidate in the 1950 and 1951 general elections, he became the prospective candidate for North Berkshire in March 1952, a seat whose current incumbent was expected to be elevated to the peerage in the near future. Though the constituency was a relatively safe one for the Tories, *They Have Their Exits*, which appeared in March 1953 under the imprint of Hodder & Stoughton, can have done Neave no harm while he was campaigning in the by-election held in June 1954 that made him an MP. The author's supporters certainly thought it important to make sure the publisher got copies into all the Abingdon bookshops.[15]

Though rather more introspective and slightly more ambitious in style than *The Colditz Story*—'whole passages have a quality of real literature', Guy Ramsey commented, rather backhandedly—*They Have Their Exits* was nevertheless an adventure-filled account, and it did quite well. Advance orders meant that the first two printings were sold out before the official publication date, it was serialized in several papers, including the *London Daily News* and the *Scottish Daily Mail*, and excerpts were read out on the BBC radio programme *Suspense*.[16]

It was quickly overtaken, however, by the sequel to *The Colditz Story*, which Pat Reid entitled *The Latter Days*. Though he himself had escaped from the castle in the autumn of 1942, the success of the first book had prompted Reid, with help from his friends Dick Howe (his successor as British escape officer), W. T. 'Lulu' Lawton, and Harry Elliott, to contact other officers who had been there and put together a picture of what had occurred at Colditz down to the point at which it had been liberated in April 1945. Though not written in the first person, *The Latter Days* was very similar in style and general content to the first book—the variety and ingeniousness of ongoing escape attempts made up the central narrative thread—and John Watton once more contributed illustrations. Worried that the public might not recognize the book as a sequel in view of the absence of the word 'Colditz' in the title, Hodder & Stoughton made the dust-jacket look as much like that of *The Colditz Story* as possible. 'Though I say it myself', Reid wrote in a letter to his publishers just before the book was launched in November 1953, 'I think it should go down with the public like nobody's business.'[17]

Critics noted that the absence of a first-person narrator made *The Latter Days* somewhat less personal in tone than its predecessor, but conceded that the tale was an inherently exciting one that Reid had told in about as gripping a fashion as possible for someone writing as a de facto historian. 'The book is alive from its first page to its last', enthused the reviewer for the *Times Literary Supplement*. Sales of the hardback edition of *The Latter Days*, priced at 15 shillings a copy, had by the end of March 1954 exceeded 12,700.[18]

The impact of the two Reid books, along with the success of earlier POW escape films, quickly prompted a production company headed by Ivan Foxwell to make a successful bid for the film rights. The fact that Colditz was now part of communist East Germany ruled out location shooting, and so a variety of exterior as well as interior sets were built at Shepperton Studios, while producer Ivan Foxwell, director Guy Hamilton, and playwright William Douglas-Home, a former officer POW himself, worked on a screenplay combining and condensing the contents of *The Colditz Story* and *The Latter Days*. Screen-time requirements meant that a lot had to be left out, and that the words and actions of various characters (all of whose names were changed, except for Pat Reid) had sometimes to be combined. John Mills was to play Reid himself, ably supported by Eric Portman as the SBO and various other actors—Christopher Rhodes, Bryan Forbes, Lionel Jeffries, and Ian Carmichael among them—playing brother officers keen on escape. Several cast members had acted in comedies or had natural comic talent, something that the director was keen to exploit. Hamilton not only wanted to highlight the adventure aspects of the story but also the schoolboy-humour elements. There would be excitement and drama aplenty, but also a strong thread of comedy. 'I was absolutely determined to show that Colditz was exceptional *and* could be very funny', he later explained. Shooting began in May 1954, and *The Colditz Story* was ready to be released by January 1955.[19]

Pat Reid (who had originally wanted Carol Reid to direct), acting as technical advisor on the set, was pleased with the results, stating in a letter to his publisher that 'my opinion is that this film will really hit the headlines'. Following the premiere at the Gaumont, Haymarket, it quickly became apparent that he was correct: *The Colditz Story* was going to be a hit. The critics almost unanimously praised the acting and admired the mixture of humour, excitement, pathos, and drama. 'There have been prisoner-of-war and escape stories [on screen] before,' Leonard Mosley opined in the *Daily Express*, '... but this one is superior in performance, in background, and in intention.' *The Colditz Story* was both 'exciting and amusing' and 'always enjoyable' (*Daily Telegraph*); throughout it represented 'not only the excitements, the failures, and the successes of the escape plans, but the dignity of the human spirit in circumstances of extreme adversity' (*The Times*). Indeed, the film 'achieved a most convincing versimilitude' in comparison to what had actually gone on in the castle (*Manchester Guardian*). Even Paul Holt, who thought it rather manipulative and hoped that the escape genre was reaching its end on screen, suggested that this 'prisoner-of-war escape film to end them all' would be a success at the box office. He was right. *The Colditz Story* was one of the top moneymaking British films of the year.[20]

Reid had every reason to be happy. But reaction among Old Colditzians outside his own circle of friends to what they saw on screen was a bit more mixed. Some understood the need to take a certain amount of dramatic licence, enjoyed particular performances, and thought that on the whole the spirit if not the letter of the place had been accurately captured. Nevertheless there were criticisms. Technical details were generally accurate but on occasion wrong. The sheer boredom of day-to-day prison life, even in a place as comparatively lively as Colditz, could not be conveyed, while the comedy elements might seem at times a bit over the top. 'I know we were silly,' Patrick Welch later commented in an interview, 'but I don't think we were quite as stupid and quite as silly as that.' Meanwhile at least one former prisoner was furious about what he had seen while visiting the cinema. Airey Neave had been the first British prisoner to make a successful home run from the castle, but in the screenwriting process his story had been axed to make way for the escape in which Pat Reid had got out, thus leaving the viewer with the impression that it was Reid rather than Neave who had first managed to escape from Colditz. Neave did not go public about what he regarded as a travesty of the facts, but through his solicitors he did insist that Ivan Foxwell insert an end credit to the film indicating that he had been the first to make it home. Relations between the authors of *The Colditz Story* and *They Have Their Exits* were apparently under some strain as a result of this contretemps.[21]

Even as the film was in production Weidenfeld & Nicolson were trying to capitalize on the growing fame of Colditz by publishing the accounts of two among the select band of special prisoners—the *Prominente*—who had been held at the castle because of their family connections. *The Privileged Nightmare*, in which Giles Romilly (a nephew of Winston Churchill) and Michael Alexander (related to the field-marshal of the same last name) stuck together their stories back to back, was first published in August 1954 and swiftly reprinted.[22]

But as Hodder & Stoughton had been anticipating, the critical and box-office success of *The Colditz Story* on screen redounded most successfully in terms of book sales on the two Pat Reid titles. The 2 shilling paperback editions of *The Colditz Story* and *The Latter Days* put out by Pan in January 1954 and November 1955 had by the end of March 1956 sold 378,871 and 172,619 copies respectively.[23]

They Have Their Exits was also issued in paperback three months after the film opened. So great had the public interest in Colditz become that not only former prisoners but also a former guard were being approached about publishing their memoirs. Reinhold Eggers wrote up his experiences as one of the camp officers at Oflag IVC (he later claimed) after Pat Reid had suggested he do so, though it was in fact Howard Gee, another Old Colditzian, fluent in German, who translated the manuscript into English. Though it took three years to find a publisher willing to risk a memoir by a former jailer rather than a escaping prisoner from the castle, after Hale published *Colditz: The German Story* in 1961 sales were such that two additional print runs had to be made to keep up with demand, and a Pan paperback edition appeared in 1963.[24]

As the 1960s progressed there were signs that interest in Colditz had passed its peak. Though new editions of the Reid and Neave books were published in the middle of the decade, no further memoirs or secondary accounts appeared. There was, indeed, a sharp drop in the publication of new books by or about prisoners of war in general, and the cycle of Made-in-England prisoner escape films also came to an end. To a large extent this was due to overexposure of the war genre in general in the 1950s. This helped fuel an anti-establishment backlash in the 1960s in which a new generation reacted against what had come before; though in the case of films the decline of the British film industry as a whole (with television-watching rapidly supplanting cinema-going) must be taken into consideration. US production companies generated several motion pictures set in British POW compounds, but in a film such as *The Great Escape* (1963) American stars took the leading roles and both the plot and dialogue were geared to the American market. The 'classic' British escape tale was seemingly a thing of the past, perhaps the greatest screen indignity coming at the start of the following decade when a made-for-TV movie, *The Birdmen*, was made in California by Universal Television, in which the story of the Colditz glider was presented in entirely fictional terms, with Doug McClure leading an all-American cast.[25]

Shortly thereafter, though, the Colditz Phenomenon would revive and grow more powerful than ever as a result of another, larger-scale, and this time Made-in-England adaptation for the small screen: the hugely successful BBC Television series *Colditz* (1972–4). Back in 1956 episodes from *The Colditz Story* and *The Latter Days*, along with other escape tales, had formed the subject-matter for Pat Reid while he was fronting half-hour episodes of *Escapers' Club*, an Associated-Rediffusion in-studio television series broadcast on ITV. But it was only at the beginning of the 1970s that Colditz finally came of age on the small screen. A documentary was mooted by the BBC TV Science and Features department, but dropped when it was discovered that the BBC Drama department was already working on a full-scale series.[26]

This was the work of writer Brian Degas and producer Gerry Glaister, who, having scored separate successes on television in the 1960s, began collaborating on a scenario that envisaged an episodic 'dramatized account' of the Colditz story in colour. The series would be 'based on' both the Pat Reid account and the big-screen version of *The Colditz Story*, but as in the film the facts would be altered for dramatic purposes. This time round all the characters were to be 'fictionalized': made-up names would be used, allowing for the personality and behaviour of the men on whom they were based to be exaggerated, downplayed, or combined for dramatic purposes. Episodes in the castle could be manipulated for the same reason, and where necessary particular characters and incidents might not be anchored to real persons and recorded events specific to Colditz at all.[27]

As the scenario for the series stressed, breaking out from the supposedly escape-proof castle would of course be the central motif. The series would be 'a record of the ingenuity . . . bravery and skill' of the prisoners who 'destroyed the reputation' of Colditz for being a place from which there was no escape. Three of the main British characters— one from each service—would differ 'in character, philosophy and background', but would share the 'common aim' of wanting to escape. Pat Reid himself was to serve as military and technical adviser to the programmes. But the creators of the series also hoped to present other aspects of life inside the *Schloss*, so as to create a more general human drama. Colditz on the small screen would serve as 'a symbol of many prisons—the prisons of class, of physical restraint and embarrassment, of despair and dejection'. The prisoners would be 'at once sharp studies of individuals and symbols of human hope, endeavour and frustration'. There would, moreover, be three main German characters to counterbalance the three main British ones: a definite contrast with the 1950s film, in which the jailers were little more than comic foils for the British. 'I went into this project with a very definite aim,' Gerry Glaister later admitted bluntly in a 1973 press interview: 'to put our boot through the myths about jolly-chap prisoners and silly old Germans.' In an earlier letter to Airey Neave the producer was more diplomatic, explaining that the overall aim of the series was 'to treat the subject a little more seriously than perhaps some escape films have done'.[28]

A co-production deal was negotiated between the BBC and Universal Television in America, in which Glaister was commissioned to produce fifteen fifty-minute episodes of *Colditz*. Brian Degas would write the first episode, but thereafter writing, like directing, would be parcelled out between half-a-dozen or so experienced hands. British character actors, including Edward Hardwicke, Bernard Hepton, and Jack Hedley, were hired for a variety of recurring parts. Two faces familiar on both sides of the Atlantic—David McCallum and the film star Robert Wagner—were also given major roles in what was essentially an ensemble work.[29]

There were difficulties that had to be overcome. Shooting extensively on location remained impracticable; but from photographs, drawings, a little filming on site, and donated objects the production team eventually were able to re-create parts of the castle to their satisfaction at Shepperton and elsewhere. There were also problems of a more creative nature. Pat Reid, it soon became clear, did not approve of the class and personality conflicts and problems present in the initial scripts, not least with respect to the character most closely resembling him. 'I think he is still hankering after those happy days of the '50's when all those POW films were made', N. J. Crisp (one of the offending writers) acidly observed. At the same time Robert Wagner was complaining to Universal about 'a tendency for the writers to revert to the stereotypes of the 1940s/50s war pictures'. However, Reid was only the technical adviser, the contract gave the BBC full creative control, and 'R. J.' himself eventually came to understand that *Colditz*, while retaining elements from an earlier genre, was a gritty drama that demanded 'a level of acting that I've never had to deliver before'. The American actor also came to understand the underlying thrust of the series. 'If you think this is a prisoner-of-war story in terms of *The Great Escape*,' Wagner publicly explained, 'you couldn't be more wrong. It's not so much a story of war and prison as of people, of humanity.'[30]

The BBC mounted a formidable publicity campaign in the run-up to the broadcast of the first weekly episode of *Colditz* on 19 October 1972. The initial reactions of television critics were mixed and somewhat cautious in tone. But after viewing the first three instalments Clive James came out in favour of *Colditz* in the pages of the *Observer*, noting that, contrary to what he and other critics had expected, it was far from being a re-run of the 1950s film, was in fact 'more realistic than any POW movie yet made', and stood a good chance of being 'an unexpected and highly interesting success'. The prediction proved to be highly prescient. On average over 7 million viewers (or over 30 per cent of the viewing public) tuned in each week to watch *Colditz*. BBC audience-research reports indicated that the majority of those who watched the programme found it thoroughly entertaining, well acted, easy to follow, but also out of the ordinary. Gerry Glaister was delighted to pass on the news that the series was 'maintaining viewing figures such as no series had reached before'. Over 8 million people tuned in to watch the last two episodes in January 1973, by which time *Colditz* had established itself as the most successful television drama series ever broadcast by the BBC. The producer, himself a veteran of the war, thought that in addition to nostalgia among older people, the younger generation, who had never known war, were curious to learn what had transpired. 'I am amazed, I simply can't account for it', a slightly stunned Pat Reid admitted.[31]

The success of the series had an immediate ripple effect. Its popular theme music, 'The Colditz March', composed by Robert Farnon, became a recording hit for the BBC. Coronet paperback editions of *The Colditz Story, The Latter Days*, and *They Have Their Exits* sold a combined total of half-a-million copies while *Colditz* was on the air. Out of print for a decade, *Colditz: The German Story* was reissued by Hale towards the end of 1972, followed in 1973 by a Sphere paperback version of *The Privileged Nightmare*, now bearing the title *Hostages at Colditz* for the sake of name recognition, as well as a compilation of stories by former prisoners and staff of the castle entitled *Colditz Recaptured* that Eggers had persuaded John Watton to edit and Robert Hale to publish. The series had appealed to younger as well as older viewers, and the toy industry was not slow to react. Vic-Toy produced a Ludo-like board game, *Escape from Colditz Castle*, in 1972, only to see it superseded by the more Monopoly-style *Escape from Colditz* from Parker Games, which bore the impressive legend: 'Devised by Major P. R. Reid, M.B.E., M.C., author of "The Colditz Story" and "Latter Days at Colditz".' Palitoy also got in on the act by producing a special *Escape from Colditz* Action Man set, containing figures dressed as a guard and a prisoner complete with Red Cross parcel. By popular demand six of the best episodes of the first series were rerun by the BBC in the spring of 1973— each episode followed by a brief interview with an Old Colditzian, beginning with Pat Reid—and plans were laid to make another thirteen episodes roughly covering the time span of *The Latter Days*.[32]

Former prisoners of war, meanwhile, including those who had been in Colditz, were sometimes rather less enthusiastic than the general public about the television series. It was they who would help spearhead what was perhaps an inevitable backlash against the BBC, on the grounds of distorting history for the sake of dramatic appeal.

Reid himself, conceding that 'this is history as well as entertainment', stated in public that he had pretty much succeeded in keeping episodes from straying too far from reality. 'I made a bit of a nuisance of myself,' he explained to the *Daily Mail*, 'ensuring that nothing crept in that would make anyone at home say: "That's sheer fiction, it's ludicrous".' Some were willing to accept a certain amount of dramatic licence, given the constraints of the medium and the recognition that this was not a documentary series. Dick Howe, successor to Reid as escape officer at the castle, made it known that while there were errors in detail, 'Gerry Glaister has captured the basic atmosphere of Colditz, the frightful, oppressive feeling'. Howe found the series made such an impression that he lost sleep as old memories resurfaced, while John Wilson, another former inmate, after watching Episode 8—in which a prisoner feigns insanity in order to be repatriated on medical grounds, but ends up going truly mad—decided that the series was a little too close to reality for comfort: 'one was enough.' Other former inhabitants, including Alan Campbell, Lord Harewood, and Jock Hamilton-Baillie, accepted that while not everything presented on screen was historically accurate, the BBC had still managed to capture the essence of Colditz. 'I found the TV dramatisation imaginatively conceived and brilliant acted,' Michael Burn wrote a year or so after the series first aired, 'and, with a few reservations, authentic as well as gripping.'[33]

There were some ex-prisoners who were simply bemused by the sight of amenities they themselves had never enjoyed and at the comparatively spick-and-span appearance of the actors. But there were also those who took lesser or greater exception to what they saw on television. 'Actually I saw only the first instalment and that was quite enough', Martin Gilliat wrote in a personal letter to an equally disgruntled David Walker. In later interviews Mike Moran called the series 'really ridiculous', while Lord Newborough dismissed it as 'completely unrealistic' and 'bloody awful', especially in relation to its positive portrayal of the Germans. Jimmy Yule, though he considered much of the first series to be relatively authentic, was annoyed enough by the presence of the entirely fictional American character played by Robert Wagner to write a letter of complaint to Glaister at the BBC. 'Look here, you know it's all very well,'

Yule later recalled himself arguing, 'but a Yank wasn't within a hundred miles of the place. I know you have to sell it to the States, and all that, but...it's a pity you had to give him such a prominent position...' Howard Gee wrote a piece for his local paper at the time complaining that 'the only thing missing from the series was Errol Flynn'.[34]

Meanwhile the BBC was preparing to air the second series of *Colditz*, starting on 7 January 1974. As part of the publicity campaign the *Radio Times* had funded the first return visit to the actual castle by four ex-prisoners—Pat Reid, Dick Howe, Rupert Barry, and Jack Best—in late 1973, and had then gone on to sponsor a special 'Escape from Colditz' exhibition at the Imperial War Museum, due to open on the same day that the first episode aired. In light of the storm that was about to break, the launch party for the exhibition, held on the previous Thursday, perhaps provided signals of troubles to come. Several hundred former prisoners had been invited, only half of whom showed up. One of the columnists from *The Times* was struck by the 'techiness' of men 'reluctant to talk about their Colditz experiences' who appeared deeply disillusioned with the world around them. Philip Howard, another *Times* man, opined that the exhibition would serve as a 'therapeutic antidote' to a TV series that he—and perhaps some of the middle-aged men he spoke to at the party—regarded as possessing too much adventurous fiction and not enough mundane fact.[35]

Howard Gee, who had attended the party, was certainly not in a positive frame of mind towards the BBC when journalist Jerry Caminada—whom Gee had known in a civilian interment camp in Germany before he was sent to Colditz—phoned him up to ask what he thought of the programmes (A: 'I don't think much of them'). The day after the first of the new episodes was aired, an opinion piece by Caminada entitled 'Killing the Charisma of Colditz' appeared in *The Times*. The central theme of the piece was that the series, the books, and indeed the whole Colditz industry was producing a false sense among viewers that the castle was a particularly difficult place in which to be incarcerated. 'The impression is abroad', he added, 'that Colditz had almost a monopoly of escapes, and that escaping from it was much more difficult than from other camps.' From what he had been told by Gee, and from the facts he had gleaned from various books, this was in fact false. Other camps were tougher to get away from, and the number of escape attempts made from Colditz was not particularly remarkable. 'So enough of Colditz', Caminada concluded. 'Let us file it away with all the camps of a generation ago, before the legend smothers us all.'[36]

If that were not enough, the same paper that day included a witty send-up review, written by Alan Coren, of the first of the new episodes that highlighted the way in which, despite efforts to make things grittier through the introduction of a nastier and entirely fictitious German character, *Colditz* drew its inspiration from books and a film in which escape was pursued with boyish enthusiasm. 'Hurrah! The Christmas hols over it was back to *The Fifth Form at St. Colditz* for a new term', the review began, after which the plot of the episode was summarized as a Greyfriars parody. 'All in all,' Coren concluded, 'I think it's going to be a whippingly good term.'[37]

This was a light-hearted jibe, of course—though funny and obvious enough to appear shortly thereafter in the form of a *Two Ronnies* comedy sketch—and a barrage of letters indicated to Caminada that his view of the Colditz phenomenon ('imprisonment by commercialism') was not widely shared, at least by readers of *The Times*. It was also fairly easy for the BBC to ignore the occasional complaint that, by inserting a truly Nazi character, the producer of the series was perpetuating wartime stereotypes about the Germans.[38]

Rather more unnerving was a full-scale assault on *Colditz* by none other than the first British prisoner to make a home run from Oflag IVC, Airey Neave. While the initial series was in production in the summer of 1972, the MP for Abingdon had been anxious to make sure that it did not perpetuate the false idea, conveyed in the film version of *The Colditz Story*, that Pat Reid had been the first British officer to escape, and had instructed his solicitors to contact the producer on the matter. In response, Glaister had given Neave what the latter took to be an assurance that the series would be 'largely fictitious' and that it would 'not portray individual escapes', either his or anyone else's.[39]

But while the producer continued to stress that 'we have fictionalised all the characters and no real names are being used',[40] the MP was not pleased when the series aired, either by what he took to be the overly bright tone—literally as well as figuratively, given the lighting needs associated with videotaping—or, doubtless, by the climactic final episodes in which the Pat Grant character (clearly based on Pat Reid rather than himself) makes it to Switzerland. Seventeen days after attending the *Radio Times* launch party at the Imperial War Museum, Neave spoke his mind at the *Sun* TV awards ceremony. 'The programme is seriously misleading,' he informed reporters, 'and does not really convey the harshness of the conditions.' Though 'a good adventure yarn', the series was too 'jolly and bright' to convey the reality of life in Colditz, and indeed almost gave the impression that the place was 'a holiday camp', what with chatty guards and well-fed, well-dressed actors in khaki who looked 'as if their hair has just been styled by Vidal Sassoon'. Making a bad public-relations situation worse was the response of Pat Reid when approached for comment at home. While arguing that it was 'nonsense' to suggest the series made Colditz out to be a version of Butlin's, the technical adviser to the series conceded that there were problems. 'Airey Neave's arguments are sound', he was reported as saying. 'I think some of the actors look too well-fed—we were thin as rakes—and their uniforms look too new', going on to emphasize that, as technical adviser to the series, 'I have had my battles with producers about accuracy'. Given the high profile the series had attained, it was not surprising that these remarks were published widely the following day in both the national and local press.[41]

This put the BBC on the defensive. 'We are as factually accurate as it is possible to be in television', a spokesman stated. 'We also try and be realistic as well and the guards are shown as human beings.' Glaister himself was more forthright. 'Colditz is an entertainment series, not a documentary', he argued. Yes, food and fuel were short, but you couldn't have actors go on a starvation diet or have them 'going round shivering all the time'. Moreover, he himself had evidence showing that conditions were not always that bad. 'I have pictures—taken by the Germans—of prisoners playing games in their courtyard and even sunning themselves in deckchairs.'[42]

The following week the BBC released copies of these photographs to the press. 'Some of the men in the photographs look extremely well fed—and one or two even have paunches', a spokesman pointed out. The series producer, meanwhile, stressed that he had taken great pains to get the general atmosphere and conditions as close to reality as possible. The release of the photographs backfired, insofar as it prompted Pat Reid to point out that the pictures were mostly German propaganda snaps. Meanwhile the press had been approaching other Old Colditzians for their impressions, the *News of the World* reporting the day before the BBC release that Reinhold Eggers, the former security officer, thought *Colditz* seriously strayed from the truth in key areas. 'Life in Colditz was never the good, clean, sentimental fun that British viewers are now being entertained with', he told reporter George Edwards. He pointed out what he thought were factual errors, and took great exception to the portrayal of the camp staff. Their characters, he insisted, owed much more to fiction than to fact. That, Glaister retorted, had been intentional.[43]

The BBC, as Neave perceived, was 'getting extremely touchy'. But the MP admitted that he was quickly 'getting quite bored with being interviewed on the subject', and the controversy slowly died down.[44] The makers of *Colditz* could in any case take comfort from the excellent viewing figures that the second series was generating. 'The strict authenticity of the series may be in question,' as the *Daily Express* put it, 'but there's no doubting the firm hold that it has on viewers.' On average over 7 million people were watching *Colditz* each week, and for the final episode, broadcast on 1 April 1974, in which the castle was liberated, the BBC estimated that a third of the UK population had tuned in. 'The perfect finish to a fine series', was the consensus verdict reached in a BBC audience poll.[45]

The success of the second series also had a knock-on effect. White Lion published a new edition of Micky Burn's *Yes, Farewell* under the title *Farewell to Colditz* in the summer, followed in November by a four-page spread in the *Observer Colour Supplement* in which the author explained why he had not tried to escape from the castle. The second Eggers volume, meanwhile, had gone into a second printing, and other authors were attempting to ride the wave of popular interest in POW escapes in general and Colditz in particular through escape-story compilations. The press continued to take an interest in everything related to Colditz—it was already being used as a metaphor for any tough institution from which the inhabitants wished to escape—including the castle itself in East Germany, and commercial spin-offs continued to generate money. Airfix, for instance, produced a model kit of the famous glider built inside its walls, while a 'Colditz Escape Map' was put out by Mars Limited with the assistance of Pat Reid as part of a promotion for Galaxy-Ripple chocolate bars.[46]

Though *Colditz* was now finished, interest in the wartime story of the castle and in escape more generally by no means disappeared in the second half of the 1970s. Pat Reid compiled a small children's book entitled *My Favourite Escape Stories*, and Robert Hale published *The Man Who Came in from Colditz*, a memoir by one of the Dutch prisoners. Adventure-mystery writer Harry Patterson (better known under the nom de plume Jack Higgins) was assumed to have used the holding of the *Prominente* at Oflag IVC as the basis for an otherwise fictional story, *The Valhalla Exchange*, put out by Hutchinson in 1976. Hodder & Stoughton published the Colditz diary of Ellison Platt, edited by Margaret Duggan, under the title *Padre in Colditz* in 1978. Pat Reid, on the jacket flap, was quoted as saying that this was a ' "must" for all enthusiasts'. Meanwhile new printings of the Colditz classics were continuing to sell briskly. The Coronet paperback version of *The Colditz Story* had by 1978 sold to the tune of 640,000 copies, while a 1977 paperback reissue of *They Have Their Exits* had within six months sold more than 170,000 copies. Neave was still receiving healthy royalties when he was assassinated in a car-bomb explosion engineered by an IRA splinter group in 1979.[47]

At the start of the following decade the Platt diary was reissued, followed in subsequent years by publication of the memoirs of several more ex-inmates—three of whom put 'Colditz' in their titles. A collection of wartime photographs of Colditz was put together by Ron Baybutt and published by Hodder & Stoughton in 1982, the same year that a paperback book of extracts from various escape stories, entitled *Catapulting from Colditz*, appeared under the Ward Lock imprint. The first computer game devoted to escape from Oflag IVC, written by Tony Barber and sold by Phipps Associates, also came on the market in the early 1980s. More consequentially, and in time to mark the fortieth anniversary of the liberation of the castle, Macmillan published a new history of Colditz by Pat Reid in November 1984.[48]

Originally titled *Challenge*, this was the end-product of a long-running collaboration between the author and a group of about half-a-dozen friends—most of whom had been at Oflag IVC themselves—who agreed that too much had been left out of the earlier books. Attempting to be as comprehensive as possible, Reid submitted a manuscript that the publisher calculated would run to nearly 500 pages of text. Macmillan refused on commercial grounds to publish a book of this length, and more than a hundred manuscript pages were eventually cut. Reid also accepted that, in order for the book to sell, name recognition would be important. *Challenge* became *Colditz: The Full Story*.[49]

Perhaps stung by criticism of the schoolboyish tone of his original account—'Possibly I overdid the humour and the fun', he admitted somewhat uneasily when questioned in the mid-1970s—Reid adopted a more impersonal style this time around. 'Pat's approach is a complete and refreshing departure from what one has been used to', as collaborator Mike Moran put it. But this did not save *The Full Story* from being criticized by the up-and-coming military historian Hew Strachan for being essentially the mixture as before. Certain omissions, he indicated in the *Times Literary Supplement*, were significant. 'Despair and depression barely feature; the tedium of a prisoner's daily round is never discussed; sexual deprivation and repression warrant [only] a misleading and inconclusive couple of pages.' But this did not stop the book from selling well enough to appear as an Arrow paperback in November 1985, marketed as 'The final classic of the Colditz trilogy', or Coronet from reissuing the first two books as a single paperback entitled *Colditz: The Colditz Story and the Latter Days at Colditz* in 1986—the same year that Virgin published a game book by Clive Gifford entitled *Escape From Colditz*, in which the reader works out how to get away. Three years later the quarterly magazine *After the Battle*, which intersperses contemporary photographs of visits to wartime sites with photographs taken during the war, devoted an entire issue to Colditz.[50]

In 1990 came the news that Colditz castle, about to become part of a reunified Germany, was planning to open its doors to tourists, shortly followed by a reunion of eighty-three of the 125 surviving former Colditz inmates held at the Imperial War Museum, with the Queen Mother in attendance, to mark the forty-fifth anniversary of the liberation of the camp. Gibson Games, meanwhile, in association with Digital Magic, was in the process of releasing an arcade version of the popular 'Escape from Colditz' board game. So great had public interest become in everything connected with the camp that the Colditz Association (the membership of which consisted of former inmates of Oflag IVC interested in keeping up acquaintance with each other) suggested in early 1991 that a new organization made up of knowledgeable enthusiasts— the Colditz Society—be created. Comic virtuoso Stephen Fry, who had grown up reading the escape tales of the 1950s, freely admitted that when writing and filming his parody of the escape films of the period, *Stalag Luft*, in 1993, he had the film version of *The Colditz Story* as well as *The Wooden Horse* firmly in mind. That same year Classic Pictures and Castle Vision released through W. H. Smith a video documentary written, directed, and co-produced by Robert Garofolo in which various Old Colditzians described their experiences on location at the castle. Anglia TV also broadcast a documentary, *Flight from Colditz*, featuring a scale model glider being launched from the castle attic in which the real glider—built but never used—had been constructed. In 1994 the BBC announced that it was reviving the *Colditz* series. The following year another Colditz memoir was published, and the British press continued to follow the trials and tribulations of local and regional governments in Germany as they tried to work out how to pay for the restoration of the castle itself. Obituaries unfailingly highlighted the fact that the recently deceased had been a prisoner at Oflag IVC, while throughout the 1990s the wartime stories and current doings of those still living were considered newsworthy.[51]

After a period of uncertainty Channel 4 gave Windfall Films the green light in the late 1990s to proceed with a three-part television documentary that, through interviews, on-site simulations, and visits by former inhabitants to the castle, would retell the story of Oflag IVC. Henry Chancellor and others involved in the production were anxious to distance themselves from what some former prisoners saw as the overly jolly picture of events painted by Pat Reid—who died in 1990—that had been further exaggerated in the 1955 film *The Colditz Story*. The sheer boredom of being a POW was stressed, along with the risk of mental instability, the presence of men not all that keen on trying to escape themselves, and an episode in which one British inmate was almost lynched as a traitor. But the central theme—albeit from a more international perspective—was still breaking out, as the overall title, *Escape from Colditz*, clearly indicated. Channel 4 underlined the point by commissioning the building of a full-scale replica of the famous glider, the test flight of which, heavily covered in the press, occurred as the new series was being broadcast. First aired in January–February 2000, *Escape from Colditz* was a success with critics and public alike. Although some reviewers acknowledged the revisionist elements in the documentary programme, others lauded its makers for underlining the ingenuity, courage, and sheer tenacity of the youthful heroes whose exploits they had read about and seen on screen for up to half a century. John Preston, writing for the *Sunday Telegraph*, found it a 'wistful, funny, and moving' evocation of the Colditz Myth. 'It's a *Boy's Own* story, of course,' he went on, '—plucky Brits, wily Frenchmen, "good" Germans—and having lapped it up in childhood I find I'm just as susceptible to it in (early) middle age.'[52]

By the autumn of 2000 the BBC was ready to broadcast its own commissioned documentary. 'I grew up with films like *The Great Escape* and vividly remember the BBC television series *Colditz*', explained Michael Davies, who wrote and directed for Hartswood Films, adding that the true story of what went on in Stalag Luft III and Oflag IVC was even more riveting than the fictional versions. Entitled *The War Behind the Wire*, this interview-centred documentary came in two parts, the first dealing with the Great Escape and the second with Colditz. Both the series and the accompanying book by Patrick Wilson were well received.[53]

Colditz continued to be a name to conjure with in the first years of the twenty-first century. Cassell published a mass-market paperback version of *The Colditz Story* in its military classics series in February 2001. 'I read this book years ago and was enthralled then', noted a satisfied customer.

'My son finds this book as gripping as I did twenty years ago.' For young teens experiencing difficulties in reading—and who therefore would find the original text too hard—Christopher Martin produced a simplified, condensed, and heavily illustrated version of the tale under the title *Escape From Colditz* that was published in April as part of the Collins Soundbites series. Henry Chancellor, the researcher behind the series for Channel 4, used his findings as the basis for a book previewed in the *Daily Mail* at the end of July and published by Hodder & Stoughton— the firm that had originally handled the first two Reid books—under the title *Colditz: The Definitive History* in August. This too proved to be a great success. 'If you are keen on history and man's ability to tough it out in the face of adversity,' as one enthusiastic reader put it, then this new iteration of the Colditz story 'has to be on your list of books that you must read.' In October 2001 Big Finish Productions released an episode of their post-BBC audio *Doctor Who* series in which the Tardis ends up inside Oflag IVC, and in December Caxton Editions published a lavishly illustrated volume entitled *Colditz: A Pictorial History*. Four months later a Coronet paperback edition of *Colditz: The Definitive History* was re-leased, followed in May 2002 by a softcover reissue of *Colditz: The Full Story*. In August of the same year Severn House released the latest popular war-is-hell novel by Leo Kessler (a.k.a. Charles Whiting), *Murder in Colditz*. Following the success of their reissue of *The Colditz Story*, Cassell put out their version of the sequel under the title *The Latter Days at Colditz* in April 2003. ITV, meanwhile, announced that produc-tion would begin in the autumn on a two-part drama that would focus on the Airey Neave escape. Almost sixty years after the existence of Oflag IVC was terminated, and even as the few remaining ex-prisoners are starting to pass away, the Colditz industry continues to thrive, complete with a range of books, home-viewing versions of films and documentaries, several types of games, and organized tours to explore the castle itself.

The reasons for, and the extent of, the popular fascination with Colditz have varied somewhat over time. In addition to nostalgia for fading glory in the 1950s, there was the 'now it can be told' factor, the public lapping up positive portrayals of heroic episodes, especially when presented in entertaining fashion, of a war about which little was yet known beyond the general outlines. During the 1960s the solid virtues the story embodied became less fashionable in an increasingly youth-oriented culture. By the 1970s there was perhaps a greater yearning after an idealized 'lost world'; nostalgia for a time when Britain was still a world power, the country was not plagued by inflation and industrial unrest, and those now in middle age were still youthful. This was matched by a new wave of interest among those too young to feel the need to rebel against the values of a bygone age. In the 1990s, just as the castle itself began to assume a more tangible form as the Iron Curtain gave way, there was a growing trans-generational realization that the time available for those who had fought in the war to renew acquaintance with old comrades and to tell their stories, whether in print, on tape, or on film, was becoming decidedly short.[55]

The core of popular interest over the decades, though, has to do with the nature of the tale itself. 'Escape stories are bound to succeed,' as one reviewer of the *Latter Days* put it, '—for the good reason that they tell of ordinary men . . . who have risen to heights of daring or ingenuity or mere bare-faced bluff in their endeavours to regain their freedom.' They were individuals who had human qualities that those who read about or watched films on their exploits could both admire and hope that they too possessed. Their stories were also straightforward morality tales, in which apparently helpless captives outmanoeuvred their supposedly omnipotent captors. This David-versus-Goliath aspect, of courage in the face of adversity and the beating of odds, appealed to the British self-image in relation to the Second World War, while the goal—personal freedom—was one with which anyone could identify.[56]

Yet this was true of all escape stories, not just those set in Oflag IVC. What was it that made Colditz *primus inter pares*? The striking exterior appearance of the castle itself, as compared to the drab if not positively identikit look of hut-and-wire compounds, may have had some influence. It may also have helped that Oflag IVC contained a relatively small number of prisoners attempting a relatively wide range of breakout methods. 'It's on a small enough scale that people can grasp it', one of the wartime inhabitants of the castle, Peter Storie-Pugh, later observed. Those who were at Colditz, however, tended to think that it was the boyish and hugely appealing way in which Pat Reid framed the story that was at the root of the Colditz phenomenon. This was a collective opinion fully supported by the objective evidence of the ongoing popularity of books first published in the early 1950s. It was the success of *The Colditz Story* and its sequel, moreover, that allowed for the making of the even more popular film version, while the success of both books and film served as the initial selling-point for the wildly popular fictionalized TV drama series of the early 1970s. In turn, the BBC's *Colditz* programmes, as well as the film seen on television and the paperbacks still being regularly reissued, spurred on those who would examine the story anew in documentary form at the end of the 1990s. Successive iterations of the story have introduced certain revisionist elements. Yet, as both critics and enthusiasts usually acknowledge, the popular image of the place remains rooted in the manner in which Pat Reid originally portrayed the castle. Indeed, there were indications that as late as 2003 his books were still outselling all others on Colditz.[57]

Hence the dominance of a particular set of images of British prisoner life in Germany within the collective imagination, in which high spirits and escape attempts are constant factors. But is this mental picture album entirely accurate? Or it is it closer to being a myth that 'abolishes the complexity of human acts' and instead 'gives them the simplicity of essences'? As the following chapters will show, the POW experience both in the Reich as a whole and inside Oflag IVC itself was quite varied, and differed significantly in key respects from what has become received popular wisdom.[58]

Notes

1. Michael Hall, *The Times*, 6 Jan. 1974.
2. UNB, MS L35, David H. Walker Papers, box 1, series 2, file 3, Moran to Walker, 17 Oct. 1981.
3. Henry Chancellor, *Colditz: The Definitive History* (London, 2001) (Chancellor distanced himself from the rather provocative subtitle—which may have been thought up by the publisher—in the preface, p. xiv); P. R. Reid, *Colditz: The Full Story* (London, 1984). Approximately 10% of all ex-POW memoirs and diaries published in the UK have been by former inhabitants of Colditz; around 30% of all published memoirs and diaries by former officer prisoners come from the men of Colditz.
4. Margaret Duggan, Introduction to *Padre in Colditz* (London, 1978), 5; see Harald Husemann, 'The Colditz Industry', in Cedric Cullingford and Harald Husemann (eds.), *Anglo-German Attitudes* (Aldershot, 1995), 141–63.
5. The Wooden Horse and (in particular) the Great Escape have drawn almost as much attention as Colditz. Early best-selling written accounts—Eric Williams, *The Wooden Horse* (London, 1949); Paul Brickhill, *The Great Escape* (London, 1950)—that remain in print were supplemented by further popular accounts over the years (see Bibliography), and reached wide audiences through the success of feature films. Stalag Luft III (Sagan) is only mentioned by name in the opening credits of the film version of *The Wooden Horse* (Wessex, 1950) and not at all in *The Great Escape* (Mirisch-Alpha, 1963). My use of the word 'myth' in this book has been influenced more by Roland Barthes than by either the classical usage or the popular definition in which the word becomes almost a synonym for falsehood.

6. See e.g. *Daily Mirror*, 22 May 1993, 30 May 1994, 5 Aug. 1994, 3 Feb. 1995, 6 Apr. 1995, 4 May 1994, 4 June 1996; 11 June 1997, 23 Mar. 1999; *Sunday Mirror*, 19 Sept. 1999; *Independent*, 8 Sept. 1992, 24 Jan. 2000; *Independent on Sunday*, 13 Feb. 2000; *Daily Telegraph*, 1 May 1991, 14 Aug. 1991, 16 Aug. 1991, 9 June 1992, 1 Jan. 1995, 10 Jan. 1995, 7 Mar. 1995; *Sunday Telegraph*, 6 Feb. 2000; *The Times*, 16 Aug. 1991, 9 Feb. 2000; *Daily Mail*, 27 Apr. 1999, 11 June 1999; 16 Feb. 2000; *Guardian*, 16 Feb. 2000, 18 May 2002; *Scotland on Sunday*, 13 Feb. 2000; see also Anon., *From Colditz to Bangladesh* (Manchester, 1996), 47.

7. *Illustrated London News*, 19 July 1941, p. 84; 26 Sept. 1942, pp. 360–1; 19 June 1943, p. 691; 30 Oct. 1943, pp. 500–1. The drawings were all passed by the German censor before being allowed to be sent to the UK. For words and images designed to reassure relatives and the general public that all was more-or-less well see, e.g. *Illustrated London News*, 13 May 1944, p. 546; War Organisation of the British Red Cross . . . , *Prisoner of War* (London, 1942); id., *The Prisoner of War*, vols. 1–4; War Office, *A Handbook for the Information of Relatives and Friends of Prisoners of War* (HMSO, 1943); Noel Barber, *Prisoner of War* (London, 1944); and D. G. Adams (ed.), *Backwater* (London, 1944). With a few exceptions the replies given to parliamentary questions about POWs were opaque. Colditz, unlike other camps, was never the subject of specific questions. See HC Parl. Deb. 5s. vols. 365–410. On efforts to avoid publicizing camps or escapes, even in fictitious guise, see e.g. Robert Murphy, *British Cinema in the Second World War* (London, 2000), 212. On telling escapers to keep silent about conditions see e.g. P. Paddon, letter, 23 Oct. 1942, in *Colditz Society Newsletter*, 3:20 (June 1999); see also M. R. D. Foot and J. M. Langley, *MI9* (London, 1979), 61. The blackout on hard news concerning POWs, generated in part by earlier public criticism of the handling of matters such as the mail, the exchange of sick and wounded, and reprisals, was such that when the first successful exchange took place in the autumn of 1943 even close relatives of the men concerned were unaware that anything was up. David Rolf, ' "Blind Bureaucracy": The British Government and POWs in German Captivity, 1939–45', in Bob Moore and Kent Fedorowich (eds.), *Prisoners of War and Their Captors in World War II*, (Oxford, 1996), 61. It is interesting to note, in an exception that proves the rule, that once in 1941 the Schloss was described—in quotation marks within a caption but without explanation—as 'the notorious IVC'. See *Illustrated London News*, 4 Oct. 1941, p. 418.

8. A. J. Evans, *Escape and Liberation, 1940–1945* (London, 1945), 45–6. Fowler was killed in action in 1944, which suggests that Evans either drew on the memories of his companions or, more likely in view of the speed with which the book was completed, condensed what he had read in MI9 escaper debriefing reports (e.g. Fowler's own—PRO, WO 208/3311, MI9/S/PG(G)994). For Michael Burn's dispatches see *The Times*, 19 Apr., 21 Apr. 1945. An account on the flight of the *Prominente* from Colditz by Captain the Master of Elphinstone was also published in *The Times*, 19 May 1945.

9. J. E. R. Wood (ed.), *Detour* (London, 1946), acknowledgements, 2; see IWMSA 4432/9, H. Gee.

10. *Manchester Guardian*, 5 Apr. 1946, p. 3; *Times Literary Supplement*, 30 Mar. 1946, p. 149; also 15 Aug. 1952, p. 531. See Michael Burn, *Yes, Farewell* (London, 1946), imprint page, contents page; BL catalogue *re* reprints.

11. *Whittaker's Books in Print* (London, 1949–90 editions); Hal May (ed.), *Contemporary Authors*, *111* (Detroit, 1984), 512; Susan M. Trosky (ed.), *Contemporary Authors*, *134* (Detroit, 1992), 80; http://www.bl.uk, catalogue entries; Husemann, op. cit., 145. The film version of *The Wooden Horse* was also a great success. See *Kinematograph Weekly*, 14 Dec. 1950, pp. 9–10.

12. P. R. Reid, *The Colditz Story* (London, 1952), 11, 19, 17; BBC, T60/9/1, K. Smith precis of talk with P. Reid, 4. That Reid sought to emulate the style of the Great War escape-story authors is suggested not only by his mentioning his favourite books in the prologue but also by the much more restrained tone employed in later books such as *Colditz: The Full Story*, published by Macmillan in 1984, and *Prisoner of War*, co-authored with Maurice Michael and published by Hamlyn the same year.

13. *Daily Telegraph*, 1 Aug. 1952, p. 6; *Manchester Guardian*, 2 Sept. 1952, p. 4; review excerpts, P. R. Reid, *The Colditz Story and The Latter Days at Colditz*, Coronet edn. (London, 1985), 1.

14. GL, MS. 16,352/8, Hodder & Stoughton, P. R. Reid file, John to Reid, 18 June 1954; ibid., *Colditz Story* sales, July 1952—Sept. 1953; ibid., H&S to Reid, 19 Dec. 1952; see *The Times*, 24 May 1990, p. 14. The *TLS* reviewer had recognized that 'these ingenious [escape] schemes are interesting enough in themselves and from them we gain a picture of the Briton at his best': *Times Literary Supplement*, 15 Aug. 1952, p. 531.

15. GL, MS. 16,352/7, letter to R. Douglas Boyd, 17 June 1953. On the election campaign see Paul Routledge, *Public Servant, Secret Agent* (London, 2002), ch. 11. On the radio adaptation see BBC, R19/1252.

16. GL, MS. 16,352/7, Sutton to Bokforlag, 17 Mar. 1953; ibid., FTFF note, E. M. Legatt, 16 Feb. 1954; *Daily Telegraph and Morning Post*, 27 Mar. 1953, p. 8.

17. GL, MS. 16,352/8, Reid to Williams, 10 Nov. 1953; see ibid. H&S to Reid, 5 July 1954; P. R. Reid, *The Latter Days* (London, 1953), 9–10.

18. GL, MS 16,352/8, John to Reid, 18 June 1954; *Times Literary Supplement*, 22 Jan. 1954, p. 60; see *Manchester Guardian*, 11 Dec. 1953, p. 4.

19. G. Hamilton in Brian McFarlane, *An Autobiography of British Cinema* (London, 1997), 274; see GL, MS. 16,352/8, Foxwell to H&S, 18 May 1954. The extent to which Hamilton succeeded in conveying the schoolboyish elements of the Reid stories is evident in an article on 1950s war films by a Film Studies academic in which the film version of *The Colditz Story* is described as 'a Billy Bunter story where Mr. Quelch is a Nazi'. Andy Medhurst, '1950s War Films', in Geoff Hurd (ed.), *National Fictions* (London, 1984), 35.

20. *Kinematograph Weekly*, 15 Dec. 1955, pp. 4–5; *Daily Herald*, 28 Jan. 1955; *Manchester Guardian*, 29 Jan. 1955; *The Times*, 26 Jan. 1955; *Daily Telegraph*, 29 Jan. 1955; *Daily Express*, 28 Jan. 1955; GL, MS. 16,352/8, Reid to Attenborough, 4 Oct. 1954; see also *Spectator*, 28 Jan. 1955; *New Statesman*, 5 Feb. 1955; *Sight and Sound*, 24 (1955), 200. In contrast to the *Guardian*

reviewer, John Minchinton thought that the film plot strayed too far from the book, but admitted that 'Dialogue and acting are in keeping with Reid's stiff upper-lip, public school account'. *Film and Filming*, Mar. 1955, p. 20. On Pat Reid wanting Carol Reid—no relation but then Britain's leading director—see GL, MS. 16,352/8, Reid–Leggatt correspondence, Dec. 1953. On Reid helping Foxwell promote the film, see e.g. LC, Michael Riviere papers, Reid to Riviere, n/d [1954/5]. On Hodder & Stoughton seeking tie-ins see GL, MS. 16,352/8, H&S to Reid, 26 Aug. 1955, H&S memo, n/d [Oct. 1954].

21. On the Neave affair see HLRO, AN/671, draft letter to G. Glaister attachment, Allen to Neave, 29 June 1972; BBC, T60/9/1, K. Smith precis of conversation with A. Neave, 6; CSVA 2, J. Yule. Reid evidently tried to make amends by having Neave relate his own escape in an episode of the 'talking head' series he began fronting for ITV, *Escapers' Club*, early the next year. See *TV Times*, 10 Feb. 1956, p. 23. On the 'silly ass' question see IWMSA 10643/3, P. Welch. On the failure to convey tedium—as well as the too-well-scrubbed-and-dressed appearance of the actors—see CSVA 11, H. Ironside. On getting technical details right see IWMSA 10643/3, P. Welch. On getting details wrong see IWMSA 4432/8, H. Gee. On enjoying the film see IWMSA 16797/4, H. Bruce; CSVA 7, P. Allan. Regarding the knock-on effects of having been a prisoner at Oflag IVC once the place became famous, another Old Colditzian happily remembered how: 'For years after the war you could dine out any day if you happened to have been a prisoner at Colditz.' Walter Morrison, *Flak and Ferrets* (London, 1995), p. viii.

22. Giles Romilly and Michael Alexander, *The Privileged Nightmare* (London, 1954), p. iv.

23. GL, MS. 16,352/8, H&S to Reid, 2 July 1956. On publicity tie-ins and the publisher's efforts to prevent the film's distributor, British Lion, from changing the title of the film during the production phase, see ibid., Leggatt to John, 7 July 1954; JA to Leggatt, 5 July 1954; Leggatt to Jones, 24 Aug. 1954; Osborne to Leggatt, 18 Mar. 1955; Lamb to H&S, 22 Mar. 1955; H&S–Murray correspondence, Feb.–Mar. 1955; H&S to Reid, 27 May 1955.

24. Reinhold Eggers, *Colditz: The German Story* (London, 1961), impressions page; ibid., Pan edn. 1963; IWMSA 4432/6, H. Gee; id. 12658/4, R. Eggers; Airey Neave, *They Have Their Exits*, Pan edn. (London, 1955). Extracts from *They Have Their Exits* also appeared as a chapter entitled 'Escape from Colditz 1942' in Fred Urquart (ed.), *Great True War Adventures* (London, 1957), 163–75. On being approached to write a memoir see IWMSA 4432/3, H. Gee. In the wake of the film even passing mention of having been at Colditz tended to be highlighted in memoir reviews. See e.g. review of Ion Ferguson, *Doctor at War* (London, 1955), in *Times Literary Supplement*, 15 July 1955, p. 403. When the enormously successful screen version of *Reach for the Sky* appeared the following year, director Lewis Gilbert and screenwriter Vernon Harris, despite cutting and condensing much of the best-selling 1954 book of the same name by Paul Brickhill—in which an

entire chapter had been devoted to Bader's time in the castle—included a Watton-style image of the exterior of Colditz with a narration voiceover explaining that Bader 'inevitably' ended up in the castle. The association of Colditz with escape was such by this point that in the original screenplay the film ended with Bader making a home run from the castle: something that, since it did not happen, Bader refused to allow into the film. John Frayn Turner, *The Bader Tapes* (Bourne End, 1986), 68.

25. The credits on the video version of *The Birdmen* (Universal Television, 1971), which was broadcast as an ABC 'Movie of the Weekend' on 18 September 1971, do not acknowledge that the plot, centring on the building of a glider in a castle, was based on events mentioned in Reid's second book. But there can be no question that 'Beckstadt' is Colditz in disguise. On this film see http://www.angelfire.com/wa/birdmen/; http://us.imdb. com/Title?0066833 (accessed 8 Feb. 2003). On the Americanization of *The Great Escape* through casting and plotting see BFI, *The Great Escape* pressbook; *The Times*, 20 June 1963. It is worth noting that in this film the camp is portrayed as being the concentration point for hard-core escapers, something true of Oflag IVC but not of Stalag Luft III.

26. BBC, 4/06869A, Bruce to Storie-Pugh, 10 Sept. 1971; GL, MS. 16,352/8, Reid file, Leggatt memo, 6 Jan. 1956; GL, MS. 16,352/7, Neave file, Leggatt note, 16 Feb. 1954 [concerning readings on the radio from *They Have Their Exits*]. Other BBC appearances included a radio interview of Reid and Eggers in 1961 at the time of the publication of the latter's book. See BBC, 4/06869A, Eggers to Reid, 23 Nov. 1971. On *Escapers' Club* see *TV Times*, 30 Dec. 1955–18 May 1956.

27. Gerard Glaister letter, *Radio Times*, 18 Nov. 1972, 94; IWM (Books), 'A one hour television series based on COLDITZ by P. R. Reid and Ivan Foxwell's film "THE COLDITZ STORY" format for television by Brian Degas & Gerry Glaister' [hereafter Degas and Glaister]. The most obvious parallel was between the character Pat Grant (changed from Patrick Bell in the original scenario) and the real Pat Reid, insofar as both were army officers who served as escape officer at Colditz and eventually made a home run.

28. BBC, 4/06869A, Glaister to Neave, 3 Oct. 1972; *Daily Mail*, 25 Jan. 1973; Degas and Glaister, 3–4, 8, 6, App. B.

29. See http://epguides.com/Colditz/guide.shtml (accessed 29 Jan. 2003). Wagner was cast as an Eagle Squadron pilot.

30. Diana Maychick with L. Avon Borgo, *Heart to Heart With Robert Wagner* (New York, 1986), 96; BBC, 4/06869A, Brolly to Glaister, 14 Apr. 1972; ibid., N. J. Crisp letter, 25 Feb. 1972; see ibid., Reid notes on episodes. On locations and authenticity see ibid., Shepperton sub-file; ibid., 'shot list', Jan. 1972; ibid., Degas to Glaister, 31 May 1972; Glaister letter, *Radio Times*, 18 Nov. 1972, p. 94; Michael Booker, 'Under the Influence of Colditz', *Colditz Society Newsletter*, 3:20 (June 1999), 2.

31. Reid and Glaister quoted in *Daily Mail*, 25 Jan. 1973; Glaister letter in *Radio Times*, 8 Feb. 1973, p. 58; *Television Mail*, 3 Nov. 1972–2 Feb. 1973; BBC, R9/7/119–21, *Colditz* audience research reports; ibid., 4/06869A, Erwin, 24 Nov. 1972; *Observer*, 29 Oct. 1972; see e.g. *Television Mail*, 27 Oct. 1972;

Daily Express, 20 Oct. 1972; *The Listener*, 26 Oct. 1972. On BBC publicity see *Observer*, op. cit.; e.g. *Radio Times*, 12 Oct. 1972.

32. On the rerun see HLRO, Neave Papers, AN 677, Whitaker to Neave, 27 Mar. 1973; *Daily Express*, 18 Apr. 1973. On the appeal of the TV series to younger generations see *Daily Mail*, 25 Jan. 1973. See Giles Romilly and Michael Alexander, *Hostages at Colditz* (London, 1973 edn.); Reinhold Eggers (comp.), *Colditz Recaptured* (London, 1973) (on which see also IWMSA 4432/3, 5, H. Gee); id., *Colditz: The German Story* (London, 1972 edn.). On the sales of Coronet versions of *The Colditz Story*, *The Latter Days*, and *They Have Their Exits* see *National Newsagent*, 24 Aug. 1973.

33. Michael Burn, *Farewell to Colditz* (London, 1974), p. i; Howe and Reid in *Daily Mail*, 25 Jan. 1974; IWMSA 15336/3, J. C. Wilson [*re* 'Tweedledum' episode]; see Campbell letter, *The Times*, 9 Jan. 1974; IWMSA 14781/3, J. Hamilton-Baillie; BBC, Harewood in 'Colditz Under Attack' unidentified newspaper clipping, Jan. 1974; *The Listener*, 2 Nov. 1972, p. 614; BBC, T60/9/1, J. Watton to BBC, 31 May 1973.

34. IWMSA 4432/7, H. Gee; CSVA 2, J. Yule; IWMSA 9721/3, Lord Newborough; ibid., 4816, TS, 44; UNB, MS L35, David H. Walker Papers, box 1, series 1, sub-series 1, file 8, Gilliat to Walker, 19 Dec. 1972. On irritation with dramatic licence see, e.g. BBC, T60/9/1, precis of K. Smith talk with P. Allan, 5; on incredulity at cleanliness and amenities, see e.g. IWMSA 15247/2, D. Hawkins; IWM, G. Betts, 149. Miles Reid thought on reflection that the series did not capture the whole story of Colditz (Miles Reid, *Into Colditz* (Salisbury, 1983), 58), and Michael Burn believed that despite its strengths the series still placed too much emphasis on escape (Burn, op. cit.; see also IWMSA 9247/3, M. Burn). Jock Hamilton-Baillie later expressed the opinion on videotape that the BBC had made Colditz out to be a much harsher place to be than it was. J. Hamilton-Baillie, *The Road to Colditz* (Applecart, 1997). Mike Moran, among others, thought the series rather superficial. See UNB, MS L35, David H. Walker Papers, box 1, series 2, file 3, *Colditz Newsletter*, 5 (Aug. 1982), 3.

35. *The Times*, 4 Jan. 1974; (Times Diary), 7 Jan. 1974, 10. On the BBC-sponsored return visit to Colditz see *Radio Times*, 3 Jan. 1974, cover, pp. 72–5. The exhibition was, apparently, among the most popular that the IWM had ever mounted. See UNB, MS L35, David H. Walker Papers, box 1, series 2, file 3, *Colditz Newsletter*, 5 (Aug. 1982), 5. It is only fair to note that others present did not appear to notice any disillusionment (see e.g. *Daily Express*, 4 Jan. 1974), and that other reunions unconnected with the series, including one at the IWM held to mark the fortieth anniversary of the liberation of Colditz, witnessed grousing by former prisoners at the state of the modern world. See e.g. Jim Rogers, *Tunnelling into Colditz* (London, 1986), 203; UNB, MS L35, David H. Walker Papers, box 1, series 2, file 3, circular letter from M. Moran, 15 July 1981.

36. *The Times*, 8 Jan. 1974, 12; IWMSA 4432/4, H. Gee. On his own experience in Germany see Jerome Caminada, *My Purpose Holds* (London, 1952).

37. *The Times*, 8 Jan. 1974, 7. On the 1955 film and Billy Bunter see Medhurst, op. cit.

38. On the anti-German living-in-the-past argument see *Sunday Telegraph*, 3 Feb. 1974 [Brook-Sheppard]; *The Times*, 14 Jan. 1974 [Furlong letter]. On the reaction to the Caminada article see *The Times*, 19 Jan. 1974 [Caminada]; see also ibid., 9 Jan. 1974 [Campbell]; HLRO, Neave papers, AN 677, Neave–Darling correspondence, Jan.–Feb. 1974. On the *Two Ronnies* sketch see Ronnie Barker, *It's Goodnight from Him* (London, 1976), 52–61.

39. HLRO, Neave Papers, AN 677, Neave to Allen, 18 Aug. 1972; see ibid., draft letter to BBC, n/d, Allen to Neave, 29 June 1972, Neave to Allen, 25 June 1972.

40. BBC, 4/06869A, Glaister to Neave, 3 Oct. 1972.

41. *Daily Telegraph*, 21 Jan. 1974; *Daily Express*, 21 Jan. 1974; *Evening Standard*, 21 Jan. 1974; *Daily Mail*, 21 Jan. 1971; see HLRO, Neave Papers, AN 677, press clippings; BBC, T60/9/1, precis of K. Smith talk with P. Reid, 4.

42. *Yorkshire Evening Post*, 21 Jan. 1974 [Glaister]; *Daily Express*, 21 Jan. 1972 [BBC spokesman].

43. *Yorkshire Evening Post*, 28 Jan. 1974; *News of the World*, 27 Jan. 1972; *Daily Mirror*, 28 Jan. 1972. Eggers did allow that the tough-but-respected on-screen security officer, Hauptmann Ulmann, as played by Hans Meyer, was 'a bit like me'. Jimmy Yule, who had liked the first series, disliked the second because of the insertion of an entirely fictional German character, Major Mohn. CSVA 2, J. Yule.

44. HLRO, Neave Papers, AN 677, Neave to Darling, 4 Feb. 1974.

45. BBC, R 9/7/128, Audience Research Report, VR74/219, Colditz, 17 June 1974; see ibid., VR 74/32, 89, 118, 202, 219; *Broadcast*, 4 Feb. 1974, 18 Feb. 1974, 22 Apr. 1974; *Daily Express*, 28 Jan. 1974. Interviews with six Old Boys broadcast immediately following the first half-dozen episodes of the second series were also well received. See BBC, T60/9/1, VR/73/318, et al.

46. On the Airfix model see *Colditz: A Pictorial History* (London, 2001), 182–3. On press interest in the castle itself see e.g. *The Scotsman*, 8 Feb. 1975; *Yorkshire Post*, 19 Mar. 1974. On Colditz as metaphor, see e.g. *The Times*, 21 Jan. 1974, p. 12. On escape compilations see e.g. Donald McCormack, *The Master Book of Escapes* (London, 1974). See Michael Burn, 'Why I didn't break out of Colditz', *Observer Colour Supplement*, 3 Nov. 1974, pp. 26–9; id., *Farewell to Colditz* (London, 1974).

47. On the bombing see Routledge, op. cit., 1–18, 303–62. On sales see Martin Gilbert, *Sunday Times Magazine*, 23 Apr. 1978, p. 83. Margaret Duggan (ed.), *Padre in Colditz* (London, 1978); Harry Patterson, *The Valhalla Exchange* (London, 1976)—on the Colditz connection see Lord Harewood, *The Tongs and Old Bones* (London, 1981), 56; E. H. Larive, *The Man Who Came in from Colditz* (London, 1975); P. R. Reid (ed.), *My Favourite Escape Stories* (London, 1975). John L. Foster, *Catapulting from Colditz* (London, 1982); Ray Baybutt, *Camera in Colditz* (London, 1982). A desire to give Colditz the kind of prominence in France it enjoyed in Britain prompted André Perrin to write *Évade de guerre via Colditz*, published by Pensee Universelle in Paris in 1975 (p 12). This was followed by a number of other memoirs by French prisoners and a popular history. See Bibliography.

48. The memoirs of the 1980s were: Harewood, op. cit.; Jack Champ and Colin Burgess, *The Diggers of Colditz* (Sydney, 1985); Miles Reid, *Into Colditz* (Salisbury, 1983); Jack Pringle, *Colditz Last Stop* (London, 1988); David Walker, *Lean, Wind, Lean* (London, 1984). See Baybutt, op. cit. On the Tony Barber Colditz computer game see http://www.lysator.liu.se/adventure/Phipps_Associates.html (accessed 19 Sept. 2002); http://www.nonwt.com/magfold/revsfol/colditz.html (accessed 17 Sept. 2002). The volume of material in English associated with Colditz by 1980 prompted several former Dutch inmates of the castle to ask Leo De Hartog to write a history of Dutch POWs, which was eventually published under the title *Officieren achter Prikkeldraad, 1940–1945* (Baarn, 1983) (see p. 11). The Colditz phenomenon was such that in the following decade it was thought that the rather less *Boy's Own*-style Belgian experience ought to be chronicled. See Didier Pontzeele, *Krijgsgevangen! Belgische officieren in het kastell van Colditz 1940–1943* (Erpe, 2000), 9.

49. UNB, MS L35, David H. Walker Papers, box 1, series 2, file 3, *Colditz Association Newsletter* 9 (Nov. 1984), 3; ibid., *Newsletter* 7 (Nov. 1983), 1, 3; ibid., *Newsletter* 5 (Aug. 1982), 3; ibid., box 1, file 6, Moran to Walker, 3 Sept. 1984.

50. *After the Battle* 69 (1989); P. R. Reid, *Colditz: The Colditz Story and the Latter Days at Colditz* (London, 1986); cover of 1985 Arrow Books version of P. R. Reid, *Colditz: The Full Story* (London, 1984); Clive Gifford, *Escape from Colditz* (London, 1986); *Times Literary Supplement*, 22 Mar. 1985, pp. 330–1; UNB, MS L35, David H. Walker Papers, box 1, series 2, file 3, *Colditz Association Newsletter*, 8 (June 1984), 6; BBC, T60/9/1, precis of K. Smith talk with P. Reid, 4.

51. See e.g. *Guardian*, 25 Feb. 1998, 27 Feb. 1992; *Guardian Weekend*, 13 Mar. 1993; *Mirror*, 28 Oct. 1998, 5 May 1995, 2 June 1993; *Sunday Telegraph*, 5 Oct. 1997; *Sunday Times*, 12 Feb. 1995; *Daily Telegraph*, 21 Nov. 1997, 14 Dec. 1995, 11 Mar. 1995, 26 Feb. 1995, 25 Nov. 1991; *The Times*, 6 June 1997, 4 Feb. 1997, 24 May 1996, 13 Apr. 1995, 3 Nov. 1993, 10 Oct. 1990. On the BBC announcement concerning the revival of the series see *The Times*, 10 Oct. 1994. The memoir was Walter Morrison's *Flak and Ferrets* (London, 1995). On Stalag Luft and Colditz see *Mirror*, 23 Oct. 1993 (see also Stephen Fry, *Moab Is My Washpot* (London, 1997), 128–9). On the origins of the Colditz Society see Michael Booker, 'In the Beginning', *Colditz Society Newsletter*, 3:25 (June 2001), 3. On the Gibson computer game see http://www.nostalgica.nu/e/escape_from_colditz.html (accessed 19 Sept. 2002); http://www.jgb.abelgratis.co.uk/data/e/escco.html (accessed 19 Sept. 2002). See *Colditz* (Classic Pictures & Castle Vision, 1993), (reissued in 1999 under the title *The Story of Colditz*). On Colditz opening its doors to tourists see *The Times*, 30 Mar. 1990; William Cash, 'Escape to Colditz', *Spectator*, 7 Apr. 1990, pp. 14–15.

52. *Sunday Telegraph*, 6 Feb. 2000; see *The Times*, 8 Feb. 2000; *Daily Mail*, 1 Feb. 2000; *Mail on Sunday*, 6 Feb. 2000; *Independent on Sunday*, 30 Jan. 2000. On the development of the programme see the *Independent on Sunday* article; http://www.cambridge-news.co.uk/archives/2002/05/03/coverstory.html

(accessed 6 Feb. 2003). On the glider see *Daily Mail*, 3 Feb. 2000; *Telegraph*, 3 Feb. 2000; *Independent*, 3 Feb. 2000; Channel 4 web pages, 2000.

53. Michael Davies preface to Patrick Wilson, *The War Behind the Wire* (Barnsley, 2000), 7; see *New Statesman*, 12 Feb. 2001, pp. 55–6; *Spectator*, 18 Nov. 2000, p. 81.

54. http://www.waveguide.co.uk/latest/news030220.htm (accessed 20 Feb. 2003); http://www.ciao.co.uk/Colditz_The_Definitive_History_Review_5286545 (accessed 6 Feb. 2003); http://www.amazon.co.uk/exec/obidos/ASIN/0304358126/qid=10446.../202-5975051-174142, Calgary reader (accessed 7 Feb. 2003). On the Chancellor book see also *Guardian*, 19 Oct. 2002; http:www.amazon.co.uk/exec/obidos/tg/stores/detail/-/books/03407.../202-5975051-174142 (accessed 6 Feb. 2003). On tours see, e.g., http://www.battlefieldtours.co.uk; http://www.chemnitz.de/colditz/ccc.htm (accessed 19 Sept. 2002). Games include *Prisoner of War* (Atari, 2002) and *Skedaddle!* (Crowhurst Games [Canada], c.1995). See P. R. Reid, *The Latter Days at Colditz* (London, 2003 edn.); Leo Kessler, *Murder at Colditz* (Sutton, 1992); P. R. Reid, *Colditz: The Full Story* (London, 2002 edn.); Henry Chancellor, *Colditz: The Definitive History*, Coronet paperback (London, 2002); *Colditz: A Pictorial History* (London, 2001); *Doctor Who: Colditz* (Big Finish Productions, 2001); Henry Chancellor, *Colditz: The Definitive History* (London, 2001); Christopher Martin, *Escape From Colditz* (London, 2001); P. R. Reid, *The Colditz Story*, Cassell Military Classics (London, 2001 edn.). On the Finnish hard-rock band 'Colditz'—a name inspired by the 1970s BBC drama series—see http://personal.inet.fi/koti/colditz/eg/band.html (accessed 17 Sept. 2002). Colditz has been enlisted too by psychotherapists. See Bill Thorndycraft, 'The Colditz Syndrome: The Need to Escape from Group Therapy', *Group Analysis*, 34 (2001), 273–86.

55. On the 1990s see e.g. Chancellor, op. cit., pp. xv–xvi; http://www.cambridge-news.co.uk/archives/2002/05/03/coverstory.html (accessed 6 Feb. 2003); Michael Farr, *Vanishing Borders* (London, 1991), 48–62; G. Davies-Scourfield in *Colditz Society Newsletter*, 3:22 (Mar. 2000), 7; 'An Afternoon with Pat Fergusson', *Colditz Society Newsletter*, 2:21 (Oct. 1999), 2. On the 1970s see e.g. *The Times*, 19 Jan. 1974, 7 Jan. 1974; *Daily Telegraph*, 23 Jan. 1974; *Sunday Mirror*, 3 Feb. 1974; BBC, Audience Research reports on *Colditz*; see also Rogers, op. cit., 203–10. On factors behind the popularity of 1950s war cinema, including POW films, see Guy Ramsden, 'Refocusing "The People's War": British War Films of the 1950s', *Journal of Contemporary History*, 33 (1998), 59; Bryan Forbes, *A Divided Life* (London, 1992), 310; Brian McFarlane, *An Autobiography of British Cinema* (London, 1997), 191, 221, 307; Murphy, op. cit., 233–6.

56. *Times Literary Supplement*, 22 Jan. 1954; see P. Storie-Pugh in *The Colditz Story* (Classic Pictures, 1993); *Telegraph*, 8 Jan. 1974; Duggan, op. cit., 5; Interviewer comment in CSVA 7, P. Allan; H. Bruce in CSVA 3; B. Norman in *Daily Express*, 2 May 2000; Ken Worpole, *Dockers and Detectives* (London, 1983), 54; Samuel Hynes, *The Soldier's Tale* (New York, 1997), 236–7. See also http://www.britishcouncil.org/studies/england/report_14.htm (accessed 20

Feb. 2003), N. Cull, 'The Great Escape of the Self-Preservation Society: Englishness in popular war and crime films', 1–2.

57. P. Storie-Pugh in *The Colditz Story* (Classic Pictures, 1993). On sales of the Reid books as against other Colditz titles see http://www.amazon.co.uk. On the influence of the Reid books and the 1955 film in spurring on Henry Chancellor see http://www.cambridge-news.co/uk/archives/2002/05/03/coverstory.html (accessed 6 Feb. 2003). On the influence of the BBC drama series on Michael Davies see his preface to Wilson, op. cit., 7. (The series also inspired an online homoerotic novel in the 1990s: see http://www.slashfic.co.uk (accessed 19 Sept. 2002), 'The First Duty'.) On the influence of Pat Reid see also David Dunn, 'A Tribute to Pat Reid', *Colditz Society Newsletter*, 1:10 (Jan. 1995), 5; *The Times*, 24 May 1990. On acknowledgement by other Old Colditzians—who were not always too happy with the results—that it was Pat Reid who was really responsible for the Colditz phenomenon see: CSVA 7, P. Allan; ibid., 11, H. Ironside; IWMSA 9247/3, C. Burn; ibid., 14781/3, J. Hamilton-Baillie. See also Champ and Burgess, op. cit., 8; On a sense that Colditz had been overwritten see IWMSA 17896/3, W. C. Purdon; ibid., 4820/2, C. Scarborough; see also Jane Torday (ed.), *The Coldstreamer and the Canary* (Langley, 1995), 54–5. Regarding the ongoing success of the Colditz Industry one might add that the fact that the Schloss was still standing at the end of the Cold War, while other camps had been destroyed or left to rot away to nothing over the years, certainly did the Colditz phenomenon no harm, allowing for on-site interviews and camera explorations for documentary purposes through the 1990s and beyond that were impossible to match. Its towering presence also offers the prospect of ready-made locations for any future motion picture, as against the costs involved in building huge sets in the manner of *The Great Escape* (on which see 'Return to the Great Escape' documentary attached to MGM DVD version of film).

58. Roland Barthes, *Mythologies*, trans. A. Lavers (London, 1972), 143.

1 Capture and Interrogation

Prisoners [on capture]...must not be threatened, insulted, or exposed to unpleasantness or disadvantages of any kind whatsoever.

(from Article 5, Geneva Convention, 1929)

No pressure shall be exercised on prisoners to obtain information regarding the situation in their armed forces or their country.

(from Article 5, Geneva Convention, 1929)

The point of departure for *The Colditz Story* is the moment at which the author begins to think about breaking out. The classic Great War yarns Pat Reid had read in his youth focused on escapes, as did the most successful of the new generation of prisoner-of-war books that appeared around the time he was writing his own memoir. And if it was escape attempts from Germany that people wanted to read about—as opposed to being caught by surprise and herded into the Reich under ignominious circumstances—then it was logical to pass over the preliminaries in silence.[1]

To completely ignore capture and the journey into captivity in the interests of the escape narrative was to go a step further than other authors of breakout tales, most of whom, while emphasizing escape, at least touched on what had gone on before. From a commercial standpoint the move proved to be sound, as the success of *The Colditz Story* both in print and on screen indicated. Skipping the preliminaries, however, also meant ignoring what were often among the most life-threatening and endurance-testing periods in the lives of captured British servicemen during the Second World War.[2]

In theory, all that needed to happen in order for a British serviceman to become a recognized German prisoner of war, with all the concomitant protections accorded him under the terms of the 1929 Geneva Convention, was to cease fighting and indicate to the opposition that he wished to surrender. In practice, this could prove to be a difficult and in some cases lethal stage in encounters with the enemy.[3]

Soldiers giving up singly or in small groups, especially while fighting in the area continued, ran a very real risk of being killed out of hand rather than having their surrender accepted. In the heat of battle it could be difficult for enemy troops to adjust to the idea that those who shortly before had been their mortal foes were now, in essence, seeking their protection.[4]

A sergeant major of the Royal Norfolk Regiment, for instance, sent out with a white flag to signal a willingness to end his company's stout defence of a farmhouse on the road to Dunkirk in late May 1940, was almost immediately mown down. In the course of the hard-fought battle for Crete a year later, German paratroopers shot dead individual soldiers and airmen as they emerged from their dugouts and trenches to give themselves up. Survivors of the sinking of HMS *Gloucester*, meanwhile, were strafed from the air as they clung helplessly to pieces of wreckage. The first attempt to surrender among the unharmed on the beach at Dieppe in the wake of the intense battle of 19 August 1942—a man stepping out from behind a wrecked landing craft, waving a white handkerchief after firing had died down—was met at once with rifle fire. In the Normandy campaign in June and July 1944, especially in periods of intense fighting, there were many documented instances of the shooting or bayoneting of wounded men in overrun positions, as well as the murder of individuals who walked forward towards the enemy with their hands up.[5]

Luckier men recalled how fortunate they had been in the first moments after a violent encounter. Second Lieutenant J. T. Stevenson (Manchester Regiment), after trying to run a German roadblock near Dunkirk in May 1940, got the impression that the panzer troops who took him and his men from their crashed truck were ready to kill. Corporal C. W. Jervis (Oxfordshire and Buckinghamshire Light Infantry), wounded by a grenade as his position was overrun in a sharp firefight in Belgium earlier the same month, escaped death by a hairsbreadth:

The Germans came over the top and one big German stopped by me, and put his rifle in my face, and I thought 'He is going to shoot me.' I then said 'Have a cigarette,' which he took and put in his pocket. He then put the rifle back in my face, so I took the tin and said 'You take the cigarettes.' He put them in his pocket, then shouted 'Churchill Swinehund'. Then he kicked me in the head . . .

Jervis 'saw stars' but was no longer in danger of his life. Conan Purdon, a Commando officer who eventually ended up at Colditz, recalled in an interview how 'touch and go' the situation was for prisoners confronted by keyed-up troops in the immediate aftermath of the St-Nazaire raid in March 1942.[6]

Even if not killed outright, prisoners could still be in grave peril in the period immediately after capture. The threat of vengeance for the loss of friends or family could be present, or it might be believed—rightly or wrongly—that the rules of war were being broken by the enemy in a way that required no quarter to be given even after surrender.

Private Frederick Ayers, captured in a farmhouse near Wattau with dozens of others from the his unit at the end of May 1940, saw the mood—hitherto quite civilized—suddenly turn ugly when a forgotten grenade was discovered in one unfortunate prisoner's pocket during the initial search. 'He was taken away and stood against a wall as the Germans were quite convinced he had left it purposely, to harm them.' Lance-Corporal George Dunning, captured the same day as Fred Ayers elsewhere in the retreat to Dunkirk, was lined up against a wall with several other hapless British soldiers by a furious German NCO who took violent exception to the eighteen-inch bayonets they had begun surrendering. The man had evidently decided that these weapons were inhumane, an unofficial stance that was shared on other occasions with respect to edged weapons in general.[7]

Especially among those unfamiliar with the nature of battle wounds and the effects on bodies of exposure, there sometimes arose the conclusion that atrocities had been committed. In the campaign in France and Belgium in 1940 some German units became convinced that the British were firing dum-dum bullets, a type of ammunition banned under international law. This was not in fact the case, but those who fell under suspicion rightly felt that they were at risk.[8]

In some cases RAF pilots who had taken to their parachutes during the Battle of Britain later in 1940 were machine-gunned to death as they hung suspended from their canopies. Some of these incidents were apparently the result of German outrage at reports of RAF attacks on German air-sea rescue planes marked with red crosses.[9]

During the battle for Crete the following year the state of bodies discovered after several days led Germans to conclude that helpless paratroopers had been unmercifully butchered and wounded men murdered. Commonwealth troops as well as Cretan civilians—some of whom had joined in the fight with great ferocity—were held responsible.

In consequence, stories began to circulate on both sides that the Germans were taking no prisoners. No such order was in fact issued, but unnecessary deaths undoubtedly occurred as a result of vengeful sentiment. Amidst the fighting for Maleme aerodrome there was at least one occasion where a furious German NCO made preparations for the execution of a group of captured RAF ground personnel; and at another point a party of forty, mostly RAF, prisoners was used as a human shield. 'We were made to line up with our hands above our heads and advance over the hill in front of the advancing Germans,' Flight Sergeant Harold Wilkinson recalled, 'who threatened us with their sub-machine guns. When we came within view of the British troops, the Germans opened fire from behind us: this fire was returned by our own troops, and I myself saw six or seven of our party killed.'[10]

Stories of Allied misconduct circulated in the Normandy campaign in the summer of 1944, including a rumour that captured panzer troops had been placed so as to prevent firing on British vehicles. Again there was talk of orders to 'take no prisoners' being issued, and this time dozens of instances in which wounded men and recently taken parties of Canadian and British troops were gunned down. Private W. J. Sudworth (Royal Warwickshire Regiment) and other survivors of a sharp baptism of fire on 7 June 1944 found themselves in the hands of SS panzer grenadiers, and had the narrowest of escapes:

They took us into a field, deprived us of all valuables and lined us up to be shot. Fortunately three of our fighter planes came over at that very minute, waggling their wings in recognition. The Germans scattered for cover, but we stood there waving, whilst the planes flew round us in a protective circle. After a while, when it became obvious what they were doing, the Germans came back, gave us our possessions, and herded us off towards their HQ. With a final waggle, the planes departed.

Others were not so lucky. One out of five fatal Canadian Army casualties in the first week in Normandy turned out to be the result of murder behind the lines.[11]

RAF aircrew, having managed to bail out of stricken aircraft, might find themselves during the latter part of the war in the hands of bombed-out German civilians and especially vengeful local officials, prepared not only to rough up captives but also in some cases kill them. After a raid in the summer of 1943, for example, Nazi Party group leader Willi Lüger had four Commonwealth airmen shot near Duisberg on the grounds that they had been bombing women and children. A post-mortem on the body of Sergeant S. J. Price, who had parachuted down from a burning

Lancaster bomber near Pockau, revealed a grisly end, apparently at the hands of a local policeman with the help of two civilians: death through repeated blows to the head from a 'blunt instrument'.[12]

In many cases it was only the intervention of cooler-headed, and usually more senior-ranking, personnel that saved men from being murdered. Fred Ayers and his comrades lived only because a corporal made a case in German that the grenade found in the soldier's pocket had been an oversight. George Dunning's group was saved by the timely arrival of an officer who countermanded the angry NCO's order to shoot. On Crete an execution was delayed, then cancelled, when a German-speaking British corporal insisted that the paratroopers get orders from an officer before they mowed down helpless men. Lieutenant-Commander Billie Stephens, who was eventually sent to Colditz, found himself lined up against a church wall along with other survivors of the St-Nazaire raid. Only the arrival of an officer 'roaring orders' to the guards menacing the group with machine-guns saved the day: 'I was very frightened', Stephens later admitted.[13] Such cases continued down to the end of the war. Private John Woods (Royal Norfolk Regiment) had a very close shave at a German first-aid post near Kervenheim in March 1945: '[One] of the Gerries standing nearby came over and flicked the safety catch on his rifle, presumably with the intention of shooting me. The officer grabbed the weapon, bawled a lot of authoritarian orders and pushed him away.'[14]

RAF aircrew, meanwhile, were often saved from potentially fatal attacks by enraged civilians, especially in or near cities, by the intervention of responsible Luftwaffe personnel. 'Fortunately,' Flight Sergeant S. C. Masters remembered, of an attempted mob assault on a group of newly captured prisoners being escorted through Frankfurt-am-Main railway station in the summer of 1944, 'the guards did not intend to let us be attacked, as loading their weapons, they told the crowd they would open fire if they didn't back off.' His was by no means a unique experience.[15]

Alas, not all authority figures thought or acted humanely when confronted with new POWs. Indeed, on occasion specific orders were issued—some from the very highest quarters—that no surrenders should be accepted and that those prisoners who were taken should be done away with rather than sent to prison camps.

There are documented cases of officers from all the German armed services engaging in such war crimes. Certain Waffen-SS officers—fanatical Nazi Party members with a long history of extreme brutality behind them—stood out, however, with respect to mass murders as acts of revenge. On 27 May 1940 a company commander in the SS *Totenkopf* division oversaw the methodical execution by machine-gun fire and bayonet thrusts of nearly one hundred soldiers of the Royal Norfolk Regiment near Le Paradis. The following day an officer from the SS *Leibstandarte* regiment witnessed the murder of a similar number of prisoners from the Royal Warwickshire Regiment with grenades, pistols, and rifles at Wormhout. Many of the smaller-scale but cumulatively comparable killings in Normandy were carried out on the orders of officers of the SS *Hitler Jugend* division.[16]

Those trying to surrender or newly in custody could also face peril as a result of vengeful instructions emanating from much higher up the ladder. A direct order to the Luftwaffe to shoot at RAF crewmen parachuting from stricken aircraft was apparently contemplated at one point, but happily never implemented; and few outright murders seem to have arisen from an instruction issued in 1942 by the chief of the submarine fleet forbidding U-boats from assisting survivors of ships they attacked, in retaliation for an incident in which a submarine on a mercy mission was sunk. 'Be harsh,' Admiral Dönitz had forcefully concluded: 'Remember that the enemy takes no regard of women and children in his bombing attacks on German cities.'[17] It was these air raids, however, increasingly destructive in the following years, which prompted efforts by senior Nazis such as Himmler and Bormann to encourage the murder of Allied 'terror fliers' once they had reached the ground. 'An eye for an eye, a tooth for a tooth', as propaganda minister Joseph Goebbels put it.[18] Some of these moves, including several by the Führer himself, were sidetracked or derailed by those in the high command and elsewhere who were worried about Allied retaliation.[19] But enough newspaper pieces and party orders were circulated to allow for a noticeable increase in the number of fatal encounters between downed airmen and local officialdom in the last year of the war. In mid-September 1944, to take just one of many documented incidents, Hans Renoth, a policeman, arrested a downed bomber pilot and then connived in having the man 'attacked and beaten with fists and rifles by a number of people'. Renoth then shot the pilot dead.[20] More than a hundred British and Commonwealth aircrew appear to have lost their lives as a direct or indirect result of such encouragement.[21]

Another group at particular risk due to orders from higher authority in the latter half of the war were members of small-scale raiding parties or those servicemen attached in a liaison or training role to resistance forces. Responding to the sometimes semi-clandestine nature and supposed underhandedness of 'so-called commandos', Hitler in the autumn of 1942 issued orders demanding that in future all such enemies of the Reich should be 'slaughtered to the last man'. This secret 'commando order', reiterated several times over the next two years, was in some instances buried in bureaucratic red tape or simply ignored by commanders on the spot. On other occasions, however, especially when it was thought that the parties concerned had somehow been acting contrary to the rules of war, the Führer's wishes were carried out. Often the military authorities simply handed captured men over to the security services for disposal.[22] The first of over one hundred Allied servicemen to be killed as a result of these orders were seven commandos taken in a raid on a power-plant at Glomfjord, Norway. In an incident not mentioned in *The Colditz Story* or *The Latter Days*, these men were moved to Germany and briefly held at Oflag IVC in early October 1942 before being handed over to the SS and secretly executed.[23] Lieutenant Michael Alexander, caught in a Special Boat Section raid along the Libyan coast, was convinced that he ended up at Colditz permanently rather than being put in front of a firing squad as a 'vulgar saboteur' only because he claimed a close blood relationship with the GOC Middle East, General Sir Harold Alexander.[24]

Happily, the majority of those servicemen who surrendered did not lose their lives. In overall terms German armed forces observed both formal and informal conventions surrounding capture with respect to the Western Allies. The odds against being killed in the heat of the moment increased dramatically if a cease-fire was first negotiated by a senior officer, and particularly when large numbers of men were involved. This was the case when it was clear that there was no chance of rescue or relief for the thousands of soldiers trapped against the sea as at, for instance, Calais and St-Valéry in 1940 or Sfakia in 1941. In all, more than 164,000 British and Commonwealth servicemen—over 10,000 of them aircrew—successfully passed into German hands in Europe.[25]

German front-line troops, once the battle had been won and the firing had stopped, could afford to be quite magnanimous in the years of victory. The standard reciting of the phrase 'for you the war is over', in English or German, could easily be followed by friendly rather than hostile gestures.[26]

As in the case of Wing Commander Douglas Bader, the famous legless air ace and future Colditz inmate brought down over France in a Spitfire during the summer of 1941, aircrew might find themselves honoured guests of local Luftwaffe units. Sergeant Richard Passmore, for instance, an air gunner whose Blenheim was downed near Wilhelmshaven in July 1940, was taken to a nearby flak unit, put up in the officers' mess, given breakfast, and shaken warmly by the hand on departure.[27]

There was also chivalry at sea. In April 1941 in the Caribbean, for example, the German raider *Vir*, having sunk the converted merchantman HMS *Voltaire*, stopped to search for survivors, her crew shooting at circling sharks, despite the danger posed to the ship by remaining in the area. After an exchange of salutes the rescued captain of the *Voltaire* thanked his opponent for 'saving our lives ... at some risk to yourselves'.[28]

Those picked up from the water were almost always initially treated as shipwrecked fellow sailors in need of aid rather than as hostile captives. Leading Telegraphist John Wilkins, who would eventually become an orderly at Colditz, remembered the treatment he and other survivors of the submarine *Starfish* received aboard a German destroyer in January 1940:

Anyone who couldn't climb on board they assisted and we were taken below ship to a large room with bunk beds. Bread, butter, bully beef and schnapps were handed out. We took it in turns to go to the engine room and dry our clothes. Later small groups of us were taken to the German officers' mess [where there were Kriegsmarine types] who gave us each a cognac. We had a good time and they were very friendly.

The following year Surgeon Commander Hugh Singer and other survivors of HMS *Gloucester*, after their ordeal at the hands of the Luftwaffe, were looked for and eventually spotted by a German rescue craft after many hours in the water. 'Once on board,' Singer later reported, 'we were told to strip off our wet things which were to be dried for us and we were each given a dry blanket. We were then sent below to a large cabin occupying most of the after part of the ship. There we were given fresh water and were able to begin the three day job of quenching our thirsts.' As Paymaster James Moran (another man who eventually found his way to Colditz) put it with reference to the crew of the destroyer that picked him and other half-dead survivors up from a lifeboat in July 1941 in the Bay of Biscay: 'they were really good ... '[29]

Surrendering soldiers could also find themselves treated courteously by their erstwhile foes, the sharing of a smoke being an encouraging sign that prisoners would not be killed out of hand. 'After a few minutes, everything was quiet,' Private R. P. Evans later wrote in reference to the surrender of a group from the Worcestershire Regiment near Dunkirk in late May 1940, 'and the Germans visibly relaxed and offered us cigarettes, which action we reciprocated.' This was a scene replicated many times on various battlefields. Private N. L. Francis of the Dorset Regiment, to take another example, instinctively guessed what would be his best course of action when his battalion commander ordered his unit to surrender at Oosterbeek in September 1944. 'I flung the bolt from my rifle into the woods and taking a packet of Woodbines from my pocket, offered one to a couple of our captors', Francis remembered of the moments after capture. 'One jerry gave me one of his fags . . . it broke the ice.'[30]

Even while fighting continued, humane considerations often governed the initial treatment extended to those rendered *hors de combat*. 'I'd been wounded twice when they dropped the paratroopers right on top of us,' Private Ahol Cook, a New Zealander, remembered of the generally quite savage battle for Crete, 'and you can imagine what a slaughterhouse it was':

A first aid station was set up under olive trees for dozens and dozens of German paratroopers and Australian infantrymen, with a German doctor who came down with the paratroopers plus our Australian doctor. They set up a surgery in a tent and carried out major operations on both German and Australian wounded. It was a wonderful example of co-operation.

This was not an isolated example. 'I am glad to say', a wounded Captain Derek Lang remembered of the period after capture at St-Valéry, 'that a lot of trouble was taken at this stage with the wounded. The German medical orderlies were as considerate as our own men would have been . . .'[31]

Sometimes, to be sure, Wehrmacht doctors were not quite so blindly Hippocratic: in some instances there was a natural enough tendency to place first aid for German wounded ahead of that of POWs.[32] Nevertheless, on the whole front-line German medical personnel behaved well. The recollections of two Colditz inmates are fairly typical in this respect. Lieutenant Edward Davies Scourfield of the King's Royal Rifle Corps, hit in the fighting for Calais, recalled in a later interview that he had been treated 'with great chivalry' by the Germans who found him after the surrender; a sentiment echoed by the wounded Second Lieutenant John Hamilton-Baillie, Royal Engineers, on the behaviour of German medical orderlies after the fighting had stopped at St-Valéry.[33]

For wounded and unwounded alike, a strong sense of military honour and *Frontkameradenschaft* on the part of the German officers and men concerned also helped, as British and Commonwealth troops usually found, to their benefit, when taken prisoner by the Afrika Korps. Lieutenant Sandy St Clair, an artillery officer, gazed in wonder at a particularly memorable example of mutual respect when the garrison at Tobruk formally surrendered in June 1942:

There, marching in columns of three down towards the crossroads, were 600 men of the Cameron Highlanders. Bayonets were fixed and gleaming from the rifles on their shoulders, and their officers had drawn swords! Colonel Duncan, the commanding officer, was at the head of his Battalion. He was flanked by two kilted pipers. All the rest were in khaki shorts. Standing to greet them were many Germans, rigidly at attention and all at the salute. Not fifty yards away was a German armoured car, with General Rommel himself in a peaked Afrika Korps cap and a black leather overcoat standing up in its turret. As the Battalion drew level with Rommel, Colonel Duncan flashed his sword up to his lips and down to his knee in salute, and Rommel raised his gloved hand in acknowledgement.[34]

A scene of this sort was exceptional, but magnanimity in victory was not all that unusual among front-line Wehrmacht troops. 'Once we had fallen into their hands,' Lieutenant Terence Prittie wrote of the period immediately after the surrender at Calais, 'they were supremely anxious to make a good impression, giving us food and cigarettes.'[35]

Even in such sympathetic circumstances newly captured POWs could rarely muster much cheerfulness. Instruction in what to expect and how to behave as a prisoner was apparently rare in the army and navy. Even in the RAF—where by 1941–2 aircrew were routinely briefed on what to do if shot down—little prior thought was given by the men concerned as to the possibility of being captured. Lectures could, in any event, do little to cushion the blow of being among the defeated in the hands of the enemy.[36]

For some officers it was hard at first to grasp this sudden new reality. Captain Robert Loder, a company commander in the Royal Sussex Regiment captured in May 1940, found the whole business somehow unreal, almost as if he was participating in an exercise. 'Oddly enough,' Jim Rogers of the Royal Engineers, a future escaper who ended up at Colditz, remembered of his surrender the same month, 'I felt no emotion at all.' This was particularly true in the wake of the physical and mental exhaustion brought about by combat, though not always. Hugo Ironside of the Royal Tank Regiment (another future inhabitant of Colditz), taken into the bag at Dunkirk, put his feelings in a nutshell: 'It was all a bit of a shock.'[37]

A sense of having put up a good fight (or, later on, of the war going well) could sometimes help make the pill easier to swallow. Those who took soldiering to be a temporary necessity rather than a long-term career might also be more philosophical than others about capture. 'I personally', reported Desmond Llewelyn, an actor turned temporary second lieutenant in the Royal Welch Fusiliers, 'had no feelings of degradation' when taken prisoner in May 1940.[38]

Most officers, though, especially career men captured in the first half of the war, were rather less insulated from the immediate mental impact of having to surrender. To feel 'absolutely shattered', 'demoralised and depressed', or even 'humiliated' to the point of 'misery' and 'despair' were not uncommon reactions among newly captured BEF officers. As Second Lieutenant Michael Duncan (Oxfordshire and Buckinghamshire Light Infantry) later explained of his anguish on becoming a POW in 1940: 'in a world of armed men, we no longer carried arms, no longer had the right to carry arms and consequently were thenceforth persons of no account whatsoever.' For Lieutenant Airey Neave, it seemed in 1940 as if 'life was over' and 'the purpose for which one was made was suddenly gone'. Looking back on the experience of being rounded up by the Germans after the fall of Tobruk two years later, Captain A. L. Nicholls, Royal Army Ordnance Corps, wrote of how deeply embarrassing it all was. Being a prisoner of war, after all, was 'not a very honourable status'.[39]

Emotional reaction on capture among those without commissions was often very similar in range. For J. C. Whelan, a Royal Marine fighting on Crete, 'the whole business of being taken prisoner was quite painless and did not involve any loss of dignity'. Many others felt rather stunned or simply numb, like Gunner Gordon Instone, captured at Calais, who found himself 'dazed with confusion and fatigue'. Ordinary soldiers could also experience a mixture of shame, anger, bitterness, and despair. Being taken without a decent fight could be particularly galling, as Leslie Moore of the South Saskatchewan Regiment recalled of his capture after blundering into German positions in Normandy. 'The disgrace and shame started to gnaw at me, right then,' he wrote in his memoirs, 'being taken prisoner without a fight.' Even if fighting had taken place, however, soldiers were often unable to be philosophical about what had happened. 'I was shattered, despondent and deflated', Stanley Rayner, a dispatch rider, remembered of the surrender at St-Valéry. At Calais, Private Jim Roberts (Queen Victoria's Rifles) found himself 'filled with despair, utterly dejected' when the end came. 'Every soldier was downcast', Ike Rosmarin of the South African army wrote of the fall of Tobruk.[40]

Being ordered to surrender by higher authority did not necessarily make the personal experience of laying down arms any easier. Such instructions did, however, provide some soldiers with the opportunity to blame others—and sometimes not without justification—rather than themselves for their predicament. 'One of our officers ordered us to throw away rifles, bayonets and ammunition', Private Maxwell Bates of the Middlesex Regiment recalled of the surrender at St-Valéry. 'No Germans were in sight. We were incredulous, then angry and disgusted.' Similar feelings were expressed over the surrender at Calais and at Dunkirk, while missing the evacuations in the Aegean the following year gave rise to much bitterness at those in charge who got away. Ian Sabey, an Australian artillery sergeant major, witnessed two cases of officers double-crossing men under their command in order to get away in Greece, while on Crete many of those left behind felt betrayed by those in charge—most of whom had gotten off the island before the end. 'Everyone felt rather savage at just being left high and dry without warning', Raymond Ryan, another Australian NCO, later wrote concerning his men's discovery on the morning of 1 June 1941 that the last order issued by his battalion HQ before evacuating itself from Sfakia had been for the remaining troops to surrender. 'We abused our leaders and bemoaned our bad luck', Peter Winter, a driver in the New Zealand Army Service Corps, remembered.[41]

Aircrew and sailors, meanwhile, had to cope with the destruction of their craft and the perils of air and sea before capture. This often more than made up for the absence of the prolonged fatigue that soldiers suffered from in the days prior to surrender. Sergeant Donald Bruce, an observer in a Wellington bomber coned by searchlights over Duisberg one night in July 1942, later recalled the chaotic moments after it became clear that the searchlights could not be shaken and that the plane was being shredded by flak bursts.

A hurried consultation between pilot and observer—then 'JUMP, JUMP, rear gunner'...no reply...he has already gone. The front gunner goes through the forward escape hatch (he has to look for his chute as it has dislodged from its stowage during the stall turn [to try and shake the searchlight beams]), the wireless operator moves forward then returns to root under his table (he was looking for his gloves!) I have removed my intercom (liable to be strangled by the leads if they catch in the chute when it opens) loosened my tie and fastened my parachute pack to the harness. I kick the wireless operator to attract his attention and point forward, he motions me past. I move to the forward escape hatch, as I pass the pilot he grins and gives me the thumbs up . . . and then I am at the opening.

Managing to get out of a mortally stricken aircraft, often in a terminal spin, was a feat in itself—but that still left the parachute descent to contend with. Flight Lieutenant Geoffrey Willatt, a bomb-aimer whose Lancaster was riddled by a night fighter and set on fire high over Mannheim one night in September 1943, bailed out through the forward hatch after the pilot was killed:

Whoosh! And there I was in mid-air, immediately followed by a sickening jerk on my groin as the 'chute opened. I don't remember pulling the cord: I was probably unconscious from lack of oxygen; anyway, I was fighting for breath. There was a horrible tearing, burning feeling between my legs, where the harness pulled, and my fur collar was clapped tightly over my face and ears. Both my boots were tugged off by the wind, and my feet were freezing cold.

Under the best of conditions it was at the very least disorienting to have oneself transformed in a matter of minutes from a crewman of an operational warplane into a fugitive in enemy territory who has narrowly escaped death. 'It was traumatic', recalled Flight Lieutenant Walter Morrison, a future Colditz inmate, of the moments after bailing out near Essen in June 1943. 'One moment I was high in the sky, free and in command, I had power at my fingertips and even a reasonable expectation of breakfast in the mess. The next moment I was standing [injured] in a German hayfield.' Mental and physical shock was not uncommon among downed aircrew. The official historian of RAF escapes, himself a former POW, argued that many of those taken into custody were secretly relieved not to have to go on making life-or-death decisions after the bail-out trauma.[42]

Navy men could also find the transition problematic. Lieutenant-Commander Peter Buckley, captain of HM Submarine *Shark*, admitted he had never thought about becoming a prisoner until he was forced to surrender in order to save the lives of his remaining crewmen after his vessel, damaged and unable to submerge, was repeatedly strafed by German aircraft off Norway in July 1940. Lieutenant-Commander Rupert Lonsdale, caught in a very similar situation with HM Submarine *Seal* two months earlier, found the mental burden of having to hoist the white flag to save the lives of his crew almost unbearable. 'Had we done everything we could to avoid this situation?', R. R. James, First

Lieutenant of an RN motor launch sunk in the Aegean in late 1944, found himself thinking some hours after being picked up by an enemy destroyer. 'Was any blame due to us by our actions that night?' Perhaps fortunately, shock was a common reaction immediately after the shooting had ceased. 'I suppose one's mental processes must become a bit numb', Billie Stephens reflected on being captured in the St-Nazaire Raid. Taken prisoner by a German landing party from the battleship *Tirpitz* on Spitzbergen in September 1943, Leading Telegraphist E. C. Dabner found the whole experience to be so unexpected that it resembled 'a dream'. All, however, were still glad to be alive.[43]

Except where sheer numbers or other circumstances made the task virtually impossible, the first indignity faced by newly captured prisoners was a search by their captors. As already noted, the discovery of weapons, and also items looted from Germans—'A sudden urge to be rid of German luger pistols, watches, cameras and binoculars manifested itself', Peter Winter remembered of the surrender period on Crete[44]—could be potentially life-threatening. Much less dangerous and more common was a tendency on the part of those searching prisoners to find souvenirs: though there were also many instances in which Germans were scrupulously correct about returning personal items.

The confiscation of military paraphernalia such as a compass or pair of binoculars was understandable:[45] German soldiers, though, in a fashion not dissimilar from most other victorious armies in the field, were often also willing to break the rules and engage in a little personal looting. Watches, rings, pens, and of course cigarettes were among the articles found to be particularly attractive to searchers. William Harding, a gunner in the Royal Artillery, remembered that in the aftermath of the surrender at Calais those British prisoners who tried to conceal items were punched in the face. Officers were by no means immune. 'Everything we possessed,' Billie Stephens wrote of being searched, 'wallets, letters, photos, cigarette cases, money, disappeared . . . never to be seen or heard of again.' RAF aircrew clothing was also coveted. 'The flying jacket will probably go to the troops on the eastern front', Eric Williams was told when his sheepskin jacket was removed after capture. Silk scarves were also likely to disappear.[46] There were other cases, though, especially if an officer was involved, when a more gentlemanly approach was taken. Walter Morrison was surprised to find that no money was taken from him, and while Jim Rogers was relieved of his penknife, his gold watch was left untouched.[47]

Once firmly in enemy hands, the next major hurdle for prisoners—again something missing from the Colditz story—was a personal interrogation, either near the battlefront or at a special interview centre. Sometimes the process could be quite painless; in other cases it was very tough indeed. Much depended on the circumstances of capture, service and rank, and above all on whether or not those in custody were thought likely to possess valuable tactical or technical information.

When a big evacuation or surrender took place, essentially bringing the battle at hand to an end, questioning might well be cursory or even non-existent. 'Interrogation was very brief,' Corporal Alan Bell wrote of his experience and that of other Yorkshire Light Infantry troops taken on 27 May 1940, '—the German officer seemed to know more about our [4th] battalion than we did!' Jimmy Yule, a signals officer and future guest of the Wehrmacht in Colditz, recalled of his own capture in the same campaign seventeen days earlier that there had been no attempt to question him at all: 'none whatsoever.' Riding the tide of victory, the Germans could afford to be—and often were—courteous when questioning officers; and once the battle was won field interrogation was often dispensed with altogether. Even in the days before the fall of Calais the surrounding enemy units seemed to be losing interest. Captain A. N. L. Munby (Queen Victoria's Rifles) was only cursorily questioned after capture along with his men at German battalion headquarters at Coquelles. 'This was a very brief affair', he later wrote. 'I was brought before the commander who asked me how many English troops there were in Calais. I replied that I didn't know and we were hustled out.' After the fall of St-Valéry some days later, even those on the staff of 51st Highland Division were apparently not considered worth examining.[48] The same was evidently true after the fall of Crete the following year, Tobruk the year after that, and in the aftermath of the 1944 Arnhem disaster, when both junior officers and men were for the most part left alone or only cursorily questioned in the days after surrender.[49]

When victory was less certain the Wehrmacht and Waffen-SS took a closer interest in those they captured in order to find out as much as possible about the units facing them. When circumstances permitted the usual technique employed at German battalion and divisional headquarters involved the interrogating officer displaying such an apparently complete knowledge of the British or Commonwealth unit concerned that the person being questioned was tricked into thinking that there was nothing he knew that the enemy did not know already. Though MI9 (one of whose tasks was to prevent the enemy from gaining valuable information from prisoners) stressed as much as possible the need to only give name, rank, and number, not all captured personnel were prepared for interrogation, especially early on in the war. When morale was low, and it seemed that there was no point in holding back on apparently unimportant matters, a few men apparently did let things slip.[50] When this technique did not work, moreover, other ruses could be used.

Captured near Venlo, Holland in November 1944, Captain G. W. Smith of the East Yorkshire Regiment was taken to the local battalion HQ for interrogation. At first the usual technique was applied—albeit poorly—starting with the offer of cigarettes.

Q) 'Now you are from the Camerons of the 15th Scottish Division?'
A) 'Am I?'
Q) 'Come now, why not admit it? Everybody admits statements which are so obviously correct, so why not save yourself a considerable amount of trouble . . .'

Eventually the interrogator noticed that Smith was wearing the wrong divisional flash on his shoulder, and called a temporary halt to the questioning. When he returned it was bearing a threat:

An hour later he returned with some unfortunate news. 'Word has just come through that whilst a party of German P's.O.W. were being escorted to the rear a Tommy opened up with a Bren. All were killed with the exception of one who was wounded. He . . . crawled into a ditch and in due course escaped back to our lines. In view of this piece of information just received, my Captain is extremely annoyed and feels that reprisals are necessary, and so, unless you can prove your identity you will be treated as a spy and shot!'

Luckily this was, as Smith guessed, merely a ruse.[51]

A more subtle technique was applied when prisoners were being held in transit camps or hospital, playing on the common desire of prisoners to let their families know they were alive. Wounded in the battle for Crete, Second Lieutenant W. B. Thomas, a New Zealander, was visited shortly after the German takeover of the dressing station in which he was recovering:

A rather fine-looking boy knelt over my stretcher and addressed me in quite flawless English.
    'Your name and rank, please.'
    'Thomas, Second Lieutenant.'
    'Your regiment and division,' very smoothly.
    'I am not required to give you that information.'
    The German smiled . . .

'You are not forced to give this information—agreed,' he replied, but should you do so I can arrange through the Red Cross to have your people advised of your safety'.

Thomas did not rise to the bait.[52]

A similar method had been used on Jim Rogers and other BEF officers after their arrival at Mainz transit camp in 1940. A suspiciously unctuous German officer, claiming to represent the Red Cross, presented them with forms supposedly designed to allow relatives to be informed that they were safe:

When we looked at the forms, they asked all sorts of questions about the place and date of capture, unit, task at time of capture etc. We had long before been told that we were required to give only our name, rank and number, and we told this to the German. He laughed merrily, which put us off even more, and said that was correct and was observed in the German army too, but this form would be seen only by the Red Cross. Our German speakers pointed out that none of us was born yesterday. The German stopped smiling and said that, if that was our attitude, he would not give any information to the Red Cross, and our families would be ignorant of our fate. And so it was.[53]

Through much of the war, especially in the case of captured army officers, field interrogations were mostly conducted in a civilized manner.[54] There were instances, however, when both Waffen-SS and Wehrmacht units did not have the information, time, or inclination to conduct an ongoing battle of wits. In some cases this made interrogation more superficial;[55] in other cases it made it a much more uncomfortable, sometimes even deadly, experience for those concerned.

Private Horace Taylor of the Dorsetshire Regiment, taken prisoner along with some comrades in Normandy in July 1944, reported that at enemy battalion headquarters 'we were hit across the face by the German N.C.O. and officer who was asking us questions about where our troops were and when we said all we had to give was our name, rank and number we was [sic] hit again . . . ' Things could sometimes get even nastier. A signals officer and a tank officer, taken during the retreat to Tobruk in 1941, found themselves being interrogated by a German *Feldwebel* armed with a Luger who demanded to know the location of their units. The signals officer gave only his name, rank, and number. The *Feldwebel*, jamming the Luger in his stomach, threatened to shoot the signals officer if he did not answer correctly. On a count of three he shot the officer dead. In June 1944 Gerhard Bremer, a battalion commander in the 12th SS Panzer Division in Normandy, was with other SS men responsible for the murder of several groups of Canadian prisoners who apparently refused to give the required information. This sort of thing was rare, but unfortunately not unique. For a soldier to do his duty in giving only his name, rank, and number, in short, though usually safe, was on occasion to court danger or even death.[56]

In land warfare the greatest need was for timely information on opposing enemy units, which was why interrogations tended to be conducted in the field. When sheer numbers were not overwhelming, small numbers of army prisoners thought to possess less time-specific information might find themselves sent to a special interrogation unit based at Stalag IIIA (Luckenwalde) in the later war years. A mixture of solitary confinement, verbal tricks, and sometimes threats occasionally yielded results for the Abwehr staff in the latter war years, though not always of a particularly useful sort. With the primary focus on field interrogation, the operation at Luckenwalde was very limited in scale in comparison to similar efforts undertaken by the other services, especially the Luftwaffe.[57]

On occasion, when the situation seemed to demand it, the German navy and air force, like the army, questioned captured personnel close to where they had been taken.[58] To a much greater extent than was true among the ground forces, however, both the Kriegsmarine and the Luftwaffe centralized their efforts in special prisoner interrogation centres in the Reich itself. There questioning could be more easily prolonged or adjusted to individual circumstances.

The German navy's main interrogation centre for much of the war, Dulag Marine Nord, was situated in the big naval base at Wilhelmshaven, where prisoners were usually placed in solitary confinement between interviews for periods of a month or more (the navy, unlike the air force, not having to worry about an overload of incoming prisoners). The experience of members of the crew of HM submarine *Seal*, captured in May 1940, revealed many of the same techniques employed by the other services being used by the navy. 'They would ask all sorts of innocent questions about my childhood, and home life, purely to gain my confidence and get me talking', Engine Room Artificer Jack Murray recalled, 'and slip in a question about where *Seal* had been, how many submarines we had lost, etc. To this type of question I gave no answer. At one stage one of them said, "Come now, if you will just answer these few simple questions we shall broadcast over the radio to England that you are safe. Your wife must be worrying about you."' Variations were played on other members of the crew.

At the start the conversation was very general [remembered R. G. Avis]. Then it became more detailed. Obviously they wanted information about our Asdic [sonar]. I was adamant that I knew nothing about this since I was a Leading Telegraphist and I stuck to this story for three increasingly lengthy sessions. At the final interrogation I was again asked if I knew anything about Asdic and, after repeatedly replying that I did not I was astonished to see the German naval captain slowly open his desk drawer and take out *Seal*'s watch-bill. He looked sadly at me and said sternly, 'I am disappointed in you, a British naval rating, you do not speak the truth.'

'I was interrogated by a German naval captain and a lieutenant [recorded John Waddington], questions and replies being recorded by a shorthand-typist. "How long had I been in submarines? When and where did I join *Seal*? How many mines did we carry and where had we laid them? What port did we sail from and when?"' To most of these questions the Germans knew the answers already.[59]

Another technique employed as the war progressed was for a 'civilian' to present the prisoner with a bogus Red Cross form. Lieutenant David James, captured in early 1943, later wrote about being presented with this document. 'Not only did the form require my name, rank, and the address of my next-of-kin . . . it also had spaces for the name of my base, the name of the captain, the number of operational flotillas there, and a hundred and one other naval details quite outside the scope of a charitable organisation.'[60]

For the most part the interrogating officers did not push matters if a prisoner refused to go beyond name, rank, and number after repeated questioning and conversational gambits had failed. 'They were very reasonable', Commander Moran recalled when questioned about his three weeks at Dulag Marine many years later.[61] On some occasions, however, a serious degree of physical or psychological pressure might be applied.

Lieutenant T. N. Catlow, taken prisoner in February 1942 (and eventually a guest of the Reich at Colditz), refused to be drawn into a discussion of the merits of British sonar. As a result, like a number of other POWs on other occasions, he was shouted at and then placed for a very long stretch in solitary confinement in an unheated room on short rations. Francis Guest, a Royal Marine commando captured in the Dieppe Raid, was dismayed to discover that his interrogator at Wilhelmshaven knew of his background, and was completely unnerved when threatened with being treated as a spy and shot. 'It has occurred to us', he was told, 'that perhaps you were landed during the operation for some other purpose—*espionage, shall we say*?' Recalcitrant sailors were also occasionally struck for insolence.[62]

The most fully developed enemy intelligence-gathering effort among recently captured POWs was that of the Luftwaffe. From humble beginnings, Dulag Luft, located at Oberusel outside Frankfurt-am-Main for most of the war, developed into a sophisticated sifting centre staffed by hundreds of Luftwaffe personnel and dozens of trained English-speaking interrogators able to process hundreds of Allied airmen each month. To take maximum advantage of the initial disorientation many downed airmen felt, the German air force also developed forward interrogation teams to process British and Commonwealth bomber crews shot down over occupied Europe before transfer to Oberusel.[63]

The basic methods employed at Dulag Luft and preliminary interrogations were variations on a few basic approaches. When possible captured airmen would be placed in individual cells for a week or more on limited rations without access to tobacco, allowed out only under guard to answer calls of nature, and prevented from communicating with each other. Prisoners would then usually be exposed to a sympathetic English-speaking figure claiming to represent the Red Cross, often bearing cigarettes as well as a long form supposedly designed to make it easier to contact relatives with news of survival (but asking for aircraft, mission, and squadron details as well as name, rank, and number). Alternatively, or in addition, airmen would be taken to an interview room for formal questioning. Here the main weapon of the interrogator would be a thorough grasp of the prisoner's background, carefully culled from intelligence files on particular squadrons and so apparently flawless that the man concerned would think there was nothing he could let slip that the Luftwaffe did not already know. A further ruse involved using bogus or blackmailed RAF types to try and gain information when a man's guard might be down.

News of the fake Red Cross form and other approaches soon got back to England and was quickly passed on to aircrew as something to watch out for. On occasion, moreover, the tables could be turned through deliberately passing on false information to the enemy. It was through the efforts of an RAF officer that the Germans were led to believe that Allied success in sinking U-boats in 1943 was due to a box that allowed aircraft to home in on a radar warning device aboard German submarines.[64] Nevertheless, prolonged isolation and hunger—the abrupt switch from British aircrew to German POW rations—coupled with skilled questioning could sometimes yield results.[65]

Sergeant James 'Dixie' Deans, who would later prove to be an outstanding leader of men, admitted that when his interrogators at Dulag

Luft read to him the details of the night bombing mission on which he had been shot down in 1940, he thought there was 'no point' in denying what they evidently knew to be true. This was also the conclusion reached by Flight Lieutenant Walter Morrison—who eventually ended up at Colditz—after several weeks of verbal sparring about the names of his Wellington crew in the summer of 1942.[66] Geoff Taylor, an Australian sergeant pilot whose Lancaster was downed over Germany in late 1943, was unnerved by the apparently complete knowledge of his interrogating officer about his squadron. 'The German was not only telling me things I knew; he was also telling me things I only half-knew and things that I had never had time to know for sure.' Nevertheless he continued to play dumb until the Leutnant seemingly lost his temper and shouted 'Will you or won't you tell me what part of the Dutch coast you crossed on your way in?', at which point Taylor rose to the bait and shouted 'No I won't!'—realizing too late that he had been tricked into giving something away.[67] An unthreatening approach could also induce prisoners to give something away on occasion. Robert Kee, a Hampden pilot shot down in 1941, at first refused to have anything to do with the bogus Red Cross form. Seeing how depressed this made his harmless-looking interlocutor, he began to waver over the more innocuous parts. 'Eventually he persuaded me to give him the name and address of my parents', Kee related. 'It was like giving a button to a blind beggar...'[68] Unfortunately this was, at least potentially, the kind of information that could be used in interrogation sessions to impress others with the extent of personal knowledge the Luftwaffe already possessed: which in turn could lead to further, superficially irrelevant revelations on the part of prisoners.[69]

A sympathetic manner and conversational virtuosity did not always work, of course, and a more coercive approach might be taken. Aircrew whose identity was in question due to loss or confiscation of identity tags might be threatened with being treated as spies (i.e. shot) if they did not play along. The man questioning Pilot Officer James Brandford of 149 Squadron, brought down in August 1943, for instance, 'pointed out that they had had a lot of trouble with spies being dropped in Germany... it was made very clear that I had still to prove my identity'. Men might be threatened with the spectre of being handed over to the Gestapo, and interrogators could in some cases also become violent. Richard Pape, an NCO navigator shot down in 1941, recalled how his questioner turned nasty after he refused to co-operate. 'Twice he spat at me, and vented his anger by slinging his ink bottle at my face.'[70]

Other forms of pressure might be applied. Prisoners could be denied access to the toilets for hours on end, wounds that were not life-threatening might not be attended to while questioning continued, and the heat in cells could be turned up or down in order to increase discomfort and wear down a man's resistance. 'It got hotter, and extremely difficult to breathe,' Squadron Leader James Cairns, a Wellington pilot, remembered of his time in cells at Dulag in April 1943; 'the metal-work on the bed got to such a temperature that it was difficult to touch.' Flight Lieutenant Jim Lang, a Mosquito pilot who had passed through Oberusel in October of the previous year, was rendered 'almost unconscious' as a result of the heat treatment. Flight Sergeant Johnny Egan, a Lancaster navigator being pushed to reveal the secrets of the latest version of the 'Gee' navigation device in 1943, found himself in a state of semi-delirium after ten days continuous exposure: 'I was in a small cell with frequent visits from an interrogator, where the temperature was at times utterly freezing.' Sergeant Percy Wilson, shot down on a reconnaissance sortie, wrote of his time at Dulag Luft: 'I would complain and the heat would be turned on so severely that I could hardly breathe. I was advised that I had only myself to blame for the discomfort of the "unpredictable" heating system, and that should I complete the "Red Cross" (bogus) form and answer some simple questions, I would be moved. However, should I continue to be un-cooperative, my stay in the cells could be very lengthy and uncomfortable.' Severely injured on landing by parachute near Stuttgart in October 1944, Flying Officer Maurice Collins, after being given the hot-cold treatment and refusing to fill in the Red Cross form, was told outright that 'I would not get medical treatment until I talked'. Dozens of British and Commonwealth aircrew reported similar encounters, and in some cases the combination of psychological and physical pressure led to the desired results.[71]

Despite this sort of thing the Luftwaffe generally behaved within humanitarian bounds during interrogation. Most aircrew passing through Dulag Luft, it is important to note, emerged unscathed.

Having negotiated the awkward transition from fighting man to prisoner of war and being questioned, captured men faced further potential challenges. Surrendering and undergoing interrogation were only the first steps in becoming a 'Kriegie' (from the German word for POW, *Kriegsgefangene*). Now prisoners had to contend with being moved to permanent camps, as well as the process of being transformed into officially recognized POWs of the Third Reich.

Notes

1. In the prologue to *The Colditz Story*, Reid indicates that most readers of escape books tended to skip the preliminaries and other 'lesser problems' in order to get down to the exciting business of breaking out. See P. R. Reid, *The Colditz Story* (London, 1952), 18. It is also possible that Reid did not wish to emphasize the fact that, while serving as Royal Army Service Corps ammunition officer with 2nd Division HQ, BEF, he and his driver had driven straight into a German armoured column on the Cassel–Dunkirk road on 27 May: 'I had no information that the enemy was anywhere near this road', he made a point of stressing in an official report made after his return to the UK (PRO, WO 208/3311, MI9/ S/PG(G)995); see also *Radio Times*, 12 Oct. 1972, p. 63; NSA 5186, *The Price of Victory* (BBC Radio 2, 7 May 1995). As Reid himself admitted in the 1980s (Pat Reid and Maurice Michael, *Prisoner of War* (London, 1984), 87–90), the journey into Germany was pretty sordid for most BEF prisoners captured in France in the summer of 1940.
2. Other books of the period that did deal with capture included David James, *A Prisoner's Progress* (Edinburgh, 1947); Ian Reid, *Prisoner at Large* (London, 1947); Oliver Philpot, *Stolen Journey* (London, 1950); W. B. Thomas, *Dare to be Free* (London, 1951); Derrick Nabarro, *Wait for the Dawn* (London, 1952); Gordon Instone, *Freedom the Spur* (London, 1953); Richard Pape, *Boldness Be My Friend* (London, 1953); Michael Duncan, *Underground from Posen* (London, 1954); James Allan, *No Citation* (London, 1955); Cyril Rofe, *Against the Wind* (London, 1956).
3. On agreement in 1939 to abide by the terms of the 1929 Geneva Convention see André Durand, *From Sarajevo to Hiroshima* (Geneva, 1984), 401–2.
4. See e.g. Richard Holmes, *Firing Line* (London, 1994 edn.), 382–5.
5. Howard Margolian, *Conduct Unbecoming* (Toronto, 1998), 58–9 and *passim*; A. Robert Prouse, *Ticket to Hell via Dieppe* (Toronto, 1982), 20; PRO, ADM1/18695, account of Surgeon Commander H. G. G. Singer; J. E. Pryce, *Heels in Line* (London, 1958), 21–2; Leslie Le Souef, *To War Without a Gun* (Perth, WA, 1980), 16–61; PRO, WO 309/736, Affidavit of Sgt. R. J. Lawrence; Anthony Beevor, *Crete* (London, 1991), 122, 168; WO 309, *passim*; A. P. Scotland, *The London Cage* (London, 1957), 79.
6. IWMSA 17896/2, W. C. Purdon; C. W. Jervis, *The Long Trek* (Elms Court, 1993), 8–9; PRO, WO 208/3298, Interview Summary for 2/Lt J. T. Stevenson.
7. George Dunning, *Where Bleed the Many* (London, 1955), 16–17; IWM (Rolf), F. E. Ayers.
8. See e.g. IWMSA 9893/3, M. Champion Jones; IWM, H. C. F. Harwood, 75.
9. Richard Hough and Denis Richards, *The Battle of Britain* (London, 1989), 231.
10. PRO, WO 309/736, Affidavit of F/Sgt H. Wilkinson; see ibid., Affidavit of Sgt. J. Lawrence; Ernest Walker, *The Price of Surrender* (London, 1992), 36–9; W. Wynne Mason, *Prisoners of War* (Wellington, 1954), 62.

11. Margolian, op cit., 123, 95, 98; IWM (Rolf), W. J. Sudworth, 4; see Alfred M. de Zayas, *The Wehrmacht War Crimes Bureau, 1939–1945* (Lincoln, Nebr., 1989), 116–18.
12. PRO, WO 309/1296, Sgt. Price case; WO 309/1106; see Victor F. Gammon, *Not All Glory!* (London, 1996), 135–6; Max Hastings, *Bomber Command* (New York, 1979), 226–7; J. Alwyn Phillips, *Valley of the Shadow of Death* (New Malden, 1991), 202.
13. IWM, W. L. Stephens, 3; Beevor, op. cit., 122; Walker, op. cit., 39–41; Dunning, op. cit., 16; IWM (Rolf), F.E. Ayers, 3.
14. John Woods, *Peace in My Time?!* (Preston, 1995), 68.
15. IWM, S. C. Masters, reel 1, 92; see IWM, G. Hall, reel 1, 31; IWM, G. H. Hobbs, 3; Geoff Taylor, *Piece of Cake* (London, 1980 edn.), 83; IWMSA 15246/2, T. Cooksey; Brian G. Hodgkinson, *Spitfire Down* (Toronto, 2000), 85–6; Pape, op. cit., 91; John Frayn Turner, *Prisoner at Large* (London, 1957), 119; Daniel G. Dancocks, *In Enemy Hands* (Toronto, 1990 edn.), 166–7; Edward Lanchbery, *Against the Sun* (London, 1955), 175; PRO, WO 309, *passim*.
16. Margolian, op. cit., *passim*; PRO, WO 309/25; WO 309/761; WO 309/26; WO 309/734; Leslie Aitkin, *Massacre on the Road to Dunkirk* (London, 1977); Cyril Jolly, *The Vengeance of Private Pooley* (London, 1956).
17. International Military Tribunal, *The Trial of German Major War Criminals* (HMSO, 1947), xiii. 230. See Karl Doenitz, *Memoirs* (Annapolis, 1990 edn.), 263–4; Clay Blair, *Hitler's U-Boat War: The Hunted, 1942–1945* (New York, 1996), 552–4. On the never-issued Luftwaffe order see Adolf Galland, *The First and the Last* (London, 1970 abridged edn.), 75–6.
18. Office of the United States Chief Consul for the Prosecution of Axis Criminality, *Nazi Conspiracy and Aggression* (Washington, DC, 1947), iv. 189; see *The Trial of German Major War Criminals*, iii. 38–40, 239; v. 289.
19. Ibid., ix. 2, 145–7, 157; x. 84, 203–4; xv. 63, 313, 367; xvi. 47–9; see Nuernberg Military Tribunal, *Trials of War Criminals Before the Nuernberg Military Tribunals, Vol. 11, The High Command Case* (Washington, DC, 1950), 169–78, 182–194.
20. UNWCC, *Law Reports of Trials of War Criminals*, ix. case 68, *Trial of Hans Renoth and Three Others* (HMSO, 1948), 76; see PRO, WO 309, *passim*; see also e.g. WO 309/559; WO 309/706.
21. UNWCC, *Law Reports of Trials of War Criminals* (HMSO, 1947), ix. 76; see iii. 23–55, 103; vii. 904; i. 81–92; xi. 74–75; PRO, WO 309, *passim*; Jonathan F. Vance, *Objects of Concern* (Vancouver, BC, 1994), 128.
22. On the Commando Order see International Military Tribunal, *The Trial of German Major War Criminals* (HMSO, 1951), iii. 239; iv. 2–5; iv. 6–11, 275; v. 286; ix. 31, 46–7, 61; xi. 25–31, 53, 256, 271; xiv. 142–5, 226, 245–6, 298, 307–8, 314–15; xv. 285, 296–305, 404–10; xix. 26–7; xxi. 91; Nuernberg Military Tribunal, *Trials of War Criminals Before the Nuernberg Military Tribunals*, xi. 73–165; UNWCC, *Law Reports of Trials of War Criminals* (HMSO, 1947), i. 22–34; v. 39–53; xi. 18–30.
23. Stephen Schofield, *Musketoon* (London, 1969). It seems likely that Reid knew about these men (contact had been made with their leader by two of

Reid's closest escape associates and the case was highlighted at Nuremberg), but decided their story would intrude on the narrative—at this point, the preparations for what turned out to be his successful escape from Colditz. In seeking to write 'the full story' two decades later, Reid did discuss the incident, which had already been used as the basis of one of the *Colditz* TV series episodes. See P. R. Reid, *Colditz: The Full Story* (London, 1984), 168–9.

24. Giles Romilly and Michael Alexander, *The Privileged Nightmare* (London, 1954), 34 ff.; see Peter Churchill, *The Spirit in the Cage* (London, 1954), 9–125; B. A. James, *Moonless Night* (London, 1983), 155, 162.

25. On prisoner numbers see Vasilis Vourtkoutiotis, 'The German Armed Forces Supreme Command and British and American Prisoners-of-War, 1939–1945: Policy and Practice', Ph.D. thesis, McGill University (2000), 55–8; Central Statistical Office, *Fighting With Figures* (London, 1995), 43; see also Chris Christiansen, *Seven Years Among Prisoners of War* (Athens, Ohio, 1994), 20; Noel Barber, *Prisoners of War* (London, 1944), 13; Paul Brickhill and Conrad Norton, *Escape to Danger* (London, 1946), 5. See in addition Maxwell Leigh, *Captives Courageous* (Johannesburg, 1992), 1; Mason, op. cit., pp. v–vi; Patsy Adam-Smith, *Prisoners of War* (Ringwood, Victoria, 1992), 89.

26. Virtually every POW narrative notes the use of these words. For evidence of German front-line self-confidence and high morale in the wake of victory see e.g. CSVA 7, P. Allan; IWM, K. J. Bowden, 47; Geoffrey D. Vaughan, *The Way It Really Was* (Budleigh Salterton, 1985), 11; Peter Winter, *Free Lodgings* (Auckland, 1993), 7–8; A. Greenshields in A. J. Barker, *Behind Barbed Wire* (London, 1974), 48. On friendly gestures see e.g. Terence Prittie, *My Germans* (London, 1983), 64–5; George Harsh, *Lonesome Road* (New York, 1971), 159.

27. Richard Passmore, *Moving Tent* (London, 1982), 21–3. On Bader see Paul Brickhill, *Reach for the Sky* (London, 1954), 292–4; Galland, op. cit., 76–9; see also IWMSA 15247/1, D. Hawkins; IWMSA 15336/2, J. C. Wilson; Nabarro, op. cit., 10, 24; Prittie, op. cit., 66; Larry Forrester, *Fly for Your Life* (London, 1960 edn.), 266–7; Hogkinson, op. cit., 52–7; Vance, *Objects of Concern*, 127.

28. Roger V. Coward, *Sailors in Cages* (London, 1967), 42–3; on the *Voltaire* sinking see IWM (Rolf), R. Mercer, 1; IWMSA 16910/1–2, J. Hoggard.

29. IWMSA 48169/2, J. M. Moran; PRO, ADM 1/18965, H. G. Singer, 9; J. Wilkins in *Colditz Society Newsletter*, 3: 27 (Jan. 2002), 4–5; see IWM, E. C. Dabner, 47–8; IWM, H. E. C. Elliott, 10–11; Pryce, op. cit., 35; Dancocks, op. cit., 146; James, op. cit., 4–5; Guy Morgan, *Only Ghosts Can Live* (London, 1945), 15 ff., 35; D. G. Butterworth in J. E. Holliday (ed.), *Stories of the RAAF POWs of Lamsdorf* (Holland Park, Queensland, 1992), 67.

30. IWM, N. L. Francis, 14–15; IWM, R. P. Evans, 29; see IWM, W. Darbyshire, 3; IWM (Rolf), J. S. Sharpe, 4; Harsh, op. cit.; Graham Palmer, *Prisoner of Death* (Wellingborough, 1990), 44; T. C. F. Prittie and W. Earle Edwards, *Escape to Freedom* (London, 1953 edn.), 12; David H. C. Read,

This Grace Given (Grand Rapids, Mich., 1984), 100; J. M. Langley, *Fight Another Day* (London, 1974), 59–60; Leslie E. Moore, *Thirty Days— A Lifetime* (Sidney, BC, 1989), 22; Frank Taylor, *Barbed Wire and Footlights* (Braunton, 1988), 17; Walker, op. cit., 54; Elvet Williams, *Arbeitskommando* (London, 1975), 9.

31. Derek Lang, *Return to St. Valéry* (Luneray, 1989), 37; David McGill, *P.O.W.* (Naenae, NZ, 1987), 15; see Graeme Warwick, *Travel by Dark* (London, 1963), chs. 1–3; Daniel Paul with John St John, *Surgeon at Arms* (London, 1958), 5–18; R. G. M. Quarry, *Oflag* (Durham, 1995), 3–4; PRO, WO 208/ 3301, W. B. A. Gaze account; IWM (Rolf), I. J. L. Lewis.

32. See e.g. A. C. Masterman, in Tony Strachen (ed.), *In the Clutch of Circumstance* (Victoria, BC, 1985), 118–19; IWM, W. A. Harding, 1.

33. IWMSA s. 14781/1, J. Hamilton-Baillie; ibid. 6367/4, E. G. B. Davies Scourfield.

34. Sandy St Clair, *The Endless War* (North Battleford, Sask., 1987), 25.

35. Prittie and Edwards, op. cit., 12.

36. On lack of preparation for being an army POW see ibid. 7; CSVA, K. Lockwood; id., H. Ironside; IWM (Rolf), G. Wilde Handley; IWMSA 4847/1, C. L. Irwin; ibid. 4747/2, E. Mine; IWM, R. A. Wilson, 9; http:// www.awm.gov.au, A. D. Crawford, TS tape 1 side A; Christopher Portway, *Journey to Dana* (London, 1955), 23; Arthur Evans, *Sojourn in Silesia* (Ashford, 1995), 11; Read, op. cit., 100; Earnshaw and Sweetman, in McGill, op. cit., 17, 20; Patrick Wilson, *The War Behind the Wire* (Barnsley, 2000), 9. See, also, however, Langley, op. cit., 29. On RAF aircrew not giving much thought to becoming a POW see e.g. F. A. B. Tams, *A Trenchard 'Brat'* (Edinburgh, 2000), 95. On official efforts to promote evasion and escape see M. R. D. Foot and J. M. Langley, *MI9* (London, 1979).

37. CSVA 11, H. Ironside; Jim Rogers, *Tunnelling Into Colditz* (London, 1986), 21; IWMSA 4827/1, R. Loder.

38. Sandy Hernu, *Q* (Seaford, 1999), 49; see Barker, op. cit., 37–8; UNB, MS L35, David H. Walker Papers, box 2, series 3, file 20, Weldon to Walker, 6 Dec. 1984.

39. IWM (Rolf), A. L. Nicholls, 3; Airey Neave, *They Have Their Exits* (London, 1953), 20; Duncan, op. cit., 45; Lang, op. cit., 37; IWM, A. N. L. Munby, 13; CSVA 4, K. Lockwood; IWMSA 4847/1, C. L. Irwin. Guilt over being a POW could linger and become a serious emotional burden in captivity. See PRO, WO 32/10950, p. 2; Douglas Thompson, *Captives to Freedom* (London, 1955), 162–3.

40. Ike Rosmarin, *Inside Story* (Cape Town, 1990), 14; J. Roberts, *A Terrier Goes to War* (London, 1998), 30; Stanley Rayner, *I Remember* (Lincoln, 1995), 102; Moore, op. cit., 21; Instone, op. cit., 39; IWM, J. C. Whelan, 3.

41. Winter, op. cit., 7; Imelda Ryan (comp.), *POWs Fraternal* (London, 1990), 55; Ian Sabey, *Stalag Scrapbook* (Melbourne, 1947), 16–17; Maxwell Bates, *A Wilderness of Days* (Victoria, BC, 1978), 15.

42. IWM, G. Willatt, 5; IWM (Rolf), D. Bruce; Walter Morrison, *Flak and Ferrets* (London, 1995), 56; see Aidan Crawley, *Escape from Germany* (London, 1956), 19–22.

43. IWM, E. C. Dabner, 47; IWM, W. L. Stephens, 3; IWM, R. R. James, 41; C. E. T. Warren and James Benson, *Will Not We Fear* (London, 1961), 137–8; IWMSA 4759/1, P. Buckley.

44. Winter, op. cit., 6.

45. See e.g. PRO, WO 209/3298, Notes on the Experiences of British Personnel Captured by the Enemy during recent Operations . . . July 1940, p. 1.

46. Eric Williams, *The Tunnel* (London, 1951), 51; IWM, W. L. Stephens, 4; William Harding, *A Cockney Soldier* (Braunton, 1989), 139.

47. Rogers, op. cit., 21; Morrison, op. cit., 57; see IWMSA 15608/1, W. Stevens; W. H. Dothie, *Operation Disembroil* (London, 1985), 37; see also PRO, WO 208/3298, Account of Escape of Maj. J. R. Mackintosh-Walker and Maj. T. G. Rennie, p. 2; ibid., Capt. S. P. Harrow, 1; ibid., 2/Lt. J. T. Stevenson, 1; Rosmarin, op. cit., 13; Quarrie, op. cit., 4.

48. PRO, WO 208/3298, Account of Escape of Maj. J. R. Macintosh-Walker and Maj. T. G. Rennie; IWM, A. N. L. Munby, 14; CSVA2, J. Yule; IWM (Rolf), A. Bell; see also e.g. Sam Kydd, *For You the War Is Over* . . . (London, 1973), 53; IWM, C. L. Irwin; IWM, C. G. King; IWM, W. K. Laing; IWM, R. A. Wilson; http://web.mala.bc.ca/davies/letters.images/stokes/collection.page.htm, D. Stokes diary, 6 June 1940.

49. In the many accounts written by ex-POWs from Greece and Crete, and the smaller number by those taken at Tobruk and Arnhem, there is almost no mention of serious field interrogation after surrender. On the cursory nature of what interrogation did take place see e.g. Jim Longson and Christine Taylor, *An Arnhem Odessey* (London, 1991), 92; Anthony Deane-Drummond, *Arrows of Fortune* (London, 1992), 108–9; Miles Reid, *Last on the List* (London, 1974), 194.

50. e.g. IWM, C. G. King, 10–11. On MI9 see Foot and Langley, op. cit. On knowledge (or lack thereof) concerning what not to do if captured see e.g. Prittie and Edwards, op. cit., 7; IWM, R. P. Evans, 29; IWM (Rolf), W. J. Sudworth, 5. On the interrogator already possessing information see e.g. IWM (Rolf), J. Hesrer; ibid, G. Upton, 6–7; IWMSA 9120/4, R. Holmes; Robert W. Calvey, *Name, Rank and Number* (Lewes, 1998), 6; G. Ellwood in Dancocks, op. cit., 40.

51. IWM, G. W. Smith, 13–14.

52. W. B. Thomas, *Dare to be Free* (London, 1955 edn.), 30.

53. Jim Rogers, *Tunnelling into Colditz* (London, 1986), 29.

54. See e.g. Ian Reid, *Prisoner at Large* (London, 1947), 244–5; Hernu, op. cit., 49; Moore, op. cit., 24.

55. See e.g. A. Moore, in Strachan, op. cit., 17; George Millar, *Horned Pigeon* (London, 1946), 44; IWM, T. Tateson, 22.

56. Margolian, op. cit., 83–7 and *passim*; IWM (Rolf), H. Taylor, 1; Paul Brickhill and Conrad Norton, *Escape to Danger* (London, 1946), 67; IWM, G. W. Smith, 13–15.

57. See Vourkoutiotis, op. cit., 327; 'Sentry', 'Shadow Life in Captivity', *Blackwood's 259* (1946), 290–1.
58. For naval interrogation outside Germany see e.g. James Spenser, *The Awkward Marine* (London, 1948), 117; IWM, R. R. James, 45–6; Warren and Benson, op. cit., 172–3; L. Burrow, in Strachen, op. cit., 202.
59. Warren and Benson, op. cit., 172–3. The *Seal* crew were in fact interviewed at Kiel, but the same techniques were applied at Wilhelmshaven once the centre was set up and running, and—after Wilhelmshaven was heavily bombed—at the naval POW camp near Bremen. See e.g. IWM, H. E. C. Elliott, 15; IWMSA 4839/2, H. F. Shipp; H. Cooper, J. L'Esperance, and R. Westaway, in Dancocks, op. cit., 149; Morgan, op. cit., 88–9.
60. D. James, op. cit., 13.
61. IWMSA 4816/2, J. M. Moran; see e.g. IWMSA 4839/2, H. F. Shipp; Chrisp, op. cit., 58–60; Morgan, op. cit.
62. Coward, op. cit., 78–9; Spenser, op. cit., 127–9; SWWEC, T. N. Catlow, 35.
63. The centre was eventually bombed out and moved into quarters in the centre of Frankfurt, becoming Dulag Luft (Wetzlar). See J. F. Vance (ed.), *Encyclopedia of Prisoners of War and Internment* (Santa Barbara, Cal., 2000), 77–8; Oliver Clutton. Brock, *Footprints on the Sands of Time* (London, 2003), ch. 2. For contrasting views of techniques employed, see Eric Cuddon (ed.), *The Dulag Luft Trial*, War Crimes Trials Series, Vol. 9 (London, 1952); Raymond E. Toliver, *The Interrogator* (Fallbrook, Cal., 1978).
64. F. H. Hinsley et al., *British Intelligence in the Second World War: Its Influence on Strategy and Operations*, Vol. 3, Pt. 1 (HMSO, 1984), 516; see also Robin P. Thomas, *Student to Stalag* (Wimbourne, 1999), 189–90. On knowing what to expect see e.g. Harsh, op. cit., 166. On being taken in see e.g. B. Filleter in Dancocks, op. cit., 19; Ron MacKenzie, *An Ordinary War* (Wangaratta, Victoria, 1995), 39–40.
65. On the rigours of short rations and isolation during interrogation at Dulag see e.g. Morrison, op. cit., 66; Geoff Taylor, *Piece of Cake* (London, 1980 edn.), 95.
66. Morrison, op. cit., 64–9; see Derek Thrower, *The Lonely Path to Freedom* (London, 1980), 14; B. Fowler in Colin Burgess, *Freedom or Death* (St Leonard's, NSW, 1994), 42; Richard Garrett, *P.O.W.* (Newton Abbot, 1981), 148.
67. G. Taylor, op. cit., 100–4; see also e.g. Edward Sniders, *Flying In, Walking Out* (Barnsley, 1999), 60.
68. Robert Kee, *A Crowd Is Not Company* (London, 1982 edn.), 61–2.
69. See also Thrower, op. cit., 14; B. Fowler in Burgess, op. cit., 42; Garrett, op. cit., 148.
70. Richard Pape, *Boldness be My Friend* (London, 1953), 99; PRO, WO 208/3274, report on escape of J. Brandford, 4. On violence see also G. Breadden in Adam-Smith, op. cit., 224. On 'shoot as spy' threats see e.g. Martin Smith, *What a Bloody Arrival* (Lewes, 1997), 112–14; IWM, G. H. Hobbs; Margarison, op. cit., 126–7; George Moreton, *Doctor in Chains* (London, 1980 edn.), 671–2; Gammon, op. cit., 172. On being threatened with the

Gestapo see e.g. Lanchbery, op. cit., 183; F. J. Crew, 'Prisoner of War', in A. E. Ross (ed), *Through Eyes of Blue* (Shrewsbury, 2002), 148.

71. PRO, AIR 40/2303, Statement of F/O M. W. G. Collins; Turner, op. cit., 129; J. Lang, in Strachen, op. cit., 89; Cuddon, op. cit., 40; see e.g. PRO, WO 208/3317, account of escape of R. M. Clinton Codner, 2; IWMSA 13573/2, A. Jones. On lack of medical attention see IWM, H. L. Martin, 109; Cuddon, op. cit., 34; PRO, AIR 40/2303; Bill Jackson, *The Lone Survivor* (North Battleford, Sask., 1993), 11. During the trial of the leading Dulag Luft staff after the war the defence claimed that overheating was the result of faulty radiators which were eventually fixed. The evidence—particularly the reluctance to immediately fix the problem or relocate cell inmates when they complained—strongly suggests a deliberate policy. See Cuddon, op. cit., *passim*. On another form of pressure see Harsh, op. cit., 168–9. On buckling under pressure see e.g. M. Smith, op. cit., 114; PRO, AIR 40/2303. The Gestapo, into whose hands airmen sheltering with the Resistance or on the run sometimes fell, tended to be much more brutal; though down to 1944–5 at least the men they caught were usually handed back after a time to the Luftwaffe. See e.g. Lawrens Adair, *Glass Houses: Paper Men* (Brisbane, 1992), 271–334; Pape, op. cit., 91–116; Harry Levy, *The Dark Side of the Sky* (London, 1996), 33–78. Airmen from Occupied Europe, Poles most of all, were often treated more roughly than British or Commonwealth aircrew. See e.g. PRO, AIR 40/2294, statement of P. Svoboda.

2 Transit and Processing

The evacuation of prisoners on foot shall in normal circumstances be effected by stages of not more than 20 kilometres per day...

(from Article 7, Geneva Convention, 1929)

Belligerents are required to notify each other of all captures of prisoners as soon as possible...

(from Article 7, Geneva Convention, 1929)

The journey from the point of capture to permanent camps within the Greater Reich is another aspect of the POW experience that has not played much of a role in the Colditz story. The reasons for this are probably similar to those surrounding the absence of much information about the circumstances of capture. Being herded into captivity lacked glamour, and for many army officers the transit experience was both depressing and sordid. It was also a phase of captivity in which escaping tended to play an ancillary role at best. Talk of transportation to stalags and oflags, in short, did not fit the Colditz profile. Yet to pass over this part of the Kriegie experience is to overlook a period that ranked for many prisoners as one of the most testing of their entire time in enemy hands.

It was in the interests of the Luftwaffe to move captured RAF aircrew to the interrogation centre at Oberusel as quickly as possible. This, along with the fact that more and more airmen were shot down over the Reich itself from 1942 onward, meant that the transportation of prisoners to Dulag Luft was usually accomplished with great swiftness and very little discomfort. Often sent under guard, usually in small groups or even individually on civilian passenger trains, British and Allied flyers reached Frankfurt-am-Main in a few hours or a day or two at most. Things were often worse on the journey from Dulag Luft to one of the permanent camps. Speed was no longer a priority, and it became economical to transport aircrew (especially of the non-commissioned variety) by special cattle-truck trains that could take up to several days to reach their final destinations. Transit conditions for captured naval personnel, meanwhile, varied on board ship from tolerable to bad, and on land from humane to atrocious. Generally speaking, the smaller the number of prisoners involved and the higher their rank the better the treatment en route became. Sailors and airmen, however, made up only roughly 8 per cent of a British prisoner population dominated by soldiers. For army POWs—along with those from other services serving on land—the transit experience was usually much worse.[1]

A number of factors were at work in making the journey into Germany for army prisoners both lengthy and arduous. Some were the result of factors beyond Wehrmacht control. Others can only be explained as arising from de facto policy choices.

Most modern armies, even when they adhere to the conventions, have not generally placed a very high priority on the upkeep of prisoners. The tendency is to plan for and place the logistical needs of one's own troops—food, shelter, transport, and so forth—ahead of those of the captured enemy, not least if fighting is still going on. Germany, more-over, at various points had to cope with very large numbers of prisoners in the wake of overwhelming victory. British prisoners, what was more, tended to be captured in the first half of the war many hundreds of miles from the Third Reich, which was where, for security and economic reasons, the POW branch of the German High Command chose to establish its permanent camps. Over the intervening distance, moreover, marking the Wehrmacht line of advance, much of the communications infrastructure had been heavily damaged in the preceding weeks. Meas-ures taken to impede the German advance, such as blowing bridges and tunnels, along with damage sustained in actual fighting, had the effect of complicating efforts to transport POWs back to Germany even after a particular campaign had ended.

Making a bad situation worse was the fact that the low-quality troops assigned to guard prisoners in transit, less self-assured than their front-line counterparts and often lacking any sense of *Frontkameradenschaft*, were more likely to bully and beat their charges. The fact that POWs were often not registered as such with the International Red Cross until they reached Germany—knowledge of their survival therefore being unknown to the outside world—added to the sense among some guards that prisoners who in some way misbehaved could be disposed of with-out consequence. All of this meant that more often than not British and Commonwealth POWs faced a *via dolorosa*.[2]

Soldiers taken during in the brief but disastrous Norway expedition in the spring of 1940 eventually achieved the dubious distinction of spending more time in enemy hands than any other group of British prisoners, excepting the handful of aircrew and sailors taken during the 'phoney war'. Due to the small size of the expeditionary force and the brevity of the fighting, however, the number of men who ended up being shipped to Germany was small (about a hundred or so). This, along with their propaganda value as the first men in khaki to be captured by the Wehrmacht, made at least parts of the journey to the Third Reich tolerable. Corporal Alan Bell of the Queen's Own Yorkshire Light Infantry remembered being escorted back on a first-class Norwegian railway carriage. Sanitary conditions deteriorated for the other ranks in a ship's hold over several days moving down the Norwegian coast and across the Baltic Sea, and once in Germany they were transported by cattle truck. This was far from pleasant but—with only forty men per wagon, and some food and rudimentary sanitation facilities provided—was still better than what was to come for those taken in France. Captured officers, meanwhile, had little to complain about at any stage of the journey from Norway. Jimmy Yule thought that 'the Germans treated us splendidly', recalling among other things that he and his fellows were moved in first-class carriages for at least part of the time in the Reich itself. Lieutenant W. K. Lang (Sherwood Foresters) was treated with great consideration, and flown with a number of other officers and other ranks from Oslo to Berlin via Copenhagen. There, on 27 April 1940, he was disconcerted to find himself part of an exhibit of British troops and equipment put on for the Führer in the Reich Chancellery garden.[3]

The common experience was rather less comfortable in Belgium and France shortly thereafter. Burdened with tens of thousands of Allied POWs in the wake of the victorious German sweep westward in the spring of 1940 for whom they were unprepared, the military authorities took a much more cold-blooded approach to dealing with the transfer of prisoners to the Reich.

The disruption of the French and Belgian transportation network meant that the unexpectedly large number of POWs taken—over 40,000 of them British—would have to be moved mostly on foot, rather circuitously along secondary roads in vast columns, generally as far as the River Rhine. In order to further minimize their effect on Wehrmacht logistics, these columns would be fed and sheltered at a very minimal level and driven hard. A combination of fatigue and hunger would make it easier for the relatively small number of troops assigned to guard the columns (rear-area types, often mounted on bicycles or motorcycle combinations) to maintain control. In order to subvert any attempt at a united front, officers would be separated from their men and nationalities played off against one another—which, in the case of the British, meant being placed at the rear of dust-choked columns and being last in line for everything. The escorts, as was made clear to the POWs, had instructions to use their weapons in earnest if thought necessary. Conducted amid great summer heat, 'The March', as it became known, was not something that the British prisoners involved would easily forget.[4]

The distance covered in each day's journey on foot could sometimes be as much as thirty miles and was rarely less than thirteen, undertaken beneath what was usually a blazing summer sun. 'Gradually men began to throw away their belongings,' remembered Private Robert Gale (Kensington Regiment) of the march away from St-Valéry, 'and even those of us in need [e.g. lacking mess tins or items of clothing] had not the strength to pick them up.' Day after day of this punishing pace left men exhausted. 'All our feet were in a terrible condition,' Gunner Gordon Instone remembered, 'and many of us could hardly stand.'[5]

At night men slept on the floor of whatever large roofed structures were close at hand, such as churches and schools, and more often than not lay in open fields under the stars. The hastily established transit cages through which POWs passed at Doullens, Cambrai, Tournai, Desvres, and other places in France and Belgium were often little better and sometimes even worse in terms of inadequate sanitary conditions. Too many men were crammed into a limited space at one time. 'The whole place smelled abominably of excreta,' Corporal James Allan remembered of the *Durchlager* at Tournai. A 'stinking, overcrowded, rat-infested sewer of a place', was how one unhappy inmate described the Cambrai cage. 'Nothing had ever been more squalid,' recorded another prisoner; 'There was no sanitation of any kind.'[6]

Whatever opportunity there was to rest, furthermore, might be interrupted by the use of POWs as casual labour. Making prisoners immediately after capture carry wounded men rearward, or dig graves and fill in shell craters once the fighting had stopped, was one thing. Forcing half-starved and exhausted men to load and unload heavy material from lorries or railway trucks was quite another; yet this too happened on occasion. At Cambrai, Gunner C. G. King remembered, he and others were detailed to move artillery shells. This was not only a violation of the Geneva Convention, which forbade the use of POWs on war-related jobs, but was also exhausting. 'By the end of the day', King recalled, 'I was . . . trembling from head to foot.'[7]

On the road or while in transit camps there was little or no opportunity to wash properly, which in turn facilitated the spread of parasites such as fleas and lice. 'I could see the blood, my blood,' recounted Stuart Brown, a private in the Royal Northumberland Fusiliers, of his discovery that he was lousy, 'through the dirty grey transparency of the bloated bodies of lice now seeking refuge in the seams of [my] shirt.'[8] Thirst and hunger made men drink from puddles and eat uncooked meat, the consequent spread of diarrhoea adding to the miseries of a march that usually extended into weeks and covered hundreds of miles.

Most critical of all was the food situation. German rations, usually in the form of very small quantities of watery soup, a few beans, or old pieces of bread, were rarely issued until the evening halt, and there were nights when nothing at all was provided. Breakfast—a rare event— usually consisted of acorn coffee, perhaps accompanied by a small biscuit. 'We were terribly hungry', as one officer recalled feelingly. After two days without food, 'men started to have blackouts and had to be supported by their comrades', remembered Private Kenneth Dyson of the East Yorkshire Regiment. Prisoners were quickly reduced to ducking the column in order to ransack abandoned shops or forage by the wayside for anything remotely edible. 'I was eating leaves from the roadside', one private bluntly admitted.[9]

Sometimes local Red Cross organizations were able to provide help. When columns passed through villages and towns, furthermore, the local population might turn out along the route offering water, milk, or food to parched and hungry prisoners. On occasion this was tolerated, but in many instances the escorting soldiers thwarted British attempts to take advantage of any largesse. The guards 'would have none of it,' Private Douglas Swift of the Royal Sussex Regiment remembered if one such incident in France, 'kicking the buckets over and shouting at the women, whilst at the same time threatening us with dire conse- quences if we made any move towards the buckets'. Those who ignored the risks faced a violent response. 'I personally was once stabbed with a bayonet', recalled Private Walter Darbyshire of the Duke of Wellington's Regiment, whilst being seen accepting food from a French girl. Peasants 'who tried to hand us bread or other food while we were on the move were nearly always clubbed with rifle-butts and driven away with parting kicks and curses', wrote Captain Terence Prittie. 'A nervous sentry was even liable to shoot at them and shoot to kill.'[10]

At the start of the march prisoners were warned that attempts to escape would end bloodily, and shots were indeed fired at the comparatively few men—most were simply too exhausted to try—who were seen making a break. Those who fell out from a moving column for any other reason, however, also ran a considerable risk of being injured or even killed.[11]

Ducking out in order to scrounge from hedgerows, gardens, or buildings was dangerous. 'I saw the cycle guards on many occasions hit British soldiers . . . when they tried to break from the ranks to get water', Lance-Corporal A. M. Garden of the Royal Corps of Signals reported in London after a successful escape. He also recorded that he himself had been beaten with a rifle butt for doing this, and that on other occasions shots had been fired at men's legs. Sometimes warning shots were fired in the air; at other times the guards could let fly in earnest from the start.[12]

Passing out from hunger and exhaustion was also potentially dangerous. In some cases men who fainted or who otherwise could not go on were picked up by an escorting truck.[13] In other instances there was a more brutal response to anyone falling by the wayside. Rifleman A. Hosington, a sixteen-year regular who eventually escaped back to England, reported that German field police 'would, as often as not, shoot [those who fainted] as they lay on the ground'. On one occasion a prisoner witnessed men who collapsed being run over by a vehicle, while others saw individuals who stopped to drop their trousers or even tie their laces being struck and killed.[14]

Even moving too slowly could invite retaliation. 'A rifle butt in the kidneys was a favourite encouragement to get a move on,' John Lawrence of the Royal Sussex Regiment remembered. 'I got threatened with a rifle butt,' a West Kent private related, 'but was sufficiently quick to dodge it.' Others were jabbed at with bayonets or had shots fired either over their heads or in their general direction.[15]

In some instances the violent behaviour of the guards might be driven by utilitarian considerations. Having to cope with very large numbers of men and very limited resources, those tasked with guarding POW columns were anxious to assert their authority and prevent escapes and the disintegration of order more generally. That this could happen was borne out by the manner in which prisoners, driven to desperation by hunger and thirst, could mob civilians offering food and drink and fight each other for whatever was on offer.[16]

In some cases, however, delight in the infliction of harm on the helpless was clearly present. Gunner Albert Paice recalled that when women came out in various villages with buckets of water for the prisoners, 'the Germans took the buckets away from the women, and threw the water over them'. At St-Pol, where women were being prevented from aiding a column of BEF prisoners, Quartermaster-Sergeant John Brown, Royal Artillery, heard a German officer say: 'Let the English swine go without—they can die of thirst and hunger for all I care!'[17] Such malice could breed atrocities. 'I saw one of the Germans fire a revolver at point blank range at the Padre's leg for no reason that I could see', a private in the Royal Scots Fusiliers reported shortly after his escape. 'I saw him fall down and the Germans did nothing to help him.' Lance-Corporal George Dunning also witnessed an action that could not possibly be justified:

I remember...the fair-haired militia boy whose bowels were giving him hell. After being repeatedly refused permission to seek relief behind a hedge, he suddenly broke ranks and, unbuttoning en route, made for the fringe of a small wood. It was glaringly obvious what he wanted, but nevertheless several guards took pot-shots at him as he crouched beneath a tree. There was an agonising scream followed by a bloodcurdling crescendo of yelps like those of a kicked puppy. We discovered later that a bullet had passed right through his eyes, through the bridge of his nose, and had blinded him.

'One incident sickened me', BQMS Brown recalled. 'A young boy ahead of me bent down to lace his boot. Instantly a German was on him, and thrust the bayonet up his arse and out his side. He was stretched out on the road as we went by: the agony on his face haunts me still.'[18]

Harsh conditions on the march naturally affected the spirits of POWs. Sometimes morale held up. Much of the time it did not. Being among men from the same unit could help maintain a sense of group identity and mutual interest, especially if—as happened only rarely—officers and other ranks who had already established a sense of mutual respect were not separated from one another.[19] Bad behaviour on the part of guards could on occasion backfire in terms of cohesion. 'We were now becoming very much a group', Jim Rogers, a future guest at Colditz, wrote of the officers in his column by the time they reached Cambrai. '[O]ur treatment by the Germans was uniting us in a spirit of strong opposition...No one's spirits seemed to be in the least daunted.' Wing Commander Basil Embry, shot down over France in late May and passed on to a POW column departing from Desvres, was struck by how, in 'marked comparison with the other nationals, the morale of the British troops was magnificent'. The ability to sing or make a joke—however grim—suggested that prisoners' spirits remained unbroken. David Read, a reserve chaplain captured at St-Valéry, wrote of how when marching through French towns 'we British prisoners always straightened up, marched in step, and sang as lustily as we could'. Gunner William Harding remembered how a German officer, stopping to view the passing column, noticed the medal ribbons on an elderly member of the Pioneer Corps. 'Englishman, you were in the 1914 war', the officer remarked; to which the man replied, 'Aye, and I'll fight you in the next'.[20]

Days and then weeks of thirst and hunger, however, took their toll on morale. This could be true for those with commissions as well as those without, as in many respects officers suffered as much as their men. 'We walked in almost complete silence', Terence Prittie wrote of his 'nightmare' journey through Artois and Picardy. By the time Second Lieutenant H. C. F. Harwood reached St-Vith he was so weakened by semi-starvation and fatigue that 'I could hardly walk and felt ridiculously giddy the moment I stood up'.[21] Most officers, however, were ferried at least part of the way across France and the Low Countries by vehicle rather than going exclusively on foot, and were less frequently shot at. As a result, and perhaps because of a stronger sense of duty, BEF officers were less likely to experience a collapse of corporate identity and discipline than were other ranks. It was in the other-rank columns that POWs began to witness the rapid evolution of a 'survival of the fittest' mentality.[22]

This was particularly true in relation to the all-consuming question of food. 'There was no thought of "fair shares"', Corporal James Allan later explained. 'Every man grabbed what he could, and if the next man got none, that was too bad.' The authority of British NCOs was either not recognized at all—everyone had been reduced to the same status insofar as they were all captives at the mercy of the enemy—or was used, some suspected, to further personal interests. 'Every man was on his own', as one private put it. This could mean every fellow for himself, both when something to eat was in the offing and when opportunities arose to engage in theft.[23]

Stealing became endemic in some columns. Portable food items were targeted, as were pieces of kit and clothing that were in short supply and possibly could be bartered for something to eat. Men found that they were particularly vulnerable while asleep. Private Keith Maxwell of the Royal Army Service Corps made the mistake of dropping off to sleep after washing his underclothes and socks in a stream at the end of a day's march and leaving them to dry. When he woke up they were gone. Some men never took off their boots over the course of the march for fear of losing them. 'You could leave nothing about,' Len Williamson (another RASC man) recalled, 'everything had to be carried on your person, even when you slept.' Sometimes even this was not enough, as men discovered when packs, boots, and other items they had used as makeshift pillows were gone the next morning. If a man woke up in time a fight would almost certainly ensue; if he lost he became, as one NCO aptly stated, yet another victim of 'robbery with violence'.[24]

Even when officers were still close enough to try and maintain order, discipline could break down. Lieutenant-Colonel Euan Miller, CO of the 2nd Battalion, King's Royal Rifle Corps, found this to be the case a couple of weeks into the march from Calais. 'I tried to organise fair distribution of food & water,' he wrote in his diary, 'but they [the other ranks] fought like beasts, stole and cheated.' As with the NCOs, there was open suspicion that officers were profiting at the expense of the men in the ranks. 'As we gave it nearly all to the men & paid for most of it ourselves this was bit hard', Miller fumed. 'I had great difficulty in stopping myself knocking one or two of them down.'[25]

Trust was definitely at a premium. 'I, certainly,' Ed Annetts later explained, 'had firmly decided in future I should only look after number one...at that stage [many days into the march] I was becoming little short of paranoid about any demonstration of friendship, for fear there was some furtive design on something I possessed.'[26] Even among officers brotherly feeling might only extend to one's immediate circle in the face of deprivation. Second Lieutenant Michael Duncan of the Oxfordshire and Buckinghamshire Light Infantry wrote of how at Doullens 'we would have given our souls for a bit of chocolate or a spoonful of jam'. A small tin of sugar he eventually acquired at Cambrai 'became my most closely guarded treasure, its contents being issued to a very limited circle of friends in a minute spoonful'.[27]

Such circles, as it happened, soon proved to be the best way for other ranks to avoid going under in the more Darwinian columns. Syndicates, even if involving only two men, could engage in the necessary foraging, bargaining, and protection of possessions more effectively than most single men. The appearance of these de facto gangs, however, might only intensify competition. Private Adrian Vincent (Queen Victoria's Rifles) recalled what happened in his column:

With the setting up of the combines, each of them with a self-elected leader, the foraging for food became a deadly business, leading to continual fights in which the weakest went to the wall, and therefore starved for most of the march.

Everybody was against everybody, with fights going on all the time. At night, one hardly dared sleep because of the night prowlers who crawled around the field, trying to steal your gas-mask container in the hope that it might contain a few scraps of bread.[28]

Those men intent on looking after number one had even less compunction when it came to relations with the masses of Allied prisoners with whom soldiers of the BEF came in contact while in transit. Widely disliked due to a mixture of chauvinism and envy at the preferential treatment they were often given by the Germans, fellow Belgian, Dutch, and French POWs—the latter by far the largest contingent—were often considered fair game among other ranks. 'We have nothing to be ashamed of,' one man insisted after he and a mate stole a Frenchman's cigarette hoard one night, 'they were NAAFI issue and we are more entitled to them than some stinking Froggie.' Fights over resources, not very surprisingly, were common.[29]

Meanwhile, insofar as they were concerned about anything beyond their immediate survival, prisoners wondered what the course of the war might mean for their future. With no hard news available, rumours—usually of a hopeful though improbable nature—ran wild among both officers and men. 'Endless rumours of peace pacts', Signalman N. R. Wylie noted in a diary he kept while at Doullens in June 1940. Padre Read remembered word spreading in his officer column, first that Turkey had entered the war, then that America had done so, and finally that 'the French were building a new army in Algeria'. Tales of sudden enemy reversals, even a likely rescue by advancing British troops, gained wide currency.[30]

Unpleasant as the trek across France and the Low Countries often was, among the worst moments for many BEF prisoners came when they reached a location in the north-east from which they could be transported into the Reich. Movement either by river or rail, it quickly became apparent, could be unpleasant in the extreme.

Many prisoners, especially those from St-Valéry, were eventually loaded onto empty 100-foot coal barges in Holland for a journey of several days down the Scheldt and Rhine tributaries into north-western Germany. Sometimes this could be bearable. More often than not, however, the bread rations provided were mouldy and insufficient, the holds were filthy and massively overcrowded—a cargo of 1,500 men was not unheard of—and both dysentery and lice were by this point rife. 'It was awful', as Dr B. N. Mazumdar, a future Colditz inmate, put it feelingly in an interview.[31]

A more universal experience involved days on end in closed railway wagons under atrocious conditions. With signs indicating accommodation for eight horses or twenty-four men, these trucks were filled to double or more their official capacity when POWs were involved. Food, water, and sanitation facilities were inadequate or non-existent. 'During the first stage of our journey we were kept in these trucks for five days without food, water, or latrine facilities', Private Charles Baker (Queen Victoria's Rifles) wrote of his standing-room-only move westward from Cambrai. 'We would urinate into our boots and excrete into pieces of linen torn from our battle-dress, and throw the substance out the slit windows.' Dysentery and heat only made matters worse. 'Several men fainted,' another QVR soldier recalled, 'but there was no room for them to fall down.' By the time this train reached its destination, Trier, two men had died in his wagon alone.[32]

Officers, meanwhile, though usually better off than the men, were having their own troubles. Lieutenant Harwood recalled the 'oppressive heat inside the lorry, the fumes coming up through the floor boards, the complete inability to get into a comfortable position', and how on the last leg to Mainz he was stuffed into a wagon with forty-nine other officers. Of the last stage of the journey through Luxembourg, Major E. Booth, Royal Engineers, recalled how his group was on the road for twenty-one hours, 'spent in the lorries in increasing discomfort, without food except for the biscuits we had brought with us in our pockets, and with one halt of five minutes . . . it was very uncomfortable and stuffy'.[33]

Once inside the borders of the Reich itself, prisoners were usually held for a few days in staging areas prior to shipment further east into permanent POW camps. Officers, by and large, seemed to have fared better than other ranks at this point. The *Offizierdulag* established in barracks at Mainz, through which most commissioned BEF personnel passed in June 1940, was something of an oasis. Rations were still often very short, and tempers sometimes ran high when attempts were made to seriously interrogate BEF officers. But the commandant was a sympathetic type, there were beds with straw mattresses as well the opportunity to shower with hot water and have one's clothes deloused, and officers were given official capture cards to fill in. The latter were legitimate and the agreed means of letting the International Red Cross, and through them the War Office and relatives in Britain, know that someone was now officially a POW. The camp at Mainz was, several officers later noted, the most well-run place they had thus far encountered in captivity.[34]

The experience for those passing through the Durchlager established at Trier for both officers and other ranks was much more variable. The first challenge, as many other ranks discovered, was the journey through the town itself.

Their uniforms and boots incomplete or in tatters, unshaven, dirty, lousy, weak, and generally in a bad way, prisoners unloaded from barges or trains were often forced to run something of a gauntlet as they were marched through the streets of Trier to a former barracks for labour-camp workers above the town. Here, as at some other locations, the civilian population was encouraged to turn out in order to gloat, jeer, and throw things as the bedraggled columns passed. 'As we marched up the hill,' Sergeant George Beeson (Royal Army Ordnance Corps) wrote of an unfortunately quite typical experience, 'some women and children spat at us while others threw stones and sticks at us; this was a terrible ordeal.'[35]

Conditions inside the wire at Trier varied from marginal (huts and bunks, a little in the way of rations, the opportunity to rest, and at least occasional access to running water) to the impossible (no shelter, no food, no sanitation). Much depended on how many prisoners were present. 'With all its drawbacks Trier was a haven', Private Wilson concluded after detailing the 'vile' sanitary conditions. 'Some peace prevailed, some food was dished out, and though there was none for us [i.e. his contingent] there was some shelter.' At a point when the camp was not overflowing Captain Munby found life there to be 'pleasantly uneventful', while Colonel Miller agreed that it was 'a pleasant change from the march—we had a fair amount of food and were only hungry, no longer practically starving'. At other times conditions were very bad. 'There were no washing facilities,' Rifleman Ewart Jones recalled, 'every wooden bunk had had two tenants (and there were about two hundred bunks, in three tiers, in each very small hut) and the latrines were very primitive.' Widespread dysentery made the situation worse. 'It was an *appalling* place', future Colditz prisoner Captain Kenneth Lockwood recalled angrily. 'The treatment meted out by the Germans was disgraceful. The soup and food was foul, and above all, the latrine arrangements were appalling.'[36]

Then there was the last leg of the journey into captivity to contend with. If only by virtue of the distances involved and what men had already been through, the final stage—shipment by rail to permanent camp locations—could rank among the roughest stages of transit in 1940.[37]

From Mainz and other locations officers spent two or three days en route to certain *Offizierlagern*, or oflags, usually located in southern Germany. In some cases, with the journey broken at a major city and local Red Cross nurses providing refreshments, this might not be so unpleasant. In other cases, too many officers were jammed into single trucks, there were few or no breaks, and not enough food was provided for a journey lasting many hours longer than scheduled. Major Booth recorded the episode in his diary as one of 'hunger, dirt, and discomfort'. Captain Irwin found it 'quite unpleasant' and Jim Rogers 'very unpleasant', the latter going on to complain that 'the crowding was just like the pictures shown after the war of Jews being taken to concentration camps'. This last comment may have been something of an overstatement but things were certainly bad. 'Although no one died,' Second Lieutenant P. F. S. Douglas of the Argylls reported after his escape on what it was like to be crowded with over sixty others in a closed wagon, 'our condition on arrival at our permanent camp was weak (my pulse was 34 for 6 weeks thereafter).' Those officers who were lucky enough to travel third class—including majors and above—were infinitely better off than those in closed wagons, but might still suffer indignities. Kenneth Lockwood remembered how during a halt at Cologne members of the public 'spat at the windows'.[38]

As in earlier stages, the other ranks often suffered more. The majority as yet were unregistered, there were far more of them to cope with, and the camps to which they were being sent—*Stammlagern*, or stalags—were located several hundred miles to the east in Upper Silesia and Poland. This usually meant train journeys, almost invariably in closed wooden goods-type wagons, of greater length than those endured by the officers.

Once again soldiers were crammed into trucks that could only hold, without discomfort, half or even a third of the number forced into them. The bread and water provided for the journey often ran out, there was usually no sanitation beyond a bucket, despite the prevalence of dysentery, halts were infrequent at best, and ventilation usually consisted of only two slit grilles high up on either side of the wagon. Where it was possible at all, those inside had to take it in turns to sit down, and even when human waste was emptied through the ventilation slits the stench was soon appalling. In some cases men went without anything to eat or drink for three days at a stretch.[39]

Sometimes, despite the hellish conditions, prisoners might manage to maintain a semblance of social cohesion, helping the worst off and even making the odd sardonic joke ('last time I travel on this railway again').

In other instances, as one private put it, 'any semblance of human dignity vanished', and men looked only to their own welfare—a matter of 'I'm all right, Jack', as another soldier explained.[40]

By the time the trains reached their destinations the survivors were in a very bad way. 'I remember having to cover my eyes when "falling" out of the wagon,' Rifleman Frank Jackson remembered, 'the legs unable to hold up.' Men had blacked out, been driven mad, or had simply been unable to stay alive any longer. 'On that journey approximately fifty people died,' Private Alex Masterson of the Argylls asserted in an interview, 'four in my boxcar.' This was by no means an isolated experience. 'It took us a very long time to forgive the Germans for that train journey', John Elwyn, Welsh Guards, later wrote.[41]

The journey to the Reich was often no better for the over 12,000 troops left behind in the wake of the battles for Greece and Crete in the spring of 1941. As before, the initial part of the trek was done on foot to and between staging points. This was rarely pleasant—the march from Sfakia to Suda Bay after the surrender on Crete being a case in point[42]— but usually lasted only a day or so, as a combination of geographical and logistical circumstances necessitated movement by other means. The need to arrange for prisoner transport, however, never a high enemy priority, meant a significantly longer period spent in overcrowded and poorly run temporary transit cages—including the notorious Dulag 183 established at Salonika, through which almost everyone captured in Greece and Crete eventually passed.

Those taken on the Greek mainland in April 1941 were usually sent to Corinth and incarcerated in a flyblown army barracks located there. There were not enough huts for the numbers involved, there were no bunks—or indeed furniture of any kind—yet plenty of bedbugs, and sanitation was so elementary and limited that the majority of prisoners were lousy and soon suffered from some form of dysentery.[43]

The guards at Corinth were also apparently not above abusing prisoners. J. E. Pryce, a survivor from HMS *Gloucester*, later wrote about how each evening fifty men were forced to undergo the 'Hop, Skip and Jump Race':

These unfortunate men were ordered to strip off their clothes and place them in piles at a distance of two hundred yards. A rifle was fired into the air and the fifty naked men would rush madly in the direction of their clothes, scramble into them and dash wildly back to the starting post. The last three to arrive back received a sharp beating up. To hasten their progress on the first stage of the race, the German fired revolver bullets into the sand behind the contestants. Prisoners might also be forced into work gangs, some of them unloading ammunition from enemy ships.

Most important of all, the daily rations provided—bread, cheese, lentils, figs, macaroni, and other items—were so small that hunger became a constant preoccupation. Sometimes items could be purchased from locals through the wire, but this was never enough to satisfy, and morale suffered. Barney Roberts, an Australian soldier, remembered catching sparrows in order to have something more to eat.[44]

The situation also soon became tough for the over 5,000 men taken on Crete who spent weeks in temporary holding cages. In such places the only shelter consisted of a few tents and some olive trees, and sanitary arrangements were of an extremely ad-hoc nature. Fleas, lice, and diarrhoea were soon rampant, while issued rations—usually little more than a cup of lentil soup each day—proved inadequate. 'After a week or so of this diet', Sapper D. W. Luckett wrote, 'a general weakness began to set in amongst us all, when to suddenly stand up after sitting or laying down, brought on a very dizzy spell for a minute or two.'[45]

Going out in work gangs whose main task was to clear up after the battle offered the opportunity to scrounge and sometimes a little extra in the way of rations. Men might initially recoil at the task of handling and burying corpses that were rapidly decomposing in the summer heat, but as Sapper Ernest Kirk recalled, 'hunger was stronger' than distaste for the job. The general situation, meanwhile, remained grim for most POWs. John Chrisp, a naval officer who was later consigned to Colditz, lost fourteen pounds in the weeks he spent here, and the more severe dysentery cases began to die at a rate of about one a week.[46]

Some men simply stole from their fellows to keep body and soul together, while others got into the trading racket (cigarettes were the key form of currency). A few tried slipping under the wire at night to forage among the locals: a practice as dangerous as stealing since, if caught, the offenders were beaten up or made to stand in the sun holding heavy objects over their heads without food or water for several days. The formation of syndicates, usually divided by nationality and unit, was often necessary but served to further fragment the prisoner community. Being an NCO meant little, those who tried to exert authority over food distribution finding themselves objects of suspicion, often ignored and sometimes attacked for alleged favouritism.[47]

Bad as things were, worse was to come when POWs taken in the spring of 1941 began to be concentrated at Salonika in preparation for shipment to the Fatherland. For some of the officers taken on Crete the initial part of the trek was by air. 'The flight to Athens in the JU52s was very pleasant', Lieutenant R. G. M. Quarry reported, before going on to describe the awfulness of the next stages. For everyone else there was a voyage of several days deep in the bowels of tramp steamers, awful halts, hour after hour in cattle trucks or lorries—often in extremely cramped and unsanitary conditions—plus an occasional forced march where bridges had been blown.[48]

It was what life was like at Dulag 183, however, that remained most vividly in prisoners' minds. As elsewhere, the local Greek population did its best to help by offering food and water as prisoners were marched through the town, despite the violent response of the escorting German soldiers.[49] Within the compounds at Salonika itself, however, the problems of inadequate shelter, poor sanitation, overcrowding, lack of food, and disease—including, by this time, conditions arising from malnutrition such as beriberi—were particularly acute, with consequent effects on mood and behaviour.

The old Turkish-built barracks around which the Germans strung barbed wire was already in a serious state of decrepitude: the floors often broken up, furniture and fixtures absent or wrecked, the water supply contaminated, and a huge population of bedbugs in residence. At any one time there were between 8,000 and 12,000 prisoners held here in the summer and autumn of 1941, 'packed [in] like sardines', as one inmate put it, so that in the barrack blocks a POW 'could not move without treading on someone when we were lying down'.[50]

The most pressing problem, as always, was lack of food. Daily rations consisted of ersatz tea at dawn, thin soup akin to greasy hot water at midday, and a small issue of bread and biscuit at about five o'clock. This last meal consisted of one-fifth to one-tenth of a small rye loaf—twelve inches in diameter and two inches thick—plus three-quarters of a biscuit ('which was the size of a large dog biscuit but tasted much worse') per man. This could mean well under a thousand calories a day, which in turn produced sudden blackouts ('Twice I passed out in the soup queue', John Chrisp remembered) and serious weight loss over time, one ambulance man losing almost fifty pounds in the three months he was at Salonika. Being detailed for a local working party outside the wire, which might involve heavy, war-related labour—unloading oil drums or loading stores onto an Italian destroyer, for example—only made matters worse. Prisoners soon began to suffer the effects of vitamin deficiencies as well as hunger. 'We were all starving', as another inmate put it succinctly.[51]

This state of affairs once more had its insidious effect on many men's outlook and behaviour. Though some officers and men managed to retain some personal dignity, for most life soon became a matter of 'survival of the fittest', according to Sapper M. E. Osborne: 'If you weakened in any way, you died.' Prisoners not only ran great risks to obtain food from Greeks outside the camp, they also bartered personal items such as rings and watches for food or cigarettes, regardless of value, and were not above stealing. In general there developed what Australian soldier Barney Roberts described as 'a single-minded sense of self-preservation which seemed to thrive on distrust and larceny'.[52]

The craving for nicotine was such that smokers battled each other for the butts thrown down by guards, often destroying the prize in the process. The same was true with respect to food, one inmate describing how men 'snarled and grovelled in the dust, clawing at a small piece of bread' that had been thrown over the wire. Conditions were so bad that mouldy cheese which even the Germans thought unfit for human consumption was sought after desperately in the dustbins when the guards' backs were turned. 'I have seen men competing for such "food" with the great rats which infested the camp', Surgeon Commander Hugh Singer reported.[53]

There was a great deal of general distrust and envy abroad in Dulag 183. Two groups in particular, however, generated more than the average amount of suspicion and dislike: non-commissioned officers and racketeers. With the officers wired off from the other ranks, senior NCOs were either given or assumed limited command functions within the main part of the camp. The best of these warrant officers and sergeants worked hard to keep up a semblance of order and defend the interests of the men in dealings with the Germans. Some, however, used their rank to further their own interests only, and at least two sergeant majors became so enthusiastic in enforcing German orders that they were widely, and perhaps rightly, suspected of having become outright collaborators.[54]

Those who appeared to do best out of the trading racket were also disliked, even by those who used their services—the Cypriots and Palestinians sometimes being thought to be particularly adept at sharp practice. The cultural-cum-racial assumptions behind such suspicion among the British long pre-dated the war, but the conditions of captivity tended to exacerbate hostility even before men arrived in Salonika, where the Palestinians were segregated but still able to trade with the rest of the POW population. According to Fritz Jordan, a German émigré, 'there was a constant tension between the Palestinian and British prisoners'.[55]

Making a bad situation worse at Dulag 183 was the attitude of the commandant. According to a senior British medical officer, this middle-aged dugout type 'took a sadistic pleasure in the misery he created inside the camp', and was responsible for the unusually high degree of brutality displayed by the guards.[56] Anyone late for the morning prisoner-count on the parade ground was liable to be beaten up, and anyone spotted moving about at night was liable to be shot. Escapers probably knew the risks they ran, but there were plenty of cases where prisoners were killed without any justification whatsoever—while hanging out washing, for instance, or using the latrines at night. The bodies were sometimes left out in the open for days as an object lesson.[57]

Finally, in the late summer and on into the autumn of 1941, enough working transport had been concentrated to allow the captured veterans of the battles for Greece and Crete to be shipped to the Greater Reich. As before, the journey was usually in overcrowded cattle trucks with insufficient attention paid to food, water, and sanitation, and this period could last from four to ten days, depending on track congestion and the final destination.

As many as seventy men might be crammed into closed wagons meant to hold forty at most, so that prisoners had to take turns to sit or lie down spoon-fashion. Diarrhoea was still very much a problem, yet prisoners were often only allowed out to relieve themselves at the side of the track once every twenty-four hours or so, and were sometimes not allowed out for days at a time in retaliation for escape attempts. As W. S. Eldred (Royal Army Service Corps) recalled, there were many men suffering from dysentery 'who literally had to sit in it'.[58]

Rations for the journey, usually consisting of one or two small tins of meat, a few biscuits, and a small loaf of black bread, were limited to begin with and wholly inadequate for journeys that were usually days longer than anticipated. Help from the Yugoslav Red Cross when trains stopped at Belgrade or Zagreb was much appreciated, but could not make up for the lack of food and also water, some prisoners going without anything to drink for days at a time. On this stage of the journey officers seem to have been no better off than other ranks. 'The days passed in a sickening haze of dysentery, the stench of urine, and unrelenting hunger in the overcrowded stifling cattle trucks', Jack Champ later wrote.[59]

On occasion the journey was just about tolerable. Most prisoners, however, remembered it as a nightmare during which, as one Australian private put it, 'everyone prayed for its end'.[60] Prisoners might be unable to climb out when the final destination was reached, and there were cases of men going mad or dying en route from the cumulative effects of what they had endured.[61]

All this did little to improve morale. The human spirit, however, can be remarkably resilient. After finishing with a truly terrible eight days in transit, a demoralized batch of POWs from Salonika ('very dirty...must have stunk to high heaven...unshaven...matted lousy hair...[sometimes] too weak to move') were escorted from the Luckenwalde train station to Stalag IIIA. Told that they were from Crete, the German civilian population jeered, spat, and threw stones as the prisoners passed. 'Then something wonderful happened [Sapper Jack Seed remembered], one solitary voice somewhere in the column had the courage to start singing "It's a long way to Tipperary". Immediately the remainder joined in singing as hard as we could, squaring our shoulders while trying to get into some sort of step.' The Germans, supposedly, were rendered speechless this display of *Engländer* defiance.[62]

Though by early 1943 it was clear that the tide had turned in favour of the Allies, there was to be one further large-scale migration of British and Commonwealth prisoners to the Reich. This occurred when over 70,000 POWs held by the Italians, mostly taken by Axis forces in North Africa, suddenly found themselves in Nazi hands after the armistice of September 1943. Their hopes of a quick release having been raised by news of Allied landings and the evident desire of their jailers to throw in the towel, prisoners in *campos* throughout Italy were bitterly disappointed to find Germans manning the camp gates and towers within a matter of twenty-four hours. A few thousand managed to make for the hills in the brief period of transition and were at liberty for greater or lesser lengths of time, but the majority soon found themselves in cattle trucks bound for the Brenner Pass.[63]

Conditions on the journey to camps in Austria and points further north were sometimes very similar to those experienced during transportation to the Fatherland in earlier years. The rations and water provided were often inadequate. Guards could and did shoot to kill prisoners 'while trying to escape'. Too many prisoners were crammed into each wagon. Halts to answer the call of nature, and other privileges, were erratic and might be withdrawn if prisoners were deemed to be insufficiently cowed. A further hazard was added in the form of Allied air superiority, which meant that trains ran the risk of being bombed or strafed. All this, on top of the sudden dashing of the common hope of imminent liberation, could have a bad effect on morale. 'I never fully regained the self-respect I lost when I found myself on a train bound for Germany', wrote Peter Winter, noting that the few among the fifty men tightly packed into his wagon who voiced thoughts of escape were prevented from doing anything by the despondent majority.[64]

All that said, prisoners shipped from Italy had certain advantages when compared to those who had entrained for the Reich in earlier years. First and foremost, those from the *campos* had in the main had time to adjust both physically and mentally to captivity. Bodies had grown used to the lower calorie intake, while Red Cross parcels had helped to provide not only more and varied food but also necessary minerals and vitamins, the end result being leanness and hunger but also a basic level of fitness. The time spent behind the wire in Italy had allowed men to develop important prisoner-survival skills. This could mean anything from how to build a 'stufa' (or 'blower', a very efficient personal cooking stove) from scratch, to knowledge of the techniques and acquisition of the tools needed to break out of confinement. Those moving toward the Brenner Pass in the autumn of 1943, in short, were generally in better shape than those transported through the Balkans or across France and the Low Countries in earlier years. Corporal John Greenwood (Royal Artillery) noted that, in contrast to newly captured RAF types placed aboard wagons in his train, soldiers like himself who had had time to adjust to the Spartan nature of POW life could find the journey from Italy tough but, in overall terms, 'not too bad'.[65]

That the prisoners from Italy were generally better able to cope showed in the relatively high number of escape attempts made. Most of those taken from the battlefields of France and Greece, including men who went on to careers as escape artists, were, at the time they were locked into cattle trucks, too mentally and physically run down to try and 'train-jump'.[66] Despite the threat of being killed, however, Desert War veterans time and again attempted to duck away during halts and drop down through holes dug in the floor of wagons when trains were moving slowly. On the train in which Lieutenant George Millar was travelling there were constant attempts to escape, the most successful being in the last wagon, where Major 'Stump' Gibbon led the entire contingent through a hole dug through the rear boards. Of the 800 prisoners distributed among twenty trucks on the train on which Sandy St Clair journeyed northward, 125 managed to get out. This sort of thing was not confined to officers. En route between PG 70 and a transit camp at Jacobstahl, 20 per cent of the other ranks on one train disappeared.[67]

The transit experience for wounded men, meanwhile, varied a good deal through the war. Those too ill or badly injured to be marched off as walking wounded with the rest occasionally struck it lucky, finding themselves transported by stages in ambulances or, better yet, on proper hospital trains. The latter were 'very good, very efficient, very efficient German staff, splendid accommodation', remembered Dr Thomas Wilson in reference to the transport of British bed cases from Lille to Germany in June 1940.[68] This was by no means the universal experience, however, and became more and more rare as German casualties mounted and medical resources became strained. Many seriously wounded cases taken at Arnhem in September 1944, for instance, were shipped to Germany in cattle trucks. Only after an RAMC doctor angrily threatened to report the field hospital commander to the Protecting Power as a potential war criminal was a 'sumptuous Red Cross train' provided for the next batch of wounded.[69]

Conditions in the ad hoc prison hospitals established en route to Germany for bed cases in the wake of major campaigns might be initially acceptable, especially if the facility concerned was a former British Army hospital now operating under new management that could draw on stockpiled medicines and equipment. On the outskirts of Athens, for example, the 26th General Hospital and 5th Australian General Hospital combined to form a large POW hospital in the wake of the German invasion in April 1941. 'We continued our work without serious interference', Dr D. L. Charters later explained, going on to assert that, all things considered, 'we had a very low death rate and the results of treatment were satisfactory'. Even this facility, however, experienced food shortages, and the sick and wounded who had to endure more makeshift arrangements elsewhere might suffer greatly. 'It was difficult trying to feed the patients at all, let alone suitably', wrote J. M. Green, a Dental Corps officer, of arrangements for the wounded at St-Valéry in the weeks after the surrender. 'Gas gangrene made its unwelcome appearance, and we had no serum, and could not get any.' Things were even worse at the overcrowded and highly unsanitary staging points across northern France. After his favourable encounter with German medical personnel in the field, Captain Lang eventually found himself lying on straw in a former casino at Forges-les-Eaux, with other wounded packed in like sardines. 'Medical supplies were virtually non-existent and, although we were fortunate in having three British medical orderlies, there was little they could do for us.'[70]

Even in the better transit hospitals overcrowding and food shortages could become a problem as time went on. The Athens POW hospital in June 1941 was operating with 20 per cent fewer physicians than was considered necessary for an RAMC general hospital with the equivalent number of patients, and men were getting as little as 1,000 calories of food a day. The orderlies were finding it harder and harder to carry out their duties due to lack of food, and the absence of vitamins and minerals was bringing on the first signs of deficiency diseases by the time the place was closed in November 1941.[71]

Much depended on the attitude of the German medical officers placed in command of transit hospitals. Some worked closely with their British counterparts in true Hippocratic fashion to do everything they could to treat the wounded and cure the sick. Others, unfortunately, proved to be more of a hindrance than an aid to good health. Among the latter was Oberstabsarzt Schott, running the transit hospital at the Salonika cage and memorably described by one who knew him well as a 'gross, bull-necked man with a shaven head and an enormous paunch'. Like his Nazi counterparts in various other places, he appeared to make up for limited medical knowledge with a mixture of bombast and vindictiveness. When a British surgeon complained about conditions in the hospital, he 'lost his temper and said that the Geneva Convention could go to hell . . . we could take what was coming to us'. This apparently meant denying the medical staff any access to captured British supplies. Even with the most rigorous economy measures, 'we were short of almost everything', reported Surgeon Commander Hugh Singer. The epidemics of beriberi and diphtheria that swept the camp and hospital could not be properly treated, only aspirin in limited quantities could be spared for cases of sandfly fever, and little could be done for those who fell ill with dysentery. Like their patients, RAMC personnel lost a lot of weight as a result of the serious food shortage and became subject to debilitating illnesses at Salonika. 'It was awful', Dr Alan King recalled feelingly.[72]

The seriously sick and wounded, in short, along with captured medical personnel, might find stages of their often more prolonged journey into the Reich just about as bad as anything encountered by fitter men in earlier weeks. Once pronounced fit enough at any temporary staging post—by a German rather than a British medical officer—patients would be placed back among their more ambulatory fellows and suffer the same rigours for the remainder of the journey.[73]

Some of the men transported rearward were sufficiently traumatized by the journey into captivity not to care what happened next. But for the vast majority, however tired and hungry they were, a nagging question loomed larger as prisoners of war were moved on foot from railway sidings to POW camps in locations stretching from East Prussia down into south-eastern Austria. Once inside, the first order of real business for their jailers was usually to register their charges as prisoners of war by taking down name, rank, and number, issuing identity discs, and snapping photographs for the files. For the unregistered there would also be 'capture cards' to be filled in and sent off as a means of notifying London, through Swiss intermediaries, that a serviceman was an official POW of the Third Reich. Finally there were efforts, especially as the war progressed, to prevent disease epidemics through a compulsory shower on arrival or daubing with disinfectant and the putting of clothing through a delousing process, supplemented in some cases by inoculations.

Amidst the mass influx of 1940 the processing of prisoners in the main army camps, particularly with reference to hygiene, could be quite haphazard. Many men had to wait weeks or even months to be deloused (often ineffectively), while officer prisoners—some suspected to add to their sense of humiliation rather than for sanitary reasons—had their heads shaved immediately on arrival at their primary destination, Oflag VIIC/H (Laufen). By the time prisoners were arriving from Greece and Italy the process was much more uniform.[74]

The experience of Fred Hill on arrival at Stalag IVB (Mühlberg) was fairly typical by the middle of the war. First the new men had their hair cut off with electric clippers. Then they were made to strip while their uniforms were fumigated. Still naked after a mass shower, they were herded into another room where disinfectant was applied to their armpits and groins by a Russian POW. 'Next,' Hill explained, 'an Italian prisoner dabbed a damp pad on my chest and arm, another stuck a syringe in my chest, and a third grabbed my arm and vaccinated me—all very efficient.' Only then were the new prisoners allowed to go through an unsorted pile of their gassed clothes and get dressed, after which they were photographed—name and number chalked on a board held at chest level—and given their *Kriegsgefangene* discs. All this was somewhat dehumanizing, what with 'the Germans shouting and screaming at us all the time', as Neville Chesterton recalled of his first day at Stalag XVIIIA (Wolfsberg) two years earlier. Nevertheless the subsequent absence of lice, albeit sometimes temporary, was appreciated. 'It was a great relief to be able to lie in bed without scratching every few minutes', Captain

Philip Kindersley remembered of the post-delousing period of his processing at Stalag VIIA (Moosburg) en route to Oflag VIIIF (Mährisch Trübau).[75]

Though almost all would find themselves moved from one camp to another within the Greater Reich over the course of time, British soldiers, sailors, and airmen given identity discs were now officially *Kriegsgefangenen*. A variety of factors would now impinge on the nature of their life as POWs—including those who ended up at Colditz—not least the type of camp to which they were sent and the nature of the Germans who ran the place.

Notes

1. For naval personnel cf. e.g. Patsy Adam-Smith, *Prisoners of War* (Ringwood, Victoria, 1992), 522; Daniel G. Dancocks, *In Enemy Hands* (Toronto, 1990 edn.), 147; David James, *A Prisoner's Progress* (Edinburgh, 1947), 5, 14–16. On variations among air force personnel cf. e.g. Richard Pape, *Boldness Be My Friend* (London, 1953), 110; Richard Passmore, *Moving Tent* (London, 1982), 27, 52; B. A. James, *Moonless Night* (London, 1983), 19, 23.

2. On the contrast between front-line and rear-area troops see e.g. IWM (Rolf), G. Adkins; ibid., J. Cocker; ibid., A. Fennel; ibid., R. Maggs, 1; ibid., H. Taylor, 1; IWM, R. A. Wilson, 15; Edwin N. Broomhead, *Barbed Wire in the Sunset* (Melbourne, 1945), 27; Michael Duncan, *Underground from Posen* (London, 1954), 45; J. M. Green, *From Colditz in Code* (London, 1971), 42–3; Miles Reid, *Last on the List* (London, 1974), 195–6, 198; James Stedman, *Life of a British POW in Poland* (Braunton, 1992), 8; Jim Rogers, *Tunnelling into Colditz* (London, 1986), 26; Edward Ward, *Give Me Air* (London, 1946), 16–17.

3. IWM, W. K. Laing, 23–27; CSVA 2, J. Yule; IWM (Rolf), A. Bell.

4. For summary accounts of some of the worst aspects of the march see PRO, WO 32/18489. Almost all first-person narratives detailing the rigours of the 1940 march suggest they were avoidable. Only a few of those involved were willing to concede in retrospect that the huge number of POWs taken in 1940 presented a real logistical problem for the Wehrmacht. See PRO, WO 208/3302, account of escape of Sgt. S. J. Fraser; David H. C. Read, *This Grace Given* (Grand Rapids, Mich., 1984), 107; IWMSA 4820/1, C. Scarborough.

5. Gordon Instone, *Freedom the Spur* (London, 1953), 47–8; Robert Gale, *Private Prisoner* (Wellingborough, 1984), 16. On distances see e.g. IWM (Rolf), E. Pickering, 12–28 July 1940; IWM, G. Jackson, 3–4; IWM, N. R. Wylie, 12–28 July 1940; J. W. Pocock, *Dairy of a Prisoner of War, 1940–1945* (Southampton, 1985), 9; Graham Palmer, *Prisoner of Death* (Wellingborough, 1990), 49; Donald Edgar, *The Stalag Men* (London, 1982), 3.

6. IWM, C. G. King, 26; Ed Annetts, *Campaign Without Medals* (Lewes, 1990), 24; James Allan, *No Citation* (London, 1955), 16.

7. IWM, C. G. King, 30; see also John Elwyn, *At the Fifth Attempt* (London, 1987), 8. On carrying the wounded, burying the dead, and generally clearing up in 1940 and 1944 see e.g. IWM (Rolf), F. Ayers, 3; IWM, J. H. Brooker diary, 6 June 1940, 29. Cases of prisoners being forced to handle ammunition also occurred—sometimes while under fire from British guns. See e.g. W. Wynne Mason, *Prisoners of War* (Wellington, 1954), 61.

8. Stuart Brown, *Forbidden Paths* (Edinburgh, 1978), 33.

9. IWM, D. Swift, 23; IWM (Rolf), K. Dyson, 4–5; Duncan, op. cit., 48. On foraging see e.g. Maxwell Bates, *A Wilderness of Days* (Victoria, BC, 1978), 31; IWM, D. Swift, 23; Sam Kydd, *For You the War Is Over...* (London, 1973), 56; Adrian Vincent, *The Long Road Home* (London, 1956), 34.

10. T. C. F. Prittie and W. Earle Edwards, *Escape to Freedom* (London, 1953 edn.), 15; IWM (Rolf), W. Darbyshire, 4; IWM, D. Swift, 22.

11. On the shooting as common see, e.g., http://www.pegasus-one.org/pow/david_parker.htm, D. Parker, 4. On threats to shoot escapers see e.g. Warren Tute, *Escape Route Green* (London, 1971), 23, 27. On being too tired to contemplate escape see e.g. IWM, E. Booth, 40.

12. PRO, WO 208/3299, account of escape of A. M. Garden, p. 1; see e.g. IWM, L. B. Shorrock, 41.

13. See e.g. PRO, WO 208/3299, Treatment of British P/W on Capture, p. 7.

14. PRO, WO 208/3303, supplement to account of escape of A. Hosington. On men who had fainted being picked up see Edgar, op. cit., 9. On men being run over, see IWMSA 12162/2, H. Esders. On men being shot or bayoneted see also e.g. IWM (Rolf), J. Copeland.

15. IWM, W. Kite, 9; John Lawrence, *2.2.9.7.* (Fontwell, 1991), 15; see Bates, op. cit., 19.

16. See e.g. IWM (Rolf), R. Low, 5; IWM, G. R. Manners, 10; Edgar, op. cit., 60; S. Brown, op. cit., 27; Gale, op. cit., 18–19. Though the majority did not try, and many were recaptured, hundreds of men broke from columns in bids for freedom. Dozens either found their way back to England or chose to blend in with the local population. See e.g. PRO, WO 208/3323, account of escape of A. Fergus; WO 208/3298, report compiled by three officers of the 30th Infantry Brigade.

17. John Brown, *In Durance Vile* (London, 1981), 23; Albert Paice and Alwyn Ward, *For the Love of Elizabeth* (privately printed, 1984), 6. On stopping civilians trying to aid POWs on the journey in general see e.g. IWM (Rolf), H. V. Davies, 3; IWM, R. A. Wilson, 18.

18. J. Brown, op. cit., 25; George Dunning, *Where Bleed the Many* (London, 1955), 19; PRO, WO 208/3299, Treatment of British P/W on Capture, 7; see FO 916/14, encl. 14A.

19. See e.g. Derek Lang, *Return to St. Valéry* (Luneray, 1989), 41; Stanley Rayner, *I Remember* (Lincoln, 1995), 107; IWM, H. C. F. Harwood, 100; IWM, E. Miller, diary I, pp. 16, 35.

20. IWM, W. A. Harding, 5; Read, op. cit., 107; Anthony Richardson, *Wingless Victory* (London, 1953 edn.), 42; Rogers, op. cit., 25; see I. Schrire, *Stalag Doctor* (London, 1956), 41.

21. IWM, H. C. F. Harwood, 85; Prittie and Edwards, op. cit., 14.

22. This term—unfortunately quite apt in more general sense—was used by a dispatch rider from the East Riding Yorkshire Yeomanry to describe the situation in the Doullens transit cage. IWMSA 12162/2, H. Esders.

23. Bates, op. cit., 16; Allan, op. cit., 17, 23.

24. J. Brown, op. cit., 26; Len Williamson, *Six Wasted Years* (Braunton, 1985), 11; IWM (Rolf), K. Maxwell.

25. IWM, E. Miller, diary II, p. 21.

26. Annetts, op. cit., 25.

27. Duncan, op. cit., 48–9.

28. Vincent, op. cit., 38–9.

29. J. Roberts, *A Terrier Goes to War* (London, 1998), 34–5. On the widespread belief that French prisoners were already packed as they marched off see e.g. IWM, W. A. Harding, 2; J. Brown, op. cit., 22–3. On French prisoners deliberately being treated better than the British see e.g. PRO, WO 208/3299, Treatment of British P/W on Capture memo, *passim*.

30. Read, op. cit., 102; IWM, N. R. Wylie, diary, 23 June 1940.

31. IWMSA 16800/1, B. N. Mazumdar.

32. IWM (Rolf), W. J. Porter, 4–5; IWM, C. Baker, 3. Those who travelled earlier or later than most prisoners could find conditions less crowded. See Norman Rubenstein, *The Invisibly Wounded* (Hull, 1989), 36.

33. IWM, E. Booth diary, 31 May 1940; IWM, H. C. F. Harwood, 84, 86; see e.g. http://web.mala.bc.ca/davies/letters.images/stokes/collection.page.htm, D. Stokes diary, 30 May 1940.

34. See IWM, H. C. F. Harwood, 88; IWM, E. Booth, diary 3 June 1940; Duncan, op. cit., 51; IWM, A.N.L. Munby diary, 8–10 June 1940; IWM, E. Miller, diary, 12–14 June 1940; IWM, R. A. Wilson, 19–20; http://web.mala.bc.ca/davies/letters.images/stokes/collection.page.htm, D. Stokes diary, 1–2 June 1940; Rogers, op. cit., 28–9.

35. George Beeson, *Five Roads to Freedom* (London, 1977), 8. For similar incidents elsewhere see e.g. S. Brown, op. cit., 32.

36. CSVA 4, K. Lockwood; Ewart C. Jones, *Germans Under My Bed* (London, 1957), 20–1; IWM, E. Miller diary, 9–11 June 1940; A. N. L. Munby diary, 5 June 1940.

37. See Alwyn Ward (ed.), *Rough Ride From Trier*, 2 vols. (Sheffield, 1987).

38. CSVA 4, K. Lockwood; PRO, WO 208/3305, account of escape of 2/Lt Douglas, 1; Rogers, op. cit., 31–2; IWM (Rolf), C. L. Irwin; IWM, E. Booth, 51–2; Duncan, op. cit., 53. For more positive experiences see e.g. E. Miller diary, 15–17 June 1940; IWMSA 4827/1–2, R. Loder.

39. IWM (Rolf), J. Copeland. On conditions for other ranks on the train journey across the Reich see e.g. ibid., K. Dyson, 5; IWM, R. P. Evans, 31.

40. IWM (Rolf), W. J. Porter, 5 ('I'm All Right Jack'); Roberts, op. cit., 38 ('any semblance'); John Castle, *The Password is Courage* (London, 1955), 33–4 ('last time').

41. Elwyn, op. cit., 32; A. C. Masterson, in Tony Strachen (ed.), *In the Clutch of Circumstance* (Victoria, BC, 1985), 120.

42. See e.g. IWM, J. Seed, 31–5; Donald Watt, *Stoker* (East Roseville, NSW, 1995), 49–50.

43. See IWM (Rolf), W. Parslow, 2; IWM, P. Jarrett diary, 1 May–5 June 1941; Jack Champ and Colin Burgess, *The Diggers of Colditz* (Sydney, 1985), 21; H. Martin Lidbetter, *The Friends Ambulance Unit 1939–1943* (York, 1993), 80; Ian Ramsay, *P.O.W.* (Melbourne, 1985), 18; M. Reid, op. cit., 198 ff.

44. Barney Roberts, *A Kind of Cattle* (Sydney, 1985), 26–8; J. E. Pryce, *Heels in Line* (London, 1958), 51; F. Cotterill in David McGill, *P.O.W.* (Naenae, NZ, 1987), 71.

45. IWM, D. W. Luckett, 6.

46. John Chrisp, *The Tunnellers of Sandborstal* (London, 1959), 46; see Neville Chesterston, *Crete Was My Waterloo* (London, 1995), 54; Peter Winter, *Free Lodgings* (Auckland, 1993), 11; IWM (Rolf), E. Kirk, 3. For segregated officers, particularly while British rations could still be ransacked and the camp was less crowded, conditions could be much better. See R. G. M. Quarrie, *Oflag* (Durham, 1985), 7–8.

47. On NCOs see IWM, D. W. Luckett, 9; IWM, J. C. Whelan, 12, 17; Winter, op. cit., 33, 35; IWM, J. Seed, 50. On combines, national divisions, and perceived variations in German behaviour towards them see Lew Lind, *Flowers of Rethymnon* (Kenthurst, NSW, 1991), 46; Chrisp, op. cit., 45–6; Winter, op. cit., 9; IWM, J. C. Whelan, 11; IWM, J. Seed, 43. On rackets, at which the Cypriots and Palestinians supposedly did best, see IWM, D. W. Luckett, 7; Ernest Walker, *The Price of Surrender* (London, 1992), 195. On stealing and foraging beyond the wire and German punishments see Chesterston, op. cit., 55; IWM, J. Seed, 37, 43; IWM (Rolf), V. E. Jones, 2–3.

48. On the journey to Salonika see e.g. Quarrie, op. cit., 9–14; IWMSA 16843/3, J. Chrisp; CSVA 8 J. Best; IWMSA 4747/2–3, E. Mine; IWM (Rolf), 2; IWM, J. Seed, 54–62.

49. Pryce, op. cit., 52–3; Walker, op. cit., 230; Watt, op. cit., 54; IWM, J. Seed, 63.

50. IWM (Rolf), R. Clark, 6.

51. Lidbetter, op. cit., 82 ('all starving'); Chrisp, op. cit., 51; Quarrie, op. cit., 16 ('dog biscuits'). PRO, ADM 1/18695, pp. 20–1; IWM, J. Seed, 66–7.

52. B. Roberts, op. cit., 35; IWM, M. E. Osborne, 10. On prisoners *not* being broken by conditions at Salonika see e.g. Elvet Williams, *Arbeitskommando* (London, 1975), 29.

53. PRO, ADM 1/18695, p. 22; Pryce, op. cit., 59–60; IWM, M. E. Osborne, 10.

54. Winter, op. cit., 43; Elvet Williams, op. cit., 21–2; Ramsay, op. cit., 25–6; Charles Robinson, *Journey to Captivity* (Canberra, 1991), 106; M. Wan, in McGill, op. cit., 68.

55. Fritz Jordan, *Escape* (Cranbury, NJ, 1970), 70–1. For British criticism of the Palestinians see e.g. Quarrie, op. cit., 16–17. For the Cypriots see e.g. IWMSA 4747/3, E. Mine. Miles Reid, commenting on the Palestinians held at Corinth, noted that while 'true to their instincts' in becoming traders, 'whatever one may feel about Jews and their trading I do not know what we would have done without them'. M. Reid, op. cit., 204.

56. PRO, ADM 1/18695, p. 18.

57. IWM, J. Seed, 68–70; IWM, D. W. Luckett, 13–14; IWM, M. E. Osborne, 9; IWM, V. West, 224; John Barrett, *We Were There* (Sydney, 1987), 261; Champ and Burgess, op. cit., 22; Chesterton, op. cit., 58; Quarrie, op. cit., 17; W. B. Thomas, *Dare to be Free* (London, 1955), 76; Watt, op. cit., 55; Charles Raymond Willoughby, *I Was There* (Brewarrina, NSW, 1994), 35.

58. IWM (Rolf), W. S. Eldred. On dysentery see e.g. ibid., W. Parslow, 3. On taking turns to lie down see e.g. Clive Dunn, *Permission to Speak* (London, 1986), 88. On the curtailment of 'call-of-nature' halts after escape attempts see e.g. IWMSA 4747/3, E. Mine.

59. Champ and Burgess, op. cit., 24. On bad conditions in officers' wagons see e.g. Quarrie, op. cit., 17–19. On rations see e.g. IWM (Rolf), W. S. Eldred; IWMSA 4747/3, E. Mine; IWM, J. Seed, 76. On help from the Yugoslav Red Cross see e.g. IWM, D. W. Luckett, 16.

60. Ramsay, op. cit., 30.

61. See Pryce, op. cit., 68–9; IWM, M. E. Osborne, 13; IWM, J. Seed, 86; IWM (Rolf), J. M. McGee, 3.

62. IWM, J. Seed, 87, 86. Though the numbers involved were much smaller, conditions in transit for British and Canadian servicemen captured in the big coastal raids at St-Nazaire and Dieppe were often almost as bad as those endured by the 1940–1 prisoners. See e.g. IWMSA 5194/2, J. Laurie; James Spenser, *The Awkward Marine* (London, 1948), 105; S. Hodgson, in Dancocks, op. cit., 41; V. Wadden, in Strachen, op. cit., 14.

63. The situation was made worse by an order, sent secretly from London and widely obeyed, for prisoners to stay put rather than strike out on their own when the Italians gave in. For the reasoning behind this order—which was not meant to result in a huge haul of prisoners for the Reich—see Foot and Langley, op. cit., ch. 7. The figure of 70,000 (a rough estimate) is from Noel Barber, *Prisoner of War* (London, 1944), 13.

64. Winter, op. cit., 106; see also George Clifton, *The Happy Hunted* (London, 1954), 309. On bad conditions in transit from Italy see e.g. IWM (Rolf), C. Allwood, 1; IWMSA 4694/2, C. Ayling; IWM, K. J. Bowden, 95–8; Philip Kindersley, *For You the War is Over* (Tunbridge Wells, 1993), 130–3. On the danger of Allied bombing see e.g. Robert W. Calvey, *Name, Rank and Number* (Lewes, 1998), 15.

65. IWMSA 4767/2, J. Greenwood.

66. On being too shocked and exhausted to make a bid for freedom in transit see e.g. IWMSA 12162/2, H. Esders; IWM, H. C. F. Harwood, 77; Duncan, op. cit., 46; Edgar, op. cit., 9; Green, op. cit., 49; Prittie and Edwards, op. cit., 16–19.

67. IWM, W. Asquith, 87; Sandy St Clair, *The Endless War* (North Battleford, Sask., 1987), 129–30; George Millar, *Horned Pigeon* (London, 1946), 159–61. The transit experience for the comparatively small number of army prisoners taken in the last year or so of the war in Europe varied from bad to almost tolerable.

68. IWMSA 11277/1–2, T. H. Wilson. Conditions on hospital trains later in the war could be fairly dire due to limited medical provisions and care. See e.g. Marmaduke Hussey, *Chance Governs All* (London, 2001), 43–4.

69. On the Arnhem episode see Daniel Paul with John St John, *Surgeon at Arms* (London, 1958), 62; Graeme Warrack, *Travel By Dark* (London, 1963), 71–2. On decent transport and superior conditions to those endured by the unwounded in transit see e.g. IWM, A. F. Gibbs, 67; John Burton, *Mirador* (London, 1986), 56. On poor conditions in transit and in hospitals in 1940 see Bertram Bright, 'Blinded and a Prisoner of War', *Blackwood's*, 257 (1945), 245.

70. Lang, op. cit., 38; Green, op. cit., 44; D. L. Charters, *Medical Experiences as a Prisoner of War in Germany* (Liverpool, 1946), 3–5. On the Athens area hospitals see also John Borrie, *Despite Captivity* (London, 1975), 24 ff.

71. Charters, op. cit., 4–6. On the doctor–patient ratio cf. Borrie, op. cit., 38 with Arthur Salisbury MacNalty and W. Franklin Mellor (eds.), *Medical Services in War* (HMSO, 1968), 111. The shortage of doctors was in part the result of the German habit of shipping off to Germany at once all medical personnel not fully occupied at a particular point in time. See e.g. IWMSA 16800/1, B. N. Mazumdar.

72. A. King in Adam-Smith, op. cit., 170; PRO, ADM 1/18695, pp. 18, 25, *passim*.

73. See e.g. PRO, WO 208/3301, account of escape of W. B. Gaze, 2; IWMSA 12162/2, H. Esders; Lang, 38; Charters, op. cit., 7.

74. On the position at Laufen see e.g. IWMSA 4827/2, R. Loder; IWM, H. C. F. Harwood, 94; IWM, A. N. L. Munby diary, 14 June 1940. On delays and problems with delousing in 1940–1 see e.g. IWM, G. R. Manners, 17; IWM (Rolf), E. T. McGill. On capture cards—which might be issued before or after arrival at a main camp—see e.g. Chesterton, op. cit., 52; IWM, G. F. Warsop, 17; http://www.naval-history.net/WW2MemoirAndS008.htm, H. Siddall, 5.

75. Kindersley, op. cit., 134; Chesterton, op. cit., 59; Fred Hill, *Prisoner of War* (London, 1994), 103–5.

3   Compounds and Commandants

Prisoners of war may be interned in a town, fortress, or other place... They may also be interned in fenced camps...

(from Article 9, Geneva Convention, 1929).

Each prisoner of war camp shall be placed under the authority of a responsible officer.

(from Article 18, Geneva Convention, 1929).

In bureaucratic terms the dozens of major POW camps and hundreds of satellite compounds within the Greater Reich differed only according to function, location, form, and the service that ran them, breaking down into five basic types. Thanks to the success of the post-war escape stories this range tends to be narrowed down even further in the popular imagination into two forms: a generic hut-and-wire image on the one hand, and the unmistakable profile of Colditz castle on the other, camps presided over by stiff-necked, authoritarian Prussians. In the real Nazi Germany, however, physical conditions varied a great deal from one camp to another, including those nominally of the same type. Quality of life, furthermore, depended a good deal not only on the attitudes and actions of the camp commandant, but also those of his security officer and *Lager* staff, which could vary from individual to individual and over time. Colditz, somewhat paradoxically in view of its fearsome wartime reputation and post-war image, was in many respects one of the better *Kriegsgefangenlagern*.[1]

Most of the prison camps in which uniformed British prisoners were held fell under Wehrmacht auspices. Oflags (short for *Offizierlagern*) were for those with commissions, stalags (short for *Stammlagern*) for those without. Each camp, whether oflag or stalag, was identified by a roman numeral reflecting the military district in which it was located and by a letter to distinguish the camps within a particular *Wehrkreis*. This was often followed, in parentheses, by the location of the camp in official correspondence. Hence Stalag IID (Stargard), for instance, or Oflag XIIB (Hadamar). From the middle of the war onward the letter-numeral combination was supplemented by a simple numerical designation: a new camp in the Lamsdorf area, for example, was known as Stalag 344. The bigger stalags, furthermore, served as administrative hubs for the hundreds of numbered work camps to which other-rank prisoners were sent until the job was completed: *Arbeitskommando* 11101 GW, for example, where prisoners sent out from Stalag XVIIIA (Wolfsberg) worked on building sites in the mid-war period.

Not all camps, however, were army-run affairs. Though on occasion RAF and RN personnel continued to find themselves held by the German army, in the second year of the war both the Luftwaffe and the Kriegsmarine were in the process of setting up their own facilities for navy and air-force prisoners.[2] To keep pace with the expanding population of aircrew prisoners, over half-a-dozen permanent camps were eventually set up by the German air force, starting with Stalag Luft I (Barth) in 1940 and finishing with Stalag Luft VII (Bankau) in 1944. The German navy, meanwhile, with only a trickle of new arrivals, contented itself with a navy-run compound at Stalag XB (Sandbostel) until the opening of a new all-navy camp, Marlag und Milag Nord at Westertimke, in 1942, where officers and ratings were kept in separate compounds.

Many of these camps were hut-and-wire affairs, though their size, age, and the type and quality of the materials used and facilities constructed were far from uniform. Various low-lying nineteenth-century fortifications in Poland were also employed at certain points to house British prisoners: and, of course, there was Colditz castle.

Located atop a steep promontory and officially designated Oflag IVC, Colditz was a high-walled, steeply gabled fortress dating back four centuries. It was the special camp (*Sonderlager*) to which officers who had made escape attempts from other camps or otherwise made themselves undesirable were sent in the early war years. It was also the place where a small group of prisoners with powerful family connections—the *Prominente*—were kept for possible use as hostages later on. Both in form and function Colditz stands out. It is worth pointing out, however, that (contrary to what has sometimes been written about the place) it was not entirely unique.[3]

Quite apart from the nineteenth-century forts already mentioned, several castles of roughly similar vintage to Colditz were used to house contingents of British officers. Oflag VIID at Tittmoning bore a particularly striking resemblance to Colditz, and both Oflag VIIC/H (Laufen) and Oflag IXA/H (Spangenberg) were principally Schloss affairs ('H' standing for *Hauptlager*, or principal camp). Oflag XIIB was also a Schloss camp, and those undergoing solitary confinement for escape attempts and other misdemeanours at Oflag VIIB (Eichstätt) might find themselves confined in the nearby Willibaldsburg castle. Persistent escapers and other 'bad boys', furthermore, were not automatically sent to Colditz. The Luftwaffe often considered that its security measures were superior to those of the army and took back many air-force prisoners into its own camps. The SS, meanwhile, came to believe that those officers who escaped from POW camps should either be executed or reincarcerated in more supposedly secure Sonderlagers attached to concentration camps such as Sachsenhausen. Even within the army the castle at Spangenberg apparently came to be seen as at least as secure as Colditz. In early 1943 several persistent escapers from Eichstätt were sent there, as were eleven engineer officers from Oflag IVC itself—apparently because Spangenberg was thought to be harder to tunnel out of.[4]

As a camp for officers, furthermore, Colditz could not accommodate the hard cases among the NCO and other-rank population. Problematic army NCOs were concentrated in their own Sonderlager, Stalag 383 (Hohenfels), in the autumn of 1942. Soldiers who were considered enemies of the Reich because of their repeated escape attempts from Arbeitskommandos could themselves be confined to the bigger stalags, often in interior compounds, or incarcerated in military prisons, sometimes Colditz-type fortresses.[5]

Finally, not all the *Prominente* were held at Colditz. The SS, typically, built up its own set of potential hostages, both civilian and uniformed, and kept them in various concentration camps. Only in the last days of the war were the various groups brought together in transit.[6]

Colditz also appears in a class by itself, however, because of its reputation as a particularly tough place to live in as well as escape from. There were rumours circulating at the time that Colditz was something of a 'hell camp', or at the very least a *Straflager* (punishment camp). Pat Reid used the latter term in his first best-seller and its sequel in the following decade, and in the course of time the word 'Colditz' became a popular synonym for any type of intensely rigorous institutional regimen.[7]

In point of fact, as the German authorities were keen to point out at the time, Oflag IVC was a Sonderlager, a special camp, rather than a

Straflager, and in 1943 even the term Sonderlager was dropped as part of the official nomenclature for Colditz. This did not, however, necessarily make it a comfortable place to be. More pertinent than bureaucratic designations were the actual conditions inside the walls of Colditz castle as compared to other camps.[8]

Things were often at their worst in the early days and again late in the war. In 1940–1 the Wehrmacht at times appeared overwhelmed by the number of prisoners that had to be housed. In 1944–5 acceptable standards of accommodation often could not be maintained, as POWs from regions under threat of being overrun had to be squeezed into a shrinking number of camps in areas still considered secure. In the intervening years conditions were usually better, but still varied over time and between locations.[9]

Oflag VIIC (Laufen), where the mass of officers from the BEF ended up in the summer of 1940, was a prime example of what could happen when far more prisoners were taken than had been allowed for. The camp, an enormous old five-storey stone edifice which gave one junior officer the impression he was being held in 'a huge asylum', was in fact an old seat of the Archbishops of Salzburg. As a camp Laufen rapidly became overcrowded, holding three times the number of prisoners that it could reasonably accommodate: a total of about 1,500 in all. 'It was *extremely* cramped', Major Charles Irwin of the Northumberland Fusiliers remembered. Up to ninety or so officers finding themselves living in a room only 45 feet by 25 feet was not unusual, each room filled with triple-tier bunks rising from floor to ceiling. Toilet and washing facilities were inadequate, and there was no laundry service. 'Conditions are almost unbearable', Michael Duncan, a second lieutenant in the Oxfordshire and Buckinghamshire Light Infantry, wrote despairingly in his diary on 29 June 1940. Though conditions improved somewhat as prisoners were eventually transferred elsewhere, Oflag VIIC—shut down in October 1941—remained a very unpleasant memory for those who had been placed there.[10]

Ordinary soldiers fared even worse in 1940. Their camps were not only overcrowded but also lacked proper shelter or anything more than the most rudimentary sanitation. Several thousand men ended up at Stalag XXIB (Schubin), where the corrugated-iron and wooden buildings were either incomplete or ramshackle, the water supply came from a single standpipe, and the latrines consisted of a trench with a pole over it in full view of outsiders. A British doctor assigned to Schubin in the autumn of 1940 found to his horror 'two thousand or more British soldiers living in utter squalor', their tents and huts as well their clothing infested with lice, fleas, and flies.[11]

Thousands more BEF men were housed in a wired-in compound in similar conditions or in hitherto more-or-less abandoned underground forts at Stalag XXA (Thorn) and Stalag XXID (Posen). Above ground, in marquee tents and huts without bunks, Gordon Manners discovered that at Thorn the ablution facilities consisted of 'just a pump from a well and a trough for the 2,000 of us'. Inside the forts overcrowding was endemic and sanitary conditions were, if anything, even more primitive. Often damp, ill-lit, and stinking, the rooms in these structures frequently held three or more times the number of men they were designed for. 'No rooms were dry,' George Beeson remembered of the fort he was in at Posen, 'as water dripped down from all the walls. The floor was wet. We were issued with straw to lie down on and soon this became wet.'[12]

Then there was the massive Stalag VIIIB (Lamsdorf). This consisted of a vast array of grey, single-storey barrack blocks dating from the First World War that eventually came to hold well over 10,000 prisoners in six compounds. Many of the buildings were dilapidated, the place developed a serious overcrowding problem, and the latrine arrangements became noxious in the extreme. As elsewhere, bedbugs and fleas were rife. 'In those days', as Sergeant Charles Coward explained to the chronicler of his time as a POW, 'Lamsdorf was a dark, dreary place . . .'[13]

As time passed conditions improved in most locations, and new army prisoners arriving en masse in later years endured bad physical conditions less frequently and for shorter periods. In camps such as Stalag IVB (Mühlburg) and Stalag VIIA (Moosburg) in 1941 and 1943, and Stalag XIIA (Limburg) in 1944, housing and sanitation problems did occur for some prisoners, but the excess numbers were soon transferred elsewhere.[14]

Much more general difficulties arose again in the last nine months or so of the war. Fuel was short everywhere throughout the final winter, and as compounds were closed out of fear they would be overrun by advancing Soviet or Allied armies, the remaining camps often found themselves bursting at the seams. The barracks at Stalag IIIA (Luckenwalde), according to one observer, were 'dank, dark and filthy', with open-trench latrines and tents (with only damp straw as bedding) for those moving in from other camps further east.[15] It was the same at Stalag 357 and XIB (Fallingbostel), Stalag XIIID (Nuremberg), and most other camps in western Germany, including Marlag und Milag Nord.[16] Nor was it just the Stammlagers that were affected by the general deterioration of the Reich infrastructure. Oflag 79 (Brunswick), for example, a former Luftwaffe barracks to which officer prisoners were transferred from Oflag VIIIF in the spring of 1944, was too small for the 3,000 new arrivals. 'Rooms constructed to hold ten people had as many as twenty-five in them', Philip Kindersley recalled. Various facilities, furthermore, soon suffered bomb damage and were never repaired.[17]

Though the worst of times for most prisoners, the mass influxes of the early and late war periods did not have the same kind of impact on Colditz as in regular camps. Oflag IVC was already an established site for Polish officers by the time the first handful of British prisoners arrived in November 1940. With only one major exception (in which foreign contingents were moved out first), new British inhabitants thereafter tended to arrive in a trickle rather than en masse. Shortages affected Colditz in the last months of the war as they did other camps, but the British contingent remained in place and, apart from the effect of a large number of French POWs in transit, Oflag IVC was not subject to the same swamping of resources that occurred elsewhere. There remains, however, the question of how Colditz compared to other camps in the years between these two traumatic periods.

Despite the relative stability of the administrative and logistical system from 1941 down through 1944, with both representatives of the Protecting Power (first the United States, then Switzerland) and the International Committee of the Red Cross (ICRC) seeking to better the conditions under which British prisoners lived, regular camp conditions still varied a good deal. Some were notoriously bad, others were extremely good—and most, over time, fell somewhere in between.

Probably the worst regular camp for officers from a physical standpoint was Oflag VIB (Warburg). Formerly an old labour camp made up of brick huts, it had been converted into a 500 by 300 yard wired-in compound into which the German authorities poured over 3,100 army and air-force prisoners from other locations in the autumn of 1941. Warburg, one inmate trenchantly put it, was 'a cross between a garbage heap and a sewer'.[18] Rooms were seriously overcrowded, few of the huts had electric light or enough carbide lamps, there was not enough coal to keep the men from feeling seriously chilled in winter, and the roofs leaked so much that bed linen was damp much of the time. Cooking facilities were inadequate and the washhouses and latrines were draughty, dirty, and quite unsanitary. Bedbugs and fleas abounded. Drainage was also a problem, so that the ground was a sea of mud much of the time. When the mud froze, so did the water supply. Former residents described Oflag VIB as a 'filthy', 'appalling', and 'disgusting' place. The ICRC representatives were blunt after they visited Warburg soon after it opened. 'This Camp is much the worst we have seen in Germany,' their official report observed, 'inadequate in every respect...' Though there were some positive changes over time, Oflag VIB was simply too small and too old to undergo significant improvement, and was closed down in October 1942.[19]

The worst main camp for other ranks in the middle war years, in terms of the scale of poor physical conditions, was probably Stalag VIIIB (Lamsdorf), a 'dirty, depressing, sprawling metropolis', in the words of a POW who experienced life in several different camps. While overall conditions were better than in 1940, and the permanent staff in particular managed to upgrade their own quarters significantly, things were still often bad in comparison to other camps for the 6,000 or more prisoners temporarily held at Lamsdorf between Arbeitskommando assignments.[20] 'The camp was not meant by the Germans to have any comfort', Donald Edgar later explained. 'It was a transit camp... In the new Germany we were constantly told there was no room for work-shy people.' All this made it 'thoroughly miserable'. Winter conditions in 1941–2 were particularly grim, new arrivals finding themselves in barracks where windows were broken and concrete walls leaked so that the floors were always damp. Even with improvements, Lamsdorf still had the reputation of being the worst camp in Germany.[21]

Ratings and marines, accustomed to the shipshape conditions of compounds run by the Kriegsmarine, certainly thought so when sent to Stalag VIIIB en route to working camps in 1942–3. 'It was infinitely worse,' Roger Coward wrote of his time there: 'greater desolation, dirt and untidiness...' Fuel was so short that the men in his compound burned the wooden bunks and were reduced to sleeping on the concrete floors. 'Coal was practically non-existent', Francis Guest remembered, which, along with overcrowding, made it 'one of the worst' places in the Greater Reich.[22]

Aircrew NCOs, confined to their own compound in the centre of Stalag VIIIB in 1941–2, also found Lamsdorf wanting, especially in comparison to conditions in Luftwaffe camps. Richard Pape, on arrival in 1941, found the place 'indescribably dirty, untidy and wretched', with 180 men to each dimly lit, poorly ventilated 80 by 30-foot barrack block: 'No wonder Stalag VIIIb was generally known as a Hell Camp.' The windows were often broken, there was not enough winter fuel, and in summer the place was fly-infested. 'That really was a terrible place', Albert Jones remembered.[23]

Things had not improved much by late 1943, when a new influx of army prisoners from Italy took up residence at Lamsdorf. 'The huts', wrote Geoffrey Vaughan, 'were . . . very dilapidated, the windows having long ago lost their glass—the apertures being covered with tatty sacking . . . ' The communal latrines by now consisted of board-covered pits in both army and RAF compounds—better than the open-trench affairs but dangerously rat-infested. 'The forty lids covering the forty holes were not intended to indicate neatness or even cleanliness', Bill Jackson recalled of the dilapidated lavatory block used by the air-force prisoners. 'They were there to keep the rats climbing out, and there were hundreds of them.'[24]

Outside observers tried to put a positive spin on conditions at Stalag VIIIB, but had to admit on occasion that all was not well. 'In comparison to the usual standard of Camps for British prisoners,' a Red Cross representative concluded after a visit to Lamsdorf in the autumn of 1943, 'this Stalag must be classed as a bad one.'[25]

Many main camps had a more variable record in the 1942–4 period. This was true for both officers and other ranks. The smallish Oflag IX A/ H (Spangenberg) was a case in point, assessments changing over time and varying between the upper Schloss and the lower compound. The lower camp, a former labour school, consisted of several barrack blocks and assorted other lathe-and-plaster buildings, and was pleasantly located next to a stream and a path adjoining the village of Spangenberg itself. 'Geese and ducks paddled about in the river, right under our windows', T. D. Calnan remembered of his brief stay there in 1941. 'On the far bank we could observe the normal bustling life of a German village.' At various points in the middle war years crowding became a problem, and exercise space was always limited: the area inside the wire was only 75 yards square, a mere ninety paces from one end to the other. Swiss observers tended to describe it in positive terms, and it undoubtedly had, as Airey Neave put it, 'a kinder atmosphere than that of the gaunt castle, perched remotely on its hill'.[26] However, despite the formidable appearance of its high walls and deep moat—'Good lord,' a new arrival remarked, 'this place is *straight* out of Grimm's'[27]— living conditions in Spangenberg castle (like those in Oflag VIID at Tittmoning, another Schloss camp used in 1940–1) were not as bad as appearances suggested. Overcrowding led to mixed assessments by neutral representatives between the third and fifth year of the war, and courtyard space in particular was extremely limited. It was, nevertheless, an improvement on Warburg. 'The conditions were definitely better and cleaner and much less rowdy and slightly more hygienic', Miles Reid remembered. The view was good, over time physical improvements were made to the lighting and facilities, an exterior sports ground that could be used by prisoners on parole was opened in 1942, and the moat was transformed into an exercise and gardening space. 'Although the camp was gloomy and most of the rooms had very small windows,' Earle Edwards noted, 'it was warm and dry.' Corran Purdon thought it 'a comfortable camp...'.[28]

Oflag VIIB (Eichstätt), the camp to which several thousand army officers were sent after the closure of Oflag VIB, also garnered mixed though ultimately positive reviews. Located in a former army barracks, it had huts of solid construction, proper lighting, tiled wash-houses, and decent toilet facilities. 'With dry rooms, electric light, running water and proper sanitation,' Terence Prittie wrote, 'these buildings were infinitely preferable to any of the Warburg huts.' There was a decent-sized football pitch, parole walks were allowed, and inside the wire Eichstätt was comparatively roomy in the early months. It left 'a very good impression' on Swiss observers after a visit in November 1942. Like many other camps, however, Oflag VIIB soon began to suffer from crowding problems, the electricity supply was cut off at night, and representatives of both the ICRC and the Protecting Power, while still regarding it as a 'good' camp, became aware of significant complaints about conditions from officers' representatives. Still, as a post-war analyst observed, conditions at Eichstätt remained superior to those in most stalags.[29]

Of the major men's camps, Stalag XVIIIA (Wolfsberg) was one of several that changed over time. In comparison to the transit camp in Salonika, from which many of its inhabitants arrived in 1941, the renovated stables that served as barracks in this hutted camp in Austria were well appointed. After visiting in August of that summer the Red Cross also found that the camp—then the base for over 5,300 Commonwealth POWs—made a good impression. By the following summer, however, after repeated requests that defects be dealt with, the Red Cross was reporting that 'the sanitary arrangements for the British are still deplorable—the running water, showers, latrines, ventilation, lighting, laundry—all have either to be created or improved.' By the spring of 1943, fortunately, the constructing of a new washhouse among other completed or promised improvements and a decrease in the camp population allowed Rudolf Burckhardt, inspecting as a representative of the Swiss government, to conclude that Wolfsberg was 'a good camp.' Living conditions appear to have remained fairly positive into 1944.[30]

Matters appear to have followed a roughly similar trajectory at Stalag XXID (Posen), to judge by visitor reports. It was 'much improved' as a result of prisoners being shipped out to working parties in early 1941, but one of the main forts still used to house POWs was 'pretty poor' when the Red Cross came calling in the autumn. 'The rooms were dark and gloomy,' Ewart Jones later wrote of this period, '[and] the stone floors cold and damp.' Crowding made bathing and toilet facilities particularly inadequate. The building of new latrines and various renovations allowed it to be labelled 'fairly good' by the autumn of 1942, and though there were still sanitary and other problems with the forts, Posen had by late 1943 become something of a showpiece. 'Taking all into consideration,' a report on the camp written by Walter Braun, a Swiss representative, concluded, 'this Stalag is one of the best for British prisoners of war.'[31]

The quality of accommodation and facilities in the working camps to which other rank prisoners were dispatched from stalags, meanwhile, varied from one location to another. Depending on the employer and the circumstances, they could be better or worse than the main camps. Arriving at a sub-camp in the Frankfurt area in March 1941 with a group of prisoners from Thorn, Private W. C. Law (Gloucestershire Regiment) was agreeably surprised, noting in his diary that 'it looks as a camp and billets as [sic] you would get in Blighty'. Blechammer, one of the largest labour camps manned by prisoners from Lamsdorf, was a good place to be. Employed by a construction company involved in the building of a synthetic fuel plant, up to 800 POWs at a time were housed in wooden huts with two-tier bunks originally built for the Hitler Youth, and provided with good hot- and cold-water washing and shower installations. It was, as a Red Cross visitor reported, 'excellent from every point of view'.[32]

Other Arbeitskommando camps in Upper Silesia were rather less salubrious. A Lager at Baurwitz, for example, where other Kriegies from Stalag VIIIB were housed while working for the owners of a sugar-beet factory, suffered from serious crowding problems according to John Elwyn:

The camp was in an old brewery and housed well over three hundred prisoners in one long, narrow room. Not only were there three-tiered wooden beds along each side of this room but there was also a row running down the middle. In between the beds were two rows of tables and benches and the only means of moving from one end of the room to the other was either under the tables or over them. We were literally packed like the proverbial sardines. The result was chaos.

There were, however, much worse places, and not just in Wehrkreis VIII. At Freiburg, where 200 men from Stalag IVF (Hartmannsdorf) were employed by a lead-mining company, British POWs were held under what a Salvation Army visitor described as 'appalling conditions': their huts were damp, and they had only one wash tap between them. Or there was Weissenfels, containing thirty Kriegies from Stalag IVB (Mühlburg) toiling in a brickworks and quarry complex, where the accommodation was literally among pigs and geese and was dirty in the extreme.[33]

Meanwhile there were also main camps where conditions were rather more uniformly good in physical terms. Oflag VB (Biberach), a converted army barracks near the Swiss frontier used in pre-Warburg days, was described by future Colditz inmate Hugh Bruce as 'a very pleasant camp', a view endorsed by others who were there. Overcrowding was not a problem, the place was clean, washing and toilet facilities were modern and up to standard for the over 700 officers in residence. The camp facilities made a 'good impression' on an American visitor in July 1941, and all in all Biberach seemed to represent 'civilisation' if not 'absolute comfort', in comparison to nastier places.[34] Oflag IXA/Z (Rotenburg), used later in the war to hold about 400 officers, was very highly thought of. It was situated in a well-equipped former girls school set in lovely countryside, and possessed amenities (such as a decent water supply) that were absent in other camps. Despite some crowding, prisoners' opinions ranged from 'not too uncomfortable' through 'really very pleasant' to 'one of the best camps in Germany'.[35] The former Czech military cadet school transformed into Oflag VIIIF (Mährisch Trübau) for the use of 2,000 officers sent from Italy was also well appointed. Oflag VIIIF was more spacious than Eichstätt, and the main buildings had central heating and good electric lighting along with modern plumbing. 'All things were good at Trubau [sic]', as a South African chaplain observed.[36]

Among the major men's camps the best in terms of living conditions was probably Stalag 383 (Hohenfels) in Bavaria. This was an ex-Wehrmacht training camp, used from the autumn of 1942 onward to hold over 4,500 army NCOs who had refused to work for the Reich. The barracks were prefabricated timber chalets, each one double-roofed and insulated with glass fibre, possessing a storm porch, and equipped with windows at both ends. Unlike in most stalags, the bunks were double- rather than triple-tier, seven to each hut. Red Cross representatives, visiting the camp in March 1943, noted that 'the installations at Stalag 383 appear to us to be excellent'. The latrines were of the proper sceptic-tank variety, and parole walks were allowed in the last nine months of the war. Sergeant Donald Edgar, arriving from Lamsdorf, was, not too surprisingly, 'very agreeably impressed'.[37]

Navy and air force prisoners, meanwhile, were united in thinking that the camps run by their equivalent German service were better than those run by the Wehrmacht. On the whole, they appear to have been right.

Stalag XB (Sandbostel) was a singularly unattractive hut-and-wire Lager in some naval prisoners' estimation. 'It was an appalling camp', Tommy Catlow remembered. This comment, however, like those of other inhabitants, was in reference to the army-run compounds in general and the predicament of Russian POWs in particular. The naval compound supervised by the Kriegsmarine was much better thought of. Containing over 100 officers and about 800 ratings, naval quarters at Sandbostel were, as two Red Cross observers discovered in the summer of 1941, of an 'excellent' sort. The officers' wooden huts all contained interior washbasins and showers as well as a separate laundry room with a hot-water supply. In winter, noted Lieutenant John Chrisp, these huts were 'reasonably weather proof and warm'. The latrines, though of the concrete cesspit variety, did not generate complaint. Arguably the only disadvantages were that officers and ratings were confined in the same compound within a stalag—'[t]he whole place was entirely unsuitable for officers', according to Lieutenant-Commander Peter Buckley—and the effect of the weather. 'Nothing', Captain G. W. F. Wilson, the Senior British Officer, reported of the place, '. . . could [make] better the driving sand storms in dry weather, or the sea of mud under foot after rain.' All in all, though, according to Leading Telegraphist Harold Shipp, transferred there from Thorn, Sandbostel was widely viewed as a 'flipping great camp'.[38]

Marlag und Milag Nord, the Kriegsmarine camp at Westertimke to which naval prisoners were transferred in the spring of 1942, was also viewed in a generally positive light despite the rather bleak and desolate surroundings. A hut-and-wire affair, with separate compounds for naval officers and men—Marlag (O) and Marlag (M)—as well as for seafarers belonging to the merchant marine (Milag), the camp made a good impression on both neutral observers and the prisoners themselves. Captain Wilson reported that 'the accommodation in Marlag (O) was

good', with no overcrowding until 1945. The well-lighted and well-venti-
lated barracks had large rooms into which eight men could fit more-or-
less comfortably, and as well as being well lit and heated were, in the
words of David James, of 'a standard wooden type, double-lined throughout and reasonably warm and waterproof'. There was less space in
Marlag (M), where there were twelve to fourteen men to a room, but
with similar amenities in the way of, for example, a canteen. It rated
highly in comparison to the stalags. 'From every point of view the Marlag
can be considered as a good camp', Red Cross representatives opined
after a visit in August 1942. 'Both the camps, "M" and "O"', a report on
a camp visit ten months later stated, 'are excellent.' Even when the ICRC
or Protecting Power rated Westertimke merely 'satisfactory', complaints
from the prisoners themselves were few and far between. Among ratings
Marlag was reputed to be the best camp in Germany.[39]

To airmen who had spent time in Wehrmacht compounds those of the
Luftwaffe were almost invariably considered a good deal better. Though
all eventually suffered from crowding difficulties, the hut-and-wire
Stalag Luft camps were mostly purpose-built, and both officers' and
NCOs' compounds were relatively well appointed in terms of accommodation and amenities. Of the five in which British and Commonwealth aircrew were held, however, it was Stalag Luft III (Sagan), built
in a Lower Silesian pine forest on flat, sandy soil in 1942, that was
supposed to be the 'showcase' camp for the air force.

Progressively expanded in size through the addition of new sections,
Luft III was made up of huts designed to hold roughly between 100 and
200 men, with separate compounds for officers and NCOs. The officers
did better in terms of the occupant–space ratio in rooms as well as
interior washing and latrine facilities; but all barracks were provided
with adequate lighting and ventilation, tables, stools, and other useful
accoutrements. Each compound, moreover, had a sports field. This was
all certainly a vast improvement over Lamsdorf. 'It was like moving off
the gutter into a luxurious hotel', Albert Jones remembered. Others
compared the space and the ablutions quite favourably with other
camps. Even relatively good places such as Stalag Luft I (Barth) and
Oflag IXA/H (Spangenberg) were inferior by comparison. There were,
of course, drawbacks. As elsewhere, crowding eventually became a
problem at Sagan, only partially solved by the opening of new compounds. With the number of inhabitants increasing, the washing facilities, among other features, became overloaded, so that six cold-water
taps had to serve for upwards of a thousand men in the officers'

compound in early 1943. The lack of ground cover meant that a sea of mud could be created when it rained and dust clouds kicked up in summer. Some prisoners, furthermore, found that the looming pine forest on every side eventually produced an 'utterly hemmed in' or 'suffocating' feeling. Nevertheless, in comparative terms Stalag Luft III, if no longer a 'model camp' after a while, was still a good place to be. As Pilot Officer B. A. James (who spent time elsewhere) accurately put it, the camp 'probably had better conditions than most others in Germany'.[40]

Then there was Colditz. Given its reputation, one might expect Oflag IVC to be one of harshest of camps in terms of physical surroundings. To prisoners being escorted up from the local railway station to the castle it certainly looked forbidding enough. 'With its high grey granite walls, barred windows, ancient towers, archways and moat,' thought Tommy Catlow as he made the approach under escort, 'it would fit naturally into the pages of a Bram Stoker novel.' Going through successive courtyard entranceways, Montagu Champion Jones wondered if 'Abandon All Hope Ye Who Enter Here' ought not to be carved over the top of the main gate. Almost everyone who made his way there agreed that Colditz castle looked very daunting. Once inside, however, conditions were far better than outward appearances suggested.[41]

Having been used at various times in the recent past as a prison, asylum, and barracks, Colditz castle was already equipped to handle residents when it became Oflag IVC. It had piped running water, indoor flush toilets, showers, washbasins, stoves for heating and cooking, electric light, and other modern conveniences. Neutral observers were generally satisfied with the quarters in which the British were housed, even as prisoners gradually increased in number. 'General impressions are favourable', an American inspector reported after a visit in late 1940. Overall the place left 'not a bad impression', according to a Swiss representative after a visit in early July 1941. And after a tour in April 1942, another Swiss observer concluded that 'the general impression of this camp cannot be called bad'.[42]

As time went by, to be sure, various problems developed, which accounts for the absence of complete enthusiasm—and indeed a growing level of dissatisfaction—on the part of neutral visitors in 1942–3. The increasing British population, in combination with normal wear and tear and a tendency among prisoners to dismantle plumbing and fixtures for escape purposes and other clandestine activities, meant that the toilets and washing facilities became strained beyond normal capacity. The crowding difficulty was to some extent relieved by the transfer of non-British prisoners elsewhere in 1943, and even with more than sixty new British POWs who were then shipped in, conditions were nevertheless 'tolerably good' again according to a Red Cross report of July 1944.[43]

Other problems, however, remained. Lack of sufficient generating capacity and poor wiring meant that while electric lighting was available in prisoners' quarters—and often necessary even in daylight because of the small size of some room windows—the actual illumination provided was so limited that at night it became difficult to read. Lack of exercise space at Colditz was also an issue, the small cobbled interior courtyard being inadequate for most sports. A fenced area had been set aside for this purpose beyond the castle walls; but this was closed more often than not in response to various escape attempts and because of general security concerns. 'The exercise facilities', Swiss representative Rudolf Denzler wrote after a visit in May 1944, 'are to all intents and purposes non-existent.'[44]

Where did all this leave Oflag IVC in comparison to other camps in physical terms? Everyone sent there had already been a prisoner some-where else, and therefore had a basis for comparison. Some thought the quarters rather cramped and the darkness of the place oppressive, but most inhabitants who left records described Colditz in positive terms. 'Obviously for us,' George Abbott pointed out an in interview with reference to SOE officers who had experienced Gestapo prisons, 'Colditz was a paradise.' Michael Alexander agreed: 'I thought we were very well off there . . . ' Some of those from regular camps were indifferent about their new surroundings—Pat Fergusson found it 'just another prison camp', and John Hamilton-Baillie later remarked that it 'wasn't all that different from other camps'—but for many Oflag IVC compared well with other places. 'I think it was the most comfortable prisoner of war camp in Germany,' Edward Davies-Scourfield remembered, 'because we weren't terribly crowded (except at the very end), [and] it was a nice castle and not a nasty hutted thing in the middle of a swamp [i.e. Warburg].' This was, to be sure, a comparison based on experience of some of the worst of the oflags. Yet those transferred from even the best of the regular camps could also rate Oflag IVC highly. Patrick Welch and Walter Morrison thought it much more comfortable than Stalag Luft III, despite the latter's good reputation among RAF officers. 'I think conditions of living at Colditz were probably better than in most other camps', Hugh Bruce, a Royal Marine officer who had spent time at Oflag VB

(Biberach), among other places, reflected in an interview. 'I think', Billie Stephens wrote of Colditz, 'that it was the best camp that I was in'— which placed it a rung or two above the well-regarded Marlag (O). As late as October 1944 a Swiss representative could report that 'the interior arrangements are as good or better than in other officer camps', going on to observe that 'rooms are less crowded [than] for instance at [Oflag VIIB] Eichstätt.'[45]

In terms of accommodation and related physical conditions, therefore, Colditz can be rated among the better places to which British prisoners of war were sent. One RAF officer, who had imagined the place to be a Straflager, found that 'it came as something of a surprise to find that Colditz was in fact the most comfortable camp in Germany'. As Michael Burn, who was there in 1944–5, observed with respect to the post-war Colditz phenomenon, the aura surrounding Oflag IVC during the war and after made it out to be 'much grimmer than it was, once it's put alongside other camps'.[46]

The character and reputation of POW camps, however, depended not only on physical surroundings but also on how they were run. On paper the administration of POWs in the Third Reich was a model of bureaucratic uniformity, and in certain respects this was true in practice. Under the umbrella of the German High Command, *Oberkommando der Wehrmacht* (OKW), a department was set up to administer prisoner-of-war affairs. One of the senior figures, Major-General Adolf Westhoff, later claimed he was doing his best to uphold the 1929 Geneva Convention governing the treatment of POWs. With some major as well as minor exceptions, the articles of the convention did indeed help shape the overall treatment of British prisoners of war in positive terms. Even after Himmler took over the direction of prisoner-of-war administration and handed it to SS Obergruppenführer Gottlob Berger in the summer of 1944, most of the rules governing treatment derived from the Geneva Convention remained in effect.[47]

More influential in day-to-day terms than the mandarins of OKW and military districts were those officers tasked with the administration of individual camps. In accordance with the Geneva Convention each camp was assigned a commanding officer, the *Kommandant*. Under him would be a group of officers and NCOs responsible for such matters as camp security, translation, and prisoner counts, their number and function depending on the size and importance of the Lager concerned. Usually too old or otherwise unable to serve at the front, German officers assigned to oflags and stalags varied in quality and competence. The best of them were men of honour who did their duty in a manner that balanced security considerations with the welfare of the prisoners. The worst were weak, bullies, or outright sadists who misused their powers in order to make life as difficult as possible for those under their control. The majority fell somewhere in between. All, however, had the power to order summary punishment such as time in cells and, in more serious cases, to initiate a formal court martial.[48]

The most important factor in determining the attitude and behaviour of a commandant was whether or not he saw his charges as worthy of respect. Those who did, and were willing to act accordingly, were often described as 'old school' by former POWs. With careers stretching back to an earlier, somewhat more chivalrous age, they truly believed in the concept of an honourable foe, and therefore in the international conventions governing the treatment of prisoners of war. Some had themselves been prisoners in the First World War. Those with less of a sense of honour, often younger and less competent men with an affinity for National Socialism who disliked the chivalric implications of the Hague and Geneva regulations, or men who simply felt threatened by prisoner complaints, could substitute vindictiveness for fairness. Less important, but still significant, was the commandant's degree of self-possession and sense of humour: those unable to see the funny side of prisoner behaviour were the most likely to lose their temper completely; sometimes with dire results.[49]

The better army commandants were remembered by ex-prisoners in surprisingly positive terms. The man in charge of Oflag VIID (Tittmoning) in the winter of 1940–1, for instance, was called 'generous and humane', while the commandant at Oflag VB (Biberach) the following summer was labelled 'very decent'.[50] Oberst Schrader, in command of Oflag IXA/H (Spangenberg) two years later, stood out through his 'correct bearing' and willingness to entertain proposals designed to make life more bearable.[51]

The colonel in command of Stalag 383 (Hohenfels), the camp for non-working army NCOs, was by all accounts something of a model commandant. Reputed to have an English wife, Oberst Felix Aufmanner was, in the words of Sergeant J. M. McGee (RAOC), 'first class, fair, impartial and [equipped] with a good sense of humour'. The latter trait was evident in an incident recorded in an Australian sergeant's diary in the summer of 1943. 'A chap presented himself at the gate with all his kit today,' wrote Raymond Ryan, 'and said that he wanted to go home. The

Comdt., however, was equal to the occasion and expressing his sympathy said the POW needed a change of surroundings—so he gave him a few days in the bunker.' Even repeat offenders did not seem to dent his good humour. 'The Comdt. met Lofty Willans as he returned from the bunker today', Ryan later recorded. 'He told him that if he attempted another escape he would put him across his knee and spank him.' Willing to take the side of prisoners regarding brutality during a Gestapo search of the barracks, the commandant was given a glowing testimonial at the end of the war by the senior British prisoner present.[52]

The Luftwaffe prided itself on treating prisoners better than the army, and a number of Stalag Luft commandants were indeed praised after the war. At Stalag Luft I (Barth), Major Von Stachelski, described as 'a humane and thoughtful man', was relieved of command for being too friendly with his charges. A successor, Major Horst Burchardt, a 'German of the old school' and reputedly a POW in the previous war, was also known to be a good sort. Pilot Officer B. A. 'Jimmy' James, cooling his heels in cells after a failed escape bid, found himself the object of a sympathy call. 'Good morning, Herr James,' Burchardt said in excellent English: 'That was very bad luck. It was a good try and a very good tunnel. Better luck next time.'[53] Oberst Freiherr Friedrich von Lindeiner-Wildau, the commandant at Stalag Luft III (Sagan), was, as his title suggested, a 'gentlemanly' and quite Anglophile officer of the old school who also enjoyed good relations with the RAF. Two recaptured escapers languishing in the cooler were somewhat startled to receive a visit from Lindeiner-Wildau during which he presented them with a bottle of whiskey as a reward for the courage they had shown in cutting through the wire in daylight. The commandant at Stalag Luft VI (Heydekrug) was a good type, more or less able to understand Kriegie humour—an unusual trait—and willing on one memorable day to buy the entire NCO population of the camp a fizzy drink from his own pocket.[54]

Some commandants were remembered less fondly, but nevertheless respected as officers who knew their job. At Oflag XIIB (Hadamar), Oberst Lap, though 'a martinet of the first order', was considered by Edward Ward, a BBC journalist consigned to the camp, as 'strictly fair and just in his treatment of us'.[55] The man in overall command of Marlag und Milag Nord, the camp for naval and merchant navy personnel at Westertimke, was for much of the war Kapitän zur See Schuer. Short, round, over 70 years of age, and sporting a goatee beard, Schuer was disliked on a personal level by some of those with whom he came into contact. 'He was a nasty little Prussian martinet', Lieutenant David James recalled. Captain G. F. W. Wilson, the Senior British Officer and as such the prisoner who met him most often, described Schuer in his diary as 'a very hot tempered, obstinate little man' with a streak of ruthlessness. The commandant did, however, have a sense of humour—he laughed when he learned that he had been nicknamed *Der Taschenshlagschiff* (the pocket battleship) by the camp dentist—and even those who found him irritating admitted that he did his job well. Lieutenant James conceded that Schuer was 'always scrupulously correct' in his dealings with prisoners. The SBO, despite numerous confrontations, admitted that 'he has done his best to provide us with decent quarters and internal amenities', and was quite sorry to see him replaced in the spring of 1944.[56]

Unfortunately there were also commandants who could make life worse for POWs. Adding to the bad situation at Oflag VIIC (Laufen), where the majority of captured BEF officers were housed in 1940–1, was the attitude of Oberst Von Frey, a tall, pompous Prussian who sported a monocle and clearly hated the British. Guards were ordered to shoot to kill to deter escape attempts and disorderly conduct. When the terms of the Geneva Convention were brought up, the commandant, who had a tendency to lose his temper and literally foam at the mouth, dismissed the document as something only 'old women and pacifists' could believe in.[57] Oberst Blätterbauer, a rather gross Nazi placed in command of Oflag VIIB (Eichstätt) in 1942, tried at first to ingratiate himself with his charges. But when that did not produce the requisite level of docility among POWs he lost his temper and imposed what one report called 'small but annoying vexations' in the way of new rules and restrictions.[58] Two years later a neutral representative was arguing that the commandant of Oflag 79 (Brunswick) was 'not at all fitted for his present post', going on to write that Oberst Strehle was 'rather petty and narrow-minded' as well as 'afraid of taking any responsibility'.[59]

Colditz was no exception to the rule that commandants could make a difference to the experience of POWs for good or ill. Though rarely seen by the prisoners themselves, the three colonels placed successively in command of Oflag IVC nevertheless helped shape life in the place. On the whole their influence can be considered to have been relatively benign, especially in comparison to some of their more vindictive counterparts elsewhere.

Oberstleutnant Schmidt, a Saxon his late sixties, was an old-school type who drove his staff hard. Though 'more of a disciplinarian than he should be', according to the report of an American observer in the summer of 1941, the commandant would not tolerate dishonesty or any bending of the rules at prisoners' expense. He once publicly reprimanded a Hauptmann for striking a cigarette—forbidden on parade—out of a British major's mouth: 'This unrestrained behaviour against an officer of higher rank was not correct.' On contentious matters, such as prisoners saluting German officers, he proved willing to negotiate with the SBO and others rather than resort to force.[60] His successor, Oberst Glaesche, who arrived in the summer of 1942, was something of a new broom at age 43. But while eager to impose his will on prisoners—midnight parades were instituted for a few nights until the camp population ceased its disruptive behaviour—he believed in the Geneva Convention and soon allowed his subordinates to pursue a more flexible approach to maintaining order in the castle. They were thus able, for example, to turn something of a blind eye to lesser infractions of the commandant's order that 'no catcalling, no hands in pockets, [and] no smoking' be allowed on parade on pain of arrest and court martial. Edgar Glaesche was replaced in February 1943, however, because from an OKW perspective he had failed to impose sufficient discipline on the camp population. As one of his staff put it, he 'lacked the aggression' some observers thought necessary to impose order on 'the unruly mob of prisoners we had at Colditz'.[61]

The last commandant, Oberst Prawitt, a man also in his forties, was a martinet, with regard both to prisoners and guards. He appeared more often than earlier commandants in the prisoners' courtyard, and insisted on being saluted at attention. In retaliation for breaches of POW discipline—deliberate on the part of the men concerned—he shut the camp theatre, curtailed exercise privileges, and even at one point turned off the electrical supply. On one occasion Prawitt was not above ordering guards to shoot at the upper windows from which POWs were shouting insults. This sort of thing gave him the reputation among prisoners of being a 'swine' (or 'smarmy shit', as Jack Best trenchantly put it). 'He aims at ruling with a rod of iron', the author of a Red Cross report from the early summer of 1943 bluntly stated. But, partly through the discretion of some of his subordinates, Prawitt too evidently learned the value of flexibility—what his security officer called a *modus vivendi*—in his dealings with the population of Oflag IVC. Nine months later another Red Cross observer was reporting that the commandant, 'although he is rather severe, behaves in a perfectly correct manner'.[62]

Commandants were not the only Germans in authority who could influence the quality of life in a particular camp. At Colditz, as in many other camps, it was the staff—the more junior officers and senior NCOs in charge of individual compounds or carrying out a particular function such as camp security—who affected day-to-day living most directly. Here too the inhabitants of Oflag IVC were, comparatively speaking, quite well off.

The authority figure with whom the greatest number of prisoners in main camps came into regular contact was the Lager officer, who commanded the count parades (*Appells*) and was responsible for maintaining order in a particular compound. As with their superiors, attitude and behaviour varied from very poor to first class.

At Oflag VIIC (Laufen) the Lageroffizier followed the example of the commandant, 'treating us extremely badly', Hugh Bruce remembered. Even when the commandant was not so bad, as at Oflag VIIB two years later, his subordinates could still prove troublesome. The officer who regularly took *Appell* at Eichstätt was a martinet who lost his temper over the casual dress of British officer prisoners and soon earned their contempt. The NCO in charge of the aircrew non-commissioned officers' compound at Stalag IVB (Mühlburg) in the last year of the war, nicknamed 'Piccolo Pete', was widely disliked for his violent tantrums. 'Put a foul-tempered old fox terrier into a pair of jackboots', wrote Flight Sergeant Geoff Taylor, 'and you have Piccolo Pete.'[63]

Those delegated to be in charge of working party (Arbeitskommando) camps, and thus not under the eyes of their stalag superiors, could sometimes behave like tyrants. The German NCO placed in charge of a 100-man peat-digging party at Konin, made up of prisoners from Stalag XXIB (Schubin) in 1940, Robert Gale remembered, turned out to be 'a dark, introspective sadist'. An Unteroffizier in command of a several hundred prisoners working in a coal-mine—popularly known as 'John the Bastard'—rapidly became notorious throughout Upper Silesia for beating and shooting prisoners, especially when drunk. 'Things have not improved', Private G. R. Manners noted at one point in his secret diary, recording that the NCO in charge of his working-party camp near Strasbourg 'has now armed himself with a piece of rubber piping for a truncheon, which he uses with the slightest provocation'. These cases were not, unfortunately, unique; not least perhaps because physical violence was one of the ways in which discipline was enforced in the Wehrmacht itself.[64]

There were also Germans in authority whose behaviour changed according to circumstances, and not always for the better. On one of the Arbeitskommandos attached to the giant Hindenburg coal-mining operation sent from Stalag VIIIB (Lamsdorf), the Feldwebel in command, remembered Fusilier Thomas Hughes, turned out to be 'a real Jekyll and Hyde':

In his sober periods he was a real gentleman, nothing was too much trouble. Whenever we had a camp concert he would help us with the lighting, and obtain what he could in the way of costumes and other necessary items. Unfortunately, these sober periods didn't last long. He would go on a drunken binge, when we wouldn't see him for a couple of days. Then he would re-appear and make his presence felt in no uncertain terms, usually at about two or three A.M. barging into the room, kicking the slop bucket over, calling us swein-hunds, heaping curses on Churchill and the Royal Family, and [saying] how much better life would be if England would capitulate, join forces with Germany and crush the Russians. Then we would all have to form up outside while we had a roll-call.[65]

One of the most notorious figures at Lamsdorf was Joseph Kussell, better known as 'Ukraine Joe', an Unteroffizier in charge first of the Straflager and then, between 1942 and 1944, the RAF NCOs' compound. Having earned a reputation for brutality in the Straf compound, he eventually began to take a pride in 'his' air-force prisoners, fiercely resisting outside interference in the running of the RAF compound and aiding in the acquisition of amenities. The threat of violence was nevertheless always present, and Kriegies were always circumspect in their dealings with a man who never forgot a face. Arriving at Stalag VIIIB in early 1943, Sergeant Bill Jackson was warned by an old lag that 'he doesn't bother us much, but if you cross him he's a bastard'.[66]

This advice was applicable to other German NCOs. 'A harsh punishment which the Germans inflicted on some of our prisoners who were incorrigible regulation-breakers [anything from not saluting to talking back],' Roger Coward noted of the ratings' compound at Stalag XB (Sandbostel), 'was to make the offender stand close to the warning wire near one of the guards' towers. He might have to stand there for twelve hours at a stretch, for up to seven days. Many collapsed from sheer exhaustion.' Sergeant Herbert Tuck recalled that at Stalag XXB (Marienburg) in 1940 even minor infringements of camp regulations would instantly result in similar retribution—'standing with arms raised near the sentry box facing the wire perimeter'. Long spells in the cells and beatings, especially of non-officer prisoners, were also possible, while manhandling a guard (even if in self defence) could result in court-martial sentences ranging from months to years in prison.[67]

Other Germans in positions of authority treated prisoners with consistent decency. John Lawrence remembered how in November 1940 the officer in charge of Fort 8, part of Stalag XXA (Posen), 'an Austrian major of the old school', personally handed out to each recipient the first letters from England. 'He was a fine old man,' Lawrence added, 'and many of us were sorry when he was transferred . . . ' Fort 13 at Thorn was also well run, Sam Kydd finding 'very well disciplined [and] pleasant officers' on staff from 1942 onward. Some of the Lager officers at Oflag IXA/H (Spangenberg) and even at Oflag VIB (Warburg), Captain John Mansel discovered, were quite sympathetic to the plight of prisoners. Later on the actions of the bad-tempered commandant at Oflag VIIB (Eichstätt) were offset to some degree by the behaviour of a sympathetic Foreign Office representative, Von Fetter.[68]

Good Germans could also be found beyond the main camps. Rittmeister Prince Waldemar zu Hohenlohe-Oheringen, responsible for one of the bigger working parties using prisoners sent out from Lamsdorf, Arbeitskommando E3 at Blechammer, was respected as an honourable and just officer. He proved willing to intercede on behalf of POWs when the demands of the civilian employer, the Upper Silesia Hydroworks, grew too great. Dismissed in 1943 for taking the side of prisoners too often, Hohenloe was popular enough to be invited to a POW reunion in London after the war. 'He was a very fair man', Fred Ayers remembered.[69]

German NCOs as well as officers could behave in a manner that generated greater respect, and even, in some cases, a degree of affection on the part of Kriegies. A sense of humour, along with strength of character and fairness, were the qualities that POWs most admired.

In a Lamsdorf-drawn Arbeitskommando attached to a synthetic fuel factory near Auschwitz, one of the smaller sub-camps, AB 21, was run by a Feldwebel nicknamed 'Romper'. An English-speaker, Romper had the rare ability to make jokes about POW transgressions. Whether warning his charges not to hang laundry on the camp warning wire—'it's not the Siegfried Line, you know'—or taking note of the Kriegie habit of dismantling the interior of huts—'you'd better be careful, this place is only Gerry built'—Romper was able to joke rather than just bawl orders. At the same time he possessed real moral authority, and could use it to effect when necessary. One day in 1943, Able Seaman Roger Coward recalled, when a parade seemed to have gone on rather longer than necessary, prisoners starting catcalling:

Romper stood this for a little while, then suddenly made a furious gesture for silence. Perhaps startled, perhaps just curious to know what he would say, the shouters were silent. The surrounding guards put 'one up the spout' to give emphasis to the order. Romper said in cutting tones, 'Churchill must have had to sweep the gutters of the British Empire to have found a crowd like you.' Which, untrue though it might be, we had to admit was a pretty good retort.[70]

Prior to the arrival of Piccolo Pete in the non-commissioned aircrew compound at Mülburg, the Lager NCO had been a youngish, previously wounded man, Unteroffizier 'Blondy' Schroder. He was initially disliked for his 'arrogance and bloody-mindedness', in particular his habit of smashing up *Verboten* shelving and laundry lines inside huts. Over time, however, a curious sense of comradeship developed between captor and captive, a baffled Blondy coming to appreciate the peculiar Kriegie sense of humour, airmen in their turn coming to respect their overseer's sense of duty and basic fair-mindedness. An episode recorded by Geoff Taylor encapsulates the curiously affectionate relationship that developed:

One wintry morning [in early 1944] we got Blondy to smile on parade. It was morning appell and a night's snow lay about us as we stood shivering, awaiting the arrival of a German officer to watch the roll-call. As seems to be the universal custom of many senior officers of the services of the world, this one was late.

Either to keep himself warm or to impress the supervising officer if he unexpectedly arrived, Blondy began goose-steeping backwards and forwards across the snow-covered parade ground. Immediately a great and not altogether derisive cheer went up from the ranks of our barrack, which was echoed by neighbouring barracks also on parade. Undaunted, Blondy kept it up, his gleaming black jackboots flicking smartly against the white snow. The more we cheered, the more he grinned.

Eventually Blondy became almost a mascot.[71]

Security people were usually another matter. Among escapers in particular, security officers and NCOs were often heartily disliked. They, after all, were the ones who made it hardest to make a successful break, and tended therefore to be objects of particular suspicion.

The officer in charge of security at Stalag Luft IV (Gross Tychow) was, according to one witness, often hysterical to the point of insanity in his hatred of RAF aircrew. His counterpart at Oflag VIB (Warburg), Hauptmann Radmemacher, was a pompous, temperamental, sometimes also hysterical man who was thought to want to 'cause as much inconvenience as possible' to prisoners during searches.[72] At Oflag

XIIB, near Hadamar, Hauptmann Förster shouted a great deal and was generally considered an unattractive character—'though in fairness to him,' BBC journalist Edward Ward reflected, 'he did no more than do his job effectively.' Among naval officers at Marlag (O) at Westertimke, Leutnant Güssefeld was described as 'a pasty-faced, anaemic-looking sleuth, always with a drip on the end of his nose', a 'ghastly man' who was 'cordially loathed by everyone for his dishonesty, his oily, sneering manners and his constant prying'. But as David James later put it, 'I am not sure he was anything worse than efficient at a job naturally unpopular with us'.[73]

Even among security staff, however, there were those with enough personal integrity, strength of character, and sense of humour to generate grudging acceptance among POWs. One of the best, in every sense, was Lagerfeldwebel Hermann Glemnitz, a tall, leathery man in his forties who was the senior security NCO at Stalag Luft III. A fluent English-speaker, talkative, observant, and patriotic, Glemnitz was both good at his job and truly concerned for the welfare of prisoners, persuading his superiors to allow them to make furniture from Red Cross parcel crates, and even in one compound to build a miniature golf course. He was always upbeat and developed his own style of wit as a counter to Kriegie humour. 'I hear that the Allies have selected Sagan as the place at which to open their Second Front', he remarked in reference to the prisoners' energetic tunnelling efforts. On noticing that a Kriegie had crept under a fire engine during a fire drill in a bid to escape, Glemnitz jumped aboard and had the engine driven round the bumpiest bits of the north compound. When the engine finally stopped at the gate, Glemnitz jumped down and said: 'Herr Cross, I hope you enjoyed the ride. You must get down from under. The rest of the journey to the cooler will be on foot.' He was also protective. One night in the spring of 1943 Glemnitz personally rescued a drunken airman who had wandered out of his hut after lights out. To break the curfew was *Verboten*, the man was yelling and paying no heed to shouted orders to stop, and guards had begun to fire at him. Glemnitz appeared and ordered the guards to cease firing as he strode in, personally grabbed the offender, and bundled him off to the cooler before he could do himself any harm. 'By war's end', Kingsley Brown wrote, 'every one of us knew Hermann Glemnitz for what he was: a loyal German soldier, an incorruptible guard, and a man of good humour, maturity and judgement.'[74]

What then of the Lager and security officers at Colditz? As much through luck as through design, Oflag IVC had more than its fair share of professional yet sympathetic officers who regularly encountered the POW population, as the proportionately large number of written and recorded recollections of the camp indicate.

The chief Lager officer at Oflag IVC in the 1940–2 period—he retired with heart problems in 1943—was Hauptmann Paul Priem. An ex-schoolmaster rather too fond of the bottle, Priem was nevertheless an easygoing but quite shrewd soul who, in Pat Reid's words, 'possessed a rare quality among Germans—a sense of humour'.[75] The latter attribute helped to produce a number of the more light-hearted moments at Colditz. In August 1941, for instance, after Lieutenant Airey Neave had been caught trying to bluff his way out of the castle in a home-made German corporal's uniform, Priem announced at the evening *Appell* that '*Gefreiter* Neave is to be sent to the Russian front', which produced gales of laughter.[76] Some of his deputies felt that he did not do enough to enforce discipline among the prisoners, but Priem could use what Padre Ellison Platt called his 'good humoured self' to advantage. In March 1942, when five British prisoners were found missing on *Appell*, Priem announced to the assembled contingent that Dick Howe, one of their number, had been shot while escaping. 'He observed our reaction to this announcement,' Platt recorded in his diary, 'and probably deduced from our merriment that an actual escape had not taken place [the five were in fact still inside the castle] . . . our laughing told him much that he wanted to know.' The following day the British held a mock funeral procession for Howe in the courtyard, which Priem watched 'with all the good humour in the world'. Priem took the joke a step further by presenting the SBO with a letter of condolence and announcing before the assembled prisoners on *Appell* the next day that in future no funerals should take place without twelve hours' notice. As Platt wrote, this sort of thing 'tickled our perverse sense of humour, and we laughed out loud'.[77]

Even better liked, though a much more serious fellow, was Hauptmann Hans Püpke, present at Colditz down to 1945. Though capable of losing his temper on occasion, he was thought to be a 'decent man' (Peter Allan), a 'reasonable sort of chap' (Pat Fergusson), and even a true 'gentleman' (Kenneth Lockwood). He made it known that he disliked giving the Nazi salute when it was made compulsory in July 1944, and was always 'very correct' (Hugo Ironside) and 'straight' (Jimmy Yule). 'One had a lot of respect for him', Jack Best remembered. 'He did his job perfectly all the time. He was a person you could admire.'[78]

Then there was Hauptmann Reinhold Eggers, the third Lageroffizier, who eventually became head of camp security. Another former schoolmaster, Eggers felt himself to be 'a teacher dealing with a lot of unruly boys'.[79] A cool, well-controlled, and intelligent man, he was widely distrusted within the British contingent as too smooth by half. Eggers appeared 'sly' (Pat Reid), 'crafty' (Kenneth Lockwood), 'smarmy' (Jack Best), 'oily' (Hugo Ironside), 'a bit two-faced' (John Hoggard), and 'a bit of a two timer' (Jimmy Yule). 'I wouldn't trust him as far as a barge pole', Peter Allan remarked.[80] The man himself put down the hostility he generated to the widespread but exaggerated Kriegie view that by fair means and foul he was personally responsible for foiling any number of escape attempts.[81] Even those who did not like him admitted that he was only doing his job (albeit rather too well for their liking). 'To give Eggers his due,' Jack Best later conceded, 'as security officer...he was always correct in his behaviour with us.'[82] Eggers refused to be intimidated by booing and catcalling from prisoners, and handled a number of potentially explosive confrontations with dignity and tact. As the war progressed, moreover, he became cautiously pro-British. 'He was shrewd enough to keep his eye on the main chance and after the war he visited England where he was warmly entertained by many of his old P.O.W.s', Miles Reid later explained. 'He had escaped any criticism of his conduct as Colditz Security Officer, which says much for his skill in steering a steady course in dangerous waters.'[83]

Senior German NCOs at Colditz, such as Stabsfeldwebel 'Mussolini' Gephard, were admired as straight types, while the camp interpreter, Herr Hans Pfeiffer, his tenuous grasp of English a source of mirth, was pleasant enough for Pat Reid to decide to initiate a correspondence after the war.[84] There were, to be sure, some angry types, such as Rittmeister Aurich, the second Lageroffizier (LO2) in the first years of the war. 'He would blow up at the least provocation, as the prisoners very soon discovered,' Eggers admitted, 'and go literally blue in the face in a moment. He suffered from mortally high blood pressure, and was all for violence against his charges.' Aurich, however, did not last long, and like other Germans inclined to blow up, was gleefully baited by prisoners. The loss of dignity that resulted was, in Eggers's view, far more significant (in terms of who was pulling the strings) than the chance for the individual concerned to let off steam.[85]

All in all, Colditz was generally well appointed and well run in comparison to other places. The Wehrmacht staff ranked among the better groups of officers and NCOs in charge of British prisoners, helping to make it, in the words of Padre Platt, 'better than other camps' he had known. 'To maintain discipline,' Platt related in his diary, 'they don't resort to a weak man's refuge, petty tyranny; but treat us—after they have taken every precaution to prevent us escaping—as gentlemen who know the meaning of honour, and possess a gentleman's dignity.'[86]

Notes

1. The five basic types were: the camps run by the German air force; the camp run by the navy; army-run officer camps; army-run other-rank main camps; and other-rank working camps. It is possible to draw further bureaucratic distinctions based on compound inhabitants and type of working party. There were separate camps for civilian internees (Ilags) and those awaiting repatriation (Heilags).

2. In addition to Oflag IVC (Colditz), to which 'bad boys' from all services could be sent, naval ratings could find themselves sent to working parties (*Arbeitskommandos*) run from army stalags, while RAF aircrew were on occasion placed temporarily in various army-run *Lagern* while in transit or while new Luftwaffe camps or compounds were under construction. The Luftwaffe interrogation centre also served as a de facto camp in the early months of the war. Fleet Air Arm crews and the occasional SAS soldier or paratrooper might also find themselves placed in the Stalag Luft system.

3. In the introduction to the first published history of the camp it is stated that Colditz 'was the only one of its kind in Germany.' J. E. R. Wood, *Detour* (London, 1946), 1.

4. Jim Rogers, *Tunnelling into Colditz* (London, 1986), 135; IWMSA 9893/5, M. Champion Jones; T. C. F. Prittie and W. Earle Edwards, *Escape to Freedom* (London, 1953 edn.), 218.

5. See e.g. James Spenser, *The Awkward Marine* (London, 1948), 240; Ian Ramsay, *P.O.W.* (Melbourne, 1985), 92–4. On Stalag 383 as *Sonderlager* see PRO, WO 2324/55A, RC report, 11 Mar. 1943, p. 1.

6. See Peter Churchill, *The Spirit in the Cage* (London, 1954), 125 ff.

7. On rumours about Colditz as *Straflager*/Hell Camp during the war see e.g. IWM, W. L. Stephens, 50–1; B. A. James, *Moonless Night* (London, 1983), 115–16; PRO, WO 224/69, report on visit of 21 May 1941, p. 1; I. Schrire, *Stalag Doctor* (London, 1956), 182; Corran Purdon, *List the Bugle* (Antrim, 1993), 52. Pat Reid evidently thought *Straflager* and *Sonderlager* were more-or-less synonymous terms: P. R. Reid, *The Colditz Story* (London, 1952), 90; id., *The Latter Days* (London, 1954), 21.

8. G. Mattielo and W. Vogt, *Deutsche Kriegsgefangenen- und Internierteneinrichtungen 1939–1945: Band 2* (Koblenz, 1987), 7. On the German desire to avoid the *Straflager* label for Colditz see e.g. J. M. Green, *From Colditz in Code* (London, 1971), 120.

9. See the comparative charts and detailed discussion contained in Vasilis Vourkoutiosis, 'The German Armed Forces Supreme Command and British and American Prisoners-of-War, 1939–1945: Policy and Practice', Ph.D. thesis, McGill University (2000), 272–306.

10. Michael Duncan, *Underground from Posen* (London, 1954), 58; IWMSA 4847/2, C. L. Irwin; Reid, op. cit., 23; see also e.g. http://web.mala.bc.ca/davies/letters.images/stokes/collection.page.htm, D. Stokes diary, 14 June 1940–9 Mar. 1941. On improving conditions see e.g. PRO, WO 224/228, summary of PP visits, March and May 1941.

11. Schrire, op. cit., 52.

12. George Beeson, *Five Roads to Freedom* (London, 1977), 10; IWM, G. R. Manners, 16.

13. John Castle, *The Password is Courage* (London, 1955), 40.

14. See e.g. PRO, WO 208/3279, p. 1, on Stalag XIIIC (Hammelburg) in 1941–2; http://users.whsmithnet.co.uk/gordonjones/page27.htm, J. G. Jones, 27, on Stalag VIIA (Moosburg).

15. Edward W. Beattie Jr., *Diary of a Kriegie* (New York, 1946), 206; see Kingsley Brown, *Bonds of Wire* (Toronto, 1989), 210; W. Wynne Mason, *Prisoners of War* (Wellington, 1954), 458.

16. Mason, op. cit., ch. 10; see e.g. Robert Garioch, *Two Men and a Blanket* (Edinburgh, 1975), 168 ff.; Robert Gale, *Private Prisoner* (Wellingborough, 1984), 178; Bill Jackson, *The Lone Survivor* (North Battleford, Sask, 1993), 148 ff.; Percy Wilson Carruthers, *Of Ploughs, Planes and Palliasses* (Arundel, 1992), 214.

17. Philip Kindersley, *For You the War Is Over* (Tunbridge Wells, 1983), 158; see PRO, WO 224/77, PP report, 7 Dec. 1944, p. 15.

18. WO 224/228, quote from report of May 1941; see e.g. http://web.mala.bc.ca/davies/letters.images/stokes/collection.page.htm, D. Stokes diary, 16 Oct. 1941.

19. PRO, WO 224/73, RC report on visit of 15 Oct. 1941, p. 3; see Prittie and Edwards, op. cit., 111–13; Miles Reid, *Into Colditz* (Salisbury, 1983), 33–4; Poole, op. cit., 144–5; T. D. Beckwith (ed.), *The Mansel Diaries* (London, 1977), 46; Jack Champ and Colin Burgess, *The Diggers of Colditz* (Sydney, 1985), 36; IWM, H. C. F. Harwood, 119.

20. Quote from K. Brown, op. cit., 155. On the feathering of nests and improving conditions see e.g. IWM, R. P. Evans, 41; IWM, PRO, AIR 40/2300, G. Johnstone, 3; IWMSA 4830/2, F. Pannett; Ewart C. Jones, *Germans Under My Bed* (London, 1957), 130–2; Adrian Vincent, *The Long Road Home* (London, 1956), 49, 53–4; Cyril Rofe, *Against the Wind* (London, 1956), 158.

21. Donald Edgar, *The Stalag Men* (London, 1983), 74.

22. Spenser, op. cit., 174; Roger V. Coward, *Sailors in Cages* (London, 1967), 114, 119.

23. IWMSA 13573/2, A. Jones; Richard Pape, *Boldness Be My Friend* (London, 1953), 113.

24. Jackson, op. cit., 37; Geoffrey Vaughan, *The Way It Really Was* (Budleigh Salterton, 1985), 43.

25. PRO, WO 224/27, RC visit, 29 Oct. 1943, p. 8. James Stedman, who arrived in 1944 after time spent in a number of other stalags, wrote that Lamsdorf 'was the worst camp I had been in'. *Life of a British POW in Poland* (Braunton, 1992), 22.

26. Airey Neave, *They Have Their Exits* (London, 1953), 23; T. D. Calnan, *Free As a Running Fox* (London, 1970), 49.
27. Oliver Philpot, *Stolen Journey* (London, 1950), 100.
28. Purdon, op. cit., 43; Prittie and Edwards, op. cit., 252; M. Reid, op. cit., 49.
29. Mason, op. cit., 365; PRO, WO 224/74, PP report on visit of 2 Nov. 1942, p. 4.
30. PRO, WO 224/45, PP report on 25 May 1943 visit, p. 4; ibid., RC report on 26 Aug. 1941 visit.
31. PRO, WO 224/51, PP report on 25–29 Mar. 1944 visit, p. 16; ibid., RC report on visit, 28 Sep. 1942, p. 6; E. C. Jones, op. cit., 120; WO 224/51, RC report on visit, Sept. 1941, p. 4.
32. PRO, WO 224/27, RC report on visit, 10 Feb. 1943, p. 5; http://www.mgb-stuff.org.uk/wcl.htm, W. Law diary 13 Mar. 1941. On Blechammer see e.g. John Borrie, *Despite Captivity* (London, 1975), 92 ff.
33. IWM, E. Ayling, 60; Fred Hill, *Prisoner of War* (London, 1994), 120; John Elwyn, *At the Fifth Attempt* (London, 1987), 70.
34. Duncan, op. cit., 94; PRO, WO 224/72, PP report, 28 July 1941, p. 9; IWMSA 16797/2, H. Bruce.
35. Ian Reid, *Prisoner at Large* (London, 1947), 278; Sandy Hernu, *Q* (Seaford, 1991), 60; IWM, H. C. F. Harwood, 120.
36. James B. Chutter, *Captivity Captive* (London, 1954), 115.
37. Edgar, op. cit., 147; PRO, 224/55A, RC report on visit, 11 Mar. 1943, p. 12.
38. IWMSA 4839/5, H. Shipp; IWM, G. F. W. Wilson, Report on the Conditions at the RN Prisoners of War Camps at Sandbostel and Marlag und Milag Nord, Germany, 1941–1945, 1; IWMSA 4759/2, P. Buckley; PRO, WO 224/101, RC report on visit, 8 July 1941, p. 10.
39. Barbara Broom (comp.), *Geoffrey Broom's War* (Edinburgh, 1993), 98; Jack Bishop, *In Pursuit of Freedom* (London, 1977), 114; Spenser, op. cit., 171, 259; PRO, WO 208/3270, p. 3; WO 224/101, RC report on visit, 28 June 1943, p. 6; ibid., 5 Aug. 1942, p. 6; David James, *Prisoner's Progress* (Edinburgh, 1947), 23; IWMSA 5194/3, J. Laurie; IWM, G. F. W. Wilson, op. cit., 1.
40. B. A. James, op. cit., 58; IWMSA 13573/2, A. Jones. On general conditions in Luft III see PRO, WO 224/53A. On the 'hemmed-in' feeling see e.g. Derek Thrower, *The Lonely Path to Freedom* (London, 1980), 92; Stephen P. L. Johnson, *A Kriegie's Log* (Tunbridge Wells, 1995), 169.
41. IWMSA 4893/5, M. Champion Jones; LC, T. N. Catlow, 53.
42. PRO, WO 224/69, PP report, 20 Apr. 1942, p. 5; id., 7 July 1941, p. 4; FO 916/16, PP report, 27 Nov. 1940, p. 6.
43. PRO, WO 224/69, RC report on visit, 6 July 1944, p. 5; see ibid., reports, 1942–3, *passim*; WO 208/3288, pp. 1–2.
44. PRO, WO 224/69, PP report on visit, 27 May 1944, p. 1; see ibid., 13 Oct. 1943, 2; PRO, WO 208/3288, p. 2; IWMSA 16797/4, H. Bruce.
45. PRO, WO 224/69, PP report on visit, 7 Oct. 1944, p. 2; IWM, W. L. Stephens, 51; IWMSA 16797/3, H. Bruce; Walter Morrison, *Flak and Ferrets* (London, 1995), 155; IWMSA 10643/2, P. Welch; IWMSA 6367/5, E. G. B. Davies-Scourfield; IWMSA 14781/2, J. Hamilton-Ballie (in a videotaped

talk, Hamilton-Baillie suggested that in terms of living conditions Colditz 'was really quite good'. *The Road to Colditz* (Applecart TV, 1997)); CSVA 10, P. Fergusson; M. Alexander in *The War Behind the Wire*, II (Hartswood Films, 2000); IWMSA 4843/3, G. W. Abbott. On more negative appraisals of Colditz as a place decades later see K. Lockwood and M. Moran in Michael Farr, *Vanishing Borders* (London, 1991), 57; Earl Haig quoted in *Sunday Telegraph*, 27 Feb. 2000.

46. IWMSA 9247/3, M. Burn; Walter Morrison, 'Colditz and Stalag Luft 3 (Sagan)—A Comparison', *Colditz Society Newsletter*, 3 : 22 (Mar. 2000), 7.

47. On POW administration see Vourkoutiotis, op. cit., 46–8.

48. For an outside observer's generally positive reflections on commandants see Chris Christiansen, *Seven Years Among Prisoners of War* (Athens, Ohio, 1994), 16–17. It should be noted that commandants tended to be on their best behaviour during visits by foreign representatives, and that Christiansen—a YMCA delegate to camps in districts II, III, and IV—who thought most commandants 'appeared to behave correctly toward the POWs in their charge' (p. 16) was right to include the qualifier 'appeared'. See Jonathan Vance, 'The Politics of Camp Life: The Bargaining Process in Two German Prison Camps', *War & Society*, 10 (1992), 109–26.

49. See Christiansen, op. cit., 16–17.

50. IWM, H. C. F. Harwood, 106; Prittie and Edwards, op. cit., 72. Not everyone saw the commandant at Biberach in such positive terms. See PRO, WO 224/72, PP report on Oflag VB, 28 July 1941, p. 9.

51. PRO, WO 224/78, PP report, 20 July 1944, p. 3. Opinions of the commandant and his staff at Warburg varied from very positive to very negative. See PRO, WO 208/3290, p. 2; WO 224/74, reports on Oflag VIB, 9 Dec. 1941, p. 4, 10 Feb. 1942, p. 6; Prittie, op. cit., 73–4.

52. IWM, R. P. Evans, 49–50; Imelda Ryan (comp.), *POWs Fraternal* (Perth, WA, 1990), 97, 92; IWM (Rolf), J. M. McGee, 11.

53. B. A. James, op. cit., 45, 30; Sydney Smith, *Wings Day* (London, 1968), 78; Thrower, op. cit., 94; A. J. Evans, *Escape and Liberation* (London, 1945), 40.

54. Calton Younger, *No Flight From the Cage* (London, 1981 edn.), 72; K. Brown, op. cit., 141, 90–1; IWM, G. A. Atkinson, 1.

55. Ward, op. cit., 128; Paul Kingsford, *After Alamein* (East Grinstead, 1992), 81.

56. IWM, G. F. W. Wilson diary, 16 Mar. 1944; D. James, op. cit., 25; Green, op. cit., 75–6.

57. IWM, A. N. L. Munby diary, 16 July, 10 July, 26 June 1940; Prittie and Edwards, op. cit., 58, 59, 71.

58. PRO, WO 208/3291, p. 2; see WO 224/44, PP report, 18 Jan. 1943, p. 7; R. G. M. Quarrie, *Oflag* (Durham, 1995), 43–4; Prittie and Edwards, op. cit., 182–3; C. Hopetoun in Wood, op. cit., 37–8.

59. PRO, WO 224/77, G. Naville report on Oflag 79, 25 May 1944.

60. Giles Romilly and Michael Alexander, *The Privileged Nightmare* (London, 1954), 85–6; PRO, WO 224/69, PP report, 26 June 1941, p. 3.

61. Reinhold Eggers, *Colditz Recaptured* (London, 1973), 227; P. R. Reid, *Colditz* (London, 1984), 184, 153–4; Reinhold Eggers, *Colditz* (London, 1961), 107.

62. PRO, WO 32/1111, RC report on visit of 9 Nov. 1943; ibid., report on visit of 13 May 1943, p. 4; CSVA 8, J. Best; IWMSA 12658/3, R. Eggers.
63. Geoff Taylor, *Piece of Cake* (London, 1980 edn.), 180; Beckwith, op. cit., 96, 112; IWMSA 16797/2, H. Bruce.
64. IWM, G. R. Manners diary, 5 Dec., 24 Dec. 1940; IWM (Rolf), A. T. M. Gant, 8, 9; Gale, op. cit., 54.
65. IWM (Rolf), T. Hughes, 5.
66. Jackson, op. cit., 33, 74–5; see also, e.g., J. Burtt-Smith, *One of the Many on the Move* (Braunton, 1992), 58.
67. PRO, WO 32/15294; IWM, D. W. Luckett, 49; Ramsay, op. cit., 102 ff.; IWM (Rolf), H. W. Tuck, 3; Coward, op. cit., 107.
68. PRO, WO 224/74, PP reports on Oflag VIIB, 24 Aug. 1943, p. 3, 5 Nov. 1943, p. 3, 9 June 1944, p. 3; Beckwith, op. cit., 41, 52, 111; Sam Kydd, *For You the War Is Over...* (London, 1973), 205; John Lawrence, *2.2.9.7.* (Fontwell, 1991), 30.
69. IWM (Rolf), F. E. Ayers, 8.
70. Coward, op. cit., 131–2.
71. Taylor, op. cit., 179–80.
72. Jack Poole, *Undiscovered Ends* (London, 1957), 150 (Warburg); Thrower, op. cit., 135 (Gross Tychow).
73. James, op. cit., 25; IWMSA 4759/3, P. Buckley ('ghastly man').
74. K. Brown, op. cit., 95–6.
75. Reid, *Colditz Story*, 106.
76. Neave, op. cit., 78.
77. Margaret Duggan (ed.), *Padre in Colditz* (London, 1978), 91.
78. CSVA 8, J. Best; CSVA 2, J. Yule; CSVA 11, H. Ironside; CSVA 4, K. Lockwood; CSVA 7, P. Allan.
79. Eggers, *Colditz*, 27.
80. CSVA 7, P. Allan; CSVA 2, J. Yule; IWMSA 16910/4, J. Hoggard; CSVA 13, J. Hoggard; CSVA 11, H. Ironside; CSVA 8, J. Best; CSVA 4, K. Lockwood; Reid, *Colditz Story*, 49.
81. See IWMSA 12658/2, R. Eggers.
82. J. Best in *The Colditz Story* (Classic Pictures, 1993).
83. M. Reid, op. cit., 66; see Michael Burn, *Yes, Farewell* (London, 1946), 433; Reid, *Full Story*, 107–8. On the reunion see *Daily Mail*, 4 Jan. 1974, pp. 16–17.
84. Reid, *Latter Days*, 15; see Reid, *Colditz Story*, 111. On Gephard see e.g. IWMSA 4432/1, H. Gee.
85. Eggers, *Colditz*, 27; see Reid, *Full Story*, 95; H. Püpke in *Colditz Recaptured*, R. Eggers, op. cit., 182.
86. Duggan, op. cit., 71.

4 Leaders and Followers

In any locality where there may be prisoners of war, they shall be authorised to appoint representatives to represent them before the military authorities...

(from Article 43, Geneva Convention, 1929)

In camps of officers and persons of equivalent status the senior officer prisoner of the highest rank shall be recognized as intermediary between the camp authorities and the officers and similar persons who are prisoners.

(from Article 43, Geneva Convention, 1929)

Important as the commandant and his staff were to prisoner-of-war life, they were only part of the overall administrative framework within POW camps. Inside the wire at Colditz and elsewhere there was a recognized Senior British Officer (SBO), who in turn had staff members serving under him as adjutants, hut or room leaders, and committee officers. In the case of stalags, where the SBO—if one there was at all—usually would be a medical officer, leadership devolved on senior NCOs, chosen hut leaders, and, especially in the work camps, an agreed-on 'man of confidence' to liaise with the Germans.

Allowing the prisoners their own staff was a practical concession for the Germans, since it allowed them to communicate via individual representatives rather than having to deal with prisoners en masse. It eased the administrative burden without, at least in theory, conceding any real authority.[1] The SBO or other camp leader would represent the interests of the prisoners to the German staff, and at the same time be responsible for maintaining a basic level of internal camp discipline in terms of implementing instructions. Therein lay the difficulty for the British staff. On the one hand they were, either through rank or popular esteem, regarded by the prisoner population as the figures who would stand up for them. On the other, they were expected by the Germans to keep order within the camps and thereby represent their captors' interests. The articles of the Geneva Convention, to which both sides claimed to adhere, and to which both senior British and German officers referred in complaining about or justifying behaviour, at best only masked the inherent ambiguity surrounding the role of senior British camp officials. Being camp leader, as an Australian soldier observed, was an inherently 'thankless job', as the figure concerned 'had to please the P.O.W.s and the Germans alike'.[2]

Complicating an already difficult situation was the uncertainty surrounding the link between rank and authority among POWs. In theory all British prisoners were still subject to King's Regulations. In fact the Germans only recognized seniority among prisoners when it suited them, which meant that ordinary Kriegies could behave more independently—even defy explicit orders if they so chose—than when free. What this in turn meant was that the leadership of camp officials rested on everything from moral authority, through commonly agreed-upon rules of conduct enforced by popular opinion and/or camp police, down to physical intimidation by the leader's minions or even (in extreme cases) appeals to the commandant.

If all that were not enough, the nature and effectiveness of British camp management varied according to several other factors. Service background, length and period of captivity, mean age, rank, social class, temperament, pre-war occupation, as well as the size of a camp—populations ranged from ten on a small Arbeitskommando to 10,000 at Lamsdorf—could all affect how prisoners responded to British as well as German authority. All of this meant that the nature and quality of British leadership could vary quite significantly. With few exceptions, it was the high standard of decision-making both at particular points and in general that prevented likely tragedy and made life better than it might otherwise have been at Colditz.

Those prisoners in positions of responsibility within the stalag system faced both opportunities and challenges. On the positive side there were the benefits associated with being able to exert some control over the running of camp or hut life. Wielding authority, however circumscribed it might be, was a major step up from being completely helpless. The ability to influence events had definite psychological value, as well as offering potential material advantages. On the negative side there lurked the spectre of being seen by ordinary Kriegies, rightly or wrongly, as a stooge for the Germans or as someone willing to feather his own nest at the expense of others. Despite the pitfalls, some leaders did a remarkably fine job of balancing the ambiguities of their position to the benefit of the prisoner population at large.

One of the peculiarities of the compounds set aside for non-commissioned personnel of the RAF was the fact that there was rarely a clear hierarchy of rank present. Aircrew tended to be sergeants of one sort or another, producing a surfeit of NCOs (as against the comparatively few other-rank ground-crew types). Combined with the comparative lack of deference toward formal RAF rank displayed by hostilities-only aircrew, this meant that camp leadership arose from, and was maintained or changed by, the compound population. Being an RAF camp leader or man of confidence was not always easy. 'If the elected [man] got on too well with the Germans he was accused of fraternising with the enemy', Sergeant Frank Taylor noted of the situation in the Luftwaffe camps. 'On the other hand, if he failed to establish good relations with the hierarchy in the Vorlager [the German administration compound] he was criticised by his fellow Kriegies for not fulfilling his function as a go-between for, and representative of, the men.'[3] It was therefore greatly to his credit that Sergeant James 'Dixie' Deans, once elected leader in the NCOs' compound at Stalag Luft I (Barth) early in the war, maintained his authority there and later at Stalag Luft III (Sagan), Stalag Luft VI (Heydekrug), and Stalag 357 (Fallingbostel) until the spring of 1945.

Deans, a fluent German speaker, was by his own admission interested in 'keeping peace and quiet in the camp', getting 'everything to run smoothly'; which on occasion could involve dressing down Kriegies who had done something that placed them in unnecessary danger. After the rifle of an unsuspecting guard was fired by a prisoner sneaking up behind and pulling the trigger, Deans ordered that such activity cease before some bright spark got killed in the act. He also tore a strip off a prisoner who, on a wager, consumed an entire Red Cross parcel in one sitting—a criminal waste in view of how vital such parcels were to long-term survival. Most of the time, however, Deans was keeping, as he put it, 'my finger on the pulse of the camp', and doing all he could through interviews with the German authorities to better the conditions of those he represented. 'His quiet but manifest honesty, purpose, and ability,' wrote Australian pilot Ron MacKenzie, 'combined with a very direct sort of charm gave him authority.' He was manifestly a patriot, working behind the scenes to further intelligence and escape work. On parade he would conduct himself in such a manner that he gave the impression that it was he rather than the Lageroffizier who enjoyed ultimate command. In one instance Deans subtly modified an order from the commandant and announced that 'whole razor blades are not to be put in the pig swill'. (The Lageroffizier was happy that Deans had endorsed the order against sabotage but could not understand why the parade was laughing so hard.) Both the prisoners and the guards respected him immensely. Calton Younger, another Australian, who spent three years with Deans, recalled that over the entire time 'I never heard a murmur against his benevolent despotism'.[4]

In army compounds, meanwhile, a greater hierarchical consciousness often existed. The wider range of ranks present in the stalags, the proportionate number of senior sergeants and warrant officers captured, along with the high degree of respect for senior non-commissioned officers encouraged within the regular army, combined to produce a more authoritarian model of command and control. In essence, many senior NCOs—though on German sufferance—behaved as if they were in charge by right behind the wire, maintaining an immaculate bearing and the belief that they were still in the business of enforcing King's Regulations.[5]

The official rationale for keeping up appearances involved issues of cohesion and morale. As the early weeks of captivity had demonstrated, severe privation could lead to outbreaks of stealing and a general sense of every man for himself. Discipline meant restoring order and preventing a return to chaos. Furthermore, when things got better, adherence to military etiquette reminded Kriegies that they could still take pride in themselves as soldiers. Smartness and military bearing might also send a message to the Germans that *Engländer* were men to be reckoned with.[6]

Not surprisingly there were suspicions in the ranks that the unofficial agenda among some senior NCOs was to improve their standard of living through helping the Germans to organize the camps, and by taking a greater share of scarce resources at the expense of the men. Cook sergeants and stores staff members were particularly likely to come under suspicion, while those who pushed too hard could be accused of being collaborationists—sometimes with justification.[7]

Yet there were plenty of sergeant majors whose manner, though ferocious, masked a genuine commitment to the welfare of ordinary prisoners. '[T]he Senior British Warrant Officer in charge of the camp was a very smart and strict, had plenty of "bull" and had his own room and his own batman', James Stedman of the West Kents remembered of his time at Stalag XXIA in 1942, going on to remark how this NCO '[g]ave you the feeling that you had to behave yourself or you could find yourself on a 252—a fizzer'. Stedman also noted, however, that this stalag 'proved to be the best camp that I was ever in'. Indeed, some of the greatest camp leaders were apparent martinets. The fearsome Bill Lord, an RSM captured at Arnhem, took control on arrival at the army compound at Stalag XIB (Fallingbostel), and ran it like a regular army camp through sheer force of personality and lungpower. 'I watched him striding across the compound toward the gate,' an RAF observer recalled, 'a fine figure of a man, every inch a Regimental Sergeant Major. The bored German at the gate suddenly snapped to attention and held the door open for Lord, whose military bearing and personality commanded immediate attention even from the enemy.' Warrant Officer Buller 'Snakebite' Cockfort of the Transvaal Scottish was a big, awe-inspiring NCO who insisted on cleanliness and orderliness in Stalag VIIIC (Sagan) while standing up to the Germans. The apparent harshness of his rule was sometimes resented by POWs, but his uncompromising willingness to confront the Germans was so irritating that he was repeatedly transferred; all to no avail, as in each new camp he set about organizing things to his liking.[8]

Other camp leaders and men of confidence, particularly in smaller settings, were less intimidating but still good at bearing their rank and representing the interests of the British over those of the Germans. Ed Annetts, another West Kents private, while on a working party out of Lamsdorf, found Troop Sergeant Major 'Flash' Emerton to be a more relaxed but equally effective camp leader. He 'could maintain easy-going discipline without recourse to the big stick, provided no-one forgot that he was, after all, a sergeant-major in the British Army'. Recalling the big Arbeitskommando at Blechammer, Captain Julius Green, a dentist, was impressed by the leaders he observed in action.

The W.O.s and N.C.O.s in general could not be faulted for their behaviour. Good-humoured, smartly turned out, ever watchful over the interests of the men under their care, they saw to it that the rations and the Red Cross supplies were distributed with scrupulous fairness. They drew a sharp distinction between breaches of military discipline and good conduct which affected their fellows, and offences against the Germans. They settled the inevitable quarrels, which are bound to arise among men thrown together for years at a time, with understanding and firmness—not always according to King's Regulations, but effectively...[9]

In the stalags too the senior staff could gain respect for the good job they did. Being man of confidence at the camp set aside exclusively for army NCOs at Hohenfels cannot have been easy, yet there was widespread agreement that Staff Quartermaster-Sergeant David MacKenzie was well suited to the task. An even tougher assignment was running Lamsdorf with its tens of thousands of inmates and hundreds of work camps; nevertheless Regimental Sergeant Major Sidney Sherriff was widely respected. Tactful yet quietly confident, Sherriff was able to wring a significant number of concessions from commandants at Stalag VIIIB. 'He was a Dunkirk prisoner,' Jack Pringle wrote, 'whose performance for five years in the administration, discipline, and welfare of the 40,000 other rank prisoners under his command was one of the finest examples of character and leadership shown by any prisoner throughout the war.'[10]

Whatever the style, on the British side it was efficiency more than seniority that often ultimately determined who remained in leadership positions in camps run by the army and navy as well as the air force. The coercive element underpinning discipline in the services was largely missing behind the wire. Appeals for German support—though they did happen on occasion—were regarded as verging on treason, while recommending demotion or pay stoppages to the War Office through the post for those who broke the rules was highly controversial. Men therefore often behaved more assertively behind the wire than they had done while on active service. 'Many people think they can come and go as they please without restraint merely because they are POWs', Staff Sergeant Raymond Ryan of Stalag 383 ruefully reflected in his diary late in the war.[11] Despite greater deference to service rules in army other-rank compounds, and within Marlag (M) as well, in comparison to those of the air force, when men of any service were dissatisfied (which could be quite often) they usually took action.

Sometimes this took the form of a complaint to neutral representatives visiting a camp, as when RSM Sherriff was falsely suspected of being involved in a kickback scheme at Lamsdorf involving the distribution of mail and Red Cross parcels. A more direct and common form of response to real or supposed injustice and ineffectiveness was for malcontents to stage a vote of no confidence when a camp leader or his subordinates became unpopular. These manifestations of grass-roots democracy could be raucous and sometimes even corrupt affairs, lacking as they did any regulatory framework. Yet the end result was generally considered decisive one way or the other: those who ignored the general will often finding themselves bypassed or even beaten up.[12]

This was why, when grumbling was on the rise, the more self-assured leaders sometimes offered to resign. When moaning increased at Hohenfels, for example, QMS MacKenzie held a referendum in which only 300 of 4,500 prisoners voted to dismiss him. Even 'Snakebite' recognized the value of this tactic. When some Australian prisoners complained about the supposed harshness of his regime at Stalag VIIIC, Cockfort climbed on a table in their barracks and shouted: 'Right, you bastards, if you want me to do so I'll step down and you can elect your own camp leader.' Knowing that there was nobody more capable of standing up to the Germans, the dissenters refused to take him up on this offer and grew quiet.[13]

The captors themselves could intervene either to get rid of a problematic camp leader or promote one who served their interests. Occasionally this might even benefit the prisoners too. In one of the stalags in Austria the camp leader, a sergeant major of the Black Watch, turned out to be ineffective. The compound lacked organization, bickering was constant, and fights were frequent. Eventually the commandant stepped in to replace him with a more effective man. But actively pro-German camp leaders parachuted in rarely lasted very long. At Stalag VIIA (Moosburg) the overtly collaborationist regime imposed on the camp and led by the infamous Sergeant Major Shanker from Corinth was overthrown after the prisoners elected their own man, and Shanker and his cronies had to be housed inside the German *Vorlager* for their own protection.[14]

The establishment, and especially the enforcement, of rules governing POW behaviour depended to a great extent on popular acceptance. Senior staff could make a difference through setting up camp police forces, investigating cases of disorderly conduct or theft, holding court, and handing down sentences. In cases involving collaboration a sanctioned murder might result; but official justice at the camp level was, by and large, humane—bearing in mind that, as we shall see in the next chapter, hut members often took matters into their own hands. In the RAF compound at Lamsdorf the humiliation of exposure for a man caught thieving (plus a warning that the matter would be taken up with the Air Ministry after the war if it happened again) was considered sufficient by the senior NCO, John Taylor-Gill, in 1941. Two years later in Stalag 383 a prisoner who was drunk and became abusive was simply made to scrub floors and cut wood for the camp hospital for six weeks. Even when stealing other men's food was involved, usually considered the worst crime short of outright treason, official sentences were comparatively lenient. At Laufen in the autumn of 1940 an officer caught filching rations was ordered by Brigadier Claude Nicholson to undergo a month of orderly duties without access to Red Cross parcels or conversation. When a prisoner was found eating his fellows' bread ration at

Moosburg in late 1944, the man of confidence, a sergeant, refused to countenance any violence. Instead the guilty party was sent to Coventry and denied access to Red Cross parcels.[15]

Even with the best men in charge, though, it was not always possible to maintain peace, order, and good government in large camps. Among the tens of thousands of army prisoners taken in 1940–1 there were, inevitably, men with shady backgrounds, including convictions for theft and assault. Especially in the early, somewhat Darwinian days of captivity, they were among the first to turn predatory. Gangs evolved, their aim being to further their own comfort through intimidation of others. The criminal element, often armed with razors, was a particular problem at Lamsdorf. The redoubtable RSM Sherriff admitted to Red Cross observers that he was encountering 'some difficulty' in preventing crime within the massive confines of Stalag VIIIB. Even after the establishment of a police force in the winter of 1943, the camp was so big that gangs dedicated to extortion, racketeering, and worse could not be fully stamped out. 'Anyone resisting the gang would be beaten mercilessly,' Private John Elwyn of the Welsh Guards observed, 'some having their faces slashed.'[16] Over time some of these men came to be wanted by the Germans for assault and even murder, but in a camp as large as Lamsdorf it was possible for individuals to go underground before being carted off. They became outlaws who no longer appeared on muster rolls but who, through a mixture of fear and reluctance to turn any man over to the enemy, lived off others.[17]

Only the strong and the brave could cope with such predators. One night a gang ransacked the possessions of a former heavyweight-boxing champion in the Black Watch while holding a razor to his throat. Unfortunately for them he recognized some of the faces:

Next day [Robert Gale remembered], accompanied by three of the toughest men in the camp, with weapons hidden about their persons, Jock called on the thieves. Standing in the doorway of their barrack-room, his henchmen solidly behind him, he said quietly, 'I want my cigarettes and quickly!' There was a long silence and then their leader smiled ingratiatingly and said, 'Sure, you'll find them under that bunk, Jock'. Jock entered the room without a word, pulled out two large suitcases of his belongings and departed with his silent bodyguards.

Other episodes of a similar sort indicated that the razor-wielders could be physically seen off or intimidated into retreat by bigger men (some of whom themselves might be less than popular with their fellows). In one camp a group of thugs who routinely pilfered Red Cross parcels before they could be distributed to the rest of the prisoners was finally brought to book after an Australian got his face slashed. 'Sergeant Alan Snedden (a district cricketer from Western Australia, and the brother of Sir Billy) led an attacking party that night,' G. R. Thompson explained, 'with two results: within four days the Glasgow [toughs] were moved from the camp, and everybody received a 50 per cent increase in their rations.' At Lamsdorf itself a group of New Zealanders eventually disarmed one of the worst of the gangs, a bunch of angry Canadians beat another Glasgow mob into submission, and with the help of an exposé in the POW-run camp paper *Stimmt*, a third extortion ring was broken up.[18] But serious crime, even murder, continued to occur at Stalag VIIIB, as Ed Annetts discovered in the last winter of the war:

A particularly disturbing incident took place one evening while I was in the loo. I heard another man come into the latrine which backed on to the one I was using. Within a few moments there was a rush of what sounded like two pairs of boots. There followed a series of dull thuds, strangled, agonised cries, and much grunting from violent exertion. Then all went quiet, except for a sudden heavy splash, as of a body being dropped into the deep, flowing trench below the seats . . . It was, for me, the blackest moment of all those years.

As the camp was being evacuated in February–March 1945, gangs were still at work. 'They go to sleeping men,' Dr John Borrie was told by Sergeant Jan Romans, 'stealing wallets and watches from under their pillows. If they resist their faces are slashed.'[19]

Despite this, however, other-rank camps—including Lamsdorf, when taken as a whole—were usually quite orderly places. The existence of the Geneva Convention, providing as it did a set of mutually agreed-upon basic conditions, plus visits from the Protecting Power (first the United States, then Switzerland) and the International Red Cross, helped a great deal. Yet without the efforts of competent and incorruptible NCOs like Deans, Sherriff, Cockfort, and others it is not difficult to imagine that life inside stalag compounds would have been far worse than it turned out to be.

According to the Geneva Convention the authority of SBOs in officer camps and compounds derived from seniority. As with non-commissioned men of confidence, however, commissioned camp leaders were in the tricky position of being seen to represent German as well as British interests. The commandant would see the SBO or his designated subordinate as a means to ease the burden of administration and control— something in the prisoners' interests too, in terms of preventing chaos and minimizing contact with armed guards. The prisoners, on the other hand, looked to the camp leader to represent their interests in the inevit-able battle of wills over everything from Red Cross parcel distribution to the creation of recreation facilities. Furthermore, as the prisoners them-selves were split on issues surrounding confrontation with the enemy, and were sometimes divided by age or background into cliques, what could be seen as a fine job by one group might be seen by another as overly aggressive or by another group as practically collaborationist. SBOs were not elected, and it was they who appointed subordinates. Nevertheless, maintaining order while at the same time earning the respect of the camp population was a task requiring leadership that rested on more than simple seniority.

Though rarely serving as SBO himself (paradoxically, because he was considered too exalted in status), Major-General Victor Fortune, the most senior British Army prisoner in successive oflags between 1940 and 1945, was in a strong position to influence affairs by virtue of his rank. First incarcerated at Laufen, General Fortune was not afraid to remon-strate over the awful conditions BEF officers faced there, nor—al-legedly—to insult the Führer in front of the commandant when for his pains he was placed under constant armed guard within the camp. According to Terence Prittie, who was with him at Oflag VIIC/H, Fortune 'was an inspiring personality, completely unwavering at all times and lending some of his own overbrimming confidence to those of us who had become slack and war-weary in mind. "The General" provided all officers with an epic example of how it should be possible to lead the life of a prisoner-of-war without loss of dignity and self respect.'[20]

Fortune was also capable of forcing the Germans to change tack, as he proved at Oflag VB (Biberach) in the summer of 1941. When a consign-ment of Canadian Red Cross parcels arrived, the commandant insisted that the tins contained in each parcel be opened to make sure there was no contraband—escape equipment—contained in them. This pre-sented enormous storage problems for the prisoners, and Fortune de-cided on a strategy designed to make the commandant reverse the policy. Jack Champ, who would end up at Colditz, described how this was done:

The directive from the Kommandant had stated that if we did not wish to draw certain items we could leave them in a store with our name on them, to be opened when we drew them out. All others were to be opened in front of us. Fortune's strategy was for each officer to claim his parcel at the store, and point out the tins required. Just as the corporal was about to open the tins, the British officer would change his mind and decide to draw out different tins. When he had finally made up his mind he would take out a piece of paper and carefully note down what tins he had deposited. This all took time, and by midday only twenty-five parcels had been drawn. As there were more than 800 of us in the camp it was obvious that they would never get through. This was pointed out to the Kommandant, and he finally consented to issue the remaining parcels with sealed tins.[21]

Victor Fortune was also a force for good at Oflag IXA/H (Spangenberg) in the middle years of the war. It was through his efforts that all-day parole walks in a nearby forest were allowed. These group outings were 'ostensibly to study trees', Captain Prittie remembered, but were 'actually to pick fruit and enjoy the sun and space that was the nearest approach to freedom that many of us experienced in nearly five years'.[22]

Forcefulness, however, was not appreciated by those who thought it misplaced. When the general was sent to Oflag XIIB (Hadamar) he found a camp population that he thought was too slack, and set about creating a more aggressive regime. Boots were to be polished and caps worn on parade to impress the Germans and improve morale, and a more aggressive attitude in general taken toward the enemy. One of the first to feel the effects was the Second Earl Haig, who was told that 'I was not smart enough on parade and that ... the son of a Field Marshal should be showing a better example'. There were also wider repercussions from the new order of things. 'Our easy democratic way of running the camp was altered, the easy relationship that had existed between the Germans and ourselves was upset', Haig later wrote. 'A rift appeared between the Camp Commandant and the new senior British officer.' This did not go down too well with some other junior officers. Edward Ward, a BBC journalist, recalled

a degree of military discipline which a good many of us found somewhat distasteful after the free-and-easy days of Italy. This was supposed to maintain 'morale'. Personally—and I know many of my fellow P.O.W.s felt the same—I felt quite capable of looking after my 'morale' myself. Discipline on our twice-daily roll-calls was so strictly observed that many of the less military-minded began to wonder whether they were supposed to be German or British parades ...

Ward and others were far from happy when it transpired that 'anyone who turned up late was given a sound telling-off by the British executive officer'.[23]

Grievances of this sort were in part simply a result of the differences in style that emerged in various camps, alternative ways of doing things that could generate friction when different groups of 'old lags' were suddenly dumped together. They were also sometimes a reflection of social and professional distinctions. At Laufen in 1940, for example, marine and army officers clashed because of different ideas about how things should be run. There were also subdivisions within army ranks. Ellison Platt, a Methodist padre, noted in his diary on arrival at Colditz in early 1941 just how cliquish army officers could be. 'In all the other officers' camps I know,' he wrote, 'certain elite sets have segregated themselves and lived in indigent but pompous isolation. At Spangenberg... the "Regulars" were exclusive to a degree. Most of them were badly bitten by the bug of which the Regular Army has never been deloused—Territorialphobia! A Territorial is some incredibly low form of life, always to be spurned...' Even among Regular officers, who had almost all gone to public schools, the Old Etonians were in a class by themselves. 'They ate together; paced the exercise ground in twos, threes or fours; attended the same lectures; and went to the *Abort* [lavatory] together.'[24]

Even more significant were differences in age and rank. At a number of oflags some of the younger officers felt that the more senior majors and colonels placed comfort and stability over duty and audacity. At Oflag VIIIF (Mährisch Trübau), for instance, James Chutter, a South African chaplain, noted that 'a group of senior officers who were said to do themselves very well were commonly known as the "U-Jack Colonels".' The older officers for their part saw their juniors as rebellious youths who refused to respect the seniority system and did not think before they acted.[25] Even a leader as admired as Victor Fortune could be, as we have seen, occasionally thought to be too much the Regular Soldier.

Another very senior officer who was lauded for doing a fine leadership job while a prisoner was Wing Commander H. M. A. Day. Shot down in October 1939, Harry 'Wings' Day was camp leader at various points in Spangenberg, Oberusel, Barth, Schubin, and Sagan, until his part in the Great Escape in March 1944 landed him in Sachsenhausen concentration camp. A man of infinite patience and considerable tact, Day was able to keep naturally rambunctious aircrew from going too far with each other or the guards, as well as imposing controls on individual activity designed to maximize the chances of successful escape.[26] Day was usually capable of getting what he wanted from the Germans too. In 1943, for instance, in return for his agreement to curtail the Kriegie habit of dropping razor blades into the pigswill and straggling onto parade, Wings was able to extract a promise from Von Lindeiner for more fresh vegetables and red meat for the prisoners' rations. 'Over the ensuing months [at Sagan],' Kingsley Brown reported, 'we ate better than we had since any of us had arrived in the camp . . .'[27]

At the same time Day made it clear that, if pushed by the Germans, he would push back. While a new compound was being built at Stalag Luft III a body of prisoners, including Day, was temporarily sent to Oflag XXIB (Schubin). When he found the Wehrmacht commandant to be 'completely unhelpful' about improving the filthy state of the ablutions and on other matters, Wings made it his business to generate as much inconvenience as possible ('we're going to get out of this place', he announced to all and sundry). German efforts to have him replaced were thwarted through popular resistance, and even when more senior RAF officers were captured, it was clear that he knew his business sufficiently well to continue as camp leader.[28]

Yet even Day and his staff did not escape occasional censure. RAF prisoners, increasingly hostilities-only aircrew, were an independent bunch, and sometimes could be suspicious of a camp social and command structure that appeared insufficiently accommodating. 'There was a definite hierarchy within [Stalag Luft III],' Martin Smith noted on his arrival there in the summer of 1942, 'with the regulars and short-service officers placing themselves above the RAFVR and the wartime volunteers.' Here as elsewhere the 'old lags' might appear to look down on 'new boys', and divisive cliques based around which camps Kriegies had come from could arise when new compounds were opened. In the NCOs' compound at Barth it rapidly became clear to Alan McKay that seniority depended on length of time 'in the bag', and that recent arrivals 'were at the bottom of the Lager's social structure'. Smith was shocked to discover at Sagan that a classmate and childhood friend of his who had been a POW since 1940 regarded him with some disdain. 'He was very senior in the camp and part of the Wings Day crowd. He obviously did not wish to know a new Kriegy pilot officer. I had the distinct impression that he would have liked me to call him "Sir" whenever our paths crossed but I did not have much time for such ego-boosting . . .'[29]

Day himself was not immune from criticism, and early on in his time in Germany was even accused of using his rank to make himself more comfortable. The permanent staff at Dulag Luft, the RAF officers who ran the compound for aircrew coming out of the interrogation block and awaiting transfer to a permanent camp, were viewed with a great deal of suspicion. To newly arrived prisoners they seemed too sleek, too comfortable, too well-fed, too much in-the-know; and it was widely believed that some, if not all, were feathering their own nests at the expense of others or even engaging in outright collaboration. This was rarely in fact the case, but rumours of shady goings-on were quickly accepted as fact. As SBO at Oberusel early in the war, Day came under suspicion, receiving an open letter from a colleague at Stalag Luft I (Barth) accusing him of hoarding Red Cross and personal parcels for his own use rather than distributing them to the permanent camps. When transferred to Barth in 1941 along with other Dulag staff members, Day was initially viewed with scorn. 'One day that summer,' B. A. James remembered, 'a tall, lean wing commander with taut upper lip and narrowed eyes strode through the gate, followed by about eighteen assorted British prisoners, to the accompaniment of some boos, snide remarks and hostile looks from a number of the onlookers.' Only when it became clear that the Oberusel party had been removed to Barth because they had tried to escape did Day come to be viewed in a generally favourable light.[30]

There were, however, still those who questioned what he did as senior man. Though Day was himself an escaping type and did all in his power to support viable schemes, at Oflag XXIB (Schubin) he probably disappointed some hard-core pioneers when he forbade the use of a tunnel. He suspected that its existence was known to the Germans, and that they were merely waiting for a break in order to shoot a few prisoners 'while trying to escape', as an example to the rest of the camp.[31] Free spirits also took exception to his supporting Roger Bushell, head of the escape organization at Luft III, who insisted that 'goon-baiting' on parade cease in case it led to measures that would make breaking out more difficult.[32] A wider constituency disagreed with Day's handling of the main trading racket at Sagan. Popularly known as 'foodacco', it was run by two enterprising young officers on a for-profit basis (cigarettes were the currency), but was nevertheless heavily used in order to obtain anything from soap to sugar. There were, however, some complaints regarding capitalistic excess, and Wings decided to hold a referendum on whether or not to 'nationalize' the business. 'It was a spirited campaign on both sides,' Kingsley Brown wrote, 'with all the overtones of the classic "free enterprise versus socialism" debate. There were soapbox speeches, a plethora of rhetoric and scathing editorials pinned to the latrine wall.' The vote went in favour of the status quo, but Day nevertheless decided to nationalize the business. The reason for this—using the profits of the new concern to help the escape committee—was not always known, and if discovered not always seen as acceptable. The action demonstrated the extent to which a hierarchy existed inside the wire, and some prisoners wondered aloud if Day was verging on megalomania.[33]

Those who grumbled about Day as dictator, however, did not know how much more aggressively interventionist an SBO could be. The Senior British Officer at Oflag VIIIF (Mährisch Trübau) was Colonel M. C. Waddilove. 'The position of SBO at a camp in Germany where there were nearly two thousand officers was not one to be envied,' wrote Philip Kindersley, 'and we were lucky to have an officer who religiously defended our rights and who refused to cooperate with the Germans unless they cooperated with us.' An example of what this meant in practice occurred when the commandant tried to institute snap *Appell*s in order to deter escape activities. Waddilove responded by instructing the camp population to ignore orders to form up other than at the normal morning and evening parades. Several officers recalled the resulting battle of wills:

The German order to form up came through at about eleven o'clock, but none of us moved out of their rooms. The German officers walked up and down, and the guards fell in to their usual positions on the stairs round the gymnasium, but no one appeared. The commandant completely lost his temper and raved at the SBO, who regretted that it was impossible for him to get the officers on parade. The Germans were kept waiting for three hours before the SBO gave the order to get on parade. The Germans never tried that experiment again.[34]

Even more pugnacious was the officer Waddilove made 'escape dictator', Lieutenant-Colonel David Stirling, founder of the SAS, under whom every aspect of camp life was controlled in the interests of escaping activity—with no exceptions allowed. For restless junior officers all this was a good thing—'a splendid example', as one among them put it, 'of the power of moral and passive resistance by unarmed men in the face of their armed enemies who also controlled their food supply'.[35] Some of the older and more senior officers, however, notably those in the Indian Army, were less than pleased at finding their creature comforts under threat and their freedoms curtailed.[36]

Not all Senior British Officers, however, were as aggressively in favour of escaping. Alan Campbell, who shortly would be sent to Colditz for breaking out of Spangenberg, recalled a conversation with the SBO in 1941. 'Are you intending to escape?' Campbell was asked, and when he indicated that he might be, the SBO made his position on the matter very clear. 'Please do not', Campbell remembered him saying. 'We are comfortable here and do not wish to lose our privileges, our parcels, our walks. That is an order.' To the senior officers concerned it was often a matter of placing the interests of the camp population as a whole over those of particular individuals. Discouraging words, moreover, could be misinterpreted to mean a sit-out-the-war policy rather than—as was at least sometimes the case—the need to submit personal breakout plans to the escape committee for approval. To restless individualists like Campbell, though, discouraging words could sound like outright cowardice.[37]

Captain Graham Wilson, RN, the SBO at both Sandbostel and Westertimke, was a case in point. In many ways he was a model British representative. 'The Senior Officer has a most difficult hand to play,' Lieutenant David James, RNVR, noted in his memoirs, 'and he played it with consummate skill. He always succeeded in getting the maximum out of the Germans consistent with the maintenance of our dignity.'[38] Wilson was a man who took justifiable pride in keeping the officers' compound shipshape. Unfortunately he sometimes went rather far in the way of controlling the conduct of junior officers. Many prisoners were ambivalent or even hostile to escape attempts because of the reprisals that they brought down on the camp population as a whole. It was, however, an officer's duty to try to escape, and by extension the SBO's business to support rather than oppose attempts to break out. Captain Wilson, however, evidently thought that certain escapers were in the same league as officers who misbehaved on parade: troublemakers who deserved to be punished for putting their own interests ahead of the camp population as a whole.[39]

In late 1941 Lieutenant Hugh Bruce, a Royal Marine who would eventually land in Colditz, was planning his first escape from Sandbostel, a low-risk venture involving switching identities with an RN rating going out on a working party. But when he took his plan to the SBO: 'I was in for a rude shock because when he'd heard this story of how I was intending to escape he told me that the camp was very stable, and pleasant, and he didn't want anything to disturb that situation.' Lacking the support of the senior officers Bruce went ahead anyway, but was recaptured. In the autumn of 1942 Lieutenant Tommy Catlow, RN, took part in a tunnel break from Westertimke. He was recaptured and, after being escorted back to Marlag (O), was told that he was being sent to Colditz. The parting words of Captain Wilson apparently were: 'Goodbye, Catlow, you've asked for it and you're going to get it.'[40]

Other Senior British Officers were known to go overboard on occasion in trying to maintain discipline behind the wire along regular service lines. In part this was doubtless just the result of failing to see that power inside an oflag was not the same as military authority in the outside world. It may also have had to do with overcompensation for feelings of inadequacy at having had to surrender command to the enemy. Failures of communication and plain bad luck also played a role. Whatever the reasons, some very questionable decisions unrelated to escape were made on occasion by certain SBOs.[41]

Due to a series of personal misunderstandings and bureaucratic errors a breakdown in relations occurred between the Senior British Officer at Stalag Luft I (Barth) on the one hand, and a party of NCOs who had been sent from Stalag Luft VI (Heydekrug) to act as officers' orderlies on the other. Angered by the 'very truculent and un-Service-like attitude' of the sergeants concerned, the wing commander in question decided to put them on a charge. This resulted in the NCOs being reduced to the ranks and, with German agreement, sent back to Heydekrug in early 1944. Friction between orderlies and officers occurred elsewhere, including at Colditz, as did overt criticism of those with commissions when it appeared that men were being 'mucked about'. In this case the available evidence suggests that, while the NCOs on charge were indeed being obstinate and generally difficult, the SBO overreacted in a major way. As far as can be ascertained, the Air Ministry did nothing to confirm his actions when news of the affair surfaced in London.[42]

Though mostly a camp for other ranks, as its title implies, Stalag VIIA (Moosburg) held over 100 British officers in a separate compound in the middle war years. Late in 1944 one of them was caught stealing food from another. This was not an unknown problem in POW camps, but in this case the SBO—a Regular Army man—chose a highly unusual course of action. After holding a formal court of inquiry, he announced that a record of the affair would be handed over to the authorities at the end of hostilities to provide evidence for court martial proceedings against the culprit. The threat of a possible post-war court marital was one thing; announcing it as a certainty was quite another. The prisoner concerned could do nothing to pay for his crime, which meant he could not reintegrate into normal Kriegie society. Worse yet, knowledge that a court martial awaited him removed the one great hope of POWs everywhere— freedom at war's end. In the words of one of those present at the time, 'nothing could have been crueller'. Even the officer from whom the man had stolen thought this action excessive, and a petition was drawn up asking the SBO to reconsider. Having announced his decision, the SBO refused to change his mind, even though the guilty man showed signs of severe mental strain as a result. The handling of this case was rightly considered 'disastrous'.[43]

Unfortunately there was an even worse course of action available to discipline-conscious SBOs, as an episode at Oflag VIIC/H (Laufen) four years earlier had already shown. One evening in their first winter of captivity a group of young officers managed to become somewhat inebriated, and in this state one of them wandered off, singing loudly. A verbal altercation with the adjutant ensued, and the matter was reported. Instead of verbally tearing strips off the offender, the Senior British Officer chose to hold a formal court of inquiry. When the man's messmates refused to testify against a brother officer, the SBO asked the commandant to intervene, resulting in several days in the cells for the unhappy chorister. To involve the Germans in internal disciplinary affairs in this way was widely regarded by officers as out of the question, and in this particular case the SBO's action was seen as simply 'unforgivable'.[44]

Fortunately, most camp leaders and those they chose as subordinates exercised their power more judiciously, and by and large acted in accordance with the general will. After an officer was shot by a guard while innocently sketching at Laufen, for example, the SBO not only protested through formal channels but also went along with the popular desire to snub the Germans at every opportunity.[45] Moreover, though they might grumble, most officer prisoners recognized that individual freedom might have to be subordinated on occasion to wider camp interests. At Oflag VIID (Tittmoning), where the German staff were decent types, it was believed legitimate for the SBO to insist that prisoners be punctual and orderly during the twice-daily *Appell* parades in order to present a military bearing in front of the enemy and free up time for other activities. Nor was it considered unbecoming for an SBO-sanctioned committee to try to regulate gambling at Oflag VIIB (Eichstätt) after officers began to get into serious debt. At Oflag 79 (Brunswick) the Senior British Officer was seen as entirely justified in protecting the power supply for the secret radio by banning the individual tapping of the camp's electricity for cooking purposes, after the commandant had threatened to turn the current off because of the power drain incurred.[46]

These, however, were all regular camps. Colditz, as a Sonderlager, a special camp, presented unique challenges for an SBO and his subordinates.

Camps and compounds containing a significant proportion of middle-aged officers captured early in the war tended to be more sedate and settled than those with younger, more energetic populations who had often been in captivity a shorter time. The contrast was strikingly evident at Oflag IXA/H (Spangenberg) and Oflag VIB (Warburg) in 1941–2, when contingents of junior RAF officers were placed among mostly senior BEF officers. The air force captives, as one of their number admitted, behaved like 'an undisciplined and unruly mob of overgrown schoolboys', while the senior captains, majors, and lieutenant-colonels appeared to some to be willing to quietly sit out the war in relative peace and comfort.[47] Differing service styles were party responsible for this, but age, length of time in captivity, and social background (school and regiment) could also produce similar contrasts of temperament and attitude in oflags where only army or navy officers were present.[48] Even in the stalag luft compounds, where the mean age was lower and the proportion of wartime officers higher than in other camps, there were clear distinctions. Some RAF types acted as though the war really was over for them, as against those who believed that everything possible should be done to inconvenience the enemy as a means of continuing the struggle. There were also plenty of social and other distinctions.[49]

Colditz, meanwhile, was in a class by itself. Almost all of its inhabitants had been sent there because they had made themselves a nuisance in other camps, primarily through escape attempts. What this meant was that, irrespective of service, those at Oflag IVC tended to be cut from similar cloth. Exceptionally restless elsewhere, they found themselves among like-minded officers in the Sonderlager.

Airey Neave, future MP and back-room brain behind the rise of Margaret Thatcher to the Conservative Party leadership, had as a prisoner been considered something of a dangerous maverick until sent to Colditz in 1941. 'It was stimulating to live in this hive of industry', Neave remembered, going on to stress how he now felt 'that I need no longer fear the indulgent smiles of those who were content to lead a vegetable existence'.[50] The legless air ace Douglas Bader, captured a few months after Neave became the first British prisoner to make a home run from Oflag IVC, proved to be an exceptionally rambunctious guest of the Reich. He was so great a troublemaker that even some of his fellow flyers were privately relieved to see him packed off. 'We were pleased to get rid of him', one pilot stated bluntly. Once in Colditz, however, Bader found himself only one of a host of *Deutschfeindlich* prisoners with energy to burn.[51]

The personal background of those sent to Oflag IVC could vary immensely. As well as service career officers, Miles Reid explained, there were 'academics, engineers, lawyers, accountants, schoolmasters, actors, industrialists, farmers and writers'. Fortunately, this diversity of pre-war employment and the concomitant implications in terms of class gradations did not seem to matter much, especially in the early years when the British contingent was small. 'My present judgement', Padre Ellison Platt happily noted in his diary shortly after his arrival at the castle in January 1941, 'is that [in contrast to other oflags] there are none who regard themselves as being of different clay from the rest.'[52] What bound the men of Colditz together and created a strong sense of camaraderie was a common refusal to passively accept their status as captives. They had almost all done something to demonstrate this already, usually in connection with escape attempts from other camps, and initially showed little sign of changing their ways at Oflag IVC. According to a Swiss observer, they comprised 'an excellent elite of remarkably strong characters, stubborn, proud and uncompromising'. New arrivals were struck by 'the electrical atmosphere' and 'cheerful aggressiveness' abroad in the castle, which they found 'stimulating' and were quick to emulate. It was this excitement that gave rise to the oft-repeated exaggeration that there was 'never a dull moment' at Colditz.[53]

What this restless atmosphere meant in practice involved, of course, a great deal of escape activity. It also manifested itself in a near-constant effort to gain the satisfaction of provoking the enemy. Goon-baiting was a pastime common to most officer camps, but evolved at Colditz into a full-time sport in the first half of the war. Naturally rambunctious, the 'bad boys' of Oflag IVC delighted in trying to provoke anger among their captors through collective and individual actions, which ranged from casual disregard of German orders and constant barracking to theft, arson, snowball-throwing, and the dropping of water bombs from the upper windows. Such pranks were undoubtedly good for morale, but were also potentially dangerous, as under extreme provocation guards were liable to use their weapons. Balancing the common desire to let off steam with the need to avert bloodshed was perhaps the most important task faced by successive SBOs at Colditz.

The first Senior British Officer, Lieutenant-Colonel Guy German, was a youngish Territorial Army officer who had landed in the castle as a result of burning copies of an enemy propaganda paper issued to POWs at Spangenberg. Though at times a stickler for the observation of military protocol between British officers, Colonel German was a quite popular camp leader, sharing the common fixation with escape and colluding in disruptive and non-cooperative behaviour.[54] Guy

German clearly thought valour the better part of discretion, and indeed was among those who found themselves doing time in cells for various offences. It was during one of these sojourns in the spring of 1941, when Lieutenant-Commander O. S. Stevenson of the Fleet Air Arm was serving in his stead, that one of the more embarrassing episodes in the history of British camp leadership came to a head.

The position of orderlies, the British other ranks assigned to work as batmen on a scale of about one ranker to every ten-to-eighteen officers, had been potentially problematic from the first. Serving as a batman was potentially a very cushy job. 'Polishing an officer's buttons beat digging spuds anytime', as Lance-Bombardier Norman Rubenstein observed after doing both. Yet at the same time, those who became orderlies knew that King's Regulations no longer in practice applied, and some-times, egged on by the enemy, grew resentful and obstreperous, espe-cially if officers behaved high-handedly and acted as if a traditional master–servant relationship existed. Colditz was by no means the only camp for officers where friction occurred; but it was one of the very few places to experience an irreparable breakdown in relations.[55]

Though coming from a variety of career backgrounds, the officers sent to Colditz were, like the vast majority of their peers, upper-middle class or upper class in origin. The orderlies were mostly from the lower classes, and had spent time in other camps and on working parties; despite their strong sense of camaraderie, many officers found the other-rank contingent rather alien. For their part the orderlies were not always impressed by the habits of their superiors—'you've no idea how much mess people make', one explained—and according to another Colditz inmate they were inclined to give the officers 'the same look of cool and devastating superiority as they gave the Germans'.[56]

By the spring of 1941 relations had deteriorated to the point where certain Colditz orderlies, as Padre Platt recorded, were openly talking 'for our benefit of revolution, parasites etc.' Some officers, for their part, thought the orderlies congenitally 'work shy' and too inclined to assume an air of equality. With Colonel German in cells, it fell to his stand-in to try to defuse the situation before things grew any worse. Stevenson, rather than finding out if any of their grievances were legitimate, chose to harangue the orderlies about their duties, addressing them, Platt stated, 'as though speaking from the bridge to the fo'c'stle with the authority of the Admiralty behind him'. This led all but three of the orderlies to down tools and refuse to do any work at all. Given his lack of real authority, Stevenson's bluff had been called, the orderlies correctly guessing that neither he nor Colonel German, who finished his sentence shortly thereafter, would appeal to the enemy for help. Instead the rebellious orderlies were forced to live apart, denied access to officers' rations, and eventually replaced by men less inclined to doubt the advantages of not having to work in the mines.

Eventually some of the new orderlies themselves grew tired of life at Oflag IVC. 'When I first got to Colditz,' remembered Alec Ross, 'I thought this is going to be a good place', noting that everyone was on first-name terms. He was less happy when the legless Douglas Bader, to whom he was assigned as personal batman, blocked his repatriation as a member of the RAMC in 1943. 'Hauptmann Püpke came into the courtyard and he called me down. "Good news, Ross," he says. "You're going home." Douglas Bader happened to be there, and he said, "No he's bloody not. He came here as my lackey and he'll stay as my lackey."' As a result, 'I had to stay another two bloody years when I could have gone home with the rest of my mates'. By January 1943, after eighteen months in the camp, the new orderlies were requesting through the Protecting Power that they be relieved and sent elsewhere.[57]

Meanwhile the liberal attitude towards disorderly conduct by officers displayed by Guy German had prompted the enemy authorities to think about exchanging him for a more senior figure. At the start of 1942 he was transferred to another oflag and replaced by Lieutenant-Colonel David Stayner, a Regular soldier from the Dorset Regiment.

'Daddy' Stayner, as his nickname suggests, was a more avuncular figure than German, yet 'cool and imperturbable', according to Jack Pringle. The new SBO had a calming influence, making clear his disapproval of unprovoked flouting of legitimate German authority without curbing escape activity in the slightest or losing the respect of those whose day-to-day lives he oversaw. 'He was quite brilliant in a very quiet way', Jack Best remembered. 'It didn't show.'[58]

This did not mean, however, that confrontations between guards and prisoners ceased. As before, there were always men in cells or due for court martial because of verbal assaults. Moreover, due to the disciplinarian regime imposed by the new commandant, Oberst Prawitt, in the early months of 1943, the intensity of incidents increased, culminating in guards opening fire to clear men from windows in the prisoners' courtyard during a visit by representatives of the Protecting Power, Switzerland. On one occasion, according to Gris Davies-Scourfield, Colonel Stayner had to step in—quite literally—to avert possible bloodshed:

I remember one incident when some of the goon-baiters were getting really wild. Everyone was shouting and screaming, and the German riot squad were ordering us back into our quarters, but it was quite difficult for us all to get back as quickly as they wanted us to. Then Daddy came forward and stood between us and these rather menacing-looking soldiers, wearing a very smart tropical uniform sent out from home. He undid the buttons of his tunic and he opened it, saying, 'Don't shoot my officers, shoot me!' It was very dramatic really, but because it was Daddy doing it we all thought it was frightfully funny.

It was probably rather less amusing for the SBO himself.[59]

Cannily, OKW decided that the removal of other nationalities—who tended towards competitiveness in goon-baiting, as in other matters— and the infusion of a large number of British officers from another camp, including a new SBO, would change the atmosphere at Colditz.[60] The other nationalities were gradually sent elsewhere, and in July 1943 over seventy officers arrived from Eichstätt. Though the majority of the new arrivals were escape-minded, the advent of the 'new boys' heralded at least a partial end to a form of camaraderie based on small numbers and shared experience in Oflag IVC. Padre Platt related in his diary the effect of this move in January 1944:

The coming of the Eichstätt boys marked the end of the British family life such as had been its characteristic from the beginning . . . Hitherto newcomers were received into the family and absorbed by it at once. But the Eichstätters came in large numbers from a large camp, were put in separate quarters, fed and lived separately, and the colonel they brought with them [W. M. 'Tubby' Broomhall] at once succeeded to the SBO-ship. They have retained the atmosphere of a large camp and, with the exception of a few of their number, have remained in small friendship circles complete in themselves and almost exclusive, hence they are described almost certainly unjustly as cliques.

'We never mixed very much with the old British contingent', John Hamilton-Baillie, one of the new arrivals, later said. 'They thought they knew all about Colditz and we were the new boys; and we thought they'd been shut up in such a small camp for such a long time that they didn't know the techniques that we did; so we didn't mix very easily.' Though equally escape-minded, the Eichstätt contingent, in the majority and with one of their own as SBO, were not as fixated on potentially dangerous acts designed to provoke the guards as seemed to be the case with some of the original inmates. As Mike Edwards explained, 'we [new boys] would try and get along with our nefarious activities without drawing too much attention to ourselves'. This created serious friction within the camp population, but apparently brought an end to riotousness. 'After July 1943,' Hauptmann Eggers recorded, 'a modus vivendi was reached.

There was no howling and whistling. The British knew very well that the dissolving of the castle was very much to their disadvantage.'[61]

In fact this conclusion was premature. Some of old lags resented what they considered Broomhall's 'policy of appeasement' toward the commandant, and as the war situation improved both old and new prisoners began a new round of disorderly conduct on parade in the autumn of 1943. As Eggers ruefully admitted, 'it was just like old times—shouts, whistles, demonstrations, indiscipline'. Relations between captors and captives were consequently once again becoming 'badly frayed'. Hence a new SBO was brought in from Spangenberg to supplant Broomhall in November 1943—Lieutenant-Colonel Willie Tod of the Royal Scots Fusiliers.[62]

The job Tod inherited was not an easy one. 'He had to withstand the constant complaints and charges of the Germans,' one of the camp doctors recalled, 'and what was probably more trying, had to control the denizens of the camp who, in many cases, were as difficult to handle as an opera house full of prima donnas.' The sheer length of the war was having a negative effect. 'I think everyone was getting a bit touchy and testy', Patrick Welch remembered. Yet the new SBO, a distinguished-looking Regular officer with a knack for charming the opposition, was soon able to restore a modicum of order and stability and have (in his own words) a 'good influence' on his fellows. Though goon-baiting did not cease, its manifestations became less frequent and thereby less dangerous. Thanks to Tod's quiet but firm diplomacy prisoners obtained parole walks outside the castle and a number of other privileges. At the same time, the last SBO at Colditz was quite willing to stand up for the rights of prisoners, and on several occasions faced down the commandant—and critics within the camp—on issues where he felt there could be no compromise. Julius Green, no shrinking violet in terms of rubbing the enemy the wrong way, was emphatic in his conclusion that Tod was a success: 'I don't think any other nation or system could have produced a man with such instincts.'[63]

British leadership within camps mattered, and both in its own right and in comparative terms Colditz came off well (except, perhaps, in relation to the orderlies at various points in time). In overall terms the place was well served by its SBOs, especially in light of the problems faced by all camp leaders inside Germany and the dangers peculiar to Oflag IVC. For much of the time, as the next chapter will show, management skills were, to the average Kriegie, of true significance insofar as they affected access to the necessities of life.

Notes

1. The Germans considered 'men of confidence', allowed for under the Geneva Convention, 'essential' to the smooth running of POW affairs. Vasilis Vourkoutiotis, 'The German Armed Forces Supreme Command and British and American Prisoners-of-War, 1939–1945: Policy and Practice', Ph.D. thesis, McGill University (2000), 194.
2. A. Passfield, *The Escape Artist* (Perth, WA, 1988), 24. SBOs tended to strike the right balance of interest with the benefit of experience. See e.g. http://www.awm.gov.au, A. D. Crawford, TS tape 1, side A.
3. Frank Taylor, *Barbed Wire and Footlights* (Braunton, 1988), 60. On the almost organic development of the POW administrative structure among RAF NCOs see Ron Mackenzie, *An Ordinary War, 1940–1945* (Wangaratta, Victoria, 1995), 43.
4. Calton Younger, *No Flight from the Cage* (London, 1981 edn.), 24–6, 50–2; IWMSA 5131/2, R. Buckingham; Mackenzie, op. cit., 51; IWMSA 6142/2, D. Deans; H. E. Woolley, *No Time Off for Good Behaviour* (Burnstown, Ont., 1990), 100–1; Richard Passmore, *Moving Tent* (London, 1982), 169; see Percy Wilson Carruthers, *Of Ploughs, Planes and Palliasses* (Arundel, 1992), 102; John Fancy, *Tunnelling to Freedom* (London, 1957), 38; IWMSA 6178/1, J. Bristow; IWMSA 15246/3, T. Cooksey; David Rolf, *Prisoners of the Reich* (London, 1988), 108; John Dominy, *The Sergeant Escapers* (London, 1974), 9.
5. NCOs of the RAF who observed army discipline were struck by how much stricter it was compared to life in RAF compounds. See e.g. Geoffrey Taylor, *Return Ticket* (London, 1972), 140; IWMSA 13573/2, A. Jones. On 'bull' and 'spit and polish' army NCOs see also e.g. Graham Palmer, *Prisoner of Death* (Wellingborough, 1990), 124–5; Jim Longson and Christine Taylor, *An Arnhem Odyssey* (London, 1991), 102; Peter Winter, *Free Lodgings* (Auckland, 1993), 113.
6. See G. Taylor, op. cit., 140; S. Sinclair in Patsy Adam-Smith, *Prisoners of War* (Ringwood, Victoria, 1992), 157; Charles Robinson, *Journey to Captivity* (Canberra, 1991), 94; Sandy St Clair, *The Endless War* (North Battleford, Sask., 1987), 197–8; George Clifton, *The Happy Hunted* (London, 1954), 341.
7. See James Allan, *No Citation* (London, 1955), 23; John Castle, *The Password is Courage* (London, 1955), 118; Neville Chesterton, *Crete Was My Waterloo* (London, 1995), 77; Douglas Collins, *P.O.W.* (London, 1970), 50; Roger V. Coward, *Sailors in Cages* (London, 1967), 89; Clive Dunn, *Permission to Speak* (London, 1986), 96; J. M. Green, *From Colditz in Code* (Hull, 1989 edn.), 327–8; H. I. Irwin in J. E. Holliday (ed.), *Stories of the RAAF POWs of Lamsdorf* (Holland Park, Queensland, 1992), 120; Ewart C. Jones, *Germans Under My Bed* (London, 1957), 23, 29, 162 ff.; Sam Kydd, *For You the War Is Over...* (London, 1973), 105; John McMahon, *Almost a Lifetime* (Lantzville, BC, 1995), 68; Passfield, op. cit., 105–6; Ian Ramsay, *P.O.W.* (Melbourne, 1985), 35–6, 56.

8. Maxwell Leigh, *Captives Courageous* (Johannesburg, 1992), 133–7; Bill Jackson, *The Lone Survivor* (North Battleford, Sask., 1993), 209; James Stedman, *Life of a British POW in Poland* (Braunton, 1992), 14.

9. Green, op. cit., (London, 1971 edn.), 112; Ed Annetts, *Campaign Without Medals* (Lewes, 1996), 114; Stedman, op. cit., 14.

10. Jack Pringle, *Colditz Last Stop* (Sussex, 1995 edn.), 120. On Sherriff see Green, op. cit., 92–3; Arthur Evans, *Sojourn in Silesia* (Ashford, 1995), 44; Robert Gale, *Private Prisoner* (Wellingborough, 1984), 147; Ike Rosmarin, *Inside Story* (Cape Town, 1990), 44; Norman Rubenstein, *The Invisibly Wounded* (Hull, 1989), 162; Castle, op. cit., 38. On MacKenzie see M. N. McKibben, *Barbed Wire* (London, 1947), 31, 41; George Beeson, *Five Roads to Freedom* (London, 1977), 27; Imelda Ryan (comp.), *POWs Fraternal* (Perth, WA, 1990), 108; IWMSA 48960/2, G. Soane.

11. Ryan, op. cit., 107; IWM, G. R. Manners diary, 24 Dec. 1940. On relying on German support see e.g. E. C. Jones, op. cit., 132.

12. See e.g. Castle, op. cit., 117–18. On the contentious nature of popular coups against camp leaders see e.g. E. C. Jones, op. cit., 162–4 (Army); F. Taylor, op cit., 65–6 (RAF); IWM, G. F. W. Wilson diary, 5 Dec. 1943 (RN); Barbara Broom (comp.), *Geoffrey Broom's War* (Edinburgh, 1993), 158–60 (RN); Elvet Williams, *Arbeitskommando* (London, 1975), 118–20. On the Sherriff case see PRO, WO 224/27, Report on Stalag VIIIB, Aug. 1941, p. 5.

13. Leigh, op. cit., 137; Ryan, op. cit., 108.

14. IWM (Rolf), J. M. McGee, 10; Ramsay, op. cit., 36, 56; J. E. Pryce, *Heels in Line* (London, 1958), 102–3.

15. IWM (Rolf), W. J. Sudworth, 15; IWM, B. A. Brooke, 8; Ryan, op. cit., 107. On camp police see e.g. IWMSA 48960/2, G. Soane; IWMSA 13573/2, A. Jones; Philip Kindersley, *For You the War Is Over* (Tunbridge Wells, 1983), 171. On the execution of traitors with the apparent sanction of senior POW authority see e.g. Colin Rushton, *Spectator in Hell* (Springhill, 1998), 86; St Clair, op. cit., 191.

16. John Elwyn, *At the Fifth Attempt* (London, 1987), 75; PRO, WO 224/27, RC report on visit to Stalag VIIIB, 12 Feb. 1943.

17. See Gale, op. cit., 143; Holliday, op. cit., 122, 141–2; Jackson, op. cit., 73–4; Rosmarin, op. cit., 74–5; IWM, W. A. Harding, 16. Though Lamsdorf had advantages in scale, Kriegies might also go underground elsewhere to avoid German retribution. See e.g. IWM, N. R. Wylie collection, 'Some Amusing Incidents', 3; Howard Greville, *Prison Camp Spies* (Loftus, NSW, 1998), 64; Passfield, op. cit., 68, 87–8.

18. Ian Sabey, *Stalag Scrapbook* (Melbourne, 1947), 104; F. Morton in Daniel G. Dancocks, *In Enemy Hands* (Toronto, 1990 edn.), 99–100; Rolf, op. cit., 148; Winter, op. cit., 113; Thompson in John Barnett, *We Were There* (Sydney, 1987), 264; Gale, op. cit., 144; Annetts, op. cit., 115.

19. John Borrie, *Despite Captivity* (London, 1975), 214; Annetts, op. cit., 160.

20. T. C. F. Prittie and W. Earle Edwards, *Escape to Freedom* (London, 1953 edn.), 69–70; IWM, A. N. L. Munby diary, 1 July, 31 July 1940.

21. Jack Champ and Colin Burgess, *The Diggers of Colditz* (Sydney, 1985), 26.

22. Prittie and Edwards, op. cit., 226.
23. Edward Ward, *Give Me Air* (London, 1946), 127–8; Earl Haig, *My Father's Son* (London, 2000), 128.
24. Margaret Duggan (ed.), *Padre in Colditz* (London, 1978), 70.
25. James B. Chutter, *Captivity Captive* (London, 1954), 121. On this sort of rift see e.g. Airey Neave, *They Have Their Exits* (London, 1953), 22; St Clair, op. cit., 181; IWMSA 4847/2, C. L. Irwin; ibid. 17896/2, W. C. Purdon; IWM, H. C. F. Harwood, 106–7, 124.
26. Sidney Smith, *Wings Day* (London, 1969), *passim*.
27. Kingsley Brown, *Bonds of Wire* (Toronto, 1989), 90–1.
28. Oliver Philpot, *Stolen Journey* (London, 1950), 118, 159; B. A. James, *Moonless Night* (London, 1983), 71, 67; IWMSA 13296/1, R. Churchill.
29. Martin Smith, *What a Bloody Arrival* (Lewes, 1997), 117; Alan Mackay, *313 Days to Christmas* (Glendaurel, 1998), 25; see Morrison, op. cit., 72; Robert Kee, *A Crowd Is Not Company* (London, 1982 edn.), 86; see also, however, IWMSA 6142/4, J. Deans. On the range of class and occupational background to be found in Stalag Luft III see R. Eeles in Robin Neillands, *The Conquest of the Reich* (New York, 1995), 224.
30. B. A. James, op. cit., 42; S. Smith, op. cit., 60–1, 74; F. A. B. Tams, *A Trenchard 'Brat'* (Edinburgh, 2000), 105. On ongoing suspicions of the Dulag staff later on see Passmore, op. cit., 138; Mackay, op. cit., 32; Eric Williams, *The Tunnel* (London, 1951), 86–7.
31. Alan W. Cooper, *Free to Fight Again* (London, 1988), 214.
32. Larry Forrester, *Fly For Your Life* (London, 1960 edn.), 285–6. Group Captain Massey also supported this policy at Luft III. See Walter Morrison, *Flak and Ferrets* (London, 1995), 82.
33. K. Brown, op. cit., 142–4.
34. Kindersley, op. cit., 151, 148.
35. Chutter, op. cit., 118. On Stirling's 'dictatorship' see Alan Hoe, *David Stirling* (London, 1992), 241 ff.
36. See St Clair, op. cit., 181; Kindersley, op. cit., 142; 'Sentry', 'Shadow Life in Captivity', *Blackwood's*, 259 (1946), 292–3.
37. A. Campbell, quoted in Henry Chancellor, *Colditz* (London, 2001), 112.
38. David James, *A Prisoner's Progress* (Edinburgh, 1947), 26.
39. Some sense of Captain Wilson's belief in the value of order can be ascertained from his diary held at the IWM. See esp. entries for 28 Aug., 20 Sept., 25 Oct. 1943, 17 Dec. 1944.
40. LC, T. N. Catlow MS, 53; IWMSA 16797/2, H. Bruce. Wilson, however, apparently did not hinder the work of the Escape Committee at Marlag (O), and when questioned by an interrogator about who had dug a tunnel he 'replied that I could give him no such information & signed a statement to that effect!' IWM, G.W. F. Wilson diary, 24 Nov. 1943.
41. See Derek Bond, *Steady Old Man!* (London, 1990), 153. RAMC doctors, usually the only commissioned personnel in men's camps, and thereby sometimes called upon to exercise the SBO role, also on occasion were seen to go too far in asserting their command authority. See Ryan, op. cit., 108.

42. PRO, WO 208/3282, Stalag Luft I (Barth)—Part IV—Officers' Camp, 1943–1945, pp. 18–25. On problematic relations between officers and other ranks (especially orderlies) see e.g. IWM, A. F. Gibbs, 87–8.

43. IWM, A. F. Gibbs, 153.

44. IWM, H. C. F. Harwood, 104–5. NCOs apparently had less compunction about using German authority to enforce discipline. See Rubenstein, op. cit., 78–9.

45. IWMSA 4827/5, R. Loder.

46. Kindersley, op. cit., 172–3; Jane Torday (ed.), *The Coldstreamer and the Canary* (Langley, 1995), 91; Jack Poole *Undiscovered Ends* (London, 1957), 162–4; Prittie and Edwards, op. cit., 72.

47. T. D. Calnan, *Free As a Running Fox* (New York, 1970), 47–8. On Spangenberg see e.g. Forrester, op. cit., 276; IWMSA 4893/5, M. Champion Jones; IWMSA 4769/2, J. Phillips. On Warburg see e.g. IWMSA 4847/2, C. L. Irwin.

48. See e.g. Clifton, op. cit., 351; Haig, op. cit., 125; Prittie and Edwards, op. cit., 125; Duggan, op. cit., 70. On differences between established senior RN officers and energetic junior wartime arrivals see e.g. LC, T. N. Catlow, 38; IWM, G. F. W. Wilson diary, 17 May 1943.

49. See Kee, op. cit., 86–7; Crawley, op. cit., 19–23; K. Brown, op. cit., 54–5.

50. Neave, op. cit., 63.

51. IWMSA 15608/2, W. Stevens; see F. Taylor, op. cit, 50–1; IWMSA 11337/4, H. Bracken; ibid. 4816/4, J. M. Moran; John Frayn Turner, *Douglas Bader* (Shrewsbury, 1995), 161, 162, 208; Mackenzie, op. cit., 54–5; LC, A. Siska tape 1527; ibid., Earl Haig interview tape 1279/80, tape 2 transcript, 7; P. R. Reid, *Colditz* (London, 1984), 178, 231; IWMSA 17585/3, J. C. Pringle; see also I. Schrire, *Stalag Doctor* (London, 1956), 193.

52. Duggan, op. cit., 71; Miles Reid, *Into Colditz* (Salisbury, 1983), 59.

53. P. R. Reid, *The Colditz Story* (London, 1952), 166; Jim Rogers, *Tunnelling into Colditz* (London, 1986), 97; IWMSA 4432/8, H. Gee; PRO, WO 224/69, PP report of 7 Oct. 1944 visit; John Chrisp, *The Tunnellers of Sandborstal* (London, 1959), 151; IWMSA 10771/1, J. Courtnay; Giles Romilly and Michael Alexander, *The Privileged Nightmare* (London, 1954), 84–5; Ion Ferguson, *Doctor at War* (London, 1955), 128.

54. Reid, *Full Story*, 126, 31; Duggan, op. cit., 116; CSVA 8, J. Best; IWMSA 16800/2, B. N. Mazumdar.

55. Rubenstein, op. cit., 71. On problems elsewhere see IWM, A. N. L. Munby diary, 21 June 1940; IWMSA 4432/2, H. Gee; Michael Duncan, *Underground from Posen* (London, 1954), 64; Prittie and Edwards, op. cit., 57–8; T. D. Beckwith (ed.), *The Mansel Diaries* (London, 1977), 7 Apr. 1941, p. 35, 15 Jan. 1942, p. 75; IWM, W. Kite, 15–24.

56. Michael Burn, *Yes, Farewell* (London, 1946), 35, 45–6; IWMSA 4432/2, H. Gee.

57. PRO, WO 224/69, PP report on visit of 25 Jan. 1943, p. 3; A. Ross quoted in Chancellor, op. cit., 251–2; IWM, J. E. Platt diary, 6 June 1941, 20 Aug. 1941, 29 Mar. 1941; see also, however, Sidney Smith, 'An Orderly Talks', in, Reinhold Eggers (comp.), *Colditz Recaptured* (London, 1973),

112–14; 'A Conversation with John Wilkins', *Colditz Society Newsletter*, 3:28 (July 2002), p. 8.

58. CSVA 8, J. Best; Pringle, op. cit., 140.
59. G. Davies-Scourfield, quoted in Chancellor, op. cit., 76.
60. See IWMSA 12568/3, R. Eggers. On courts martial see e.g. IWM, P. W. Dollar folder; IWM, J. E. Platt diary, 19 Feb. 1943.
61. IWMSA 12658/3 R. Eggers; M. Edwards in Chancellor, op. cit., 242; IWMSA 14781/2, J. Hamilton-Baillie; Duggan, op. cit., 223; see Reid, *Latter Days*, 207; CSVA 10, P. Fergusson; CSVA 8, J. Best.
62. Reinhold Eggers, *Colditz* (London, 1972), 133, 154.
63. Green, op. cit., 122; PRO, WO 224/78, PP report on visit to Oflag IX A/H, 28 Apr. 1944, 3; IWMSA 10643/3, P. Welch; Schrire, op. cit., 195; see Corran Purdon, *List the Bugle* (Antrim, 1993), 55; M. Reid, op. cit., 59–60; Chancellor, op. cit., 293, 313–4; Reid, *Full Story*, 233–5, 241, 245, 263, 271, 275–8, 285, 288–9, 292, 295; IWMSA 4432/9, H. Gee; CSVA 8, J. Best. See PRO, WO 224/72, PP visit, 28 July 1941, p. 4. Concerning Broomhall and a 'policy of appeasement' see IWM, J. E. Platt diary, 24 July 1943.

5 Body and Soul

The food ration of prisoners of war shall be equivalent in quantity and quality to that of depot troops... The use of tobacco shall be authorized... Clothing, underwear and footwear shall be supplied to prisoners of war by the detaining power... Each camp shall possess an infirmary...

(from Articles 11–13, Geneva Convention, 1929)

Prisoners of war shall be permitted complete freedom in the performance of their religious duties... Belligerents shall encourage as much as possible the organization of intellectual... pursuits... letters and cards shall be sent by post by the shortest possible route...

(from Articles 16–17, 36, Geneva Convention, 1929)

Though the layout of particular camps and the behaviour of individual German and British leaders could generate real differences in life behind the wire, the more immediate problem for the ordinary Kriegie was simply to keep body and soul together. Certain periods were worse than others, but throughout the war POWs had to cope with the reality of near-constant deprivation. The shortage or complete absence of what had previously been taken for granted—everything from food to privacy—was something with which every prisoner had to come to terms, both physically and mentally. Those who went to Colditz were no exception. To understand what went on at Oflag IVC, however, it is first necessary to examine the general situation with respect to physical and mental health among British POWs.

Regarding the necessities of life, every prisoner of the Reich had to undergo the harsh transition from comparative plenty to relative want. According to the Geneva Convention the detaining power was supposed to provide for prisoners on a level comparable to that of its own garrison troops. In the case of Nazi Germany the requisite articles were more

honoured in the breach than in the observance. The rations, clothing, footwear, and everything else given to POWs were inadequate both in quantity and in quality. Outside supplies, provided chiefly through the International Red Cross, were of inestimable value; but their timely arrival could not always be depended upon, especially when existing supply routes were suddenly disrupted. When the enemy had to be relied on exclusively for support, as was the case for most prisoners in 1940–1 and again in 1944–5, the ability of bodies to keep on functioning came into serious question.

For the small number of servicemen captured in the first months of the war the situation with regard to food, clothing, and other necessities was generally not too bad at first. Black bread and acorn coffee (among other *ersatz* delicacies) were unappetizing, but the stew still tended to have meat in it. Furthermore food parcels, mail, and packages from relatives soon began to arrive from Britain via Belgium under the auspices of the Red Cross.[1] The situation changed radically in the summer of 1940, however, when German victories in the West first broke the existing route for mail and parcels and then produced a mass influx of prisoners into the Greater Reich. It would take months to establish new and rather more circuitous routes for material sent from Britain to Germany via Switzerland or, on a smaller scale, Sweden (using Lisbon, Marseilles, and Gothenburg as neutral entry ports). In the meantime the forty-odd thousand British prisoners would have to subsist on what the enemy was able and chose to provide. In practice POWs in the Third Reich always tended to rate below the high standards set by the Geneva Convention with regard to upkeep, and in any event what could be provided per man in the context of the huge number of new prisoners was inevitably going to be limited. The end result was deprivation so severe that if it had continued unabated men would have begun to die in large numbers. The latter months of 1940 were extremely bleak ones for British prisoners in German hands.

The most immediate necessities of life are food and water. For the officers and men of the BEF, along with the as-yet small number of air force and navy prisoners taken, there was precious little to be had of either—especially food—at this point in the war. Running water was a rarity at places like Lamsdorf, Thorn, and Schubin in the early days. Meanwhile the daily rations for captured soldiers usually consisted of mint or strawberry-leaf tea, crushed acorn or barley coffee, plus a ladle of soup, a slice of black bread, or perhaps a hard-tack biscuit. The soup— made from boiling potatoes, beets, or other root vegetables with the

occasional bone, shred of fat, or piece of offal thrown in—was invariably thin, while the tea was so weak that it could be used in place of hot water for shaving. Hungry to begin with, men quickly found the question of fair shares becoming an obsession.

The soup was ladled out from big vats, where the solids tended either to float on top or sink to the bottom, and men soon began to suspect—fairly or not—that the British cook sergeants were favouring some men over others as part of a racket.[2] The division of the loaves of bitter-tasting black bread was even more of a fixation. Depending on its size, a single loaf had to feed between five and ten men. Identity tags were often used as a measuring device, the designated cutter being watched hawk-eyed to make sure the slices were even. Once a loaf had been cut, those it was meant to feed received their particular slices based on the luck of the draw, men cutting cards, drawing lots, or using other 'blind' methods to divvy up the results. 'It was a serious business indeed when with hungry suspicious eyes the little groups of men watched the cutting of the loaf', Gunner William Harding remembered of the early months at Stalag VIIIB; 'And many arguments and fights started up when one slice was thinner than the others; there was even a scramble for the crumbs with the licked finger off table and floor. A sparrow would have starved to death in that place.'[3]

On occasion a dab of fish-paste, runny cheese, ersatz margarine, or perhaps even a slice of sausage or piece of dried fish might be added to the standard fare, but never in any quantity. Prisoners who volunteered for working parties in the autumn of 1940 in the hope that rations would at least improve ('anything seemed better than this', as Sergeant Donald Edgar put it in reference to the prevailing hunger at Lamsdorf) were often disappointed. The little extra that might be forthcoming from the employer was more often than not counterbalanced by the manual labour that *Kriegsgefangenen* were expected to carry out.[4]

Prisoners at best were getting only about two-thirds of what they needed in the way of calories, and even less in the way of vitamins. The overall result was malnutrition and incipient starvation. 'Frequently someone would get up to go somewhere,' a QVR prisoner later wrote of the situation at Thorn after several weeks, 'and then just without any warning collapse unconscious.' Wasting bodies developing boils and sores, and faces became 'painfully gaunt and haggard', as a West Kent soldier remembered. 'One chap of about 20 years lost all his teeth, his hair went grey and he walked about staring at the ground', another soldier recalled of the initial period at Stalag VIIIB. 'I saw pre-war

guardsmen literally fold up, their big frames couldn't exist on the meagre rations.' To survive, men might filch food where they could from friend and foe alike, and were not shy about rooting through rubbish bins for potato peelings and other discarded items. Those caught stealing were usually dropped into latrine pits or beaten to within an inch of their life.[5]

The food situation was little better for officer prisoners at Laufen, where stealing also occurred but justice tended to be less summary. The type of rations issued at Oflag VIIC were similar to those in the big stalags, with the addition—soon commonplace everywhere—of a few small potatoes. At Laufen, however, these were in many cases rotten, apparently due to the machinations of the German quartermaster. 'Only a small part of each potato was edible; the rest was just revolting', wrote future Colditz inmate Jim Rogers. Hence those with army commissions also soon began to rapidly lose weight and suffer the effects of a deficient diet by way of gastrointestinal problems and boils. Dropping sixty pounds was not unheard of, and prisoners regularly fainted on parade. 'One became so weak that even walking up stairs grew to be to be an effort,' Desmond Llewelyn recalled, 'and sometimes such exertion caused blacking out.'[6]

Officers were only marginally better off in other camps. Pilot Officer B. A. James later described the situation in this period at the newly opened Stalag Luft I at Barth:

We subsisted on the German rations for a non-working civilian: a cup of Ersatz coffee, made from acorns, in the morning, a bowl of soup, usually Sauerkraut, with a few potatoes at mid-day, and one fifth of a loaf of black bread with a pat of margarine and a small piece of sausage or cheese in the evening, supplied on a room basis and divided up by the room 'stooge' for the day—very accurately as he had to wait until the others had chosen their portions! These rations accounted for barely 800 calories per day, less than half the optimum for an adult human being. The pangs of hunger were ever present.

'We lost weight and any exercise was exhausting', J. M. Green, a dental officer whose future lay in Colditz, wrote of his time in Oflag VIID (Tittmoning) in 1940–1. 'Climbing stairs was an effort, you took two or three steps and then stopped to get your breath back. I found that if I stood up too quickly I felt faint and some of us had legs swollen from famine oedema.'[7]

Little could be done for those who fell ill. Captured RAMC doctors usually had almost nothing with which to treat such common complaints as dysentery and leg ulcers. A teaspoon of charcoal for an intestinal complaint was about the best most soldiers could hope for, and some men died who might otherwise have been saved.[8]

Food, meanwhile, was not the only thing the body might crave. For heavy smokers the absence of nicotine was also a great torture. In the stalags and work camps men were seen begging guards for their fag ends and—true of oflags as well—grubbing about in the dirt for those that were dropped. Some soldiers even volunteered to clean German quarters just so as to be able to get at the contents of ashtrays. Officers and men alike smoked anything that might give the illusion of a fix—dried leaves, grass, coffee grounds, potato skins, even manure—in home-made pipes or hand-rolled tubes of whatever paper (e.g. bible pages) was available. 'Some leaves are not nearly so bad to smoke as one would think', Captain A. N. L. Munby reflected in his Laufen diary in July 1940. The craving for nicotine could be so great, however, that those affected might be willing to trade part of their meagre food ration or pay in exchange for the opportunity for a deep drag or two.[9]

In the eastern working camps and later on in some canteens, *Junaks*— a type of Polish cigarette consisting largely of cardboard—sometimes could be obtained for money or through the selling of personal possessions. These, though, were a far cry from Players and Woodbines. 'They were *revolting*', according to Kenneth Lockwood. Yet 'no matter how evil the smell or foul the taste, we were always happy to puff a Junak when nothing better was available', Stuart Brown remembered, hastily adding: 'But it was always as a last resort.'[10]

As the months passed and winter approached, clothing and footwear also became a problem. Uniforms were often incomplete to begin with. 'Very few have hats,' Captain Munby noted of his fellow officers at Laufen in July, 'many have no underclothes, a few no shirts or jackets.' What there was, furthermore, especially footwear, wore out through continual use, and prisoners became more and more tramp-like in appearance. 'We were like scarecrows', John Elwyn recalled of his working party in Upper Silesia in the autumn of 1940. The Germans eventually provided in limited quantities bits and pieces of captured European uniforms, along with sabots (wooden clogs) and foot-rags in place of boots and socks. Clothing size, however, was irrelevant, and the sabots problematic. 'The clogs were terribly uncomfortable and chafed the feet badly', R. P. Evans wrote. 'The best we could manage was a shuffle.'[11]

Added to physical misery was psychological stress arising from defeat and lack of hard news about the war situation. It was easy enough to dismiss what appeared in the German press or *The Camp*—the English-language paper for British POWs that began to appear in the summer and, among other things, made an excellent substitute for non-existent toilet paper—as enemy propaganda, but anxiety remained. Rumours, ranging from imminent peace treaties to aerial Armageddon at home, ran unchecked. The absence of letters from loved ones did nothing to improve the situation.[12]

In the face of all this it was natural that many should turn to God for spiritual comfort. 'There is a very large congregation,' Lieutenant G. B. Wright noted in his diary of the communion held at Laufen on 30 June 1940, 'probably 500.' Captured clergymen of the Army Chaplains' Department, alas, were not always able to meet the need for spiritual solace. Since padres in the British Army were dressed as officers they tended to be concentrated in Laufen rather than spread around the stalags. What was more, even when attached to other camps they did not often display the kind of moral leadership through example that was expected of them. 'Most of the chaplains that we met in France, and subsequently in Germany, were completely useless and hopeless', an RAMC orderly attached to various POW hospitals subsequently wrote: '—the less said about them the better.' Having eighteen chaplains at Oflag VIIC did little to improve spiritual matters, as most apparently spent much of their time lying on their bunks arguing about denominational issues rather than going out and ministering to their de facto flock.[13]

In both stalags and oflags it was laymen—Toc-H members, for instance—who often seized the initiative and began to organize communal worship. 'One of the chaps started holding a church service on Sundays in one of the big tents on the sandy floor', a private in the Sussex Regiment recalled of the early days at Stalag XXIB (Schubin). 'It became packed and I believe men were getting solace from it.' Similar scenes occurred elsewhere. At Stalag XXA (Thorn) a lay preacher organized a service which, according to an observer, 'did a lot to comfort many who were feeling lost, who had perhaps not been used to, or had not felt the need of, God's help before'.[14]

Prayers and hymns, however, could do little to ease the prevalent physical distress. 'It is impossible now, after several decades . . .', RAF Sergeant Richard Passmore wrote of the early months at Barth, 'to describe to outsiders the constant misery, almost despair, of the time.'[15] All in all it was a bad period in which to be a British prisoner of war in Nazi Germany, and spirits naturally suffered. A small number of men gave up and either actively committed suicide or simply lay down and died.[16] Everyone wished that the war would end, some even if it meant defeat. John Elwyn, a Welsh Guardsman, recorded the following incident at Lamsdorf that occurred in the third week of June 1940:

That evening we were bombastically harangued by an English-speaking officer who informed us that news had just been received of the capitulation of France and that we might all be home for Christmas. This was received by prolonged and tumultuous cheering. I asked a man next to me why he was cheering. He replied, 'Didn't you hear him say we'll be home by Christmas?'
    'But don't you realise that the fall of France means that Germany has won the war [*sic*]?'
    'What the hell do I care who's won the war? All I want is to get home.'

This was not an isolated case. Sergeant Douglas Collins remembered overhearing an exasperated Cockney grumble in the same camp three months later: 'if we're going to 'ave the Nazis, let's 'ave 'em and get it over wiv. It don't make no difference to me 'oo's in Whitehall.' Nor was it just the other ranks who might want to get the whole thing over and done with. That autumn at Laufen a very senior officer made no secret of his belief that England was finished, and there was also defeatist talk at Spangenberg.[17] Though a few special extras in the way of food were provided and most Kriegies did their best to keep up Yuletide appearances, there was precious little to celebrate as a British POW in Germany on Christmas Day 1940.[18]

Happily for those concerned, the future would be rosier than the experience of captivity thus far had suggested. It is no exaggeration to say that the arrival of Red Cross parcels, first in an irregular trickle, then in a more-or-less steady stream from 1941 through 1944, saved the lives of many thousands of men and generally made life bearable where it had verged on the intolerable. As a New Zealand doctor in German hands put it, a decent diet 'was essential to health and morale', and Red Cross food parcels made this possible.[19]

    Even when all other details had been forgotten, ex-Kriegies could recite with great precision the contents of standard food parcels. Those made up in the United Kingdom were oblong cardboard boxes weighing between ten and eleven pounds and containing a host of packed and tinned items unavailable in prisoner rations. Cheese, milk, biscuits, margarine, some vegetable, syrup, jam, sausages, bacon, oatmeal, tinned meat or stew, beef cubes, rice pudding, marmite, custard, chocolate, sugar, and—of course—tea were among the necessities and luxuries that might appear. Parcels along similar lines came from Canada—especially prized for the meat roll and tins of dried milk (Klim) that they contained—and in some instances from the United States (the latter often including peanut butter, a novelty to most British servicemen). There were also occasional bulk issues, often hailing from Argentina: 'Fray Bentos bully beef, large round flat hard tack biscuits, slabs of dark bitter cooking chocolate, and raisins', wrote RAF Sergeant Frank Taylor over forty years on, displaying the total recall typical of ex-Kriegies when remembering Red Cross food.[20]

Faced with the collapse of the original dispatch and routing system and a vast increase in the number of prisoners in enemy hands, it took some time for the Red Cross to develop and organize a new way of getting consignments to Germany. Some parcels got through to camps in the second half of 1940, but rarely with any frequency or on nearly a sufficient scale. At Thorn sixty-seven parcels arrived at one point in July, by which time there were over a thousand prisoners in the stalag. At Laufen there were a couple of limited issues in July, then nothing until November. Many camps did not receive any parcels at all into the late autumn, and even when they did, there were never enough to go round. In the autumn months at Oflag IXA/H (Spangenberg) parcels were arriving on a scale of about one per officer per month. The first parcel issue at Stalag VIIIB did not occur until December, when every four men had to divide the contents of a parcel designed for one. That was better than at Stalag XXA, where the scale was one parcel for every twenty men. Satellite working camps tended to be worst off in terms of delays, as parcels went first to the main stalags before going out to *Arbeitskommandos*. They often did not get any parcels at all until the first quarter or so of 1941.[21]

By the late spring of that year, thankfully, the parcel flow had become much more regular in scope and scale. It took much less time—though there was still a gap in which men suffered real privation—for the Red Cross to respond to the arrival in the Third Reich of the tens of thousands of men captured in Greece and Crete, or those transferred from Italy two years later. By the summer of the third year of war most Kriegies were starting to experience the comparative luxury of between one half and a whole parcel each week. Delight and relief were present in equal measure for those who had been facing starvation. 'When I came to open my [first] parcel I was overwhelmed to the point of tears—like all the others—and we were a tough bunch of men by now', Donald Edgar wrote. 'The whole hut went mad!', Robert Gale explained in reference to his working party. 'I have never seen so many hysterical men in my life.'

It was the same for those from Greece and Crete who had been trying to survive on German rations for weeks or even months. 'Only one who has shared the experience could remotely gauge the impact of that first issue of one parcel for every two men', Elvet Williams later asserted. 'No class of Mixed Infants can ever have shown the ecstasy and unashamed pleasure displayed throughout the compound during the next couple of hours as treasure after treasure was revealed, drooled over, fondled and sampled.'[22]

Naturally enough the arrival of Red Cross parcels had a very positive effect on health and morale. Over and over again Kriegies would later remark that they made the difference between life and death, not least because the German authorities took the opportunity to cut their own ration issue. 'There is little doubt that if we had been dependent on German rations only,' RNVR Lieutenant David James asserted in reference to one of the better-run camps, Marlag (O), 'we should have died.'[23]

Food parcels, moreover, were not the only packages arriving via the Red Cross. Invalid parcels for the sick, along with some medical equipment and drugs, were also arriving in quantity by the middle years of the war, and special Christmas fare was also dispatched towards the end of each year. And whatever the long-term health effects, the arrival in tins of cigarettes on an authorized scale of fifty per week did wonders for nicotine addicts. 'I can still remember the intense sensual pleasure we enjoyed when opening a sealed tin of fresh cigarettes and deeply inhaling the aroma of tobacco', Squadron Leader Tommy Calnan rhapsodized. This, of course, was just the build-up to the main event, especially for those who had not seen real tobacco since capture: 'I opened my tin of Players [wrote a BEF man] and had my first English cigarette for six months or so. The ecstasy! I did not wish to speak; I did not wish to move an inch; I just wanted to inhale the fragrance and feel the sense of well-being that spread from my head to my toes ... Perfection, fulfilment.' 'I lit one up and took a big drag', another soldier remembered of his first smoke; 'my head spun around and I almost lost my senses in sheer delight.'[24]

The clothing situation also improved. Parcels with essentials like socks and underwear sent by relatives could now get through to Germany on the scale of up to four a year. Replacement uniforms and boots were also sent out, the Allied authorities eventually deciding that prisoner needs and the propaganda value of well-dressed British and Commonwealth servicemen moving about within sight of ersatz-clad

Germans outweighed trying to make the enemy live up to its obligations. (In addition to providing inadequate replacement clothing, the Nazis had started to take sheepskin flying-boots and jackets away from RAF prisoners in an effort to provide winter wear on the Eastern Front.) Kriegies no longer had to look like beggars. 'It was really great to be properly dressed as British soldiers once more', Gunner Albert Paice recalled.[25]

The resulting transformation in appearance and outlook for those who had been living on the verge of collapse was dramatic. 'Young men became young men once more, backs straightened, drooping shoulders were raised, heads were lifted again', as Welsh Guardsman John Elwyn put it. 'The pleasure of a little extra food, good British food, with a smoke to follow was absolute joy visible on every face,' another BEF man remembered, 'and at last we had something to smile about.' Sergeant Collins, returning to Lamsdorf in 1941, was struck by the change from 1940. 'Gone were the hangdog stances of the ragged and starving, the moods and suspicions that erupted into bitter fights, the deaths rooted in hunger and misery. Men sported brand new battledress and boots. Faces were fuller.'[26]

Just as important, at least from a psychological point of view, was a noticeable improvement in the mail situation. It took time for the International Committee of the Red Cross in Geneva to receive, process, and forward prisoner registration information, and—as with parcels—for a new mail route to be worked out. By late 1940 and on into early 1941, however, most of those men already taken were beginning to receive letters from home and being allowed to send up to four postcards and two letters a month. Subsequently a combination of proportionately fewer new names to deal with (even when POWs were taken and transferred en masse, as in the spring of 1941 and the autumn of 1943) and greater practical experience meant that prisoners could reasonably expect mail to arrive within six weeks of dispatch. This link with home was a huge boon, especially for men who had heard nothing for many months.

'The first letter from one's family was terrific', Lieutenant-Commander P. N. Buckley remembered. 'I am right on top of the top of the world now,' Signalman Gordon Manners scribbled in his diary on 7 December 1940 after receiving mail from his family, 'now that I know for certain that they know what has happened to me, and I know that they are safe and well—as although the letters were written three months ago they are just as good as if they were written yesterday!' First letters only stoked anticipation for more. As RAF Sergeant Richard Pape explained:

Mail from home was our greatest joy; the token of reality in an insane and unreal world. Whenever mail from home came into the barrack for distribution a rallying yell penetrated to every corner, a clarion call of 'Mail up!... Mail up!' by the Barrack Commander. Confusion and noise abruptly ceased and as if by magic a tense silence gripped the 180 men. Precious letters from wives, mothers, sweethearts, from those near and dear, were handed out. Hard countenances and grim expressions relaxed, anticipatory feelings too strong to conceal appeared.

'These letters [from home] were a comfort and a blessing,' wrote Lance-Corporal K. J. Bowden; 'I really can't find adequate words to describe what they meant to me.' Major Jack Poole was unequivocal in his Eichstätt memoirs: 'Mail day was a golden one.'[27]

General news was also more accessible in the middle war years. New prisoners found themselves deluged with questions upon arrival in main camps.[28] Special coded war situation reports sent out in the mail to camps by MI9 were not a success. 'Only a very few officers remarked on the value of the news letters,' a post-war report on the situation at Oflag VIB (Warburg) concluded, 'and all seemed to be of the opinion that although the letters were welcomed, most of the information contained therein was usually too out of date to be of very much interest.'[29] This was because, especially in the main camps, POWs were able to obtain up-to-date news through the use of illicit radio sets tuned to the BBC.

Parts with which to build crystal or valve receivers were improvised, stolen, or obtained through barter with guards or civilians (cigarettes and the luxury contents of Red Cross parcels often proving an irresistible lure). Sometimes entire radio sets were smuggled into camps, great care being taken to keep them hidden from the German security people while *in situ* or when the inhabitants were moved from one place to another. Though a number of receivers were eventually discovered, most oflags and stalags, along with the Luftwaffe and Kriegsmarine camps, soon possessed at least one and usually several secret sets in cunningly designed hides. Those responsible for radio news, driven by the same security concerns, tended to develop similar patterns. While a careful watch was kept for roaming guards, someone would take down the BBC news in shorthand during the short time the set would be switched on. Copies of the bulletin in longhand would be made, and these would subsequently be passed along and read out—before being destroyed—in each barrack. The situation in the sergeants' compound at Barth was fairly typical:

Our radio was a masterpiece of ingenuity [wrote Richard Passmore]. Our highly skilled radio mechanics used the most everyday things in the construction of the innards of their gadget. Condensers were made by interleaving India-paper Bibles with the metallic foil of a particular brand of cigarettes. Coils were wound to specification, using stolen wire . . . Components which could not be contrived were smuggled in from the outside, using a mixture of bribery and blackmail. Each night a small squad extricated the 'canary'—our code-name— from its current place of concealment, assembled the various bits, tuned in to the BBC European service, took down the news in shorthand and carefully packed the set away again. The following day three copies of the news were made. Each block was allocated a newsreader who went from room to room, while scouts kept watch at doors and windows.

Down to the end of 1942 the news was often far from good, but access to a trusted information source lifted spirits enormously. 'It was a great morale booster', Sergeant McGee recalled of the radio news at Hohenfels. Held at Stalag IVB in 1943–4, Corporal John Greenwood found that the BBC reports 'used to cheer us up immensely'. Pilot Officer Martin Smith, recalling life behind the wire in Stalag Luft III, went even further: 'Without this outside contact I'm sure we would all have gone crazy.'[30]

The relatively stable situation between 1941 and 1944 allowed POWs to think ahead more than had been the case in the past about matters both corporeal and mental. Lean-but-not-starving bodies and better spirits meant that activities previously often felt to be too difficult could now be undertaken.

In addition to sports (discussed in the next chapter) non-working Kriegies—mostly officers, aircrew of all ranks, and senior NCOs— were now in a position to engage in a certain amount of physical exercise without running the risk of collapse. Compulsory drilling was occasionally instituted and parole walks were sometimes allowed. In hutted camps of all types there was always what RAF types dubbed 'circuit bashing' (i.e. strolling round the perimeter multiple times).[31]

There was also a fair amount of attention paid to acquiring one of the consumable luxuries the Red Cross did not provide, namely alcohol. Prisoners in one or two places, using their meagre earnings converted into special currency (*Lagergeld*), could on rare occasions buy weak beer or cheap wine in addition to the more commonly available range of shoddy combs, hair oils, shaving gear, tooth powders, and various knick-knacks stocked in main camp canteens. Rather more common was the practice of mixing sugar or illicit yeast in with mashed-up fruits or vegetables (anything from Red Cross raisins to ersatz jam) to create a 'brew' that would be allowed to sit and, hopefully, ferment. More ambitious types went a stage further and constructed secret stills from used tins, stolen piping, and various metal containers, using similar ingredients to boil up liquids of often very high alcoholic content. The goal, in many cases, was to have something with which to celebrate Christmas and New Year's Eve. Errors and after-effects aside, 'Kriegie Brew' or 'Jungle Juice' seemed to yield the desired result when swallowed—i.e. near-immediate inebriation. In the north compound at Stalag Luft III the stuff available on Christmas Eve 1943 was so potent that, according to Flight Lieutenant Geoffrey Willatt, 'drunks wandered around for three days!'[32]

A decent Red Cross parcel supply was also a precondition for another common activity: trading. Prisoners, especially those who worked, sometimes had the opportunity to barter items rarely seen in the wartime Reich. Real soap, chocolate, coffee, tobacco, and sugar could be parted with in exchange for fresh eggs and extra bread offered by civilians or even guards (who might also be blackmailed into providing even more *Verboten* items such as passes, real money, and maps). In the bigger camps there would often be enterprising prisoners who would set themselves up as shopkeeper middlemen in domestic trade in which cigarettes served as currency. While supplies lasted 'the rackets' could play a quite positive role in camp life. Non-smokers, obviously, were in a position to sell their tobacco issue for something else; but in theory anyone who wanted an item (a razor, perhaps) could shop for it by trading some item they did not need (say an extra watch) for cigarettes, that could in turn buy what was wanted. 'With enough cigarettes,' one Lamsdorf entrepreneur boasted, 'anything except freedom could be bought.'[33]

Matters of the mind and spirit were also explored. In material ways those interested in organized worship were best off in the middle war years. Space was set aside in many of the main compounds for a chapel that might become, as one RAF sergeant put it, 'the centre of camp life'. Bibles and hymnbooks arrived through the post, and chaplains were allowed more freedom to move about and minister to men both in main and satellite camps. 'In some camps I found flourishing Christian fellowships', Salvation Army Major Fred Hill reported. Some of the padres, moreover, proved that they could fully live up to their vocation in the secular sphere. Father Philippe Gadreault, for example, was widely admired in Stalag Luft III. 'His relationship with the prisoners was mostly one of easy, informal comradeship', Kingsley Brown later wrote admiringly. 'He never preached [figuratively speaking]. He spent most of his days sitting in on bull sessions, swapping stories, chatting about the news and answering the not infrequent questions about religion and philosophy. He enjoyed no special privileges, [and] shared our privations.' A protestant padre by the name of Ledgerwood was equally admired for his work at Stalag XVIIIA. 'He was such a good sport,' Eric Fearnside recalled. 'On his way to take Communion on a Sunday it was typical of him that he would see perhaps four or five Australians playing pitch and toss and he would sit on the ground and play with them, then persuade all of them to come to Communion.' Those who refused repatriation as a non-combatant in order to stay with their flock had a tremendous moral impact. 'These visiting Padres were certainly saints', Private W. J. Sudworth argued from the perspective of men in satellite camps. 'They travelled all over the country with a solitary German guard, braving the dangers of rail travel [after Allied bombing started in earnest], just to bring us a little comfort. They were always cheery and nothing ever got them down. We truly appreciated their visits.' OKW was less enthusiastic, noting that after sermons the working prisoners tended to become less docile. Methodist chaplain Douglas Thompson, among others, found himself temporarily banned from preaching for having 'incited the men to unrest'.[34]

For non-working POWs, at least, there was also the opportunity to expand one's mind. In the middle war years educational activity developed into one of the major features of Kriegie life in many main camps. The first major attempt at developing a teaching programme had started at Oflag VIIC in the dark days of 1940. Officers were invited to lecture on their pre-war interests and hobbies, which in practice could mean anything from a foreign language to bee-keeping. As a means of passing the time, what was eventually dubbed the 'University of Laufen' was a great success, but, as with a similar programme in the NCOs' compound at Barth, suffered from a lack of essentials such as writing material and, above all, texts. Books of any kind were a rarity in the early months, and consisted almost exclusively of novels that the prisoners themselves had had on their person at the time of capture. Amongst RAF non-commissioned aircrew at Stalag Luft I there were only five books among 450 men. 'A paperback book was like a bit of gold dust', Private Frank Pannett remembered of Lamsdorf in this period, going on to remark that those who possessed one had to be careful it was not stolen.[35]

The resumption of the parcel flow, however, allowed for books to be sent from England, and with time sometimes quite extensive camp libraries were built up from the over a quarter-million volumes dispatched through the Red Cross and YMCA. In addition arrangements were made with various professional bodies to allow for prisoner-students to engage in a programme of study, along with courses put together with the help of the Universities of London and Oxford, both culminating in matriculation-level or pre-professional standard exams. By the spring of 1944 over 250 official subjects could be studied, a figure which does not include the topics brought up in organized debates and one-off lectures. Progress tended to be stronger among officers and non-working NCOs, who had more time and ended up with more resources than the rank-and-file Kriegie. At Oflag 79, for instance, an estimated 60 per cent of the camp was involved in one course of study or another by late 1944. But even in the main stalags it was still possible, as one corporal put it, to hear lectures or debates on virtually 'everything under the sun'. Studying helped ease the acute boredom of life inside the wire, and with books and courses increasingly available, the number of prisoners officially recorded as studying rose from 450 at the end of 1940 to over 13,000 in the late summer of 1944. The success rate in exams was 75 per cent, with the occasional feat such as that of a captain in the Gordon Highlanders who studied then sat for, and was *in absentia* called to, the Bar.[36]

There was also a fair amount of spontaneous and, more occasionally, staged political debate. These discussions tended, in very rough terms, to mirror the leftward shift in British public attitudes that occurred during the war, and ranged from 'guilty men' outrage to mildly reformist sentiment. 'Why should we take any further risks to maintain titled layabouts, stock-exchange gamblers, and chair-borne warriors and other rich parasites in the positions which, they would have us accept, were theirs by divine right?' Sergeant Richard Passmore raged inside Stalag Luft I in 1941. Meanwhile Marxism was being seriously discussed across the way in the RAF officers' compound at Barth, and a year or two later questions such as 'Should the Public Schools be Abolished?' were being debated among the mostly hostilities-only officers held at Stalag Luft III. 'We have been having a number of lectures and debates on social reform and the Beveridge Plan', Captain Roger Mortimer, a professional officer in the socially exclusive Coldstream Guards who had been captured in 1940 wrote to his father from Eichstätt in February 1944:

most people are pretty progressive except for one or two hide-bound landowners and a few R.C.'s. I think many of the reforms are long overdue and to oppose them would be short-sighted and ungenerous, and perhaps a cause of serious trouble. Certainly the Conservative party will almost certainly cease to exist if it continues to show such half-hearted enthusiasm for what is a general and reasonable demand.

Forced contact with more recently captured middle-class officers with temporary commissions, argued James Chutter, a senior South African chaplain, was exposing even upper-class professional soldiers to unaccustomed ways of thinking about society. At Brunswick the result was the popular sponsorship of a Boys' Club in the East End. Meanwhile in the stalags and Arbeitskommando camps middle-class lads were living cheek-by-jowl with working-class veterans of the dole queue, resulting (at least sometimes) in a similar sense that change was necessary. A mock by-election held at Wolfsberg produced a result in which the Conservative representative came dead last behind the Labourite, the Liberal, and even the Communist candidate. 'I found myself able', Donald Edgar remembered of his time at Hohenfels, '. . . to foresee a flowering of a better society after the war—if we would only take some action when we returned. Perhaps I was doing my bit in a P.O.W. camp towards the landslide victory of the Labour Party in 1945!'[37]

Whether or not those concerned thought about politics as such or racked up a professional qualification, reading, lectures, classes, and debates all helped to pass the time and combat mental stagnation. 'Having missed out on a university career,' Derek Bond wrote of his time at Moosburg, 'I found it very stimulating and enriching.'[38]

In comparative terms, therefore, POW life in the Greater Reich was better in the middle war years than it had been in 1940 (or, as we shall see, would be again in 1945), thanks largely to the re-establishment of a lifeline to the United Kingdom. But it would be a grave error to imagine that being a Kriegie was ever anything other than hard. There were still plenty of factors that could make daily existence inside the wire very tough indeed.

For one thing, the official German ration scale was reduced by one-third starting in December 1941, on the premise that the contents of Red Cross parcels would more than make up the difference in calories. Both parcels and letters, however, did not always arrive regularly or in sufficient quantity even in good years. There were systemic shortages due to the breakdown of one of the chartered cargo ships sailing between Lisbon and Marseilles, and then due to the main supply route having to be switched to Gothenburg after Marseilles became a war zone. There were also gaps, sometimes lasting a month or more, whenever prisoners were transferred en masse from one camp to another. Sometimes the supply could not keep up with the increase in a camp's population, as happened at Stalag Luft III in early 1942. 'We often felt slightly giddy when we got up too suddenly', wrote Oliver Philpot. At other times there was no obvious explanation for an interruption that was none the less all too real. 'The issue of Red Cross parcels was by no means a regular, weekly ritual', Sergeant Bill Jackson took pains to point out in reference to his time in the RAF compound at Lamsdorf in 1943. 'There were breaks of many weeks when we had to depend solely on the meagre German rations only.' Early in 1944, to take another example, there was a serious shortage at Hohenfels. Arbeitskommando camps, meanwhile, had to rely on the staff at the main stalag to send along parcels and mail with regularity. Due to the administrative complexities involved in keeping track of thousands of men in hundreds of big and small satellite camps—plus some occasional corruption on the part of certain racketeers and guards—this did not always happen. 'I had learned from my own experience', explained one Company Sergeant Major in reference to conditions in the summer of 1941 after nine months *Arbeitskommando* work administered through Stalag XXB, 'that many of the [several hundred] working parties scattered throughout Prussia and Poland would undergo long stretches with no Red Cross food or clothing...' According to Charles Baker, it took two years for the first Red Cross parcels to reach the small working party to which he was attached via Thorn, and there is evidence to suggest that some other groups never received any shipments at all. Fred Hill, visiting the satellite camps of Stalag IVF (Hartmannsdorf) in his capacity as a Salvation Army representative, came to a little place where the men were almost too weak to carry the coffin of one of their fellows who had just expired. 'They were thin and ill, and wore old Russian clothes', he noted with horror. 'Holes were in their boots and they had no underclothing. Even my guard said he had not seen Englishmen in such a state.'[39]

The danger of a sudden shortfall made it necessary to keep a proportion of food parcels at the main camps in storage, which in turn meant that it was comparatively rare for prisoners to receive the designated rate of one parcel per week even in the fat years. The Red Cross reckoned that half a parcel plus rations would suffice to maintain health. From the start Kriegies had formed what were variously dubbed 'combines', 'syndicates', or 'messes', in which groups of men pooled their food resources and culinary efforts in order to make the most of meals. Later on in many camps fuel-efficient 'blowers' or 'stoofas' (hand-cranked forced-air water boilers) or, more rarely, 'throbbers' (illicit immersion cookers tapped into the camp electricity supply) were developed that provided more flexibility in the all-important 'brewing up' process. Tins were fashioned by metal-bashers into a variety of productive eating and cooking utensils when, as was often the case, the German issue of spoons, plates, pots, and other essentials proved inadequate. In one or two camps POWs were allowed to develop vegetable gardens or raise rabbits to supplement their meagre diet. Despite all this, however, the wretchedness of camp rations and the relative scarcity of Red Cross parcels made hunger a continual and major factor in Kriegie life. Matters were perhaps worst for heavy smokers, who in times of shortage might trade bread for cigarettes ('a cigarette was more of a pacifier than a piece of bread, mentally', Arnold Hanes later commented on his choice of tobacco over food at Heydekrug), but everyone suffered. Ron Mackenzie, an Australian airman, reckoned that he lost a stone in weight each year between 1941 and 1944. 'The overwhelming preoccupation of every prisoner was with food', Colonel W. H. Bull, a New Zealand medical officer, rightly observed, and stealing—often dealt with summarily by the men affected rather than by the camp leader—continued to occur.[40]

What was true of food was also true of clothing. Replacement uniforms and footwear did not always get through in a timely fashion, and German quartermasters could be niggardly about handing out new articles from stores. The occasional Guardsman might go to great lengths to keep up appearances, but many prisoners grew used to appearing more slovenly than they perhaps realized, in a mixture of service dress, private clothing, and German-issue foreign uniform parts and clogs.

Oliver Philpot, observing his fellow airmen on their way to Sagan in 1942, was forced to admit that standards had fallen somewhat. 'Had anyone ever seen such a down-at-heel lot as we were?' he wrote. 'We wore odd coats and jackets, different sorts of shirts; some had ties, most didn't; some had hats, some didn't; all were dishevelled and filthily dirty. We all had young beards.' With both soap and washing facilities in short supply, a change into a clean outfit became a rare occurrence, as Pilot Officer Stephen Johnson explained in his diary: 'There are two methods of attacking the problem [of clothing hygiene]. Firstly one can wash one's clothes as soon as they become dirty and so keep them all clean. Secondly one can let them all get very dirty and wash a minimum number when one wants to put on clean clothes. This is by far the most popular method.' One or two Kriegies gave up the battle entirely, neither washing nor—given the razor shortage—shaving. Combined with the dark, cluttered, and generally warren-like appearance of barrack-blocks without partitions, the visual effect (not to mention the smell) could be quite shocking to newly captured aircrew. 'Jesus!' Geoff Taylor remembered one new arrival exclaiming on entering a hut at Stalag IVB (Mühlberg): 'where's Fagin?' Nor was scruffiness exclusively an RAF phenomenon. The Second Earl Haig, as noted in the previous chapter, was dressed down in Oflag XIIB (Hadamar) at one point by General Fortune because of his not-atypical less-than-smart turnout. 'We had never bothered about our personal appearance,' Tommy Calnan later reflected, 'we were always scruffy and untidy and made no attempt to dress correctly.'[41]

Medical provisions and equipment sent by parcel were welcome, and on occasion German doctors could help to develop first-class treatment. Much of the time, however, not enough medicine and instruments arrived through the Red Cross, camp sickbays and hospitals were often lacking in everything from X-ray machines to anaesthetics, only a small percentage of working prisoners would be permitted to go sick at any one time, and British MOs were placed in the unenviable position of restricting access to the few beds available. Necessary operations might be delayed, could take place without the right kind of anaesthetic or specialist, and drugs and ointments used simply because that was all there was available. 'It was not unknown for an aching tooth to be yanked out unceremoniously without anaesthetic, general or local,' medical orderly H. L. Martin recorded, 'and I once witnessed the removal of a circular piece of sequestrium (detached bone) from the centre of a man's skull with no more than a pair of long forceps and a very strong surgeon's wrist!' At one point staff at a hospital attached to Stalag IXC were reduced to picking rose-hips because there were no vitamin tablets with which to help working prisoners suffering from tuberculosis, an increasingly deadly disease. RAMC doctors and other captured medical personnel, with the help of their more sympathetic German counterparts inside the Reich, worked tirelessly to keep the mortality rate down to about 5 per cent. But some Stabsärzte were incompetent or unhelpful ('any results we had were achieved largely in spite of him', Dr D. L. Charters noted in reference to the German placed in charge of one hospital), treatment was necessarily limited, and otherwise preventable deaths did occur in the middle war years.[42]

Letters were always awaited eagerly, but not infrequently as the war dragged on could contain news that a sweetheart or wife had taken up with another man. Such 'Dear John' notes, better known to air force prisoners as 'messpots' (from similar missives received by RAF types serving in Mesopotamia in the 1920s), caused a good deal of anguish. A sense of being one among many, as when it became a de facto camp policy to make the contents of such letters known to all, thus making them the subject of much grim and sardonic collective humour, could sometimes help. Though a few men were apparently indifferent and others put on a great show of bravado, there is no question that news of this kind was for the majority of recipients a serious blow to morale. 'It was a really callous thing to do,' Geoffrey Vaughan thought, 'to tell a man in captivity that all his hopes and waiting had been in vain.' Suicides sometimes resulted.[43]

News bulletins produced less extreme, but still sometimes negative, reactions. It was good to know what was happening, but down to the end of 1942 much of the information was bad. Some Kriegies could maintain a degree of detachment—'[f]or three years the war was just a large scale Radio thriller', RAF pilot Robert Kee recalled—but for most the progress of the war (and by extension how long they were likely to remain captive) was a subject of intense personal interest. 'When the news was good our spirits rose accordingly', as an officer at Luft III put it. 'When the news was bad we were sometimes rather depressed.' The prevalence of rumour as well as BBC-drawn fact added to uncertainty and swings between optimism and despair. The D-day landings of June 1944 raised hopes that prisoners would be home for Christmas; but then such hopes were dashed by news of enemy success, first at Arnhem and then in the Ardennes. 'Morale sank to an all time low,' Gunner Bernard Piddleston observed of his working party, 'I've never seen prisoners of war so disheartened as they were then.'[44]

The manufacture of wine, beer, and spirits, though overall a positive contribution to the psychological well-being of prisoners, also had a down side. While drunk, a man could exercise dangerously poor judgement (as when an RAF prisoner decided to pay a visit to another compound and tried to climb over the intervening wire). Crashing hangovers the morning after were inevitable; and in a limited number of cases the effects of home-made alcoholic beverages could be far worse. By inadvertently poisoning themselves Kriegies could go blind, insane, or even die. The dangers involved were vividly illustrated to one group of would-be distillers at Stalag Luft IV, after their ultimate concoction was left overnight in a tin washbasin. 'The whole area around our bed was damp and smelled vaguely of disinfectant', Sergeant

Herbert Woolley related. 'I picked up the basin. It was pitted and corroded, full of tiny pinprick-sized holes.' Little wonder that in at least two camps the senior British MO fully supported the German ban on amateur alcohol.[45]

Trade, meanwhile, although meeting certain individual needs and a significant sign that small material surpluses existed, had its own problems. Especially in times of relative scarcity—that is, when parcels were not coming through—free-market capitalist trade within camps led to suspicions of sharp practice and price gouging by those in 'the rackets', as well as serious cigarette-currency inflation.[46] Combined with pressure from escaping officers for the camp authorities to exert control of trade with guards as a means of efficiently obtaining needed escape equipment, this could produce sometimes successful calls for price controls or the outright 'nationalization' of internal and/or external trade in the bigger camps. At Oflag VIIC (Laufen) and Oflag XXIB (Schubin), for instance, a fixed points system was developed, while at Stalag Luft I the SBO audited the traders' books in the last year of the war and insisted on each block having a designated trade representative. At Stalag Luft III (Sagan) a non-profit management system was eventually imposed. In some of the army stalags, however, the impression remained that racketeers were prospering at the expense of ordinary Kriegies.[47]

The influence of organized religion in the middle war years was perhaps not as great as was sometimes imagined. Cyril Scarborough, a Catholic chaplain who eventually ended up at Colditz, argued that 'it's a mistake to think that POWs are good at practising their religion—they're not'. As far as services went the numbers tended to decline to normal (i.e. civilian) levels in times of relative prosperity. 'A cynic once remarked to me that the attendance at our church services was inversely related to the number of parcels arriving in the camp', an observation to which Church of England chaplain David Head had no satisfactory response. Padres tended to become popular because of their self-sacrifice rather than as a result of pure godliness. Conversely, whatever their spiritual state, they could be despised if they appeared to place their own physical comfort ahead of their flock's needs, as apparently happened on occasion at Lamsdorf.[48]

There were also limits to expanding the mind while behind barbed wire. Some POWs worried that paying too much attention to texts could result in a warped sense of reality and be the first step on the path to losing one's mind. A rather more obvious problem was that working prisoners—meaning the majority of Kriegies—usually did not have either the time or, spread out as they usually were in satellite camps, the resources to undertake courses of study at all. For the exam system to work, furthermore, the mail had to be fairly regular, and flexibility (i.e. a willingness to tailor what was done to the circumstances in a particular place) had to be shown by the examining bodies concerned. Unfortunately this was not always the case, as Arthur Gibbs, a medical orderly at a POW hospital attached to Stalag IXC, found out:

In the latter half of 1942, I had written to the School of Accountancy asking for a correspondence course in preparation for the Certified Accountants examinations. At the same time I wrote to the New Bodleian [Library], Oxford, asking for a correspondence course in shipping. The School of Accountancy wrote advising me to apply directly to the Certified Accountants Association to request exemption from the preliminary examination covering general subjects... The Association duly received my letter and sent a form to complete which I returned in March 1943—so that by this time 9 months had elapsed. The New Bodleian had replied saying that they were sending a book on Shipping Law and a Pittman's Shipping course. These arrived in June 1943 via the British Red Cross who had posted them in October 1942!

While sheer numbers allowed for courses to be taken other than solo in the bigger camps, lack of space meant that there were few places to read and work quietly: 'there is always noise', Martin Lidbetter complained in a letter home from Stalag VIIIB in April 1942.[49]

Crowding was in fact a more general difficulty. Lacking any personal privacy and living on top of one another for weeks, months, and then years, even the most tolerant individuals could eventually feel claustrophobic and grow irritable. 'Sometimes you would find yourself hating all the other men in your room with a great and all-destructive loathing', an officer at Sagan remembered. 'You would lie on your bunk and think of each man in turn and remember his particular nasty habits and the shortcomings which you could bear no longer.' Kriegies did their best to be tolerant of each other's foibles, but over time this became more and more difficult. Heated arguments could break out over the most trivial of questions, and solo time in cells for one *Verboten* activity or another might even be welcomed. 'I suppose in an ordinary life to be given ten days solitary confinement in the cooler would be a nasty experience', Dick Churchill, another Luft III prisoner, reflected in a television interview. 'If on the other hand you were always in a room with six or eight people, then you had peace and quiet for once, it wasn't such a hardship at all.'[50]

Captivity could take a serious psychological toll over time. Everything remained the same day after day, there was nowhere to go, and time passed excruciatingly slowly. For those without the inner resources to find ways to fill their waking hours—anything from reading and games to working on escape schemes—the tediousness of Kriegie life behind the wire could weigh heavily. 'If you have never had the experience you can never imagine what it is like to get up in the morning to face a long empty day with nothing whatever to do except what you do yourself', an officer captured in 1940 commented.[51] Some men lived from day to day, trying not to think about how much longer they would be behind the wire. Other long-term Kriegies, though, especially non-working men, could find it harder and harder as time went on to avoid becoming withdrawn and seriously depressed. 'I would stand on parade during roll call,' Canadian air gunner Andrew Cox later wrote of his worst bout of low spirits, 'snow pelting into my face and a biting, arctic wind blowing through my unbuttoned vest, not feeling the cold, just wishing that my life would end...' Other men simply turned their face to the wall and refused to emerge from under their blankets for days or weeks other than for *Appell*.[52]

The true extent of the problem may never be known. 'One continually heard stories of people who had "gone round the bend"', Guy Morgan wrote of life at Marlag (O), 'but who, on closer inquiry, turned out to be exhibiting no more than harmless eccentricity.' Morgan himself thought that the incidence of mental illness was actually lower behind the wire than in wartime civvy street, and a study based on discharge figures compiled by the Department of Army Psychiatry suggested that Kriegies were in fact less likely to suffer from hysteria and manic-depression than their free counterparts. On the other hand, the line between eccentricity and madness could be a fine one, especially given that mental illness was something many preferred to ignore. The same army study found a much higher percentage of anxiety neurosis among POWs. While many sufferers managed to pull themselves together, others found the strains of captivity too much and in effect lost their minds.[53]

Some of these men were eventually repatriated in the course of the war, but sometimes too late for effective treatment and—as with the physically crippled—too few in number. Disputes between the respective governments over how many POWs should be included in particular exchanges and over treatment of prisoners, along with routing difficulties, meant that only four transfers occurred relatively late in the war (October 1943, March and September 1944, and January 1945). Worries over numerical reciprocity and the fear that some cases were in fact sane men trying to wangle a ticket home meant that a fair number of truly ill prisoners remained behind wire. Though men who became seriously delusional or depressive were often hospitalized or watched over by their fellows, it was not always possible to prevent desperate men from hanging themselves, cutting their own throats, or—as happened in several camps—suddenly climbing the wire in full view of guards under orders to shoot.[54]

Improvements in the middle war years, in short, tended to be relative. What was more, conditions sharply deteriorated in the last six months or so of the war. The intensification of Allied bombing of the Reich and consequent ever-more serious disruption of the transportation network meant that it was harder and harder to maintain the supply of the all-important parcels to the camps. Local food supplies were increasingly under strain, and fuel sources practically vanished in the last winter of the war. The sight of massed formations of Allied aircraft was good for morale, as was the end of fighting coming into sight. There were growing concerns, though, that Hitler might order the execution of POWs, especially aircrew, in a last act of desperate vengeance rather than allow prisoners to be liberated. And in the meantime an increasingly acute shortage of parcels, food, and fuel, combined with the influx of prisoners from the periphery into the contracting centre of the Third Reich, meant that life was again becoming very precarious.

Arbeitskommandos were often the first to feel the pinch. Geoffrey Vaughan, out on one of the working parties from Lamsdorf, found that by the end of 1944 rations had been cut by a quarter, and by early 1945 the all-important Red Cross parcels had ceased to arrive entirely. In a satellite camp attached to Mühlberg, another soldier recalled, the Red Cross parcel supply 'dropped from once a fortnight to once a month, and eventually to none at all'. Those in the main camps also suffered as reserves ran low. By February 1945 there were no parcels left at Stalag IIIA (Luckenwalde). The camp population had ballooned to 16,000, rations were more and more meagre, and dysentery was rife. There was virtually nothing that the camp doctors could do, and in the opinion of one observer everyone 'was slowly starving'. In Hohenfels men were once more blacking out on parade and spending most of their time in bed trying to endure the combination of acute hunger and cold. By the end of 1944 at Oflag 79 there were no Red Cross parcels and daily rations consisted of little more than a cup of acorn coffee, two thin slices of black bread, two small boiled potatoes, and a bowl of thin soup. Not surprisingly, cases of famine oedema began to appear in early 1945. In

Oflag VA (Weinsburg), where conditions remained better longer than in many other camps, Lieutenant A. F. Powell nevertheless noted that between April 1944 and January 1945 he lost twenty-three pounds in weight over and above what he had shed after capture back in 1941. Everywhere the price of cigarettes as well as Red Cross food items had shot up astronomically as outside sources dried up. 'Two colonels and a padre were admitted to hospital suffering from malnutrition,' Philip Kindersley noted, 'simply because they had exchanged what little food they had for cigarettes.'[55]

Dwindling supplies and increasing privation also led to more stealing. Those caught might find themselves up on a charge before the senior man and awarded punishments such as close confinement for several weeks. Most of those caught, however, were dealt with summarily and rather more harshly by their fellows. In practice this meant being beaten up, dumped in a cesspit, and/or flogged. As an officer who admitted to having stolen potatoes later wrote, what happened was a 'situation brought about by continuous and unbroken hunger', and showed 'vividly the moral deprivation one can suffer as a result of acute malnutrition'.[56]

What then of Colditz? As in other spheres, the experience of prisoners at Oflag IVC with regard to body and soul was a mixture of the typical and the unique.

British officers did not begin to arrive at this Sonderlager until late in 1940, by which time the shortages brought about by the events of the spring and summer had begun to abate. The first Red Cross issue arrived by Christmas ('The excitement had to be seen to be believed', Pat Reid reported), and by the time ICRC delegates inspected the camp in the spring of 1941 the German rations, similar in composition to those elsewhere, were dubbed 'sufficient but not abundant'. Though the supply was sometimes intermittent, enough Red Cross parcels arrived to allow for at least between one and two parcels per person every three weeks. 'With regard to Red X parcels the camp is remarkably well stocked,' Lieutenant Michael Riviere assured his mother in a letter dated April 1944, 'stuff has been pouring in from Switzerland over the last few months, & we have supplies till the end of September.' Small vegetable plots on the castle slope were also eventually sanctioned. Even before tins of cigarettes began to arrive in the usual large quantities, prisoners at Colditz who were truly desperate could buy Junaks from the canteen. Though the weak beer that could be purchased in the early months soon disappeared, a number of enthusiastic officers acting solo or in combination built brewing apparatuses and constructed stills. Using bottles, tins, boxes, and bits of lavatory piping enterprising men were able to produce alcoholic concoctions such as 'firewater' or 'jam alc' that aided in making occasions such as Christmas and New Year's Eve in captivity merrier affairs than they would otherwise have been: they 'had an enormously good effect', Peter Storie-Pugh commented. As elsewhere domestic trade soon began to flourish.[57]

Basic medical care was adequate at Colditz, with several RAMC doctors and medical orderlies in residence along with a German MO to oversee the camp sick quarters, and a system in place whereby serious cases could be transferred elsewhere for treatment. At times, indeed, there was a veritable surfeit of physicians. 'Four doctors and two dentists,' Geoffrey Ransom wrote in a letter sent home in March 1944, 'in a camp of 200 odd are not needed on medical grounds!' Most of the medical personnel had ended up at Colditz because they were troublemakers rather than because of a pressing need for physicians. But while in theory certain individuals were not recognized as camp doctors by the German authorities, they nevertheless continued to dispense medical advice and examine patients. The overall result was quite positive. 'On the whole the physical health amongst the officers was very good', Dr Ion Ferguson observed.[58]

Spare uniform parts were at first in very short supply at Oflag IVC, but by early 1941 enough parcels were getting through to allow for the issue of liberal amounts of clothing as and when required. Most members of the British contingent, however, apparently encouraged by Colonel German, continued to dress rather like vagabonds. 'It was common for a Britisher to appear on parade', Pat Reid recounted in his first book, '... wearing a woollen balaclava or no cap at all, a khaki battledress blouse, blue R.A.F. or red Czech army trousers, home-knitted socks of any colour, and trailing a pair of clogs on his feet.' This puzzled other nationalities, but was in keeping with the general lack of attention and respect paid to the Germans by the British on *Appell*. 'Though many of them were distinguished soldiers,' Earl Haig noted on his arrival at Colditz, 'the variety of their dress showed they did not suffer from regimentation.'[59]

Letters—which had to be diverted for each new arrival—were allowed in and out on the usual scale. As far as news was concerned, British prisoners at Colditz were at a disadvantage for the first twenty months in not having their own secret radio set. 'Whenever a new arrival came into the gates he was assailed for news', Corran Purdon noted. However, information was relayed by the French contingent, which had radio receivers, and in the summer of 1943 a set was passed over when the French were cleared out. Taking care to keep its location a secret, those responsible for the radio introduced a version of the standard procedure for the taking down and dissemination of war information. 'The feeling of being in touch with the outside world through the reception of the B.B.C. news broadcasts and other broadcasts', a summary report on Colditz asserted, 'was of inestimable value in maintaining morale throughout the period.'[60]

Religious needs were generally well catered for at Colditz, there being both a Church of England and a Methodist chaplain in residence from early on and a purpose-built chapel in which to worship (though this was closed in the summer of the third year owing to the discovery of a tunnel). Catholics received communion at Polish or French services until the winter of 1943, when a Roman Catholic chaplain took up residence. Education also took hold. By 1941 lectures were under way, a good library was being built up, and needed equipment was arriving courtesy of the YMCA. 'Most prisoners accepted their fate,' thought Peter Allan, '[and] got down and studied.' Debates—sometimes of a political nature—were set up, and as elsewhere, professional examinations could eventually be taken. At least one officer at Colditz qualified as a chartered accountant.[61]

Despite all this, and a tendency on the part of several former residents to portray their time there as cheerful and uplifting, it should not be thought that being a prisoner at Oflag IVC was akin to successive terms in a particularly boisterous public school. Life was still very difficult, and though physical conditions were better than in many places, there were aspects to the experience that were just as bad—sometimes even worse— than in other POW camps.

'"Never a dull moment"', Pat Reid wrote in his first book, 'might well have been the motto on the armorial bearings of Oflag IVC.' For some prisoners, certainly, there was enough activity within the walls for them to claim that they were never at a loss for something to do and always possessed an optimistic outlook. 'I was never bored', Hugh Bruce categorically stated in an interview, while Jimmy Yule claimed that his and most others' morale in Colditz was 'absolutely wonderful' right down to the last days of the war.[62]

This was not true, however, of everyone. Food, for one thing, remained a major preoccupation and a gnawing problem. German rations in this camp were poor in quality throughout the war, with little in the way of green vegetables and no fresh milk. Red Cross parcels staved off actual starvation, but the desire for food remained. In March 1941 Ellison Platt recorded in his diary that an officer had been caught hoarding bread at the expense of his messmates. Pat Reid, on reviewing the situation in Colditz after his own escape, had to admit that without enough vitamins and protein men became 'physically weak' and that many 'took to their beds for long periods of the day'. Using cigarettes and chocolate from parcels, POWs were able to bribe guards for eggs, onions, and other extra food items, but demand was so great on the British side that massive inflation soon occurred. In early 1944 the SBO ordered that free trade should cease and enforced strict price controls through a designated quartermaster. This was the right thing to do, but it was not greeted with universal enthusiasm. Since the basic problem (scarcity) still persisted, there were those who continued to trade il-legally. 'You are always hungry,' Billie Stephens later wrote, 'which means that you spend most of your time thinking about food.'[63]

There were activities and pastimes that could fill in the empty hours. But these were sometimes dangerous, not available, or difficult to stick to. The alcohol created at Colditz had the usual after-effects in terms of crashing hangovers. Padre Platt noted down a sign posted on the med-ical inspection room door the day after a particularly raucous drinking party: 'If any British officer thinks he feels worse than the MOs, will he please visit them in their room.' The stuff could also be on occasion quite toxic—'it took the fillings out of your teeth', as Corran Purdon put it. One officer developed serious cirrhosis of the liver from drinking the fluid he had distilled, while others went temporarily blind. 'I stored it in an enamel mug, one of my most valued possessions,' Miles Reid wrote of some raisin wine he had gotten a hootch-king to distil in 1944, 'but it ate its way through both a crack in the enamel and the iron underneath and luckily leaked away in my cupboard before I could poison myself by drinking it for Christmas.' Little wonder that Colonel Tod came to take an extremely dim view of hootch celebrations.[64]

The opportunities to move about and stretch one's legs in Colditz were very limited, what with the prisoners' courtyard being only about the size of a tennis court, the outside exercise field often being closed off because of escape attempts, and parole walks being restricted. Though less crowded than in many oflags, prisoners in Colditz were still living in very close proximity to one another: so much so that, even if no blow-ups occurred in quarters, there were those who found a few days or a week or two in cells a welcome break. 'One really quite relished the peace and quiet and having a room to oneself', Gris Davies-Scourfield explained.[65]

In some respects harmony was easier to maintain at Colditz than at other camps because the population was small and the background and outlook of prisoners were more uniform than elsewhere. Practically every officer there had demonstrated a marked antipathy to quietly sitting out the war—hence their presence in the Schloss. Most were youngish men captured in the first years of the war, with many shared experiences. 'Of course, the other thing you've got to remember is this,' Hugo Ironside stressed in an interview, 'that the majority of us had been to public schools.' Haig, tellingly, found Colditz rather more socially exclusive than other camps: 'I did find a very large percentage amongst the British people there who came from my own walk of life', he explained; 'the whole atmosphere was very much, you know, the country gentleman set up.' Though the men of Colditz were individualists to a man, and collectively quite unregimented (at least compared to their peers elsewhere), a common background and attitudes did produce a dominant—though perhaps largely unconscious—system of values that alienated the few truly odd men out.[66]

Birendra Nath Mazumdar was not the only doctor to be sent to Colditz for complaining too much about the poor medical conditions in POW camps, and once there not allowed to practise. But he was the sole Indian prisoner to darken the doors of the castle, and—partly as a result of his own fierce independence and nationalist sympathies—soon began to feel excluded and looked down upon by Anglo-Indian officers in particular and much of the camp population in general. Life became so 'unbearable' for Mazumdar at Oflag IVC that he staged a successful hunger strike to force the Germans to transfer him elsewhere.[67]

The Methodist chaplain Ellison Platt, despite his initial enthusiasm, eventually grew disenchanted with some of his fellow prisoners. Other padres at Colditz recognized that matters of the spirit did not necessarily take precedence over matters of the flesh. But Platt refused to turn a blind eye to what he saw as 'perverted' pseudo-erotic activity (see following chapter): 'he was censorious of much of our behaviour, and said so!' Tommy Catlow recalled. Platt, needless to say, considered 'excitable' in his turn, had not been to boarding school.[68]

There was also a minority who disliked the prevailing Tory political ethos. Both by background and temperament, most prisoners at Colditz appeared out of sympathy with the left-wing trend in politics. 'Many had been prisoners since 1940', wrote Michael Burn, along with Giles Romilly one of the few openly pro-Left POWs; 'it cannot have been pleasant to have some smart newcomer instructing them that England had changed, was changing, and ought to be changed more.' A Marxist study group and public lectures on the virtues of Socialism were tolerated, but only just. While some of the more retrograde opinions of certain titled officers might give rise to vocal derision during well-attended debates on, say, the future of the monarchy or the Beveridge Report, the overall political atmosphere at Colditz was apparently far from radical. 'I was told that one senior British officer forbade his subordinates to attend,' Burn recalled, 'and that another wished to have me tried for treason after the war.' Little wonder that the fictionalized account of life as a Kriegie that Burn wrote while at Colditz is filled with alienation.[69]

Whatever one's politics, study could be difficult, especially for the restless. Ennui was still hard to avoid—'there were still times when you were absolutely bored', admitted Jack Best. The war news, meanwhile, might be 'pretty bleak', as Mike Harvey put it, and there was of course the uncertainty—particularly tough on restless and energetic young men feeling left out of things—as to when exactly it would end. The winter of 1943–4 was particularly trying on morale. 'Our cross is the curse of waiting', read the heartfelt opening line of the last verse of a poem written by Alan Campbell while incarcerated at Colditz.[70]

As the war dragged on year after year a proportion of the inhabitants of Colditz—by that very fact more restive than most prisoners—were having trouble coping mentally with captivity within the walls of the Schloss. The proportion of officers who sat and passed exams in 1943–4 was much lower than in other places, suggesting that organized study was less of a balm at Oflag IVC than in most other officer camps.[71] Dr Ion Ferguson reported that while physical health was generally sound, in very many cases 'mental health bordered on the psychotic side of normal behaviour'. There were at least four officers who became unbalanced enough to be hospitalized, and several others who teetered on the edge of insanity. 'I suddenly realised I was going round the bend,' Jack Best remembered, after which 'I took myself, metaphorically, off to the corner of the room, and gave myself a good dressing down.' Not all were able to cope alone, however, and a characteristically British tendency to ignore the realities of psychiatric illness did nothing to help. One officer tried to hang himself, while the sudden dash to scale the wire in the exercise park that resulted in the shooting death of Mike Sinclair in September 1944 was widely regarded—albeit perhaps erroneously—as the product of a spontaneous breakdown in reason. 'I remember seeing one chap going demonstrably off his rocker at an appell (roll call),' Jack Champ recalled, 'crying and pleading with the guards to shoot him.'[72]

Matters were not made easier by the extreme reluctance on the part of OKW to allow one of the mixed medical commissions that chose suitable cases for repatriation from among the severely ill or wounded to visit Colditz. Only twelve months before the end of the war did a visit occur, and even then Colonel Tod had to push hard for all worthy cases to be examined. Not all those passed by the Swiss doctors, moreover, were allowed to go home.[73]

Things became worse for everyone in the winter of 1944–5. It was clear that the war was not going to be over by Christmas. The supply of Red Cross parcels slowed and then stopped altogether. Daily rations declined to an estimated 1,300 calories—'a diet that would ensure loss of weight even if one were just lying in bed all the time', according to dentist Julius Green—and then to an estimated 1,000 calories. Starvation loomed, and it was not uncommon for prisoners to be seen scouring the cookhouse rubbish for possible edibles. 'After we'd peeled a turnip,' as orderly Syd Smith put it, 'we used to peel the peelings.' Suspicions grew that some men were getting more food than others, and there was mounting concern that Hitler might order the execution of the prison population—all *ipso facto* defined as enemies of the Reich—rather than see them liberated. Anxiety levels rose considerably in the last months, even as morale increased.[74]

All in all, prisoners at Oflag IVC enjoyed most of the same benefits and suffered many of the same body-and-soul hardships as their counterparts elsewhere. There was an unusually strong sense of camaraderie among the 'bad boys' of Colditz—at least down to 1943—but morale did at times suffer, and sheer restlessness meant that prolonged captivity was probably harder to bear psychologically for Schloss inmates than it was for the average Kriegie. Bottled-up stress could not be worked off through physical labour, since under the Geneva Convention officers were considered gentlemen and therefore above menial work. But, as we shall see, the men of Colditz could and did play hard.

Notes

1. On rations in 1939–40 see e.g. Sydney Smith, *Wings Day* (London, 1968), 31. On Red Cross parcels via Belgium see Hilary St George Saunders, *The Red Cross and the White* (London, 1949), 29.
2. See C. W. Jervis, *The Long Trek* (Elms Court, 1993), 14–15; Ewart C. Jones, *Germans Under My Bed* (London, 1957), 23; Sam Kydd, *For You the War Is*

Over... (London, 1973), 105; Adrian Vincent, *The Long Road Home* (London, 1956), 49; SPM, S. Watson; see also Robert W. Calvey, *Name, Rank and Number* (Lewes, 1998), 7.

3. IWM, W. A. Harding, 16–17; see e.g. IWM (Rolf), H. S. Bowers, 3–4; Arthur Evans, *Sojourn in Silesia* (Ashford, 1995), 18; Len Williamson, *Six Wasted Years* (Braunton, 1985), 14; SPM, S. Watson.

4. Donald Edgar, *The Stalag Men* (London, 1982), 16; see also e.g. Graham Palmer, *Prisoner of Death* (Wellingborough, 1990), 67–70. On work counterbalancing rations see e.g. IWM, O. Dover, 5. For a more positive assessment on rations outside main camps see e.g. Robert Gale, *Private Prisoner* (Wellingborough, 1984), 44.

5. On summary retribution for stealing see e.g. IWM (Rolf), R. Low, 7; Gale, op. cit., 37. Quotes: IWM, W. A. Harding, 29; Ed Annetts, *Campaign Without Medals* (Lewes, 1990), 38; J. Roberts, *A Terrier Goes to War* (London, 1998), 42. In theory German rations provided about 1,500 calories per day (Noel Barber, *Prisoner of War* (London, 1944), 25–6, 82). In fact the average caloric intake in 1940 was less than this total (see e.g. B. A. James, *Moonless Night* (London, 1983), 29), a total which in any case was below what German depot troops received. ICRC, *Report of the International Committee of the Red Cross on its Activities During the Second World War (September 1, 1939–June 30, 1947): Vol. I, General Activities* (Geneva, 1948), 254.

6. Sandy Hernu, *Q* (Seaford, 1999), 50; Jim Rogers, *Tunnelling into Colditz* (London, 1986), 34. Stealing also occurred at Laufen. See http://web.mala. bc.diaries/letters.images/stokes/collection.page.htm, D. Stokes diary, 6–13 July 1940.

7. J. M. Green, *From Colditz in Code* (London, 1971), 54; B. A. James, op. cit. These rations were, in fact, less substantial than non-working German civilians were receiving.

8. See I. Schrire, *Stalag Doctor* (London, 1956), 53, 57–8, 59; Betram Bright, 'Blinded and a Prisoner of War', *Blackwood's*, 257 (1945), 246; A. C. Masterson, in Tony Strachen (ed.), *In the Clutch of Circumstance* (Victoria, BC, 1985), 121; Annetts, op. cit., 39; Kydd, op. cit., 123–4; Eric Williams, *On Parade for Himmler* (Hull, 1994), 10–11; IWM, H. E. C. Elliott, 18; IWM, R. P. Evans, 35; George Beeson, *Five Roads to Freedom* (London, 1977), 10.

9. IWM, A. N. L. Munby diary, 19 July 1940.

10. Stuart Brown, *Forbidden Paths* (Edinburgh, 1978), 51; CSVA 4, K. Lockwood.

11. IWM, R. P. Evans, 34; John Elwyn, *At the Fifth Attempt* (London, 1987), 39; IWM, A. N. L. Munby diary, 18 July 1940.

12. See John Brown, *In Durance Vile* (London, 1981), 36; Edgar, op. cit., 22; B. A. James, op. cit., 32. On *The Camp* see IWM, O. Dover, 15; IWM, G. R. Manners, 18; IWM (Rolf), H. S. Bowers, 3; ibid., E. B. Davis, 21; Kydd, op. cit., 110; Maxwell Bates, *A Wilderness of Days* (Victoria, BC, 1978), 83; Vincent, op. cit., 66; Roberts, op. cit., 80. On its usefulness for non-reading purposes see e.g. IWMSA 5831/2, R. Buckingham; http://www.naval-history. net/WW2MemoirAndS009.htm, J. Siddall, 1. On rumours see e.g. IWM, L. B. Shorrock, 94.

13. IWMSA 4827/4, R. Loder; IWM, G. B. Wright diary, 30 June 1940.

14. IWM, G. R. Manners diary, 21 Aug. 1940; IWM, D. Swift, 31.

15. Richard Passmore, *Moving Tent* (London, 1982), 75.

16. See Douglas Collins, *P.O.W.* (London, 1970), 53; John Castle, *The Password is Courage* (London, 1955), 42.

17. John Elwyn, *At the Fifth Attempt* (London, 1987), 34; Collins, op. cit., 19. On the senior officer at Laufen see IWM, H. C. F. Harwood, III; also IWMSA 4847/2, C. L. Irwin; David Wild, *Prisoner of Hope* (Lewes, 1992), 18. On morale at Laufen in general see IWM (Rolf), C. L. Irwin; IWMSA 4827/4, R. Loder. On defeatist talk at Spangenberg see IWM, J. W. M. Mansel diary, 14 Feb. 1941, 21 Feb. 1941.

18. See e.g. James Stedman, *Life of a British POW in Poland* (Braunton, 1992), 12; Williamson, op. cit., 17.

19. W. H. Bull in David McGill, *P.O.W.* (Naenae, NZ, 1987), 93. On the parcel work of the British Red Cross see St John Saunders, op. cit., ch. 3. On the international dimension see ICRC, *Report of the International Committee of the Red Cross on its Activities During the Second World War (September 1, 1939–June 30, 1947): Vol. III, Relief Activities* (Geneva, 1948).

20. Frank Taylor, *Barbed Wire and Footlights* (Braunton, 1977), 84.

21. Palmer, op. cit., 137; Henry Veis Suggitt, *Reluctant Guest of the Reich* (London, 1992), 44; Vincent, op. cit., 16; J. Roberts, op. cit., 52–3; Kydd, op. cit., 110, 131; Collins, op. cit., 5; Jervis, op. cit., 16–17; Edgar, op. cit., 58; Elwyn, 40; IWM, J. E. Platt diary, 7 Nov. 1940; IWM, A. N. L. Munby diary, 10 July, 21 July 1940; IWM, C. G. King, 49. On the problems faced by the Red Cross see St John Saunders, op. cit., 30–1; David Rolf, ' "Blind Bureaucracy": The British Government and POWs in German Captivity, 1939–45', in Bob Moore and Kent Fedorowich (eds.), *Prisoners of War and their Captors in World War II* (Oxford, 1996), 50–2.

22. Elvet Williams, *Arbeitskommando* (London, 1975), 43; Gale, op. cit., 47; Edgar, op. cit., 58.

23. David James, *A Prisoner's Progress* (Edinburgh, 1947), 27. On the life-versus-death issue see e.g. Oliver Philpot, *Stolen Journey* (London, 1950), 102; A. Robert Prouse, *Ticket to Hell via Dieppe* (Toronto, 1982), 43; Passmore, op. cit., 102. On the cutting of German rations see ICRC, *Report of the International Committee of the Red Cross on its Activities During the Second World War (September 1, 1939–June 30, 1947): Vol. I, General Activities* (Geneva, 1948), 255.

24. Stedman, op. cit., II; Edgar, op. cit., 58; T. D. Calnan, *Free As a Running Fox* (London, 1970), 56.

25. Albert Paice and Alwyn Ward, *For the Love of Elizabeth* (privately printed, 1984), 32.

26. Collins, op. cit., 77; IWM, O. Dover, 8; Elwyn, op. cit., 40.

27. Poole, op. cit., 164; IWM, K. J. Bowden, 109; Richard Pape, *Boldness Be My Friend* (London, 1953), 155; IWM, G. R. Manners, 39; IWMSA 4759/5, P. Buckley.

28. See e.g. IWMSA 4759/5, P. Buckley; IWMSA 5194/4, J. Laurie; IWMSA 4933/2, W. Reid; John Chrisp, *The Tunnellers of Sandborstal* (London, 1959),

63; John Fancy, *Tunnelling to Freedom* (London, 1957), 76–7; John D. Harvie, *Missing in Action* (Montreal, 1995), 126, 129; ; F. A. B. Tams, *A Trenchard 'Brat'* (Edinburgh, 2000), 105–6; Geoff Taylor, *Piece of Cake* (London, 1980 edn.), 135; Calton Younger, *No Flight from the Cage* (London, 1981 edn.), 22.

29. PRO, WO 208/3290, p. 9.

30. Martin Smith, *What a Bloody Arrival* (Lewes, 1997), 124; IWMSA 4767/4, J. Greenwood; IWM (Rolf), J. M. McGee, 11; Passmore, op. cit., 120–1. On sets and distribution elsewhere see PRO, WO 208 camp reports. See also e.g. William James Hunter, *From Coastal Command to Captivity* (Barnsley, 2003), 76. On radio news helping morale see e.g. WO 208/3281, 11; IWMSA 4847/3, C. L. Irwin; ibid. 15608/1, W. Stevens.

31. On circuit bashing see e.g. IWMSA 15587/2, E. Boyd. On drilling see e.g. IWM, G. R. Manners, 18. On parole walks see PRO, WO 32/9912.

32. Geoffrey Willatt, *Bombs and Barbed Wire* (Tunbridge Wells, 1995), 57.

33. Ike Rosmarin, *Inside Story* (Cape Town, 1990), 52. On trade shops inside camps see e.g. Kingsley Brown, *Bonds of Wire* (Toronto, 1989), 142–3; Robert Garioch, *Two Men and a Blanket* (Edinburgh, 1975), 118–19; M. N. McKibbin, *Barbed Wire* (London, 1947), 43–4. On outside trade see e.g. IWM (Rolf), W. J. Sudworth, 18; Derrick Nabarro, *Wait for the Dawn* (London, 1952), 35; Maxwell Leigh, *Captives Courageous* (Johannesburg, 1992), 141. On cigarettes as currency see also e.g. Harry Levy, *The Dark Side of the Sky* (London, 1996), 112.

34. Douglas Thompson, *Captives to Freedom* (London, 1955), 142, 147–8, 151; Vasilis Vourkoutiotis, 'The German Armed Forces Supreme Command and British and American Prisoners-of-War, 1939–1945: Policy and Practice', Ph.D. thesis, McGill University (2000), 106–7; IWM (Rolf), W. J. Sudworth, 16; Eric Fearnside, *The Joy of Freedom* (Burton-in-Kendel, 1996), 74–5; K. Brown, op. cit., 107–8; Fred Hill, *Prisoner of War* (London, 1994), 158; Leslie Le Souef, *To War Without a Gun* (Perth, WA, 1980), 213; Passmore, op. cit., 110. On the development of organized worship in main camps see PRO, WO 208, PP and RC reports. The better padres, it should be noted, usually tended to try to avoid openly antagonizing the German camp authorities. Cf. e.g. PRO, WO 224/27, PP report on Stalag VIIIB, Aug. 1941, p. 4, and IWM, N. R. Wylie collection, CSM Fulton, 'Organisation of Stalag XXB from the point of view of prisoners of war', 3, with WO 224/45, PP report on Stalag XVIIA, 3 June 1942, p. 4.

35. IWMSA 4830/2, F. Pannett; Passmore, op. cit., 67. On the situation at Barth see PRO, WO 208/3282, pt. 2, p. 6. On the early days at Laufen see e.g. IWMSA 4893/5, M. Champion Jones; ibid., 4847/2, C. L. Irwin; IWM, A. N. L. Munby diary, 26 June 1940; http://web.mala.bc.ca/davies/letters. images/stokes/collection.page.htm, D. Stokes diary, 4–11 Aug. 1940.

36. St John Saunders, op. cit., 43–4; IWM, G. W. Smith, 59; IWMSA 4767/6, J. Greenwood.

37. Edgar, op. cit., 165, 162–4; Chutter, op. cit., 163; Jane Torday (ed.), *The Coldstreamer and the Canary* (Langley, 1995), 114 (see also St Clair, op. cit., 235–7); Philpot, op. cit., 181 (see also Thompson, op. cit., 167); Passmore,

op. cit., 139–40. On the Wolfsberg mock election see Fearnside, op. cit., 60–1. On the Boys' Club see IWM, A. R. Prebendary, 4 ff.; *The Times*, 28 Apr. 1945. On the influence of socialism at Sagan see e.g. Tom Slack, *Happy Is the Day* (Penzance, 1987), 103–4. For even more radical sentiment see e.g. IWM, A. F. Gibbs, 87–88. There were, of course, as Mortimer's letter suggests, still conservatives about. Micky Burn, for example, experienced hostility to his left-wing talks at Spangenberg; (Michael Burn, *Turned Towards the Sun*, (London, 2003), 152), though Victor Fortune refused to censor him, while at Stalag Luft I (Barth), for instance, John Dodge, a pre-war Tory candidate, made no secret of his pro-capitalist views (B. A. James, op. cit., 54), and the majority of RAF prisoners were outraged when news reached them of the coal-miners strike in June 1944. 'A few voices spoke in the miners' favour, saying that a right to strike was one of the freedoms for which we were fighting', Ron Mogg recalled. 'They were shouted down by the majority whose opinion was that there was a time and place for everything and it was certainly not in the middle of a bitter life-and-death struggle.' Victor F. Gammon, *Not All Glory!* (London, 1996), 177. For a tentative assessment of Kriegie political sentiment see David Rolf, 'The Education of British Prisoners of War in German Captivity, 1939–1945', *History of Education*, 18 (1989), 264–5.
38. Derek Bond, *Steady, Old Man!* (London, 1990), 154–5.
39. IWM, N. R. Wylie box, CSM Fulton report, 'Organisation of Stalag XXB', 1; Hill, op. cit., 159; IWM, C. Baker, 9; Bill Jackson, *The Lone Survivor* (North Battleford, Sask., 1993), 48 (see also H. I. Irwin, in Holliday, op. cit., 120); Philpot, op cit., 123. On OKW cutting rations once Red Cross parcels arrived see Vourkoutiotis, op. cit., 88. On the importance of Red Cross parcels and the negative effect of interruptions see e.g. Guy Morgan, *Only Ghosts Can Live* (London, 1945), 120–1.
40. McGill, op. cit., 93; Ron Mackenzie, *An Ordinary War* (Wangaretta, Victoria, 1995), 60; A. Hanes, in Daniel G. Dancocks, *In Enemy Hands* (Toronto, 1990 edn.), 88. On stealing and punishment in the middle war years see e.g. IWMSA 4767/4, J. Greenwood; Neville Chesterton, *Crete Was My Waterloo* (London, 1995), 63; Frank Taylor, *Barbed Wire and Footlights* (Braunton, 1988), 57; H. E. Woolley, *No Time Off for Good Behaviour* (Burnstown, Ont., 1990), 36. On ongoing vigilance over the division of rations see e.g. Harry Buckledee, *For You the War Is Over* (Sudbury, 1994), 31. On blowers see e.g. George Dunning, *Where Bleed the Many* (London, 1955), 47. On the throbber see e.g. Philip Kindersley, *For You the War Is Over* (Tunbridge Wells, 1983), 172. On combines see e.g. IWMSA 6142/2, J. Deans. On tin-bashing see e.g. Stephen P. L. Johnson, *A Kriegie's Log* (Tunbridge Wells, 1995), 132. On making an effort to appear spic-and-span see e.g. George Clifton, *The Happy Hunted* (London, 1954), 341. On vegetable gardens see e.g. IWMSA 4759/4, P. Buckley. On rabbits see e.g. McKibbin, op. cit., 34–5. See also Vourkoutiotis, op. cit., 84–5, 206.
41. Calnan, op. cit., 314; Earl Haig, *My Father's Son* (London, 2000), 128; G. Taylor, op. cit., 132; Johnson, op. cit. 152, 157–8; Philpot, op. cit., 116.

42. D. L. Charters, *Medical Experiences as a Prisoner of War in Germany* (Liverpool, 1946), 4, 11 ; IWM, H. L. Martin, 28. On the death rate see John R. Pritchard and Sonia Zaide (comps.), *The Tokyo War Crimes Trial* (New York, 1981), vi., fr. 12863. On medicine and equipment shortages see e.g. David Kidd, *POW!* (Pontefract, 1986), 10, 28; Calnan, op. cit., 198–9; Clive Dunn, *Permission to Speak* (London, 1986), 107; John Borrie, *Despite Captivity* (London, 1957), 102; John Burton, *Mirador* (London, 1986), 44; Green, op. cit., 65; Mackenzie, op. cit. 75. On TB see IWM, A. F. Gibbs, 81, 144; George Moreton, *Doctor in Chains* (London, 1980 edn.), 148. On German reluctance to expend resources on POW treatment see e.g. PRO, WO 208/3274, App. D, p.6; Norman Rubenstein, *The Invisibly Wounded* (Hull, 1989), 47; IWM, D. W. Luckett, 46; IWM (Rolf), J. M. McGee, 10c; IWM, H. L. Martin, 78, 89, and *passim*. On the experience of RAMC doctors in captivity, both positive and negative, see e.g. PRO, ADM 1/18696, pp. 3–5; Burton, op. cit.; Charters, op. cit.; Ion Ferguson, *Doctor at War* (London, 1955); Le Souef, op. cit.; Schrire, op. cit. On making hard choices about who to look at see e.g. Edgar, op. cit., 43; Schrire, op. cit., 78, 83; E. Jones, op. cit., 257. On specialists in one branch of medicine having to try their hand at another see e.g. Charters, op. cit., 12; http://www.pegasus-one.org/pow/bruce_jeffrey.htm, B. Jeffrey letter to mother, 5 Dec. 1944; Marmaduke Hussey, *Chance Governs All* (London, 2001), 47. On patient appreciation of MO efforts under difficult conditions see e.g. IWM, D. Swift, 64; IWM (Rolf), F. A. Robertson, 7; Robert Harding, *Copper Wire* (Dublin, 2001), 106; R. Thomas, op. cit., 258. On patient condemnation see e.g. IWM (Rolf), H. S. Bowers, 9. British doctors carried out four-fifths of operations on POWs in Germany. See IWM (Books), Harold Satow, *The Work of the Prisoners of War Department During the Second World War* (Foreign Office, 1950), 21, 23–4.
43. Geoffrey Vaughan, *The Way It Really Was* (Budleigh Salterton, 1985), 54.
44. IWMSA 4661/3, B. Piddleston; Johnson, op. cit., 167; Robert Kee, *A Crowd Is Not Company* (London, 1982 edn.), 70. On D-day and the later dashing of hopes see IWM, G. F. Warsop, 187; Percy Wilson Carruthers, *Of Ploughs, Planes and Palliases* (Arundel, 1992), 152; William W. Hall, *Flyer's Tale* (Braunton, 1989), 25; Francis S. Jones, *Escape to Nowhere* (London, 1952), 241–2; Poole, op. cit., 171; Ward, op. cit., 146–7. On rumours drawn from wishful thinking see e.g. IWMSA 4830/5, F. Pannett. Rumours were, it should be noted, sometimes based on fact. See e.g. Imelda Ryan (comp.), *POWs Fraternal* (Perth, WA, 1990), 115.
45. Woolley, op. cit., 142. On the ban see IWM, R. P. Evans, 50; McKibbin, op. cit., 59; Brickhill, op. cit., 136. On blindness and insanity see IWM, I. P. B. Denton, 35–6; Chesterton, op. cit., 79; Roger V. Coward, *Sailors in Cages* (London, 1967), 154; Elwyn, op. cit., 104; R. Thomas, op. cit., 253; Vincent, op. cit., 115. On drunks wandering into the wire see e.g. Harvie, op. cit., 174. On deaths see J. Brown, op. cit., 49–50; F. Jones, op. cit., 263.
46. See e.g. Gant, op. cit., 92; Moreton, op. cit., 107; Barbara Broom (comp.), *Geoffrey Broom's War* (Edinburgh, 1993), 120; IWM, R. P. Evans, 42;

Robert Garioch, *Two Men and a Blanket* (Edinburgh, 1975), 124, 150–1. On the problems of nicotine addiction see e.g. Dancocks, op. cit., 88–9.

47. See e.g. Garioch, op. cit., 124, 150–1; Johnson, op. cit., 149; Leigh, op. cit., 141. On the fixed points system see IWMSA 4827/3, R. Loder; Williams, *Tunnel*, 124–5. On Luft I see PRO, WO 208/3283, pt. iv, 5; Barry Keyter, *From Wings to Jackboots* (London, 1995), 236. On Luft III see WO 208/3283, pt. I, 5. The War Office supported the nationalization of external trade for escaping purposes. See M. R. D. Foot and J. M. Langley, *MI9* (London, 1979), 106–7.

48. Moreton, op. cit., 93–4, 99–100, 198; David H. C. Read, *This Grace Given* (Grand Rapids, Mich., 1985), 106; IWMSA 4820/1, C. Scarborough. On fine padres see e.g. http://www.naval-history.net/WW2MemoirAndS009.htm, H. J. Siddall, 24; Le Souef, op. cit., 213; Edward Howell, *Escape to Live* (London, 1947), 48; A. Passfield, *The Escape Artist* (Perth, WA, 1988), 100.

49. Martin H. Lidbetter, *The Friends Ambulance Unit 1939–1943* (York, 1993), 91; IWM, A. F. Gibbs, 123; See e.g. Wild, op. cit., 65, 67. On concerns about study and mental stability see B. James, op. cit., 81; Tams, op. cit., 108; Williams, *Tunnel*, 115 ff. On difficulty concentrating see e.g. David Walker, *Harry Black* (Cambridge, Mass., 1956), 107.

50. D. Churchill in *The Great Escapes of World War II: 1. The Great Escape* (Greystone Productions, 1997); Johnson, op. cit., 167. On crowding causing irritation see e.g. Alan Mackay, *313 Days to Christmas* (Glendaurel, 1998), 27 On the pressures of close living see e.g. IWM, J. W. M. Mansel dairy, 7 Feb. 1941. On efforts to avoid confrontation see e.g. Buckledee, op. cit., 29. On welcoming time alone see e.g. IWMSA 6178/1, J. Bristow; http://www.awm.gov.au, A. D. Crawford, TS tape 2 side A. Not everyone, of course, liked solitary, especially after a few days. See e.g. CSVA 8, J. Best.

51. A. J. Barker, *Behind Barbed Wire* (London, 1974), 88.

52. Bond, op. cit., 147; Andrew B. Cox, *Our Spirit Unbroken* (Port Elgin, Ont., 1999), 38. On living from day to day see Vincent, op. cit., 168.

53. F. A. E. Crew, *The Army Medical Services: Administration, Vol. I* (HMSO, 1953), 450; Morgan, op. cit., 134–5 (see also R. Thomas, op. cit., 197). On not taking mental illness seriously enough see e.g. IWMSA 4432/8, H. Gee.

54. On suicide attempts see e.g. IWMSA 13573/3, A. Jones; Younger, op. cit., 62. On the growth of mental problems over time see e.g. PRO, WO 208/3294, p. 2; Moreton, op. cit., 207; J. E. Pryce, *Heels in Line* (London, 1958), 187–8.

55. Kindersley, op. cit., 180 (see also Le Souef, op. cit., 326); IWM, A. F. Powell, ch. 8, p. 3; Sandy St Clair, *The Endless War* (North Battleford, Sask., 1987), 239; Le Souef, op. cit., 224–5; Davies, op. cit., 148; IWM, T. Tateson, op. cit., 50; Vaughan, op. cit., 59–61. On the effect of shortages on medical treatment in this period see e.g. WO 208/3257, p. 8.

56. St Clair, op. cit., 240; See e.g. A. Partridge, *That Split Eternal Second* (London, 1995), 101.

57. P. Storie-Pugh in *The Colditz Story* (Classic Pictures, 1993); Reid, *Colditz Story*, 90–1; LC, M. Riviere letter, 11 Apr. 1944; PRO, WO 224/69,

ICRC report on visit, 13 May 1941, p. 1. On rations see Reid, *Colditz Story*, 90–1. On alcohol and trade see ibid. 169–72, 189; P. R. Reid, *The Latter Days* (London, 1953), 129–31; IWMSA 4432/5, H. Gee; M. Reid, op. cit., 79; Michael Farr, 'Chateau Colditz', in Reinhold Eggers (comp.), *Colditz Recaptured* (London, 1973), 116–17; Margaret Duggan (ed.), *Padre in Colditz* (London, 1978), 82, 228, 233, 251. On Junaks see CSVA 4, K. Lockwood.

58. Ferguson, op. cit., 131–2; NRO, MC 695/12, 40, 14 Mar. 1944; see PRO, WO 208/3288, pp. 17–18; WO 224/16, *passim*.

59. Earl Haig, *My Father's Son* (London, 2000), 130; Reid, *Colditz Story*, 124; see WO 208/3288, p. 69; Reinhold Eggers, *Colditz* (London, 1961), 28; Green, op. cit., 125; Henry Chancellor, *Colditz* (London, 2001), 59.

60. PRO, WO 208/3288, p. 69; Purdon, op. cit., 56; see CSVA 3, J. Yule; LC, T. Catlow, 71.

61. CSVA 7, P. Allan; see LC, T. Catlow, 73; PRO, WO 208/3288, p. 16; Green, op. cit., 122.

62. CSVA 2, J. Yule; IWMSA 1697/5, H. Bruce; Reid, *Colditz Story*, 19, 166; see e.g. Rogers, op. cit., 97; IWMSA 16797/5, H. Bruce; CSVA 10, P. Fergusson; IWM, W. L. Stephens, 51; CSVA 7, P. Allan; J. Best in *The Colditz Story* (Castle Pictures, 1993).

63. IWM, W. L. Stephens, 19; Reid, *Latter Days*, 25; Duggan, op. cit., 87–8; see LC, POW item 12, H. Bruce, 'Lingering Thoughts'; *The Guardian Weekend*, 13 Mar. 1993, p. 28. On trading see PRO, WO 208/3288, p. 7; Reid, *Latter Days*, 133; Michael Burn, *Yes, Farewell* (London, 1946), 403–4.

64. M. Reid, op. cit., 79; C. Purdon in *Escape From Colditz: 3. Eureka!* (Windfall Films, 2000); Duggan, op. cit., 234. There were also, of course, massive hangovers. See e.g. Reid, *Latter Days*, 131.

65. E. G. Davies-Scourfield in *The Colditz Story* (Classic Pictures, 1993); see Duggan, op. cit., 171, 268; CSVA 7, P. Allan. On the negative effects of crowding see Lord Harewood, *The Tongs and Old Bones* (London, 1981), 61; Jack Champ and Colin Burgess, *The Diggers of Colditz* (Sydney, 1985), 136; IWMSA 17896/2, W. C. Purdon; ibid. 10643/2, P. L. E. Welch. Jimmy Yule, on the other hand, testified that 'in the entire time I was a POW I think I only saw one chap lose his temper'. CSVA 2, J. Yule. On limits to exercise see PRO, WO 208/3288, p. 15.

66. LC, Earl Haig interview transcript, tape 2, page 7; CSVA 11, H. Ironside; see IWMSA 4432/6, H. Gee; Chancellor, op. cit., 247; *The Times*, 11 Apr. 1995, p. 15. On unity of outlook and background see Airey Neave, *They Have Their Exits* (London, 1953), 63; CSVA 7, P. Allan; J. Best in *The Colditz Story* (Classic Pictures, 1993); IWMSA 16797/3, H. Bruce; id. 6376, E. G. B. Davies-Scourfield; CSVA 4, K. Lockwood. Though see also LC, T. Catlow, 56; CSVA 8, J. Best.

67. IWMSA 16800/2–3, B. N. Mazumdar; see Ferguson, op. cit., 130–31.

68. IWMSA 9893/6, M. Champion-Jones; LC, T. Catlow, 66; IWM, J. E. Platt diary, 22 Apr. 1941, 18 Nov. 1941, 6 Dec. 1941.

69. Michael Burn, *Farewell to Colditz* (London, 1974 edn.), preface, p. v (though see also *The Times*, 11 Apr. 1995, p. 15, and *Observer Colour Supplement*, 3 Nov. 1974, p. 29, in which Burn indicates that, at least among his

upper-class messmates his radicalism was tolerated to a surprising degree); See *Yes, Farewell*, 430 and *passim*.; Edwin L. Robinson, *We Fell On Stony Ground* (Lewes, 1998), 103, 111–12; LC, T. Catlow, 74. Cyril Scarborough, the Roman Catholic chaplain, evidently took exception to the atheistic bent of those who argued for a Brave New World. See C. P. Scarborough, 'Utopias', in J. E. R. Wood (ed.), *Detour* (London, 1946), 32–3.

70. Alan Campbell, *Colditz Cameo* (Ditchling, 1954), 25; M. Harvey in *The Colditz Story* (Classic Pictures, 1993); CSVA 8, J. Best; see IWMSA 10643/3, P. L. E. Welch; Giles Romilly and Michael Alexander, *The Privileged Nightmare* (London, 1954), 89; Burn, *Yes, Farewell*, 27; Ferguson, op. cit., 135. On the winter of 1943–4 see PRO, WO 208/3288, p. 17. On (repeatedly dashed) expectations that the war would soon be over see the predications in the 1943–4 letters of Geoffrey Ransom: NRO, MC 695/12/23, 27, 40, 43, 45.

71. BL, BRC, Educational Books Section, *Results of Examinations, Prisoners of War Camps, 1 July–31 December 1943* (Oxford, 1944); ibid., *January 1–June 30, 1944* (Oxford, 1944). Geoffrey Ransom, for one, was evidently worried that too much study might be a recipe for mental imbalance. NRO, MC 695/12/43.

72. Champ and Burgess, op. cit., 11; CSVA 8, J. Best; Ferguson, op. cit., 131–2; see Chancellor, op. cit., 214; IWMSA 9247/3, M. Burn; ibid., 4432/5, 8, H. Gee; PRO, WO 208/3288, p. 18; IWM, J. E. Platt diary, 10–11 Feb. 1941, 6, 8 Aug. 1942, 21 Feb. 1943, 19 June 1943; Chrisp, op. cit., 163; André Perrin, *Évadé de guerre via Colditz* (Paris, 1975), 121. On the public-school tendency to ignore madness see IWMSA 4432/8, H. Gee; Chancellor, op. cit., 215–16.

73. Reid, *Full Story*, 232–5. This was tough not only on the mental cases but also on those with severe physical disabilities for which proper treatment could only be received in the UK. See e.g. IWMSA 4816/5, M. Moran, discussing the case of Dan Hallifax. On the mixed medical commissions see ICRC, *Report of the International Committee of the Red Cross on its Activities During the Second World War (September 1, 1939–June 30, 1947): Vol. I, General Activities* (Geneva, 1948), 386.

74. *Guardian Weekend*, 13 Mar. 1993, p. 28; Green, op. cit., 146; see Harewood, op. cit., 56; Burn, op. cit., 403–4; W. Morrison in *The War Behind the Wire, Part II: The Road to Colditz* (Hartswood Films, 2000); Haig, op. cit., 134; Walter Morrison, *Flak and Ferrets* (London, 1995), 176; Rogers, op. cit., 188; LC, T. Catlow, 66; IWMSA 16797/5, H. Bruce; IWMSA, 4816/7, M. Moran; IWMSA, 10771/1, J. Courtnay; CSVA 4, K. Lockwood; A. Siska, in *Colditz Society Newsletter* 3: 27 (Jan. 2002), 8. On weight loss see also http://www.awm.gov.au, A. D. Crawford, TS tape 1 side A.

6 Work and Play

Belligerents may employ as workmen prisoners of war who are physically fit, other than officers or persons of equivalent status, according to their rank and their ability.

(from Article 27, Geneva Convention, 1929)

Belligerents shall encourage as much as possible the organization of intellectual and sporting pursuits by the prisoners of war.

(from Article 17, Geneva Convention, 1929)

The single most significant difference in the POW experience of other ranks, as against that of officers, related to employment. Under the terms of the Geneva Convention, those with commissions, as well as many non-commissioned officers, were exempt from the provision that prisoners could be compelled to engage in non-war-related work by the detaining power while in captivity. As a result, while officers spent almost all their time behind the wire, most other ranks found themselves labouring for the Reich.

Opinion differed as to whether it was better to be in a main camp or out on a working party. Officers and non-working NCOs, feeling cooped up and bored to distraction, might envy what they imagined was the comparatively varied and incident-filled life led by working prisoners. Those who had no choice but to labour often saw things rather differently. Jobs could be immensely tedious and fatiguing, a world away from the concerts, games, and other recreational pursuits working men imagined were available to 'Stalag Wallahs' and those confined in oflags. In overall terms it was probably better for both body and soul to be working than to be idle; but this did not prevent many Kriegies from strenuously seeking to avoid the former in favour of at least a period enjoying the latter.[1]

Whether working as members of an *Arbeitskommando* (a working party employed by a contractor at a particular location) or a *Bau und*

Arbeitsbattalion (one of the mobile pioneer parties that, over time, became virtually indistinguishable from more static groups), POWs were in theory protected by the Geneva Convention. Under its terms prisoners were to be fed, paid, and worked at rates comparable to civilian workers, and employed on projects that were neither dangerous nor directly contributing to the German war effort. The hope of better conditions than those found in the stalags after the mass arrival of POWs led many to 'volunteer' for work that, so they were told, would be an improvement. But as new Kriegies soon discovered, neither enemy promises nor international law necessarily determined what working life would be like in a state increasingly short of home-front manpower as the war dragged on.[2]

Physical conditions could vary a good deal from one working camp to another, as we have seen. So too, depending in part on what was deducted for upkeep and what type of work was being done, could rates of pay. The length of the working day and week might differ both between and within one industry or area and another, along with the working rations made available. Parties ranged in size from less than a dozen to over a thousand men, and prisoners usually found themselves moved either as individuals or en masse from one job location to another at least once and perhaps as many as nine or more times in the course of their captivity. Nice or nasty civilian overseers could and did cause marked improvement or deterioration in the quality of working life. Prisoners who had been white-collar workers before the war had more of an adjustment to make to the general type of work they were ordered to undertake—mostly of the heavy manual variety—than working-class men who had been similarly employed in civvy street. Amidst all these variables, and in spite of occasional German efforts to deceive POWs as to what kind of work they were being sent out to do, over time Kriegies built up a fairly uniform and accurate picture of the best and worst type of Arbeitskommando based on the type of work being done.[3]

The best place to work, it was widely reckoned, was on the land. 'The great prize', Sim Watson recalled, 'was to be sent to a farm.' The working day might continue from dawn to dusk in season, but there was fresh air and greater relative freedom in the fields, and—importantly—the prospect of acquiring more food than elsewhere. In some cases Kriegies became de facto members of the household. 'The main occupation in winter was the lounge where the ladies would spin wool and we prisoners would shell peas and beans', Reg King fondly recalled. 'Some of the prisoners liked their jobs so much and got on so well that they stayed with their farm for the duration of the war', asserted Sam Kydd. Not all among the approximately 20 per cent of British prisoners employed in agriculture found conditions quite so idyllic. Overseers could be harsh, and men might be injured or even killed while carrying out unfamiliar tasks. However, most postwar accounts of life on the land suggest that Kriegies were right to prefer this kind of Arbeitsko-mmando.[4]

Forestry work, though occasionally dangerous, was also generally considered a good option. Road and railway repair gangs and building-site parties had a more variable reputation, as did the majority of Arbeitskommandos that involved loading and unloading material in hundreds of mills, foundries, and factories of various kinds, where the majority of Kriegies laboured. Cement works were disliked because of the dust, while chemical plants on occasion produced fumes that proved injurious or even lethal. (In 1944–5 a new danger was added to work at synthetic-fuel installations and transport sites by USAAF bombing raids.) Carpenters, bricklayers, electricians, and other skilled workers were envied by their less fortunate fellows for having evaded the heavy work of those given picks and shovels, to the point where men might claim knowledge of a trade that they did not in fact posses. Prisoners not surprisingly preferred relatively light jobs (such as road-sweeping) to heavy labour (such as rock-quarrying), especially in light of the fact that they were given significantly less in the way of rations than German civilians.[5]

The worst jobs, it was widely accepted, were down the mines. Digging coal was hard, claustrophobic, and dirty work, the hours were usually very long, and German overseers were often brutal. For those who had never gone below ground before, their first experience could be trau-matic. 'I believed I had arrived in hell itself', wrote Ewart Jones of his first day in the tunnels:

[T]he cavern was full of foul smoke. Pit props with flickering little lights on them leaned drunkenly out of the murk, and rows of naked black arms wielding shovels moved back and forth, back and forth in the abysmal gloom. Above a metal trough shook up and down, hurling lumps of coal back towards the conveyor belt, and the noise of rock against metal, coupled with that of the compressed air engine, was absolutely deafening.

Safety precautions below ground—especially where prisoners or slave workers were concerned—were minimal, and gas inhalation as well as injury from unsafe equipment and roof-falls a constant danger. Men returning in a steady stream with smashed limbs and pulped faces were noted at Lamsdorf, and most prisoners would have agreed with the assessment of the International Red Cross that the worst conditions for working POWs were to be found in the German mining industry. 'When a prisoner became a miner,' as Peter Winter put it, 'he had reached the end of the line.'[6]

Variable conditions only increased the natural tendency for prisoners to avoid work and seek better conditions where possible. Since refusing outright to leave a stalag to join an Arbeitskommando usually meant a jail sentence, Kriegies developed alternative avoidance tactics. NCOs were supposed to work only in a supervisory capacity. As it took time for the enemy to check up on ranks and establish true identities, especially in big places like Lamsdorf, enterprising soldiers tacked stripes to their arm or altered pay-books in a game of self-promotion designed to allow them to steer clear of pick-and-shovel work. Other options included making friends with camp staff to ensure being sent to a pleasant location and—particularly if being sent to the mines seemed likely—trying to appear too ill to go out. Periodically, though, the Germans would conduct comb-outs of stalag staff personnel. If the sick parade grew too large, even sympathetic British MOs might be forced to turn shirkers away in order to find bed-space for the truly ill, while German doctors were known to pass men as fit even after they had resorted to swallowing carbolic soap.[7]

Faking or exaggerating injuries and sickness in order to rest or be relocated once in an Arbeitskommando was also possible. Francis Jones remembered with admiration the successful techniques employed by newly arrived veteran cases on a quarry party late in the war:

The first day three of the new recruits reported sick. Being expert at this kind of thing, they stayed sick and Wertzig [the overseer] never saw them. Jock, a tiny Glaswegian, rubbed ersatz butter into a cut in his arm, and developed a minor skin infection. Curly, from Bow Bells, had a swollen wrist. He tapped it with the back of a spoon for half an hour before it swelled sufficiently, but he knew that five minutes a day after that would be ample. Harry, the third invalid, was out of action with a bad foot. It didn't bother him until the Germans were around, but he wouldn't disclose details. 'It's a professional secret,' he said.

Another successful ruse involved the drinking of a special concoction designed to temporarily raise the body temperature to 100° Fahrenheit.[8]

British camp leaders and medical personnel in the satellite camps devised sick rosters that allowed healthy men to have a few days off as sick on a rotation basis, while (as long as genuinely ill men were not put at risk) British MOs in stalag hospitals were willing to fudge diagnoses and practise 'looking-glass medicine' in order to fool German doctors and keep comparatively fit men unemployable. A minor racket developed involving 'necessary' circumcision operations followed by a prolonged recovery period of several weeks.[9]

Unfortunately, dodging the column by going sick did not always work. On the tougher Arbeitskommandos only 4 per cent of the workforce might be allowed off at any one time, and then only for the really serious cases such as those with broken bones. In such circumstances the more desperate Kriegies might resort to the self-infliction of real injuries. The aim was to produce 'Krankers'—conditions serious enough to necessitate at least temporary removal from the mines or other unpleasant work. Knee or wrist bruises would be nursed into fluid-filled horrors by repeated tapping; festering sores could be created through sanding or rubbing dirt and other matter into razor cuts; burns would be induced through pouring boiling water over a hand or rubbing in caustic soda. A more common practice, indicative of how bad conditions might be, was to have a mate break fingers or toes (or even do the deed oneself).[10]

Fortunately there were usually less painful ways of dodging the column on many job locations. In some instances, especially where large numbers of men and big industrial concerns were involved, it might be possible simply to hide either in camp or at the work-site and go to sleep. There was, however, always the risk of being caught napping, as Robert Gale learned from a friend at Lamsdorf who had been working in a coal-mine. 'Steve had managed to discover a technique to avoid working for the enemy', Gale reported; 'he simply hid in a disused working, blew out his lamp, and went to sleep. However he did this once too often for he awoke one day to find himself surrounded by Germans with their lamps shining on him and they gave him such a thorough beating that he had been unfit for work for three days.' Some men, however, always seemed to manage to find a way of eluding detection while 'Doing a Churchill', as hiding was sometimes patriotically called.[11]

Wandering off and taking a break for cigarettes or tea when backs were turned was another possibility. '[T]he guards found themselves involved almost hourly in a game of hide-and-seek with some prisoner or other who had left his job for a quiet stroll around the factory', Adrian Vincent wrote of daily life at a quarry and cement works early in the war. 'When caught he always had an answer—an order had been misunderstood; he was looking for a better shovel or for the foreman to discuss a problem that had arisen about the unloading of some wagons.' An enterprising pair of Geordies managed to avoid real work for several days by studiously carrying a plank from one spot to another before being caught out. Opportunities were even greater in the largely unsupervised crating department of a paper mill in 1942, as Donald Edgar fondly remembered: 'We brewed up tea or made coffee on a little stove and had a cigarette more or less as we felt like it.' A similarly comfortable environment was established in the machine shop where G. F. Warsop was left alone in 1944: 'most of my 12 hour shift was whiled away, chatting to my mates in the various shops, or holding meetings in the latrine.'[12]

Even on outside jobs in small groups it might be possible to avoid doing very much actual work, since supervisors and guards could not keep an eye on every prisoner for every minute, and some at least grew tired of constant chivvying. Spades and pickaxes might turn into props rather than tools. As Gordon Manners commented in relation to road-building, 'it's surprising how busy one can look by merely leaning on a shovel when you have learned how'. An apparent unfamiliarity with tools and the mantra phrase *'Nicht Verstehen'* ('I don't understand') sometimes came in useful as a means of prodding the German trying to explain a job into doing most of it himself. British officers out for a parole walk in 1944 observed how this game might ideally operate:

I vividly recall [Frederick Corfield related] . . . when we passed a party of British other ranks supposedly working on a drainage project but in fact giving a splendid example of typical British bloody-mindedness . . . by studiously playing the 'idiot boy'. Whatever the efforts the Germans made to explain what was required they were greeted by a row of totally blank faces murmuring 'nicht verstehen' . . . until in desperation the Germans themselves took off their jackets, rolled up their sleeves, and leapt into the trench to demonstrate—a wag amongst our troops commenting, 'That's right; you are the master race; you do it'! Although we were hurried along by our escort, it must have been a further twenty minutes or so before our 'working party' was out of sight. They were still standing, arms folded, watching the Germans hard at work with pick and shovel.

According to Stuart Brown, working on a farm in 1941, 'a steady stream of *"nix verstehens"* [sic] usually meant that the unpleasant tasks could be sidestepped'.[13]

Enemy impatience at the slowness with which POWs went about their daily tasks could be put to use in another way: the negotiation of piece-work quotas with overseers. In return for doing a specified amount of true work each day—filling a certain number of skips, say—prisoners would be allowed to knock off early. 'This way the foreman got more work out of us,' Cyril Rofe explained of the de facto contract agreed to on his transport gang in 1942, 'and we were generally back in our billets by midday.' Similarly favourable terms might be obtained on occasion through either bribery or blackmail of guards using Red Cross parcels.[14]

If the negotiating process failed, then prisoners might choose to withdraw their labour services altogether. Parties would go on strike for better conditions or in protest at having to carry out war-related tasks. As can be imagined, the results were not always to the prisoners' liking.

Sometimes strikes seemed to work. Faced with unexpected truculence and perhaps intimidated by being outnumbered in semi-isolated locations, guards or foremen might give way. 'Jack's gang went on strike one evening when they were told to load another skip at 20 minutes to 6', a road-building signaller recorded in his diary in September 1940. 'They got away with it, and not another word has been said.' Efforts to intimidate strikers were common, but standing firm produced occasional successes. 'At the end of November no clothing had been issued and the whole camp struck work', Sergeant J. Prendergast reported in connection with the working party to which he was sent in 1941. 'We were put on half rations for a week as punishment. A German officer was then sent from the Camp H.Q. [Stalag IIID], and we explained the reason for the strike.' French uniforms were then issued. Led by their camp leader, the men of a quarrying Arbeitskommando to which John Lawrence was attached struck in protest at the deteriorating food situation in early 1944:

The Goons threatened, they shouted, they yelled, they called us everything except legitimate. They said, 'No work, no food!' So naturally we replied by reversing the saying to 'No food, no work!' They again tried everything, short of violence, but ably led by Bill McGuiness we stuck it out, until, one day, the 'Kontrol Offizier', a kind of District Kommandant, gave the order that we would pack up, and move back to Lamsdorf.

A similar food-related 'hunger strike' in 1942 at another quarry manned by prisoners from Stalag VIIIB had resulted in complete official capitulation.[15]

Most strikes, however, collapsed in the face of enemy pressure. The denial of rations tended to have an effect after several days, while making Kriegies stand to attention outdoors if the weather was bad might induce second thoughts even sooner. 'All the other men passed out through heat exhaustion,' Albert Paice related of an attempted strike for more food at a quarry in the late summer of 1941, 'and we [those who remained upright] had no option but to give in.'[16] Threats to unleash savage guard dogs often made men think twice, as did guards who 'waded in with the butts of their rifles', as Frank Pannett put it. Even more intimidating were NCOs or officers who picked out hostages or lined strikers in front of armed guards and announced that they would start having men shot if work was not resumed. 'You don't have much choice when guns are pointing at you', Elvet Williams commented pointedly in reference to a failed sawmill protest in 1942. Calling the enemy's bluff was perilous. In 1942 men of a working party attached to Stalag XVIIIA refused to go out to work one Sunday, and under orders their guards 'went into the billet and shot one of the prisoners as he lay in bed and also killed and wounded several prisoners who were in the billet'.[17]

Nevertheless, British prisoners of war were generally poor workers whether in field or factory. The pay was miserable, most of the jobs were repetitive and tiring, and of course there was always the knowledge that the employer was the enemy, both literally and figuratively. Deliberate sabotage aside (see Chapter 9), Kriegies usually went out of their way to do as little real work as possible. OKW issued a string of directives designed to make POW labour more efficient, but to little effect, judging by the fact that the first was dated March 1941 and the last was distributed only five months before the end of the war. ' "Faul Arbeiter" (lazy worker) was an accusation we heard very often', Corporal Harry Buckledee remembered of his time at an I. G. Farben works. The commandant at Stalag XXID estimated that a single German worker was more efficient than five British prisoners: the latter figure was too low, in the opinion of the British camp doctor.[18]

Recreation was something that working prisoners enviously tended to associate with the long-term occupants of main camps—administrative types, officers, non-working NCOs and aircrew—and pleasures ranging from sport to sunbathing. 'In Stalag they had it all', John Lawrence complained, comparing the ample leisure time and facilities at Lamsdorf with the Spartan life on an Arbeitskommando. It was true enough that those in well-established stalags, like the inhabitants of oflags, tended to have more time, space, and resources to devote to the development of outdoor sports-grounds and indoor theatre stages than was the case in smaller and more transitory satellite camps. The games and sports equipment that the YMCA and other organizations provided through the Red Cross, moreover, went to main camps and were not always distributed to the working parties on an equitable basis. Those confined behind wire twenty-four hours a day, meanwhile, were faced with the serious problem of filling up 'a wilderness of time', as one RAF sergeant lamented, and lacked what can be seen as one of the main recreational compensations available to those on some working parties—the chance to interact with the opposite sex.[19]

Outdoor play served two main functions for POWs. First, once men were getting enough food, it helped keep bodies fit. Second, and more importantly in the main camps, it helped to pass the time for those with little or nothing to do. Whether as active participants or relatively passive spectators, Kriegies could focus their attention on games and perhaps forget for hours at a time where they were. As Desmond Llewelyn explained, 'competitive sports acted as a balm to utter boredom'.[20]

Lack of space was a serious problem in the Schloss camps, and even in the big hut-and-wire jobs finding enough ground sometimes could be difficult. Commandants, however, could usually be prevailed upon if pressed enough times to extend the area where prisoners could move about and allow for the creation of fields and pitches. The arrival in main camps of large YMCA parcels containing everything from balls to bats allowed for a host of sports to be played, including cricket, rugby, field hockey, boxing, and netball. Dominion troops introduced their own games, including Australian-rules football, Canadian-inspired softball, and—on rare occasions in winter—ice hockey. In the larger camps intramural and international sporting events were arranged, up to and including test match series. In places where both the commandant and other conditions allowed for them, as described in an official report on Stalag Luft VI (Heydekrug), sports-grounds 'were in constant use from dawn until dusk except during roll calls and meal times'.[21]

The primacy of particular sports could vary from place to place over time, with field hockey coming into its own among officers at Warburg and Eichstätt in 1942–3, and boxing tournaments drawing crowds of between 5,000 and 6,000 spectators at Lamsdorf in 1944. But the single most popular recreational sport for British POWs was soccer. Association football was of course massively popular at home, and in Germany was a game that even the unskilled could play and that required only a single item of equipment to keep dozens occupied for hours at a time. 'The great stand-by was soccer,' David James recalled in reference to sports in Marlag (O), 'which went on practically the whole year round.' In German eyes British prisoners were simply football-mad. Danish YMCA delegate Chris Christiansen recalled a telling incident:

In the field hospital at Königswartha I often called on some one hundred British POWs who had contracted tuberculosis. One winter day one of the [British] doctors and a [British] chaplain broke up our conversation by saying, 'You must excuse us, but we have an appointmke to play football in ten minutes.' There was a heavy snowfall outside, but that didn't prevent twenty-two of the fittest men among the patients from turning up for a football match and many more from watching it, standing around in the slush and sludge. This made the German doctor in charge of the hospital and the commandant exclaim in one voice: 'Yes, they are absolutely crazy, these British. They have to be fatally ill not to play football. But try teaching them how to peel potatoes, that's impossible!'

In Stalag IVB (Mühlberg) alone there were twenty-two separate soccer teams at the start of 1944.[22]

In times of real food shortage the interest in—and tempo of—outdoor games naturally tended to diminish. Even when Red Cross parcels were flowing with comparatively regularity, an inordinate number of calories might be burned up through too much vigorous physical activity. In the officers' compound at Westertimke the touch-rugby matches were limited to twelve minutes each way, while among the NCOs at Hohen-fels each half in football matches was only thirty minutes in length, 'since Stalag rations did not make for stamina', as one Kriegie aptly put it.[23]

Among the more restless of the camp-bound prisoners in the mid-war period, however, neither a limited diet nor the dangers posed by grounds that were hard-packed earth rather than grass-covered turf were necessarily a deterrent to heavy tackling. The netball played on top of Fort 13, Thorn, was, in the words of Sam Kydd, 'a good deal rougher than would normally be allowed', while in a large Arbeitskommando camp in the same general region Jim Roberts found that the mixture of netball and rugby commonly played 'was no game for the squeamish'.[24]

Other pursuits of a less vigorous nature helped fill up the hours, especially in bad weather or after lights-out when men were confined to their quarters. Tin bashing to make utensils and wood and metal modelling of the arts-and-crafts variety might flourish where the time and materials were available. Main camps, and through them some Arbeitskommandos, received parcel consignments of chess sets and board games such as Monopoly. Card decks, since they were easily portable and the source of a variety of games, became a ubiquitous feature of Kriegie life.[25]

Everything from patience to poker was played. But especially among officers it was contract bridge—socially acceptable and wonderfully time-consuming—that became the dominant activity. 'The standard of bridge was fairly high,' Philip Kindersley wrote of his fellow players at

Mährisch Trübau, 'as many prisoners devoted a considerable period of their captivity to mastering the various conventions...' True aficionados at Stalag Luft I (Barth) were observed devoting from ten to twelve hours each and every day to the game. Peter Buckley later conceded of his time at Marlag (O) that 'most of the day was [spent] playing cards'.[26]

Sometimes there were cigarettes, sterling IOUs, or other valued items at stake. At Oflag VIIIF a casino was created where players could try their luck two nights a week on faro or card roulette, while at Oflag VIIB rival syndicates offered the chance of a win at roulette or blackjack. Where the placing of wagers was concerned, however, cards might not necessarily take pride of place. In Stalag 383 the most popular form of betting involved 'two-up', a simple game introduced by the Australians that involved tossing pennies or dice on the heads-or-tails principle. There and in other camps bets might also be placed through self-appointed bookies on upcoming sporting events. When men were not competing then other creatures might be enlisted. At Barth bets were placed on the endurance of 'flycraft'—bluebottles with loads attached to their bodies by thread—as well as earwig and beetle races and frog-jumping competitions. The excitement associated with gambling, the chance to relieve the tedium of Kriegie life for even a brief period in the main camps, could drive some men to wager on practically anything. In Stalag Luft III bets were placed on whether an RAF sergeant could crawl round his compound inside thirty minutes, and whether or not a Scottish NCO could consume a Red Cross parcel in two hours without vomiting. 'Gambling was a great way of relieving boredom for many', as Martin Smith noted of life at Sagan. 'Be it cards, two flies on a window, or the speed one could walk round the camp', the punters 'would take a bet on it.'[27]

Over time the wagers placed could get out of hand. In the summer of 1942 at Warburg the SBO was forced to step in and cancel personal gambling debts that were running into the tens of thousands of pounds. 'Gambling was a pastime in every camp,' Jack Poole conceded, 'but in Eichstätt in 1944 it raged like a fever, reaching a dizzying maximum.' Wins and losses were skyrocketing, and some players were getting into real debt (having exchanged their *Lagermark* script for sterling IOU slips). A middle-aged schoolmaster, unable to pay the £80 he owed, was reduced to mending other men's socks at 5 shillings a hole. Eventually the SBO stepped in to try to regulate the industry and at least prevent punters from being cheated, but bets made on the basis of 'settlement after the war' could still result in significant monetary losses.

Though gambling was officially forbidden at Oflag 79 (Brunswick) in the same period, here too matters got out of hand. 'It will be appreciated, I hope,' the SBO explained in a report to the War Office:

that under conditions of prison life, it has been quite impossible entirely to prevent 'underground' gambling; there is no doubt that this has taken place, and I have strong reasons for believing that certain officers have either won or lost considerably larger sums of money than they could afford to pay for. I also have strong reason to believe that certain officers have covered their losses with 'provisional' cheques on notepaper, which they are going to be unable to honour.[28]

Another fairly common means of punctuating the humdrum nature of POW life that could be viewed as a form of sport involved deliberate efforts to hoodwink, baffle, or anger to the point of loss of composure—and thereby dignity—German guards, NCOs, and staff officers. This provided a morale boost through upsetting the natural balance of the captor–captive relationship. The enemy would always be in charge in a physical sense, by virtue of the act of surrender and possession of arms. But success in baiting or playing mind-games with the Germans with whom Kriegies came in contact was a means of suggesting that at the psychological level Britons would in truth never be slaves. Indeed, success suggested that they were in fact superior in terms of intelligence or character to the members of the master race assigned to guard them. The latter were, after all, foreigners. 'I noted once more how we all, perhaps instinctively, behaved with the usual British air of superiority, not to say arrogance', mining engineer Jim Rogers noted of the group of escapees he was with while being escorted to Colditz in June 1941. 'I had noted this in British tourists before the war—how they walked around as if they owned the place. It was not just a trait among the officers; the troops had it too.'[29]

Use of the term 'Goons'—apparently deriving from particularly thick-witted creature-characters resembling the missing link in a pre-war cartoon strip—as a synonym for guards was a small but telling indication of mental one-upmanship. Swearing at and using derogatory nicknames in front of Germans who did not understand English were sources of considerable mirth and pleasure for soldiers. Overly deliberate or nonchalant salutes by British officers were a means of demonstrating their slight regard for German staff in various places. *Appell*s could turn into scenes of mild indiscipline accompanied by cat-calls, whistling, singing, barnyard noises, and derisive cheering as men hid, wandered on and off parade, smoked or read, and dodged between files so as to cause the guards to miscount and have to start again. Just about anything that might make the enemy look uncomprehending and uneasy, or better yet foolish, and—for the more daring types of goon-baiter—angry to the point of loss of temper (and thereby dignity and 'face'), was tried somewhere at some time.[30]

Mind-games involved deliberately eccentric behaviour by Kriegies designed to leave onlooker Germans with baffled expressions and—in the best-case scenario—uneasily wondering if they were being mocked in some way that they did not comprehend. Such games took time to organize and, even if did not always have the desired effect, were a pleasant time-waster for the men involved.

Odd dress and deportment was one option widely practised. At Barth daily *Appell*s were undisciplined affairs, RAF sergeants slouching onto parade, often in intentionally ridiculous clothing. One day in the summer of 1943, amidst roars of laughter from the already assembled prisoners and puzzlement and fear of mockery among some of the guards, a squad of men bizarrely dressed either as boy scouts or girl guides—accounts differ—marched onto the parade ground to the sound of fife and drum. In the same period in the centre compound at Sagan leg-pulling on *Appell* took the form of bizarre haircuts—everything from devil's horns to five-of-dice patterns—that made men look so peculiar that the German authorities finally imposed a ban on the practice. The RAF aircrew prisoners responded with a new manifestation of craziness. As Richard Passmore explained, weird haircuts were succeeded by pebble-pushing—'a race in which the contestants pushed a pebble along the ground with their noses, always when there was a party of visiting Germans nearby'. The event always involved a throng of noisy supporters cheering on their favoured pusher. When the first goon pushed his way through the mob to see what was going on this time, he was rendered speechless. 'Either we were quite, quite mad or this, too, was some subtle move to convey criticism and scorn.' It was a great day when pebble-pushing was also forbidden by the camp authorities.[31]

At Warburg in 1942, after the reading of books on parade was banned by order of the commandant, British officers suddenly began to knit on *Appell*. One morning when the Lageroffizier appeared, Miles Reid recorded, 'we all concentrated our eyes on his fly-buttons, moving our heads as he moved, until at last he made a surreptitious swoop with his hand to make sure he had not disgraced the German Army'. The resulting titters were apparently so embarrassing that the officer fled and never appeared at *Appell* again.[32]

Props were optional. 'One day, for instance,' J. H. Witte remembered of his time at a railway stock repair shop in the Leipzig area in 1944:

four lads ... marched on to a wide open space ... and took up imaginary billiard cues. They began going through the motions of playing snooker, putting the balls in the frame, going off, potting the colours, snookering each other and marking the scores. Every so often one of them would chalk up his imaginary cue, whilst another would walk round the imaginary table looking for the best way to play a difficult shot.

The amazed looks on the faces of German onlookers made the whole exercise thoroughly worthwhile. Several years earlier Douglas Swift had witnessed similar spontaneity while working on a farm in Poland:

I think it was Walt Newcombe who started it, he came from the West Country. He went out into the compound and started casting an imaginary fishing rod, as though he was fly fishing. Kept casting and reeling in, then getting a bite. He gently played the fish whilst reeling it in. Working the fish to the bankside before putting the net underneath it to lift it out on the river bank—all imaginary, of course. The guards looked and looked, putting their fingers to their heads, saying '*Farouk*' [*Verückt*—crazy].

Kriegies staring intently into an empty sky or walking imaginary dogs produced further bafflement.[33]

The largest-scale and most sustained of such efforts to baffle and confuse the guards through leg-pulling occurred at Stalag 383 during what became known as 'crazy week'. This began one hot day in the fourth summer of the war, when a guard was observed watching two army NCOs testing a kite that one of them had made. Intuiting that the goon in question thought that kite-flying was not a adult activity, the two men started to act like squabbling children, complete with shin-kicking and howls of anguish when the kite got caught in the perimeter wire. More guards came to stare in wonder, which in turn prompted other prisoners to engage in childhood regression, playing ring-a-ring-of-roses and making daisy chains—all, as M. N. McKibbin reported, 'just for the sight of the Hun reaction'. The results, varying from 'dumb amazement to suspicious scowls', were enough to generate further peculiar behaviour in the following days. Individuals were observed riding invisible bikes and leading invisible dogs round the perimeter, passing by stationary figures dressed as Napoleon or Nelson, and groups of grown men playing marbles: 'doing anything, in fact, to get the Huns bewildered.'[34]

The high point of happy invention came with the appearance of the Hohenfels 'Train to Blighty'. Pretending that eight huts and a cookhouse facing the wire were in fact railway carriages and an engine, men in increasing numbers and over several days began to act out increasingly elaborate imaginary scenarios. Passengers assembled and boarded the train under the direction of a stationmaster and his minions amidst goodbyes from well-wishers and arguments over seating and fares, followed by the sounds of a steam-engine pulling out and men waving hankies and calling out farewells from the windows. 'The train got the Jerries really ga-ga', McKibbin wrote. The watching Germans could not make it out at all. 'What is all this about? What is all this about?' George Beeson remembered the guard sergeant anxiously repeating. The commandant, worried that he was witnessing scenes of mass psychosis, asked the camp leader what might be done: to which MacKenzie, thinking on his feet, replied with a list of needed amenities that included parole walks and a bigger sports-ground.[35]

On occasion German puzzlement, unease, and embarrassment at such play-acting could turn to outrage and fury. The commandant at Oflag VIIIF, according to one witness, 'completely lost his head' when, at the start of a scheduled visit to the prisoners' compound, his arrival was heralded by the blowing of a hunting horn, whistling of the Dead March, ironic cheers, the singing of 'Why was he born at all?', and—as if all this was not enough—a British officer suddenly appearing with an imitation hand-cranked film camera and pretending to record the progress of the august Teutonic presence.[36]

Several years earlier at Stalag VIIA there had been a much-heralded visit by senior dignitaries, among them, at least reputedly, Himmler himself. At one point in the proceedings four Australian NCOs broke ranks and ran in front of the advancing retinue. The four then stopped and began going through the motions of setting up and loading an imaginary Vickers machine-gun. While the Germans were still too confused to take action, the leading Aussie gave the order 'Fire!' After that all hell broke loose as, amid wild cheering from the parade, the crew sprinted away with furious guards in hot pursuit. The one man caught got fourteen days in cells, while the rest of the prisoners were denied Red Cross parcels and full rations for a week. The entertainment value of the incident was thought to have outweighed the subsequent restrictions.[37]

German worries about what the prisoners were up to inside the wire in the way of escape preparations sometimes brought irresistible opportunities for mischief. Protected by the thickness of the Schloss walls, officers at Laufen poked dummies they had sewn together out of exterior windows to draw German fire. If a guard's aim was poor and the bullet meant for the 'escaper' thudded into the wall, a green flag—the rifle-range signal for 'clean miss'—was waved on the end of a long stick. 'Indulging in a favourite and often successful game,' Frank Taylor wrote of the RAF compound at Lamsdorf, 'we used to walk out of the barrack, look around furtively, put a hand in a pocket, pretend to take something out, scrape a hole in the ground and bury the non-existent object, then walk away, whistling nonchalantly. As often as not, guards with shovels and sniffer dogs would appear and start digging and searching'. Searches for contraband articles conducted by the camp authorities or by the local Gestapo often proved to be occasions in which the enemy lost more in the way of stolen hats, wallets, pens, and coats than he gained in the way of escape equipment or hidden radios. Flying Officer Stephen Johnson recalled a further leg-pull during a search of his hut in Stalag Luft III in 1943:

One night a man said in a loud whisper, 'I hope they don't search John too well, he's hiding some important stuff.' An English speaking German overheard him, so when it came to John's turn [to be searched] they gave him a proper going over. They found nothing at first, so they made him strip and searched his clothes and shoes, but still found nothing. They then searched him again and in the very last place they looked they found a little piece of paper. On it was written 'Heil Hitler!'

At Stalag IVB in 1944 much enjoyment was derived from watching a 'ferret'—a member of the security officer's team whose job it was to uncover contraband and signs of escape—excitedly follow a strand of wire that ran from a hut roof down into the ground. This, when dug up, proved to lead only to a buried chamber pot: 'they were quite annoyed about that', John Greenwood commented.[38]

Goon-baiting was not without its detractors. Some thought that childish pranks undermined prisoners' dignity and only reinforced a sense of superiority among the Germans. Others argued that, in keeping the enemy alert and non-complacent, unruly behaviour hindered serious efforts to escape from camps. It was for these reasons that senior British officers at Oflag VIIC/H and Stalag Luft III sought to clamp down on the practice. Moreover, if provoked sufficiently guards could react with painful and sometimes tragic consequences. Cheekiness might result in a savage kick, a blow from a rifle butt, or even a bayonet thrust (as when a Scottish soldier, after too openly insulting a sentry, was jabbed fiercely in the bottom at a synthetic oil factory). Worse yet, triggers might be pulled. 'Some of the boys undertook adventures beyond what was considered reasonable provocation', Percy Carruthers admitted of the aircrew NCOs at Stalag Luft I. Despite what another inhabitant described as 'incredible' enemy restraint, shots occasionally rang out here and elsewhere. It was fear of this happening with fatal results at Luft III that led 'Dixie' Deans, the elected leader, to persuade his fellow RAF sergeants to desist from stunts such as sneaking up behind a guard and pulling the trigger of his loaded rifle. 'In passing, and from the hindsight of many years on,' Richard Passmore reflected in his memoirs, 'I am surprised—if no more—at our arrogance and astonished at the self-control of our captors . . . '[39]

Many prisoners nevertheless derived a good deal of enjoyment, not only from needling the enemy but also from involvement in what amounted in many cases to a form of public theatre. This was not surprising given the great interest in the more conventional performing arts that POWs displayed. As either performers or as part of the audience, Kriegies found that music, the stage, and even dance—perhaps all together in a variety show—were a pleasant way of passing the time and dispelling, however temporarily, the threat of ennui and the crushing sameness of everyday life in captivity. 'You became absorbed in the music,' former Stalag Luft III prisoner Dick Churchill rhapsodized in an interview fifty years on, 'the surroundings recede into the background, you can imagine you weren't there for a while.'[40]

At first there might be little more than the human voice to work with. Those BEF men imprisoned in Stalag XXA in late 1940 were only able to organize a sing-song accompanied on a mouth organ, followed by 'Pennies from Heaven' played with a comb and piece of tissue paper; while their officers held at Laufen were confined to small vocal recitals accompanied by a piano already *in situ*. Over time, though, instruments arrived from Switzerland in increasing volume. Listening to men learning to play was rarely pleasant, but over time and with the help of veteran players the standard of sound improved to semi-professional levels. Even on the smaller Arbeitskommandos it was possible to, say, arrange to purchase with *Lagergeld* enough instruments to equip a trio. By late 1941 an orchestra had been created at Thorn, while a year later at Eichstätt, where many of those officers once held at Laufen ended up, a fifty-piece orchestra was up and running. Sailors in Marlag (M) developed a brass band, a dance band, and a small string orchestra to boot. Oflag 79 possessed no less than five bands and orchestras, as did Stalag 383: two dance bands, a pipe band, a Spanish band, plus a mouth-organ band. 'By February 1944,' reported Richard Garrett, 'Oflag VIIB had become so well equipped with musical instruments, sheet music and sufficiently talented inhabitants, that the occupants were able to stage a

"Musical Festival" lasting two weeks.' A total audience that numbered well in excess of 6,000 prisoners listened to thirty-three separate performances involving a total of over 100 musicians and singers.[41]

Recorded music was also popular, but despite shipments of discs and gramophones though Switzerland, always remained in short supply. By the end of the war the ratio of prisoners to phonographs at Stalag VIIIA (Görlitz) and its satellite camps was a hundred to one. Where there was a gramophone, however, records—everything from Bing Crosby to Beethoven—would be played till they broke, wore out, or the war ended. An RAF sergeant who received a set of five discs from his wife in 1941 estimated that by 1945 they had each been played about a thousand times.[42]

In the main and bigger working camps the stage also came to play an important part in Kriegie life. The construction of costumes and scenery as well set and lighting design and cast rehearsals could take up the time of dozens of men, while hundreds more could enjoy themselves immensely for a few hours a week as members of the audience. 'To make our way down to the theatre to see the latest show', Bill Jackson remembered of life at Lamsdorf, 'was the highlight of our miserable day-to-day existence and I saw some prisoners actually trembling with excitement at the thought of a couple of hours' return to a happier life.'[43]

For the most part the camp authorities viewed the theatre as a good way of keeping prisoners busy, and commandants were helpful in providing space and, sometimes, building material to supplement what could be done with Red Cross crates. Tools were loaned out on parole with which Kriegies could construct rows of tiered seats, orchestra pits, and proper stages. Much ingenuity went into the development of often quite elaborate sets and costumes from local resources, and on occasion prisoners were even allowed to obtain some of what they needed from outside *costumiers*. As with concerts and recitals, the scope and scale of theatrical activity, along with the overall quality, tended to expand and improve with time. At Oflag VIIC/H in 1940 amateur theatricals were by necessity rather crude, small-scale, and generally makeshift. By 1944 at Oflag 79 there were two separate stages with their own companies, to whose efforts up to 500 officers were said to contribute everything from lighting to set design. At Stalag 383, where there were also two stages with several hundred seats, each of the 6,000 prisoners could look forward to 'doing [i.e. watching] a show' about once a fortnight.[44]

The majority of those involved continued to be amateurs, but true theatre people who had found their way into the services and subsequently been captured helped to raise production values. The professionalism of Denholm Elliott helped the quality of Shakespeare plays put on at Lamsdorf, for example, while the efforts of fellow-actors Desmond Llewelyn, Michael Goodliffe, and Dan Cunningham added to what was achieved at Eichstätt and Rotenburg in 1943–4.[45]

Everything from *Macbeth* to *The Mikado* was staged at one time or another in Germany, though the overall trend seems to have been away from darker fare. *French Without Tears* was put on in many camps, along with other West End hits like *Blithe Spirit* and *Rookery Nook*. Interspersed with the light comedies and shows were whodunits and popular melodramas, along with locally produced revues and pantos, often of a deliberately lowbrow variety.[46]

One obvious problem that Kriegie theatre faced was the complete absence of actresses. The solution was for producers to enlist young men for female roles. Fresh-faced types were in high demand, even if they sometimes had deep voices and big feet. 'When I reflect on it,' Walter Morrison noted of being chosen as the leading lady for *French Without Tears* at Sagan, 'I think that the obvious conclusion was that I was a pretty boy.' Some of these young men turned out to be very successful at playing members of the opposite gender, and were always cast in female roles. Having the right looks, however, was not enough. 'To perform the parts properly they had to learn to walk rather mincingly, and use female mannerisms', R. P. Evans remembered of Hohenfels. A certain number of this select group 'began to permanently acquire those mannerisms when walking about the camp', and be identified by the names of the roles they played—'there were various Dollies and Maisies scattered around the camp,' recalled another officer at Stalag Luft III.[47]

These youths might be so convincing that, in places where men might not have seen a real women in years, they acquired devoted admirers. 'Any person who played the lead role in the camp theatre was considered to be a heart-throb', George Moreton wrote of Lamsdorf. '"She" had more fans and more people dreaming about "her" than "she" would ever imagine. When "she" walked down the road, eyes would follow "her" adoringly.' Such fans had more than acting on their mind. 'The first time he slunk on to the stage, wearing a convincing evening gown,' Richard Passmore wrote of one successful 'actress' at Sagan, 'the spontaneous wave of enormous lust which arose from the audience was so perceptible as to make him stagger back slightly before he recovered his self-control.' Graham Palmer, another Lamsdorf prisoner, thought that

Kriegies playing girls 'really needed protection going "home" to their barracks after the shows'.[48]

Not all prisoners were affected in this way. 'I must say that even after sampling a good amount of the fiendish brew from our distillery together with some Schnapps,' an observer of an Arbeitskommando pantomime commented, 'my imagination still wouldn't stretch to having lustful thoughts about the principal boy or any of the chorus girls.' For others sexual feelings had no connection with, for example, the dances that were held in some places: 'the fact that one [man] took the ladies [sic] part had no implications whatsoever', one soldier later stoutly asserted. What ardour there was might cool in the cold light of day, when the beautiful temptress of the night before turned out to be just another blue-chinned Kriegie. Persistent attentions might be deflected with a few sharp words from the recipient ('watch it mate—it was only an act').[49]

In some quarters it was believed that 'chorus-girl' types were generating what in practice were homoerotic longings. A blind or tolerant eye was turned toward homosexual liaisons in some compounds, even when 'wingers' were pretty much all the way out of the closet. But in an age when homosexuality was very much a closet affair, it is not surprising that some men were shocked. A 'hell of a lot of men seem to be affected here', Geoffrey Broom wrote in his diary at Marlag (M) in the autumn of 1944, '– some of them quite obvious. It's all more or less beyond me and quite out of control!' Others were both scandalized and—for a mixture of moral and practical reasons—determined to take action. In the mid-war period at Lamsdorf the camp paper, *Stimmt*, ran an editorial campaign denouncing theatre 'pansies' and their bitchy admirers as well as same-sex dancing as degenerate. In his memoirs Roger Coward explained why the unusual measure of asking the German authorities to step in was taken at AB 21 (a large Arbeitskommando out of Lamsdorf):

While the padres and some of the wiser heads did everything possible to keep the youngsters from the older perverts, many of the boys, from sheer boredom as well as natural sexual urges and lack of the society of girls, became contaminated with this vice. Open pursuit of vice led to increasing outbursts of violence because of jealousy and 'unfaithfulness'. From screaming and scratching they soon went on to passionate hysterics and drawn knives. These perverted 'show-offs' would kill, by day as well as by night, what peace there was in the rooms they occupied. In the end things got to such a pass that our M.O. had to appeal to the *Kommandant* to break up the pairs by moving one man of each to some other camp.

At about the same time the MO at Hohenfels ordered a crackdown on 'the girls' after Red Cross items began to be exchanged for sexual favours and more and more young men were said to be 'tempted to become transvestite whores'.[50]

Jokes about 'home or homo' by Christmas aside, the extent of active homosexuality among British POWs is open to debate. Most prisoners could not recall any at all throughout their captivity, or only very occasional signs. There was the social stigma to contend with, and just as importantly, the fact that main camps were very crowded places with virtually no privacy. Ron Mackenzie reckoned that the number of overt homosexuals was less than 0.33 per cent of the total population at Sagan and elsewhere. On working parties the opportunities were greater—not least because prisoners were in contact with civilians of other nations—and there were a few places where a modus vivendi with guards extended into the sexual sphere. Here too, however, the available evidence suggests that gay men were comparatively rare. 'Homosexuality was not as common an occurrence as one might think', Adrian Vincent commented, after describing how young Polish male workers offered sex to men on his mining party in exchange for cigarettes. 'There had been no evidence of it on my other working parties, and by all accounts it was rare on all working parties.'[51]

Heterosexual activity was another matter. When health and opportunity allowed, a significant number of British working prisoners appear to have established physical relations with members of the opposite sex.

When food parcels from the Red Cross were absent or in short supply, it was food that occupied men's attention rather than sex. 'A hungry man's thoughts are concentrated on the area around the belt, not that below the belt', as a South African sergeant put it. 'If you had the choice between the most beautiful women in the world and a cheese roll,' Syd Smith explained in reference to his time in the mines, 'you'd pick the cheese roll.' One prisoner from Crete recorded a telling incident early on in his captivity at an Arbeitskommando. 'We were at work on this particular morning . . .', wrote D. W. Luckett, 'overlooking the road that led into the village, when a young girl of about twenty was seen walking along the road, she was quite attractive and smartly dressed, carrying a string bag that held a round loaf, something like 35 pairs of eyes followed her progress in silence then a very Aussie voice was heard to remark,—"Bloody Hell! Look at that loaf!"'[52]

Even when hunger was no longer quite so overwhelming, prisoners in main camps found that over time, in the absence of contact with women (and on what always remained a restricted diet), their sex drive seemed to diminish or vanish entirely. 'It's a funny thing, but I have no sexual appetite at all', a BEF medical officer complained to another RAMC doctor in 1944. 'Prison life has neutered me and I'm wondering what my wife is going to say when I get home.' In Oflag VIIIF and Oflag 79 it was generally conceded that officers who had spent years behind wire tended not to think or talk about women at all. 'Libido seemed dead', a senior South African chaplain later wrote.[53]

For many young men, however, the effect of Red Cross parcels was to make the opposite sex loom large in Kriegie thought and conversation. 'One had the feeling that when prisoners were not talking about sex they were thinking about it', Kingsley Brown wrote of officers at Sagan. 'Women were always a favourite topic', Sergeant John Fancy confirmed in reference to Barth. RAF types and others closely confined to main camps had to content themselves with secret or articulated yearnings, and—when privacy and inclination permitted, which was not often—a certain amount of what was once known as self-abuse as a means of relief. There was general hilarity when a German order was read out at places like Eichstätt, Hohenfels, and Sagan to the effect that fraterniza-tion with *Frauen und Fräulein* was a punishable offence.[54]

For working prisoners, on the other hand, this warning might have direct relevance. British soldiers on Arbeitskommandos, using a mixture of parcel contents and native charm, were not slow to establish relations with the opposite sex at the workplace once they were no longer quite so hungry. On farms male conscription meant that wives and daughters were sometimes susceptible to Kriegie blandishments. Clandestine li-aisons were also established with women in factories where the supervi-sion was not too stringent. In some instances it also proved possible to slip away at night to local brothels set up for foreign guest workers. Such desirable Arbeitskommandos were not that common, though, and fear of venereal disease kept many men celibate in any case. Nevertheless a large proportion of ex-POWs remembered having witnessed or partici-pated in illicit sex with local women. As one former prisoner explained, 'it was difficult but it could be arranged'.[55]

There was certainly enough of it about to prompt the German author-ities to start issuing dire warnings about the consequences of being caught *in flagrante*. Consorting with female members of the *Herrenvolk* carried by far the stiffest penalties. A man might get a spell in the cooler merely for being seen chatting with a German woman. To be seen kissing was to invite a prison sentence of nine or more months. An actual affair, as explained in OKW pronouncements read out to Kriegies, was a capital offence.[56]

In fact no executions seem to have occurred—transfers followed by lengthy prison sentences became the de facto penalty—but many Kriegies agreed with Geoffrey Vaughan that the announcement that prisoners would be shot for undermining the purity of the distaff members of the Master Race 'meant exactly what it said'. Anglo-German liaisons continued to occur, especially in rural areas, but most would-be Lotharios made a conscious choice to steer clear of *Frauen und Fräulein*: a decision that could be justified on both patriotic and practical grounds. Though still *verboten*, parcel-fed romances with foreign workers were subject to far less draconian penalties, and were avidly pursued.[57]

Fortunate Kriegies could find themselves working in proximity to Poles, Ukrainians, Czechs, and women of other nationalities who were forced to work for the Reich. Alexander Gant, sent from Lamsdorf to a plant in Upper Silesia in 1943, recalled what happened after 200 Ukrainian women arrived: 'within two days romances were blossoming everywhere.' Kriegies might make efforts to plaster down hair, polish boots, and generally look smart; but it was the luxury items to which they had access—everything from face soap to long-johns—that proved the truly irresistible lure. 'After a week or so, we all had a girl friend except the misogynist', Jock Ferguson reported of his party's initial contacts with the Polish factory women. 'Every one of them [South African POWs] was firmly established with one or other of the Polish girls who worked at the factory', Ed Annetts discovered, on being transferred to a sugar-beet processing centre in 1944. There were even a few known cases of soldiers escaping in order to try and live out the war quietly with their girlfriends.[58]

Due to their rank, British officers sent to Colditz did not work, and therefore did not have much opportunity to meet members of the opposite sex (though one Czech RAF officer did apparently manage to turn a dental appointment into a brief romantic encounter with a female hygienist whom he had charmed while in transit to the castle).[59] Some of them thought that, quite apart from the question of escape, other ranks on Arbeitskommandos must *ipso facto* lead better lives than officers cooped up in the castle. The orderlies at Oflag IVC for the most part disagreed, insofar as the castle was viewed as a cushy billet compared, say, to a Silesian coal-pit. 'After the copper mines,' Syd Smith explained, 'Colditz was a holiday camp.' There is some evidence that soldiers sought out postings to the castle and that the majority of orderlies—at least for a time—wanted to stay. The consequences arising from a group of malcontents confronting the British camp authorities have already been described. Protests directed at the German authorities at Colditz appear to have been rare, though when one orderly refused to obey the orders of a *Gefreiter* in September 1943 the commandant made his position on industrial action crystal-clear. 'If a PoW does not obey orders,' Oberst Prawitt shouted at his officers while banging his fist on his desk, 'repeat the order and push your rifle in his back. If he continues disobeying shoot him on the spot!' (The man in question, thankfully, got off with a stretch in the cells on bread and water.)[60] Meanwhile those men the orderlies looked after were forced to channel their restlessness in a variety of other ways.

Lack of space for outdoor sports was one of the major inconveniences of incarceration at Colditz. With the exercise field below the walls closed for much of the time as a reprisal measure, inmates were forced to fall back on the prisoners' courtyard. This was mostly in shadow, was entirely cobbled over, and in terms of area was little more than the size of single tennis court. 'The courtyard was impossibly small', remembered Billie Stephens. Despite its drawbacks, this space was used for volleyball, rather cramped versions of cricket and soccer, and—most famously—a game peculiar to Oflag IVC called 'stoolball'.[61]

Apparently derived from public school creations such as the Eton wall game, stoolball involved two teams of between about eight and thirty men contending in a scrum for possession of a ball in order to run with it rugby fashion (and occasionally bounce it basketball style), the ultimate aim being for a player to touch one of the two stools at either end on which a goalkeeper sat. There was no referee and no rules limiting what form tackling might take in the ten-minute-a-side matches. 'It was the roughest game I have ever played,' wrote Pat Reid, 'putting games like rugby football in the shade.' Those involved in these exciting, no-holds-barred events were later amazed that there were no serious injuries. Stoolball was always played 'with reckless abandon', according to Jim Rogers, '—a reflection of the mood of the camp'. The game did, however, serve a purpose. 'It all looked highly dangerous, and the Germans were convinced that the players were insane,' Dr Ion Ferguson reflected in his memoirs, 'but it was a good way of working off energy for fit men who were allowed to do no work.'[62]

Above-average restlessness was evident in the way in which new arrivals could be greeted in the middle war years. John Chrisp, arriving with a party of naval officers in September 1942, was startled by the huge noise that greeted the group as they were escorted into the prisoners' courtyard—all around Colditzians were 'screaming and cheering and yelling, singing and blowing bugles and banging drums and clattering cans' from the windows. 'From an upper window a tiny parachute came floating down. In it a tiny white mouse sat motionless as an ivory statue. He landed almost at [another officer's] feet. We picked him up, and read the label attached to his neck—"Welcome to Colditz." '[63]

The 'men of spirit' in Colditz could also on occasion burn up energy on pranks directed at 'new boys'—a form of introduction common to many public schools but rare in POW camps. Pat Reid later wrote up an account of the way in which the naval party was put in its place before its members had had time to digest who was who and what was what:

The Colditz 'old lags' decided to have some fun at the new boys' expense. Howard Gee, who spoke German perfectly, was togged out in the best pieces of home-made German officer's uniform, converted from a Dutch uniform for the occasion (and removed from its hiding place). He was accoutred as the German camp doctor, complete with stethoscope, accompanied by his medical orderly, alias Dominic Bruce, in white overalls, carrying a large bowl of blue woad— mainly theatre paint—and a paintbrush. No sooner were the fifteen new arrivals let loose in the British day quarters than Gee and Bruce entered. Gee, in a stentorian voice, demanded that the newcomers parade before him. He inspected them, condemned them as lice-ridden, bellowed at them to remove their trousers, condemned them again in insulting language as being ridden with crabs and indicated to his orderly that the offending body and other excrescences be painted with the blue liquid, permeated with high-smelling lavatory disinfectant.

Convinced by their fellow prisoners that this indignity had to be endured for fear of dire retribution from the Germans, the naval party found their private parts generously daubed with the blue stuff while they held their trousers at half-mast. After a final harangue on the bodily habits of the English, the 'doctor' retired.[64]

So much fun was had that the trick was repeated on members of the Eichstätt contingent when they arrived ten months later. 'We arrived like new boys at a school', Pat Fergusson recalled:

We were taken one by one down to the medical room, where we were interviewed by a German doctor in a white coat. We were told to do all the usual things—drop your trousers, cough. Then a bucket of purple paint appeared, which was duly slapped on in the appropriate places, and we were told to get the hell out of there. All the time the German doctor was shouting loudly and rudely at us; and, of course, he wasn't a German. We fell for it and felt quite silly...

Other members of the same group were taken in by a stunt mounted by Harry Elliot. He formally introduced these unsuspecting types to the one

'Chinese naval officer' in residence—in reality a Dutch Indonesian—who completely fooled his audience and managed to get them into a position where the national anthem was sung at attention by all as he left the room.[65]

Far more effort, though, went into attempts to put the enemy in his place. 'The game was "goon baiting",' Jack Champ recalled of Colditz, 'and this was practised at every possible opportunity.'[66]

The daily counts, which occurred four times a day rather than the usual two, were often fractious affairs. 'If parade discipline had been bad in other camps,' Miles Reid reflected, 'in Colditz it was practically non-existent.' Dressed any way they pleased, British prisoners would shamble down to the courtyard, assemble in an untidy clump, smoke, chat, wander about, and voice rude remarks about the guards, the castle, and the Third Reich in general. The Germans did not appreciate having *Appell* treated like a music-hall turn, and even after the SBO called the contingent to attention saluting was always casual in the extreme, and enough shuffling might occur to foul up the count and force a repeat performance. 'Indiscipline, I can truly say,' a chagrined Lageroffizier Reinhold Eggers later wrote, 'was the unspoken order of the day on their side; indiscipline often amounting to plain personal insolence, or at least studied offhandedness.'[67]

There was a certain amount of fairly innocuous leg-pulling designed to make the captors look foolish. The embarrassment caused by a goon suddenly finding that his cap or other items (half a ladder in one famous instance) had disappeared while his back was turned gave rise to mirth. When a sentry was heard complaining that he had missed his lunch while a search was on, Peter Tunstall, an RAF officer, proffered a coin—which the searchers had clearly missed—with the words, 'Here you are my good man, go out and get yourself a good meal'. The sentry replied '*Nein, Danke, Nein*', and retreated in considerable confusion. There was also the case of the Oflag IVC Spitfire, related by Miles Reid in his memoirs:

There was a nimble-handed young R.A.F. officer in Colditz who made a perfect model of a spitfire with a wingspan of about eighteen inches. Once, on a parole walk, he caught a very vicious-looking hornet and took it back into the castle in a matchbox and, just before running down to take his place on parade on a very hot day, when the heat from the basalt was rising, he loosed the hornet from his window with the toy spitfire attached to it by a piece of cotton tied round its thorax. With the lift from the rising current, this insect towed this perfect aerodynamic toy round and round the courtyard, to the amusement of everyone except the Germans trying to count us. Then the hornet's engine failed, or he got tired, because he nose-dived straight on to Hauptmann Pupka [*sic*]. Thinking it was a wasp and not wishing to show curiosity about the laughter, he made a sweeping gesture without raising his eyes from his score sheet, only to get his hand caught up in the middle of a cotton towrope with a hornet on one end and the toy plane on the other.

'Anything which rattled us', Hauptmann Eggers noted, 'was a point in the prisoners' favour.'[68]

Goon-baiting did sometimes have a more malicious and combative quality at Colditz. A fire was deliberately started using a pile of wood-shavings at the bottom of the staircase leading to the British quarters during one *Appell* in June 1942, for instance. While the Germans were trying to put it out amid cheers and barracking from the assembled officers, an RAF officer ducked up the stairs and dropped a water bomb that soaked the nearest sentry. Snap parades, searches, and VIP inspections might be accompanied by a variety of sound effects— screaming, booing, whistling, animal noises, bugles, and shouted insults. If the prisoners were ordered back to their rooms they might then launch water and sometimes excrement bombs (made from newspapers folded into cocked hats), plus, on occasion, potatoes (presumably when Red Cross parcels were plentiful), and lob other items from the windows into the courtyard. Conan Purdon wrote of the pandemonium that accompanied German efforts to fingerprint new arrivals in the courtyard in June 1943: 'The Germans had two tables in the yard, each placed below windows, and German officers sat there to take our particulars, photograph us and so on. To my amazement water bombs rained onto the tables, and then a blazing palliasse thrown down out of an upper window. Grinning faces looked down, roaring insults at our captors.' The commandant himself narrowly missed getting soaked while conducting a tour of the castle at about this time.[69]

Incidents of this sort certainly made Colditz a livelier place than some of the more sedate oflags. Not all officers, however, especially those transferred in 1943, agreed with the philosophy that 'anything to irritate the Germans is a good thing', as Jimmy Yule put it. 'I personally felt rather embarrassed', admitted Michael Alexander in relation to some of the more schoolboyish antics. 'There's no point in making a fool of yourself all the time just to prick a few Germans', Patrick Welch later commented. John Chrisp, thinking about a particular water-bombing incident many years after the war, had to admit that the goons put up with far more aggravation than he would have done in their place. If an individual was identified as having thrown something or made an insulting remark he ran the risk of a court martial. There were further dangers in goading the sentries to the point where they were ordered to fire warning shots in the vicinity of windows, as at least one French prisoner in the castle maimed by a ricochet could attest. The guards at Colditz exercised a fair amount of restraint in their use of firearms—far more than the British would admit to during visits by the Protecting Power—but their patience was not limitless. 'After a few days in Colditz I came to the conclusion that the Germans were being teased beyond reasonable measure,' wrote Miles Reid, who arrived in September 1943, 'and that sooner or later the Wehrmacht staff would be strengthened by SS troops; then there would be trouble and someone would get shot.' Colonel Stayner evidently sought to place limits on provoking the enemy in 1942–3, when goon-baiting was at its height, and when things looked to be getting out of hand again Willie Tod, as SBO, took a firm line after arriving in May 1944. He publicly berated a junior officer in June whose rudeness towards the guards overstepped the mark; and in October, in view of the war situation, issued orders that even the usual *Appell* annoyances were to stop.[70]

The taunting that went on by the 'men of spirit' should not be taken to mean that more sedentary games were not pursued at Oflag IVC. Chess became an obsession for some, officers being known to stay up all night to allow a game to continue uninterrupted. Here, as in other officer camps, playing cards became a major part of daily life for most prisoners. 'Some men took to playing cards as though it was their religion', Ion Ferguson noticed. Close quarters meant that the constant patter of players could irritate those trying to do something else, and even some of the players themselves might grow fed up with bridge and poker. Rather more serious was the gambling that took place in the later war years. 'There was in the camp a Poker School of rich young officers who played for high stakes', Tommy Catlow wrote in his memoirs. 'I don't think it mattered to them whether they won or lost, but they were joined by one or two less rich officers to whom it mattered a lot if they lost—and they did. I heard one chap lost £7,000, even today not a minor sum.'[71]

Music also helped to pass the time at Colditz. Prisoners brought instruments with them from other camps or obtained them through the canteen or the Red Cross. The comparative lack of outdoor space meant that the sounds generated by those learning to play were not always appreciated, but eventually a small orchestra was formed that, in the words of the War Office report on the camp, 'provided a certain amount of entertainment once or twice a week'. Gramophone recitals were also undertaken (though the substantial number of records built up seems to have diminished after it was realized that MI9 was smuggling contraband in them, and a large number were broken to see if they contained money or maps).[72]

The stage was another diversion actively pursued in the castle on those occasions when the theatre was not closed as a retaliatory measure. 'The productions were ham but fun,' wrote Tommy Catlow, 'and filled a gap in one's time with make-believe.' Plays ranging from *Hay Fever* and *Tonight at Eight-Thirty* to *Gaslight* were staged, but most memorable were the musical-comedy revues dreamt up by the prisoners themselves. These, often presented in the form of Christmas pantomimes, were full of lowbrow puns and innuendo, but were great fun for all concerned. 'Like all prison pantos,' Michael Riviere wrote to his father about the Christmas 1944 production, 'it's a good hotch potch and includes Snow White, her Prince, a wicked duke, an American Detective, a Witch, an A.D.C., a Japanese torturer, and so on.'[73]

A tradition had been started in late 1941 with the revue *Ballet Nonsense*. 'It is difficult to say whether, in a normal atmosphere,' Airey Neave wrote of his own contribution to the show, a sketch entitled 'The Mystery of Wombat College', 'this wretched little piece would be regarded as funny, but it was an uproarious success in the all-male atmosphere of Oflag IVc.' Among other over-the-top sketches staged was one involving a pure-of-heart maiden and a lascivious moneylender. *Faux* melodrama was punctuated by *faux* dance numbers. 'The underlying theme of *Ballet Nonsense* was provided by a *corps de ballet* consisting of the toughest-looking, heaviest-moustached officers available,' Pat Reid proudly recalled, 'who performed miracles of energetic grace and unsophisticated elegance upon the resounding boards of the Colditz theatre stage attired in frilly crépe paper ballet skirts and brassières.' The show was a huge success. 'It was escapism, without a shadow of a doubt', Jimmy Yule—who wrote the lyrics and music for this and later revues—affirmed in an interview: 'I make no apology for that at all.'[74]

One of the few British audience members not amused by *Ballet Nonsense* was Ellison Platt, the Methodist padre. This was mainly because he was already worried about what he thought were incipient cases of sexual perversion among British officers. 'Since the beginning of March homosexualism has occupied an increasingly large place in contemporary prison humour', he wrote in his diary in April 1941. 'Jocular references to masturbation too, are freer than is usual among healthy minded adults.' Oscar Wilde and Frank Harris literature was encouraging 'perverse sexualism', as was the presence of a young man attractive to those 'susceptible to homosexual inclination' in the close confines of a POW camp. Platt did not think matters had progressed beyond the level of 'coarse humour', but he was clearly worried that Colditz might become the new Sodom. *Ballet Nonsense* did nothing to quiet his fears: 'It was primarily the production of sex-starved, virile, young men whose minds perforce, inclined towards abuse as an anti-dote.' Neave's sketch was 'redolent of a master's perverted interest in small boys', and the Methodist minister had doubts about cross-dressed men playing prostitutes. 'This fight against nature,' he reflected in anguished tones, 'against tortured bodies and imagination that has become perverted with longing in a battle no young man should be required to fight'.[75]

By the end of the year Padre Platt was certain that talk had been supplemented by action. 'A small mutual masturbation group hold what they hope are secret sessions!' This was apparently widely known and—to his chagrin—quietly tolerated, along with homosexual talk. In early January 1942 the padre decided that he would have to act. 'I must attempt as difficult a task as has yet come my way', wrote Platt. 'Some of those to whom I propose to speak will deny all knowledge of anything of the kind; while one, I imagine, will tell me to mind my own business! But this happens to be my business!' What action Platt actually took, if any, is not recorded. Thereafter there are few references to sexual matters in his diary; though at the end of 1943 he noted that 'perversion' was still a lively topic of conversation.[76]

Platt, it must be said, may well have misunderstood and exaggerated in his own somewhat fevered imagination what was actually going on at Colditz. Sex was certainly not absent from men's minds when Red Cross parcels were available. 'The castle was full of randy young men', Hugo Ironside remembered. As in other camps, those who regularly took on female roles in the theatre might produce a certain amount of confusion. 'The leading ladies were incredibly convincing', George Drew admitted on camera. 'They really did try and make up to look like proper women. I remember feeling quite sort of, er, embarrassed, to find oneself stand-ing up behind one of these chaps in the shower, because they all had long hair, and er, one began to wonder what was going on.' Active liaisons between men, though, were another matter. Most recalled no sign of homosexuality at all. 'I think there was probably an element of homo-sexual feelings at times but never practicing that I know of', Lord Haig reflected. Diminished libido and fear of discovery aside, there was simply not much opportunity to engage in homosexual activity. 'It might be guessed that homosexuality became rife,' wrote Michael Burn, 'but this was not so. Even if desire had retained its strength, the crowded conditions and a general censure would have made satisfaction almost hopeless.' As Tommy Catlow observed, 'there wasn't any space for it to occur in!' Masturbation, which does seem to have happened, may well have been fuelled by the same heterosexual urges that prompted the making of telescopes (commonly known as 'lecherscopes') with which to observe young women in the town below the castle.[77]

Though others might display a greater degree of inventiveness, and some—especially those incarcerated in RAF compounds—might occasionally manifest similar tendencies, many officers at Colditz took goon-baiting to a level of rambunctiousness bordering on sometimes outright violence that was rare in most camps. The caged souls at Oflag IVC worked hard at playing, and for some of their transgressions against enemy authority would pay the penalty in the form of German retaliatory actions. Yet relations never deteriorated to the extent feared by some, and Colditz in fact turned out to be the very opposite of a Straflager, insofar as most of its inhabitants avoided the mass reprisals imposed on the men of other oflags or stalags. In a paradoxical way, being a prisoner at Colditz turned out to have its rewards.

Notes

1. On the relative mental and physical value of work over idleness see Chris Christiansen, *Seven Years among Prisoners of War* (Athens, Ohio, 1994), 34; IWM, A. F. Gibbs, 161; James B. Chutter, *Captivity Captive* (London, 1954), 123; Pat Reid and Maurice Michael, *Prisoner of War* (London, 1984), 156, 157. For envy of non-working prisoners by working men see e.g. John Lawrence, 2.2.9.7. (Fontwell, 1991), 71–2. For envy of working prisoners by non-working POWs see e.g. Guy Morgan, *Only Ghosts Can Live* (London 1945), 131.

2. Section III of the 1929 Geneva Convention covered POW labour. On the *Arbeitskommando* and *Bau und Arbeitskommando* distinction see J. M. Green, *From Colditz in Code* (London, 1971), 90–1. On the hope of better conditions in working camps see e.g. IWM, L. B. Shorrock, 54; http://www.pegasus-one.org/pow/jack_bird.htm, J. Bird, 6. It was in the interests of the Reich to get as many prisoners as possible into the labour force, which was why, for example, British Army NCOs who stood by the terms of the convention in the early war years were sometimes pressured into 'volunteering' through the withholding of privileges, and conditions in at least some

main camps kept Spartan so that both soldiers and NCOs would want to be elsewhere. 'I was informed', the man of confidence at Stalag XXB was told by the commandant in 1941, 'that it was not the intention to make the camp in any way comfortable for the prisoners of war because they might refuse to go out to work on farms if the camp was too comfortable.' IWM, N. R. Wylie collection, CSM Fulton, 'Organisation of Stalag XXB', 2.

3. On POWs learning from each other what the best and worst jobs were see e.g. George Moreton, *Doctor in Chains* (London, 1980 edn.), 100; Ike Rosmarin, *Inside Story* (Cape Town, 1990), 47. On adjusting to manual labour see e.g. Stuart Brown, *Forbidden Paths* (Edinburgh, 1978), 46; Adrian Vincent, *The Long Road Home* (London, 1956), 65–6. On multiple moves from one job to another see e.g. John Elwyn, *At the Fifth Attempt* (London, 1987), *passim*; Robert Gale, *Private Prisoner* (Wellingborough, 1984), *passim*. Prisoners commonly worked six days a week but sometimes only got one Sunday off each month (see e.g. IWM, E. Ayling, 49 ff.), despite regulations to the contrary (see Vasilis Vourkoutiotis, 'The German Armed Forces Supreme Command and British and American Prisoners-of-War, 1939–1945: Policy and Practice', Ph.D. thesis, McGill University (2000), 197–8). Daily time on the job could range from eight hours to up to fourteen hours—especially on farms in summer. See e.g. IWM, R. P. Evans, 33; IWM (Rolf), K. Dyson, 14; IWM (Rolf), A. T. M. Gant, 8. Daily pay could range from as little as 7 to over 80 *Lager Pfennig*s per day. See e.g. Richard Pape, *Boldness Be My Friend* (London, 1953), 164; Vincent, op. cit., 63–4. For deductions to cover accommodation and other costs see Vourkoutiotis, op. cit., 208–10.

4. Sam Kydd, *For You the War is Over...* (London, 1973), 102; R. King in Patsy Adam-Smith, *Prisoners of War* (Ringwood, Victoria, 1992), 158; SPM, S. Watson. On the percentage of POWs on the land and positive conditions see A. J. Barker, *Behind Barbed Wire* (London, 1974), 100. For accounts of farm life see e.g. Clive Dunn, *Permission to Speak* (London, 1986), 123–4; J. E. Pryce, *Heels in Line* (London, 1958), 88 ff.; Barney Roberts, *A Kind of Cattle* (Sydney, 1985), 134 ff.; Charles Raymond Willoughby, *I Was There* (Brewarrina, NSW, 1994), 38 ff. On negative experience see e.g. Pape, op. cit., 246. On unfamiliar agricultural work and casualties see e.g. Jonathan Vance, *Objects of Concern* (Vancouver, BC, 1994), 128.

5. Summaries and lists of some of the types of work POWs were expected to do are contained in Barker, op. cit., 98–100; David Rolf, *Prisoners of the Reich* (London, 1988), 64–8; Maxwell Leigh, *Captives Courageous* (Johannesburg, 1992), 146. On casualties from bombing plants see e.g. IWM, E. G. Laker, 30 ff.; ibid., J. H. Witte, 179–80; John Borrie, *Despite Captivity* (London, 1975), 203; Neville Chesterton, *Crete Was My Waterloo* (London, 1995), 106; Colin Rushton, *Spectator in Hell* (Springhill, 1998), 109. On the dangers of fumes and related safety issues see ICRC, *Report of the International Committee of the Red Cross on its Activities During the Second World War (September 1, 1939–June 30, 1947): Vol. I, General Activities* (Geneva, 1948), Part III, 333. On low POW worker rations see ibid. 335. On road-sweeping over rock-quarrying see Chesterton, op. cit., 65. On skilled trades and

claiming skills see e.g. IWMSA 4747/5, E. Mine. On differing opinions about, for instance, working in sawmills see Peter Winter, *Free Lodgings* (Auckland, 1993), 110; Moreton, op. cit., 100. On chemical fumes see Vance, op. cit.

6. Winter, op. cit., 116; Ewart C. Jones, *Germans Under My Bed* (London, 1957), 183; see ICRC, op.cit., 329; IWM (Books), Harold Satow, *The Work of the Prisoners of War Department During the Second World War* (Foreign Office, 1950), 35; IWM (Rolf), A. T. M. Gant, 8; ibid., D. S. Bailey; IWM, J. H. Witte, 154; Graham Palmer, *Prisoner of Death* (Wellingborough, 1990), 81; Charles Portway, *Journey to Dana* (London, 1955), 44–6; Cyril Rofe, *Against the Wind* (London, 1956), 97. See also, however, IWMSA 4661/2, B. Piddleston. British POWs also worked in salt and iron-ore mines. See e.g. http://www.wartime-memories.fsnet.co.uk/pow/stalagixc.html, 4; PRO, WO 208/3278, p. 1; Maxwell Bates, *A Wilderness of Days* (Victoria, BC, 1978), 43, 49; Frank Taylor, *Barbed Wire and Footlights* (Braunton, 1988), 33.

7. On sick-list problems in stalags see I. Schrire, *Stalag Doctor* (London, 1956), 78, 83–4; E. Jones, op. cit., 181. On dodging the column by reporting sick see e.g. http://www.pegasus-one.org/pow/david_parker.htm, D. Parker, 7; Dunn, op. cit., 122. On stalag field promotion see IWM, L. B. Shorrock, 165; E. Jones, op. cit., 181, 199–200; Robert Garioch, *Two Men and a Blanket* (Edinburgh, 1975), 116; A. Passfield, *The Escape Artist* (Perth, WA, 1988), 203; Norman Rubenstein, *The Invisibly Wounded* (Hull, 1989), 93–4. On getting friendly with the British NCOs administering working-party rosters in stalags see e.g. James Allan, *No Citation* (London, 1955), 22. On prison sentences see Barker, op. cit., 99.

8. Francis S. Jones, *Escape to Nowhere* (London, 1952), 245, 258.

9. See Vincent, op. cit., 126–7; Schrire, op. cit., 105; Moreton, op. cit., 143; Philip Newman, *Safer Than a Known Way* (London, 1983), 57–8; Passfield, op. cit., 201–2. On 'looking glass medicine' more generally see John Burton, *Mirador* (London, 1986), 76, 77–9, 82. On Arbeitskommando sick rosters see e.g. John Castle, *The Password is Courage* (London, 1955), 157; Charles Robinson, *Journey to Captivity* (Canberra, 1991), 146.

10. See Rolf, op. cit., 74; IWM, S. J. Doughty, 33; Vincent, op. cit., 127–9; Winter, op. cit., 119–20. On the Germans limiting the number of sick by fiat and being brutal about sending injured men to work see e.g. IWM, W. A. Harding, 13; Rushton, op. cit., 64. OKW had been made aware of the fact that some of the sick were faking illness to get off work. See Vourkoutiotis, op. cit., 101.

11. Gale, op. cit., 150–1.

12. IWM, G. F. Warsop, 185; Donald Edgar, *The Stalag Men* (London, 1982), 113; Vincent, op. cit., 68.

13. S. Brown, op. cit., 60; SWWEC, F. Corfield, 41; IWM, G. R. Manners, 26.

14. Rofe, op. cit., 79.

15. Lawrence, op. cit., 56; PRO, WO 208/3272, p. 4; IWM, G. R. Manners, 27; see IWM, J. Freeman, 59.

16. Albert Paice and Alwyn Ward, *For the Love of Elizabeth* (privately printed, 1984), 24.

17. PRO, WO 310/46, R. J. Doggett affidavit; Elvet Williams, *Arbeitskommando* (London, 1975), 38–9; IWMSA 4830/2, F. Pannett. On actual and threatened shooting and killing see e.g. C. Dhillon, *Guardian*, 6 Nov. 2002; IWM, L. B. Shorrock, 98–9; IWM, W. Asquith, 97; IWM (Rolf), E. B. Davis, 16–17; Ed Annetts, *Campaign Without Medals* (Lewes, 1990), 71–2; Jim Longson and Christine Taylor, *Arnhem Odyssey* (London, 1991), 117; Pryce, op. cit., 106–8; Rolf, op. cit., 71, 72. On beatings see e.g. IWMSA 4661/2, B. Piddleston. On dogs see e.g. IWM, J. H. Witte, 156. Even when strikes appeared to succeed, troublemakers might find themselves quietly transferred elsewhere. See e.g. A. King in Adam-Smith, op. cit., 150; Borrie, op. cit., 100–1. On striking for the hell of it see Fearnside, op. cit., 40–1.

18. Schrire, op. cit., 76; Harry Buckledee, *For You the War Is Over* (Sudbury, 1994), 39; Vourkoutiotis, op. cit., 186–93. It should be noted that some prisoners did, on occasion, work hard for the sheer pleasure of accomplishment. See e.g. I. Munckton in J. E. Holliday (ed.), *Stories of the RAAF POWs of Lamsdorf* (Holland Park, Queensland, 1992), 149.

19. Richard Passmore, *Moving Tent* (London, 1982), 72; Lawrence, op. cit., 71. On the differences between main and satellite camps in the way of recreational facilities and opportunity cf. the inspection reports in PRO, file WO 224. On sunbathing at e.g. Stalag Luft III, see IWM (Rolf), R. H. Eeles, 9.

20. Sandy Hernu, *Q* (Seaford, 1999), 50.

21. PRO, WO 208/3286A, p. 15. On German obstructionism with respect to outdoor sports facilities see e.g. WO 224/45, PP reports, 26 Aug. 1941, p. 4, 3 June 1942, p. 4; WO 208/3282, pt. I, 9.

22. Leigh, op. cit., 125–6; David James, *A Prisoner's Progress* (Edinburgh, 1947), 31; Christiansen, op. cit., 51. On boxing tournaments at Lamsdorf see PRO, WO 224/27, PP report, Sept. 1944, 9. On hockey at Warburg and Eichstätt see Quarrie, op. cit., 131. On the primacy of football see also e.g. Jackson, op. cit., 58; CMAC, RAMC 1787, A. V. Tennuci, 18.

23. McKibbin, op. cit. 78. On touch rugby at Westertimke see D. James, op. cit., 32. On lack of food limiting interest in vigorous sporting activity see also e.g. IWM (Rolf), R. C. Clark, 21; D. Arct, *Prisoner of War* (Exeter, 1988), 64; T. C. F. Prittie and W. Earle Edwards, *Escape to Freedom* (London, 1953 edn.), 66.

24. J. Roberts, *A Terrier Goes to War* (London, 1998), 84; Kydd, op. cit. 214; see Rubenstein, op. cit., 165.

25. See e.g. B. A. James, *Moonless Night* (London, 1983), 55; IWMSA 4759/2 and 4, P. Buckley; IWM, G. R. Manners, 78; J. Barnes in David McGill, *P.O.W.* (Naenae, NZ, 1987), 78. On the details of tin-bashing (mostly creating utensils) and modelling see e.g. Robin P. Thomas, *Student to Stalag* (Wimbourne, 1991), 224–35.

26. IWMSA 4759/4, P. Buckley; J. Barnes in McGill, op. cit., 74, 77; Philip Kindersley, *For You the War Is Over* (Tunbridge Wells, 1983), 147; see also, e.g., Steve Darlow, *Lancaster Down!* (London, 2000), 165–6.

27. Martin Smith, *What a Bloody Arrival* (Lewes, 1997), 123. On wagers at Sagan see Imelda Ryan (ed.), *POWs Fraternal* (Perth, WA, 1990), 74. On betting at Barth see John Fancy, *Tunnelling to Freedom* (London, 1957), 52.

On 'two-up' and betting at Hohenfels see McKibbin, op. cit., 79; IWM (Rolf), J. M. McGee, 15. On the casino at Oflag VIIIF see Kindersley, op. cit. On the gambling syndicates at Oflag VIIB see Jack Poole, *Undiscovered Ends* (London, 1957), 163. On gambling at Spangenberg see T. D. Calnan, *Free As a Running Fox* (London, 1970), 62.

28. PRO, WO 208/3292, Report of the SBO Colonel W. D. E. Brown R.A., n.d. [May 1945?]; Poole, op. cit. On gambling at Warburg see IWM, I. P. B. Denton, 33. The SBO's efforts to regulate gambling in the Belaria compound of Stalag Luft III were apparently more successful. See Edward Sniders, *Flying In, Walking Out* (Barnsley, 1999), 144.

29. Jim Rogers, *Tunnelling into Colditz* (London, 1986), 84. On the origin of the term 'goons' see R. Thomas, op. cit., 191. On Germans who could not understand the English language or Britain as a country and were therefore, ipso facto, a bunch of stupid foreigners, see e.g. CSVA 7, P. Allan; Borrie, op. cit., 73; Kydd, op. cit., 222; Miles Reid, *Into Colditz* (Salisbury, 1983), 53–4.

30. On the goal of making the Germans feel angry or foolish enough to lose their tempers and their dignity see e.g. IWMSA 4827/4, R. Loder; M. Reid, op. cit., 31.On 'offensive' saluting among British Army officers and acting in a superior manner see e.g. IWMSA 4893/4, M. Champion Jones. On name-calling and swearing in English by other ranks see e.g. Kydd, op. cit., 130. On confusing the count and generally playing up see e.g. PRO, WO 208/ 3274, App. D, 6.

31. Passmore, op. cit., 167–8. On the scout/guide affair see Percy Wilson Carruthers, *Of Ploughs, Planes and Palliasses* (Arundel, 1992), 104; Derek Thrower, *The Lonely Path to Freedom* (London, 1980), 107–8.

32. M. Reid, op. cit., 37–8.

33. IWM, D. Swift, 45; IWM., J. H. Witte, 169; see e.g. IWM(Rolf), D. B. Palmer, 7.

34. McKibbin, op. cit., 75–6.

35. George Beeson, *Five Roads to Freedom* (London, 1977), 43–7; McKibbin, op. cit., 76.

36. Kindersley, op. cit., 150–1.

37. IWM (Rolf), J. M. McGee, 10a.

38. IWMSA 4767/4, J. Greenwood; Stephen P. L. Johnson, *A Kriegie's Log* (Tunbridge Wells, 1995), 144; Frank Taylor, *Barbed Wire and Footlights* (Braunton, 1988), 25. On the Laufen dummies see Jim Rogers, *Tunnelling into Colditz* (London, 1986), 34. On stealing during searches see e.g. Andrew B. Cox, *Our Spirit Unbroken* (Port Elgin, Ont., 1999), 93.

39. Passmore, op. cit., 169, 115; Carruthers, op. cit., 102. On the bayoneting incident see IWM (Rolf), F. Edmunds. On the case against goon-baiting see Calton Younger, *No Flight From the Cage* (London, 1981 edn.), 50; Walter Morrison, *Flak and Ferrets* (London, 1995), 154; Prittie and Edwards, op. cit., 72; R. Thomas, op. cit., 247.

40. D. Churchill in *The Great Escapes of World War II: 1. The Great Escape* (Greystone Productions, 1997). See e.g. J. Hartnell-Beavis, *Final Flight* (Braunton, 1985), 39.

41. Richard Garrett, *P.O.W.* (Newton Abbot, 1981), 150.

42. Cox, op. cit., 56; Leigh, op. cit., 105.

43. Jackson, op. cit., 47.

44. On theatre at Stalag 383 see McKibbin, op. cit., 84–7; at Oflag 79 see Chutter, op. cit., 137; at Oflag VIIC see Prittie and Edwards, op. cit. On help from the Germans see e.g. PRO, WO 208/3270, 3.

45. Hernu, op. cit., 58, 60; R. G. M. Quarrie, *Oflag* (Durham, 1995), 134–5; Jackson, op. cit., 47; Borrie, op. cit., 201; Buckledee, op. cit., 45; Susan Elliott with Barry Turner, *Denholm Elliott* (London, 1994), 29–33; http://dspace.dial.pipex.com/jgoodliffe/mg/pow.

46. On what was staged see e.g. IWM, C. N. S. Campbell, 9–10; CMAC, RAMC 1787, A. V. Tennuci, 18; Carruthers, op. cit., 105; Gant, op. cit., 105; D. James, op. cit., 29; McGill, op. cit., 71; Quarrie, op. cit., 135, 137; Rosmarin, op. cit., 49; Stedman, op. cit., 15; F. Taylor, op. cit., 62, 78–9; R. Thomas, op. cit., 218.

47. A. Cassie and W. Morrison in *The War Behind the Wire: 1. The Great Escape* (Hartswood Films, 2000); IWM, R. P. Evans, 45.

48. Graham Palmer, *Prisoner of Death* (Wellingborough, 1990), 179; Passmore, op. cit., 141; Moreton, op. cit., 96; see also e.g. J. Burtt-Smith, *One of the Many on the Move* (Braunton, 1992), 59.

49. Alan Mackay, *313 Days to Christmas* (Glendaruel, 1998), 42; Roberts, op. cit., 102–3. On dances see e.g. IWM (Rolf), K. Dyson, 15; IWM, R. P. Evans, 44; McKibbin, op. cit., 66–7.

50. Edgar, op. cit., 156; Roger V. Coward, *Sailors in Cages* (London, 1967), 153–4; Ian Sabey, *Stalag Scrapbook* (Melbourne, 1947), 105, 117. On the view that homosexual relationships were linked to the theatre see e.g. Robert Kee, *A Crowd Is Not Company* (London, 1982 edn.), 75; IWMSA 4827/5, R. Loder. On active homosexuals being (albeit sometimes uncomfortably) tolerated see e.g. John Barrett, *We Were There* (Sydney, 1987), 265; IWMSA 4839/5, H. F. Shipp; Fred Hill, *Prisoner of War* (London, 1994), 146.

51. Vincent, op. cit., 113; Ron Mackenzie, *An Ordinary War* (Wangaratta, Victoria, 1995), 63. On lack of opportunity see e.g. IWMSA 4827/5, R. Loder; Sandy St. Clair, *The Endless War* (North Battleford, Sask., 1987), 255. On antagonism toward active homosexuals see e.g. Robert W. Calvey, *Name, Rank and Number* (Lewes, 1998), 48–9; Rubenstein, op. cit., 119–20, 163. When questioned on the matter during interviews conducted by Imperial War Museum sound archivists, former POWs almost always did not recall any homosexuality. See also IWM (Rolf), R. Dexter, 21. On a working camp where sex with guards was apparently common see Elwyn, op. cit., 95–6. On the 'home or homo' comment see James Stedman, *Life of a British POW in Poland* (Braunton, 1992), 76.

52. *Guardian Weekend*, 13 Mar. 1993, p. 28; IWM, D. W. Luckett, 28; Leigh, op. cit., 90.

53. Chutter, op. cit., 143–4; John Burton, *Mirador* (London, 1986), 65.

54. Fancy, op. cit., 59; Kingsley Brown, *Bonds of Wire* (Toronto, 1984), 131, 120–1. On the libido boost provided by Red Cross parcels see e.g. IWM,

R. P. Evans, 39; IWM (Rolf), R. Dexter, 21; L. Ray Silver, *Last of the Gladiators* (Shrewsbury, 1995), 139.

55. 'It was difficult . . .', Warren Tute, *Escape Route Green* (London, 1971), 52. On the relative scarcity of workplaces where women could be contacted see Garioch, op. cit., 122. On VD fears see F. Jones, op. cit., 232. On brothels see e.g. IWM, E. Ayling, 199; John Brown, *In Durance Vile* (London, 1981), 83. On factory romances see e.g. E. Jones, op. cit., 201 On farm liaisons see e.g. James Spenser, *The Awkward Marine* (London, 1948), 198–9.

56. See Vourkoutiotis, op. cit., 138, 150–51; Geoffrey Vaughan, *The Way it Really Was* (London, 1985), 53–4; J. Brown, op. cit., 55; Dunn, op. cit., 105; PRO, WO 32/15294, 69A, Shore case; IWM (Rolf), K. Dyson, 15.

57. Vaughan, op. cit., 53–54. On prison sentences instead of executions see Rolf, op. cit., 69–70. On the patriotism question see McKibbin, op. cit., 62–3; S. Brown, op. cit. 99–100. On continued liaisons with German women see e.g. IWM, J. Glass, 29 ff.; B. Roberts, op. cit., 151–2; J. Roberts, op. cit., 90–1.

58. Annetts, op. cit., 144; Barker, op. cit., 133; IWM (Rolf), A. Gant, 7; ibid., E. H. Drysdale, 1–3. On 'living out' see e.g. Tute, op. cit., 52; Kydd, op. cit., 171; IWMSA 4839/5, H. Shipp. On the role of parcels see e.g. IWM, L. B. Shorrock, 118; IWM (Rolf), K. Dyson, 16; Kydd, op. cit., 194, 197, 203, 232.

59. Henry Chancellor, *Colditz* (London, 2001), 311.

60. *Guardian Weekly*, 13 Mar. 1993, p. 26; IWM, R. Eggers, Colditz Register, 7 Sept. 1943. On differing opinions of life for officers and other ranks see Burn, op. cit., 305–6. On ORs seeking to be transferred to Colditz see IWM, R. A. Wilson, 113–14. On what appear to have been positive experiences once there see Philip Silvester, 'A Commemoration of Gerald Neal', *Colditz Society Newsletter*, 2:16 (June 1998), p. 5; Colin Burgess, 'Shortcut to Captivity', *Colditz Society Newsletter*, 3:25 (June 2001), 10; IWMSA 12163/1, S. Smith.

61. IWM, W. L. Stephens, 53; see PRO, WO 208/3288, 15.

62. Ion Ferguson, *Doctor at War* (London, 1955), 134; Rogers, op. cit., 95; P. R. Reid, *The Colditz Story* (London, 1952), 98–9.

63. John Chrisp, *The Tunnellers of Sandbostal* (London, 1959), 150–1.

64. P. R. Reid, *Colditz: The Full Story* (London, 1984), 160–1.

65. P. R. Reid, *The Latter Days* (London, 1954), 210–15; P. Fergusson in Chancellor op. cit., 241.

66. Jack Champ and Colin Burgess, *The Diggers of Colditz* (Sydney, 1985), 129.

67. Rheinhold Eggers, *Colditz: The German Story* (London, 1991 edn.), 64; M. Reid, op. cit., 59.

68. Eggers, *German Story*, 31; M. Reid, op. cit., 72. On the coin incident see P. R. Reid, *Full Story*, 143. On slight of hand see e.g. P. R. Reid, *Latter Days*, 140–3. On leg-pulling as a major source of mirth see G. Davies-Scourfield in *The Colditz Story* (Classic Pictures, 1993).

69. Corran Purdon, *List the Bugle* (Antrim, 1993), 53.

70. M. Reid, op. cit., 59–60; IWMSA 16843/4, J. Chrisp; ibid. 10643/3, P. Welch; M. Alexander and J. Yule in *Escape From Colditz: 2. The Best of British* (Windfall Films, 2000).

71. LC, T. N. Catlow, 77–8; Ferguson, op. cit., 136.
72. On the orchestra and gramophone recitals see PRO, WO 208/3288, 16; CSVA 2, J. Yule. On breaking records see J. Hamilton Baillie in *Escape From Colditz: 2. The Best of British* (Windfall Films, 2000). On irritation caused by the sounds of practice see e.g. Reid, *Colditz Story*, 163–4.
73. LC, M. Riviere letter, 18 Nov. 1944; ibid., T. Catlow, 76.
74. CSVA 2, J. Yule; Reid, *Colditz Story*, 94–5; Airey Neave, *They Have Their Exits* (London, 1953), 82–3; see IWM, J. E. Platt diary, 18 Nov. 1941; Eggers, op. cit., 61; J. Yule in *Escape From Colditz: 1. The Escaping Academy* (Windfall Films, 2000).
75. IWM, J. E. Platt diary, 18 Nov. 1941, 22 Apr. 1941.
76. Ibid., 5 Jan. 1942, 6 Dec. 1941.
77. Chancellor, op. cit., 312; LC, T. Catlow, 73; Michael Burn, *Farewell to Colditz* (London, 1974), pp. ii–iii (though see also id., *Turned Towards the Sun* (London, 2003), 157); LC, Earl Haig interview, tape 2, transcript, 2. On the absence of homosexuality see also IWMSA 16797/5, H. Bruce; Chancellor, op. cit., 218. On telescopes see Walter Morrison, *Flak and Ferrets* (London, 1995), 170. On self-abuse see Michael Burn, *Yes, Farewell* (London, 1946), 17. One of the orderlies seems to have gone a step further when, in the immediate aftermath of the liberation of Colditz, he started a relationship with a female Polish worker in the town below. *Guardian Weekend*, 13 Mar. 1993, p. 28.

7 Reprisals and Rewards

All forms of corporal punishment, confinement in premises not lighted by daylight and in general, all forms of cruelty whatsoever are prohibited. Collective penalties for individual acts are also prohibited.

(from Article 46, Geneva Convention, 1929)

Belligerents shall be required to send back to their own country, without regard to rank or numbers, after rendering them in a fit condition for transport, prisoners of war who are seriously ill or seriously wounded.

(from Article 68, Geneva Convention, 1929)

Under the terms of the Geneva Convention individuals in enemy hands were subject to well-defined penalties for acts of misconduct that mirrored those in place within the captor's armed forces. At the same time certain categories of prisoner—chiefly medical personnel and the severely injured—were supposed to be repatriated to their home country as quickly as practicable after capture. For British prisoners of war in Nazi Germany, however, the process of apportioning reprisals and rewards would be mostly rather more complex and often fraught with peril than was allowed for under the provisions of an international agreement concluded in time of peace by a defunct regime. One of the principal features of the POW experience as a whole was the sameness of day-to-day life behind the wire. Yet individuals, groups, and even on occasion the population of entire camps could find their condition worsened or improved on the basis of events that were not always of their own making. As in other respects, the inhabitants of Colditz were often better off, but also sometimes worse off, than their contemporaries incarcerated elsewhere in the Third Reich.

Apparent or real insubordination (which was mentioned as sufficient cause for disciplinary action in Article 45 of the Geneva Convention, yet might encompass everything from talking back to outright mutiny) was what got most individual Kriegies into trouble. Whether involving an on-the-spot response by a guard or NCO, the penalty meted out by a commandant, or a full-blown court martial at army district level, enemy justice from the perspective of the recipients was sometimes clearly fair and honest, but at other times seemed extreme to the point of savagery.

On working parties and in main camps the more brutish NCOs and guards could resort to violence if other-rank prisoners appeared unwilling or slow to carry out orders. Slaps, kicks, being hit with a rifle butt, or even jabbed with a bayonet amidst a stream of high-pitched invective might result, as well as field punishments such as being made to stand rigidly at attention facing the wire, possibly for days at a time, with hands above the head while holding a rock.[1] Summary brutality of this kind— as against being put on a charge or court-martialled—was not commonly directed against British officers, but they too ran the risk of being shot for acting in ways that guards thought—or were under orders to assume— involved insurrection or escape. On the comparatively rare occasions that this happened, the results were often fatal.

Near or actual tragedy might occur as the result of a simple misunderstanding or an argument with a trigger-happy German who felt his authority or dignity was being threatened. In the first year of the war shots were fired at a group of officers in the grounds of Laufen by a guard who alleged that the prisoners had been laughing at him. Luckily he missed his mark, but other human targets were not so fortunate. On a working party out of Posen several years later a soldier was fatally wounded after misunderstanding the direction a guard wanted him to walk in and being shot in the back. Getting into a fight could end bloodily, as when two apparently drunken soldiers were shot and bled to death after an altercation with an NCO on a working party sent out from Wolfsberg in April 1944. A point-blank refusal to work could lead to bloody results. One cold winter day a corporal on a working party out of Lamsdorf was shot dead by an Unteroffizier for refusing to climb a steel-girder pylon without proper boots and gloves. On other occasions it took virtually nothing for a guard to become enraged enough to open fire. In December 1941 a lance corporal was shot in the stomach and died for having the temerity to ask the guard in charge of his Arbeits- kommando from Thorn to allow the men on his gang to take shelter from the rain while they were stacking and loading beets.[2]

Armed civilian foremen might be just as bad, especially as the bombing of Germany increased in the second half of the war and the

Nazi propaganda machine started to foster a lynching mentality among the population. A private in the Green Howards heard about a particularly nasty incident in another work gang that was part of his coal-mine Arbeitskommando out of Mühlberg late in the war:

The victim was an Australian who, by tragic coincidence, was celebrating his birthday that day. It seemed that the civilian guard had seized one rather small and weak prisoner and was physically ill treating him. The Australian came to the assistance of his fellow prisoner and demanded that the German leave him alone. For answer, the German drew a revolver and shot the Australian in the chest at point blank range. It took him about half an hour to die, during which time the German refused to let anyone come near him to render first aid, nor did he allow anyone to send for help.

Eric Laker, another Stalag IVB man working in another colliery, noted a similar tragedy in his diary on 23 September 1944. 'Incident at mine with night shift, at 2200 hrs. Chap from our room, shot in neck, and *left lying until 0300 hrs.* in the pouring rain. The Germans cannot take all this bombing and are beginning to get very nasty towards us.'[3]

In main camps the majority of shooting incidents seem to have occurred as a result of guards following standing orders to the letter. In hutted camps prisoners were warned that guards were under orders to shoot without warning from the watch-towers if prisoners were spotted outside their barracks after evening lock-up, and that the same applied during the day if they touched or crossed the warning wire laid around the inside perimeter of the camp a few yards from the main fence. Technically three warning shouts were to be given before shots were fired during the day, but such verbal cautions were not always heard or made.[4]

Sometimes shooting incidents were the result of poor communication. In the East Compound of Stalag Luft III, in the summer of 1942, an RAF officer narrowly missed being hit by a bullet fired by a guard who had not been told that prisoners were now being allowed to leave their huts to go to the latrine just before dawn. On other occasions sufficient warning was given but—as in the case of a mentally disturbed Fleet Air Arm officer who clambered up the main fence in broad daylight in the spring of 1943 and was shot dead—tragically was not heeded. At other times guards (either by accident or design) fired wide of the mark when Kriegies sought to retrieve balls and other items from beyond the warning wire without first obtaining permission, or were particularly slow in returning to their barracks at lock-up time.[5]

There were, however, a number of instances where prisoners were either wounded or killed by guards whose aim was truer and whose scruples were fewer. Incidents multiplied as the war dragged on, the prisoner population expanded, and enemy tempers shortened amidst Allied bombing and a deteriorating war situation; but the first fatal shooting occurred within eleven months of the outbreak of hostilities.

At Laufen orders were issued by the commandant that prisoners were not to lean out of the Schloss windows, on pain of being shot at by guards. In November 1940 a *Posten* took careful aim and killed without warning a British lieutenant who was seen sketching from a window, but who was apparently not leaning out at all. One day, while a party of British POWs were temporarily housed in a camp full of French POWs in the spring of 1941, everyone was ordered back to their huts. After several hours a Scots sergeant went outside and gesticulated to the guards that he wanted to fill his canteen from the pump near the wire. What response he got is not clear. The aggressively anti-British commandant claimed that he had been warned several times not to come out, while the man of confidence asserted that this was a lie. Whatever the truth of the matter, the sergeant set off for the pump and within sixty seconds lay mortally wounded. In the late summer of the same year British POWs were confined to barracks during the day as well as at night at Stalag IVB (Mühlberg) because of a suspected diphtheria outbreak. A Royal Marine shouted to a passing French POW one day to throw him some cigarettes: when he leaned out the window of his hut to retrieve them he was instantly shot through the head by a guard.[6]

A particularly nasty episode occurred one night in the RAF compound at Lamsdorf in January 1942. An air gunner, having observed some loose timber just beyond the compound fence, crept out to retrieve it for use as fuel. The notorious and sometimes violent NCO known as Ukraine Joe spotted him, walked up, and deliberately fired a bullet from his pistol into the unfortunate man's stomach. 'The victim writhed on the ground and screamed "mother, mother, mother!"' according to Sergeant Richard Pape, who observed the scene from the barracks. Ukraine Joe then stepped back a few paces and fired three more bullets, two into the head and one into the chest, to make sure the wounded man died.[7]

In the autumn of 1943 one of the army sergeants at Hohenfels was wounded in the leg while picking dandelions for his rabbits from under the warning wire. At about the same time a South African officer was shot and badly injured at Oflag XIIB (Hadamar). 'A courtyard was used for the purpose of recreation and exercise', a war-crimes memo on the episode explained, 'which was surrounded by an apron wire fence, inside which was a trip wire':

During September 43, in the course of a Basket Ball game, the ball went out of play hitting the outside wire, rebounding and coming to rest under the trip wire, a little to the wrong side of it. Lieut. Gordon BROWN went to retrieve the ball which he succeeded in doing by inserting his hand underneath the trip wire, and when he had walked back about 4 paces towards the scene of play, [a guard named] NEULIST fired at him with his rifle from the raised sentry tower from a range of about 15 yards; this shot missed. Lieut. BROWN hesitated, then went on and was about to throw the ball in from a position near the back of the field of play when NEULIST fired again, this time the bullet struck Lieut. BROWN in the left shoulder and has resulted in the disablement of his left arm.

Ten seconds elapsed between the first and second shots.[8]

In the first months of 1944 there was further evidence that at least some guards were intent on shooting to kill at the first opportunity that presented itself. In January an RAF prisoner in 'A' compound at Stalag Luft VI (Heydekrug), contrary to regulations, threw some English cigarettes to a Russian prisoner working nearby. While the RAF man was walking towards his hut a machine-gun in one of the towers opened up on him. He only just managed to round a corner before a hail of bullets struck the end of the hut, narrowly missing several other prisoners inside. An even more disturbing episode occurred at Oflag VIIB (Eichstätt) the following month. When the air-raid siren wailed one day and officers seemed to be dawdling in returning to their huts, as they were supposed to when the sirens started, an apparently off-duty guard raised his rifle in a menacing gesture. Amidst the mad rush for the doors one lieutenant paused to look up for the planes. He was promptly shot dead. A friend then came out of the nearest hut with his hands over his head, nodding to the prone body in the expectation of being allowed to carry the man inside in case he was only wounded. Instead the second officer, with his hands still in the air, was shot in the head at point-blank range. At Stalag Luft VII (Bankau), a guard calmly shot dead a Canadian prisoner who emerged prematurely from his hut after a raid had finished. In March, again at Stalag IVB, an RAF flight sergeant was fatally wounded when guards fired into a coal shed inside the camp that a number of prisoners were raiding. Later an officer in the Belaria compound of Stalag Luft III was shot in the hand because he had allegedly brushed it against the warning wire. In the summer of 1944 an Indian prisoner at Oflag 79 (Brunswick) was killed outright by a bullet from a sentry's rifle after apparently leaning over the trip wire to retrieve a fallen item. In none of these instances did witnesses notice any verbal warnings before shots were fired.[9]

Matters did not improve in the last six months of the war. In January 1945, for instance, once again at Stalag IVB (Mühlberg), a sentry shot and wounded an RAF man caught at night climbing through the wire between compounds. The man was left to bleed and freeze to death, the sentry resuming his beat, and the prisoners had to face the sight of a corpse on the wire—presumably as an object lesson—the following day. Marlag, which by the end of the war housed hundreds of men who had marched in from Sagan, as well as naval personnel, was the scene of another shooting the following month when an RAF officer was hit twice—in the arm and the liver—after being spotted crossing the warning wire in order to trade for eggs with someone in a neighbouring compound.[10]

Prisoners trying to break out not only ran the risk of being fired at if spotted going through the wire, but also—assuming they were successful in getting out—acts of personal retribution on the part of those who arrested them if they were unlucky enough to be recaptured. These could range from beating up and torture (in the case of the Gestapo) to 'shot-while-trying-to-evade-arrest' type executions (in the case of ordinary police, soldiers, and even civilians). Gestapo officials, not surprisingly, often showed little compunction in keeping the military authorities ignorant of escaped POWs who fell into their hands while they were severely interrogated, especially if they were not officers and particularly if they were thought to have had contact with underground resistance movements. In the latter stages of the war the local chief might simply execute ('shot while trying to escape') those who came into the local jail or make them disappear into the *Konzentrationslager* system.[11]

Yet it was not just members of the Gestapo who took matters into their own hands. There was always the danger of misunderstandings between newly recaptured prisoners and trigger-happy police or armed-forces personnel leading to tragedy.[12] Beyond this, moreover, angry soldiers, acting either on their own initiative or with the support of a superior NCO, sometimes chose to inflict their own form of retributive justice on escapers.

On one of the Lamsdorf Arbeitskommandos it was widely believed that two prisoners whom the Germans claimed were killed in the act of escaping had actually surrendered but were then deliberately shot by guards, their bodies being left in the open for two days *pour encourager les autres*, in March 1941. About a year later two privates made a break from their iron-quarrying working party administered through Wolfsberg. They were picked up at a railway junction and two guards shortly arrived to escort them back to camp at Radner. One of the two recaptured men, Trooper W. J. Lawrence, explained what happened next in a war-crimes deposition:

I do not know the names of these two guards but as soon as they got us out of the police barracks they started calling us names and slapping our faces with the backs of their hands. We were taken about a quarter of a kilometre down the road and were then met by the commandant of the camp [a senior NCO] and four other guards. The commandant ordered the guards to tie our hands behind our backs and then Davis's hands were tied tightly to mine so that we had to march back to the camp, a distance of about nine kilometres, in this fashion. This was very painful as we were tied by means of the string used to tie Red Cross parcels and the flesh of our wrists was badly cut. We kept falling down and we were kicked, punched, hit with rifle butts and hit with the flat side of the guards' bayonets across the back and legs. I was only semi-conscious towards the end of the journey and Davis partly carried me. This ill-treatment was all carried out on the instructions of the commandant who was present for the whole of the journey. He had his Luger pistol and he hit me on the back of the neck with it several times. He did the same to Davis. We were knocked down by him several times, owing to the blows from his pistol, and each time we fell down he and the guards kicked us to our feet and threatened to shoot us.

Once back behind the wire the two men were further beaten about the face, arms, and legs by an enraged junior NCO with planks of wood. Early in 1943 when two Palestinian escapers from an Arbeitskommando in Upper Silesia were recaptured, a railway policeman shot one of them dead without provocation. According to another member of the same party, this was not a unique case. ' "Shot while trying to escape after recapture" was the stock formula used by the Germans to cover up murder', Cyril Rofe asserted.[13]

Though other ranks were perhaps more prone to be physically assaulted by Wehrmacht personnel than officers on recapture, the latter were not altogether exempt from the threat of enraged guards. In August of 1942 two captains managed to break out of Oflag IXA/H, but were retaken by civilians within two miles of the camp. Two guards from Spangenberg came running up, the first of whom immediately started to strike one of the officers with the butt of his rifle, beating him to the ground with such force that his rifle broke and the man's skull was fractured. This seemed only to enrage the guard further, and he then proceeded—covered by the raised rifle of his companion—to beat up the other officer with his broken weapon.[14]

Thankfully this sort of ad hoc corporal punishment or shooting was comparatively rare (at least until the last fourteen months of the war, when the extra-judicial killing of escapers came to be widely sanctioned by the state authorities). The common practice was to treat escape attempts as one of a range of camp disciplinary infractions. The length and severity of imprisonment for problematic individuals in a Kriegie cell-block (sometimes known as the cooler) or a special disciplinary compound for POWs (*Straflager*) was the responsibility of the commandant. The maximum penalty he could impose under Article 54 of the Geneva Convention for offences ranging from insolence to escape was thirty days. At first disciplinary retaliation often tended to be mild. Multiple offences, however, along with increasing pressure from OKW to punish offenders and deter emulation as the war went on, led to harsher awards and efforts to circumvent the spirit if not the letter of international law.

In 1940–1 at Stalag Luft I (Barth) the penalty for a first escape attempt was five days in cells, the second attempt ten days in cells, and for any third attempts the full thirty days. By the spring of 1941, however, the price of failure had begun to increase as the Germans sought both to punish and deter through sending offenders to the cooler for fourteen days without access to Red Cross parcels and amenities. Alex Masterson, who broke out of one of the forts of Stalag XXA (Thorn) in April, on recapture was immediately slapped in cells for the full thirty days, even though this was his first bid for freedom. For refusing to reveal how he had broken out in his first escape attempt, RAF Sergeant Derrick Nabarro was punished with the full thirty days, on top of the four days he had already spent in a cell while under interrogation at Stalag IXC (Bad Sulza). Holding men 'pending investigation' before they started their official time behind bars became a popular tactic at Stalag Luft III (Sagan), and by 1942–3—encouraged by OKW—camp commandants were often not counting time spent in local jails while in transit back to camp, and were using add-on offences such as 'destruction of Reich property' (damage done to fences, walls, furniture, and items of infrastructure) and even forgery (using faked passes and documents) to lengthen camp disciplinary awards. Sergeant George Beeson, who had already spent nine days under close arrest in the hands of the Gestapo and in a Straflager, found himself awarded twenty-eight days of solitary confinement when he arrived back at Hohenfels. The days spent en route back to Stalag XVIIIA and waiting in the local Straf compound in October 1944 were not deducted from the twenty-one days Percy Carruthers spent in cells after recapture. Sometimes allowances were made. At Stalag Luft III eleven days were deducted from the fifteen-day

1. Captain Pat Reid (played by John Mills) takes advice from the SBO, Colonel Richmond (based on Guy German and 'Daddy' Stayner, and played by Eric Portman) in the film version of *The Colditz Story* (Ivan Foxwell, 1955).

2. Some of the main characters from the first series of the BBC TV drama *Colditz* (1972). Top row: The SBO, Lieutenant-Colonel John Preston (Jack Hedley); Lieutenant Dick Player (Christopher Neame); Pat Grant (Edward Hardwicke). Bottom row: Flight Lieutenant Phil Carrington (Robert Wagner); Flight Lieutenant Simon Carter (David McCallum).

3. Pat Reid in person, showing off a recent product of the Colditz Industry at the Brighton Toy Fair, 1973.

4. Into the bag: A pair of army officers and a corporal undergoing a search by their Afrika Korps captors, Agedabia, January 1942.

5. Wire in every direction: A winter view from Stalag VIIIB (Lamsdorf).

6. This shot of Hut 16b at Lamsdorf taken around Christmas 1943 shows how cramped quarters equipped with three-tier bunks could be for Other Ranks and RAF NCOs.

7. Still cramped but better off: A room for army officer prisoners at Oflag VIIIF (Mährisch Trübau), January 1944.

8 (*above*). The rat-infested 'forty holer' at Lamsdorf.

9 (*left*). Colditz was not the only Schloss camp for British officers—others included Spangenberg castle.

10 (*left*). A clandestine shot of 'Ukraine Joe' during *Appell* in the RAF NCOs' compound at Lamsdorf.

11 (*below*). Squadron Leader L. W. V. Jennens, adjutant to the SBO, argues with the amicable *Hauptmann* Pfeiffer at Stalag Luft III, 1942.

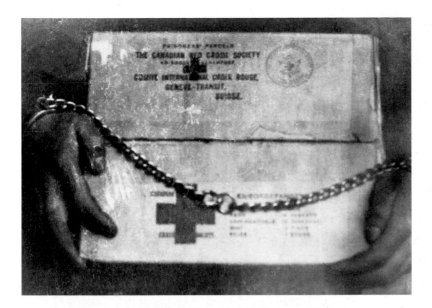

12 (*above*). Manacled Kriegie holding Canadian Red Cross parcel.

13 (*left*). A 'blower' in operation at Stalag VIIIB.

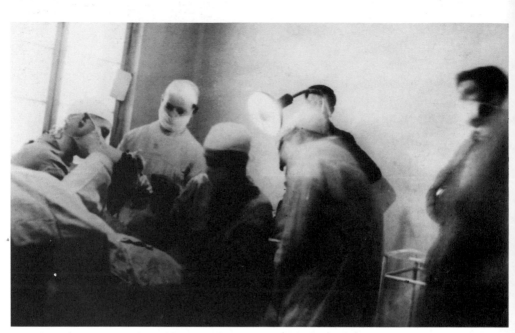

14. RAMC doctors operating with minimal support, Lamsdorf camp hospital.

" *Mad? Why, you're no more mad than I am!!*"

15. A humorous look at a serious subject.

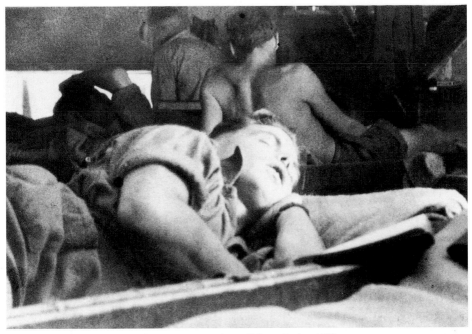

16. Reading giving way to sleep in cramped conditions, Stalag VIIIB.

17. Transcribing the BBC news heard via a clandestine radio, Oflag 79 (Brunswick).

18. Circuit bashing on a cold day, Stalag Luft III.

19. The results of skilled tin-bashing, Oflag 79.

20 (*above*). Mass being conducted in the courtyard at Colditz, 1942.

21 (*left*). Sikh soldiers of an *Arbeitskommando* under guard, Wehrkreis IV.

" *All the world's a stage . . .*

. . . and one man in his life . . .

. . . plays many parts."

22. When boys must be girls . . .

23. The cast of 'Ballet Nonsense', Colditz, 1941.

24. Not all would make it home: Funeral of Private Frank Smith, April 1942.

25 (*right*). Lance-Corporal W. C. Britten, Royal Warwickshire Regiment, in British Free Corps uniform, 1944.

26 (*below*). Neutral inspectors escorted around Stalag Luft III by the commandant and his staff.

To all Prisoners of War!

The escape from prison camps is no longer a sport!

Germany has always kept to the Hague Convention and only punished recaptured prisoners of war with minor disciplinary punishment.

Germany will still maintain these principles of international law.

But England has besides fighting at the front in an honest manner instituted an illegal warfare in non combat zones in the form of gangster commandos, terror bandits and sabotage troops even up to the frontiers of Germany.

They say in a captured secret and confidential English military pamphlet.

THE HANDBOOK OF MODERN IRREGULAR WARFARE:

". . . the days when we could practise the rules of sportsmanship are over. For the time being, every soldier must be a potential gangster and must be prepared to adopt their methods whenever necessary."

"The sphere of operations should always include the enemy's own country, any occupied territory, and in certain circumstances, such neutral countries as he is using as a source of supply."

England has with these instructions opened up a non military form of gangster war!

Germany is determined to safeguard her homeland, and especially her war industry and provisional centres for the fighting fronts. Therefore it has become necessary to create strictly forbidden zones, called death zones, in which all unauthorised trespassers will be immediately shot on sight.

Escaping prisoners of war, entering such death zones, will certainly lose their lives. They are therefore in constant danger of being mistaken for enemy agents or sabotage groups.

Urgent warning is given against making future escapes!

In plain English: Stay in the camp where you will be safe! Breaking out of it is now a damned dangerous act.

The chances of preserving your life are almost nil!

All police and military guards have been given the most strict orders to shoot on sight all suspected persons.

Escaping from prison camps has ceased to be a sport!

27. German poster warning against escapes, 1944.

28. Ex-Kriegies prepare to board the Lancasters that will fly them to England, 11 May 1945.

HOME AT LAST

" . . . *funniest thing I ever heard ! ! . . .*"

29. Adjusting to civilian life could take time . . .

award given to Kingsley Brown because he had switched identities with a soldier at the Lamsdorf hospital and had already spent days in the Straf compound at Stalag VIIIB after a failed escape bid from a working party. But in other cases men could spend five weeks behind bars for using a forged pass, sometimes—though not always—under quite harsh conditions.[15]

Individual commandants might also impose sanctions on the camp population as a whole for escape activity, goon-baiting, and other forms of insubordinate behaviour—and, on occasion, as revenge for RAF bombing. The theatre might be closed, access to the sports field denied, water shut off for much of the day, extra roll-calls and searches instituted, and the mail supply interrupted. Many of these actions were explained to neutral observers as being the result of technical difficulties unconnected with POW behaviour—the Geneva Convention, after all, specifically forbade the imposition of collective punishments—but there was no doubt in prisoners' minds that they were being subjected to reprisals.[16]

In response to escape attempts from Stalag Luft I (Barth) in the early war years, the men of the officers' compound were subjected to twenty-eight successive days of searches—during which their barracks and possessions were turned upside down—as well as the shutting off of the electricity supply at night. After a group of men broke out of Stalag IIIE (Kirchhain) in late 1941 the remaining inmates were paraded in front of a horde of armed guards, made to discard their socks, shoes, and boots and slip on clogs. They were then forced to run round the compound by a pistol-wielding officer for almost three hours while guards watched with guns at the ready. By the time this 'clog dance' ended the barracks had been ransacked, many men had bleeding feet, and several had fainted from pain and exhaustion. 'No afternoon tea by order of the Kommandant,' Captain John Mansel noted in his diary on 3 October 1942 at Oflag VIIB (Eichstätt), concerning a more typical level of reprisal, 'because he was laughed at on search parade yesterday.' Evidently the camp had not learned its lesson, for on 18 March 1943 the same officer was recording that 'the Kommandant has ordered the Canteen to be closed for 10 days and we are to be shut in our huts at 7.00 p.m. for 7 days as a punishment for laughing and jeering and quack-quacking yesterday'. Meanwhile, in Stalag VIIIB at Lamsdorf privileges were being curtailed, searches increased, and parcels withheld for escape attempts and destruction of Reich property.[17]

Vindictiveness towards prisoners could also manifest itself in relation to Red Cross parcels. Containing luxury items such as real coffee and cane sugar unobtainable in Germany, these parcels became a natural source of envy and a focal point for personal retaliation by camp authorities. Red Cross parcels were not tampered with in England for fear of the consequences if the Germans imposed an outright ban, but the fact that MI9 was known to be sending maps, money, and other contraband items in parcels under the guise of various bogus philanthropic organizations made searching Red Cross packages before they were handed over to the recipients a justifiable exercise. Furthermore, the use of tinned food for escapes—it could be stored for later use in a way that perishables could not—and of the tins themselves as anything from earth scoops to parts of a tunnel ventilation system—legitimized the piercing of newly arrived tins and the confiscation of emptied tins under orders from OKW.[18] The way in which this was done, however, indicated whether the commandant and his minions were or were not framing their actions in terms of a reprisal.

The better camp administrations proved willing to do deals in which restrictions as to the use of tins were agreed to in return for a certain degree of flexibility in implementation. It was not until 1942 that OKW issued instructions that tins were to be confiscated, not just pierced, and for months afterward—as the high command discovered to its annoyance—there were commandants who continued to allow unopened parcels to be issued. In some compounds there were special parcel stores where a prisoner could come to withdraw an individual tin and have it opened in front of the Germans, before the contents were passed over to him in an open receptacle. Unfortunately there were also those who saw upholding security as a beautiful cover for retaliating against the *verdammt Engländer*. 'On one occasion in the early days [at Laufen],' Jim Rogers recalled, 'the Germans opened all my tins, took my bowl and emptied everything into it—the meat and two veg stew, loose biscuits, cheese, chocolate, powdered milk, etc.—stirred them all together and handed the mess to me with a smirk.' Unfortunately this was not a unique incident. 'I shall never forget the expression on the face of Angus McCombie,' recalled J. E. Pryce of a post-escape incident at Lamsdorf in 1943, 'as he watched one of the guards empty a tin of Quaker oats into his basin [under orders] and then maliciously cover it with a layer of powdered coffee.'[19]

Area bombing of German cities, in combination with Nazi propaganda, could also on occasion drive those in command to acts that were apparently not officially sanctioned by higher authority, against RAF prisoners in particular. The day after the massive night raid on

Hamburg in late July 1943—smoke from which could be seen in the camp—prisoners at Barth suddenly found themselves being locked into their barracks with shutters placed on the windows at four o'clock in the afternoon. Protests to the Protecting Power brought this particular incident to an end shortly thereafter, but a far worse form of retaliation was to come elsewhere.[20]

Angered by the refusal of many RAF sergeants to salute and by their complaints about food, the commandant at Stalag IVB (Mühlberg) decided to teach them a lesson by sending one group of troublemakers to a local concentration camp at Jacobstahl. 'They were a subdued and quietly horrified crowd when they returned', an observer noted. Geoff Taylor, an NCO Lancaster pilot in the RAAF, made the mistake of suggesting to a Scottish NCO who had returned from this place that surely it could not be much worse than Stalag IVB. 'The Scot turned his head, staring at me. Suddenly, I could have been a total stranger. "Worse than this? You bloody fool. You don't know what worse is." '[21]

In mid-July 1944 Stalag Luft VI, located at Heydekrug in Lithuania, was evacuated to prevent the prisoners from being liberated by the approaching Red Army. The three-day sea journey from Memel to Stettin in an old coaster, with men packed in like sardines, battened down below decks, and subject to air attack, was bad enough, as was the next three-day leg of the journey in closed cattle trucks without food or water and handcuffed in pairs. It was the journey on foot from the train station to Stalag Luft IV at Gross Tychow, however, that proved most frighteningly memorable for the approximately 2,000 NCOs involved.

Formed up in one large column, the prisoners were uneasily aware from comments thrown in their direction that the large number of escorting guards—a mixture of naval cadets and young Luftwaffe pioneer and signal troops—were mostly bombing victims of one sort or another. Before the actual march began the officer in command, practically frothing at the mouth, harangued his audience into an even uglier mood with talk of how these *Terrorflieger* types were no better than gangsters on whom revenge should be wreaked for the killing of innocent women and children. Still handcuffed and suffering from hunger, thirst, and heat exhaustion, the prisoners were forced to jog along the uphill road leading to the new camp for several kilometres. Meanwhile the escort thrust at the outer files of the column with bayonets and rifle butts, and ferocious dogs were unleashed to snap and bite at legs and arms. Shots were heard, kit had to be abandoned willy-nilly, and anyone who fell down was immediately pounced on and beaten further, as were those who stopped to try and help. Some accounts mention that machine guns and cameras were spotted in the woods on either side of the road, the aim being to force prisoners to break ranks and scatter to avoid the blows raining down on them, and thus provide a convenient excuse—recorded on film—for murder under the guise of 'shot while trying to escape'. Luckily the Kriegie leadership, notably Sergeant Vic Clarke, recognized the danger and warned their fellow prisoners to stick together at all costs. In the end no one was killed in the infamous 'run up the road', but many dozens of men had been wounded to a greater or lesser degree by the time they passed through the gates of Stalag Luft IV.[22]

A further sign of the times came during the following month, when over 150 recently captured Allied aircrew evaders and others were evacuated from Paris before the Allied advance caught up with them. Instead of being passed on to the Luftwaffe, these prisoners were sent by the local Gestapo chief to Buchenwald concentration camp, where they were treated as *Terrorfliegern*. It was a small miracle that the senior Allied officer managed to smuggle a message out to a nearby airfield and thereby allow the Luftwaffe—who knew nothing of these men up to that point—to demand that the SS hand them over for proper registration and incarceration in Stalag Luft III. The airmen spent only two months at Buchenwald and were not treated quite as abominably as the civilian inmates of the camp. They did not receive Red Cross parcels, however, were given the standard and entirely inadequate concentration camp food, shelter, and clothing, and were seriously threatened by disease through a combination of malnutrition, lack of sanitation, and severe overcrowding. Their chances of ultimate survival if they had stayed at Buchenwald much longer would likely have been slim, given their already emaciated state on arrival at Sagan.[23]

An even narrower escape occurred seven months later, in the wake of the aerial destruction of Dresden. In late February 1945 all the RAF prisoners held at Stalag IVB (Mühlberg) were taken to a compound where six-foot deep trenches had been dug and machine-gun equipped motorcycle combinations lay in wait, apparently under the command of an SS officer. The assembled NCOs waited in ranks for several hours, fully expecting to be mown down. In the end, however, cooler heads prevailed and they were told to disperse.[24]

Except when individuals or local commanders took matters into their own hands without authorization, matters that were considered too grave to be dealt with through disciplinary awards meted out by the commandant and his staff (which in practice could mean anything from abusing individuals in a letter home to murdering someone on a working party) became the subject of judicial proceedings—i.e. courts martial—at *Wehrkreis* or divisional level. According to witnesses, courts martial were generally conducted in accordance with Wehrmacht regulations, though this was little comfort for the several hundred men receiving sentences ranging from months in military prison to death by firing-squad. Penalties became more lenient in the latter half of the war, and no judicial executions seem to have actually taken place—though at least half-a-dozen Kriegies were on 'death row' until the end of the fighting. For the first three years convicts were sent to the detention barracks at Torgau. At the end of 1942 the inhabitants were shifted to another fortress prison, this time at Graudenz. In line with the Wehrmacht disciplinary philosophy, daily life in these prisons was strict and condi-tions very severe. There was a serious overcrowding problem, inad-equate clothing and footwear, as well as—until March 1944—no access to Red Cross parcels. A New Zealand MO noted that after six months or so at both places he had lost four stone and was suffering from scurvy, and others were known to have developed beriberi.[25]

Then there were the reprisals imposed on hundreds of prisoners by the leadership of the Reich. Many of these were in retaliation for the mis-handling—both supposed and real—of German POWs under British and Commonwealth control.

The first major reprisal action, instigated by OKW, came in the spring of 1941 after reports reached Berlin that German officers were being held under unacceptably primitive conditions at Fort Henry in Canada. In retaliation, several hundred British officers were transferred from Laufen and Spangenberg to two forts at Posen and Thorn dating back to the nineteenth century. Much of the space in these semi-ruined and hitherto largely abandoned structures was below ground level. Men were crowded into unfurnished rooms where moisture dripped from every crevice, light was inadequate, water was provided through a single hand pump, and sanitation arrangements in general were primitive in the extreme. 'We caught all sorts of nasty diseases and infections', Hugh Bruce recalled. 'It really was a wonder we didn't catch typhus because we were infested with lice which we couldn't get rid of.' Heating was practically non-existent, and to add to the jail-like atmosphere the guards carried rubber truncheons. Dartmoor prison, speculated a captain in the Coldstream Guards, was simply not in the same league.[26]

Luckily for the officers concerned, it became clear to Berlin after three months that in fact conditions at Fort Henry were not as bad as initially thought, and in June 1941 the two forts were closed and their inhabitants moved back to Spangenberg and Warburg. Retaliation against British prisoners for perceived outrages against German prisoners, however, had far from run its course.[27]

Perhaps the most unfortunate of the individuals to feel the effects of retaliatory actions arising from decisions made at state level in the first years of the war were seriously sick and badly wounded Kriegies. The Geneva Convention specified that exchanges of such men should take place, and in the summer of 1940 negotiations between the British and German authorities commenced, mediated by Switzerland. Progress was slow but steady, and by the spring of 1941 mixed medical commissions—two German doctors and two physicians from neutral countries—had toured most camps and identified over 1,200 prisoners whose condition justified repatriation. In September 1941 the chosen few (who included some medical personnel and padres, as well as the disabled) were concentrated at Bad Sulza. Their spirits rising, members of the repatriation party boarded a special hospital train bound for a camp at Rouen, the last staging post before the cross-channel journey from Le Havre. Everything thus far suggested that the exchange was in the bag. However, the much smaller number of Germans in British hands meant that there were only 150 cases suitable for repatriation from the United Kingdom. Despite earlier tacit acknowledgement that a swap would have to be proportionate to the number of men held, at the beginning of October 1941 the Reich Foreign Office suddenly announced that only a man-for-man exchange would be acceptable. Shortly thereafter the commandant at Rouen regretfully announced that the whole thing had been called off. 'I suppose most of us have experienced disappointments in life, but at that moment, there could not have been a more dejected lot of men than us', G. A. Griffin, whose shoulder had been shattered by machine-gun fire in May 1940, later reflected. 'We slunk back to our barracks and I know that I cried my eyes out, [and] many of my comrades did the same.' George Dunning, working as an RAMC orderly, described the effect of this blow on men who had expected to be home for Christmas:

Some of us went to the hospital wards to give what assistance we could [to the bed-ridden men]. It was painfully evident that the patients already knew that there would be no Christmas in England for them. They lay there—withdrawn, passive, unresponsive—indifferent to our ministration. One youngster, with stumps for arms, was fighting to hold back the tears he could no longer wipe away. Another, his glazed eyes fixed on the ceiling, muttered over and over again, 'Jesus Christ! Jesus Christ!'

Around the end of the year the entire party was sent back to Germany.[28]

The year 1942 was a bad one for tit-for-tat reprisals. At Stalag XXID prisoners' boots were confiscated for six weeks in retaliation for the same thing being done to German prisoners in a camp in Canada after an escape attempt. Incoming mail was interrupted at Oflag VIB for a time in response to problems German POWs sent to Australia were encountering in receiving letters from home. In the spring news arrived in Berlin of a disastrously mishandled transfer of Afrika Korps prisoners from Egypt to South Africa aboard the transport ship *Pasteur*. Largely due to the actions of an army officer clearly unsuited to be in command, efforts to forestall an apprehended POW insurrection had led to prisoners having all utensils confiscated and much of their personal kit and possessions looted or damaged. To force the British government to apologize officially and make restitution OKW decided to institute conditions similar to those on the *Pasteur* at Oflag IXA/H. On 30 September 1942 the personal belongings of all officers in the castle, including books, extra clothing items, towels, and razors, along with scissors, knives, forks, and all utensils, were confiscated. Badges of rank and campaign ribbons were also removed from uniforms, and it was announced that the camp orderlies would be moved elsewhere. The officers, from Major-General Victor Fortune on down, were therefore left, as Captain W. Earle Edwards explained, 'with no means of washing, shaving, combing our hair, cutting our nails, no utensils with which to eat, no clothes into which we could change and with nothing to read'. Satisfied by the eventual response from London, OKW brought this regimen to a close at the end of November.[29]

Unfortunately by this time a much bigger reprisal was in progress elsewhere. In the late summer of 1942, in the wake of the large-scale raid mounted against Dieppe by Canadian and British forces in August, evidence had come to light that German prisoners taken in this action had been tied up and blindfolded. From the German perspective this was a flagrant violation of the terms of the Geneva Convention, and OKW announced on 2 September 1942 that, unless an apology was forthcoming from the British government, all Canadian and British prisoners taken at Dieppe would be tied up. This threat was reiterated, with a twenty-four-hour time limit attached, in the wake of a smaller commando raid on Sark at the start of October, when German prisoners were again tied up and a few later found shot dead while still tied. Whether or not the tying-up of prisoners in the battle zone was contrary to the terms of the Geneva Convention was open to interpretation, and according to British reports the men killed on Sark had been shot while trying to escape. With retaliation looming the matter was pushed up to War Cabinet level, where Churchill compelled his colleagues on 8 October 1942 to agree to a bullish response, warning the Germans that if they carried out their reprisal His Majesty's Government would take similar measures against an equal number of German POWs.[30]

By this point OKW had already started its reprisal against Dieppe prisoners. At noon on 8 October over 1,300 Canadian and British officers and other ranks in a variety of camps were paraded and had their hands bound together. It was announced on 9 October that if the British government carried out its threat then at least three times this number would be incapacitated in a similar manner. The British went ahead anyway, and on 10 October over 3,000 Kriegies—concentrated mostly at Lamsdorf, Hohenfels, and Eichstätt—suddenly found themselves victims of a new round of retaliation. At first string was used to tie up hands, but police handcuffs separated by a short length of chain were soon the standard means of manacling the affected prisoners from 9 a.m. to 9 p.m.[31]

Most of those affected responded with the standard Kriegie reaction to bad news—laughter, singing, ironic cheering, goon-baiting—when told they were to be tied up, and there were some prisoners who remained apparently untroubled by being manacled. 'I didn't mind in the least', Alec Masterson, a BEF veteran, remembered. 'It was better than working in the sand quarries.' But for many Kriegies the reprisal represented both a humiliation—'somehow I felt dirty and degraded', RAF Sergeant Bill Jackson remembered—and a new set of challenges. 'One does not realise how essential hands are,' George Moreton, another RAF sergeant, later reflected, 'until deprived of their functions...' Everything from walking to lighting a cigarette and eating proved a challenge.[32] Even with one man in ten left free to help the others, the shackling reprisal might have seriously affected the welfare and health of thousands of men, given that it took over a year to fully resolve the confrontation between the two governments most directly concerned. Lamsdorf seems to have been particularly bad. Here the school, theatre, church, and sports facilities were closed; and, in an act described as one of 'pure malice', Red Cross parcels were also withheld.[33] The initial tying of hands was carried out with considerable severity—'*It's Hell!*' one prisoner recorded in his secret diary—and men asking to be freed in order to go to the *Abort* sometimes brought out the sadistic streak among the guards. 'They deliberately took their time to perform this,' Stoker Harold Siddall remembered, 'and there must have been some near misses among the lads, who quite frequently reached the bursting point.'[34] At first the guards were strict about exposing and punishing prisoners who had freed themselves by manipulating cords or using a nail or meat-tin key to unlock steel manacles. Officers at Eichstätt were threatened with arrest, NCOs caught out at Hohenfels were given three days standing at attention from dawn till dusk in the guardroom, and at Lamsdorf guilty parties were made to stand with their nose against the wire for eight hours with their hands chained behind their back.[35]

Over time, nevertheless, a combination of practical considerations—prisoner-of-war camps were not, after all, panoptic dream facilities—and efforts by the British and Dominion governments to defuse the crisis (by accepting ICRC and Swiss mediation and through freeing German prisoners) produced a less rigorous atmosphere. 'During the winter of 42 [at Stalag 383],' Sergeant J. M. McGee later explained, 'it became the done thing to remain in bed and await the arrival of the guard festooned with handcuffs.' The guard would handcuff the men and then withdraw, it being tacitly understood by all concerned that the cuffs would be then taken off. 'We used to hang the handcuffs on a hook in the back of the door,' R. P. Evans remembered, 'and when the guards came in at night, they merely reached round the door and took off the handcuffs and carried them away.' It took longer for an accommodation to be reached at Oflag VIIB, but by the spring of 1943 here, as elsewhere, shackled prisoners were subject to less supervision (which meant they wore re-straints only in the presence of a guard), and were no longer isolated from their fellow Kriegies. Eventually 'the Germans gave up and settled for a roll call with handcuffs and nothing more', Jack Pringle recalled. 'Most prisoners did not bother even to do that,' Tony Strachen argued, 'merely carrying the manacles and swinging them nonchalantly as their hosts tried to count them.' Even at Stalag VIIIB life gradually improved. 'Each morning the handcuffs were brought to our compound and handed out to the prisoners who put them on themselves', wrote Private Robert Gale. 'After roll-call we went into our respective barrack-rooms, took off the handcuffs and slipped then under the towels at the end of our bunks. The German NCO in charge of our compound knew quite well what was going on', but turned a blind eye. At first prisoners who had unlocked their cuffs and went outside carried them about, ready to slip them on if an untamed guard was sighted. After a few months it became possible to leave the chains and shackles in the hut, only to be worn if an officer was about. By the autumn, as at Hohenfels, reprisal prisoners were no longer segregated, and were only made to wear hand-cuffs when senior military dignitaries were visiting. But it was only in November 1943 that the reprisal quietly came to an end.[36]

While this mass reprisal was still going on, moreover, a smaller-scale retaliatory action had taken place. In the summer of 1942 news reached Berlin that German POWs had been mistreated in a transit camp in Palestine. OKW responded by transferring eighty-two Palestinian NCOs and sixty-eight other British Kriegies to a special Straf camp at Cholm. Eventually it was made clear to Berlin that the offending camp at Latrun no longer held German prisoners, and in May 1943 the reprisal party was moved to normal Kriegie surroundings elsewhere.[37]

Smaller-scale reprisals initiated at state level continued into the last year of the war. News that German prisoners in British hands had been chained while in transit caused Berlin to insist in April 1944 that officers being transferred en masse by train from Oflag VIIIF to Oflag 79 be handcuffed during the journey. In May reports of the separation of Austrian and German prisoners in Allied hands apparently led to a limited segregation of Irish from other British Kriegies. Later in the year members of the 22nd New Zealand Battalion found themselves locked up, apparently in response to complaints from wounded German repatriates over the unit's behaviour during the hard-fought battle for Crete. Then came news that German prisoners at Camp 306 in Egypt had been forced to sleep on sand by Jewish guards. In mid-January 1945 all bedding and furniture were removed and the theatre and canteen closed at Oflag VIIB (Eichstätt), Stalag VIIIC (Sagan), and Stalag 357 (Fallingbostel), a reprisal that lasted into March and made life very uncomfortable, given that the majority of bed-boards had already been used to shore up tunnels or for fuel.[38]

The treatment of German POWs, then, played a central role in many of the reprisals directed against groups of British prisoners. The reprisal with the greatest long-term impact, however, had nothing to do with how German prisoners were treated, and was in fact carried out by the Gestapo rather than OKW. This was the deliberate murder of fifty of the seventy-six officers who had broken out of Stalag Luft III through a tunnel in March 1944. The 'Great Escape' was the fourth successful

mass British breakout in twenty-five months, and fears had been growing in high circles that POWs might be making contact with underground movements and be preparing to lead uprisings. When the news
reached Hitler that over seventy British airmen were loose in the Reich
he flew into a rage, and ordered Himmler to execute a suitable number
of those recaptured as a deterrent to future escapes. These deaths,
conducted in secret, were officially passed off as the result of officers
being killed while trying to evade recapture. But once the death toll was
reported neither the British government nor deeply shocked Kriegies at
Sagan and elsewhere had any doubt that a deliberate and very bloody
reprisal had been orchestrated. Five of the surviving recaptured officers,
including Wings Day, were sent to a Sonderlager. When Jimmy James
arrived and saw Day he said, 'Hello, Sir, is this Colditz?' He learned that
in fact they were in a special compound at Sachsenhausen concentration
camp under SS control.[39]

As well as reprisals, there were rewards. At various junctures the
German authorities made moves to allow selected groups of prisoners
various privileges—sometimes in special settings designed for the purpose—denied in average day-to-day life within regular POW camps. The
rationale for these rewards tended to be opportunistic rather than altru-
istic in nature, but for those Kriegies able to take advantage without
compromising themselves, they were a welcome change from the restrictions and austerities of normal life behind the wire.

Among the first to be presented with the possibility of better conditions were the Irish. Members of the IRA in Germany had claimed from
the start of the war that there would be POWs who, with a little incentive
and the right propaganda exposure, would agree to fight against Britain
in the name of a united Ireland. Over the winter of 1940–1 agents of the
Abwehr made visits to various camps to interview those identified as of
Irish parentage and, in promising cases, hold out the possibility of
transfer to a special Lager where there would be more opportunity
to talk politics as well as greater freedom to soak up German *Kultur*.
Often handled clumsily and to the point of farce, these efforts yielded
little in the way of positive return for the Germans, but did provide
some Irishmen with a welcome break in routine and an opportunity to
make mischief.

Little account seems to have been taken by some of the Germans
involved that, while there was a strong Anglo-Irish element within the
commissioned ranks of the British Army, the families concerned were

Protestant rather than Catholic. Unbeknownst to the civilian recruiters, those few officers who seemed in sympathy with the ideas they were putting forward were moles. The officers had been instructed by the British camp authorities to find out what the enemy was up to and seek to undermine their efforts. About half-a-dozen or so were taken to a special 'holiday' compound attached to Stalag IIIA (Luckenwalde) outside Berlin at the start of May 1941. Once there, H. C. F. Harwood explained, he and his fellows 'got more freedom' and 'certain privileges' as part of a softening-up process prior to the full sales pitch. Terence Prittie later wrote at greater length on what it was like:

At Luckenwalde we were given immensely better treatment [than at Tittmoning]. We lived in three small, perfectly comfortable rooms. There was very much more and better food . . . We were allowed to go out for walks almost every day under armed escort, and could go wherever we wanted . . . Twice a week we were allowed into the town for shopping or for visits to the local cinema . . . In the camp itself there was as much beer and wine as we wanted.

It took about three weeks for the Abwehr to realize that it was they rather than their charges who had been hoodwinked. Almost all of the supposed IRA sympathizers, having been rewarded for false sentiments, were sent off to the Straf camp at Thorn.[40]

The situation was little better among the fifty other ranks who had been concentrated in a Stalag XXA Arbeitskommando at Friesack. Many of them were Liverpool Irish who had told their interrogators what they thought they wanted to hear, in hope of gaining more food and freedom but without any intention of turning traitor. The few Irish officers with them, including the SBO, John McGrath, were double agents whom the Abwehr had failed to spot. A delay in the forwarding of Red Cross parcels did little to win the men over, and in the end the Friesack experiment yielded a paltry number of men whose trustworthiness and interest in matters other than wine, women, and song were seriously open to question. Later efforts to segregate Irish soldiers in a 'holiday camp' atmosphere were undermined by prisoners exchanging identities. When attempts were then made to recruit—this time aiming to get Irishmen to fight against Russia rather than England—the subjects became so incensed at the propaganda they were being fed that they were reputed to have burned down their barracks.[41]

Despite the lack of success with Irish POWs, rewarding prisoners in advance of anticipated gain was a policy that the German authorities continued to pursue. Efforts to convert soldiers to the Axis cause among the over 1,000 Indian Army prisoners concentrated at Stalag IVD/Z

(Annaberg) in the spring of 1941 and on into 1942 seem to have involved the stick rather more than the carrot. A much more seductive approach, however, was taken in June 1943 with the setting up of two 'holiday camps' for British Army personnel, both administered through Stalag IIID (Steglity) in the region of Berlin.[42]

Established on the initiative of the Foreign Office rather than military intelligence, these camps were set up with a good deal of forethought and run with comparative subtlety. Officers and men would be handled separately, groups of each being sent respectively to a converted villa at Zehlendorf (eventually replaced by Schloss Steinberg in Bavaria) and a former grain warehouse at Steglitz (later moved to huts at Genshagen), on the pretence of offering several weeks of relief for long-term Kriegies from the normal privations and restrictions of POW life in Germany. Prisoners would be allowed greater freedom of movement and access to more recreational facilities, and exposure to German propaganda would be mostly of a rather indirect variety. Depending on their responses to all this, Kriegies would either be returned to their previous camps after several weeks of 'holiday' or examined more closely with the aim of recruiting for propaganda or espionage purposes and a new SS unit dubbed the British Free Corps.

Those sent to the holiday camps were generally happy with what they encountered, not least with respect to rations. RASC driver R. S. Kerridge, who was sent to the other-ranks camp from a Stalag XXB (Marienburg) working party, recalled a variety of other welcome privileges. If there had been a bombing raid on Berlin the night before, inmates were allowed to sleep in until ten o'clock in the morning. Visits were arranged to tourist sites such as the Olympic Stadium and Potsdam, and in camp the music and theatre facilities were of a superior variety. 'There was plenty of recreation at the camp,' he added, 'and if we wanted to go for a walk we only had to ask a guard and he had to take us.' If anything, conditions were even more pleasant for officers in the 'country house' setting at Schloss Steinberg, where there were special concerts, magnificent views, a swimming pool, and plenty of opportunity to go for rambling walks. 'Some of the sick, very worn prisoners,' Brigadier George Clifton, a New Zealander who spent time there in September 1944, later wrote, 'especially those who went into the bag so early in Norway and France, benefited very much from their month or six weeks' complete change of air, scenery and conditions.'[43]

The Reich Foreign Office had chosen both the regime and the staff (both German and British) for these camps with great care. Once again, however, it was the captives rather than the captors who were doing much of the outfoxing. The suborning of officers was made unlikely by the British insistence that the SBO rather than the Germans chose who did and did not get to go to Steinberg. Even though the Foreign Office representatives apparently tried on occasion to get round this, the fact remained that no officer there ever switched sides. As for the other ranks, the NCO the Germans had chosen to help run the camp at Genshagen turned out to be a double agent. Though BQSM John Brown was outwardly very much a Nazi sympathizer—he was considered a traitor by many of his fellow Kriegies at the time—he not only feathered his own nest but also improved the material conditions of those who passed through the camp, while undermining recruiting efforts for the British Free Corps to the point of complete failure.[44]

Holiday camps probably made those who passed through them somewhat less ill-disposed toward the Third Reich than they might otherwise have been. Lieutenant Stewart Walker, who would shortly be transferred to Colditz, was disconcerted to discover at Steinberg in May 1944 that the majority of his fellow prisoners, especially the senior officers, thought it wrong to try and make a break from this scenic idyll, and condemned—though without betraying plans to the enemy—those who tried. ('By Jove, chaps, bad show, this, play the game, you cads, not bad fellows these Germans!') Nevertheless, assuming that traitorous behaviour rather than a slightly more benevolent attitude was the desired object, actually rewarding prisoners without a quid pro quo clearly did not work very well for the Germans, especially when British countermeasures were in play. The real beneficiaries of the holiday-camp idea were the prisoners lucky enough to be sent to them.[45]

Attempts to incite divisions between prisoners from Britain and those from other Commonwealth countries by rewarding certain nationalities but not others were also unsuccessful. 'The Germans are unchaining the Australians and have issued us with passes stating we are "Nicht zue [sic] fesseln" [not to be shackled]', Sergeant Raymond Ryan noted in his Lamsdorf diary in early 1943. 'By unanimous vote all the Australians have decided to hand all the non-chained passes back to the Germans and tell them we do not wish for preferential treatment...' Threatened with additional reprisals unless they accepted their good fortune, the Aussies gave in and accepted the passes. But they had made it quite clear that they would not allow Commonwealth unity to be undermined by the enemy.[46]

Canadians proved to be equally obdurate. In February 1944, in the wake of positive reports on the conditions among German POWs in

Canada, the Führer issued orders that Canadian prisoners were to be allowed special privileges. Canadian aircrew NCOs would be segregated in superior huts, while Canadian soldiers would get to work exclusively on farms and be concentrated at Stalag IID (Stargard), where temporary inmates and permanent staff would enjoy better rations and more freedoms than in regular camps. Canadian officers, meanwhile, would enjoy a substantial increase in their mail privileges and parole walks. Ottawa immediately recognized that the real intent was to divide rather than to reward, and lodged a protest through the Protecting Power. In the meantime, however, it fell to the prisoners themselves to decide how best to respond.

At Marlag (O), the senior Canadian naval officer approached the SBO for advice. 'I told him that as a general principle I considered that officers were justified in accepting any specific privilege offered to them,' Captain Wilson recorded in his dairy, 'always assuming that it did not react adversely on the rest, but in this case they must act as they thought best.' Wilson was nevertheless glad when the prisoners concerned decided to reject what was on offer. 'In a right and generous spirit the Canadians refused all concessions that were not given to all in the Camp.' Canadian army officers at Eichstätt reached a similar consensus, aircrew NCOs spurned temptation—'they couldn't understand why we wouldn't take preferential treatment', Ross Elford recalled of the response at Stalag Luft VI—and soldiers refused to make themselves pawns to meet enemy objectives. 'This offer was turned down flatly by the Canadian representative', Robert Prouse, held at Stalag IVB (Mühlberg), recalled. Angered by this ingratitude, the authorities in some camps insisted on segregating the Canadians and giving them more mail and parcels than anyone else. A clear and unambiguous message nevertheless had been sent to those hoping to encourage rifts within the POW community.[47]

The one body of Kriegies from whom nothing was expected in return for better treatment was the seriously sick and wounded. By the summer of 1943, with the tide of war turning, the numbers of POWs respectively in British and German hands was much closer than it had been almost two years earlier when the first repatriation scheme had broken down. With the resolution of the shackling crisis coming into sight, a new effort to organize an exchange of about 4,000 British *grands blessés* and medical and other protected personnel took hold. Mixed medical commissions of German and Swiss doctors toured the camps to identify worthy cases, and this time those sent out on hospital trains to the Danzig area did not have their hopes dashed. In mid-October 1943 they boarded ships bound for Gothenburg in Sweden, whence they were transhipped to other vessels bound for Liverpool. This was followed by a second repatriation exchange in May 1944 conducted through Barcelona, and then a third via Gothenburg in September of the same year involving over 1,500 Allied POW cases. The final large-scale Anglo-German exchange, which involved the 2,500 men concerned being sent to Switzerland, occurred in early 1945. Technically the beneficiaries were just being treated in accordance with the Geneva Convention, but for most it had taken an unconscionably long time to happen, and seemed more in the nature of a reward than a right. Those still behind wire did not begrudge amputees and madmen the opportunity, yet understandably felt the odd pang of jealousy. 'It gave me a queer sensation to watch this party leave', Philip Kindersley reflected, on waving off repatriates from Oflag 79 in September 1944. 'They were walking away to home and freedom, while we stayed the other side of the wire like a lot of caged animals. In a way it hurt, but on the other hand everyone was delighted that these people who had suffered so much should be going home at last.'[48]

As in other spheres, being at Colditz as against other camps proved to be a mixed blessing with respect to reprisals and rewards. On the one hand there were more *Kommandantur*-imposed sanctions than in other places and far less likelihood of being granted rights and special privileges. On the other, the men of Oflag IVC were not subject to some of the major state-level retaliatory actions imposed elsewhere.

Given the high level of goon-baiting and escape-related activity at Colditz, it was not surprising that Lager officers found themselves responding with a large number of disciplinary punishments—i.e. awarding time in cells for troublesome inmates. Billie Stephens was pleasantly surprised to get only ten days in solitary for the escape that landed him in the castle in September 1942 ('really an extremely light sentence'), though as elsewhere the Germans exceeded the twenty-eight-day limit set by the Geneva Convention by holding men for a week or more 'pending investigation' before sentencing them. Eventually the waiting list for cell-time in the castle led to the use of the jail in the town below to accommodate the overflow. There was also no shortage of fines for damage to German property or of courts martial for insulting remarks and indiscipline—Peter Tunstall alone was sent to Leipzig for trial no less than three times. Though not always announced as such, reprisal action also took the form of shutting off the hot water supply and halting access to the chapel, theatre, and the sports-ground below the walls.[49]

Yet prisoners were usually guilty of the offences for which they were being individually disciplined or tried (albeit that collective reprisals were inherently unfair and banned by the Convention). Thanks to the Bar talents of Lieutenant A. R. 'Black' Campbell, furthermore, court martial verdicts might still go in favour of the accused. More importantly, there was less overt vindictiveness on the part of the Germans at Colditz than elsewhere.

When the initial group of British prisoners had been sent to the Schloss in November 1940 the first three to arrive—all, as it happened, Canadian airmen from Spangenberg—were told by their new guards that they would be shot at dawn. It turned out, however, after the three had been marched out at daybreak and lined up against a wall, that this was only a goon prank—they were in fact being given exercise—rather than a terminal reprisal for escaping. The joke was undoubtedly in rather questionable taste; nor did it in any way reflect the high degree of correctness, restraint, and personal discipline displayed by most members of the castle garrison for the majority of the time. It was true that Stabsfeldwebel 'Mussolini' Gephard, the senior NCO at Oflag IVC, on one occasion attacked a cheeky British orderly with his ceremonial sword while drunk in March 1941. This, however, was an isolated case, in which damage was done to beds and furniture but nobody was hurt. Tins in Red Cross parcels were punctured and their contents turned out as a security measure, to be sure; but this was done in front of the recipient in the parcels office, without any mixing or deliberate spoiling of items.[50]

It was also true that shots were fired at various moments of upheaval and confusion when the riot squad was called into the courtyard, or an escape was under way and suddenly discovered. In the one case where a prisoner was wounded from shots fired in the courtyard, however, the firing was accidental. The guards let fly that day in the summer of 1942 because, as they brought their rifles to the present position, the cacophony was so loud that it was assumed the NCO in charge—who was speaking at the same moment—had shouted 'Feuer!' when in fact the prisoners had been shouting 'higher!' Similarly, in the famous 'Franz Josef' escape attempt one night in September 1943, Mike Sinclair, dressed as a German NCO, had been wounded because he refused to put his hands up. He was still trying to pass himself off as the genuine article, and in the darkness seemed to a panicky and rather confused

Obergefreiter to be about to snatch something from his holster. 'Big Bum' Pilz, who was too worked up to realize that it was extremely unlikely that a British officer in a fake uniform would have a pistol about his person, panicked and fired his own weapon before his opponent could draw. Sinclair was shot dead after climbing over the wire in the exercise park one year later, but not in cold blood: 'Sentries cried "Halt"', Hauptmann Eggers recorded. 'He did not stop. So shooting started.' Missed several times as he continued to dash away from the park, Sinclair was finally hit by a bullet that most unluckily ricocheted off an elbow directly into his heart.[51]

The presence of the *Prominente* in particular and the maximum-security Sonderlager status of the castle in general meant that both Berlin and London took a keen interest in what happened at Oflag IVC. Successive commandants and their staff officers were therefore under scrutiny, OKW exerting pressure on the camp administration to prevent escapes and avoid incidents between captives and captors that might have wider repercussions than elsewhere. Though some of the German officers at Colditz favoured aggressive retaliatory action in cases of mass indiscipline, Hauptmann Eggers, with the support of Hauptmann Püpke, successfully argued that resorting to violence would be playing into the enemy's hands. He himself was not above making dire threats. While trying to find out where the entrance to a tunnel lay, for example, Eggers was faced with two British prisoners known to be involved who refused to divulge any information. He tried to intimidate the two officers by having them lined up against a wall in front of a mock firing squad. But as one of the two officers put it: 'he wasn't fierce enough [to make the threat credible]; none of them were.'[52]

A desire on the part of OKW to avoid potentially embarrassing incidents at Colditz also meant that tit-for-tat reprisals were apparently applied only once to the British and Commonwealth prisoners held there. In the summer of 1942 the amount of outgoing mail was cut down because of complaints about the length of time it was taking for mail from German POWs in Canada to reach the Reich. Oflag IVC was conspicuous by its absence, however, from the list of camps where prisoners were tied up, handcuffed, and shackled in 1942–3, and was not subject to any of the later OKW reprisals.[53]

This is not to suggest that the men of Colditz were entirely insulated from vindictive individual acts or reprisal decisions taken at senior levels outside the walls. They had all come from other camps, and some had experience of how vicious certain members of the *Herrenvolk* could be if sufficiently enraged. Peter Storie-Pugh, a lieutenant of the West Kents, was recaptured in late December 1940, after a successful breakout that would shortly land him in Oflag IVC. In a truck sent to fetch him back to his original oflag, Storie-Pugh was held down and bayoneted through his cheeks by guards enraged at having their Christmas cheer interrupted. And while comparatively safe once inside the castle itself, prisoners who broke out in the latter part of the war were subject to the same risk of mortal reprisal as other escapees. It is likely that the Canadian officer Bill Millar, the last man to make a successful break from the camp (in January 1944), was quietly murdered by the SS. 'One always thought that that happened or could happen,' Hugo Ironside commented, 'and one was surprised it didn't happen more often, to be honest.'[54]

There was also growing concern among the 'bad boys' of Colditz that they would be shot before they could be liberated. 'It was a *Sonderlager*, the Special Camp,' wrote David Walker, ' . . . and if the enemy, desperate in defeat, should seek a target among prison camps, Colditz was the obvious bulls-eye.' As de facto hostages the *Prominente* were particularly worried. As Dawyck Haig recalled, he and his fellows all 'knew that we weren't there for nothing and our continued residence on the planet was not necessarily guaranteed'. That no killing in fact occurred was due in part to a fear of Allied retribution by the SS general in charge of prisoner affairs and, more specifically, the fate of the *Prominente* during the final stages of the war, Gottlob Berger. It was also due to the recognition on the part of the prisoners themselves that the Wehrmacht at Colditz were much less likely to engage in wholesale slaughter than the SS or other security forces of the Reich. Hence the efforts of Colonel Tod, first to prevent the move of the *Prominente* and then of the entire camp population in April 1945. In the former case he failed, but in the latter he was successful. It had simply become much safer to be inside Colditz than out.[55]

In terms of avoiding high-level reprisals, being inside the walls of Oflag IVC had its advantages. The inmates of Colditz, to be sure, never had the opportunity of spending time at a 'holiday camp'—the security risks alone were too great—and neither the Canadians nor any other nationality were offered special privileges as a reward for the treatment of German POWs. Camp rewards usually came only as the result of a promise not to escape, as when twenty-five officers gave their parole in order to be allowed to play football on some flat ground below the castle walls in the summer of 1942.[56] What was more, the inhabitants strongly suspected that they were discriminated against in connection with the repatriation of *grands blessés*.

There was certainly evidence to support this belief. In July 1942 the names of five officers had been put forward for examination by a mixed medical commission by the senior British MO at Colditz, but of these only two were allowed to travel outside the castle to where the commission was then working in October. In June 1943 Flight Lieutenant Dan Hallifax, whose face was badly burned when he was shot down, had been allowed to visit the commission and had been passed as eligible for repatriation. Despite protests, however, the authorities would not let Hallifax take part in the 1943 or the subsequent repatriation, on the grounds that he was a security risk. Hallifax was not alone. When the mixed medical commission was finally permitted to pay a visit to Colditz itself on 6 May 1944, it was announced that of the twenty-nine names put forward by the British for examination, six were not to be allowed the chance to make their case for repatriation before its members. With the overt support of the SBO and the rest of the prisoners, the remaining twenty-three refused to come forward to meet with the commission. Despite the riot squad being called in and much haranguing from Eggers, the milling mass of Kriegies in the courtyard would not give way. The Swiss members of the commission, suspicious as to why the first cases were not being brought to them in the *Kommandantur* section of the castle, asked to speak to Colonel Tod. Apprised of the situation by the SBO, the Swiss doctors demanded an explanation. The commandant agreed to phone Berlin, and OKW finally agreed that all twenty-nine cases could be examined. Over a dozen were passed at this point, and more after a group was sent for examination elsewhere in October 1944. At Oflag IVC, however, being passed by the commission did not guarantee a place in an exchange. Though Hallifax and four others finally went home in January 1945 after more pressure from Tod, a few inhabitants who were supposed to be exchanged remained in the Sonderlager until the end of the war because of security and other concerns.[57]

The difficulties surrounding repatriation from Colditz should, however, be kept in perspective. Almost all of the prisoners at Colditz had made escape attempts and—with the obvious exception of the irrepressible Douglas Bader—were not missing limbs or otherwise physically incapacitated. In other words, Oflag IVC was not the sort of camp where those with encumbering serious wounds to the body sustained in battle were to be found. Mental problems could and did develop inside the walls, as did internal sicknesses such as tuberculosis. Yet given the proclivity for breakout attempts among the inmates, the Germans were understandably cautious about allowing those who might be working their ticket home through faking illness—whether physical or mental—to make their case in front of a mixed medical commission. Three men were unjustifiably held back entirely from going home even after they had been passed for repatriation, and even allowing for the small size of the Colditz contingent relative to other camps and the POW population as a whole, German foot-dragging meant that officers who might have gone home in the autumn of 1943 or spring of 1944 lost out. The percentage of those from Colditz who did get to Britain in late 1944 and early 1945, however, was comparable to the overall percentage of Allied personnel exchanged.[58]

In overall terms, the inmates of Oflag IVC were not so badly off in relation to reprisals, if not rewards. And as we shall see, they also had the opportunity to interact in a stimulating fashion with a variety of foreign nationals.

Notes

1. See e.g. PRO, WO 224/27, IRC report, 11 Dec. 1941, p. 6; IWM (Rolf), H. Tuck, 3; Roger V. Coward, *Sailors in Cages* (London, 1967), 107; C. M. Jervis, *The Long Trek* (Elms Court, 1993), 21; Richard Pape, *Boldness Be My Friend* (London, 1953), 145; Len Williamson, *Six Wasted Years* (Braunton, 1985), 16; http://www.mgb-stuff.org.uk/wcl.htm, W. C. Law, 5. On the official OKW line on physical violence, which sometimes seems to have been more honoured in the breach than in the observance, see Vasilis Vourkoutiotis, 'The German Armed Forces Supreme Command and British and American Prisoners-of-War, 1939–1945: Policy and Practice', Ph.D. thesis, McGill University (2000), 157, 299.
2. For the Posen AB incident see PRO, WO 311/163. For the Lamsdorf AB incident see John Castle, *The Password Is Courage* (London, 1955), 162–3. For the Wolfsberg AB incident see WO 310/36. For the Posen incident see IWM (Rolf), R. Low, 14. For the 'they were laughing at me' incident see IWM, A. N. L. Munby diary, 10 July 1940.
3. IWM, E. G. Laker diary, 23 Sept. 1944; IWM, T. Tateson, 54.
4. On OKW standing orders see Vourkoutiotis, op. cit., 156.
5. PRO, WO 208/3283, Stalag Luft III: East Compound, 10–11; WO 208/3287, Stalag 387 (Thorn/Fallingbostel), 6–7; WO 208/3286A, Stalag Luft VI, pt. I, p. 17.
6. IWMSA 4747/4, E. Mine. On the shooting of the Scots sergeant see Donald Edgar, *The Stalag Men* (London, 1982), 71–3. On the Laufen shooting see PRO, WO 309/972; http://web.mala.bc.ca/davies/letters.images/stokes/collection.page.htm, D. Stokes diary, 17–24 Nov. 1940, 22–7 Jan. 1941.

7. Pape, op. cit., 140.
8. PRO, WO 309/212, brief to apprehend ex-Oberstleutnant Lapp and ex-Gefrieter Neulist, 18 Jan. 1946. On the Hohenfels episode see Imelda Ryan (comp.), *POWs Fraternal* (Perth, WA, 1990), 96; IWM, R. P. Evans, 50.
9. PRO, WO 309/24. On the Belaria incident see PRO, WO 208/3283, pt. V, p. 4. On the shooting at Stalag IVB see WO 309/980. On the shooting at Bankau see Russell Margerison, *Boys at War* (Bolton, 1986), 140. On the Eichstätt double shooting see WO 311/52; WO 208/3291, p. 1. On the Heydekrug episode see WO 208/3286A, p. 17.
10. Barbara Broom (comp.), *Geoffrey Broom's War* (Edinburgh, 1993), 190; Geoff Taylor, *Piece of Cake* (London, 1980 edn.), 207.
11. See e.g. T. Mottram in David McGill, *P.O.W.* (Naenae, NZ, 1987), 140 ff.; Donald Watt, *Stoker* (East Roseville, NSW, 1995), 78 ff.; Cyril Rofe, *Against the Wind* (London, 1956), 83; George Beeson, *Five Roads to Freedom* (London, 1977), 26; George Dunning, *Where Bleed the Many* (London, 1955), 53 ff.
12. See e.g. PRO, WO 208/3285, p.25.
13. Rofe, op. cit., 93. On the Radner case see PRO, WO 309/364, W. J. Sillence deposition. On the Lamsdorf AB case see WO 224/27, PP report, Aug. 1941, 6.
14. See PRO, WO 309/131.
15. David James, *A Prisoner's Progress* (Edinburgh, 1947), 63; Kingsley Brown, *Bonds of Wire* (Toronto, 1989), 164; Beeson, op. cit., 43, 65–6; Percy Wilson Carruthers, *Of Ploughs, Planes and Palliasses* (Arundel, 1992), 132; T. C. F. Prittie and Earle Edwards, *Escape To Freedom* (London, 1953 edn.), 212–17. On the changing award system at Barth see PRO, WO 208/3282, pt. I, p. 6. On 'held while pending investigation' at Sagan see WO 208/3283, 8. On progressively tougher sentences for repeat offenders see e.g. A. Passfield, *The Escape Artist* (Perth, WA, 1988), 17, 31, 64. On OKW support for tougher awards see Vourtkoutiotis, op. cit., 132–3. On *Straf* compounds and prisons see e.g. Neville Chesterton, *Crete Was My Waterloo* (London, 1995), 102–3; Ewart C. Jones, *Germans Under My Bed* (London, 1957), 162; George Dunning, *Where Bleed the Many* (London, 1955), 59; Ian Ramsay, *P.O.W.* (Melbourne, 1985), 92 ff.
16. See e.g. IWMSA 4759/3, P. Buckley; ibid. 4827/5, R. Loder; PRO, WO 208/3283, p. 12; WO 224/73, PP report, 11 July 1942, 6; Oliver Philpot, *Stolen Journey* (London, 1950), 179; Calton Younger, *No Flight From the Cage* (London, 1981 edn.), 35–6. OKW officially supported the Geneva Convention ban on collective punishments. Vourkoutiotis, op. cit., 130.
17. On Lamsdorf see Graham Palmer, *Prisoner of Death* (Wellingborough, 1990), 152–3; J. E. Pryce, *Heels In Line* (London, 1958), 155. On Eichstätt, T. D. Beckwith (ed.), *The Mansel Diaries* (London, 1977), 85, 90. On the Kirchhain 'clog dance' see PRO, WO 208/3319, MI9/S/PG(G)1833; John Dominy, *The Sergeant Escapers* (London, 1974), 49–50. On Barth see WO 208/3282, pt. I, p. 10.
18. See Vourkoutiotis, op. cit., 90; M. R. D. Foot and J. M. Langley, *MI9* (London, 1979), 107.

19. Pryce, op. cit., 156; Jim Rogers, *Tunnelling Into Colditz* (London, 1986), 48. On commands and camp leader negotiating compromises see e.g. R. G. M. Quarrie, *Oflag* (Durham, 1995), 124; Stanley Rayner, *I Remember* (Lincoln, 1995), 153; Michael Duncan, *Underground from Posen* (London, 1954), 76; PRO, WO 208/3283, 60; IWM, G. F. W. Wilson diary, 4 Jan., 7 Mar. 1945.

20. On the Hamburg reprisal at Stalag Luft I see Frank Taylor, *Barbed Wire and Footlights* (Braunton, 1988), 71.

21. Geoff Taylor, *Return Ticket* (London, 1972), 37–8; see id., *Piece of Cake*, 166; IWMSA 12093/3, A. Topliss.

22. See e.g. Carruthers, op. cit., 152–77; Tony Johnson, *Escape to Freedom* (Barnsley, 2002), 140–2; Derek Thrower, *The Lonely Path to Freedom* (London, 1980), 123–31; H. E. Woolley, *No Time Off For Good Behaviour* (Burnstown, Ont., 1990), 128–37; Daniel Dancocks (ed.), *In Enemy Hands* (Toronto, 1990 edn.), 172–6; IWMSA 6175/2, S. Arthur.

23. On the Buchenwald episode see Colin Burgess, *Destination Buchenwald* (Kenthurst, NSW, 1995). A similar incident seems to have occurred in February 1943. See IWM (Books), Sir Harold Satow, *The Work of the Prisoners of War Department During the Second Word War* (Foreign Office, 1950), 9–10.

24. IWMSA 15113/2, W. Hart. It is just possible that this was a 'joke' (mock firing squads had been assembled elsewhere for the benefit of individuals and small parties of prisoners), and that the trenches were for shelter during air raids: but it is worth noting that this was the period in which *Terrorflieger* propaganda was at a fever pitch and Goebbels was urging Hitler to shoot a number of airmen equal to the fatal casualties in Dresden. H. Trevor Roper (ed.), *The Goebbels Diaries: The Last Days* (London, 1978), 78. Commandants, on the other hand, might recognize that the war was lost and that being more lenient rather than harsher towards prisoners might be in their own best interest. See e.g. http://hompepage.ntlworld.com/longley/pow4.htm, H. R. Town, 2.

25. Ramsay, op. cit., 136–46; W. Wynne Mason, *Prisoners of War* (Wellington, 1954), 395–6. On sentences see PRO, WO 32/15294, 1941–42, tables; Satow, op. cit., 45. On the adherence to legality in courts martial see e.g. Paul Kingsford, *After Alamein* (East Grinstead, 1982), 81. The man of confidence at Stalag XXB (Marienburg) discovered that briefing accused soldiers on court layout and procedure, along with a smart appearance, could lead to less severe sentences. IWM, N. R. Wylie box, CSM Fulton report, 'Organisation of Stalag XXB', 2. It was also possible to appeal a sentence through the protecting power. See e.g. WO 208/3325, MI9/S/ PG(P)2824, p. 2. One private, though he thought his court martial on a charge of having struck an SS man was far from fair, was in fact very lucky to be given a year rather than sentenced to death even in 1944. See Eric Williams, *On Parade For Himmler* (Hull, 1994), 46–50.

26. Jane Torday (ed.), *The Coldstreamer and the Canary* (Langley, 1995), 51; IWMSA 6797/2, H. Bruce. See Charles Rollings, *Wire and Walls* (Hersham, 2003), ch. 5. Earlier in 1941 there had been an effort to make the SBO at Laufen sign a daily muster roll confirming that all prisoners were present,

apparently in response to reports of a similar tactic being tried in certain camps in Canada. See PRO, FO 916/14, p. 28.

27. PRO, WO 366/26, f. 65. The German staff at Thorn apparently did their best to alleviate conditions almost from the first. See IWM, J. W. M. Mansel diary, 10–11 Mar. 1941.

28. Dunning, op. cit., 68–9, 62 ff.; IWM, G. A. Griffin, 35.

29. Prittie and Edwards, op. cit., 253. On the *Pasteur* incident see Bob Moore, 'The Last Phase of the Gentleman's War: British Handling of German Prisoners of War on Board HMT *Pasteur*, March 1942', *War & Society*, 17 (1999), 41–55. On the confiscation of boots at Posen see IWM, G. A. Griffin, 43. On the letter reprisal at Warburg see Torday, op. cit., 67; http://web.mala. bc.ca/davies/letters.images/stokes/collection.page.htm, D. Stokes diary, 10 Aug. 1942.

30. On the origins, nature, and outcome of this reprisal see S. P. MacKenzie, 'The Shackling Crisis: A Case-Study in the Dynamics of Prisoner-of-War Diplomacy in the Second World War', *International History Review*, 17 (1995), 78–98; Jonathan F. Vance, 'Men in Manacles: The Shackling of Prisoners of War, 1942–1943', *Journal of Military History*, 59 (1995), 483–504.

31. Other camps where some POWs were manacled included Stalag XVIIIA (Wolfsberg), Stalag IXC (Bad Sulza), Stalag XXA (Thorn), and Marlag. Commandant Von Lindeiner reputedly refused to allow anyone at Stalag Luft III to be chained (see Younger, op. cit., 42), and the need for productive labour meant that men on Arbeitskommandos generally were not affected (see e.g. Rayner, op. cit., 151; J. Roberts, *A Terrier Goes to War* (London, 1998), 79). Dieppe officers at Eichstätt were segregated and confined in Willibaldsburg castle. See J. H. Roy and J. E. R. Wood, in J. E. R. Wood (ed.), *Detour* (London, 1946), 153 ff.

32. George Moreton, *Doctor in Chains* (London, 1980 edn.), 86; Bill Jackson, *The Lone Survivor* (North Battleford, Sask., 1993), 34; A. Masterson, in Tony Strachen (ed.), *In the Clutch of Circumstance* (Victoria, BC, 1985), 124–5.

33. Ryan, op. cit., 76–7.

34. http://www.naval-history.net/WW2MemoirAndS009.htm, H. Siddall, 2; IWM, L. H. Harcus diary, 16 Oct. 1942.

35. Jackson, op. cit., 34, 43–46; Ryan, op. cit., 85; Beckwith, op. cit., 88; IWM, J. E. Platt diary, 6 Nov. 1942.

36. Robert Gale, *Private Prisoner* (Wellingborough, 1984), 148; Strachen, op. cit., 68; Jack Pringle, *Colditz Last Stop* (London, 1995 edn.), 102; IWM, R. P. Evans, 44; IWM (Rolf), J. M. McGee, 18.

37. Yoav Gelber, 'Palestinian POWs in German Captivity', *Yad Vashem Studies*, 14 (1981), 115–6; PRO, WO 366/26, p. 65.

38. On the Camp 306 reprisal see e.g. IWM, F. J. Stewart diary, 15 Jan. 1945; http://web.mala.bc.ca/davies/letters.images/stokes/collection.page. htm, D. Stokes diary, 18 Jan. 1945. On the New Zealander reprisal see Ryan, op. cit., 119. On the Irish segregation see ibid., 116. On the transfer from Oflag VIIIF to Oflag 79 see e.g. Philip Kindersley, *For You the War Is Over* (Tunbridge Wells, 1983), 199.

39. Jimmy James in *The War Behind the Wire: Part I, The Great Escape* (Hartswood Films, 2000).

40. Prittie and Edwards, op. cit., 73–6; IWM, H. C. F. Harwood, 104–6.

41. IWMSA 4767/5, J. Greenwood; see M. N. McKibbin, *Barbed Wire* (London, 1947), 81. On the Friesack experiment see Adrian Weale, *Renegades* (London, 1995 edn.), 79 ff.; Carolle J. Carter, *The Shamrock and the Swastika* (Palo Alto, Cal., 1977), ch. 10.

42. On the 'holiday camps' see Weale, op. cit., 102 ff. On Annaberg see Milan Huer, *India in Axis Strategy* (Stuttgart, 1981), 583.

43. George Clifton, *The Happy Hunted* (London, 1952), 354; IWM (Rolf), R. S. Kerridge, 5. On the Steinberg camp as 'country house' see IWM, G. F. W. Wilson diary, 26 July 1944. On its predecessor see D. James, op. cit., 62; IWM, G. F. W. Wilson diary, 5 July 1943. On conditions for the other ranks see e.g. John Borrie, *Despite Captivity* (London, 1975), 160; John Brown, *In Durance Vile* (London, 1981), 98 ff.; Barney Roberts, *A Kind of Cattle* (Sydney, 1985), 96 ff.; Maxwell Leigh, *Captives Courageous* (Johannesburg, 1992), 161–5.

44. Weale, op. cit., ch. 7.

45. S. Walker in Wood, op. cit., 102. On prisoners hoping to take advantage of softer conditions without the slightest intention of being hoodwinked see e.g. Norman Rubenstein, *The Invisibly Wounded* (Hull, 1989), 95–6.

46. Ryan, op. cit., 86; see IWM, H. L. Harcus diary, 1 Mar. 1943.

47. A. Robert Prouse, *To Hell Via Dieppe* (Toronto, 1982), 131; R. Elford in Dancocks, op. cit., 98; IWM, G. F. W. Wilson diary, 18 Feb, 21 Feb. 1944.

48. Kindersley, op. cit., 169. On the repatriation exchanges see Satow, op. cit., 51–6. On the repatriate experience see e.g. http://www.awm.gov.au, A. D. Crawford TS tape 1 side A; Marmaduke Hussey, *Chance Governs All* (London, 2001), 50–1.

49. Henry Chancellor, *Colditz* (London, 2001), 14, 122, 198, *passim*; PRO, WO 208/3288, pp. 13–14, 18–19.

50. On tins see PRO, WO 208/3288, p. 61. On the Gephard sword-wielding incident see P. R. Reid, *The Colditz Story* (London, 1952), 118. On the mock execution see Chancellor, op. cit., 9.

51. IWM, R. Eggers, Colditz Register, 25 Sept. 1944; see Chancellor, op. cit., 325–6, 234–5, 9; see also PRO, WO 208/3288, 17; WO 311/145; TS 26/405 on the 'Franz Josef' shooting.

52. Chancellor, op. cit., 300–1. On OKW interest in Colditz see e.g. Hans Püpke, 'No Easy Job', in R. Eggers (comp.), *Colditz Recaptured* (London, 1973), 183–4; IWM, R. Eggers, Colditz Register, 3 Oct., 24 Oct. 1942. On the unusually strong British interest in this particular camp see PRO, WO 32/11110.

53. Foot and Langley, op. cit., 153. On the mail reprisal see Margaret Duggan (ed.), *Padre in Colditz* (London, 1978), 196–97. On the opening of Red Cross food-parcel tins see PRO, WO 208/3288, p. 61.

54. CSVA 11, H. Ironside; see Chancellor, op. cit., 307–8. On Storie-Pugh see Rogers, op. cit., 140–1; PRO, FO 916/16, PP report, 27 Nov. 1940, p. 6.

55. Earl Haig, *My Father's Son* (London, 2000), 139; David Walker, *Lean, Wind Lean* (London, 1984), 145. On Tod's negotiations with Prawitt over moving out see Chancellor, op. cit., 353, 372–3. On concerns about executions at the last moment see also IWMSA 4843/4, G. W. Abbott; ibid. 16797/4, H. Bruce; LC, tape 1527, A. Siska; Lord Harewood, *The Tongs and Old Bones* (London, 1981), 56, 58; Pringle, op. cit., 143. On Berger see Robert Kübler, *Chef KGW* (Lindhorst, 1984).
56. Duggan, op. cit., 200.
57. Chancellor, op. cit., 290–2; J. M. Green, *From Colditz In Code* (London, 1971), 135; P. R. Reid, *Colditz* (London, 1984), 232–6; PRO, WO 224/69, PP visit report, 13 Oct. 1943, p. 3; ibid., RC visit report, 9 Nov. 1943, p. 6; ibid., RC visit report, 6 July 1944, p. 4; ibid., PP visit report, 7 Oct. 1944, p. 4; ibid., RC visit report, 24 Nov. 1944, p. 3; see also ibid., PP visit report, 23 Jan. 1945, p. 3.
58. The OKW tally at the start of 1945 shows the Reich holding just under 226,000 British and American POWs. 10,760 prisoners were repatriated between 1943 and January 1945. Given a total number of registered prisoners held by Germany to be in the region of 308,000 (including those exchanged), approximately 3.49% per cent were sent home. The number of British and Commonwealth POWs at Oflag IVC at this point was 330. A total of ten men were repatriated from Colditz. Thus approximately 3.44% were sent home. Colditz figures are drawn up from: Reid, *Colditz*, 302–10—including those listed as gone as of 7 January 1945 who are not labelled as repatriates but were (e.g. Miles Reid); PRO, WO 32/11111, PP visit, 6 Feb. 1945, p. 1. Overall figures were drawn up from: Vourkoutiotis, op. cit., 58; Jonathan F. Vance, *Objects of Concern* (Vancouver, BC, 1994), 7. The small size of the Colditz officer population at the end of 1944 relative to the number of British officers held in the Reich (3.68%), not to speak of the British prisoner population as a whole (0.15%), can be gathered from German tallies. See NARS, T-120, roll 5012, Vr. Kr. 26, Nr. 15, frames L414001, L414004.

8 Allies and Aliens

Belligerents shall as far as possible avoid bringing together in the same camp prisoners of different races or nationalities.

(from Article 9, Geneva Convention, 1929)

Prisoners of war... shall also have the right to communicate with the representatives of the protecting Powers in order to draw their attention to the points on which they have complaints to make with regard to the conditions of captivity.

(from Article 42, Geneva Convention, 1929)

The Geneva Convention indicated that prisoners from different countries were to be housed in different locations. Yet as one new arrival put it, Oflag IVC was 'desperately international!' Along with prisoners from the British Isles, Commonwealth, and Empire, there were at various times contingents from Poland, France, the Netherlands, and Belgium, plus a handful of Americans and the occasional Yugoslav officer inhabiting the castle. 'Colditz was the only camp of this kind in Germany', Pat Reid proudly explained in *The Colditz Story*, a true community of nations solidly allied. In point of fact there were many other camps where British POWs interacted with their counterparts from other nations, and while these did not include some of the other contingents in the castle, the 'society of the tower' in its turn had much more limited contact with certain types of foreigner. The British in Oflag IVC, furthermore, were not always as internationalist in outlook as legend suggests.[1]

Though many smaller camps contained prisoners of only one nationality, there were places other than Colditz where POWs from more than one country were housed in the same location. There were also camps that contained various nationalities in different but adjacent compounds, where in some cases prisoners from different parts of the Lager were allowed to mix during daylight hours. This was especially true of very large camps such as Lamsdorf and Wolfsberg. Commonwealth and many Empire prisoners were considered for administrative purposes to be British, and therefore normally placed in the same compounds as Kriegies from the United Kingdom. In the middle war years US aircrew and naval officers in particular might also be housed with their British counterparts until their numbers might justify a separate American compound. Prisoners of war from other European countries were encountered at various times and in various locations, while the sheer number of captured Soviet troops meant that it was almost impossible for any British prisoner not to have some exposure to their unhappy fate. Those on working parties might also bear witness to the treatment of slave workers and concentration camp inmates. All this contact produced a wide range of opinions.

Numerical odds meant that among the Allied prisoners taken in the first year of the war it was the French—over a million taken into captivity—with whom British prisoners most often came in contact. To many Kriegies 'the frogs' were a thoroughly bad lot, a combination of selfishness and complacency. As early as June 1940 at Oflag IXA/H it was noted that French officers captured in the Saar refused to share the parcels they were still receiving at a time when no parcels were arriving from Britain. The evacuation from Dunkirk, the French armistice with Germany, and the British sinking of the French fleet made matters much worse, each side accusing the other of letting down the Allied cause, while the British suspected that French POWs were being rewarded for surrendering with ease. At Stalag XXA (Thorn) the cheering by Frenchmen that greeted news of the armistice so incensed British prisoners that they broke ranks and started throwing punches—'although in all honesty we were so weak that we couldn't have broken the skin of a rice pudding', one participant admitted. 'They were well housed in proper barracks, enjoyed reasonable rations, were allowed wine and had cigarettes', Donald Edgar wrote of conditions in a French oflag through which British other ranks were passed later in 1940. Mutual hostility was often palpable, and relations had clearly not improved when another group of British soldiers passed through another French-run camp in the spring of 1941:

We were marched straight to the 'transit' camp [remembered John Lawrence], already inhabited by French POWs, who, as always, resented we British coming into the place which they had reorganised most comfortably for themselves. About 100 of them had had to leave their barracks and move in with their colleagues in the other huts. As they had more space per man in their huts than we had between five in previous camps, I was not too sympathetic, and when we entered our new homes, my sympathy vanished completely. They had smashed up all the benches and tables, overturned the stoves, and strewn straw from the palliases over the floor, while, in the lavatories, they had smeared excreta over the walls and seats. Vive la France![2]

Not all encounters were so negative. Guy Morgan, recalling his arrival in Oflag VIIIF (Mährisch Trübau) in January 1944, had a much more favourable—if still somewhat chauvinistic—impression of the previous occupants: 'The French officers who had occupied the camp for two or three years had left little evidence of their tenure. In fact, except for Gallic inscriptions on the lavatory walls and a faded German standing order in the main entrance hall forbidding "the separation of the hind legs of living frogs," we might have been the *Oflag*'s first tenants.' Victor West remembered that on arrival at Mühlberg from Greece in August 1941 the Frenchmen who ran the camp 'gave us a grand reception, good soup, mass gifts of biscuits, and a feeling of solidarity'.[3]

But there remained a feeling in many quarters that these erstwhile allies had been irretrievably corrupted by defeat. 'We didn't like [the privileges apparently enjoyed by French prisoners],' John Greenwood explained in an interview concerning his experience at Stalag IVB in 1943–4, 'we didn't have a lot to do with the French...we didn't get along with them.' Shortages of food and fuel in 1945 only accentuated suspicion and hostility. 'The French, with very few exceptions, were bastards', RAF pilot Stephen Johnson wrote concerning Anglo-French relations in Stalag IIIA (Luckenwalde), going on to assert that the French had enjoyed 'extremely soft billets' for a very long time yet refused to share food when shortages occurred.[4]

Contact with the French was nevertheless sporadic throughout most of the war, and out of sight usually meant out of mind. The same could not be said of the several million Red Army captives who appeared in neighbouring compounds from late 1941 onward. From the RAF prisoners at Barth up near the Baltic in Pomerania to the Commonwealth POWs down at Wolfsberg in southern Austria, from the men at Lamsdorf in Silesia as far westward as the officers at Warburg in Westphalia, British Kriegies probably saw more citizens of the Soviet Union than prisoners from any other single nation.[5]

Regarded as subhuman by their captors, prisoners from the USSR were treated with appalling brutality. By the time a million and more men who survived the journey were herded into compounds inside the

Third Reich, several million others had already died in the east or in transit, from a combination of starvation, exposure, and disease. Those who made it were ambulatory skeletons, dressed in brown rags that had once been uniforms, and most were dying by inches. Soviet POWs did not get Red Cross parcels and German rations were below subsistence level, to the point where there were constant rumours of cannibalism. A recaptured British escapee accidentally sent into a compound for Soviet prisoners, where there was no medical treatment, massive overcrowding, and survival was a matter of every man for himself, succinctly described the place as 'Hell'. Graham Palmer was extremely lucky to have been recognized as British by a man in an adjacent compound after a few months and sent back to the comparatively civilized world of the British compounds at Stalag VIIIB—but there were Red Army survivors at Lamsdorf too, in an adjacent compound. 'It was not uncommon to see a Russian drop dead from sheer hunger and exhaustion', Raymond Ryan remembered. Typhus outbreaks in 1941–2 raised the death toll even further. 'They were very, very badly treated,' Hugo Bracken recalled of the Soviet prisoners held in a Lager near Oflag VIB in 1942. 'Terrible. They died like flies.' Even in subsequent years, when efforts were made to use Red Army prisoners as slave labour, conditions remained appallingly bad. 'When it came to being prisoners,' Ed Annetts reflected in reference to what he observed of life in a Soviet labour camp near his Arbeitskommando in 1943, 'the Russians were in a completely different league to us ... They were treated by the Germans as inferior beings, who merited less consideration than the slaves of old, to be used at will, an expendable commodity. Whose departure from this mortal coil was of less consequence than the death of a louse.'[6]

The initial British reaction to the appearance of, and enemy behaviour toward, Red Army prisoners was outrage. 'I was utterly appalled that such terrible conditions existed, and found it difficult to believe that a so-called civilized nation could stoop to treat other fellow human beings with such degradation', Percy Carruthers recalled after seeing Russians at Stalag VIIA (Moosburg). 'One would never have treated vermin in this way', a furious George Moreton wrote of how the guards behaved towards the Russians at Stalag VIIIB (Lamsdorf). Protests were lodged with camp authorities here and elsewhere, and in several camps efforts were made to pass on German rations or even portions of Red Cross parcels to men who were clearly in extreme need of nourishment.[7] In most cases, either because they were concerned about security or simply did not care whether Soviet captives lived or died, the German authorities refused to allow an orderly compound-to-compound transfer. That left the option of smuggling food or throwing bread and other items over the wire. Such acts of kindness were common (especially at first) in a variety of camps, but sometimes became problematic for those involved.

At Lamsdorf and Mühlberg shots were fired when Kriegies tried to toss cigarettes and food to their new neighbours. There and elsewhere there was also the shock of seeing what happened when items landed on the other side of fences. 'One day,' Frank Taylor wrote of his time in the RAF compound at Stalag VIIIB, 'we threw some cigarettes over the wire to the "Russkies" and were appalled to see ill-clad soldiers, garbed in tattered green uniforms, stuff the fags into their mouths and ravenously devour them.' It was the same in other camps. 'We threw some small loaves of bread over the wire to them [at Moosburg] and watched them fight like wild beasts to get a few crusts', Sandy St Clair remembered. 'To see human beings in that state, fighting each other', an observer at Lamsdorf noted, was a harrowing reminder of what starving men could be reduced to. The same sort of thing happened when the Germans passed in their meagre rations, and though conditions slightly improved in the latter part of the war there were still nasty sights. Moved to Stalag 357 (Fallingbostel) in the summer of 1944, Australian pilot Calton Younger was horrified to see a skeletal Red Army work party outside the wire suddenly catch sight of a pile of empty tins from Red Cross parcels and, despite being beaten by guards, break ranks and rush over. '[T]he Russians fell upon their knees before the dump, as if the mound of old tins housed a god. Their crab-fingers and cat-licking tongues winkled out every smear of food.' It was all too obvious, furthermore, that what was being transferred by British Kriegies was not going to be enough to keep men who looked like 'walking broomsticks' alive. 'It used to distress us that there was so little we could so about it', Charles Irwin commented on the wretched conditions of Soviet POWs at Oflag VIB. 'You could only smell death', Wilfred Hart remembered of the Russian compound at Mühlberg.[8]

'In such an atmosphere, with all this savage barbarism going on a few yards away from us,' Donald Edgar reflected on the situation at Lamsdorf in 1942, 'it was difficult for anyone with a shred of humanity, let alone sensitivity, not to be profoundly depressed.' What was happening to Soviet prisoners was a nasty reminder of what life had been like initially for men of the BEF, and might be again without Red Cross parcels and the protection of the Geneva Convention. Too often for comfort the long-term reaction was to begin to loathe their presence. 'It was easier to pretend they were not there,' T. D. Calnan wrote of the emaciated Russians who worked at Stalag Luft III, 'much as one crosses the street to avoid a beggar.' Derek Thrower noted that at Stalag Luft I, despite efforts to help, the psychological burden of seeing Red Army prisoners held in the recreation field was very great. 'It was almost with a sense of relief that we woke one morning to find that they had gone.' When Russian prisoners were first observed at Warburg in December 1941 there was a whip-round for soap and cigarettes to pass over to Britain's new allies. Soon, however, worried about the spread of typhus, the SBO at Warburg insisted to the commandant that a party of Russians being held in the reception area of the camp in 1942 be moved. 'They departed two days later much to everyone's relief,' R. G. M. Quarrie noted, 'and at the time we really didn't give a damn what had happened to them.' Callousness might manifest itself in other ways. According to Ian Ramsay, some of his fellows at Wolfsberg 'couldn't care less for Russians', viewed their passing with indifference, and thought it only a mild curiosity that, when the arrival of Red Cross parcels allowed British prisoners to dispense with the gritty grey-green German-issue soap and pass it along to their neighbours, the Red Army men concerned were so starved that they immediately ate the bars for their tallow content. A very small percentage of British prisoners actually began to bait the terrible-looking Soviet POWs, derisively laughing at the animalistic scramble that occurred when an empty bully beef tin was tossed across the wire. 'It was not good to look at the Russians', Geoff Taylor, incarcerated at Stalag IVB, admitted.[9]

Sometimes rather more humane instincts prevailed. On a Lamsdorf sawmill Arbeitskommando in the winter of 1942–3 British prisoners not only smuggled Red Cross food to their Soviet counterparts but also made it clear that they would not tolerate beatings. A guard engaged in flogging one of the Russians, Roland Gant noted, 'seemed quite non-plussed when every Englishman in sight stopped work and came running up, shouting and threatening to have him hanged after the war was over'. A party of South Africans arriving in Lamsdorf late in 1943 from Italy were briefly billeted in one of the Soviet huts. Observing their pitiful condition, the Afrikaners, as yet unregistered, decided to adopt as many Soviet prisoners as they could by passing on bits of their own clothing. Though the task of selecting men who could pass as South African in appearance from hundreds of desperate men was a heartbreaking task, this selfless action apparently saved twenty Russian lives. 'Collections were organized whenever Red Cross parcels were issued [at Moosburg between 1943 and 1945],' Derek Bond noted, 'and I am proud to say that every syndicate contributed generously, although we had so little to spare.'[10]

At the other end of the scale in material terms were the Americans. Shot-down Eagle Squadron pilots had been sent to RAF compounds in 1941–2, but it was not until 1943–4 that captured American servicemen began to arrive in Germany in significant numbers, often mixing with British prisoners in transit and (until there were enough to justify separation) in the Stalag Luft system. Inevitably a certain amount of national stereotyping occurred, based on preconceived ideas about Americans as well as observed behaviour. To the more reserved, stiff-upper-lip types it seemed that the Yanks—'full of enthusiasm and exuberance', as a rather more sympathetic RAF officer put it—complained too much about the level of deprivation they encountered as Kriegies, while exhibiting worrying signs of material waste and both moral and physical laziness. 'They looked like a defeated army', one Guards officer disdainfully noted of the casual way in which American prisoners at Moosburg approached matters of dress and deportment in comparison to the British. 'They were easy going and much less disciplined than the British airmen', Andrew Cox noted of USAAF non-commissioned officers at Heydekrug. 'An empty food tin was more likely to hit the floor and be kicked under the bed than be put in a garbage can.'

It was quite a contrast to compare [the British and American compounds] on a cold winter's day. In the British compound hundreds of men could be seen walking around the camp, beating a path in the snow, their breath forming a misty cloud around their heads as they stepped out vigorously to get the benefit of some exercise. In the American compound the only noticeable movement was the smoke curling from the chimneys; not one footprint could be seen in the snow.

'They all spit', an irritated Geoffrey Willatt noted in his Sagan journal in October 1944, going on to describe those Americans he had met as 'very noisy' and 'immature'. At Stalag IVB the SBO took great exception to a colonel from the Deep South calling the Maori officer running the Red Cross parcel store a 'godammed Nigger!', and at Fallingbostel towards the end of the war there was what one British soldier described as 'nearly an international incident' when American POWs refused to share their US Red Cross parcels at a time when no others were arriving.[11]

Anglo-American friction, though, should not be overemphasized. American servicemen usually did their best to be friendly, and—aside from a rather crusty older element—their British counterparts quickly disabused themselves of most of their Hollywood-fed assumptions. 'There were differences of opinion, of course,' Ron Mackenzie explained of non-commissioned British and USAAF aircrew at Stalag Luft III, 'but there were very few problems and an enormous benefit to both groups: new points of view to disagree with, new stories to hear, new jokes, a new language, and new games.' The situation was similar among air force officers, notably in the North Compound at Sagan where both groups helped to dig the tunnel (one of three) that, many months after the Americans had been transferred to their own compound, British and Commonwealth airmen would use in what became known as the Great Escape. 'We got on very, very well with the Americans', Hugo Bracken commented. Attempts to exploit Anglo-American differences by the Germans were always rebuffed, and at Barth relations between senior RAF and American officers were close enough to allow USAAF Colonel Hubert Zemke to assume overall command of the Kriegie population as Senior Allied Officer in 1944.[12]

As a general rule relations with prisoners from the Commonwealth and Empire were also quite amicable. Australians, Canadians, New Zealanders, and South Africans serving in their own forces were normally placed in the same compounds as the British servicemen with whom they had been captured, and, as indicated in the previous chapter, occasional enemy efforts to undermine British Commonwealth solidarity through selective rewards met with no real success. As with the Scots, Welsh, and Irish, there was a tendency in some camps for Kriegies from the same region and background to band together in the same huts and combines, and there was occasional grousing about cliquish behaviour. Some of the Canadian soldiers captured at Dieppe, furthermore, apparently maintained a grudge against British prisoners at Lamsdorf who had fleeced them in trading when they had first arrived and were desperately short of food and cigarettes. But on the whole there were few real complaints about men who had volunteered to fight alongside Britain in the common cause.[13]

There were also a few groups where national or racial stereotyping generated a certain amount of mutual hostility. Differences in language and working habits sometimes meant that South African prisoners of Dutch extraction were viewed with suspicion. The trading acumen of some Cypriots and Palestinians might conjure up 'swarthy Levantine' imagery, and Indian POWs could be seen as lesser mortals than white-skinned soldiers of the King. Open conflict was rare, but fights did sometimes occur.

Edward Ward, a journalist, noted the development of a gulf between Afrikaner prisoners and the rest at Oflag XIIA (Hadamar). 'We had a majority of South Africans there,' he later wrote:

many of whom naturally talked to each other in their own language, Afrikaans. This, quite unreasonably, irritated many other P.O.W.s who, the longer they remained in the bag, became increasingly unreasonable. But it had the effect, broadly speaking, of splitting the camp into two factions, South African and non-South African. The South African members of the camp certainly tended to stick together rather on their own in a way which Australians and New Zealanders never did.

There was also a sense among other ranks on some working parties that the Boers were more co-operative with the enemy than they ought to have been. 'This was something that created a tremendous amount of bad feeling,' Bernard Piddleston remembered of a sugar-beet factory Arbeitskommando administered from Stalag VIIIC, 'because they would work like stevedores for the Germans.'[14]

There was also residual resentment towards Cypriots who, because they could speak Greek, had been able to converse with civilians outside the wire at Suda Bay and Salonika and engage in lucrative trade. In conditions of privation this led to envy and the suspicion that the Cypriots were cheating their fellow inmates when acting as go-betweens. 'Most of the selling was done by Cypriots,' V. E. Jones remembered, 'who cornered the market and forced up the prices.' Tempers grew short, harsh words were exchanged, and occasional knife-fights ensued. Though at Dulag 183 several Cypriots were shot by the Germans while trying to escape—and left hanging on the wire as an example to others— and on at least one Arbeitskommando it was the Cypriots who took the lead in 'go slow' working policies, the loyalty of Cypriot POWs was still sometimes called into question in the Third Reich.[15]

Friction also occurred between British POWs and some of the over 1,500 Palestinians serving as pioneers who were captured in Greece and on Crete. Adeptness at trading in transit camps had a tendency to exacerbate anti-Semitic opinions among British troops. At Corinth, in the words of Fritz Jordan, 'there was a constant tension between the Palestinian and the British prisoners'. British troops held at Salonika, seeing those involved in local working parties amass small fortunes by acting as black market go-betweens, derived satisfaction from the ultimate outcome, according to R. G. M. Quarrie. 'We were amused to hear that when the Palestinians left [for Germany], the Germans confiscated all their money!'[16]

Anglo-Palestinian relations were more limited in the Greater Reich itself, in part because in some camps the Palestinians were segregated (or in their own separate Arbeitskommandos), and in part because there was less of a scarcity of resources. A certain amount of ill-feeling and suspicion, sometimes with an anti-Semitic dimension, was nevertheless present in those camps where mixing occurred. The loyalty of the comparatively small number of Arabs among the Palestinians was called into question because of defections to the German-sponsored cause of the Grand Mufti. Meanwhile, the fact that many of the Palestinian Jews were pre-war émigrés from Germany or Austria, and could therefore converse and trade easily with the guards or take on jobs as interpreters, was not always held in their favour. 'They, the Jews, soon began to display one of their national traits, by setting up stalls and trading in all sorts of things', R. P. Evans wrote of the non-working army NCOs' camp at Hohenfels set up in 1943. 'They even started buying bread from the Germans', he claimed, 'for cigarettes, and selling it for a profit. This didn't please some sections of the community...' At Lamsdorf they were labelled 'the Jordan Highlanders'—' "Only a nose we bring you", was their march past, we said' (R. A. Wilson). The German authorities did their best to foster and exploit anti-Semitic sentiment, and as Ike Rosmarin recalled, when there was a shortage of Red Cross parcels at Stalag 344 tempers frayed and British prisoners sometimes lashed out.[17]

On the other hand, as with other groups, there were plenty of indications that British POW leaders refused to see Jews as anything other than British servicemen when the enemy was involved. When a Palestinian sergeant died at Lamsdorf and was denied a proper military burial—here as elsewhere the authorities were usually quite punctilious about funeral honours—the protest was so great that the Germans had to reverse their position. Sidney Sherriff actively opposed attempts to segregate Jews from other prisoners at Stalag VIIIB. When efforts were made to prevent Palestinian POWs from picking up British Red Cross parcels, the redoubtable SBNCO announced that his men would refuse parcels altogether if the ban was not lifted—a threat that caused the camp authorities to back down immediately. When segregation was announced at Warburg nobody inside the wire would communicate with any German until the plan was quietly dropped. Similar efforts to segregate Jews at Stalag Luft VI on parade one day met with strenuous objections from Dixie Deans. The men concerned were members of the RAF, he reminded the camp authorities, and in the Royal Air Force 'even bloody tree-worshippers'—a dig at the ancient Aryan cult being promoted by Himmler—would be treated the same as everyone else. Again the Germans backed down.[18]

Kriegies of all ranks who were against any form of passive collaboration could not but be impressed by the way in which Palestinian working parties refused to be intimidated by the Nazis' overt and extreme hostility to their faith and people. And for some Gentiles it might be an outright bonus to have a Yiddish speaker around to act as a trader with the locals. 'A Jewish lad called Issy Gorsevitch, who came from Glasgow, had been captured with us in 1940', Lance-Corporal David Parker of the Durham Light Infantry explained of one particular Arbeitskommando. 'He was a great bargainer and from about 1943 we used to give him a few cigarettes and he would get things for us.'[19]

The re-emergence of extreme privation in the last months of the war, unfortunately, could still stir up expressions of anti-Semitic prejudice. 'I don't wonder at Hitler hating them,' RAF air gunner R. Watchorn angrily wrote in his diary at Fallingbostel in March 1945, 'they haven't a good trait in them, they pander to the Germans, and with their knowledge of the German tongue they are able to control all the rackets in the camp and they are a bad lot . . . ' When the Gestapo searched the camp and one of the Palestinians asked him for a crucifix so he could pose as a Roman Catholic, Watchorn turned him down flat.[20]

The pattern was also mixed with respect to Indian prisoners. Thousands of Sikhs, Pathans, Punjabis, and Gurkhas captured in North Africa were transferred from Italy to Germany, mostly in 1943, adding their numbers to the few hundred Indians who had been taken by the Wehrmacht in 1940–1. Most were held in a separate camp at Annaburg, but there were also Indian huts at Lamsdorf and Sagan and Indian officers at Mährisch Trübau. Indians, in the minds of some other ranks at Stalag VIIIB, were allied aliens rather than true friends. Cheating them in the course of trade transactions was not considered a particularly heinous crime in certain circles, and disputes between British and Indian POWs could sometimes end in physical violence—the 'wogs were getting uppity', one Kriegie remembered another saying amidst a tit-for-tat set of individual attacks and counter-attacks at Lamsdorf in the summer of 1943.[21]

On the other hand, when the water supply to the Indian Lager broke down men in the neighbouring RAF compound cut a hole in the intervening wire and organized a bucket chain. Bill Jackson, a Canadian, recalled what happened when the guards found the gap in the wire and stopped the hand-over-hand bucket transfer:

A British army corporal was watching as the Sikhs returned with their empty buckets. He was attached to their regiment, they were his boys and they were being poorly treated. Without further ado he grasped two buckets in each hand and advanced determinedly on the offending guards...He came to a halt a couple of feet in front of a guard and addressed him in German, the guard shook his head and yelled at the insistent corporal, the corporal yelled back and up came the rifle butt—where it hurt. The stalwart 'brown job' never retreated an inch, no sir, not in front of a crowd of 'brylcream boys'. His knees sagged a little but up came four metal buckets, two on each side of the guard's ears. There were two clunks, a loud yell from the surprised guard and a cheer from the 'brylcream boys'.

Honour satisfied, the corporal sprinted off and dived through a hut widow before the guard, having had a misfire, could reload his weapon and shoot again. 'They were a decent lot and we got friendly with them', Harry Buckledee, incarcerated in the RAF compound at Lamsdorf, remembered of the adjoining Indian soldiers. Relations between British and Indian prisoners at Oflag VIIIF and Stalag VIIIC, meanwhile, appear to have been generally amicable.[22]

As the incident related above suggests, inter-service rivalry was not entirely absent from POW life in Germany. The main problems arose when soldiers rubbed shoulders with the RAF. To aircrew NCOs at Lamsdorf and other stalags the degree of internal discipline practised in the army compounds could seem excessive, and even a little pro-German. Meanwhile the stuffiness and formality of senior army officers in particular came as something of a shock to RAF officers billeted for periods at Warburg and various other oflags. BEF veterans, for their part—along with senior RN officers—might resent the overly provocative and schoolboyish behaviour of those in air force blue, many quite new to captivity. The apparent failure of the RAF to protect troops at Dunkirk angered some men, and the fact that non-commissioned aircrew were automatically promoted to the rank of sergeant also rankled some among the army other ranks (who thought stripes ought only to come after long years of service). There was also a certain amount of class difference, Royal Air Force volunteers in very rough terms falling somewhere between the lower-class professional soldiers and more upper-class professional army officers in terms of social background. 'At times it seemed as if we did not belong to the same nation', army sergeant Donald Edgar commented on the contrast at Stalag VIIIB.[23]

Conversely, junior army officers could find the exuberance of their air force counterparts a breath of fresh air. 'Morale went right to the top', Charles Irwin wrote of the RAF presence at Warburg. Inter-service friction did not prevent soldiers from agreeing to do identity switches with air force types wishing to go out on working parties (and thereby increase their chances of making a successful escape), nor stop army administrative NCOs, despite occasional grumbling, from cooking the books to facilitate such exchanges. Some of those who exchanged khaki for air force blue grew homesick for their comrades, but others found the change—which, among other things, meant not being posted to a bad job—a positive one. Raymond Ryan remembered that he and a friend at Lamsdorf in 1942 'found life with the "boys in blue" much more pleasant than in army compounds. The barrack leaders and the others did not have the domineering manners of the British WOs and best of all there were no rackets.' At no point were the Germans able to exploit differences between air force and other prisoners.[24]

Confined as they were behind wire except during transfers or escapes, officer prisoners and RAF aircrew of all ranks had little opportunity to interact with ordinary Germans. 'I had absolutely no contact with the German civilian population', Charles Irwin explained in reference to his captivity in successive oflags from June 1940 through May 1945. For those in main camps, furthermore, a combination of personal preference, the language barrier, regulations—both German and British—limiting contact, and disparity in numbers severely curtailed opportunities for contact with the ordinary *Posten*; most of whom were, in any case, ten or more yards away on the other side of the wire. On Arbeitskommandos, on the other hand, the chances for inter-action were much greater, both with soldiers and with civilians at the workplace.

Even Kriegies in main camps could observe their captors at leisure and, on the comparatively rare occasions when personal inclination and opportunity arose, engage in conversation and assessment. At first there was often a perception of swaggering arrogance, and on Arbeitskom-mandos it was something of a lottery through much of the war whether individual guards were comparatively benign or highly dangerous. As the war progressed, however, and older or less fit men replaced the younger guards being sent to the front, the average *Posten* appeared much less threatening, sometimes almost likeable.

George Soane thought the guards 'pretty good' at Hohenfels by 1944: 'They were no longer as tough as they were before.' The guards in charge of Oflag IXA/H prisoners in the last stages of the war were, according to Terence Prittie, 'on the whole, sympathetic' figures. Most of them by this point had traded with prisoners through the black market, and they 'were nearly all oldish men, of fifty to fifty-five', who 'were sick and tired of the war and wanted only to get back to their homes, families, and civilian occupations'. This was apparently true for Kriegsmarine and Luftwaffe guards as well as those serving the Wehrmacht. 'Our guards were always of a friendly disposition', Jack Bishop wrote of the *Posten* at Marlag (M). 'They were all German Marines who had passed the age limit for their service and were therefore more responsible and less trigger-happy than the younger guards.' Guy Morgan remembered that at Marlag (O), as the *Posten* grew older, they 'lost all traces of arrogance' and became friendly to the point of semi-servility at times. 'One was almost tempted to pity these pathetic old posten, in their threadbare ill-fitting uniforms, with their pince-nez and their pot-bellies and their rheumatism, their over-large steel helmets almost resting on their collarbones . . . ' Russell Margarison's assessment of the guards at Stalag Luft VII (Bankau) was similarly fair-minded. 'Generally speaking,' he later reflected, 'our guards being rather older than the frontline troops, acted in a reasonable manner, most of them longing to get home to their wives and families at the earliest possible moment.' Similar opinions were expressed about guards at other camps, especially as the war drew to a close.[25]

Individual soldiers could come in for special praise. Stanley Rayner was impressed by the restraint displayed by a friendly guard whose house was struck by RAF bombs:

He was given leave to go home for a week, to sort things out. On his return, despite the severe damage done, he never took it out on us. In fact, later on in 1943–4 his entire home and garden was completely flattened. Once again, he had home leave. I remember it was a time when we [prisoners] had no cigarettes at all. When he returned he gave each of us a packet of tobacco and papers so that we could roll a fag. One good Jerry.

Others had similarly positive relations with particular Germans. 'He was older than most of the other guards,' Arthur Dodd recalled of a Wehrmacht soldier on a industrial Arbeitskommando in 1944, 'and treated the men [i.e. British prisoners] with the respect he felt they deserved as fellow soldiers.'

He was once leaving the camp to go home to Cologne on leave and was presented with a package by the men. Knowing how hard times were for ordinary Germans, they had presented him with two packets of cigarettes, two bars of chocolate and a block of soap [from a Red Cross parcel]. Aware of how much they needed these rations for themselves, the man was overcome and cried in front of them.

'Dare I say it', BEF prisoner James Stedman reflected on another very helpful older guard he met on a working party in the latter war years, '—he was the sort of fellow I would have loved to have shaken hands with if I had met him after the war.'[26]

It was also possible, romances aside, for working prisoners to grow close to particular enemy civilians with whom they worked. 'I always got on well with the Austrians I met,' Neville Chesterton recalled of the Alpine Arbeitskommando to which he was sent from Stalag XVIIIA (Wolfsberg), 'as they always seemed honest, hard-working and decent people.' Donald Edgar remembered the sympathy he and others felt for the personal losses of ordinary Germans they knew, recalling in particular how two fellow Kriegies had tried to comfort an old women when she began sobbing over the death of her son, killed at Stalingrad.[27]

The extent of such fellow feeling, however, should not be overestimated. Kriegies on working parties were often exposed to the brutal way in which workers from the east in general, and Polish civilians in particular, were maltreated. This was something that—especially given the generosity displayed by the Poles towards British prisoners—did not endear the Germans to the British. Many hundreds, moreover, had seen concentration camp victims while working in the I. G. Farben works and other factories surrounding Auschwitz. Continual exposure to atrocity did, to be sure, sometimes generate a high degree of callousness. 'One of the significant and terrible things about being in daily sight and contact with such horrors,' J. M. Green unhappily admitted, 'was that one became inured to it. I had to keep reminding myself that this was *not* normal, that these poor wretches were fellow human beings, often fellow Jews.' It was, however, difficult to forget who was responsible for the appalling way in which *Untermenschen* were treated, and although those British POWs who actively tried to help through passing along food and even colluding in escapes were in the minority, for those witnessing such treatment or hearing about it at second-hand, the realities of Nazi rule limited the degree of sympathy felt for ordinary Germans. Even the most pathetic cases could not shake the basic belief that, while there might be an individual Good German or two, the Nazis were still the enemy, and there seems to have been little compunction about engaging in shady trading practices when the recipient was German. Sergeant Edgar noted that after the old lady the two British soldiers had comforted for the loss of her son was out of earshot, a comment was made that produced a chorus of assent—'Mind you, serves these Nazi bastards right! They started it all. Now they're learning what it's like to be on the receiving end!'[28]

In a class by themselves were the neutral representatives of the Protecting Power and the International Committee of the Red Cross. Inspections were always arranged in advance, and camp authorities naturally tended to spruce up facilities and improve the scale or quality of rations to give a sometimes overly positive impression of what life was like behind the wire. In turn the prisoners might complain that their privations and difficulties were greater than in fact was the case. The representatives themselves had to appear both credulous and rigorously impartial, which inevitably tended to annoy one side or the other in particular camps at various junctures. Kriegies, though universally thankful for the Geneva Convention and for Red Cross parcels, could draw contradictory conclusions about the efficacy of neutral visits.

Albert Pooley thought that conditions improved somewhat in the wake of an American visit to Stalag XXIB in late 1940, while Richard Passmore was impressed with the tough questions put to the Germans by the US Embassy representative during a visit to Stalag Luft I some months later. In 1942, after complaining to Swiss representatives that the work POWs were being asked to do at a particular steelworks involved munitions manufacture and was therefore contrary to Article 31 of the Convention, Robert Gale was delighted to learn that prisoners were being withdrawn from this particular works because of queries by the Red Cross. 'They brought warm, friendly smiles and handshakes,' John Borrie later wrote of a Swiss visit to Blechammer in May 1942, 'talked English, noted our many problems, and gave us the feeling that someone cared.' Others were less enthusiastic in their assessments. Reflecting on an ICRC visit to his Arbeitskommando in 1943, another soldier remembered that, despite complaints, 'we didn't get any encouragement and certainly nothing changed'. Geoff Taylor thought that neutral visits to Stalag IVB in 1944 achieved little, despite the taking of lengthy notes and promises of action. Nothing much changed from one visit to another, since 'the delegation from Geneva was in no position to enforce its recommendations'.[29]

Colditz was both unusual and yet in some ways quite typical with respect to foreigners. Both the variety and proximity of Allied contingents in the castle during the early and middle war years was unique. No other camp held significant numbers of Polish, French, Dutch, and Belgian prisoners of war alongside British and Commonwealth POWs for such length of time, in such close quarters, and in such varied combination. Later in the war British Kriegies might share a compound with or be neighbours of US servicemen in certain stalags as well as the Luftwaffe camps and Marlag, but Colditz was apparently the only Wehrmacht oflag where British and American army officers—albeit only a handful in the latter case—were placed permanently under the same roof. Few places could match Oflag IVC for the unity of spirit generated through the inhabitants, whatever their nationality, having all ended up in the castle as enemies of the Reich. At the same time, compared to those in hutted and working camps, the officers incarcerated in the castle had less opportunity to observe the fate of Jews and other victims of Nazi Germany. Yet the attitudes and actions of British prisoners at Oflag IVC sometimes reflected—albeit often in modified form—many of the preconceptions and prejudices common to British POWs in Germany as a whole.

In contrast to other camps, there was plenty of opportunity for British Kriegies to get to know Polish servicemen at Colditz. One hundred and forty Poles were already in residence when the first British officers arrived in the castle in November 1940, and the warmth of their welcome, combined with their evident disdain for the Germans, rapidly won them many friends. 'They were wonderful crowd, those Poles', Kenneth Lockwood reminisced; 'Marvellous chaps.' According to Peter Allan, these spirited allies were 'absolutely magnificent', and 'liaison [between the two contingents] was excellent'. By the spring of 1941, Pat Reid recorded of his time as British escape officer, the Poles had become 'old and trusted comrades'. As with other nationalities, Polish and British prisoners paired off for language lessons, while the Polish contingent as a whole benefited from money and parcel contributions made by British prisoners, who knew that Germany, claiming that Poland no longer existed as a state, did not allow them normal Red Cross and Protecting Power privileges. Enthusiasm for parcel donations did, to be sure, decline somewhat over time. There were also lingering worries—not without foundation, as it turned out—that there might be a traitor among the Poles who was betraying escape plans. But relations were undoubtedly warm, and there was genuine sorrow expressed when the Poles were moved out in the summer of 1943.[30]

By the autumn of 1940 almost all of the 15,000 POWs from the Netherlands had gone home after agreeing not to take up arms again against Germany. The sixty-eight Dutch officers who refused to give their parole, or were otherwise considered problematic, ended up being sent to Colditz in July 1941. At first there was some suspicion of the Dutch because of their rather Germanic-looking uniforms and stiff, very formal manner, especially on parade. It rapidly became apparent, however, that far from being 'model prisoners' (as Reinhold Eggers initially concluded), the Dutch were very serious about escaping and no friends of the master race. Close co-operation between the British and Dutch contingents was established in matters of action, especially breakout attempts. Nevertheless, among the foreigners the Dutch were considered the most humourless.[31]

Opinions of the largest contingent through to the middle of the war, which consisted of over 260 French officers, were generally positive. Kenneth Lockwood judged them a 'a wonderful crowd'. Peter Allan thought the Frenchmen at Colditz 'excellent, not the rabble we had seen before [on the road into Germany]'. Pairs of British and French POWs learning each other's language were a common sight. Nevertheless, there was still clearly something of a cultural divide between the British and the French. *Les Anglais* could appear peculiarly Spartan in their attitude to convenience and comfort, and bafflingly Stoic in their reactions to outside news. 'The frogs', in turn, might be viewed as rather disorganized, too loquacious and anxious about the fortunes of war, and perhaps even overly interested in both physical and mental contentment. There was also a little lingering distrust arising from the 1940 debacle, and questions concerning security connected with splits between Pétainist and Gaullist supporters among the French. According to Jimmy Yule, British officers had to be careful about inviting Frenchmen into British quarters if escape-related activity was under way within.[32]

An additional source of unease was the French attitude towards Jews. Some of the British officers were not entirely free of cultural prejudice themselves. The East End orderly Solly Goldman was sometimes seen in a rather stereotypical light, while the equally voluble dentist, J. M. Green, was later described by one of the chaplains as 'a clever devil, like most Jews'. Nevertheless it came as a shock when senior French officers supported the idea of segregating French Jews in 1941. 'We didn't approve of that at all', Lockwood remembered. Though some British officers remained neutral on the issue, Airey Neave among others made a point of visiting the new quarters the Germans had designated for *die Franzosen Juden* and inviting round some of the inhabitants for tea.[33]

The British regretted that the French, along with the other foreign contingents, were eventually moved out, missing not only the language lessons but also the rivalry that had spurred on escape efforts and goon-baiting. This was made up for to some extent by the range of people arriving from the British services and their Commonwealth counterparts. 'We were a tremendous mixture from all over the British Empire', Jack Best remembered fondly. Except for 'Jumbo' Mazumdar, who felt he was being discriminated against as an Indian on the basis of race, there seems to have been more to draw men from different regions and backgrounds within the King's dominions together than drive them apart. Tommy Catlow felt the 'wealth of bizarre characters' who ended up in the castle was stimulating, and George Abbott thought relations 'pretty good, I would say very good', in 1944–5. For those who missed foreign tongues, there was the chance to interact with a small number of Czechs wearing RAF blue, along with a few French Canadians from Dieppe, a growing Free French contingent, and in the last months of the war Poles from the Warsaw Uprising as well.[34]

Relations were not as good when it came to the thousand-plus tired, hungry, and bedraggled 1940-vintage French prisoners who arrived on foot from Oflag IVD (Elsterhorst), over 60 miles away, during the fourth week of February 1945. 'The British took them generally in hand', Pat Reid stated in his second book, wording that suggests the friendly provision of order and aid. Reid, however, was not actually there at the time—he had successfully escaped in October 1942—and some of those who were remembered a fair amount of friction.

By this point the British were themselves very short of essentials, and the arrival of the French forced several shifts in quarters. There was an undercurrent of resentment to individual British contacts with the new arrivals: 'damned sorry for them, but when they start scrounging they're a bloody nuisance'—'reduced to hawking frying pans and dirty post-cards for bread, poor b[ugge]rs'—'Marseilles...exactly what one saw'—'not very spiritual types', were some of the more charitable comments. 'I suppose we weren't on such good terms with the French,' Cyril Scarborough later admitted, 'didn't want to share our grub with them.' Colonel Tod called a general meeting of British prisoners to discuss what should be done to help. It was eventually agreed, after much debate, that the stock of Red Cross parcels in the camp should be donated to the obviously *in extremis* French, but that other items, such as cigarettes, should only be pooled if the men concerned in a particular combine all agreed. The passing over of Red Cross parcels improved relations somewhat, though there were still indications that in British eyes the French were seen as inconvenient and dirty house-guests, and that in French eyes the British were rather too obviously assuming the command position. Open friction returned a week later after a large consignment of French parcels suddenly arrived. Seeing no signs of reciprocity for earlier British charity, Colonel Tod raised the matter with the senior French general. 'You've always been known as a nation of shopkeepers,' the general haughtily informed the SBO, 'and a nation of shopkeepers you remain.' Mutual recrimination was once again the order of the day, though some newly established personal friendships might remain immune from the generally hostile atmosphere.[35]

Some of the British officers sent to Colditz from late 1941 onward may have already seen the state of prisoners from the USSR, and for those who had not, a party of them came into the castle to be deloused in the spring of 1942. From them it was learned that there were 300 or so Soviet POWs being used as labour in the town below. Shocked at their skeletal appearance, the SBO made efforts to transfer Red Cross parcels to the Russians that ultimately proved fruitless because of OKW opposition. There were, however, limits to what British prisoners at Oflag IVC would do or believe with reference to Nazi crimes. When a collection for the Russians had first been mooted, some had thought it enough to 'chuck in an old toothbrush', and out of sight seems to have meant out of mind, to judge by memoirs and related literature. Cut off in the castle as they were, many officers dismissed harrowing stories of concentration camps and occupation policies passed on by witnesses as false or highly exaggerated. It was only when the castle was liberated in April 1945 and a nearby KZ Lager containing Hungarian Jews was discovered that opinions seriously changed. 'A few of [the British contingent] went off to see for themselves,' J. M. Green related, 'and told me that they hadn't altogether believed what I had told then about the atrocities I had seen in Silesia [inflicted on Jews used as slave workers in factories].'[36]

As for the Americans, there were really too few—only eight in all—arriving too late at Colditz for them to leave much of a mark. Nevertheless they seem to have made a good impression overall, especially among the more outgoing souls within the British contingent. 'We liked these three Americans,' Douglas Bader recalled of the first arrivals in August 1944, 'they were our type.' The senior US Army officer, Colonel Florimond Duke, did boast about American construction knowhow and complain about the snail's-pace driving of the British in a public lecture; but he took in good spirit a fair amount of ribbing about his improbable first name (as well as the nature of the secret mission to the Balkans which had eventually landed him in Colditz), and as SAO apparently got on well with Willie Todd. 'They added a freshness and a new outlook to our lives', Bader noted.[37]

Befitting its status as a maximum-security prison camp, the ratio of guards to prisoners at Oflag IVC was far higher than elsewhere. From a low of about 200, the castle garrison increased to a high of around 500, which meant that most of the time there were fewer inmates than there were guards. Paradoxically, however, there was less contact between *Posten* and *Kriegsgefangenen* than in most other camps. Much of the garrison was occupied in guarding the grounds below the walls and parts of the Schloss to which prisoners normally did not have access. The high walls themselves meant that the kind of over-the-wire exchanges and conversations that might occur in a hutted camp could not take place. 'You didn't see them', Jimmy Yule observed. As for those guards posted in the inner courtyard, they were under strict orders not to fraternize. News of the execution of a soldier caught trading with the prisoners confirmed for the rest that, in the words of *Posten* Alfred Heinrich, 'it was very dangerous to talk to prisoners'. The British escape committee, for its part, tried to limit contact to a few men fluent in German who could be relied upon to engage in blackmail to obtain escape equipment. The end result, though illicit trading operations continued to take place between particular individuals and goon-baiting remained popular, was comparatively restricted real contact between the average guard and the average inmate inside the camp. 'The prisoners avoided them and they avoided the prisoners', as Michael Burn put it.[38]

Those few prisoners allowed out for parole walks might encounter German civilians. Padre Platt noted after one such perambulation in September 1943 that 'some of the villagers nodded in a friendly fashion, and some of the tiny flaxen-haired children, too young to know if their daddies were fighting or not, or to know anything of the artificial barriers between nations and classes, smiled at us and chattered happily'. From the windows of the castle the sight of elderly and very young refugees fleeing the advance of the Red Army elicited a high degree of sympathy. On the whole, however, inmates saw even less of the German civilian population than they did of the guards.[39]

A certain degree of ambivalence existed here as elsewhere concerning neutral visits. On the one hand the inspections on behalf of the Protecting Power and International Red Cross were welcomed as an opportunity to complain about conditions and German behaviour. On the other, there was the sense that nothing much changed as a result, and on certain occasions signs that particular visitors were out of sympathy with the prisoners' ethos. Padre Platt, like everyone else in Colditz, was dumbfounded at the faux pas committed by a new American Embassy representative in early April 1941. 'In spite of his six-foot, fourteen-stone figure, a pea would have bowled the Colonel [Guy German] over when, in reply to our "moan" that five hours' exercise is not sufficient, the American said, "You would get more exercise, and other privileges too, if you gave up the idea of escaping. Anyway, it is impossible to get out of Germany, no matter how hard you try."' There was also annoyance expressed toward those visitors who appeared completely out of touch. 'The bi-monthly American Embassy visit occurred today,' Platt wrote on 14 May 1941:

an old man suffering from some kind of paralysis which made the lifting and lowering of his legs and feet, and indeed his arms also, a very uncertain and slow process. His idea of helping to ameliorate our lot was expressed in the momentous enquiry: 'Have you any difficulty here [at Colditz] over getting married by proxy?' He was obviously displeased with the mirthful answers he got, but a question more remote from our needs it would be difficult to find.

The Swiss Embassy, which took on the job after US entry into the war against Germany in December 1941, seems to have been rather more professional in its handling of visits, but there were times when it seemed nothing much was achieved. 'The Swiss came today!' Platt noted in his diary on 25 January 1943. 'All the usual complaints were brought up and several new ones. Each three-month visit brings us the same answers to the same questions—"We will take up the matter again with the OKW"!... "We are awaiting reply from the O.K.W."!'[40]

All in all, international relations in Colditz were more typical of the British experience as a whole than the 'one of a kind' legend suggests. Some ex-inmates other than Pat Reid did indeed remember 'complete solidarity', or at worst 'friendly rivalry', and ipso facto those sent to Oflag IVC tended to have much in common. Yet, as we have seen, some stereotyping did occur in the castle, there was atypically limited exposure to certain groups, and international frictions familiar to Kriegies elsewhere were by no means entirely absent. Hugo Ironside may have come close to describing the true situation when he observed that liaison between the different nationalities at Colditz often left a lot to be desired, but that the resulting friction 'wasn't too difficult' to tolerate and that relations with allies 'just bobbed along gently'. The same could not be said of interaction between the majority of POWs here and elsewhere who remained loyal and the very small minority who turned traitor, as the next chapter will show.[41]

Notes

1. P. R. Reid, *The Colditz Story* (London, 1952), 124–5; LC, M. Riviere letter to Mrs Riviere, 27 June 1943. The 'society of the tower' was the phrase used as the title of chapter 5 by Giles Romilly and Michael Alexander in their joint memoir *The Privileged Nightmare* (London, 1954).
2. John Lawrence, *2.2.9.7.* (Fontwell, 1991), 37; Donald Edgar, *The Stalag Men* (London, 1982), 44. On the fight at Thorn see J. Roberts, *A Terrier Goes to War* (London, 1998), 51–2. On the situation at Oflag IXA/H in June 1940 see IWM, W. K. Laing, 30.
3. IWM, V. West, 229; Guy Morgan, *Only Ghosts Can Live* (London, 1945), 65.
4. Stephen P. L. Johnson, *A Kriegie's Log* (Tunbridge Wells, 1995), 181; IWMSA 4767/3, J. Greenwood. For negative assessments see also e.g. Leslie Le Souef, *To War Without a Gun* (Perth, WA, 1980), 195–6; Russell Margarison, *Boys at War* (Bolton, 1986), 172, 172–3; George Millar, *Horned Pigeon* (London, 1946), 195–200; Derek Nabarro, *Wait for the Dawn* (London, 1952), 65–6; Richard Passmore, *Moving Tent* (London, 1982), 87–8; Sandy St Clair, *The Endless War* (North Battleford, Sask., 1987), 161; I. Shrire, *Stalag Doctor* (London, 1956), 64; CMAC, RAMC 1787, A. V. Tennuci, 19. For more positive reactions and experiences see e.g. IWMSA 4694/2, E. Ayling; http://www.naval-history.net/WW2MemoirAndS009.htm, H. J. Siddall, 19; Derek Thrower, *The Lonely Path to Freedom* (London, 1980), 72–8; Ron Mackenzie, *An Ordinary War* (Wangaratta, Victoria 1995), 83; Edward Ward, *Give Me Air* (London, 1946), 114 ff. There was also sometimes unease with and ill-feeling toward Italian prisoners—formerly allies of Germany—on the few occasions when they were encountered between late 1943 and 1945. On varying reactions see Clive Dunn, *Permission to Speak* (London, 1986), 113; Le Souef, op. cit., 210; Charles Robinson, *Journey to Captivity* (Canberra, 1991), 157–8; Norman Rubenstein, *The Invisibly Wounded* (Hull, 1989), 115–17.
5. Other camps where Soviet POWs were seen and commented on by British inhabitants include Sandbostel, Moosburg, Mühlberg, Wagna, and Heydekrug.
6. Ed Annetts, *Campaign Without Medals* (Lewes, 1990), 100; IWMSA 11337/5, H. Bracken; Imelda Ryan (comp.), *POWs Fraternal* (Perth, WA, 1990), 79; Graham Palmer, *Prisoner of Death* (Wellingborough, 1990), 112–20. On German behaviour towards Soviet prisoners see, by way of introduction to an extensive literature, Rolf-Dieter Müller, 'Die Behandlung sowjetischer Kriegsgefangener durch das Deutsche Reich 1941–1945', in Günter Bischof and Rüdiger Overmans (eds.), *Kriegsgefangenschaft im Zweiten Weltkrieg* (Ternitz-Pottschach, 1999), 283–302.
7. See e.g. IWM, F. W. Telfer, 32; Derek Bond, *Steady, Old Man!* (London, 1990), 144; George Moreton, *Doctor in Chains* (London, 1980 edn.), 105; Percy Wilson Carruthers, *Of Ploughs, Planes and Palliases* (Arundel, 1992), 99–100.
8. IWMSA 15113/2, W. Hart (also 'walking broomsticks'); ibid., 4847/3, C. L. Irwin; Calton Younger, *No Flight From the Cage* (London, 1981 edn.), 169;

Lawrence, op. cit., 61 ('to see human beings...'); St Clair, op. cit., 156; Frank Taylor, *Barbed Wire and Footlights* (Braunton, 1988), 24. On incidents where shots were fired see Edgar, op. cit., 105; Moreton, op. cit., 105–6; IWM, J. H. Witte, 146. On German refusals to allow transfers of food see e.g. Sam Kydd, *For You the War Is Over...* (London, 1973), 295; Len Williamson, *Six Wasted Years* (Braunton, 1988), 30. On occasion, especially from 1943 onward, the authorities either accepted transfers of food or turned a blind eye. See e.g. Maxwell Leigh, *Captives Courageous* (Johannesburg, 1992), 170–1; Ike Rosmarin, *Inside Story* (Cape Town, 1990), 77. On smuggling see e.g. Richard Passmore, *Moving Tent* (London, 1982), 125. On the degradation witnessed when German rations were passed in see e.g. IWM, N. L. Francis, 23–4; Geoff Taylor, *Piece of Cake* (London, 1980 edn.), 137; John Barrett, *We Were There* (Sydney, 1987), 260.

9. G. Taylor, op. cit., 137; Ian Ramsay, *P.O.W.* (Melbourne, 1985), 53, 71; R. G. M. Quarrie, *Oflag* (Durham, 1995), 34; IWM, J. H. Sewell diary, 3 Dec. 1941; Derek Thrower, *The Lonely Path to Freedom* (London, 1980), 105; T. D. Calnan, *Free As a Running Fox* (London, 1970), 236; Edgar, op. cit., 106.

10. Quarrie, op. cit.; Robert Gale, *Private Prisoner* (Wellingborough, 1984), 142, 130. At Warburg, too, efforts were made to get food to the Russians. See Terence Prittie, *My Germans* (London, 1983), 78.

11. B. A. James, *Moonless Night* (London, 1983), 70; Geoffrey Willatt, *Bombs and Barbed Wire* (Tunbridge Wells, 1995), 87; Andrew B. Cox, *Our Spirit Unbroken* (Port Elgin, Ont., 1999), 95. On the 'international incident' at Fallingbostel see IWMSA 4767/4, J. Greenwood. On the 'nigger' incident and 'defeated army' comment see Bond, op. cit., 165, 151. On seeing the Americans as overindulged and undisciplined complainers see e.g. IWM, I. P. B. Denton, 47; IWM, D. Swift, 86; Barrett, op. cit., 313. As loud and overly voluble see e.g. Tony Johnson, *Escape to Freedom* (Barnsley, 2002), 94; Sydney Smith, *Wings Day* (London, 1968), 115–16. The vast contrast between the treatment and condition of American and Soviet POWs is described in Barbara Steltzl-Marx, *Zwischen Fiktion und Zeitzeugenschaft* (Tübingen, 2000).

12. Hubert Zemke as told to Roger A. Freeman, *Zemke's Stalag* (Washington, DC, 1991), 27 ff.; IWMSA 11337/5, H. Bracken; Mackenzie, op. cit. 63. On Anglo American co-operation in preparations for the Great Escape see e.g. Jonathan F. Vance, *A Gallant Company* (Pacifica, Cal., 2000).

13. See e.g. IWM (Rolf), E. B. Davis, 7, 18; Edgar, op. cit., 150; Ramsay, op. cit., 155; Rosmarin, op. cit., 63; Bond, op. cit., 165; James Stedman, *Life of a British POW in Poland* (Braunton, 1992), 24; IWM, H. L. Martin, 46; id., W. A. Harding, 31; id., D. W. Luckett, 5; http://www.pegasus-one.org/pow/walter_collins.htm, W. Collins, 6. On the Canadian grudge see Rubenstein, op. cit., 165–6.

14. IWMSA 4661/2, B. Piddleston; Edward Ward, *Give Me Air* (London, 1946), 127. South Africans did, however, have British admirers. See Bond, op. cit., 167; Lawrence, op. cit., 32.

15. IWM, V. E. Jones, 9. On the shooting at Salonika see Jack Champ and Colin Burgess, *The Diggers of Colditz* (Sydney, 1985), 23. On not working hard for the Reich see Francis F. Jones, *Escape to Nowhere* (London, 1952), 229. On suspicions about the loyalty of Cypriots in Germany see IWMSA 4820/1, C. Scarborough.

16. Quarrie, op. cit., 16; Fritz Jordan, *Escape* (Cranbury, NJ, 1970), 70; see Yoav Gelber, 'Palestinian POWs in German Captivity', *Yad Veshem Studies*, 14 (1981), 93.

17. Rosmarin, op. cit., 63, 76; IWM, R. A. Wilson, 83; IWM, R. P. Evans, 42. On suspicions of Arab POWs see Ramsay, op. cit., 143; Cyril Rofe, *Against the Wind* (London, 1956), 31. On the Grand Mufti's efforts see Klaus Gensicke, *Der Mufti von Jerusalem, Amin el-Husseini, und die Nationalsozialismus* (Frankfurt-am-Main, 1988), 108 ff.

18. On the Stalag Luft VI episode see John Dominy, *The Sergeant Escapers* (London, 1974), 99. On the Warburg episode see IWM, I. P. B. Denton, 38; Prittie, op. cit., 73. On Sherriff at Stalag VIIIB see Gelber, op. cit., 111–12. On the funeral episode see Rofe, op. cit., 31. Segregation of British Jews did apparently take place at Stalag Luft I in January 1945. See Barry Keyster, *From Wings to Jackboots* (London, 1995), 269.

19. http://www.pegasus-one.org/pow/david_parker.htm, D. Parker, 13; On Palestinian working parties see J. M. Green, *From Colditz in Code* (London, 1971), 103; John Borrie, *Despite Captivity* (London, 1975), 121; Rofe, op. cit., 31, 196. On Palestinians being treated the same as other British prisoners see also Robert Gale, *Private Prisoner* (Wellingborough, 1984), 153; Henry Vies Suggitt, *Reluctant Guest of the Reich* (London, 1992), 101. Relations between the Arabs and Jews at Lamsdorf varied: see Gelber, op. cit., 111; Tony Strachen (ed.), *In the Clutch of Circumstance* (Victoria, BC, 1985), 75.

20. IWM, R. Watchorn, Book 2, p. 47.

21. IWM, R. A. Wilson, 166; see IWM, H. L. Harcus diary, 2 June 1943. The Sikhs were apparently moved away from Lamsdorf at the request of British prisoners who suspected them of homosexual advances. See Rubenstein, op. cit., 163. See also, however, Harry Levy, *The Dark Side of the Sky* (London, 1996), 115–16. The smaller number of captured black African troops could also be viewed sometimes in stereotypical terms, especially in times of privation. See e.g. http://www.pegasus-one.org/pow/jack_bird.htm, J. Bird, 9. See, however, e.g. Rubenstein, op. cit., 163–4.

22. Bill Jackson, *The Lone Survivor* (North Battleford, Sask., 1993), 72; Harry Buckledee, *For You the War Is Over* (Sudbury, 1994), 44. On Oflag VIIIF see e.g. Philip Kindersley, *For You the War Is Over* (Tunbridge Wells, 1983), 142. On Stalag VIIIC see e.g. http://www.pegasus-one.org/pow/jack_bird.htm, J. Bird, 5.

23. Donald Edgar, *The Stalag Men* (London, 1982), 103; see IWMSA 5131/2, R. Buckingham; ibid., 4767/3, J. Greenwood; ibid. 13573/3, A. Jones; IWM, R. A. Jones, 160; IWM, R. Watchorn, Book 2, p. 24; Fred Hill, *Prisoner of War* (London, 1994), 107; B. Jackson, op. cit., 86; Rofe, op. cit., 26–7, 160–5; Frank Taylor, *Barbed Wire and Footlights* (Braunton, 1988), 30;

G. Taylor, op cit., 39–40; H. E. Woolley, *No Time Off For Good Behaviour* (Burnstown, Ont., 1990), 34.

24. Ryan, op. cit., 69; IWM (Rolf), C. L. Irwin.

25. Margarison, op. cit., 140; Morgan, op. cit., 168; Jack Bishop, *In Pursuit of Freedom* (London, 1977), 115; T. C. F. Prittie and W. Earle Edwards, *Escape to Freedom* (London, 1953 edn.), 384; IWMSA 48960/2, G. Soane. On guards as better, especially in the latter stages, see e.g. IWMSA 4827/4–5, R. Loder; http://www.pegasus-one.org/pow/fred_moore.htm, F. Moore, 1; http://www.pegasus-one.org/pow/david_parker.htm, D. Parker, 12; John Burton, *Mirador* (London, 1986), 119; Robert Gale, *Private Prisoner* (Wellingborough, 1984), 70–2, 129; Alan Mackay, *313 Days to Christmas* (Glendaruel, 1998), 94; Jack Poole, *Undiscovered Ends* (London, 1957), 137–8; James Spenser, *The Awkward Marine* (London, 1948), 268; Geoffrey D. Vaughan, *The Way It Really Was* (Budleigh Salterton, 1985), 47.

26. Stedman, op. cit., 22; Colin Rushton, *Spectator in Hell* (Springhill, 1998), 84; Stanley Rayner, *I Remember* (Lincoln, 1995), 160.

27. Edgar, op. cit., 119–20; Neville Chesterton, *Crete Was My Waterloo* (London, 1995), 85.

28. Edgar, op. cit., 120; Green, op. cit., 122. On stiffing the enemy while trading see e.g. IWM, O. Dover, 16. On reactions working alongside Auschwitz inmates see e.g. John Castle, *The Password Is Courage* (London, 1955), 148 ff. On the spread of news about the treatment of concentration camp inmates see e.g. Barbara Broom (comp.), *Geoffrey Broom's War* (Edinburgh, 1993), 139. BEF men and later Kriegies greatly admired the way in which Polish civilians, despite their own troubles and the risks involved, did their best to assist British prisoners through gifts or trade. See e.g. IWM, J. V. Brown, 15; IWMSA 48960/3, G. Shipp; John Elwyn, *At the Fifth Attempt* (London, 1987), 68; Ewart C. Jones, *Germans Under My Bed* (London, 1957), 31; Adrian Vincent, *The Long Road Home* (London, 1956), 107.

29. Taylor, op. cit., 165; J. Roberts, op. cit., 98; John Borrie, *Despite Captivity* (London, 1975), 100; Gale, op. cit., 126; Passmore, op. cit., 82–3; Cyril Jolly, *The Vengeance of Private Pooley* (London, 1956), 97. On 'cleaning up' and issuing better rations prior to and/or during neutral visits see e.g. T. D. Beckwith (ed.), *The Mansel Diaries* (London, 1977), 81; Christopher Portway, *Journey to Dana* (London, 1955), 102. On visits in general see Jonathan F. Vance, 'The Politics of Camp Life: The Bargaining Process in Three German Prison Camps', *War and Society*, 19 (1992), 109–26. Neutral visitors could be particularly credulous concerning conditions in camps early in the war. See e.g. PRO, FO 916/14, encl. 14A. On the varying quality of Swiss representatives see e.g. David Wild, *Prisoner of Hope* (Lewes, 1992), 176.

30. Reid, *Colditz Story*, 129; CSVA 7, P. Allan; CSVA 4, K. Lockwood. On regret at the Poles and other nationalities leaving see Margaret Duggan (ed.), *Padre in Colditz* (London, 1978), 223.

31. Reinhold Eggers, *Colditz* (London, 1961), 29. On the Dutch contingent see Giles Romilly and Michael Alexander, *The Privileged Nightmare* (London, 1954), 99; Henry Chancellor, *Colditz* (London, 2001), 58, 60;

IWMSA 4432/9, H. Gee; John Chrisp, *The Tunnellers of Sandborstal* (London, 1959), 151.

32. CSVA 2, J. Yule; ibid. 7, P. Allan; ibid. 4, K. Lockwood; see also Romilly and Alexander, op. cit., 90–2; CSVA 11, H. Ironside; Michael Burn, *Yes Farewell* (London, 1946), 36–7; Chancellor, op. cit., 33. The term 'frogs' was used by Jack Courtnay in a post-war interview, though not in a disparaging manner. See IWMSA 10771/1, J. Courtnay. The thirty-five Belgians (at the opposite end of the spectrum from the Dutch in terms of military attitude and bearing) seem to have had no problem at all striking up amicable conversations with anyone of any nationality. See Romilly and Alexander, op. cit., 89, 99–100.

33. CSVA 4, K. Lockwood; see Airey Neave, *They Have Their Exits* (London, 1953), 68; Chancellor, op. cit., 31–2. For the comment on Green see IWMSA 4820/2, C. Scarborough. On Goldman see IWM, J. E. Platt diary, 22 Feb. 1941; see also Reid, *Colditz Story*, 119–20.

34. IWMSA TS 4843, G. Abbott, 36; LC, T. N. Catlow, 56; CSVA 8, J. Best. On relations with the Czechs and Free French making up for the loss of the main foreign contingents in 1943 see Rogers, op. cit., 164. On the original 'international effect' see e.g. CSVA 7, P. Allan. On regret at the original departure see e.g. CSVA 4, K. Lockwood. On Mazumdar see IWMSA 16800/2, B. N. Mazumdar.

35. For the 'shopkeepers' episode see LC, T. N. Catlow, 67. On comments on the 1945 French and debates about sharing see Romilly and Alexander, op. cit., 157–8; Champ and Burgess, op. cit., 215; G. Davies-Scourfield in Chancellor, op. cit., 351; IWMSA 4820/2, C. Scarborough; CSVA 4, K. Lockwood; IWM, J. E. Platt diary, 19 and 28 Feb. 1945. For the 'taken in hand' comment see P. R. Reid, *The Latter Days* (London, 1953), 269. For personal friendships see e.g. Earl Haig, *My Father's Son* (London, 2000), 137–8.

36. Green, op. cit., 148–9; see LC, T. Catlow, 83. For the 'old toothbrush' comment see Romilly and Alexander, op. cit., 158. On trying to help the Russians see Chancellor, op. cit., 127–8.

37. D. Bader in Florimond Duke, *Name, Rank, and Serial Number* (New York, 1969), p. x. On the lecture see Romilly and Alexander, op. cit., 154–5.

38. Burn, op. cit., 27; A. Heinrich in Patrick Wilson, *The War Behind the Wire* (Barnsley, 2000), 180; CSVA 2, J. Yule.

39. IWM, J. E. Platt diary, 26 Jan. 1945, 15 Sept. 1943.

40. Ibid., 23 Jan. 1943, 14 May 1941, 6 Apr. 1941; see ibid., 17 Jan. 1941, 23 July 1943; PRO, WO 224/69.

41. CSVA 11, H. Ironside. The 'friendly rivalry' comment was by Kenneth Lockwood. See *Escape from Colditz: 1. The Escaping Academy* (Woodfall Films, 2000). The 'complete solidarity' comment was by Peter Allan. CSVA 7, P. Allan.

9   Patriots and Traitors

Prisoners of war shall be subject to the laws, regulations and orders in force in the armed forces of the detaining Power. Any act of insubordination shall render them liable to the measures prescribed by such laws, regulations, and orders...

(from Article 45, Geneva Convention, 1929)

Prisoners who refuse to reply [to enemy demands] shall not be threatened, or exposed to any unpleasantness or disadvantage of any kind...

(from Article 5, Geneva Convention, 1929)

In relation to the war around them, British POWs in Nazi Germany existed in a curious state of limbo. They were still recognized members of the armed forces of the Crown. Yet through the process of surrender and official recognition as prisoners of war, Kriegies had assumed a non-belligerent status. They were like chessmen removed from the board—still in one piece but out of the game. Under international law, only if a prisoner escaped back to his home country could he legitimately become directly involved again in the war effort and re-enter the fray. There were those, however, who chose not to accept a passive role while in enemy hands. As the next chapter will indicate, escape was one way of getting back into the thick of things—but there were other avenues that could be pursued to help the war effort. Acts of sabotage could be undertaken, efforts made to undermine enemy morale, and intelligence gathered for transmission back to the United Kingdom in code letters. At the opposite end of the spectrum was the much smaller number of prisoners who broke out of limbo by choosing to actively co-operate with their captors as spies, propagandists, or even as soldiers. In short, some Kriegies could continue to serve their country while in unfriendly hands, while others might end up serving the enemy. The situation in Colditz regarding patriots and traitors was, as we shall see, surprisingly unexceptional.

The opportunities for sabotage were greatest on Arbeitskommandos. Kriegies could not be closely supervised all the time, had tools in their hands, and could decide to act destructively rather than constructively in whatever tasks they were employed on. There were risks involved, as being caught in the act could mean anything from on-the-spot beatings to long stretches in a military prison. On the other hand, there was great satisfaction to be derived from the knowledge that, despite being a captive, a prisoner was not entirely helpless and that he was secretly undermining rather than contributing to the captor's war effort. A mixture of apathy and fear caused many POWs to confine their defiance to lack of industriousness, and sometimes a billet seemed just too cushy to risk by gambling that acts of sabotage would remain undetected. Stuart Brown, despite having done some agricultural sabotage else-where, decided in 1942 that on one farm he and his fellow Kriegies 'were too well treated to risk jeopardising our chances of staying where we were'. Meanwhile the more active Kriegies learned how to appear half-witted and cover their tracks when eroding the quality of their overt work.[1]

Ditch-digging or navvy work could present opportunities to demon-strate a gang's sabotage skills. Drainage pipes could be broken as they were laid, and covered with earth before anyone in authority noticed. 'We spent a lot of time digging holes where they were not wanted,' Cyril Rofe remembered of a canal drainage project he worked on in 1942, 'invariably managing to let the water in at the wrong moment. We had a great time and generally contrived to do the wrong thing.' Made to dig and line a fire-fighting reservoir in 1944, James Stedman and his fellows derived a strong sense of job satisfaction from the end result. 'We had made sure it would not be water-tight by shoddy work', he later wrote. 'By the next day [after completion] the reservoir was half-empty. Good old British workmanship.' Road maintenance could also become an exercise in futility. 'To anyone observing—even if they were interested—our labours on some outlying perimeter,' Ed Annetts wrote of the repair job on the track surrounding an airfield he and his mates undertook in 1941, 'it would look as if we were just the usual gang mending pot-holes. In fact, we were actually making them . . . we simply moved holes from one section of road to another.'[2]

Agriculture offered its own set of opportunities for mischief. Sugar, the end-product of beet harvesting and processing (common seasonal tasks for Kriegies), proved ideal for arson purposes. A fire started in a small cardboard box could be stuffed into a vat of loose sugar that would in turn smoulder for hours before the whole load—by then many miles away in railway wagons—burst into flames, apparently as a result of spontaneous combustion. Cabbages could be planted the wrong way up, wheatsheaves could be positioned so that much of the seed would germinate, and threshing could be brought to a halt by slipping unbound sheaves of corn into the milling machinery until it jammed. Other mechanical devices, including harvesters, could be rendered useless through the removal or damaging of key parts.[3]

Quarrying and mining could also be the scene of sabotage. Ore and coal might not be separated properly from broken rock, and conveyor trucks overloaded or otherwise damaged. John Lawrence fondly remembered what happened after he and others from Lamsdorf began work at a limestone quarry in 1941. 'When two skips were full they were let down the steep slope,' he explained, 'on a miniature railway line':

The skips were linked together, and connected by a huge wooden 'bremser' [bremse—brake]. As the two wooden skips went down, two empty ones came up on the other end of the cable. At least, that was in theory, until the English 'Kriegies' arrived. It was amazing how many times poor old 'Slim' [the elderly German operator] lost control of his Bremser and sent two empty skips careening back into the yard, sending all and sundry scurrying to escape the shower of 50 lb rocks, which flew everywhere when the skips finally came to a rest.

The civilian foreman guessed that prisoners were to blame and made dire threats, but without hard proof he could do nothing but fume.[4]

There was often a variety of possibilities for undermining work on building sites. Washers might be removed as plumbing was installed, hinges could be misaligned or left too loose when doors and windows were put in, and everything from nails to glass left lying about waiting for an accident to happen. 'Filling pipes with rubble and loosening nuts after work had been inspected and passed was a regular trick', Arthur Dodd recalled of work at an I. G. Farben plant near Auschwitz. 'The men deliberately miscounted when mixing concrete and ensured the mix was too heavy with cement causing cracks in the structures that were built.'[5]

Putting prisoners to work on transport-related jobs was simply asking for trouble. A visiting RAMC doctor was impressed by the level of Kriegie inventiveness he observed at a lorry depot:

At the repair shops for damaged motor vehicles our mechanics were engaged in reconditioning trucks and cars. The electrical faults which developed in the majority of vehicles once they had left the shops must have proved a sore trial to their drivers. One Sapper who had worked in a motor factory before the war was particularly skilled in loosening the nut connecting the oil outlet of the sump so that it would fall off after about a hundred miles travel, when the oil would escape and the engine seize up.

Jobs in railway marshalling yards provided a range of options for brave and inventive types. Everything from ashes to pebbles and sand could be surreptitiously dumped into the axle grease of rolling stock, contents and destination labels could be switched from one wagon to another, dry goods 'accidentally' exposed to the elements, and the track itself rendered dangerous by camouflaging the surreptitious removal of ballast or secretly switching points.[6]

Those confined to oflags and stalags obviously had less opportunity to engage in sabotage activity. To wreck the plumbing, electricity, or heating supply inside camps would adversely affect the prisoners more than the guards. Nevertheless, when the authorities attempted to introduce devices—loudspeakers or sound detectors—that clearly benefited the captors rather more than the captives, the more aggressive POWs were not averse to a little malicious sleight of hand. When in 1941 hidden microphones were discovered at Stalag Luft I, for instance, enterprising Kriegies connected up the wiring to the main electrical supply. The result, B. A. 'Jimmy' James recalled, was 'an electrical tour de force which undoubtedly caused considerable confusion in the Vorlager'. At Barth as elsewhere an added ingredient took the form of bits of used razor-blades placed in the cookhouse swill, destined to be consumed by pigs on surrounding farms. The resulting porcine deaths, however, could be traced back to their source once autopsies were performed. 'The threats uttered then', Richard Passmore recorded, 'were serious enough to make us desist forthwith.'[7]

RAF prisoners were also responsible for the unfortunate consequences of what might be classified as a semi-intentional act of sabotage at Stalag IVB (Mühlberg) in April 1944. After Ju 88 aircraft from a nearby airfield began buzzing the camp, Kriegies responded with the usual mixture of jeering and barracking reserved for German intrusions into normal camp life. Various hand signals, rude and official, were used to indicate to the pilots of the Ju 88s that they were not flying *really* low over the compound. One day a Luftwaffe pilot, thereby encouraged to make a particularly low dive-bombing pass, pulled up too steeply, allowing the tail to hit the ground, practically decapitating one prisoner and severely wounding another. The aerial visits stopped, but the price of success, all agreed, had been too high.[8]

Undermining enemy morale was another tack that could be taken in continuing the war effort behind the wire. The abundance represented by Red Cross parcels and cigarettes was designed to depress the Germans as well as support POWs, and MI9 courses in the middle war years encouraged those who might fall into enemy hands to flaunt Allied victories. Air force prisoners were well to the fore in the psychological warfare game. German-speakers at Stalag Luft I made a point of trying to sow doubt concerning Nazi victory in the minds of the *Posten* they encountered. At Stalag Luft III the chief mover in the Great Escape, Roger Bushell, took time to orchestrate a carefully planned conversational campaign designed to depress the guards in the North Compound. Both at Sagan and at Barth 'flycraft' were employed to carry short but nasty messages to nearby villages and farms. Canadian pilot Kingsley Brown found his first encounter with Wing Commander 'Taffy' Williams, the officer in charge of propaganda in the East Compound at Stalag Luft III, quite memorable:

He was seated at a table by an open window. He appeared to be busy with some kind of hobby that involved old empty jam jars, pieces of paper, scissors and other assorted odds and ends. He turned to greet me.

'Good show! You're just in time to lend me a hand. We've got a propaganda job. Something to break the morale of the civilian population, you know. Sow doubt and all that. Not much we can do at the present time [summer 1942], but we do have to make a start, don't we? Small beginnings, eh what? I'm sure you can be of help. We need professional people. Now let me show you . . .'

He swung back to the table and picked up one of the jam jars. An elastic band held a piece of cheesecloth over the top of the jar. As he picked it up, there was an angry humming sound.

'Bumblebees,' he said, handing me the jar.

They were bumblebees, all right—about a dozen of them, all trying their best to escape.

'Oh, I have a team of the boys out collecting them. They find them over by the cookhouse and among the weeds. There's more of 'em.' He pointed to two more jars on the windowsill, 'Very well. Now let me show you the rest of the business.'

I handed back the jar of bees, and in return he passed me a tiny slip of paper. It was almost tissue paper, not unlike the paper used for airmail letters. It was about four inches in length, and had been cut in the triangular shape of a pennant. On one side of it, it said DEUTSCHLAND KAPUT. On the reverse side it said HITLER KAPUT.

The nature of our propaganda effort suddenly dawned on me. The bumblebees were to carry our devastating message to the German populace.

'I'm afraid it's the best we can do right now, old boy,' said Wings. He handed me a gentleman's light leather glove for my right hand.

'Now, what we do is this. I attach this thread to the pennant, see? With a running noose at the end. Now, when I make a little opening in the jar, you'll grab the first bee that comes out.

'You'll have to be careful—gentle, you know. We mustn't hurt the little devil or he'll be no good to us, will he? You must hold him gently by the wings while I slip the noose over his backside and make it fast—but not too tight, mind you. And just where his thorax and abdomen meet. And, after that, well, the best way to begin is to begin, what?'

About an hour later, the jar was empty. One after another the bees had been pinioned and harnessed to their banners and released out the window. The wing commander was delighted to see how well they handled their burden.

'Just the right wing loading, what? Had to figure that out. Any more weight and they couldn't maintain altitude. Thanks old boy. That's it for today. How about tomorrow morning, right after *Appell*?'

The effectiveness of this propaganda campaign is open to question, but it was satisfying for those involved, and at Barth the local townspeople complained to the camp authorities after encounters with hornets towing paper cylinders with *Germany kaput* and *Hitler niche goot* inscribed on them.[9]

Efforts were also made to sabotage enemy propaganda efforts. Loudspeakers had been set up in a number of main camps to broadcast 'Lord Haw Haw' announcing German victories and Allied setbacks, sandwiched between bursts of marching songs such as *Wir fahren gegen England*. The result was not what the Propaganda Ministry had hoped for. 'Unfortunately from the German point of view, this open air concert of recorded martial music did not have the desired effect,' Lamsdorf prisoner Frank Taylor noted, 'for far from being cowed, browbeaten, and subdued, we "mad British prisoners" took to the compound goose-steeping, "Heil Hitlering" and flinging out Nazi salutes with gay abandon—all in time to the music.' At Wolfsberg the wiring for the loudspeakers was cut, and when this produced unacceptable reprisals a campaign was started to convince the commandant that Lord Haw Haw was giving away information valuable to the RAF in his broadcasts.[10]

Gathering and passing along intelligence was a clandestine but potentially much more important way of contributing to the war effort. Much time and effort was expended on communicating information of potential importance to London by interested parties.

In the early war years in particular, Kriegies who wished to pass on war-related information through letters that would not be stopped by the German censors might think up their own codes. Arthur Gibbs, an RAMC orderly working in the hospital of Stalag IXC, discovered that a private soldier wanting to alert the RAF to various armaments factories in the vicinity had developed a plan. '[H]e started writing letters home using a code which was the one where the first word of the first sentence, for example, starts with the "W" and the first word of the second sentence starts with "E" etc. etc. and the person at the other end reads "WE" and so on—a very simple code but he thought this would fool the German censor...' It did, but proved useless because the recipient did not recognize what was being attempted and was simply left puzzled as to why the letters read so oddly.[11]

MI9 had been established as an arm of the Secret Service in November 1939 to provide information and tools for both potential and actual escapers and evaders. A code section was established in the spring of the following year, and within six months had developed a letter code (HK) that newly captured prisoners could in turn teach to other Kriegies. Use of this and later official codes (such as the air force 'Amy' code) gradually expanded through the camp system as new men arrived and passed on their knowledge to trusted comrades. Two-way communication was thereby established with many main camps, supplemented in the latter war years by coded broadcast messages received on illicit radios. Much of the traffic concerned issues related to escape, but there was also a fair amount of emphasis on intelligence gathering.[12]

The two-or-more month time-lag involved in sending a request and receiving an answer, along with the fact that many prisoners spent most of their time behind wire in particular locations, meant that much of the requested intelligence was of a general kind: 'Nothing very precise or detailed', Dixie Deans recalled. Information on enemy morale, the state of the harvest, and general bomb damage were among the common questions posed, along with information from newly arrived aircrew on German air defences and interrogation techniques. Details were also forwarded by code writers on other items of interest that were seen in transit or from inside the wire. Depending on the location, activity observed around factories, railway lines, or airfields could be carefully noted down and passed along to London.[13]

Just how useful this type of activity really was remains open to debate. Some camps never established contact with MI9, and in those that did, the Kriegies involved might have difficulty mastering a code or grasping what was required in the way of contents and security needs. 'The dispatch of information ... by means of code-letters was not exploited fully', a summary report on intelligence efforts in Stalag IIIE determined. MI9 queries in turn might appear to be irritatingly irrelevant or dangerously amateurish to camp decoders. 'Code messages were sent out to us on certain [radio] programmes', Jack Poole related of his time at Oflag IXA/H; 'they took hours to decode, and were often of such a futile nature that they were not encouraged.' In the same camp code letters were received bearing telltale signs that would have shown, if the German censors had being paying attention, that they had not in fact come from real relatives—including one with the word 'CODE' pencilled on the envelope and bearing a British censor's stamp. And even under the best of circumstances, the time-lag involved in exchanging secret messages meant, as an in-house summary of MI9 activity conceded, that 'the information [received in London] may be of value only on a long-term policy [basis]'.[14]

On the other hand, the Germans never seem to have worked out any of the codes, confining their attention to possible use of invisible ink. Moreover, sometimes the information passed on spontaneously by a particular code writer did prompt specific requests that in turn produced specific answers. London was understandably keen to keep tabs on traitors, and encouraged reports on the personnel and progress of the British Free Corps (on which more below). The crews of the 'X'-craft mini submarines captured while attempting to sink the battleship *Tirpitz* were debriefed inside Marlag, and their opinions as to the damage done passed along. Descriptions of V-weapon test firings were also encouraged, and confirmation sought on occasion that a particular factory was indeed producing a certain item. Sometimes there were subsequent signs of cause and effect.

At Sagan it was believed by those in the know that the information provided at London's request on rocket launches led to the RAF raid on the Peenemünde testing site in 1943. The intelligence organization at Oflag 79 (Brunswick) was asked via a radio message in mid-June 1944 to ascertain whether or not a factory about half-a-mile from the camp was turning out 88 mm anti-aircraft guns. Through conversations with a guard this was confirmed, a code letter reply was sent, and six weeks later a raid by USAAF bombers obliterated the place. Whether or not there was a direct connection between certain POW intelligence reports and particular Allied actions, the gathering, encoding, and sending of information gave those involved—usually no more than a dozen men in most places—a sense of purpose and patriotic meaning to Kriegie life.[15]

A very different path to a more active existence was chosen by those prisoners who, through a mixture of avarice, gullibility, ideological inclination, or simple fear, agreed to work for the enemy. Turncoats were needed by the German authorities for several, sometimes overlapping, roles. These included disseminating propaganda, usually over the radio; spying, mostly on fellow prisoners; and, depending on their origins, joining enemy-sponsored fighting units: the Free India Legion, the Arab Legion, and the British Free Corps. None of these units amounted to much, and the propagandists added little to what was being achieved—or rather not achieved—by civilian traitors. Those employed as stool pigeons inside POW camps, on the other hand, proved to be a serious threat to the security of clandestine activities.

The Free India Legion was the creation of Subhas Chandra Bose, the militant Indian nationalist leader who had eluded British surveillance and made his way to Berlin in early 1941. He argued for the raising of a liberation force from among the thousands of Indian Army soldiers recently captured in Libya, and in the autumn OKW—foreseeing the collapse of the USSR and a road opening up to the subcontinent through Afghanistan—agreed to allow full-scale recruitment to begin. About 1,000 Indian other rank and NCO prisoners were concentrated at Oflag IVE—which became Stalag IVD/Z—at Annaburg awaiting a visit by Bose, who apparently anticipated that his personal charisma would win men who had fought as 'mercenaries' for the British over to the Free India cause. The Netaji, or leader, was in for a rude shock. Pro-British elements began coughing and barracking as soon as he began to speak, drowning out most of Bose's words and making it abundantly clear where their sympathies lay. 'I thought it was a complete fiasco,' one of his civilian lieutenants admitted, 'and that there was no possibility of starting the Legion, as it was called at the time, with that particular batch.' Efforts to recruit officers, if anything, met with even greater hostility. The most likely prospects were brought together in a special low-security working camp in a residential section of Berlin, and addressed first by William Joyce ('Lord Haw Haw') and then by a representative of Bose who made an 'inflammatory and nationalistic' speech on behalf of the militant cause. BQMS John Brown, who observed the scene, later described how, as soon as the speeches were finished, one of the Indians stood up to respond:

'As Senior Officer here I speak for my fellow officers. We regard *you* as a traitor not only to England but to our own dear land. We will have nothing to do with your foul schemes. England has promised us that as soon as the war is over we shall be free. We have no reason to doubt her word. I give you five minutes in which to leave this room. After that I will not be responsible for my fellow officers.'

This was greeted with a storm of applause, followed by the hasty departure of the recruiters.[16]

Subsequent efforts were initially more successful. The defiant elements were separated out and a carrot-and-stick approach taken with the remaining sepoys. Potential recruits, subjected to a regimen of short rations and propaganda, were promised better food and more freedom if they volunteered for the Legion. Two hundred and eighty of the more amenable Indian POWs were moved in the summer of 1942 to a camp at Königsbrück, where they were given German uniforms with a special arm-badge showing a leaping tiger superimposed on the Indian national colours and the legend *Freies Indien*. But the oath of allegiance they had sworn, along with more material worries such as loss of pensions, slowed the pace of recruiting. Moreover, though German officers and NCOs did their best to train volunteers in the use of Wehrmacht weapons and tactics, the civilian leadership cadre that Bose appointed to oversee the growth of the Free India Legion managed to mishandle sensitive issues of caste and religion. Morale remained low, relations with German personnel were distant, and when in April 1943 news arrived that the Legion was to serve as part of the Atlantic Wall garrison in the Low Countries, elements in all three battalions mutinied. The ringleaders were sent off to detention camps and the newly designated Infantry Regiment No. 950 was transferred, first to Belgium and then to France. Bose himself had gone to the Far East, where his efforts to establish an Indian National Army from among Indian prisoners of the Japanese proved rather more successful. Meanwhile the *Freies Indien* volunteers in Europe felt increasingly alienated. Two smaller-scale mutinies occurred, and morale and discipline collapsed as the unit retreated eastward in the face of the Allied advance in the autumn of 1944. Two hundred men defected back to the Allied side via the Resistance. By now part of the Waffen-SS, what remained of the Legion was rounded up by American forces near Lake Constance in April 1945, only having fought in self-defence against the French Resistance.[17]

The much smaller Arab Legion was the brainchild of the Grand Mufti of Jerusalem, Haj Amin al-Hussaini, who like Bose had arrived in Axis Europe seeking aid in expelling the British from his homeland. He lobbied for a unit to be raised from the Arab population under Axis control—including the Arab Palestinians in POW camps—that would serve in the Middle East. The proposal was eventually accepted, and in 1942 recruiting began for the *Deutsche-Arabische Lehrabteilung*, later known as the *Arabischer Freiheitkorps*. The pool of potential recruits for the Legion numbered only in the hundreds, and though there were those who chose to wear German uniforms with 'Free Arabia' patches on their sleeves who served on the lines of communication in the Balkans and elsewhere, the Legion achieved nothing of significance. Like its Indian counterpart, it apparently suffered from low morale and poor discipline. An Australian POW encountered a recruit while serving a sentence at the military prison at Graudenz. 'He was an Arab who had fought for the Germans with the Arab Legion at the insistence of the Grand Mufti of Jerusalem', Ian Ramsay later wrote. 'This Arab had been sent to the Russian front and, finding it too cold for his liking, had decided to stab his German officer and desert.'[18]

Last and in some ways least was the British Free Corps. John Amery, the renegade son of the Secretary of State for India, had ended up in Berlin in 1942, where, in addition to engaging in propaganda broadcasts, he had urged the creation of a 'British Legion of St George' to join the fight against the Bolsheviks. Though Amery himself was soon sidelined from the project—he was clearly something of a loose cannon—the idea of raising a unit from among British prisoners was taken up at the end of the year by the Foreign Office and the SS. Even a small number of British servicemen fighting on the Eastern Front would be a major propaganda coup and a serious embarrassment to Anglo-Soviet relations. Turning the concept into a reality, however, was to prove highly problematic.

Assembling known fascist sympathizers and other likely prospects in a special 'holiday camp', where they could be exposed to a combination of good treatment and anti-communist propaganda before any outright recruiting took place, was in theory a fine idea. The man chosen as camp leader at Genshagen, however, was in fact playing a double game. Despite pre-war links with the British Union of Fascists and suspicions among fellow Kriegies that he was endeavouring to cosy up to the Germans, BQMS John Brown was secretly collecting intelligence and sending it to London by code letter. Brown managed to persuade his masters, after the first batch of Kriegies had passed through Genshagen in 1943, that the camp ought to be dedicated to instilling pro-German sentiment and that further attempts to persuade POWs to join the Legion would simply turn them further against the Reich. A few prisoners had already come forward for ideological reasons or simply to improve their living conditions, and these were supplemented in the last months of 1943 by a handful of more recently captured men who were essentially browbeaten at the Luckenwalde interrogation centre into signing on. Yet by the start of 1944, when the unit was officially taken under the wing of the Waffen-SS as the British Free Corps (BFC), it consisted of only eight men.[19]

Field-grey service uniforms were issued, along with special insignia—a Union Jack shield worn on the sleeve and later three embroidered silver lions on a collar patch—and basic training commenced at Hildesheim. It was obvious, however, that if the BFC was ever to take the field it would have to reach at least platoon strength. Further recruiting efforts were therefore launched. In addition to the apparent resumption of subtle efforts at Genshagen, the drive took the form of visits to camps by members and their minders, the posting of notices inside the wire, and the distribution in huts of leaflets announcing the formation of the British Free Corps.

Happily for the historian, soldiers sometimes saved these missives as souvenirs. The main section read as follows:

1. The British Free Corps is a thoroughly British volunteer unit conceived and created by British subjects from all parts of the empire, who have taken up arms and pledged their lives in the common European struggle against Soviet Russia.

2. The British Free Corps condemns the war with Germany and the sacrifice of British blood in the interests of Jewry and international finance, and regards the conflict as a fundamental betrayal of the British people and British Imperial interests.

3. The British Free Corps desires the establishment of peace in Europe, the development of close friendly relations between England and Germany and the encouragement of mutual understanding between the two great Germanic peoples.

4. The British Free Corps will neither make war against Britain or the British Crown, nor support any action or policy detrimental to the interests of the British people.

Volunteers would be considered for spot promotions on joining the BFC and would receive a priority passage home when the war was won.[20]

The reaction to the leaflets was, by and large, either complete disgust or hilarious incredulity. Even the guards who distributed the recruiting notices often seemed embarrassed, hastily dumping them en masse in huts, stuffing them in greatcoat pockets, or claiming that they had been dropped by the RAF. The latter excuse was something of a stretch at Thorn, where the 'air dropped' leaflets were found held down by stones to stop them blowing away. It was obvious to most Kriegies that joining the BFC meant becoming a traitor. When the leaflets were found at Marlag (M), Harold Shipp remembered, 'they told them where to stick them'. The reaction to the appearance of a BFC recruiting poster at a working camp run through Stalag XVIIIA was not atypical. 'Once everyone had read it,' recalled D. W. Luckett, 'it was torn down and burned.' In other places the leaflets were simply considered a huge joke. 'The Russians didn't mean all that much to us,' wrote Francis Jones, 'but at least we weren't on fighting terms with them.' The war was expected to end in victory for the Allies by the end of the year, and in any case winter conditions to the East were already the stuff of legend. At Lamsdorf a notice appeared on one of the huts: 'Recruiting Office—Join the Free Corps and see the Eastern Front.' Apart from the souvenir factor, leaflets were valued mainly as something on which to write and as toilet paper.[21]

Recruiting visits by BFC members in person were no laughing matter, however. 'The Kom. informed me that two members of the "British Free Corps" . . . had orders from Berlin that they were to visit the camp', the SBO at Marlag recorded in his diary on 14 May 1944. 'I replied that I did not wish any traitors to come into the camp.' In this case the BFC party never got beyond the Vorlager. One day a German officer accompanied by someone wearing BFC uniform visited one of the Stalag XXA Arbeitskommandos. 'We soon discovered that he was an Australian who had been taken prisoner in Crete,' a QVR private recorded, 'and that the main purpose of his visit was to encourage as many Allied prisoners as possible to join this newly formed unit to fight alongside the Germans against the Russians.'

When this became obvious the prisoners were furious and several made threatening moves toward the Australian, calling him some unprintable names and telling him in no uncertain terms exactly what they would do with him when they got hold of him . . . the guards had to fix bayonets and more or less keep the prisoners at bay whilst the German officer and the Australian beat a hasty retreat out of the camp.

In Fort 13 at Thorn itself an earlier visitor had been called 'a bloody traitor' to his face, and there had been talk of killing him if the opportunity arose. When the Free Corps came to Wolfsberg the inmates were assembled and given a recruiting speech that stressed the material benefits of joining the BFC. 'When one of these British conscripts had to use the toilets,' Neville Chesterton remembered, 'two Aussies followed him and threw him into the stinking pit. He had to be pulled out, looking very sorry for himself, and smelling to high heaven.'[22]

On the whole the recruiting efforts for the BFC proved not worth the effort expended. There were, however, a handful of men who were sufficiently gullible (or were facing the alternative of time in jail for various offences) to sign on. 'Some of the more simple and politically unsophisticated prisoners still harboured the idea that these leaflets had really been sent with the authority of the British government,' wrote Robert Gale, 'and that, if things became too bad at the stone quarry, they could always get away by volunteering to join this anti-communist unit.'[23] One recruit, Thomas Freeman, joined with the express purpose of wrecking the BFC from within. In June 1944 he managed to get fourteen of his twenty-three fellow recruits to sign a petition requesting that they be sent back to stalag, forcing the SS to place Freeman and company in an isolation camp and hope that more recruits would come forward. Poor leadership and a slump in morale following the successful D-day landings in Normandy led eight more volunteers to withdraw their services thereafter. Transferred to Dresden, the BFC reached a peak strength of twenty-seven in January 1945. Morale and discipline, however, continued to crumble, and anyone in doubt about the course of the war was disabused by the destruction of the city from the air the following month. Talk of desertion led the Gestapo to arrest all members of the BFC it could find and send them to Berlin. Dragooned into the defence of the German capital, but never actually confronted by the Red Army, the remaining members of the British Free Corps slipped away amid the collapse of the Third Reich in April 1945.[24]

Many of those Britons who agreed to do propaganda work for Germany were civilians of one kind or another. There were, however, a small number of POWs who agreed to help with radio broadcasts and engage in related activity aimed at undermining British morale at home or the front. A handful of Kriegies helped to glean information from newly captured prisoners at interrogation centres by concealing the fact that they were co-operating with the Germans. There were also recently captured personnel who broadcast messages to the effect that they were safe, a propaganda victory insofar as it drove families to listen in to enemy broadcasts in the hopes of hearing news of someone known to be missing.[25]

In June 1940, with the Anglo-French war effort in tatters and conditions in the camps near their worst, William Joyce was successful in persuading eight men from Stalag XXA (Thorn) to join the broadcasting effort in return for a change of identity, civilian clothes, private accommodation, and a salary. Efforts thereafter were far more sporadically successful, with one junior Merchant Navy officer along with one RAF officer and NCO eventually being persuaded to undertake propaganda work. Meanwhile servicemen were being warned in England not to broadcast under any circumstances if captured, and in real terms the effect of German radio propaganda, especially after 1940, was negligible.[26]

There was also a handful of Kriegies who assisted the enemy through agreeing to get involved in the Katyn affair. The discovery in April 1943 of the bodies of thousands of Polish officers in the Katyn Forest, murdered by Soviet security forces three years earlier, presented the German propaganda machine with a unique opportunity to sow discord between Britain, the Polish government-in-exile, and the USSR. To prove that the Katyn massacre was not a fabrication an international medical commission was formed to investigate the site, and British medical and senior officers invited to view the remains. From General Fortune down, most of those prisoners asked to go refused to do so, recognizing that, whatever the truth of the affair, their presence would make them tools of the Nazi propaganda machine. Three other ranks, an RAMC doctor, and a lieutenant-colonel in the South African forces did travel to the site in May, but there are indications that these men were already on the road to becoming German pawns.[27]

Then there were the dozen or so traitors who assisted their captors in interrogating other prisoners, chiefly at the air force and army interrogation centres. Soldiers who agreed to help extract information from prisoners by posing as fellow Kriegies at Luckenwalde mostly did so as a result of intimidation and blackmail. In 1943 Stoker H. H. Rose, for instance, was threatened with death as a spy after he exchanged identities with an agent provocateur, and eventually agreed to help in interrogation work. Private John Welch of the Durham Light Infantry, meanwhile, signed on in exchange for not being court-martialled after having been caught *in flagrante* with a German woman.[28]

The motives of those airmen who worked for the enemy at Oberusel, posing as 'friendly' fellow airmen in whom newly captured RAF aircrew could confide, were a little more complex. The Luftwaffe wanted volunteers who were more-or-less willing rather than simply coerced into the job.

Everything from poor judgement and ideological affinity to fear of retribution and mental instability helps explain why certain aircrew did what they did. Flight Sergeant Raymond Hughes, an air gunner shot down in August 1943, for example, appears to have been afraid of the consequences of being captured in civilian clothes (he had been on the run). He was also blissfully unaware of the dangers of stating more than his name, rank, and serial number, and gullible enough to think that if an RAF officer he met was already working at Dulag Luft then it could not be the wrong thing to do. The officer in question was Squadron Leader Fitz-Boyd Carpenter, a Mosquito pilot of such garrulous boastfulness that he not only talked about his own job but also agreed to work on radio propaganda. Flight Sergeant Frank Tipton briefly became a pawn of the Germans at about the same time, through what the RAF Special Investigation Branch decided was a case of temporary derangement. The actions of Squadron Leader Railton Freeman, who eventually did radio propaganda work and assisted the camp authorities at Oberusel to a limited extent in 1940–1, were governed by his strong anti-Jewish and anti-Communist views.[29]

By far the most dangerous group of traitors from the Kriegie perspective consisted of those who accepted work as stool pigeons. A variety of *Verboten* activities and objects, especially those related to escape, could be compromised by a turncoat inside the wire learning what was going on and spilling the beans to the camp authorities. Bribed, bullied, or blackmailed into betraying their comrades, these hidden traitors were the assumed cause of a range of major and minor setbacks, and operated in lagers large and small. 'In no camp in which I lived while a p.o.w.', Richard Pape, an RAF navigator who spent years behind wire in six different locations, later reflected, 'did I find 100 per cent loyalty.'[30]

The havoc wrought in 1943 by a turncoat at Oflag IXA/Z (Rotenburg) and then Oflag IXA/H (Spangenberg) was, unfortunately, probably not atypical. Later thought to be either a private soldier or NCO masquerading as a lieutenant, the individual in question pushed hard at Rotenburg in the spring to be let in on escape plans. After being dressed down by the SBO for his refusal to abide by escape committee security rules, he was suddenly whisked out of the prisoners' section of the camp by the German security officer. 'He gave everything he knew about escape plans, contacts with Great Britain and the like', Peter Harwood, the camp escape officer, later recorded. Once again masquerading as an officer, this stool pigeon was then placed in Spangenberg in July and then suddenly taken away—so the Germans claimed—for medical treatment. 'No series of coincidences could explain the sudden discovery within forty-eight hours of five separate hides [containing escape equipment and, in one case, a radio] which had withstood countless German searches', Terence Prittie explained. There were also signs that the traitor had found out enough to lead the Germans to uncover tunnels at both Rotenburg and Spangenberg.[31]

In an effort to thwart this sort of thing, those responsible for security matters behind the wire in the more highly organized compounds did their best to uncover plants by interrogating every new prisoner entering the camp to establish bona fides. In the early war years an officer's stated identity and background was relatively easy to confirm through cross-checking with others who were known to have been to the same places. Officers, especially those captured early in the war, either knew each other or shared enough background to make this comparatively easy. As Sandy St Clair explained of the interrogations conducted at Oflag VIIIF, 'most of us had been to a relatively small number of public schools in England together or to major universities like Oxford and Cambridge before the war'. If this failed, 'your other means of checking was your regiment or your OCTU'. Those who could not be vetted in this way stood out, and further questioning could reveal that the man was in fact a plant. In the North Compound at Stalag Luft III, an Egyptian arrived in 1944 who claimed to have been shot down while serving with the RAF in the Middle East. But nobody could vouch for him, and under close questioning his cover story fell apart. He finally revealed that he had agreed to work as an agent of the Germans under the auspices of the Grand Mufti.[32]

There were nevertheless limits to what could be done to foil spies. The other-rank population was so large that it was only after repeated incidents in various locations that word spread through the Kriegie grapevine about the unreliability of particular soldiers. The line between being a racketeer or odd man out and being a traitor was sometimes difficult to be sure of, and hearsay evidence could condemn a man unjustly. Some of the POWs suspected of assuming false identities turned out to be SOE and other secret agents whose very survival depended on cover stories designed to fool the Germans not being blown. The wartime expansion in the armed forces made it increasingly difficult in the latter war years to find people who knew, or knew of, newly captured officers, especially with respect to the RAF.[33]

Once a stool pigeon had been identified as such, there remained the question of what to do with him. In the case of the Egyptian and several other plants the line taken was to inform the camp authorities that unless the offender was removed at once his survival would be in serious jeopardy. In other cases Kriegies sought a measure of retribution before handing a man over. Francis Jones observed what happened after a group of Australians set a trap that netted an informer who was subsequently confronted in a bathhouse at Stalag IVB (Mühlberg):

I pushed through to see what was going on. From the [traitor's] point of view it was more than enough. A tall Australian was standing over him. 'You yellow German [*sic*] ba-astard!' he snarled. The lovely Australian long 'a' was twice its length. 'You'd squeal would you? Well start now!' A succession of open-handed smacks landed on the informer's already puffed face. He moaned, gibbered, and began to collapse, but it didn't work. The Australian was at fever pitch. 'Get up, you swine!' he hissed, 'there's more yet!' The informer staggered up again, with a hobnailed boot helping him. Then it happened. The Aussie gripped him in one hand and inflicted such murderous punishment with the other that before he was finished I had to turn away: and my stomach wasn't a queasy one.

In the end, eyes blackened, teeth missing, and face unrecognisable, he was flung to the ground . . . I thought he might die, but he didn't. About an hour later, he staggered up and lurched to the First Aid centre; but there was nothing doing there. Nobody would lift a finger to help him. He reeled away, managed to reach his own hut, and was promptly cuffed and kicked out again.

In this particular case the camp leader stepped in to prevent the informer from being subsequently lynched. But in several instances those in charge agreed with those who not only wanted revenge but also thought that death would prevent a traitor from being taken out and used elsewhere.[34]

On an Arbeitskommando near Auschwitz a new arrival claiming to be from the Green Howards arrived one day. Enquiries back at Lamsdorf revealed that nobody in that regiment recognized his name, and Sergeant Charles Coward had no compunction in ordering that this mysterious stranger be secretly killed and dumped in the latrine pit. In Stalag VIIIB those suspected of being stool pigeons might not live long. A decomposed body in British battledress was discovered during an early thaw in one of the reservoirs kept filled with water in case of fire. The identity of this mysterious corpse was never confirmed, but it was strongly rumoured that RSM Sherriff had ordered an execution in the wake of a particular tunnel being blown. Several months later James Stedman was among the Kriegies detailed to empty one of the latrines at Lamsdorf. 'We had to empty the contents of one the cesspools into a big metal container on wheels,' he remembered, 'and once when I looked down I saw a body floating on the top. I was quickly told by an old hand to give it a push under, as it was most likely a German stooge who had been sent into the camp, dressed in battledress, to spy and try to find out where tunnels were dug.' At Dulag Luft one of the permanent staff in 1941 was marked for death by three NCO aircrew who were convinced that he was a traitor. 'Three of us waited for him one dark night', Richard Pape remembered. 'As he crossed from one barrack to another we fell on him with bricks. A roving searchlight saved his skull from being fractured beyond all repair...' Roger Bushell, the mastermind behind the Great Escape from Stalag Luft III, was strongly in favour of ordering the execution of an officer who had wobbled a bit at Dulag and was now trying to get himself repatriated as insane in early 1944. 'This man...must be eliminated, bumped off if necessary...He will sell the tunnel for a repatriation. It's a completely unacceptable risk. He has to be got rid of!' Wings Day eventually persuaded Bushell that the officer in question was not an incipient traitor.[35]

In the immediate post-war decades it was popularly assumed that the British contingent at Oflag IVC contained only super-patriots. It was the camp for bad boys, the dumping ground for officers who demonstrated their desire to continue the fight by attempting to escape or otherwise making life difficult for their captors. The revelation in the latter 1970s that intelligence had been sent to MI9 through code letters from the castle only added to the patriotic aura, while news of a British traitor—a detail left out of *The Latter Days*—was seen as the exception that proved the rule. In fact the Germans had their eye on at least two other potential turncoats in the castle who wore British uniform, and the intelligence being sent on activity outside Colditz appears to have been no more than typical of that sent from other camps.

Baiting and escaping were the prime means through which the more restless souls cooped up in the castle sought to demonstrate that they had not given up and were still at war. However, there was also some sabotage undertaken, attempts at psychological warfare, and—as noted above—intelligence work not directly connected with breaking out.

Since Colditz was not a working camp there were not very many opportunities for sabotage; restless souls nevertheless devised ways of carrying the war to the enemy. Swiss visitors on occasion were given the impression by prisoners that conditions in the camp were worse than they really were, in turn prompting queries, complaints, explanations, and investigations, and thereby thoroughly wasting the time of the OKW administrative staff concerned. Razorblade pieces and shards of glass were added to the cookhouse refuse due to become pigswill on local farms, a practice that had to be abandoned in the face of general reprisals and threats by the commandant. A longer-term war strategy was pursued by Harry Elliott. He collected insects during exercise in the park and placed them in holes he had bored in various wooden key beams within the castle in the hope that termite-style structural damage would eventually ensue.[36]

Psychological warfare was also a feature of life at Oflag IVC. As in other camps in the early war years, prisoners were subjected to periodic special radio news bulletins (*Sondermeldungen*) announcing the latest German triumph over a loudspeaker system. The bad boys of Colditz responded by shouting, whistling, banging utensils, blowing musical instruments, and generally creating such a cacophony that the Sonder- meldung was drowned out. At the same time tallies were kept of the losses announced and the impossibility of some of the totals pointed out gleefully to guards. Hornets were harnessed to carry messages of the *Deutschland Kaput* variety, and in the later war years—by which time the radio bulletins had long been abandoned—attempts were being made to generate anxiety among the guards by posting notices with the words 'Are *you* on the list?' In exchange for co-operative behaviour in the last months of the war, *Posten* were offered specially printed cards indicating that the bearer had treated prisoners humanely.[37]

Confined as they were to a castle in Saxony, the useful information Kriegies at Colditz could pass on to London concerning outside events was rather circumscribed. Those involved in intelligence and code work nevertheless assiduously passed on news from new prisoners and what was seen, for instance, during individual trips to and from Leipzig for courts martial. That this information, along with whatever might be observed from within the Schloss, was of rather limited importance is suggested by the fact that when caught trying to pass a message on bombing effectiveness—his handwriting was identified behind the sep- arated backing of a photograph—Douglas Bader was lectured about the perils of espionage but otherwise let off. On occasion, however, the code group at Colditz was able to respond to specific MI9 queries through careful questioning of guards or newly arrived prisoners. Kenneth Lock- wood, for example, was able to discover whether or not there was a balloon barrage around Dresden through drawing out a friendly guard in conversation.[38]

Ill-informed as to what kind of a place they were visiting, recruiters for the British Free Corps arrived at Oflag IVC in June 1944. No doubt guessing that their charges would assault Britons dressed in German uniform, the camp authorities did not allow the BFC men any face-to- face contact with prisoners. Instead, recruiting leaflets were passed along with the regular mail issue, which produced a strong protest from the

SBO and an abject apology from the commandant. A few leaflets were kept as souvenirs; the rest were burnt.[39]

The *Deutchefeindliche* inmates of Colditz were inherently unlikely to inform on one another, though as security officer Eggers did do his best. 'One of the British orderlies wrote repeatedly in his letters home that he was sick of acting as servant to officers and wished he could go and work in the mines', the Hauptmann later explained. A censor brought this soldier to his attention and he was brought in for an interview. 'I could send you away, you know,' Eggers told him, 'but I should want some information in exchange—as to what is going on inside the camp.' The orderly stoutly replied: 'I may not like it here but I am still British.'[40]

Shortly thereafter an effort was made to plant a stool pigeon in the camp. Sub-Lieutenant Walter Purdy, a pre-war member of the British Union of Fascists who had been captured as an engineering officer aboard an armed merchant cruiser, had been broadcasting alongside Lord Haw-Haw in Berlin and getting involved in setting up one of the holiday camps. Having made himself *persona non grata* within the propaganda fraternity by going absent without leave, he was sent into Colditz in March 1944 to act as a spy. 'What an opportunity!' Eggers reflected. Unfortunately an inmate recognized Purdy from his Marlag days, and under intense questioning he more or less admitted that he had been working for the Germans. The question then arose of what to do about this traitor. The escape officer, Dick Howe, thought Purdy should be hanged, and brought together a group of volunteers in one of the rooms to carry out the deed. 'Right,' Gris Davies-Scourfield remembered Howe saying, 'we're all here because we agree that it is our very painful duty to carry out the hanging of the traitor Purdy. We know what he's doing here, he's admitted to it, came here as a stool pigeon, so quite clearly it's our duty to, isn't it?' Nobody, however, was willing to be the hangman, and instead the SBO informed the commandant that Purdy should be removed from British quarters for his own safety—which he was.[41]

Walter Purdy, however, was neither the only nor the first British officer sent to Colditz suspected of harbouring potentially dangerous pro-Axis sympathies. B. N. Mazumdar had been transferred to Oflag IVC in August 1941, after complaining too frequently about the inadequacies of German medical and other treatment of POWs. 'Jumbo' Mazumdar was a rather prickly character and, as the only Indian prisoner inside the walls, something of a loner. When it was revealed that he was being sent to Berlin to meet Subhas Chandra Bose, some of the officers assumed the worst. 'That bloody Mazumdar's a spy', Harry Elliott was heard to remark. Though an admirer of Bose and a firm Indian nationalist, Mazumdar refused to take up the offer of a commission in the Indian Legion and was returned to Colditz. 'We never expected to see him again', Davies-Scourfield admitted. 'I hold a British commission,' Mazumdar explained, 'and therefore I owe my loyalty to the King whatever my political views and my private feelings may be.' Elliott apologized, but Mazumdar was still sufficiently alienated to stage a Gandhiesque hunger strike in order to achieve a transfer elsewhere.[42]

Ultimately just as disappointing for the Germans were attempts to capitalize on the fact that the mother of Australian Lieutenant Ralph Holroyd was a citizen of the Third Reich. Both mother and son expressed a desire to meet, and after an exchange of letters and a stay in the capital facilitated by the German authorities, Holroyd had been sent to the Sonderlager as a special prisoner. However, despite the anxieties of some prisoners, Holroyd evidently gave nothing away in exchange for his mother being allowed to visit him at Colditz with Hitler's blessing in March 1944. Two years earlier Holroyd had confided in BQMS John Brown in Berlin 'his intention to play along until asked to do something then tell them to go to hell'.[43]

In the last year of the war, nevertheless, the escape committee at Colditz harboured suspicions that another plant might lurk within the castle walls. When the first infantryman from New Zealand arrived in the summer of 1944 he was treated with great suspicion. It apparently took some effort by a New Zealand medical officer to convince the acting adjutant, Martin Gilliat, that the rather quiet new arrival was in fact Captain Charles Upham, VC and Bar.[44]

There were more captives at Colditz actively hostile to the Reich than in most other camps. But what they achieved in the way of intelligence and sabotage work was by and large typical of patriotic officers elsewhere. Both the type and level of intelligence work were generally similar to what was undertaken in many other camps. As for traitors, while it was true that the BFC got no recruits from Colditz, the response was the same in other oflags: the only officer to volunteer for the corps was in a mental hospital at the time, and was repatriated shortly thereafter suffering from schizophrenia. As far as stool pigeons were concerned, the suspicions that gathered around certain individuals, whether justified or not, were typical of the anxieties felt in all other Lagers. J. M. Moran, involved in the security side of camp administration in the castle, later commented that 'in every camp' there were those who were never trusted.[45]

The matters discussed so far, though significant, have not included the activity that lies at the heart of the Colditz phenomenon. If there had been no daring and ingenious breakout attempts to narrate, no 'home run' statistics to cite, Colditz would never have achieved its near-mythical status in British popular culture. Escaping, however, as with other aspects of the Kriegie experience, needs to be seen in context.

Notes

1. Stuart Brown, *Forbidden Paths* (Edinburgh, 1978), 92. On varying attitudes to sabotage and work see e.g. Peter Winter, *Free Lodgings* (Auckland, 1993), 117. On court-martial sentences associated with sabotage see e.g. PRO, WO 32/15294, William Westbrook, Victor Brehme, Wilfred Johnson cases.
2. John Castle, *The Password Is Courage* (London, 1955), 119; Ed Annetts, *Campaign Without Medals* (Lewes, 1990), 77; James Stedman, *Life of a British POW in Poland* (Braunton, 1992), 20; Cyril Rofe, *Against the Wind* (London, 1956), 76.
3. See Richard Pape, *Boldness Be My Friend* (London, 1953), 252; Brown, op. cit., 60; Geoffrey D. Vaughan, *The Way It Really Was* (Budleigh Salterton, 1985), 49; IWMSA 4661/2, B. Piddleston.
4. John Lawrence, *2.2.9.7.* (Fontwell, 1991), 42–3.
5. Colin Rushton, *Spectator in Hell* (Springhill, 1998), 81.
6. I. Schrire, *Stalag Doctor* (London, 1956), 76; see e.g. IWM, D. W. Luckett, 60; IWM (Rolf), R. C. Clark, 11; Ron Mackenzie, *An Ordinary War* (Wangaratta, Victoria, 1995), 65; Colin Burgess, *Freedom or Death* (St Leonards, NSW, 1994), 100.
7. Richard Passmore, *Moving Tent* (London, 1982), 131; B. A. James, *Moonless Night* (London, 1983), 30.
8. IWMSA 4767/4, J. Greenwood; ibid. 15587/3, E. Boyd; PRO, WO 208/3274, App. C, 4.
9. Kingsley Brown, *Bonds of Wire* (Toronto, 1989), 57–8; see Andrew Cox, *Our Spirit Unbroken* (Port Elgin, Ont., 1999), 56; M. R. D. Foot and J. M. Langley, *MI9* (London, 1979), 180; PRO, WO 208/3282, pt. I, p. 65; WO 208/3283, pt. I, pp. 83–4; ibid., pt. II, pp. 50–1.
10. Frank Taylor, *Barbed Wire and Footlights* (Braunton, 1988), 25. On Wolfsberg see J. E. Pryce, *Heels In Line* (London, 1958), 84–6. On counter-propaganda re Lord Haw Haw elsewhere see http://www.pegasus-one.org/pow/david_parker.htm, D. Parker, 9.
11. IWM, A. F. Gibbs, 126.
12. On MI9 and code communication see Foot and Langley, op. cit., 53–4, 109–10, 114, 123, 173–5. On intelligence gathering see also PRO, WO 208/3242, Historical Record of IS9, p. 86.
13. IWMSA 6142/3, J. Deans; see WO 208/3273, p. 10; WO 208/3279, p. 8; WO 208/3280A, p. 4; WO 208/3285, p. 33; WO 208/3283, pt. I, p. 58, pt. III,

p. 49; WO 208/3290, p. 10; WO 208/3292, p. 2; WO 208/3294, p. 12; Foot and Langley, op. cit., 175–7.

14. PRO, WO 208/3242, IS9 record, p. 87; WO 208/3293, p. 10; Jack Poole, *Undiscovered Ends* (London, 1957), 168; WO 208/3285, p. 33. For camps where no contact with MI9 was established see WO 208/3271A, p. 8; WO 208/3275, p. 4.

15. Sandy St Clair, *The Endless War* (North Battleford, Sask., 1987), 221–2. On intelligence and the Peenemünde raid see Sydney Smith, *Wings Day* (London, 1968), 136–7. On V-weapons intelligence see PRO, WO 208/3287, p. 20; WO 208/3270, p. 9; Lord Harewood, *The Tongs and Old Bones* (London, 1981), 53; Mackenzie, op. cit., 81. On *Tirpitz* see WO 208/3270, p. 9; IWMSA 4759/3, P. Buckley. On another apparent instance of cause and effect see Howard Greville, *Prison Camp Spies* (Loftus, NSW, 1998), 71. On intelligence concerning the BFC see WO 208/3272, p. 8.

16. John Brown, *In Durance Vile* (London, 1981), 78; Abid Hasan Safrani, 'A Soldier Remembers', *The Oracle*, 6 (1984), 29–30. On Berlin, Bose, and the Free India Legion see also Milan Hauer, *India in Axis Strategy* (Stuttgart, 1981), 365 ff.; Leonard A. Gordon, *Brothers Against the Raj* (New York, 1990), 456 ff.; Agehananda Bharati, 'Bose and the German INA', *New Quest*, 26 (1981), 73–85.

17. Hauer, op. cit., 583–9; Bharati, op. cit., 78–80; IOR, L/WS/1/1363, WO 33215/7, p. 7.

18. Ian Ramsay, *P.O.W.* (Melbourne, 1985), 143. On the Grand Mufti and the Arab Legion see Klaus Gensicke, *Der Mufti von Jerusalem, Amin el-Husseini, und die Nationalsozialisten* (Frankfurt-am-Main, 1988), 108 ff.; Philip Matter, *Mufti of Jerusalem* (New York, 1988), 104; Joseph B. Schechtman, *The Mufti and the Fuehrer* (New York, 1965), 135.

19. Adrian Weale, *Renegades* (London, 1995 edn.), 54–123.

20. A. Robert Prouse, *Ticket to Hell Via Dieppe* (Toronto, 1982), 124–5; Jim Longson and Christine Taylor, *Arnhem Odyssey* (London, 1991), 115; IWM, R. R. Bull, TS of BFC recruiting leaflet.

21. On latrine and other uses see e.g. CMAC, RAMC 1787, p. 13. On the Lamsdorf notice see Imelda Ryan (ed.), *POWs Fraternal* (Perth, WA, 1990), 118. 'The Russians . . .', Francis S. Jones, *Escape to Nowhere* (London, 1952), 247. On the leaflets as funny see e.g. IWM, R. A. Wilson, 180; IWMSA 4839/6, H. Shipp; Jack Bishop, *In Pursuit of Freedom* (London, 1977), 118. On the 'air drop' incident at Thorn see IWM, G. R. Manners, 131. On distribution and the reactions of guards see Adrian Vincent, *The Long Road Home* (London, 1956), 183, 185; IWM (Rolf), T. Hughes, 9; S. Brown, op. cit., 97; Robert Gale, *Private Prisoner* (Wellingborough, 1984), 135.

22. Neville Chesterton, *Crete Was My Waterloo* (London, 1995), 78; Sam Kydd, *For You the War Is Over . . .* (London, 1973), 222–3; J. Roberts, *A Terrier Goes to War* (London, 1998), 87–8; IWM, G. F. W. Wilson diary, 14 May 1944.

23. Gale, op. cit., 135–6. To prevent this sort of woolly thinking, MI9 sent out coded messages warning Kriegies against joining the BFC. See PRO, WO 208/3279, p. 8.

24. Weale, op. cit., 128–43, 159–84. Even the original six recruits had apparently not thought they would ever have to face the Red Army. See e.g. PRO, AIR 40/2297, p. 12.

25. See Weale, op. cit., 27 ff., 114 ff.; PRO, AIR 40/2295–2297.

26. Weale, op. cit., 47, 51–3, 149; see also PRO, AIR 40/2297. On failure to persuade newly captured servicemen to broadcast see e.g. IWM (Rolf), T. Berry, 3; Graeme Warrack, *Travel by Dark* (London, 1963), 67–9.

27. John H. Lauck, *Katyn Killings* (Clifton, NJ, 1988), 90; Weale, op. cit., 108. On refusals to visit Katyn, despite sometimes considerable pressure, see e.g. IWMSA 4820/1, C. Scarborough; IWM, J. W. M. Mansel diary, 9–10 May 1943; IWM, N. R. Wylie collection, CSM Fulton, 'Katyn Forest Mystery', 3; John Borrie, *Despite Captivity* (London, 1975), 146–7; Miles Reid, *Into Colditz* (Salisbury, 1983), 55.

28. Weale, op. cit., 114–15.

29. Ibid. 144–50; PRO, AIR 40/2295; AIR 40/2296; AIR 40/2297; Smith, op. cit., 142–3.

30. Pape, op. cit., 109; see also Oliver Clutton-Brock, *Footprints on the Sands of Time* (London, 2003), ch. 16. On bribing someone to be an informer see e.g. Douglas Collins, *P. O. W.* (London, 1970), 38. On being bullied and blackmailed into becoming a stool-pigeon see e.g. Arthur Evans, *Sojourn in Silesia* (Ashford, 1995), 55.

31. Terence Prittie and W. Earle Edwards, *Escape to Freedom* (London, 1953 edn.), 223, 310; IWM, H. C. F. Harwood, 122; see Poole, op. cit., 153–4.

32. Smith, op. cit., 143; St Clair, op. cit., 190.

33. See Smith, op. cit., 79–81, 143–5; Prouse, op. cit.; William H. Hall, *Flyer's Tale* (Braunton, 1989), 19–20; Gale, op. cit., 95–6.

34. F. Jones, op. cit., 206.

35. Smith, op. cit., 145; Pape, op. cit., 291–2; Stedman, op. cit., 22. On the famous 'body in the pool' see e.g. Robert Garioch, *Two Men and a Blanket* (Edinburgh, 1975), 131; Bill Jackson, *The Lone Survivor* (North Battleford, Sask., 1993), 72; John McMahon, *Almost a Lifetime* (Lantzville, BC, 1995), 160. On Coward and executions see Colin Rushton, *Spectator in Hell* (Springhill, 1998), 86.

36. IWMSA 16843/3, J. Chrisp; IWM, R. Eggers, 'Colditz Register', 8.

37. M. Reid, op. cit., 73; P. R. Reid, *The Colditz Story* (London, 1952), 101; John Chrisp *The Tunnellers of Sandborstal* (London, 1959), 170.

38. CSVA 4, K. Lockwood; see Green, op. cit., 161–85; IWMSA 4432/9, H. Gee; ibid. 4816/8, J. M. Moran; PRO, WO 208/3288, pp. 65–7, 73. On the photograph episode see John Frayn Turner, *Douglas Bader* (Shrewsbury, 1995), 114–15.

39. Margaret Duggan, *Padre in Colditz* (London, 1978), 252–4.

40. Reinhold Eggers, *Colditz* (London, 1961), 141.

41. G. Davies-Scourfield in *Escape From Colditz: 2. Best of British* (Windfall Films, 2000); IWM, R. Eggers, 'Colditz Register', 10; see David Walker, *Lean, Wind Lean* (London, 1984), 165; LC, T. N. Catlow, 62; Duggan, op. cit., 236–7; Weale, op. cit., 51; see also PRO, CRIM 1/1738.

42. IWMSA 16800/2–4, B. N. Mazumdar; Henry Chancellor, *Colditz* (London, 2001), 208–9.
43. J. Brown, op. cit., 68; see P. R. Reid, *Colditz* (London, 1984), 223; Borrie, op. cit., 80–1, 82; Duggan, op. cit., 235.
44. Kenneth Sandford, *Mark of the Lion* (New York, 1953 edn.), 243–4.
45. IWMSA 4816/8, J. M. Moran. On the psychiatric patient see Weale, op. cit., 139. On (sometimes) false suspicions of traitors elsewhere see e.g. PRO, WO 208/3282, pt. II, p. 18; WO 208/3292, p. 4.

10 Abiding and Escaping

When belligerents conclude an armistice convention, they shall normally cause to be included therein provisions concerning the repatriation of prisoners of war.

(from Article 75, Geneva Convention, 1929)

Prisoners of war . . . may be required not to go beyond certain fixed limits . . . they shall not be confined or imprisoned except as a measure indispensable for safety or health, and only so long as circumstances exist which necessitate such a measure.

(from Article 9, Geneva Convention, 1929)

The narration of successful escape attempts underlies the success of British prisoner-of-war stories in print and on screen in the post-war decades. Breakouts always involved an element of risk, and in the case of many of the more successful bids were the end result of much fore-thought and a good deal of ingenuity. In the hands of those who knew how to wield a pen effectively, escape accounts could and did become real-life adventure stories in which the protagonists, and by extension British POWs in general, were shown as clever and brave young men who refused to accept defeat. The second half of the twentieth century witnessed a more or less steady stream of popular publications and screenplays associating Kriegie life with escape. 'There is a kind of nostalgia about escaping', reflected author and former POW Richard Garrett in the late 1980s, noting with a certain degree of bitterness—he himself was not an escape artist—that it had become 'one of the war's fringe entertainments'.[1]

Colditz is commonly portrayed as *primus inter pares* among the camps from which British POWs escaped. Books on the Wooden Horse and the Great Escape may have rivalled the Colditz Story in terms of sales and cinematic potential, but these were about particular escapes rather than the overall record of the camp where they took place. Not only did the 'bad boys' prove the Germans wrong about the castle being escape-proof, they also set the record for persistence, ingenuity, and consequently breakouts. 'The impression is abroad that Colditz had almost a monopoly on escapes,' a South African journalist interned in Nazi Germany during the war observed several decades later, 'and that escape from it was much more difficult than from other camps.' The precise figures cited have varied over time, but the overall thrust has remained constant: there were more escape attempts and more home runs from Oflag IVC than from any other camp in Germany.[2]

The reality is rather more complex. Though escapes are at the heart of popular perceptions of prisoner-of-war life in general and life at Colditz in particular, the truth is that a great many captives were willing to wait out the war rather than try to make it home. Even at Oflag IVC there were those who chose discretion as the better part of valour, and while the proportion of dyed-in-the-wool escape artists was higher at Colditz than elsewhere, there are reasons to question the validity of an unqualified belief in the castle always topping the escape league table. Contrary to popular belief, nothing was attempted there in the way of breaking out that had not been thought up and often tried elsewhere. Moreover, despite the formidable defences of the castle, being inside the walls in the early war years provided a number of advantages in terms of escape that were either not available at all or less common in other prison camps. A close look at the escape record of British prisoners suggests that—while unquestionably impressive—what was done at Colditz was not an achievement *sans pareil*.

One of the great myths surrounding British POWs in the Second World War is that planning and carrying out daring escapes dominated every waking hour. Generated largely through the success of the print and celluloid versions of *The Wooden Horse*, *The Great Escape*, and of course *The Colditz Story*, this is in fact a false assumption. Most Kriegies consciously or unconsciously decided to wait for the war to end rather than to try to make it home while fighting continued.[3]

There were a variety of reasons for this. In the years of Axis triumph there might seem no reason to break out, since the enemy was soon going to win anyway. 'In the early days of the war,' Signalman Peter Oates reflected on life inside Wolfsberg in 1941–2, 'when Jerry was winning and going from strength to strength, the vast majority of our blokes would not have liked to rock the boat.' Conversely, once it became clear that the Allies were going to emerge victorious in the latter war years, many Kriegies justified inaction on the grounds that escape had become superfluous. 'The most ardent escape merchants were prepared to return home in a normal manner,' Philip Kindersley wrote of the post D-day 1944 atmosphere at Oflag 79, 'and the tunnellers laid down their tools for good.' Why stage a break when the war was soon going to be over?[4]

Some POWs thought that they had done enough for King and Country, without also risking life and limb in trying to escape. Those who were seen trying to get away might well be fired at and, when caught, beaten up. 'Others of us,' Herbert Woolley wrote of the non-escapers inside the RAF compound at Lamsdorf, 'of a more philosophical nature, or perhaps less adventurous, were content to adapt to the situation, to make the best of it, to wait it out and accept the relative security of camp life in preference to the unknown but real danger of escape attempts.' That escaping could be a potentially life-threatening business was underlined by a German poster announcing that soldiers and police in certain unspecified areas of the country had orders to shoot first and ask questions later. In the wake of the massacre of fifty men who had used a tunnel to get clear of Stalag Luft III, even MI9 made it clear that captured servicemen were no longer duty-bound to try to escape from Germany, given the odds against survival.[5]

Older men, less restless and less fit than their juniors, were often cautious, and sometimes even dismissive, about the possibility of escape. This seems to have been particularly true of certain army officers, who decided that the odds against success were so great that it was best to 'settle down and make the best of it'. Having decided to wait out the war themselves, these prisoners were rather jaundiced about younger men who did not share their outlook. 'They thought it [escaping] a form of exhibitionism,' Jack Poole explained with reference to some of the senior figures he met in various oflags, 'a shocking waste of time and anyway why irritate the Germans?'[6]

Concern over what a breakout would mean for those not involved was a major issue in places where a degree of material stability and personal comfort had been achieved. Though collective reprisals were banned under the Geneva Convention, escape attempts always brought about retaliation in the form of the withdrawal of various 'privileges'. 'Why the hell do you want to escape when we're all having such a cushy time?' a young corporal angrily asked J. E. Pryce when he announced his intention of escaping from a working party in 1941. 'They never think of those left behind,' as one badly wounded soldier plaintively remarked, 'Red

Cross parcels stopped, no letters from home, treated like [dirt] . . . ' In some camps there was a good deal of peer pressure not to rock the boat that might include even the camp leader or SBO. At Stalag XXA, for instance, it was alleged in an official report that there were 'several senior W.O.s who discouraged all escape talk, as such activities would lead to the Germans imposing restrictions, and curtailing any existing comforts'. On occasion, hostility based on fear of reprisals could mean that attempts were made to sabotage escape plots by fellow prisoners. At Eichstätt someone never identified left notes on lavatory doors falsely claiming that a tunnel that was about to be put to use was known to the Germans, and that those who used it would be shot as they emerged. 'Whenever they discovered some escape plan,' Michael Duncan later wrote of a number of his fellow officers at Biberach, 'they would discuss it in loud voices and scathing tones and many a promising plan failed through lack of security.' At Thorn a number of senior NCOs were thought to have betrayed two successive escapes to the enemy before they could be attempted.[7]

Though Arbeitskommandos were easier to get away from than main camps, other ranks could argue initially that they were too weak to undertake the rigours of life on the run, and later that they did not possess the necessary linguistic skills—and that therefore the odds against success were too high. 'The question of escape creeps up from time to time,' G. R. Manners wrote in his diary in early October 1940, 'but I have decided it's too long a shot.' The frontiers were distant and guarded, and in any case he could not speak German. It was claimed by some that in a working camp Kriegies lacked the time and resources to manufacture forged passes, maps, compasses, and other pieces of escape equipment, and in any case were deep in enemy territory without any clear idea of their exact location. Proportionately there were far fewer escapes by other ranks as compared to officers. 'The question of escape did not arise in any real sense', one soldier admitted in writing about his time working for the Reich.[8]

Even those who had initially been keen on escape might eventually give up the idea. For prisoners captured in the middle and late war years, it was disheartening to discover that every scheme they thought up had already been tried and that security measures were consequently tighter. 'We were extremely keen at first,' Mosquito pilot Stephen Johnson, who arrived at Sagan in early 1943, later related, 'but it gradually dawned on us that it was just about impossible to think of an original idea that would be passed by the Escape Committee. After a while most of us came to the conclusion that the chances of getting out were slim.' His own hopes 'gradually evaporated'. After one or more failed attempts, captives taken earlier in the war might eventually conclude that it could not be done.[9]

Others began to worry that focusing on escape for years on end was having a bad effect on their mental stability. Terence Prittie, who had been trying to make a home run since he was first incarcerated at Laufen, later wrote at length about why he and several other officers decided to cease their breakout activities after being transferred to Spangenberg Castle in the summer of 1943:

For thirty-two months most of us had concentrated all our energies on planning escape. As a subject for talk and action it afforded tremendous scope for physical and mental endeavour. But single-minded concentration on outwitting the Germans definitely began to tell on the nerves of all of us. I found myself becoming short-tempered, absurdly secretive, and muddle-headed about the details of ordinary life. In nearly three years I had used my brain in what might be termed an 'underground' capacity... I noticed in others the effects of escape-psychosis. They became moody, vaguely and meaninglessly mysterious, almost morbidly self-interested. Often they seemed to be only 'half-there', for their thoughts were nearly always periscoped round the corner of the castle battlements or down through the flagstones of its courtyard into the bowels of the earth. Their eyes tended to become shifty and unhappy, and their slouched shoulders gave a curious impression that they were always listening...

Hard-core escape artists, in short, might eventually risk their minds as well as their bodies.[10]

Nevertheless there were prisoners almost everywhere willing to gamble—or at least help others do so—in pursuit of freedom. Like the majority who chose to wait out the war, the minority who decided to engage in escape planning did so for a variety of reasons.

Guilt over capture sometimes played a role among officers, but more common was the belief that it was a man's duty to try to return to his unit and resume a fighting role. Moreover, even if achieving a home run seemed unlikely, a breakout would force the Germans to divert police and paramilitary forces to hunting down those at large. Figures ranging from four to ten Germans being occupied for every one Briton on the loose were confidently bandied about inside the wire. Even if an escape attempt failed to breach the camp defences, it was a signal to the enemy that he could not diminish the resources devoted to guarding POWs. 'We continued to fight in Colditz', Pat Reid proudly proclaimed over forty years after his own successful break. 'We were the besiegers within and we were holding down a large number of troops outside.'[11]

In the case of mass escapes, tying down human resources even took precedence over getting men home, since unlike small-scale breaks, the absence of more than one or two men could not be concealed on *Appell* and breaks involving more than ten or so persons automatically triggered a nationwide manhunt. Not all agreed with this emphasis, not only because it lessened the chances of a home run, but also because it gave too many Germans too much practice in the art of detecting future escapers on trains and roads. 'Mass escapes—of over about a dozen prisoners—were bad news in this respect', commented Hugh Bruce. Adherents of the big break school, however, were undeterred by the very high proportion of men from mass escapes who were caught before they could reach neutral soil. Against the failure to make home runs, they argued that even if nobody got home big breaks were, in the words of Jack Champ, 'a tremendous nuisance' to the Germans. A tunnel at Schubin through which forty officers got out was said to have involved a search by 5,000 enemy personnel. The Eichstätt tunnel break in May 1943, involving over sixty escapers, reputedly tied down over 50,000 Germans.[12]

Both sides in this debate could agree, however, that prisoners getting clear of the wire in numbers large or small forced the Germans to beef up camp security, usually in the form of more guards who might otherwise have been employed on tasks more directly related to the war effort. Knowledge that prisoners had escaped, moreover, could provide an important morale boost for all but the determined non-escapers. The planning and execution of escape schemes, in short, could be seen as a form of patriotic endeavour, keeping up spirits and carrying on the war behind the wire.[13]

There were also more personal motives at work. Some men were keen to get home for entirely private reasons, while most of the hard-core escaping types simply could not stand the restrictive boredom of long-term incarceration. RAF sergeant John Fancy found life in Stalag Luft I a trial almost from the moment he arrived: 'the confinement was killing me', he later wrote. 'My active nature revolted at the meaningless daily routine which brought my restless body to a halt at the warning fence and limited my thinking powers to one obsession, how to get beyond the warning wire!' Such restless souls might make repeated escape attempts and never give up trying. Fusilier John Evans, captured in May 1940, made five unsuccessful attempts before he achieved freedom on his sixth try in January 1945. It took Private Lawrence Marks, another BEF soldier, seven attempts to achieve the same result. Fancy himself, though he never made the longed-for home run, was involved in no fewer than eight separate escape schemes.[14]

These hard-core types, however, were a minority within the escaping fraternity. Wings Day estimated that even in RAF compounds—where the proportion of men interested in escape was thought to be higher than the norm—only 5 per cent could be counted as true fanatics, the kind of man Hugh Bruce described as 'totally dedicated' to getting away. The majority of those involved also hoped to get home, but found the means as satisfying as the anticipated ends.[15]

For some Kriegies the adventure of playing at being a fugitive was as important as winning the game. 'Many looked on escape as a sport', Cyril Rofe found in the RAF compound at Lamsdorf in 1942. 'It broke through the monotony. They did not expect to succeed; they merely wanted something to do. The planning passed the time, and the escape was a great adventure. When they were recaptured they would do a few days in the cooler, then return to start planning once more. A dangerous sport, certainly...' A similar atmosphere was detected elsewhere. 'Escape', Sandy St Clair explained of the prevalent attitude at Oflag VIIIF prior to the Sagan massacre, 'had been treated as a kind of special—but dangerous—sporting event. Hazardous at the moment of breakout, and again at the moment of capture, but essentially an adventure.'[16]

To the more cynical this sort of enthusiast was simply indulging in *Boy's Own*-style fantasies. Robert Kee claimed that at Stalag Luft III prisoners might 'spend all day wandering happily round and round the camp musing on the possibility of a hole in the wire there, a tunnel dug there, or an assault with scaling ladders somewhere else', though very few were willing to risk their lives. 'Many people took this game of make-believe to fantastic lengths,' he added, 'going through the whole elaborate business without the slightest intention of ever carrying it out.' Others were more passive, daydreaming about escape but not doing much about it. Michael Duncan found that at Biberach in 1941 there were many officers 'who, in theory, would like to escape but who waited for someone else to make the plans and who passed the time in the vague hope that someday someone would invite them to join an escape party'. Wings Day estimated that 50 per cent of RAF prisoners were willing to make an escape bid only 'if it was handed to them on a plate'.[17]

Many of these men, however, while not hard-core escapers, were a valuable component of schemes that involved a lot of work. Tunnels, for example, usually required not only diggers and people to help hide the soil, but also men to stand watch. There were also Kriegies whose skills at forgery, tailoring, trading, and blackmailing made them more prized inside the wire than out. To get seventy-six men out in the Great Escape, for example, had involved the efforts of several hundred other prisoners.[18]

Furthermore, whether serious or not about breaking out and getting home personally, those who became involved at some level in escape schemes had found a good antidote to the pervasive tedium of camp life. On working parties there were men who walked away simply because they were bored and wanted a change of scene (and thereby perhaps access to the opposite sex), rather than because they thought they might do a home run. In main camps even true escapers might admit that, even if a scheme stood little chance of developing to the point of getting clear of the wire, it served a purpose to be involved: it was, as Jack Poole put it in reference to younger oflag prisoners, 'a physical outlet from their life of boredom'. Hugh Bruce, who would soon find himself in Colditz, guessed that a tunnel being planned at Oflag XXIB was not going to work because the water table was too high. 'However,' he confessed in an interview, 'that is something that I quite enjoyed—going out at night, messing about on the roof [of the fort in order to get to a casement room next to the moat from which the tunnel was to be dug]—so I continued even though I knew it would never get to fruition.' Though being a hard-core escape artist might eventually take a toll, there was little question that in the short and medium term there were potential psychological as well as physiological benefits to being a member of the escaping club. 'At Spangenberg,' reflected fighter pilot T. D. Calnan, 'I had...come to realise that to devote all my mental and physical energy to the problem of escape had a very beneficial, therapeutic effect. The difficulties and variations of the problem were so challenging that I was always fully occupied.' Jim Rogers admitted that 'we felt rather lost' after a tunnel escape at Laufen on which he and friends had been working was blown: 'It had provided the centre of our interest and thinking for so many months there seemed nothing to do.' The cure, of course, was to start in on a new breakout scheme.[19]

The level of difficulty involved in getting away varied from place to place and over time, though the general rule was that security precautions rose in proportion to the military value of the prisoners and the number of escape bids made. Officers therefore tended to be confined more closely than other ranks, through persistent bids for freedom and other

Deutschfeindlich behaviour by non-commissioned personnel might result in them being kept permanently inside the wire.

Castles and forts were generally considered the hardest places to escape from, but even in hut-and-wire camps the defences could be formidable, and grew more so as security officers duelled with escapers in 'high-activity' compounds such as those containing valuable—because highly skilled—RAF prisoners. Basic security features usually included two wire perimeter fences twelve feet or more in height, topped with inward-facing barbed wire, the space of several yards between being filled with barbed-wire coils. At night the fences would be lit up by electric lamps, while the interior of the camp would be swept by searchlights mounted in towers built at strategic intervals along the perimeter. Guards would man these towers around the clock, and armed sentries would patrol the outside fences. In some cases Alsatian and other guard dogs would be let loose in the compounds at night after prisoners were confined to barracks. Those wishing to escape might also be in a compound that was not located next to the perimeter wire—as was the case for the RAF at Lamsdorf—which in turn meant that other compounds had to be crossed first. Often at least one section of the fenced perimeter separated prisoners not from the outside world but from the German administrative buildings. Security innovations introduced in the course of the war included buried microphones to detect tunnelling and specially trained guards—derisively known to the prisoners as snoopers or ferrets—whose job it was to roam about the interior of Kriegie compounds looking for signs of escape activity. A perimeter trench could be dug to deter digging under the wire, and heavy vehicles or a roller driven or dragged round to force the collapse of suspected tunnels. Prisoners would be counted at least twice daily, and whatever type of camp was involved, there would be intermittent searches of Kriegie quarters for contraband material, the most destructive usually conducted by plain-clothes police (commonly thought to be Gestapo) brought in for the occasion. Even on working parties, where the wire and other deterrents tended to be far less formidable than in main camps, escape attempts led to men's boots and trousers being removed at night as a precaution. The enemy, in short, went to some trouble to keep restless types at bay.[20]

Difficult though it might be, getting beyond the wire was only the first part of the home-run equation. Beyond the confines of the camp there remained the tricky business of travelling hundreds of miles incognito in a hostile police state, and either crossing the border into a neutral country or linking up with a resistance group in occupied Europe.

With millions of foreign nationals to keep track of—not to speak of the German population itself—the Reich security services introduced a shifting array of identification cards and passes designed to separate legitimate travellers from escapees and deserters. The civilian population was constantly urged to be on the lookout for suspicious characters, and as the war continued frontier guards grew more and more vigilant. The great majority of those who made it clear of their camps were sooner or later caught inside Germany. Of the 200 RAF aircrew personnel who got out through tunnels in various camps in the course of the war, for example, only eight men escaped recapture and made it home.[21]

Those who overcame the formidable odds against ultimate success owed a lot to simple good fortune. But in many cases careful planning and preparation played an important role, which in turn tended to reflect the input of more than one or two individuals. At first this was not appreciated, and lone, pair, and small-group schemes were hatched and carried out independently; but in the main camps it soon became apparent that there were problems with such a laissez-faire approach to escaping. Someone might undertake a hare-brained effort that not only stood virtually no chance of success but also, when it failed, might alert the Germans to more thought-through efforts along the same lines that had not had a chance to come to fruition. Those recaptured en route to safety also became acutely aware that escapees stood little chance unless they had a disguise, a cover story, some identification papers, food, and money, plus basic geographical and route information. The best way of obtaining all the prerequisites and maximizing the chances of success was to pool information and resources by establishing an escape committee.

The form, nature, and role of escape bureaucracies varied over time and place. Some compounds, particularly those associated with the smaller and less permanent working camps, never organized escape committees. The influence of others, especially where representatives from camp leader on down were elected—that is, among the NCO and other-rank population—was often somewhat limited. Particularly in the early years, there might be competing committees in a camp, or one so apparently ineffectual that hard-core escapers continued to think they were better off working on their own. Over time, however, particularly in camps where there was a Senior British Officer to grant it official legitimacy and authority, a powerful organization led by a strong escape officer could develop that might take precedence over all other bodies. At Oflag VIIIF (Mährisch Trübau), for example, the 'cloak and dagger' men led by David Stirling clearly ruled the roost, while in the North Compound at Stalag Luft III (Sagan), Roger Bushell and his extensive and powerful 'X' organization brooked no dissent concerning its decisions in 1943–4.[22]

Some escape committees might confine themselves to the 'aid and advise' role pursued in the RAF officers' compound at Barth, where the only proviso for complete support was that a new scheme should not put one already under way in jeopardy. Several others, including those mentioned above, insisted on a rigorous vetting process before allowing a plan to proceed. The following Air Ministry report on the process developed in the East Compound at Sagan makes clear what someone seeking support had to go through before getting it in 1942–3:

A prisoner who had plans for escaping would tell the Escape representative of his barrack, who would send him to the appropriate member of the Planning Staff. The prisoner would explain his plan, and the advisor would help him work it out in detail. The advisor would then explain it to the Head of the Escape Committee, who would make the final decision whether or not it should be carried out. If the plan was approved and had not already been suggested or used by another P/W, the proposer was given first chance to use it. If it had already been used or suggested, the head of the EC would choose who should attempt it . . . The P/W chosen would then attend a meeting of the Committee where there would be representatives of every department which would be involved in his plan. Details would be worked out . . .

And this, it should be noted, was 'a free for all' in Walter Morrison's opinion, compared to the even more centralized and bureaucratic escape system subsequently imposed by Roger Bushell in the North Compound.[23]

For many escaping types this was all well and fine as long as the bureaucrats delivered the goods. The three officers who got away in the famous Wooden Horse escape, for instance, conceded that it had only been possible as a result of the manpower and material support provided once the escape committee in the East Compound at Stalag Luft III had been won over to the plan. Mass escapes, furthermore, were impossible without a high degree of co-ordination in planning and preparation, and few men could organize on their own the clothing, rations, and papers necessary for an escape to stand a chance once beyond the wire. The Great Escape, which involved the secret digging of three very deep and very long tunnels, and the preparation of escape equipment for hundreds of men, would not have been possible if the 'X' organization had not drawn in by choice or coercion virtually every prisoner in the North Compound. The equally strong hand exerted by the NCO committee at Heydekrug in matters such as trading could also be justified by the way in which it developed an escape line to Sweden once men had got outside the wire, as well as its success in equipping designated escapers. 'They did sterling work', Sergeant John Fancy commented, adding that the escape organization at Luft VI had by 1944 'reached such a state of efficiency and self-support that it became their proud boast that they could supply a P.O.W. with food, money and clothing, and equip him with a complete set of papers permitting him to travel, and obtain work, in any part of Germany'.[24]

Not everyone, however, was happy with certain escape committees. Some aspirant escapers were less than impressed with the way the escape bureaucracy in their particular camp functioned. Inevitably there were some proposals that were turned down and others that were altered (particularly concerning who got to participate in the actual break), acts of interference that did not go down terribly well with the more independent-minded types. In some camps, what was more, escape committees could be dominated by older men who seemed more interested in devising and enforcing rules than in getting prisoners home. The army committee at Spangenberg was seen by some of the RAF types in 1941 as overly hierarchical and cautious to the point of timidity. Its counterpart some miles away at Rotenburg developed the reputation of being so intricately organized and fussily bureaucratic that it hindered the task of escaping as much as it helped. The escape committee at Marlag could and did provide help for particular schemes, but the Senior British Officer in particular took an extremely dim view of officers who engaged in 'unauthorized' escapes. Impatience with the system was by no means confined to the oflags. Foot-dragging by senior figures and members of the escape committee drove a number of men to try their hand independently at Stalag IVB, and an apparently 'Buggins' Turn' approach to escape at Stalag 383 was highly annoying to those who thought the committee was only going through the motions. 'I couldn't see why I should ask some silly bugger what I could do and when I could do it,' R. A. Wilson wrote, 'especially someone I thought hadn't a clue.'[25]

Red tape, in short, could be a problem. Yet there can be no question that, in overall terms, the stronger the escape committee the greater the resources that could be devoted to a particular effort, both in terms of getting out and getting home. In camps where escaping was not a priority there was far less chance, for example, of escape aids surreptitiously sent from Britain being recognized and put to good use. Recognizing that the chances of escape were greater if POWs possessed money, maps, ink, compass parts, hacksaw blades, and sundry other useful items, MI9 made a large-scale effort from 1941 onward to smuggle such contraband material into Germany. Packages from bogus organizations, such as the Licensed Victuallers Association and the Local Ladies Comfort Society, as well as various fictitious individuals, were sent out containing escape equipment carefully hidden in everything from playing cards and records to tins and blankets. The quantity of equipment dispatched was quite staggering; but it had to be, not only because the security staff in some locations learned what to watch out for, but also because people inside the wire could not be depended on to recognize or take advantage of what was being provided. In general terms, the better the escape organization in a particular camp, the more likely it was that contraband would be found and used. Though there were variations in efficiency and effectiveness, those camps with coherent escape committees clearly did better than those without. There is no record, for example, of the arrival at Stalag VIIIC (Sagan)— housing over 2,800 Commonwealth soldiers from late 1943 until early 1945, but lacking an escape committee—of any of the over 7,000 Reichsmarks, eighty-two maps, twenty compasses, sixteen passes, and six magnetized razorblades sent by MI9.[26]

Whether acting independently or seeking official sponsorship, those who were serious about escaping back to Britain had to begin by thinking up a way of breaking out. On many Arbeitskommandos this could be a comparatively simple matter. A prisoner might unobtrusively duck out of a column when the escort was not looking, while en route to or from the job or at the worksite, or if that seemed impossible then work out how to get through the comparatively meagre defences of sleeping quarters—sometimes just a locked door, and very often not more than a single encircling fence that was not patrolled at night. This was why over a dozen officers and a slightly larger number of air force non-commissioned types—specifically those held in Lamsdorf, where the RAF compound was surrounded by army enclosures—began their ultimately successful escape bids by exchanging identities with soldiers. Three times as many disguised aircrew NCOs made it back via this route as compared to those who broke out of stalags. Over 85 per cent of those soldiers who got home from Germany before the end of the war began their trek by slipping away in this manner. By the war's end, indeed, over

50 per cent of all recorded 'home runs' by Kriegies had begun with a break from an Arbeitskommando.[27]

Most commissioned officers, however, along with plenty of others incarcerated in those locations where there was no regular inflow and outflow of working prisoners, did not have the opportunity to switch identities and prepare a break from a low-security Arbeitskommando. This meant that thought had to be given to working out a way of getting past the much more substantial obstacles mentioned above, designed to prevent escape from the main camps. For these prisoners, plans for escape boiled down to variations on three possible approaches: over, through, or under the perimeter defences.

Climbing out of a main camp was attractively direct, but also highly dangerous. If those concerned could get over the fences or walls without being spotted and without leaving obvious traces of their exit method, then it might take several hours or even days for the camp authorities to realize that an escape had taken place, especially if only one or two men got out and their absence could be covered for on *Appell*. The odds in favour of being caught in the act, however, were very high. Guards on the ground and those in watchtowers scanning the perimeter would almost certainly spot someone attempting to climb over the wire or scale a wall during the day, while the cover offered by darkness was limited by floodlights, tower-mounted searchlight sweeps, and in some cases guard dogs left to roam the compound after lockup. If seen, moreover, anyone halfway up or down a fence or wall ran a serious risk of being shot at by sentries, especially since climbing made it virtually impossible to accomplish the usual raising-of-arms surrender gesture. Acting on the impulse to climb over the wire to freedom, indeed, became one of the accepted signs that a prisoner had lost his grip on reality and gone 'wire-happy'.[28]

Despite the risks involved, there were those among the escape-minded who thought they knew how to beat the odds against success using the 'up-and-over' approach. It was just a matter of careful observation, meticulous planning, and—above all—perfect timing.

Those who decided to climb their way to freedom, either acting singly or in pairs, had first to work out how to avoid being seen while they negotiated their way over the perimeter. The cover of darkness was usually considered essential, though heavy snowfalls or fog might be used as alternate or additional cover. Most important of all, soft spots in the defences had to be identified: points where there was less wire to cross, fewer lights to dodge, and where sentries did not venture often or could not easily gaze—underneath the guard towers they manned, for instance. In the first years of the war, especially in hutted camps, stealthy exits over the wire (often preceded by hiding out in a secluded spot near the main wire or in an adjacent and less well-defended compound) were relatively popular, as they did not require special equipment—i.e. wire-cutters—and it became clear that perimeter security was not as tight as the enemy assumed. In separate bids mounted in different camps in the course of 1941, two pairs of RAF sergeants managed to slip out unobserved by clambering up the poles and cross-struts supporting a guard tower (in one case in broad daylight). At Stalag Luft I a total of seven attempts were made to actually climb the wire itself in various parts of the camp between 1940 and 1943, all but one of which succeeded in getting one or two men away.[29]

It was at Oflag VIB in the summer of 1942, however, that the single most spectacular fence-hopping escapade took place. In ambition and scale of execution the Warburg Wire Job would dwarf all other attempts to go over the wire.

As in other camps, the sentries at Oflag VIB relied on static perimeter lighting and searchlights mounted in towers to help guards spot anyone moving about outside after curfew. A means of fusing the relevant electrical circuit from inside the camp was discovered, and plans for Operation Olympia drawn up. Requiring a great deal of advance preparation and split-second co-ordination, this escape involved sending four ten-man teams out from huts near the wire on the night of 30 August 1942, with specially constructed hinged ladders that would be used to climb up and over the fences once the lights had gone out and while the guards were too confused to react effectively. 'So far as we could see,' one of the officers involved reported after getting back to England, 'the operation went like clockwork.' In fact one team only got two men across before it became necessary to withdraw to safety, and in another only seven men succeeded; but that still meant that twenty-nine officers were out, seventeen of whom evaded immediate recapture.[30]

Nevertheless, the attractiveness of over-the-wire schemes seems to have diminished over time as the Germans learned how to strengthen their defences, and longer-term but less risky types of escape plan were developed. In the more carefully constructed Stalag Luft III at Sagan, for example, there were only three planned attempts to climb the wire executed between 1942 and 1945. And, rather fortunately in view of the risk of mass slaughter in the opinion of some involved, plans laid at

Schubin and Mährisch Trübau to carry out mass breaks similar to Operation Olympia were never implemented.[31]

Getting over the defences of a medieval Schloss (or, for that matter, a nineteenth-century fortress) was often more difficult than climbing up wire fencing, as walls and moat facings tended to be high and without much surface purchase. Nevertheless, where the will existed a way might be found, as illustrated by the ingenuity of successive bids to escape from Spangenberg castle.

The greatest obstacle to overcome at the upper camp at Oflag IXA/H was a dry moat surrounding the castle that included a stone-clad outer wall that rose to a height of thirty feet topped by a fence. Dick Lorraine, while a prisoner at Oflag IXA/Z (Rotenburg), had formulated an escape plan whereby, at an opportune moment when sentries were elsewhere on their beat, a steel beam—scrounged from a bricked-up lift shaft that he had discovered—would be placed on rollers, steadied by cables running up to two upper windows, and pushed out of a lower window over the wire immediately surrounding the stone walls of this former school. The escaper would lie on this metal bridge beam as it was pushed out, lower his body to the ground from a rope once over the wire, and be clear of the camp. Unfortunately the Sydney Harbour Bridge, as it was known, was discovered during a trial run and confiscated. After he was sent to Spangenberg, Lorraine, with the support of a number of other majors, devised a variation on the bridge theme. The new plan involved a tubular boom, resembling a fishing rod—made from trestle-table ironwork and capable of being assembled and dismantled in a hurry—being thrust over the moat and onto the fence while being guided and supported by attached ropes leading up to two upper windows on either side. The rod would have hanging from its far end a rope made from knotted sheets that escapers—already lowered by rope into the moat—would use to climb out. Unfortunately, when an attempt was made to escape this way one night in the summer of 1942 a guard appeared unexpectedly, and the attempt had to be aborted without a chance to withdraw the rod or ropes. Undeterred by this failure, the escapers went back to the drawing-board and the following year a new moat-scaling scheme was developed. This time a grappling hook with a long ring rope attached would be thrown from a window and catch on the fence beyond the moat wall. Then a rope ladder, after being hooked vertically to the lower line of the ring rope, would be sent across the moat by pulling the main rope through a metal ring attached to the grapple itself—in best washing-line fashion—until it rested against the wall and could be used by escapers already hiding in the moat. This time the plan worked, two majors getting away from Spangenberg castle in October 1943.[32]

One alternative to trying to get across wire or wall was to work out ways of passing through rather than over the defences. Breaking out at ground level was one possibility. Another was to develop a means of exiting via the gate, through either concealment or bluff. Both options would be tried repeatedly and in a variety of forms in camps across the Greater Reich.

The main problems associated with penetrating camp perimeters at ground level, if gates were being avoided, were the tools required and the amount of time it often took to break out. Files and wire-cutters could either be made or obtained through bribery and blackmail, but they always remained in short supply. The process of cutting through a succession of wire fences and obstacles while trying to avoid noise or movement that would attract the attention of guards and perhaps also dogs, moreover, could take anything from seven minutes to several hours to accomplish. Even making the best possible use of cover and camouflage—for example, by operating only at night and wearing colours designed to blend with the darkness—the chances of escapers being caught in the act in this type of operation were very great.

The odds improved slightly if blind spots could be identified—that is, points on the perimeter where a man working at the wire would be less likely to be spotted by sentries in particular guard towers, because of the angles of sight involved and the presence of intervening structures—or if an escaper could first manage to get himself into a part of the camp where the defences were weaker than elsewhere. The latter requirement was indeed practically *de rigueur* in castles or forts, where the thickness and positioning of brick and masonry walls made breaking through the fences and lumber of a hut-and-wire camp appear an easy option. Hence the decision by John Hamilton-Baillie to escape from Tittmoning by cutting through the wire of the exercise ground situated beyond the castle itself, where weeds and diversions allowed him the necessary cover and minutes to crawl out. Here, as in the case of three officers who got through the wire at Warburg, much depended on the ability of fellow-prisoners to distract the attention of patrolling sentries by one means or another.

The chances of being caught in the act and fired at, however, remained great. Though there were well over half-a-dozen successful attempts—including one break in which a dozen aircrew got out of Stalag IIIE (Kirchhain) one night by crawling through a hole made in an outward-facing barrack wall, and another in which thirteen soldiers managed to get through a gap created in the wire at Lamsdorf under cover of a thunderstorm—the number of wire-or-wall cutting schemes attempted in main camps seems to have been comparatively small. Even in the Luftwaffe camps only about fifteen attempts were made to cut through wire, of which three came off more-or-less as hoped.[33]

Rather more attractive were those schemes that involved going through the camp gates. In addition to the chance of getting out and getting home, there was the peculiar psychological satisfaction involved in trying to pull the wool over the enemy's eyes—along with the comforting knowledge that anyone spotted in the act would be within arm's length of arrest by the gate sentries, and therefore less likely to be fired at by a patrolling guard or a *Posten* in a tower.

In some instances those intent on escape might have a legitimate reason in German eyes to be allowed outside the wire or into an area of the camp from which an easy exit could then be made. In most cases, however, varying degrees of subterfuge or concealment were necessary to make gate attempts.[34]

Volunteering for day-work parties operating out of stalag compounds was a comparatively simple means of walking out for other ranks intent on escape. No less than twenty-four Royal Air Force aircraftsmen and NCOs got away from local working parties in the Barth area between 1940 and 1941, while in 1942—the year that OKW decided that even those aircrew prisoners with no previous escape record should not be allowed out on day-work for security reasons—two RAF sergeants located elsewhere successfully made their way home after volunteering for local jobs. All of the successful home runs from Thorn and Posen in 1942–3 began with the seven Kriegies concerned getting out of the forts under the pretence of going to work at some local concern and then slipping away.[35]

Officers, however, were not supposed to work at all, and along with those NCOs and others identified as likely escapers, were usually only allowed outside high-security compounds while on parole (that is, after having given their word that they would not attempt to escape). This meant a resort to two basic forms of subterfuge on which many variations were played: hiding in outward-bound vehicles or containers, and walking through the gates in a variety of disguises designed not to arouse suspicion.

Every cart and lorry that entered and exited POW compounds was scrutinized by escapers as a possible means of transport to the outside world. Impromptu attempts to quietly climb aboard and hide inside the back of a vehicle leaving the camp were hard to resist if the opportunity suddenly arose: yet they were unlikely to succeed (in view of security checks at the main gate) and potentially quite risky (given the way guards tended to use their bayonets for investigative prodding of soft cargo). Numerous hopefuls jumped onto carts and buried themselves under the foliage debris and tools that were being regularly transported out of the newly constructed East Compound at Sagan after it was opened in April 1942, but none got beyond the gate. 'They were lucky not to have been bayoneted', J. M. McGee reflected on an impulsive dive into the exiting refuse cart by two NCOs at Hohenfels later in the war: 'the guards, thrusting into the rubbish, turfed them out.' A real chance of success involving transport usually demanded thought and a fair degree of preparation.[36]

Carefully hiding under piles of clothing carried outside in hampers for laundering or some other purpose was an option pursued by a number of officers in various camps, while several escapers also tried secreting themselves inside individual palliasses hidden among piles of old straw mattresses due to be moved elsewhere. Even less salubrious but more commonly possible were efforts to take advantage of the regular departure of refuse-disposal carts. Dedicated escapers proved willing to hide amidst rubbish or even in sewage whose odour alone might deter guards from thoroughly examining an outward-bound cart. With sufficient ingenuity it also proved possible to take advantage of piles of empty tins from Red Cross parcels collected for outside disposal. At Barth an escaper was hidden under the false bottom built into the wooden box used to carry discarded tins out of the officers' compound, while the following year at Warburg two intrepid souls wore home-made suits of armour that offered protection from probing bayonets after they had been hidden under a pile of tins about to be carted through the camp gates. It also proved possible on occasion to try hiding in shipping boxes when the population of a camp was moved from one location to another. Tried in one form or another in at least ten different locations, such attempts mostly ended in discovery and arrest at the gates. There were nevertheless enough successful breaks—around a dozen—to keep stow-away schemes popular into the last year of the war.[37]

More popular yet were schemes whereby prisoners might, through bluff and sheer nerve, simply walk their way out of captivity. A. J. Evans, who had himself escaped from Germany in the Great War and worked for MI9 in the Second World War, described in 1945 the manner in which a pair of enterprising soldiers had apparently escaped from a busy stalag:

By chance these two soldiers found a pot of white paint and two brushes. There was only one exit from the camp, and that was through the main double gates. From the Commandant's office inside the wire, a road led directly to the main gate. Starting from the office, the two soldiers, as though on fatigue duty, proceeded to paint a white line down the centre of the road. They took their time about it, the guards got used to seeing them on this work. At last they reached the gate, and seeming in no hurry, stood there chatting and smoking until someone opened the gates for them and told them to get on with the job. The same thing happened at the outer double gate. Outside the camp they continued to paint a line down the centre of the road till, seizing the opportunity of a convenient corner, they unobtrusively disappeared.[38]

The vast majority of walkout attempts, however, were much more elaborate. Involving as they almost always did the prior fabrication of *Posten* uniforms or alternate disguises (mostly civilian labourers and working prisoners of various nations), the forging or procuring of pass documents, the building up of detailed knowledge as to enemy habits and exit procedures, and preferably the incorporation of at least one participant who could speak German, walkout attempts from main camps usually required a great deal of preparation and support. There were, nevertheless, a significant number of such attempts, of which an unusually high proportion succeeded in getting escapers beyond the confines of the camp.

This was particularly true in the early war years. Walkouts were staged no fewer than nine times between July 1940 and April 1942 by officers at Stalag Luft I, and eight times the men involved got away. Of the six attempts made at Oflag VIB between the date the camp opened in 1941 and the point at which it closed in 1942, four enabled escapers to get outside the wire. There were also successful gate schemes mounted in this period at Biberach, Bad Sulza, and Spangenberg. Over time, though, the chances of success diminished as security improved. Hence, after the move to the East Compound at Stalag Luft III only two of the eight walkout schemes staged by RAF officers in 1942–3 came off successfully. Fewer attempts seem to have been made in the second half of the war, and with a lower rate of success. Four disguise-based escape attempts were made in the North Compound at Sagan in 1943, two of which failed. Similarly, of the three gate tries made by RAF officers at Barth between 1943 and 1945, only one came off.[39]

Increased vigilance on the part of sentries, however, tended to be confined to compounds where successful walkout attempts had already occurred, which meant that in newly established camps skill and luck might still favour escapers. In November 1942, for instance, five army officers got out of Eichstätt by doing a good impression of French prisoners under escort who had supposedly arrived earlier in the day to visit the English dentist, while in August 1943 a pair of army sergeants equipped with false passes managed to bluff their way out of the main gate at Hohenfels dressed as sentries.[40]

Even in high-risk camps, furthermore, more official scrutiny might be countered successfully by greater ingenuity on the part of would-be escapers. Impersonating military or civilian figures who visited the compound on a semi-regular basis, rather than just playing a generic sentry or worker, could add to the chances of the bluff working, as might figuring out ways to avoid gate guards who would be on the lookout for fake passes.

Careful impersonation, for example, lay behind the success of Pat Leeson in getting beyond the wire. Taking note of the appearance of a Polish chimney-sweep working on an intermittent basis at Barth, and managing one day to 'borrow' the man's pass long enough for a reasonable facsimile to be produced, Leeson made himself a version of the man's clothing and equipment—complete with battered top hat made of cardboard, coat and trousers covered in soot, and something resembling a chimney brush—and after the real sweep entered the compound one day in mid-March 1942, exited in disguise without incident through the main gate while the real sweep was still inside the camp. Only the ill-luck of running into the German staff members they had thus far successfully impersonated prevented two other RAF flight lieutenants from achieving a similar result at Barth at about the same time and the North Compound at Sagan a year later. The arrival of a party of Swiss inspectors at Warburg was used as cover in July 1942 to successfully stage the carefully pre-planned exit of Captain Terence Prittie and others dressed up to resemble their neutral visitors—a remarkable feat of group impersonation thought to have been carried off previously in other oflags.[41]

Making use of disguises to get away from some point other than a main gate also resulted in a number of notable breaks, especially in the later war years. Guards escorting parties to delousing sheds or bathhouses outside the main compound were more easily fooled than gate sentries, since anyone walking away from these locations dressed as someone other than a POW would not have to produce a pass or undergo scrutiny at close range. It was even possible to avoid the gate by successfully bluffing one's way over the wire, as George Grimson demonstrated in the NCOs' compound at Sagan in June 1943 by dressing as a civilian electrician, equipping himself with a ladder, and doing a brilliant job in fluent German of pretending to be on official business testing telephone wires that ran out from a sentry tower.[42]

The alternative to trying to get over or through a camp perimeter by one means or another was to try to go under it. Though time-consuming (usually months of hard digging), materiel-intensive (the need to shore up shafts), hard to mask (entrance camouflage and dirt disposal), and potentially lethal (roof falls), tunnelling proved to be popular across a wide band of the escaping fraternity. Tunnels were an obvious means of getting out, and also offered more opportunities than other methods to stage mass escapes. Furthermore they were much safer—in terms of risking being shot at—than having a go at the wire. In the early months tunnels were in fact the single most common form of escape effort for the RAF in hutted camps.[43]

Tunnelling could not be pursued everywhere. Fortresses might be built on stone and often had masonry floors and foundations that were enormously difficult to chisel through. Some of the hutted camps might be on land where the water table was very near the surface or on soil that was loose enough to be a serious underground hazard. Even under the best conditions, more in the way of engineering skill was required for tunnels than early enthusiasts imagined, and the longer they took to dig, the greater the chances of discovery by increasingly expert security staff. 'The amount of labour devoted to tunnels in this war is really astounding,' A. J. Evans reflected, 'but relatively few have been successful.' The majority were either written off or discovered—over sixty in the East Compound at Stalag Luft III alone—and only one in thirty-five starts ended in a usable exit in RAF camps in general.[44]

On the other hand, experience and ingenuity could help overcome both natural and man-made obstacles to successful tunnelling. Over time better camouflage techniques were developed for shaft entrances, and ways were found to begin a tunnel close to the wire, as with the famous Wooden Horse affair (in which a vaulting-block was used as cover for sinking a concealed shaft) and related but more quickly dug 'moler' schemes. Alternatively, a combination of engineering skill and co-operative effort might allow in later years for tunnels deep enough to evade discovery by sound detectors or ground probing, yet buttressed with enough timber to minimize the danger of sudden collapse, as with the Tom, Dick, and Harry shafts of Great Escape fame. Given enough time and willing labour, man-size holes could even be sunk into apparently impermeable rock, as an ultimately unsuccessful (but nevertheless very impressive) tunnel dug at Schloss Spangenberg demonstrated.[45]

Those shafts that got all the way from under a hut to a point beyond the perimeter, moreover, could pay off spectacularly. In September 1941 twenty-six officers exited through a tunnel at Biberach, followed eight months later by fifty-two prisoners held at Kirchhain. In March 1943 thirty-three men got away from Schubin, followed in June by another sixty-five from Eichstätt. And, in the most famous tunnel break of the war, a grand total of seventy-six officers escaped from the North Compound at Sagan in March 1944. Especially if the primary aim was to get as many men out as possible in one go, and thereby cause maximum inconvenience to the enemy—without knowledge, of course, that Hitler would become infuriated enough to order the execution of fifty recaptured men in the wake of the Great Escape—then tunnels were undoubtedly a worthwhile option.[46]

For those willing to seize opportunities when they were offered, it also proved possible on occasion to make breaks while in transit under guard from one location to another. 'It is difficult to envisage a more desperate or dangerous means of escape than leaping from the window of a train travelling at high speed with absolutely no protection,' Jack Champ reflected on those who tried on the journey from Warburg to Eichstätt, 'and with the full knowledge that one could easily jump straight into an oncoming pole, tunnel, or the many railway utilities that border a track.' Dropping through a hole in the floor of a cattle truck was just as dangerous, given the high risk of being crushed under the wheels. Nevertheless, and in spite of a number of deaths and the inherent unlikelihood of being at liberty for long—anyone train-jumping would have little in the way of escape kit—transit breaks were popular among hard-core escapers.[47]

Time spent recovering in hospitals might also be seen as an opportunity to escape. Some staff doctors and other officers were rather ambivalent about this form of exit, feeling that an escape would be likely to bring reprisals down on the heads of men who were suffering to begin with. Individual attempts were nevertheless made, plus a fifteen-man break from the transit camp at Rouen where those passed for repatriation were being held after the collapse of the negotiations over the first Anglo-German exchange of sick and wounded in the autumn of 1941.[48]

Even more controversial than hospital breaks were attempts to fake a serious illness (either physical or mental) and thereby be repatriated in an exchange. Especially in light of the heroic self-denial of men such as Group Captain H. M. Massey who had pointedly refused to be repatriated on medical grounds, trying this particular dodge was, for some, 'humiliating and smacking of cowardice and therefore rather infra dig', in the words of Flight Lieutenant Paddy Denton. The main problem with this type of escape, though—a route home which is completely ignored in official reports—was that a man pretending to be sick might displace a prisoner who really was seriously ill: hence the insistence by British medical officers at Oflag IXA/Z that the SBO issue orders that genuinely serious medical cases should take precedence over anyone thinking of a try-on prior to the visit of the mixed medical commission in the latter stages of the war.[49]

Especially at first, though, before it was clear that there would be limits on the numbers sent home, there was much less moral or official resistance. At Lamsdorf, for example, some of the British medical staff encouraged those with comparatively inconsequential complaints to have a go. Even after the precedence question began to arise, moreover, there were many prisoners—including some doctors—still desperate enough to try faking their way home.[50]

This, however, was more easily imagined than accomplished. Complaints that could not be linked to serious maladies got nowhere, and wounds of sufficient seriousness to warrant an interview with the mixed medical commission—say a shattered or missing limb—could not be self-inflicted. Attempts to mimic the signs of tuberculosis by swallowing soap and tinfoil or painting iodine patches on the skin prior to the taking of a chest X-ray all proved at best only partially successful; and ingesting foreign substances might in any event be genuinely harmful. Sam Kydd knew of a Kriegie who ate twenty cigarettes on the assumption that this would have an impressive effect on his heart rate: 'but all it did was make him violently sick and give him a nicotine complexion!' It was easier to pretend to be partially blind or to have gone deaf, but close examination by German or Swiss doctors usually indicated that there was nothing really wrong. One soldier who seemed to have lost his hearing in an industrial accident was eventually sent before the commission and appeared genuinely deaf, but failed at the last moment when, in response to a parting question by one doctor while walking out, he involuntarily turned round: 'just in time to see the president tearing up the certificate.'[51]

There were nevertheless some successes. Those with genuine medical problems might convince the commission that their health was far worse than it was, and with sufficient knowledge, preparation, and skill even healthy prisoners might be passed as physically incapable. Having learned that the symptoms included yellow skin and swollen ankles,

Richard Pape was able to mimic acute nephritis (kidney disease) at Heydekrug. He induced the necessary swelling through having his ankles flicked with a wet towel for several hours, dyeing his skin, and obtaining a urine sample from a real case before being first examined. Just to be on the safe side Pape subsequently added symptoms of pleurisy (through smoking dried sunflower seeds for three days straight) and tuberculosis (by having a friendly German orderly substitute a chest X-ray of a real case for his own). He was passed for repatriation and returned home in the autumn of 1944.[52]

Mental illness might also be faked successfully. With the help of a former medical student, Paddy Bryne was able to develop all the outward signs of someone going slowly insane in the North Compound at Sagan—lack of appetite, insomnia, memory loss, plus increasingly odd remarks and general incoherence in word and deed. He was eventually passed as mentally incompetent, and while waiting to be repatriated ran a one-man Lunacy School that helped four other RAF officers successfully fake psychological problems. Knowledge that some of those who came before the commission were trying to work their ticket home might lead to a certain amount of scepticism, however, and posing as a lunatic required so much effort over so much time that it was feared that a Kriegie initially pretending to be mad might devolve into someone genuinely in trouble. 'My biggest worry now', a young soldier quietly remarked after being passed for repatriation, 'is to be able to prove that I'm sane when I arrive [home].'[53]

In the meantime, for those thinking about breaking out rather than being sent home among the incapacitated, getting beyond the wire was only the beginning. There then arose the awesome prospect of crossing hundreds of square miles of enemy territory in search of a safe haven. Once again the odds against ultimate success were high to begin with and grew more so with time. In a totalitarian state eventually awash with foreign workers, those at large ran a serious risk of being arrested by policemen of various sorts on the lookout for anyone suspicious, and both ports and frontiers were increasingly well guarded. Once the authorities realized that a break had taken place, moreover, an alert would bring about a heightened state of security and, in the case of mass escapes, active searching by up to 50,000 home guard, police, and Hitler Youth members. Of the 200 aircrew prisoners who successfully broke out of tunnels, only eleven made it to safety.[54]

Beyond the problem of getting beyond the wire, several essential questions confronted potential escapers and escape committees. Was it possible to make a break secretly? What country should escapers make for? And how should they try and get there?

There was no way to cover up a mass break for more than a few hours at most, but the absence of individuals or pairs could be at least temporarily masked on *Appell* by various means. The simplest way was to have men quietly dodge from one place to another during the count so that the ultimate tally showed all present and correct. More sophisticated means included hiding men inside the camp, thereby giving the Germans the impression that an escape had already taken place and allowing the *Appell* numbers to genuinely match when a real escape was staged and the 'ghosts' re-emerged, and constructing head-and-shoulder dummies that could be held up and be counted in the middle ranks on parade—as at Marlag (O), where 'Albert' did yeoman service.[55]

As for where to aim for, there were a number of possibilities, none without its hazards. The USSR was close for those escaping from the eastern stalags in 1940–1, and indeed over 14 per cent of all successful escapers crossed the border into the Soviet Union. Even before the Nazi invasion abruptly put an end to this route in June 1941, however, it had become evident that fleeing Britons would not receive a warm welcome in Stalin's Russia. Escapers heading east risked being shot by border guards, and those who made it were almost invariably arrested and imprisoned under terrible conditions.

Throughout the war Switzerland was a natural choice—over 18 per cent of home runs involved crossing this border—but the frontier was closely watched and several unhappy escapers were caught just inside Germany. Almost 30 per cent of successful escapers got home through Sweden, but this route usually involved stowing away on a Swedish ship at a German port where quays were patrolled, vessels searched, and captains faced dire consequences if they were caught hiding anyone. Unsympathetic masters might even turn back once at sea if a stowaway was discovered. Travelling into occupied Europe—a route taken by 47 per cent of ultimately successful escapers—opened up the possibility of being helped by underground resistance movements, but also increased the chances of being at best interned under prison-camp conditions in places such as Vichy France and Hungary, and at worst being executed by the Gestapo for having consorted with illegal enemies of the Reich.[56]

A method of travelling across Germany without getting caught in transit also had to be decided on. Here too there were a number of options open to escapers, with opinions differing and evolving as to the most reliable.

Especially at first, it was assumed that walking cross-country in darkness and hiding during the day would be best, since this was the way a number of famous First World War escapes had been accomplished, and because money, passes, and disguises were not necessary. 'To move only by night, choosing a sparsely inhabited route, and to remain well-concealed during the hours of daylight: those were our maxims', Major A. S. B. Arkwright explained of the plans he and his fellow escapers had made for travel after getting over the wire at Warburg. Yet more often than not, those who tried this option either singly or in pairs found themselves in serious difficulty. Due to a combination of lack of stamina arising from the limited camp diet and uneven terrain, distances covered were less than anticipated and escape rations therefore ran out sooner than expected. Hunger and fatigue, combined with constant exposure to the elements, took both a physical and psychological toll. In a bid to make up for lost time marchers might decide to try the roads, where they were far more likely to be picked up. Others eventually reached the stage where they were ready to give in. 'The *Stalag* floated in our minds, a mirage of fellowship and ordered routine', Douglas Collins wrote of how he and his escaping partner felt after several weeks on the run. 'Maybe it wouldn't be so bad to be caught, whispered the inner voice.' The end result was a host of failed night treks, though there were also a few successes.[57]

Stealing bicycles was one alternative favoured in certain circles at Lamsdorf and elsewhere. Cyclists ran the risk of being stopped on the roads, but could cover much greater distances in much less time than men on foot and thereby increase their chances of success. Thomas Speed, for instance, after slipping away from a Stalag IXC Arbeitskommando in May 1943 and acquiring a succession of bikes, got to the Swiss border—which he crossed by other means—within five days. Many pilots, not surprisingly, dreamt about stealing an aeroplane and flying to freedom (a hope encouraged by MI9 when it secretly sent out cockpit layout plans for various types of enemy aircraft), and indeed on several separate occasions between 1941 and 1945 escapers came very close to success on German airfields.[58]

An escaper could not count on finding a bicycle, of course, and only pilots could think about stealing a plane—and even the most successful of the latter group never managed to get beyond the stage of trying without success to start the engine of an unfamiliar aircraft. The obvious alternative, if speed was the aim, was to travel by rail.

Though successful home runs were achieved by soldiers who climbed aboard goods trains, this method of transport could be dicey, since the ultimate destination might not be known. Routes and timetables for passenger trains might be obtainable by various covert means, but tickets required money, mainline stations were heavily patrolled, and express trains in particular were subject to constant security checks. Anyone thinking about riding the rails in relative comfort with any hope of success, in short, usually needed not only Reichsmarks but also a good disguise (with cover story and fake identity papers to match) and enough German (or at least a partner who spoke the language) to back up the false paperwork indicating that the traveller or travellers concerned were, say, foreign workers authorized to be on the move. The skills and materials necessary to prepare with this degree of thoroughness were rarely available on working parties, and even in those main camps where escape committees were well organized and supplies from MI9 were available, a great deal of time, ingenuity, and collective effort had to be put into equipping escapers for train journeys. 'The railways came to be urged not because they were easy,' Hugh Bruce explained, 'but because eventually we found that this was overwhelmingly the best method of travel.' In all, around sixty home runs from camps in the Greater Reich involved passenger trains at some point in the journey—roughly a third of the overall total—as against about seventeen that involved goods wagons.[59]

Success or failure in getting out and getting home, though, was not entirely dependent on the degree of planning and preparation put into an escape. Fortune also had a role to play. A promising tunnel might be discovered quite by accident; a disguised escaper might run into the guard he was trying to impersonate or some other German who recognized him; someone could find himself arrested within sight of the Swiss border or aboard a Swedish vessel that had already left its moorings. On the other hand, a sergeant might steal a succession of bicycles without incident, cycle his way leisurely to the Baltic, and stow away aboard a ship and get to Sweden without once being challenged; an escaper who spoke no German might still end up bluffing his way through security checks on trains; or a pair of escapers without papers or civilian clothing might locate and be able to cling to the underside of a train destined for Switzerland. 'Luck is the most essential part in an escape', David James wrote shortly after the war, an opinion reflecting not only both his own failed and successful attempts at Marlag—in the former he had the nerve to travel for several days disguised as 'Ivan Bagarov' (i.e. 'Bugger-Off') of the Bulgarian navy—but also the accounts of other prisoners he had read on his return to England. Hugo Bracken, a Fleet Air Arm officer interviewed about his experiences at Stalag Luft III and other camps several decades later, agreed: 'there was a hell of a lot of luck in it . . .'[60]

It took more than luck, to be sure, for the men of Colditz to establish their enviable escape record. The OKW goal was to secure their bad apples, escapers in particular, in one very special basket. Schloss camps were hard to get out of to begin with, and the security precautions taken at this Sonderlager, including four roll-calls a day and a garrison that outnumbered the prisoner population, were to be much more stringent and extensive than elsewhere. Oflag IVC was indeed a tough nut to crack—but there were inherent flaws in the policy of concentration that help to explain why, fortune aside, Colditz came to be anything but escape-proof. With their common background as troublemakers, an unusually high proportion of the inhabitants favoured escaping from Oflag IVC in principle and supporting it in practice. 'All of us were escape minded', Kenneth Lockwood later stated emphatically, going on to assert that this 'was *always* the spirit in Colditz'. Even those slightly less desperate than others to get away from the castle recognized the need 'to present oneself to the rest of the chaps as being that sort of chap', as James Moran put it. Placing the known escapers in one place further meant that a greater store of knowledge about types of breakout and methods of travel could be built up than was the case in other camps. The castle became a hive of creative activity, in which a wide range of escape possibilities—including the famous Colditz glider—were actively explored. In consequence, the number of escapes relative to the number of inhabitants was actually greater at Colditz than elsewhere. Well in excess of a hundred direct and indirect British escapes were attempted, thirty of which succeeded in setting men loose and eleven of which resulted in a total of fifteen men getting home. Thus the Sonderlager came to possess, in the words of Tommy Catlow, 'the highest successful escape record of any POW camp in Nazi Germany'.[61]

Colditz as escape capital of the Third Reich is nevertheless a vision that ought to be kept in perspective. Even at Oflag IVC, the reasons for and level of commitment to escape varied between people and over time, and the home-run record in particular needs to be qualified and placed in a comparative dimension. What happened at Colditz was unquestionably impressive, but was less *sui generis* than is popularly supposed.

Though it is easy to see why some former inmates could assume the contrary—there was no openly anti-escape faction at Colditz of the type that existed in other camps, and collective morale was boosted by successful breaks—commitment to escape was in fact far from absolute within the castle walls. 'Generally escaping was limited to the keen types', Jim Rogers remembered of the sixteen-odd men he dubbed the Kings of Colditz. 'It would have been too difficult for me to escape from Colditz,' Lieutenant John Watton candidly admitted of his time in Oflag IVC from August 1941 onward, 'as I did not consider myself competent to achieve the skill and effort required . . .' A willingness to pitch in and help assist in breakout bids was practically de rigueur, especially in the early war years, but age or other limitations led many officers to conclude early on that they ought to be spear-carriers rather than protagonists in the great drama of escape. 'I wasn't involved in it much', Major Montagu Champion Jones, who arrived at Colditz in the summer of 1941, pointed out in an interview. 'I hadn't any abilities that way, particularly—I didn't speak German—and I thought "my role is better helping those with a chance of getting out, really."' Pitched into the castle a week later, Jimmy Yule subsequently recalled that while willing to help the cause, he thought others had a greater claim to escaping and admitted that the support he gave 'was a gesture more than anything else'. Those who actually tried to get out numbered only in the low dozens, with the proportion of attempts (both absolute and in relation to the size of the British contingent) significantly dipping in the later war years. 'I would be surprised if more than a quarter really wanted to [break out], if that', Michael Burn, who arrived in the summer of 1943, later commented in reference to his decision to give up trying to escape. Entering the courtyard at about the same time, Major Miles Reid, in his early forties by this point, neither contemplated a breakout nor was asked to help others do so. By 1943–4 even some of the keenest types were coming to accept that most exit methods had already been tried, and that, as Kenneth Lockwood put it, 'Eggers was getting very good at blocking exits'. In the early years at Colditz the British contingent had viewed escaping as a morale-boosting game of wits. By the summer of 1944, with a notice having been posted announcing the creation of 'death zones' in which strangers would be shot on sight— 'escape from prison camps is no longer a sport!'—and news of the Sagan massacre circulating within the castle, Hugh Bruce decided 'it was pretty clear that escaping was no longer in any way a reasonable risk'. The SBO ordered a halt to breakout attempts—an order confirmed by MI9—and though escape planning continued, only Mike Sinclair actually tried to beat the odds in his ill-fated leap over the exercise enclosure wire in September 1944. After that the field was left to Francis 'Errol' Flinn, who, with the help of one of the doctors, finally managed to convince the Germans that he had gone insane and ought to be repatriated.[62]

It might also be argued that those involved in escape plans at Oflag IVC were no more ingenious than their counterparts in other camps, and indeed that a number of escape innovations usually associated with Colditz were in fact pioneered elsewhere. Hiding someone in an old palliasse was tried successfully not only at Colditz in May 1941 but also at Biberach at around the same time. Walking out of the gate in disguise, as Airey Neave tried to do at Oflag IVC in September of the same year, was a method already attempted by officers at both Stalag Luft I and Oflag VB. Concealing an escaper in a box of prisoners' belongings due to be carried out of camp was accomplished at Colditz in the autumn of 1942, but was nevertheless a means of exit that had been first used four months earlier at Marlag. 'Ghosting' was pioneered at Spangenberg about eighteen months before it was introduced at Colditz in late 1942, while the idea of making oneself up to pass for a particular member of the guard—the Franz Josef affair of May 1943—was something that had been attempted more than a year earlier at Barth. Even the famous two-man glider, built in the course of 1944 in an attic but never used, was not a unique concept. The glider idea had first been mooted at Sagan and was also apparently examined at Spangenberg.[63]

Colditz was unquestionably a difficult place to break out from, but it is worth remembering that those aiming for home runs from the castle had a few advantages denied to many of their counterparts elsewhere. Overall they had better access to money, maps, and other contraband material covertly sent from Britain to POW camps in Germany. Even more significantly, down until the last two years of the war they could obtain help from foreign prisoners who possessed escape-related material or skills that they themselves might lack.

Though exact comparisons are difficult to make in view of the varying types of data presented in reports, it nevertheless appears that more MI9 escape aids reached prisoners at Oflag IVC compared to many other officer camps. Of the 'special' parcels sent out from Britain in 1941–2, for instance, the escape committee at Colditz seems to have received about double the number received by Barth—despite the fact that there were well over three times as many British officers incarcerated in Stalag Luft I during this time than at Oflag IVC. Although those involved complained of the difficulties of smuggling contraband parcels past vigilant security, and the majority of material dispatched was intercepted at Colditz as elsewhere, it is worth noting that whereas no mention is made of receipt proportions in the official narratives of other camps, the report on the history of Oflag IVC confirms that the escape committee here 'acquired a great deal of escape material' from MI9.[64]

Being in the one multinational camp in which prisoners from different nations could easily mix proved to be of no small significance in relation to various aspects of escape. At a general level a healthy competitive spirit developed between the various contingents, the successes of one nation spurring the others—not least the British—to new feats of inventiveness and daring. In more specific ways, both the Poles and the Dutch in particular could offer the British at Colditz special advantages that increased the chances of successful escapes. Having mastered the art of castle door-lock picking before the British came, members of the Polish contingent were happy to teach the new arrivals their secrets. Pairing an Englishman with a Pole for an escape attempt was advantageous, insofar as it would be easy for the Polish officer to pose as one of the hundreds of thousands of Polish labourers at work in the Greater Reich and thereby offer cover for a 'silent partner' on train journeys that would be entirely absent if, say, two Britons who did not speak the language tried to pass themselves off as foreign workers. The Dutch were even more useful, since their greatcoats, caps, boots, and other uniform parts could be easily altered to resemble the German equivalent and—most importantly and in marked contrast to most British prisoners—they could speak practically flawless German. Though all five Anglo-Polish break-out attempts failed, three of the eight joint ventures with Dutch prisoners got the pairs involved well beyond the perimeter, and two were home runs in which the ability of the Dutch officer to communicate in German proved vital, thereby accounting for two-thirds of the successful British breakout escapes starting from inside the castle and ending in a neutral country.[65]

The British home-run figures have themselves been subject to a certain amount of popular oversimplification. Though fifteen British prisoners held at Colditz made it back to England, the fact was that only six of them—in three separate breaks—actually escaped from inside the castle. Five others either arranged transfers to, or in one case took advantage of, moves to less secure camps, while the remaining four faked physical or mental illnesses that got them repatriated from the Schloss itself. Even without including the repatriation route, there were other camps that either surpassed or equalled the Colditz record. If escapes from satellite working camps are included then Lamsdorf was the place from which the largest number of Kriegies—over forty—made it back.

If only breaks from main camps are included then Thorn emerges as the clear winner, with ten men getting home. Both Stalag Luft III and Oflag VB came close to matching the Oflag IVC record in terms of getting men to England via breakouts from the more closely guarded officer compounds. What was achieved at the Schloss was still impressive—about one-fifth of all those who escaped and made it home from officer compounds broke out from the Sonderlager—but it is time to stop assuming that Colditz was in a league of its own.[66]

For an increasing number of prisoners it seemed that Allied victory was the most likely way in which freedom would be achieved. Even at Colditz the prospect of liberation rather than escape eventually came to dominate thought and action. As enemy defeat began to loom, however, so too did questions about what the captors might do with their captives as the Third Reich began to crumble.

Notes

1. Richard Garrett, *Great Escapes of World War II* (London, 1989), 3.
2. Jerome Caminada in *The Times*, 8 Jan. 1974, p. 12. On the Colditz escape record see e.g. LC, T. Catlow, 55; Airey Neave, *They Have Their Exits* (London, 1953), 73; P. R. Reid, *The Latter Days* (London, 1953), 22; id., *The Colditz Story* (London, 1952), 18.
3. See Hugh Bruce, 'Patterns of Escape', *Colditz Society Newsletter*, 8 (1994), 5; Sydney Smith, *Wings Day* (London, 1968), 81; Michael Duncan, *Underground from Posen* (London, 1954), 99; A. Passfield, *The Escape Artist* (Perth, WA, 1988), 36–7.
4. Philip Kindersley, *For You the War Is Over* (Tunbridge Wells, 1983), 163; P. Oates, in Patsy Adam-Smith, *Prisoners of War* (Ringwood, Victoria, 1992), 200–1.
5. H. E. Woolley, *No Time Off For Good Behaviour* (Burnstown, Ont., 1990), 23. See M. R. D. Foot and J. M. Langley, *MI9* (London, 1979), 291–2. See Sandy St Clair, *The Endless War* (North Battleford, Sask., 1987), 196; Richard Passmore, *Moving Tent* (London, 1982), 139; Jack Pringle, *Colditz Last Stop* (London, 1995 edn.), 125; Ewart C. Jones, *Germans Under My Bed* (London, 1957), 201.
6. Jack Poole, *Undiscovered Ends* (London, 1957), 13; Jim Rogers, *Tunnelling into Colditz* (London, 1986), 143.
7. PRO, WO 208/3281, p. 4; Duncan, op. cit.; George Dunning, *Where Bleed the Many* (London, 1955), 79; J. E. Pryce, *Heels in Line* (London, 1958), 93. On the Eichstätt note see David Walker, *Lean, Wind Lean* (London, 1984), 88–90; Jack Champ and Colin Burgess, *The Diggers of Colditz* (Sydney, 1985), 113. Material demands on camp resources by escaping types could

also be resented. See e.g. J. Lyon, in Anton Gill, *The Great Escape* (London, 2002), 127.

8. IWM, T. Tateston, 58; IWM, G. R. Manners diary, 6 Oct. 1940. It should be noted, however, that despite the obvious problems involved it was still sometimes possible to arrange for main-camp escape committees to send escape aids to Arbeitskommando locations from which someone wanted to make a break. See e.g. http://www.binternet.com/~stalag18a/jimbennett. html, J. Bennett, 2. It has also been suggested that the reason for the comparatively low number of escapers among the other ranks had to do with the fact that officers (and NCOs) had already displayed the intelligence and initiative necessary to be an escaper through being promoted (see Foot and Langley, op. cit., 103), and that for similar reasons the highest proportion of escapers was to be found among RAF Kriegies (see Aidan Crawley, *Escape from Germany* (London, 1956), 26). A survey of 'home run' escape reports in relation to the POW population suggests that those with commissions were roughly five times as likely to make it back to the UK from Germany than those without (PRO, WO 208/3305–3327; Vasilis Vourkoutiotis, 'The German Armed Forces Supreme Command and British and American Prisoners of War', Ph.D. thesis, McGill University, (2000), 58, n. 180).

9. Stephen P. L. Johnson, *A Kriegie's Log* (Tunbridge Wells, 1995), 124.

10. T. C. F. Prittie and W. Earle Edwards, *Escape to Freedom* (London, 1953 edn.), 220; see also e.g. J. D. Rae, *Kiwi Spitfire Ace* (London, 2001), 125.

11. Michael Farr, *Vanishing Borders* (London, 1991), 61; see Crawley, op. cit., 24; PRO, WO 208/3279, p. 3. On escaping as a patriotic duty see e.g. IWMSA 13296/2, R. Churchill; IWM, R. A. Wilson, 170; Sam Kydd, *For You the War Is Over...* (London, 1973), 170; Walter Morrison, *Flak and Ferrets* (London, 1995), 82. There were also personal reasons for trying to escape, such as the desire to be reunited with a wife or girlfriend and regaining the sense of being in control of one's destiny. See e.g. UNB, MS L35, David H. Walker Papers, box 1, series 2, file 6, Moran to Walker, 3 Sept. 1984; ibid., box 3, file 84, Tomes to Walker, 27 Nov. 1984.

12. Champ and Burgess, op. cit., 125; Bruce, op. cit. On the Schubin tunnel numbers see Paul Brickhill, *The Great Escape* (London, 1950), 19. On the Eichstätt numbers see Foot and Langley, op. cit., 246. For the case in favour of big breaks see also e.g. IWMSA 15558/3, A. Cole; Brickhill, op. cit., 157, 163; J. Lyon, in Gill, op. cit., 171. For the case against big breaks see e.g. T. D. Calnan, *Free As a Running Fox* (London, 1970), 181–2; Passfield, op. cit., 24.

13. On forcing the enemy to beef up security see e.g. PRO, WO 208/3282, pt. IV, p. 49. On the morale boost see Champ and Burgess, op. cit.

14. John Fancy, *Tunnelling to Freedom* (London, 1957), 44, *passim*; PRO, WO 208/3327, MI9/S/PG(G)3009; ibid., MI9/S/PG(P)3119.

15. Bruce, op. cit.; Smith, op. cit., 81–2; see Crawley, op. cit., 26. In Stalag Luft III there was also a minority who had to be coerced into helping support escapes. See e.g. George Harsh, *Lonesome Road* (New York, 1971), 196.

16. St Clair, op. cit., 196; Cyril Rofe, *Against the Wind* (London, 1956), 33.

17. Smith, op. cit.; Duncan, op. cit.; Robert Kee, *A Crowd Is Not Company* (London, 1982 edn.), 77.

18. See Gill, op. cit.; Jonathan F. Vance, *A Gallant Company* (Pacifica, Cal., 2000).

19. Rogers, op. cit., 75; Calnan, op. cit., 155; IWMSA 16797/2, H. Bruce; Poole, op. cit., 138. On soldiers escaping from Arbeitskommandos (and even main camps) out of a desire for greater stimulation see e.g. PRO, WO 208/3275, p. 3; IWM, T. Tateson, 58; Clive Dunn, *Permission to Speak* (London, 1986), 105; Barney Roberts, *A Kind of Cattle* (Sydney, 1985), 75.

20. On trousers and boots being removed see e.g. PRO, WO 208/3275, p. 3; Dunn, op. cit., 98. On the thickening up of camp defences see e.g. WO 208/ 3270, p. 5; WO 208/3282, pt. I, p. 4; WO 208/3282, pt. III, p. 7; ibid., pt. IV, p. 6; WO 208/3283, pt. I, pp. 6–8; WO 208/3286A, pp. 7–9.

21. Crawley, op. cit., 133.

22. On Bushell and the 'X' organization at Sagan see PRO, WO 208/3283, pt. III, pp. 7 ff. On the 'cloak and dagger' group at Mährisch Trübau see WO 208/3292, pp. 4 ff. On fragmented escape bureaucracy see e.g. WO 208/ 3281, p. 3; WO 208/3317, MI9/S/PG(G)1629, p. 4. On prisoners ignoring camp escape organizations see e.g. Champ and Burgess, op. cit., 28. On the absence of organization see e.g. WO 208/32943, p. 3; WO 208/23282, pt. II, p. 8. On the lesser authority of NCO camp leaders concerning escape organization as against SBOs see e.g. WO 208/3283, pt. II, p. 16.

23. Morrison, op. cit., 82–3; PRO, WO 208/3283, Pt. I, pp. 17–18; WO 208/ 3282, pt. IV, p. 28.

24. Fancy, op. cit., 99; see PRO, WO 208/3286A, pp. 20 ff. John Dominy, *The Sergeant Escapers* (London, 1974), 64 ff. On virtually everyone being involved in the Great Escape see IWMSA 15558/3, A. Cole. On escape committee support for the Wooden Horse tunnel see Eric Williams, *The Wooden Horse* (London, 1949), 37 ff.

25. IWM, R. A. Wilson, 170. On Stalag IVB see PRO, WO 208/3274, p. 3. On the SBO at Marlag see LC, T. N. Catlow, 53; IWMSA 16797/2, H. Bruce. See also, however, David James, *A Prisoner's Progress* (Edinburgh, 1947), 46. On the escape committee at Rotenburg see Foot and Langley, op. cit., 247. On the escape committee at Spangenberg see Calnan, op. cit., 67, 69, 70; Oliver Philpot, *Stolen Journey* (London, 1950), 97, 106.

26. PRO, WO 208/3277, pp. 3, 6. To compare the dispatch and receipt record of MI9 material in a variety of camps see WO 208/3270–96. On not recognizing that an item contained escape aids see e.g. John D. Harvie, *Missing in Action* (Montreal, 1995), 158. On the development of clandestine escape aids see Foot and Langley, op. cit., 55–6, 107–8; Clayton Hutton, *Official Secret* (London, 1960); Charles Fraser Smith with Gerald McKnight and Sandy Lesberg, *The Secret War of Charles Fraser-Smith* (London, 1981).

27. PRO, WO 208/3305–27. The figures are based on those of all ranks who escaped from camps (or in transit between them) inside the Third Reich. Not included are the dozens of Kriegies who slipped away from marching POW columns or temporary facilities in 1945 and eventually reported in to

MI9. On the importance of being able to switch identities at Lamsdorf see Crawley, op. cit., 99.

28. See e.g. IWMSA 13573/3, A. Jones; Robert Garioch, *Two Men and a Blanket* (Edinburgh, 1975), 121; Alan Mackay, *313 Days to Christmas* (Glendaruel, 1998), 26; A. Robert Prouse, *Ticket to Hell Via Dieppe* (Toronto, 1982), 46–7; Eric Williams, *The Tunnel* (London, 1951), 247.

29. PRO, WO 208/3282, pt. I, pp. 34–6, pt. II, p. 33, pt. III, p. 35. On using the guard towers as climbing frames see Fancy, op. cit., 64–7; WO 208/3278, MI9/S/PG(G)891, p. 1; Derrick Nabarro, *Wait for the Dawn* (London, 1952), 42–6.

30. PRO, WO 208/3290, App. B, p. 2. On Operation Olympia see WO 208/ 3311, MI9/S/PG(G)974–976; Crawley, op. cit., 142–4; A. S. B. Arkwright, *Return Journey* (London, 1948), 27 ff.; Champ and Burgess, op. cit., 37–47; Walker, op. cit., 16 ff.

31. PRO, WO 208/3283, pt. I, p. 51, pt. II, p. 36, pt. III, p. 41; see Edward Sniders, *Flying In, Walking Out* (Barnsley, 1999), 74–80. On plans for mass over-the-wire breaks at Schubin and Mährisch Trübau respectively see B. A. James, *Moonless Night* (London, 1983), 69; Kee, op. cit., 96 ff.; Philpot, op. cit., 162; Pringle, op. cit., 113.

32. PRO, WO 208/3293, p. 5; Prittie and Edwards, op. cit., 319–22; Rogers, op. cit., 152; WO 208/3994, p. 4.

33. PRO, WO 208/3282, pt. I, p. 34, pt. III, pp. 36 ff., 39 ff., 40; pt. IV, pp. 50, 52, 53; WO 208/3283, pt. I, pp. 48–50; see Crawley, op. cit., 35, 65–9. On the escape from Lamsdorf see IWM, R. A. Wilson, chs. 16–17. On the escape from Kirchhain see WO 208/3285, p. 22. On the Hamilton-Baillie escape from Tittmoning see IWMSA 14781/1, J. Hamilton-Baillie. On the Warburg escape see Prittie and Edwards op. cit., 137–9.

34. On the relative popularity and success of bluffing one's way out see A. J. Evans, *Escape and Liberation, 1940–1945* (London, 1945), 15.

35. On the 1943 home-run from Stalag XXID (Posen) see PRO, WO 208/3314, MI9/S/PG(Poland)1393. On the three home-run escapes from Stalag XXA (Thorn) in 1942–3 see WO 208/3313, MI9/S/PG(Poland)1189; WO 208/ 3315, MI9/S/PG(Poland)1499–1500; WO 208/3316, MI9/S/PG(Poland) 1520–1, 1514. On aircrew breaks from Barth local working parties and the 1942 ban see WO 208/3282, pt. II, pp. 15–18. On 1942 home-run escapes via local work from other locations by non-commissioned RAF aircrew see WO 208/3314, MI9/S/PG(G)1316; WO208/3311, MI9/S/PG(G)947.

36. IWM (Rolf), J. M. McGee, 16. On the failure of the attempts made in the two weeks after the opening of the East Compound at Stalag Luft III see PRO, WO 208/3283, pt. I, p. 51.

37. On 'moving' efforts see e.g. PRO, WO 208/3282, pt. II, pp. 14–15. On 'tin pile' escapes see Champ, op. cit., pp. 50 ff.; WO 208/3282, pt. I, p. 39. On other waste-disposal attempts see e.g. WO 208/3294, p. 5; M. N. McKibbin, *Barbed Wire* (London, 1947), 98. On palliasse escape attempts see WO 208/3282, pt. III, pp. 42–3; Prittie and Edwards, op. cit., 81. On laundry-basket and related schemes see e.g. WO 208/3283, pt. I, p. 51; Kindersley, op. cit., 148; Corran Purdon, *List the Bugle* (Antrim, 1993),

44 ff. On other vehicle attempts see e.g. WO 208/3282, pt. I, p. 39; WO 208/3290, p. 3.

38. Evans, op. cit. Though he clearly believed it, this escape story may have been an apocryphal tale told to Evans by liberated or escaped Kriegies who had heard it themselves second-hand at some point in their captivity. If so it reflects the psychological lure of any scheme—real or supposed—that involved pulling the wool over the captor's eyes and making him look foolish.

39. On disguise/walkout attempts by officers at Barth, 1943–5, see PRO, WO 208/3282, pt. IV, pp. 49–50. On same from the North Compound at Sagan see WO 208/3283, pt. III, pp. 40–1, 43–4; Harsh, op. cit., 180–5. On same from the East Compound, 1942–3, see WO 208/3283, pt. I, pp. 43–7. On the gate escapes at Biberach see IWM, H. C. F. Harwood, 107–9; Champ and Burgess, op. cit., 28–9; Prittie and Edwards, op. cit., 81 ff. On same at Bad Sulza see Nabarro, op. cit., 70 ff. On same at Spangenberg see Philpot, op. cit., 105. On bluff escapes and attempts from Warburg see Prittie and Edwards, op. cit., 119–21, 147–9; Strachen, op. cit. On walkouts by officers at Barth between 1940 and 1942 see WO 208/3282, pt. I, pp. 24–31.

40. On the walkout from Hohenfels see George Beeson, *Five Roads to Freedom* (London, 1977), 49–53. On the dentist scheme at Eichstätt see Prittie and Edwards, op. cit., 187–93.

41. On the Swiss Commission escape from Warburg see Prittie and Edwards, op. cit., 140–52. Oliver Philpot was told of this bluff being carried off at Spangenberg castle (see Philpot, op. cit., 105), while Paul Brickhill reported the same thing occurring at the officers' compound at Barth (see *The Great Escape*, 10): unfortunately there seems to be no supporting evidence for these claims. On the impersonation attempts that ended with a confrontation with the real McCoy see PRO, WO 208/3282, pt. I, p. 30; WO 208/3283, pt. III, p. 45. On the chimney-sweep escape see WO 208/3282, pt. I, pp. 29–30.

42. PRO, WO 208/3283, pt. II, pp. 36–8. On the mass escape via the delousing shed in the North Compound that took place shortly thereafter see ibid, pt. III, pp. 43–4; Morrison, op. cit., 99 ff. On the bathhouse bluff escape from Biberach see Prittie and Edwards, op. cit., 81. On the bathhouse escapes from Marlag see D. James, op. cit., 67 ff., 116, 118, 123 ff.

43. Crawley, op. cit., 33. The high water table at Barth, for instance, made for extremely difficult tunnelling conditions (see PRO, WO 208/3282, pt. I, p. 24, pt. II, p. 10), while sandy ground was a major problem at both Sandbostel and Sagan (see John Chrisp, *The Tunnellers of Sandborstal* (London, 1959), 69–70; Crawley, op. cit., 162). Heavy rains and burst water-pipes could also cause irreparable flooding, as at Warburg, the lower camp at Spangenberg, and Hohenfels: see on Oflag VIB, Prittie and Edwards, op. cit., 132; Jane Torday (ed.), *The Coldstreamer and the Canary* (Langley, 1995), 66; Miles Reid, *Into Colditz* (Salisbury, 1985), 36: on Oflag IXA, IWMSA 4769/2, J. Phillips; on Stalag 383, IWM (Rolf), J. M. McGee, 16; Beeson, op. cit., 35.

44. Beeson, op. cit.; Evans, op. cit., 14; Philpot, op. cit., 124.

45. On the Spangenberg tunnel see PRO, WO 208/3293, p. 5; Prittie and Edwards, op. cit., 220–1; Rogers, op. cit., 149. On the Tom, Dick, and Harry tunnels and the Great Escape see e.g. WO 208/3283, pt. IV. On the Wooden Horse escape see WO 208/3317, MI9/S/PG(G)1618–19; Williams, *Wooden Horse*; Philpot, op. cit. On 'moler' tunnels see e.g. Crawley, op. cit., 90–1; Calnan, op. cit., 159, 161–7; Fancy, op. cit., 82–4; Garioch, op. cit., 139.

46. On the Sagan tunnel see WO 208/3283, pt. IV. On the Eichstätt tunnel see PRO, WO 208/3291, p. 2. On the Schubin (Oflag XXIB) tunnel see Sydney Smith, *Wings Day* (London, 1968), 120–2. On the Biberach tunnel see Michael Duncan, *Underground From Posen* (London, 1954), 98–129.

47. Champ and Burgess, op. cit., 91; see e.g. IWM, W. L. Stephens, 46; Kindersley, op. cit.

48. On the Rouen break see PRO, WO 208/3308, MI9/S/PG(F)771, 952–3, 51–2.

49. George Clifton, *The Happy Hunted* (London, 1954), 349–50; IWM, I. P. B. Denton, 76. On Massey see Harsh, op. cit., 194.

50. See Cyril Rofe, *Against the Wind* (London, 1956), 30; IWM, H. L. Martin, 46; Harry Levy, *The Dark Side of the Sky* (London, 1996), 141–2.

51. Eric Fearnside, *The Joy of Freedom* (Burton-in-Kendal, 1996), 75; Kydd, op. cit., 216.

52. Richard Pape, *Boldness Be My Friend* (London, 1953), 304–7.

53. IWM, N. R. Wylie, CSM Fulton report, 'Some Amusing Incidents', 1. On the lunacy school see Smith, op. cit., 144. See e.g. K. W. Mackenzie, *Hurricane Combat* (London, 1990 edn.), 148.

54. Crawley, op. cit., 23; Foot and Langley, op. cit., 246.

55. On dummies see e.g. PRO, WO 208/3270, p. 6. On 'ghosting' see e.g. WO 208/3274, App. D, pp. 7–8.

56. On home runs by destination see PRO, WO 208/3242, p. 79. On execution for consorting with enemies of the Reich see e.g. John Dominy, *The Sergeant Escapers* (London, 1974), 108–11. On internment see e.g. WO 208/3301, MI9/S/PG(FG)188, p. 4. On the dangers of seeking sanctuary in the USSR see Foot and Langley, op. cit., 227–8.

57. Douglas Collins, *P.O.W.* (London, 1970), 90; Arkwright, op. cit., 15. On hunger, fatigue, and taking unnecessary risks on foot see Hugh Bruce, 'Patterns of Escape', *Colditz Society Newsletter*, 8 (Nov. 1994), 5. On night-trek success see e.g. PRO, WO 208/3305, MI9/S/PG(G)433, p. 447.

58. On attempts to steal aircraft see e.g. PRO, WO 208/3308, MI9/S/PG(G)1717, p. 3. On stealing bicycles see e.g. WO 208/3326, MI9/S/PG(G)2929, pp. 3–4 (Speed).

59. PRO, WO 208/3298–327 (breaks from columns and transit cages in 1945 are excluded); H. Bruce, op. cit.

60. IWMSA 11337/4, H. Bracken; D. James, op. cit., 42. On clinging to the underside of a train that crossed into Switzerland see PRO, WO 208/3276, account of escape of Edwards and Lang. On speaking no German but getting away with it and bicycling without being stopped see Evans, op. cit., 18–19. On being caught aboard a Swedish ship already under way

see e.g. A. McSweyn in Alan W. Cooper, *Free to Fight Again* (London, 1988), 215. On being caught after thinking the Swiss frontier had been crossed see e.g. Donald Watt, *Stoker* (East Roseville, NSW, 1995), 77. On an impersonator being caught by the German he was impersonating see e.g. WO 208/3282, pt. I, p. 30. The accidental breaking of a water main led to the discovery of a major tunnel at Hohenfels (see Beeson, op. cit., 33–5), while a fault in the tunnel-light wiring led to the death by electrocution— and hence by necessity the uncovering of the shaft—of a digger at Warburg (see Champ and Burgess, op. cit., 78–9).

61. LC, T. Catlow, 54; IWMSA 4816/6, J. M. Moran; CSVA 4, K. Lockwood. The escape figures are derived from the list provided in Henry Chancellor, *Colditz* (London, 2001), App. 1. On everyone either trying to escape or feeling obligated to help others at Colditz see also e.g. IWMSA 16843/3, J. Chrisp.

62. *Sunday Times*, 6 Feb. 2000, p. 4 (Flinn); IWMSA 16797/4, H. Bruce; CSVA 4, K. Lockwood; M. Reid, op. cit., 69; IWMSA 9247/2, M. Burn; CSVA 2, J. Yule; IWMSA 9893/5, M. Champion Jones; Rogers, op. cit., 110; John Watton, 'Goodbye Colditz', in R. Eggers (comp.), J. Watton (ed.) *Colditz Recaptured* (London, 1973), 172. For references to escaping as a morale-boosting form of sport at Colditz in earlier years see e.g. B. Paddon, letter, 23 Oct. 1942, reproduced in *Colditz Society Newsletter*, 2:20 (June 1999), 6; IWMSA 6367/5, E. G. B. Davies Scourfield.

63. On the Spangenberg glider idea see Crawley, op. cit., 30. On the origins of the Colditz glider idea at Sagan see IWMSA 10643/3, P. Welch; Kee, op. cit., 77. On the 'Colditz Cock' see Chancellor, op. cit., ch. 17. On the Franz Josef affair see ibid., ch. 11. On the Charlie Piltz attempt at Barth see PRO, WO 208/3282, pt. I, p. 30. On ghosting at Colditz see P. R. Reid, *Colditz* (London, 1985), 183 ff. On ghosting at Spangenberg see Calnan, op. cit., 65–6. On the moving box escape from Colditz see Chancellor, op. cit., 180 ff. On the similar escape from Sandbostel see Chrisp, op. cit., 131 ff. On the Neave disguise attempt see Neave, op. cit., 75 ff. On the earlier disguise attempt at Barth see WO 208/3282, pt. I, p. 25; at Biberach see Prittie and Edwards, op. cit., 81.

64. PRO, WO 208/3288, pp. 62, 35; WO 208/3282, pt. I, p. 19; see e.g. WO 208/3295, p. 3; WO 208/3294, p. 6; WO 208/3293, pp. 7–8; WO 208/3291, pp. 3–4. Jock Hamilton-Baillie later implied that having a former prisoner who had escaped from the castle in an important position in MI9—Airey Neave—meant that requests from Colditz for escape material were given particular attention. *The Road to Colditz* (Applecart TV, 1997). The large amount of MI9 material smuggled into Colditz, it should be added, was in part due to the great ingenuity displayed by the relevant members of the escape committee—so that it is also possible to argue that they simply got what they deserved. On the other hand it is worth noting that, in contrast to reports on other oflags, no figures for materials dispatched to Colditz were appended to the report on Oflag IVC. On MI9 material being put to good use in Colditz escapes see e.g. N. Crockatt, quoted in Lloyd R. Shoemaker, *The Escape Factory* (New York, 1990), 9.

65. See Chancellor, op. cit., 34, 44, 86–90, 178–9, App. 1. On international escaping rivalry see PRO, WO 208/3288, p. 17; see also e.g. K. Lockwood in *Escape from Colditz: The Escaping Academy* (Windfall Films, 2000).

66. PRO, WO 208/3297–327; Chancellor, op. cit., App. 1.

11 Exodus and Liberation

No prisoner may at any time be sent to an area where he would be exposed to the fire of the fighting zone...

(from Article 9, Geneva Convention, 1929)

Representatives of [Red Cross and related] societies shall be permitted to distribute relief in the camps and at the halting places...

(from Article 78, Geneva Convention, 1929)

How soon the war would come to an end had been a major preoccupation for most prisoners since capture, and had certainly become the dominant question since the D-day landings. Early estimates had proved overoptimistic, but as 1944 gave way to 1945 it was clear even to the most jaundiced Kriegie observers that Germany was about to be overrun. In the eastern camps the rumble of Red Army artillery could be heard, while further west it was clear that Allied forces would soon be over the Rhine. In overall terms the imminent collapse of the Third Reich was something that the vast majority of prisoners eagerly looked forward to; but anticipation was often tinged with anxiety. Members of the British Free Corps and other turncoats were of course frightened about their future, but so too—albeit for different reasons—were other Kriegies. Ideally, the enemy would allow POW camps to be peacefully liberated as the front advanced. Unfortunately, rather less agreeable possibilities also sprang to mind among the more forward-looking captives.

One source of worry was the possibility that Hitler would order the murder of some or all prisoners by SS units as a final act of *Götterdämmerung*-style vengeance. This was of particular concern to those POWs already marked out as enemies of the Reich, such as officers sent to Colditz and the bomber crews long vilified in the Nazi press as *Terrorflieger* gangsters. A related concern, particularly acute among the *Prominente*, was that Kriegies would be moved before they could fall into friendly hands and be used as hostages within whatever area the Nazis chose to make their last stand. Even if prisoners were left where they were, there was no guarantee that camps would not become fought-over battlegrounds as the front moved through the area.[1]

The latter prospect was not made easier by the fact that the majority of Kriegies were located in the eastern half of the Greater Reich and would be most likely overrun by the Red Army. While some prisoners were not bothered by this prospect at all, others were distinctly worried. The Germans clearly expected Soviet troops to engage in an orgy of pillage and destruction as they drove westward, and many Kriegies were worried that the Red Army would care little for their safety and welfare. 'We had heard stories about what the Russians did to POWs that they found,' H. S. Bowers, a Lamsdorf Arbeitskommando veteran remembered, 'such as using them as a human shield in front of their advancing troops.' Overblown or not, such concerns added to the uncertainty among POWs as the shooting war drew inexorably closer.[2]

It soon became apparent, however, that the German High Command had no intention of allowing Kriegies to be liberated by enemy forces of any country while it still possessed the means to prevent it. The Geneva Convention specified that prisoners of war were to be kept clear of the fighting zone, which was a convenient rationale for trying to conserve a large body of captured personnel who might still be of value as workers or bargaining-chips. Despite the huge logistical problems bound to be created by setting hundreds of thousands of prisoners on the move in the context of a transport and supply situation that was already under critical strain, OKW insisted that camps be evacuated once in imminent danger of being overrun. The first to be affected were those prisoners held in Poland and Silesia in the course of January and February as the Red Army advanced, but by March and April many of the camps as far west as Hanover and Franconia—to which many refugee Kriegies from the east had ultimately been dispatched after weeks or even months on the road—were also being hastily abandoned in the face of advances from the west by Allied forces. The overall result was a series of marches that few of those involved would soon forget.[3]

Though working prisoners were more used to sustained exertion than those men kept permanently behind the wire, few POWs by 1945 were physically or mentally prepared to suddenly start slogging on foot from dawn to dusk for days on end, loaded down with their worldly possessions. Red Cross parcels had been in short supply for some time, and bodies had become progressively weaker. More often than not—though rumours might have been circulating for some time—very little notice was given that an evacuation was about to take place and no hard information was provided about the form or length of the march, leaving Kriegies, unused to any speedy activity, with as little as sixty minutes to work out what to leave and how to carry what they decided to take among their few but highly prized possessions. 'Complete panic!' was how Geoffrey Willatt remembered the reaction to the news that Stalag Luft III was about to be evacuated in late January 1945. Sling bags, backpacks, wheel carts, and sledges were hastily thrown together to ease the carrying burden, but in almost all cases Kriegies found that they had overestimated their strength and stamina as well as the effectiveness of their load-bearing contraptions. Some main-camp types became so fatigued that they abandoned much of their kit within hours. Men like submariner Jack Bishop might perceive that a heavy haversack would necessarily 'get lighter as I consumed the contents', but a desire to lighten the load often took precedence above all else when Kriegies started walking. 'Many of them', Percy Carruthers observed of his fellow NCOs after less than a day's march from Stalag Luft IV in February, 'had already resorted to what I considered absolute folly; throwing away the heaviest items which happened to be tins of food.'[4]

In defence of such behaviour it should be noted that few men guessed that their journey might last more than a short time before they were liberated. 'It was like a holiday!' Hugo Bracken recalled of the buoyant mood at Stalag Luft III amidst the chaos of last-minute departure preparations. 'Walking out through the gates I felt like shouting and dancing', remembered Martin Smith. Unhappily, most prisoners found themselves trekking—moving up to twenty or more miles a day at times—for anywhere from a week to several months, with the official supply system clearly unable to cope with the job of feeding hundreds of thousands of prisoners moving in hundreds of columns, large and small, across the secondary and tertiary road network. 'We lived from hand to mouth', Frank Taylor explained in connection with the 800 kilometre march from Stalag Luft IV to Fallingbostel, 'and never knew from one day to the next what rations, if any, would be forthcoming.'[5]

Acquiring something to eat soon became a major preoccupation as days stretched into weeks. Sheltered at night more often than not in barns and other outbuildings, and sometimes given rest-breaks during the day in villages and hamlets, prisoners regularly sought to obtain food through barter with the locals. Luxury items from Red Cross parcels were useful when available, but after these ran out—always assuming the extra load had not been discarded early on—more desperate measures were necessary. Having already traded a bar of soap for bread earlier in the trek from a Lamsdorf working camp, Harold Siddall found himself ducking into a baker's shop and exchanging his long-johns for two loaves of bread in the depth of winter. With acute hunger spurring them on, Kriegies might beg farmers for food or more commonly simply grab whatever edibles they could lay their hands on unobserved. Root vegetables might be scavenged from frozen fields or roadside clamps, while animal feed, pigswill, and sometimes even mice would be surreptitiously consumed in barnyards at night. One sailor clearly remembered watching another POW successfully wrestle with a barnyard dog to obtain the table scraps it had been given. The comrades of a South African sergeant went one step further by killing and cooking the dog itself. 'I well remember eating some cow biscuits that I found on one of the farms,' Lance-Corporal Jack Bird noted of the march from Stalag VIIIC, 'and though they were full of maggots they still tasted good to me.'[6]

At first guards and farmers might attempt to stop such pillaging, but as the end came nearer (and the roles of captive and captor seemed likely to be reversed in the very near future) POWs were often in practice allowed to live off the land relatively unimpeded. 'Prisoners of war could put locusts to shame,' observed Alan McKay of the march out of Falling-bostel in April. 'Once we were out,' Richard Passmore confirmed, 'we moved across the countryside like a ravaging Mongol horde', looting crops, stealing chickens, and breaking and entering buildings where food was likely to be stored. 'I suppose we were worse than Vandals, really', Albert Jones later reflected on what he saw as an absolutely necessary process. Even so bartering might still be necessary, and sometimes items that would not normally have been considered fit for animal—let alone human—consumption were ingested to try to assuage the ever-present pangs of hunger. Passmore and his friends, for instance, did not hesitate to wolf down bits of a decomposing carcass when they came across a dead horse one day.[7]

Civilians were not the only victims of theft. In conditions of extreme privation it became increasingly common for Kriegies to steal from one another as well. 'As conditions deteriorated and hunger became a reality one was forced to hide one's bread,' James Davies recalled of a march from Bankau to Luckenwalde, 'and on one occasion I witnessed a group of men, once disciplined, fighting like animals around a dump of frozen sugar beet.' In some cases an every-man-for-himself mentality might develop in which personal survival at almost any cost was the order of the day. Adrian Vincent, in a column out of Lamsdorf, found that 'the lack of food had turned men into something like wild beasts', willing to fight and rob each other for the contents of a swill-bucket or a crust of bread. Acts of charity toward others were rare, since, as Maxwell Bates bluntly put it in reference to the exodus from a Stalag IXC working camp in March 1945, 'every man cared only for himself and his syndicate'.[8]

It was under such difficult circumstances that those in charge within the Kriegie administrative hierarchy tried to maintain a semblance of moral order through a mixture of persuasion and leadership. Men who seemed intent on imposing their authority for its own sake or appeared too chummy with the enemy often got short shrift. To be a true 'man of confidence', the prisoner in question had to lead by example and force of personality. Through sheer will and character, a single sergeant major might manage to prevent a party of 150 desperate men from turning on each other, while a padre of exceptional quality, such as the Revd John Collins, could jolly along aircrew NCOs who were near the end of their tether. With long experience of coaxing occasionally truculent Kriegies as well as the German authorities, a camp leader of the calibre of Jimmy 'Dixie' Deans could continue to exert quiet influence. He constantly cycled back and forth between columns marching out of Fallingbostel in April 1945 to check on their welfare, negotiated in fluent German with the local authorities over the provision of food and shelter, and made every effort to ensure their safety. 'It was impossible not to admire Deans', a Canadian sergeant later wrote. The best senior officers, meanwhile, might instil confidence simply by being themselves. 'Occasionally he would wave his stick in the air as if he was leading a charge', a junior officer remembered of Group Captain D. E. L. Wilson as Sagan was evacuated. 'He was a half-ridiculous, half-inspiring figure and I felt better for seeing him.'[9]

The degree to which such leaders could influence the situation depended in part on the attitude of the escorts, many of whom came from the same camps and work-sites as the prisoners themselves and remained with them throughout the march. By this point most guards were old and unfit men, relatively few in number (approximately six *Posten* for every 100 POWs in the case of the columns out of Stalag Luft III), who found life on the road almost as tough as did the prisoners themselves. Coupled with the growing recognition that the total destruction of the Third Reich was imminent, this might mean that Kriegies were treated with some degree of sympathy. A blind eye might be turned when prisoners scrounged from fields and farms, the daily pace and number of rest-breaks might be set at what the prisoners themselves believed was not unreasonable, and orders to shoot to kill in the case of escapers ignored. Indeed, a hitherto unheard-of degree of tacit collaboration might develop en route, with food and burdens being shared between captives and captors. One private recalled how a group of prisoners and their guards heading away from Lamsdorf had on one occasion conspired to steal a civilian wagon in order to carry everyone's packs. Maxwell Bates, a POW since 1940, considered that the *Posten* escorting his working party in 1945 were 'remarkably good from our point of view'.[10]

By the spring of 1945, indeed, the balance of power between captors and captives was sometimes beginning to reverse itself. 'They knew the end was near,' Francis Guest wrote of the *Posten* accompanying his column away from Marlag (M) in April, 'they knew they would be "for it" if there was any kind of ill-treatment of us now.' Kriegies elsewhere were not slow to take advantage of this shift through a growing disinclination to obey enemy orders, and in some cases the escort simply gave up any semblance of imposed authority. By the time Guest and his fellows crossed the Elbe they found that the 'guards, including their officers, were now growing so polite, so positively servile . . . that we knew the end—and liberation—could not be far off'.[11]

Not all sentries, however, adapted well to changing circumstances. Kingsley Brown noted that while some of the guards from Sagan took 'a fatherly interest in our physical welfare', others displayed 'inflexible adherence to orders'. Marching from a mining camp further east, a New Zealand soldier could not help noticing that while some Germans 'did what was expected of them in a reasonable way', others 'never lost the opportunity to harass and bully us'. Prisoners who wandered from columns or campsites in search of food or shelter would do so at their peril, and in some cases guards became desperately militant rather than passively philosophical if their diminishing authority was apparently challenged in some way. An air force NCO remembered that when he and his fellows were moved out of Fallingbostel the sentries 'were edgy, ill-tempered and violent'. They still had rifles, and they could still beat or even shoot prisoners if they so chose.[12]

Robert Buckman recorded the following incident on the march from Marlag (M) in his 11 April diary entry:

We were ordered into a field about 6:30 last night. While establishing our campsite, we spotted two haystacks in the adjoining barnyard, and with thoughts of a straw mattress under our bedrolls, a half-dozen of us jumped the fence to gather hay. Suddenly a guard appeared, stepping from behind a stack, and levelling his rifle, shouted and immediately fired into the midst of our group.

In this case two of the men received bullet wounds in the leg.[13] In other instances the resort to firearms proved fatal. One Kriegie might be shot dead without warning as he ducked out to scavenge from the roadside; another could be beaten and killed for being too slow in getting to his feet one morning; and a third might be hit for being seen to accept food proffered by Czech civilians. Sometimes a prisoner could be fired upon for no discernable reason at all.[14]

Despite such occasional violence, the majority of POWs thought it better to stick with the group than duck out and strike off on their own. Many of the German farming families and villagers Kriegies encountered were now anxious to appear friendly and helpful, providing food or water free of charge as well as trading and generally behaving in a sympathetic manner. Others still remained hostile, though, and more importantly there was the knowledge that paramilitary and other Nazi forces were at large, enforcing order through terror within what remained of the Third Reich. Once on the road, it was not uncommon for Kriegies to witness the way in which SS escorts displayed no hesitation about dispatching any starving concentration camp inmates and Soviet POWs who fell by the wayside from their own columns. Indeed, there were a number of incidents in which British prisoners were murdered by passing SS men even while in column. Though escaping itself might now be comparatively easy, getting out of enemy territory seemed more hazardous, and for most men it became a case of better the devil you know. Senior figures were in a quandary about what to advise about escaping while on the march, the SBOs at Stalag Luft III and Marlag going so far as to issue orders—later rescinded—that prisoners should refrain from making breaks, given the high risk of sudden death at enemy hands.[15]

Nevertheless, some of the more impatient and restless Kriegies did eventually decide that now was the time to take matters into their own hands. Quietly ducking away from the line of march, evading the few sentries who might have been posted around campsites, or hiding out and waiting for everyone else to depart in the morning, often proved surprisingly easy. That there nevertheless did exist a real danger of being murdered if subsequently picked up is demonstrated by the reports of those who only narrowly escaped this fate. But by mid-April 1945, as guards began simply to give up and Allied forces closed in, what had hitherto been a trickle of en route escape became a small stream, most men now intent on simply hiding out for the few days it would take for their location to be overrun by friendly forces.[16]

Getting to that point, however, was an uphill struggle. Inclement weather did nothing to make the march easier for men who were soon in a state of semi-starvation. The diary of Flight Lieutenant Robert Buckman (RCAF) for 29 January 1945 records a scene that was quite typical for prisoners moving from camps in Poland and Silesia in winter:

Our line of march was revealed to us, winding to the horizon. The wind in our faces was now mingled with driving snow. From midday on we marched in below-zero temperatures. Food froze in tins. Bread snapped into granular chunks. The column trudged on throughout the endless day, covering an estimated 36 kilometres as feet froze and limping marchers became commonplace.

'The cold was intense,' a Royal Sussex private recalled, 'our boots froze solid if we took them off at night.' When billeted on farms, Kriegies came to value the relative warmth of cowsheds or even pigsties as compared to draughty barns. On those occasions where no shelter at all was available, it was often necessary not only to build a fire but also stay up all night next to it so as to avoid freezing to death in one's sleep. Temperatures dropped to minus-twelve degrees centigrade or lower still. As Harold Cole later commented, 'conditions were quite ferocious'.[17]

The weather inevitably grew milder as winter gave way to spring, but the thaw brought its own problems. Ice sleds became quite useless, and the omnipresent slush soaked through boots that were often already falling to pieces. Even when the seasons had changed completely, continued exposure to the elements might be less than pleasant. 'It's so easy to accept rain as a natural hazard,' commented I. P. B. Denton about a march from Nuremberg to Moosburg in April 1945, 'but when you are conveying everything you have in the world and become sodden in the process you also become aware that not only does water penetrate but [it] also adds considerably to the burden you are transporting.'[18]

With the German railway network overstrained and under heavy attack, relatively few prisoners were moved anywhere by train. Those who did spend time aboard cattle trucks, however, did not count themselves lucky. The wagons were freezing in winter, and men were often crammed into each one to the point where it was impossible for them to lie down. 'We were packed in like sardines,' an RAF air-gunner later wrote of a nightmare rail journey from Görlitz through Hanover, spent mostly in sidings and without the doors ever being unlocked, 'and we had to "go" where we sat and tough luck on your neighbour.' Transport of this kind was particularly hard on those hospital cases too ill to be moved from camps on foot.[19]

Not surprisingly, sickness soon began to take a serious toll on marchers. Frostbite during the winter was a constant threat, coupled then and later by widespread dysentery and other intestinal problems brought on by consuming whatever was available, no matter how rotten or filthy. Pneumonia and tuberculosis also spread, as did problems associated with malnutrition such as boils and ulcers. Sick rates of 60 to 80 per cent in columns were not unheard of. Unable to take off, much less wash, their clothes, most men soon became louse-ridden. Overwhelmed by fatigue or illness, Kriegies would suddenly buckle at the knees and keel over. 'People begin to drop out in scores,' an air force officer recorded in his diary entry for 29 January 1945, 'just sitting in the road at the wayside with a glazed look in their eyes and going to sleep where they sit.' Sometimes those too exhausted and ill to carry on were either abandoned to their fate or carried between the shoulders of slightly fitter men. In many cases prisoners who collapsed by the roadside were later picked up by carts stationed at the rear of columns, but this was not something to look forward to in the depths of winter, given the higher risk men who were not moving ran of freezing to death. 'Soon nobody wanted to ride in the cart', one sailor recalled of the march away from his Silesian Arbeitskommando. Doctors and medical orderlies did their best to help the sick, but there was little they could do without medical supplies. Having the afflicted swallow the charred detritus from campfires was one of the few means of treating dysentery. The attrition rate through illness and exhaustion therefore tended to be high. Within eighteen days of leaving Gross Tychow, at least nine men in one RAF column had died; and it was estimated that of the 1,800 Kriegies who began the march from one working-camp in Poland in January, only 1,300 were present by the time the column reached Bavaria in April.[20]

As if all this was not enough to contend with, POWs also had to worry about being bombed or strafed from the air by their own side. Attacks by Soviet aircraft whose pilots could not distinguish friend from foe were not unknown, but it was the Allied air forces that turned out to pose the most serious threat to life and limb.[21]

Marching columns of prisoners were commonly moved through the countryside, which meant they were unlikely to be caught in the kind of mass heavy-bomber raids that had already reduced most German cities to rubble. Yet prisoners were still sometimes killed by bombs falling wide of the target area, and on one occasion heavy casualties were incurred: in mid-April 1945 a large party of Kriegies on the banks of the Danube suddenly found themselves caught beneath hundreds of tonnes of USAAF bombs meant for a railway bridge and the nearby town of Regensberg. As many as 100 men who had marched all the way from Poland were left either dead or seriously wounded. 'The scene was ghastly', a sickened witness remembered.[22]

Potentially more dangerous, because they roamed everywhere in search of something to shoot up in the last month of the war, were Allied fighters and especially fighter-bombers. Efforts were made to warn pilots where prisoners were likely to be found, and Kriegies themselves might try to indicate their friendly status by laying down strips of towel and other material on the ground or even carts to spell out 'P.O.W.' Nevertheless, there were numerous cases of mistaken identity in which 'friendly' aircraft attacked moving or resting groups of prisoners behind enemy lines, sometimes with quite horrific results.

A few days before the Regensberg incident the rear of a column marching away from Westertimke was suddenly strafed by a pair of US Thunderbolts aiming at a cart. One man was killed outright, another two died shortly thereafter from injuries sustained, and a fourth was severely wounded. Three days later American fighters, whose pilots thought the khaki-clad figures below were in Hungarian uniform, spent half an hour strafing a party of officers who had just been evacuated from Eichstätt. This time seven Kriegies died outright, two more expired later the same day, and forty-five sustained serious injuries. 'Christ, it's murder', a deeply shocked Geoffrey Wright confided to his diary. Five days after that a column of aircrew NCO prisoners was bounced by a squadron of RAF Typhoons near Gresse. By the time the attack had finished several dozen men had been wounded and more lay dead—'you were passing bodies with smoke coming out of 'em', recalled Sergeant Thomas Cooksey.[23]

Eventual arrival in camps that served as de facto transit or reception centres lessened the odds of having to endure such 'friendly fire' incidents, and provided a respite from marching. At the same time, so many prisoners were coming in that facilities were often quickly strained beyond capacity. Stalag VIIIA, through which many Kriegies from Lamsdorf passed in early February, was described in a war-crimes deposition as seriously overcrowded, the barracks 'indescribably filthy' and awash with mud and water, and the heating arrangements in a state of collapse. Worst of all, rations were at the starvation level. 'It was not an unusual sight to see some prisoners poking about in the garbage pails to see if there might be anything therein worth salvaging and eating', recorded RASC Sergeant Alexander McCaskill. Air force men from Sagan coming into Stalag IIIA at about the same time found Luckenwalde already massively overcrowded—16,000 prisoners and climbing—and in a state of terminal decay. Men were jammed into huts that had earthen floors and leaky roofs, the camp latrines were awful beyond description, there was little running water, and food reserves were on the point of exhaustion. Similar, though sometimes worse, conditions prevailed inside the wire at popular destinations to the west such as Stalag 357, Stalag XIB, and Stalag VIIA. The population of Moosburg was estimated at 100,000 by mid-April, putting critical pressure on the water supply and cooking facilities. There were no Red Cross parcels at Fallingbostel by this point, and daily rations had fallen to something like one loaf between ten men along with half a pint of very thin soup. The latrines had ceased to function and there was no way of preventing the spread of lice or—medical supplies having already been exhausted—treating the sick. 'Things had more or less broken down by the time we arrived', one British Army officer remembered of Moosburg at this time, 'and it was a case of "*sauve qui peut*".'[24]

At camps like those outside Fallingbostel utter collapse was only narrowly averted through the nick-of-time arrival of convoys of ICRC trucks carrying vital Red Cross supplies from neutral territory. 'Just as the situation was really desperate for us a miracle happened', Robert Gale later wrote of the situation at Stalag XIB. 'A fleet of huge white lorries marked with the Red Cross emblem drew up outside the camp and were admitted.' The so-called White Angels also provided very welcome aid to men on the march. As with camp visits, though, road encounters were irregular and the supply chain necessarily erratic, given the poor state of the roads and communications, a finite number of trucks, and constant uncertainty about where prisoners were at any particular moment.[25]

By the spring privation existed everywhere, but by happy accident of geographical location there were a few camps where the inhabitants did not have to endure the rigours of the march. In the east there had been working-camps that were overrun by the Red Army before they could be evacuated. Further west and to the south there remained a few main camps that were distant enough from the main lines of advance for the order to evacuate to arrive too late—or in other words, at a point in April–May where the commandant was more concerned about possible reprisals being meted out by the enemy on the doorstep than about the reaction of OKW and the Gestapo to a refusal to obey orders.

When such instructions arrived at Stalag Luft I, USAAF Colonel Hubert Zemke, the senior Allied representative, persuaded the commandant to cable OKW to report that the prisoners at Barth refused to move and he did not have the personnel to force them to flee the Soviet advance. Shortly before this Colonel W. D. E. Brown had flatly refused to go along with an evacuation order when it was clear the Americans were within a few days of liberating Oflag 79. 'The SBO, we heard afterward,' Sandy St Clair reported, 'had told the Commandant we had a radio transmitter in the camp, and that if he made us move he would radio London to treat the Commandant as a war criminal.'[26]

The outcome was similar at Colditz. In the second week of April the Senior British Officer had been unable to prevent the evacuation of the Prominente under SS guard, because the commandant had received the order from Himmler and feared that any attempt to derail the departure would result in an immediate SS assault on the castle. A couple of days after the Prominente left, however, by which time shellfire could be heard and occasionally seen, Oberst Prawitt eventually gave in when Lieutenant-Colonel Tod and other senior representatives flatly refused to go along with an OKW order to evacuate the camp in its entirety. It was agreed that the inhabitants of Oflag IVC would remain where they were until the Americans arrived, with sentries only mounting guard as a means of disguising from SS troops in the town below the fact that the roles of captor and captive had been reversed inside the Schloss.[27]

Elsewhere, whether in the open or once again behind barbed wire, a fairly common precursor to liberation in the last two weeks of the war was the sudden disappearance or surrender of the escorts and sentries a few hours or days before friendly forces hove into view. 'May 1945 dawned and we were still marching,' one private heading west from a mining camp later recorded, 'but the next day the guards told us to go home—just like that—with a wave of their arms in the direction of England... [They then] formed up into a company and marched off.' More usually prisoners woke up one morning to find that some or all of the enemy personnel had vanished during the night. Those who remained, officers included, might need little or no persuading to be convinced that it was in their interest to exchange places with their charges. 'One morning the German guards, Kommandant and all, marched up to us, stood rigidly to attention and asked us to take them over', John Brown wrote of the surrender inside Stalag 383. The hope of those involved was that, already disarmed and in Kriegie hands, those wearing German uniform would run far less risk of being killed by advancing troops than if they were still bearing arms and manning posts when contact occurred. As C. N. S. Campbell later noted with reference to the sudden handing over of rifles by the guards in charge of a large RAF party outside Lübeck on 2 May, amidst rumours of a British Army scout-car sighting, this 'was obviously so that when the British troops appeared the German themselves would be prisoners and there would be no likelihood of them being shot'.[28]

Amidst rumours of nearby friendly forces, columns and camps, Colditz included, might start to seethe with repressed excitement. However, the actual moment of liberation—heralded by the arrival of American, British, or Russian reconnaissance parties—produced mixed reactions.[29]

Some prisoners maintained their *sang froid* to the end. When US tanks crashed the gates at Moosburg on 29 April 1945, Tony Strachen noticed that his army officer hutmates, many POWs since 1940, continued to recline on their bunks reading as if nothing much was happening. 'Finally,' he related, 'one of them put aside his copy of Plato. "I suppose," he murmured, "that we're technically free."' Other prisoners were genuinely puzzled to discover that the arrival of friendly forces seemed oddly unreal or left them curiously flat. 'It was surprising how calmly our liberation was received', Jack Bishop wrote of the naval officers and ratings he was with in a former barracks near Lübeck on the day the British Army arrived. 'There was complete silence, as if the situation was beyond our comprehension.' Other suddenly free men recorded a similar lack of demonstrative acknowledgement elsewhere. 'There was no wild cheering or anything like that', H. S. Bowers wrote of the point at which American troops drove into view and freed his party on the road in Bavaria. 'It was an event that for years had seemed so impossible and remote that, when it happened, we couldn't believe it.' An RAF officer whose party was liberated with a mere 'shrug of the shoulders' on an estate in the Lübeck area reached a similar conclusion. 'I think', C. N. S. Campbell reflected in his diary at the end of the second day of May 1945, 'we were a little afraid as to whether it had actually happened.'[30]

Inside the wire in particular, however, most Kriegies reacted to the appearance of friendly troops with spontaneous enthusiasm, bordering at times on hysteria. The reaction to the arrival of the first US Army jeep at Oflag 79 on the morning of 12 April was recorded vividly in the YMCA logbook of Captain G. W. Smith:

There was a sudden deathly silence—then a murmur, a shout, a cheer, then a stampede towards the main gate where a large crowd of us collected: cheering, laughing, crying in our excitement... We were free! In a flash the gate was open, and as they drove in they were mobbed by an ever-increasing crowd of officers and men, who, in their show of emotion, shook the Yanks by the hand, smacked them on the back, [and] hugged them...

'For the next hour everything was chaos and jubilation!' Sandy St Clair later confirmed. 'Prisoners dashing meaninglessly in all directions; some of us weeping, laughing, shouting, and slapping each other on the back.' The result was almost identical when a mounted Red Army patrol entered Stalag IVB eleven days later. 'The barrack, when I walked back into it from the compound,' Geoff Taylor recalled after witnessing the wild cheering that greeted the event, 'was a tumultuous, laughing riot of back-slapping and hand-shaking.' What was described as a 'yelling, maddened throng' greeted the first US Sherman tank and jeep to arrive at Moosburg on 29 April. 'I have sworn to keep calm', Geoffrey Wright, captured back in 1940, noted in his diary. But when the moment arrived he found officer-like composure impossible. 'I get up, I start to walk, I start to run, I nearly fall down a trench and break my blasted neck... I let out a strangled yell—I am yelling and roaring and waving my arms—so much for my resolution.' Similar scenes were played out across Germany as British POWs were overrun, not least when the liberators turned out to be British themselves. Robert Buckman noted down in his diary the reactions he observed in a transit camp outside Lübeck occupied by RAF prisoners when armoured vehicles rolled up on 2 May and a tank crewman dressed in a familiar shade of khaki opened up his turret hatch and waved: 'A roar of cheers; crudely made flags waving; laughter and tears mingling; men climbing the wire to run to the tanks; men embracing each other, shouting incoherently; men kneeling to pray... thousands of men in a state of blessed, hysterical relief.'[31]

When the first GI walked into the prisoners' courtyard at Colditz on 16 April 1945 he was received with similar effusiveness. 'A great cheer went up,' Hugh Bruce remembered, 'and the bewildered and uneasy soldier stepped back as the jubilant crowd surged forward to embrace him.' He and those who followed were given an 'ecstatic welcome', according to Corran Purdon, their presence tangible confirmation that the castle inmates were no longer in danger of being moved or done away with. Though at least one British prisoner later thought that it had been the American ex-POWs who did most of the back-slapping and hugging, there was little doubt that for British as well as American inmates the moment was one of considerable emotion. As Hugo Ironside explained to an interviewer decades later, the liberation of Oflag IVC 'was one of the highlights of my life, as you can imagine'.[32]

The liberators themselves often left an enduring impression on men cut off—often for upwards of five years—from first-hand experience of the evolving outside world. Whether Russian, American, or even British, the soldiers with whom Kriegies came into contact were undoubtedly different from anyone they had met for a long time.

Ex-prisoners were often unnerved by the sometimes rather motley appearance and often extremely ruthless as well as reckless behaviour of Soviet troops, and struck by the presence of armed women soldiers. The men seemed to be highly undisciplined, firing their machine guns into the air with abandon, often appearing drunk, and blatantly lacking any scruples whatsoever about looting and raping their way through the German countryside: 'like brigands', as one inhabitant of Stalag IVB put it. Senior officers at Luckenwalde were startled by an on-the-spot suggestion that newly liberated RAF prisoners pick up some weapons join the Red Army advance on Berlin.[33]

Just as shocking, albeit for somewhat different reasons, were first encounters with men of the US Army. 'I noticed a striking contrast between the strong, healthy, dusty, tanned faces of the GIs,' John Watton noted at Colditz, and the 'pale pink, bony' faces of his liberated comrades. British ex-prisoners were in general surprised by the friendliness and largesse of GIs, who seemed to have an unending supply of goodies to distribute. 'They were something else, those Yanks', Ed Annetts remembered of the American soldiers he met after the farm in which he was hiding was overrun. 'After the years of austerity to which we and the Germans had become accustomed, these garrulous, confident, super blokes seemed to have everything. They were like an enormous, bottomless Red Cross Christmas parcel and they shared their bounty with a generosity beyond belief.' 'Their friendliness and generosity were overwhelming', agreed Ike Rosmarin, liberated at Stalag XIIIC; though as one British private put it, 'the way they threw their cigarettes away only half smoked seemed sacrilegious to us'.[34]

Even British troops might appear quite odd to men who remembered the BEF and had not seen a free British Army soldier in a very long time. Unfamiliar vehicles festooned with equipment of a type and on a scale unknown in 1940, men with odd-looking berets and jacket sleeves covered in divisional and other flashes, and the confidence of troops who knew they were fighting their way to victory could be disorienting. Robert Gale recalled how at Fallingbostel he had been struck by how 'gigantic' the liberating tanks of the 8th Hussars had seemed, and how startled he had been by the contrast between their crews and the POWs. 'Suddenly [a tank] stopped,' Gale wrote, 'and a soldier appeared from the conning tower—such a man as I had never seen before—a superman with bronzed face, flashing white teeth and sparkling eyes.' It took him a moment to realize that he had not seen a truly healthy man in years.[35]

One of the first consequences for former captives of being taken under the wing of friendly forces was the opportunity to turn the tables on their erstwhile captors. After years of deprivation, fear, and occasional brutality, at least some British ex-prisoners were keen to exact a degree of revenge. 'The Germans had made us suffer,' as Leonard Beard put it, 'now it was *their* turn.' Micky Wynn, having escaped from Colditz by faking a medical condition in 1944, proved eager to be at the forefront of liberating forces in the north because, as he later put it, 'I wanted to get my own back' against a hated security officer at Marlag. Men in this frame of mind might shed few tears if former guards and local civilians were abused or even killed by liberating troops. When the Red Army arrived at Mühlberg and two of the remaining guards emerged from hiding with their hands up, they were immediately gunned down—'and this was something that nobody cared one bit about at the time', RAF wireless operator Wilfred Hart reflected, going on to emphasize in an interview that 'we weren't sorry for the Germans in any way'. GIs made it clear that they would execute, no questions asked, anyone deemed by ex-Kriegies to have committed a war crime. At Moosburg this resulted in the execution of a *Posten* who had shot a prisoner during the recent march, and there were several other recorded instances where, as J. H. Witte put it, guards 'were summarily executed by Americans merely on the words of ex-P.O.W.s who had a grudge'. British troops were also willing to impose retribution on any German deemed by a former captive to have maltreated prisoners in the past. When Westertimke was overrun, Flying Officer Robin Thomas recalled how an ex-guard, fingered as having earlier killed a prisoner in cold blood, 'was summarily dealt with by being escorted on a one way trip into the woods by a couple of our liberators'. When Ron Buckingham tracked down a notably vicious Feldwebel in a holding cage, he was told to 'do what you like' by the officer in charge and immediately offered a revolver by the provost sergeant. At Colditz itself several officers, in contravention of orders, managed to join the GIs who were still clearing the surrounding area.

This was a way of expressing long-pent-up frustrations, and it worked: 'It certainly made the two of us feel good', reported Corran Purdon on his own and Dick Morgan's reactions.[36]

Many ex-prisoners, though, were taken aback by the violent way in which fighting troops and sometimes ex-Kriegies could treat helpless Germans. It was one thing to glean satisfaction from seeing the shoe on the other foot, and even to hit former guards who refused to obey orders; but it was quite another to revel in men being gunned down or women being raped. Some were horrified by American behaviour at Moosburg and elsewhere, and others actively sought to avoid giving GIs with itchy trigger-fingers any excuse to bump off a German. At Colditz, where women were raped and the surrendered castle staff treated none too gently, David Walker had to explain quickly that when he said he wanted to 'take care of' the popular Püpke—'You wanna take care of a Kraut officer? Hell, Scottie, we'll do that, a real pleasure'—he did *not* mean he wanted the Hauptmann killed. A disgusted US soldier called the inhabitants of a liberated other-rank camp 'chicken-livered sons of bitches' because they refused to give him the go-ahead to do away with the guards (Q: 'How have these sons of bitches been to you?' A: 'Oh, they're all right'). Ron Buckingham himself found he did not have the stomach to use the gun offered to him, and evidently felt slightly ashamed after he allowed the subject of his rage to be menaced by the sergeant—'We're going to take him round the back. Coming?'—and given a hard punch by a provost corporal. A Methodist chaplain was struck by the way in which members of his RAF party, marching from Westertimke to the Lübeck area, ended up shielding their former captors on the day of liberation from the wrath of the British Army. 'That evening R.A.S.C. men, fresh from Belsen's relief, came up,' Douglas Thompson wrote, 'and it took all our ingenuity to protect our guards from them. We found our sympathies all tied in knots, for some of these aged Marines who guarded us had become friends.'[37]

Paradoxically, another consequence of liberation involved placing limits on the freedom enjoyed by ex-Kriegies. Supreme Headquarters Allied Expeditionary Forces (SHAEF) wanted to keep prisoners where they were found so they could be fitted into a comprehensive repatriation-and-interrogation plan administered by a special section devoted to ex-Kriegies (PWX) and kept out of trouble. 'Generally speaking,' opined A. J. Evans in his role as a PWX advance man within 21st Army Group, 'prisoners of war are not fit to be given uncontrolled liberty—certainly not during the intense excitement which follows the liberation of a camp.' It was the fear that an intoxicating sensation of freedom would go to the heads of ex-POWs, causing them to wander off on their own and behave like irresponsible individuals rather than trained servicemen awaiting due processing, that led to the issuing of secret instructions to camp leaders to the effect that they should make preparations to reimpose military discipline as soon as an enemy collapse created a power vacuum behind the wire.[38]

Having begun to make secret contingency preparations to take over and defend camps if push came to shove with the enemy, SBOs and other senior figures in the last weeks of the war also developed scenarios for a peaceful transfer of power. After the Lager authorities had disappeared or surrendered, the task of administering the camp would be taken on by the Kriegie hierarchy, which would, among other things, deploy a security force to maintain order and stability. 'The last thing the committee [of senior POW representatives led by RSM Lord at Stalag XIB] wanted', Robert Gale recorded, 'was for the prisoners to get out of the Stalag and roam about the district causing havoc while the British army advanced and they certainly did not want any local Nazi Party Leaders getting into the camp to hide in British or Russian uniforms.'[39]

In some cases, soon-to-be or newly minted ex-Kriegies were pointedly reminded that they were still wearing the King's uniform. 'Our officers had warned us days before that from the moment we were liberated we should be "back in the Navy"', Marine Francis Guest recalled, 'and that there was to be no looting, no rape, no rioting, nor even drunkenness.' In case anyone had missed the message, the day the British Army arrived 'the Senior British Officer addressed us', remembered submariner Jack Bishop, 'and informed us that we were no longer prisoners of war and henceforth would be subject to the Naval Discipline Act.' Similarly, the night before the Americans liberated Colditz, the SBO issued a directive stating that King's Regulations would be enforced from the next day forward. 'Extraordinary how [camp discipline] changed,' Montagu Champion Jones reflected on the way in which, after the arrival of the first few GIs in the castle courtyard the following morning, military protocol had to be fully observed: 'that day we went back to calling each other "Sir" and that sort of thing.' Colonel Tod was adamant that his orders be obeyed. 'Nobody was to leave the camp until he gave the all clear', Jim Rogers explained. 'When we were allowed out we were to behave ourselves.'[40]

Especially at first, some ex-prisoners were heartened by such authoritative pronouncements. 'We were very lost in new found freedom and were looking round for someone to tell us what to do next', Graham Palmer remembered of the initial position at Fallingbostel. Philip Kindersley thought that the first order to stay inside the wire at Brunswick was not unwelcome. 'Most of us were so dazed that that we had no desire to go out', he later wrote. But there were others who did not take kindly to being ordered about in best military style from the start, and their numbers grew with each passing day. 'At present it is much more trying being a prisoner of the British than a prisoner of the Germans', Geoffrey Wright angrily complained in his diary five days after Moosburg was liberated, 'and I have just about had enough of these British bureaucrats who will not allow a British officer out of the camp . . . ' It was difficult to accept that going beyond the hated wire could be potentially problematic. 'We have been liberated,' as Robert Buckman glumly put it the day after the arrival of British troops at Lübeck, 'but we are not yet free.'[41]

In practice, the 'stay put' policy proved impossible to implement and enforce throughout Germany. Orders to remain *in situ* did not reach all those who were overrun while still on the march or, for that matter, every camp before VE day. After the first friendly troops had passed through them, columns of liberated men might find themselves living much as they had done previously—roaming the countryside in order to obtain food—while awaiting follow-on support. The pressing need to keep body and soul together in the absence of well-organized logistical arrangements on the part of liberating forces—a particular problem where the Red Army was concerned—meant that it was impossible for many camp leaders to do without authorizing a certain amount of forced requisitioning of local civilian resources. What was more, front-line troops did not always see the need for men to continue to be kept behind wire, and could on occasion surreptitiously or openly undermine SBO instructions. Against orders, the Scottish soldiers stationed in the vicinity of Stalag 357 (following the departure of the 8th Hussars) allowed prisoners in and out of the camp through holes the former Kriegies had made in the fences. Meanwhile, at Stalag IVB a succession of visiting senior Red Army officers undermined efforts by the British camp authorities to maintain order and keep ex-Kriegies inside the wire. 'Men who have been prisoners have the right to move freely now', a visiting Russian officer apparently stated, after ordering that camp police be removed from the gates several days after Mühlberg was liberated: 'they do not wish to be guarded by their own comrades.'[42]

This was certainly true, judging by the fairly large number of men who either never received or simply ignored instructions to remain where they were in the aftermath of liberation and went out touring the villages and towns in the vicinity. 'Prisoners of war, as soon as they are liberated,' as A. J. Evans censoriously observed after visiting Marlag, Stalag Luft I, and Stalag IIA, 'cannot resist the urge to commandeer any vehicle they find, and drive it round the countryside.' Joyriding about in abandoned enemy cars, motorcycles, and lorries, with fuel supplied by passing friendly troops, was sometimes an end in itself; but newfound freedom also offered the opportunity to acquire things without paying for them. 'I suggested to Tom that now we were free,' H. E. Trinder wrote candidly of a conversation with his mate after running into US troops in the field in March 1945, 'we should get some transport, a German car or light truck, go into towns after they had been taken by the Americans and have a good loot.' Pigs, chickens, rabbits, eggs, beer, wine, and other consumables were often uppermost in men's minds when they set out, but a vast range of souvenirs—everything from cuckoo-clocks to machine-pistols—were also picked up. What amounted to a form of kleptomania in abandoned homes seems to have been fairly widespread in the open and in the vicinity of camps where authority was not asserted firmly from the start: though the drive-and-collect stages were sometimes reversed. 'The usual thing that happened was that the men helped themselves to the things they fancied and then looked for some kind of vehicle on which to fetch them back to the camp', Robert Garioch wrote of the post-liberation days at Moosburg. 'They came on bicycles and motor cycles, or pushing handcarts or milk delivery barrows.' Nor was this behaviour confined to other ranks. Officer ex-prisoners at Oflag 79 commandeered cars and drove about extorting food and other desired items from local farms ('the bloated German farmers produced their goods without any argument', commented Philip Kindersley), in addition to liberating the wine cellars in Brunswick.[43]

Even at Colditz, certain officers seemed determined to play hard now that the war was over. 'Oh, it was great,' Dominic Bruce remembered of the day after the castle was overrun, 'it was pure wild west, and we all got guns and went off and liberated chickens and bottles of wine which had been suffering under Hitler. Had a great time.'[44]

In many places, to be sure, service discipline was successfully imposed through the acquiescence of the majority of ex-POWs from the day of liberation onward; though not always without a certain amount of privately expressed irritation. 'One naturally resents it,' Major A. T. Casdagli confided to his diary at Oflag XIIB, 'however, it keeps the brigadiers amused.' It was recognized that preventing newly liberated prisoners from rampaging about was not unreasonable, given the need to keep tabs on the population, the risk of setting off booby traps, and the high likelihood of road accidents. The drivers, after all, were men who had not been behind the wheel in years and who might easily forget that on the Continent people drove on the right.

Unfortunately not all of the orders issued by ranking figures were quite so sensible. 'Small wonder that some senior officers, who had had no opportunity to exercise a wholly independent judgement for years, made some mistaken decisions at the crisis of liberation', the historians of MI9 explained.[45] Not everything went smoothly at Colditz, for example. Jim Rogers was aghast to find himself brusquely ordered by the senior officer of engineers to clear the mines below the castle the morning after the Americans arrived at Oflag IVC:

I said, 'The Germans put them in. Let the Germans take them out.' The reply was that, according to the Geneva Convention, prisoners of war cannot be put in a position of danger. I then suggested that a herd of goats be driven through the minefield. This suggestion was dismissed, because meat and dairy products were in short supply. And what about me? I asked. Was I less than a German goat? The officer looked at me with a stony stare. Then I flew in the face of discipline and said: 'I'm beggared if I'm going through five years of war and end up blown to pieces in a bloody minefield.'

Under threat of arrest and court martial, the mining engineer finally acquiesced and, with invaluable advice from Jock Hamilton-Baillie, worked out how to disarm the mines and started doing so; only to be interrupted by another senior sapper who insisted—again on pain of arrest and court martial—that he go to work on what was thought to be a booby-trap in one of the guardrooms. To his credit, when Colonel Tod finally learned what was happening he immediately put a stop to it. 'I only wish I had gone to him in the first place', Rogers reflected in his memoirs.[46]

Meanwhile, with repatriation looming, ex-prisoners might begin to speculate about life outside the wire. Going home was something that every Kriegie had dreamed about from the day of capture, but now that it was about to become a reality some of the more thoughtful types were inwardly a little worried. 'After three and a half years how would I cope when forced to deal once again with handling money, buying train tickets, ordering a meal in a restaurant, conversing with members of the opposite sex?' Canadian pilot Herbert Woolley recalled himself wondering inside Fallingbostel. 'The prospect was terrifying!' Ike Rosmarin felt much the same in the aftermath of the liberation of

Hammelburg. 'I was so used to the p.o.w. existence that I actually found myself scared to leave', he later admitted. 'It is difficult to explain, but possibly I was frightened of the future.' Roger Mortimer found himself similarly anxious at Oflag 79. 'The artificial life we laboriously built up over five years has collapsed', he privately confided to Tony Strachen. 'I'm *dreading* going home.'[47]

In Colditz too there were signs of uneasiness. Life inside the castle had become familiar, and some officers showed signs of what Hugh Bruce described as 'mild anxiety' about the future. Indicative of this rarely articulated concern about what freedom might bring was the fact that, when a group of officers was allowed down into the town after the Americans arrived, several of them found themselves ill at ease and almost eager to go back inside the Schloss. 'The castle had become a habit with them', Michael Burn explained in his semi-fictional account of life at Oflag IVC. 'They knew it, and they were afraid of going places they did not know.' Here as elsewhere, there were question-marks hanging over the journey home. How would wives and families seem after years in the bag? What would life in the open world be like for men who had been away from it for so long?[48]

Notes

1. M. R. D. Foot and J. M. Langley, *MI9* (London, 1979), 290–1.
2. IWM (Rolf), H. S. Bowers, 18.
3. See John Nichol and Tony Rennell, *The Last Escape* (London, 2002).
4. Percy Wilson Carruthers, *Of Ploughs, Planes and Palliasses* (Arundel, 1992), 200; Jack Bishop, *In Pursuit of Freedom* (London, 1977), 120; Geoffrey Willatt, *Bombs and Barbed Wire* (Tunbridge Wells, 1995), 93.
5. Frank Taylor, *Barbed Wire and Footlights* (Braunton, 1988), 108; Martin Smith, *What a Bloody Arrival* (Lewes, 1997), 133; IWMSA 11337/5, H. Bracken.
6. http://www.pegasus-one.org/pow/jack_bird.htm, J. Bird, 9–10; see Desmond Hawkins (ed.), *War Report* (London, 1946), 368; http://www.naval-history.net/WW2/MemoirAndSo10.htm, H. Siddall, 2–3, 6.
7. IWMSA 13573/4, A. Jones; Richard Passmore, *Moving Tent* (London, 1982), 217, 221–3; Alan Mackay, *313 Days to Christmas* (Glendaruel, 1998), 129.
8. Maxwell Bates, *A Wilderness of Days* (Victoria, BC, 1978), 97; James Arthur Davies, *A Leap in the Dark* (London, 1994), 144; Adrian Vincent, *The Long Road Home* (London, 1956), 175.
9. Robert Kee, *A Crowd Is Not Company* (London, 1982 edn.), 205; Andrew B. Cox, *Our Spirit Unbroken* (Port Elgin, Ont., 1999), 107, also 104. On Canon Collins see Davies, op. cit., 144–5. On the British Army sergeant-major see Roger V. Coward, *Sailors in Cages* (London, 1967), 229–33.

10. Bates, op. cit., 93. On the wagon-stealing incident see Stedman, op. cit., 27. On ignoring orders to shoot to kill see e.g. Johnson, op. cit., 175–6. On guards allowing an easy pace see e.g. IWMSA 5131/3, R. Buckingham. On looking the other way when scrounging see e.g. PRO, AIR 40/ 2300, p. 3. On sharing burdens and rations see e.g. IWM, C. N. S. Campbell, 39.

11. James Spenser, *The Awkward Marine* (London, 1948), 286–7, 271.

12. Mackay, op. cit., 128; Peter Winter, *Free Lodgings* (Auckland, 1993), 126; Kingsley Brown, *Bonds of Wire* (Toronto, 1989), 198.

13. Robert Buckman, *Forced March to Freedom* (Stittsville, Ont., 1984), 60; see IWM, C. N. S. Campbell, 35.

14. On unprovoked shooting see e.g. IWM, N. R. Wylie, Report of Itinerary Completed by British Prisoners of War from Marienburg, Stalag XXB, 2 May 1945, p. 2.

15. On orders against escape see Foot and Langley, op. cit., 294. On the dilemma faced by authority figures see IWM, H. C. F. Harwood, 126. On deciding that making a break was too dangerous see e.g. IWM, T. Tateson, 60. On shooting incidents see e.g. IWM (Rolf), W. Southern, 5. On hostile civilians see e.g. IWM, I. P. B. Denton, 82. On friendly civilians see e.g. K. Brown, op. cit., 197–8.

16. On the comparative ease with which this could be accomplished see e.g. R. G. M. Quarrie, *Oflag* (Durham, 1995), 106–8. On close calls while on the run or hiding out see e.g. WO 208/3326, MI9/S/PG(G)2977, pp. 6–8.

17. IWMSA 15558/4, H. Cole; IWM, D. Swift, 77; Buckman, op. cit., 20.

18. IWM, I. P. B. Denton, 78.

19. Bill Jackson, *The Lone Survivor* (North Battleford, Sask., 1993), 192.

20. http://www.naval-history.net/WW2MemoirAndSo10.htm, H. Siddall, 2 ('Soon nobody wanted to ride . . .'); Willatt, op. cit., 102 ('People began to drop out . . .'). The attrition figures are from IWM, A. Scales, 16 Apr. 1945, 1; Victor F. Gammon, *Not All Glory!* (London, 1996), 201. On the charcoal remedy see James B. Chutter, *Captivity Captive* (London, 1954), 216. On 60–80% sick rates see IWM (Books), Sir Harold Satow, *The Work of the Prisoners of War Department During the Second World War* (Foreign Office, 1950), 31. On British medical staff doing their best see e.g. Stedman, op. cit., 26. On being unable to change or wash see e.g. IWM, D. Swift, 86. On lice see e.g. IWM, H. E. Trinder, 13. On malnutrition see e.g. H. E. Woolley, *No Time Off for Good Behaviour* (Burnstown, Ont., 1990), 158. On pneumonia see e.g. Carruthers, op. cit., 210. On dysentery see e.g. A. Robert Prouse, *Ticket to Hell Via Dieppe* (Toronto, 1982), 143. On frostbite see e.g. Albert Paice and Alwyn Ward, *For the Love of Elizabeth* (privately printed, 1984), 41

21. On Soviet air attacks see e.g. IWM (Rolf), D. B. Palmer, 18.

22. IWM, A. Scales, 3; see IWM (Rolf), T. Hughes, 10; id., R. L. Maggs, 6; Vincent, op. cit., 187–8.

23. IWMSA 15246/4, T. Cooksey; IWM, G. B. Wright diary, 14 Apr. 1945. On the strafing outside Eichstätt see e.g. IWMSA 4847/3, C. L. Irwin; http:// web.mala.bc.ca/davies/letters.images/stokes/collection.page.htm, D. Stokes

diary, 19 Apr. 1945. On the strafing near Westertimke see PRO, WO 208/3270, Report on transfer of Marlag . . . to Lübeck, 7; Harvie, op. cit., 212–13.

24. Jane Torday (ed.), *The Coldstreamer and the Canary* (Langley, 1995), 158; PRO, WO 309/931, Affidavit of A. McCaskill, 3. On Fallingbostel see e.g. Robert Gale, *Private Prisoner* (Wellingborough, 1984), 178. On Luckenwalde see e.g. IWM (Rolf), F. East, 4–5.

25. Gale, op. cit., 79. On the timely arrival of 'White Angels' see e.g. Moreton, op. cit., 227, 229, 324; IWM, A. Scales, 16 Apr. 1945, 10.

26. Sandy St Clair, *The Endless War* (North Battleford, Sask., 1987), 246; see Hubert Zemke, *Zemke's Stalag* (Washington, DC, 1991), 75–6.

27. Henry Chancellor, *Colditz* (London, 2001), 353, 372–3. On the flight of the Prominente, which ended without loss of life in northern Italy, see ibid., ch. 18; PRO, WO 32/11110, encl. 174B.

28. IWM, C. N. S. Campbell, 36; John Brown, *In Durance Vile* (London, 1981), 139; IWM, D. Swift, 92. On guards vanishing on the road see e.g. IWM (Rolf), R. S. Kerridge, 17. On guards disappearing from camps see e.g. IWM, O. Dover, 26. For guards surrendering to POWs on the road see e.g. Donald Edgar, *The Stalag Men* (London, 1982), 190. For staff surrendering to POWs in camps see e.g. IWMSA 11277/2, T. H. Wilson.

29. On the excitement of anticipation see e.g. IWM, G. F. Warsop, 221. On tension and excitement at Colditz, where prisoners had a bird's-eye view of the battle between advancing US troops and the SS and Hitler Youth defending the town below, see e.g. CSVA 13, J. Hoggard.

30. IWM, C. N. S. Campbell diary, 2 May 1945; Bishop, op. cit., 123; IWM, J. S. Bowers, 20; Tony Strachen (ed.), *In the Clutch of Circumstance* (Victoria, BC, 1985), 78.

31. Buckman, op. cit., 92; IWM, G. B. Wright diary 29 Apr. 1945; Geoff Taylor, *Piece of Cake* (London, 1980 edn.), 291; St Clair, op. cit., 248; IWM, G. W. Smith, 48.

32. CSVA 11, H. Ironside; Corran Purdon, *List the Bugle* (Antrim, 1993), 61; LC, POW item 12, Hugh Bruce, 'Lingering Thoughts', 5.

33. Rolf, op. cit., 175. On the offer at Luckenwalde see e.g. Russell Margerison, *Boys at War* (Bolton, 1986), 182. On Red Army hooliganism see e.g. CMAC, RAMC 1787, A. V. Tennuci, 43. On noticing women in the Red Army see e.g. IWMSA 15587/4, E. Boyd.

34. IWM, D. Swift, 96; Ike Rosmarin, *Inside Story* (Cape Town, 1990), 95; Ed Annetts, *Campaign Without Medals* (Lewes, 1990), 186; John Watton, 'Goodbye Colditz', in R. Eggers (comp.), J. Watton (ed.), *Colditz Recaptured* (London, 1973), 174.

35. Gale, op. cit., 181.

36. IWMSA 17896/3, W. C. Purdon (see also Kenneth Sanford, *Mark of the Lion* (New York, 1953), 251); IWMSA 5831/3, R. Buckingham; R. Thomas, op. cit., 289; IWM, J. H. Witte, 201; IWMSA 15113/2, W. Hart; id. 9721/2, Lord Newborough (see Henry Chancellor, *Colditz* (London, 2001), 383–4); IWM (Rolf), L. Beard, 19.

37. Douglas Thompson, *Captives to Freedom* (London, 1955), 186 (see also Harvie, op. cit., 223–4); IWMSA 5831/3, R. Buckingham; J. Elworthy in David McGill, *P.O.W.* (Naenae, NZ, 1987), 136; David Walker, *Lean, Wind Lean* (London, 1984), 172–3, 180. On disgust at the rapes occurring in Colditz town see IWMSA 4816/9, J. M. Moran. On Colditz guards being roughed up by the Americans see Reinhold Eggers, 'The Other Side of the Fence', in *Colditz Recaptured*, 198. On outrage at US behaviour at Moosburg see IWM, I. P. B. Denton, 90–1. On being rather shocked by the willingness of front-line British troops to rough up or kill Germans see e.g. David Rolf, *Prisoners of the Reich* (London, 1988), 171. On satisfaction at seeing the shoe on the other foot see e.g. J. Brown, 139. On striking uncooperative former guards see e.g. Moreton, op. cit., 239. On disapproval of ex-Kriegies bullying helpless former guards see e.g. IWM, D. Swift, 93. On drawing the line at lynching see e.g. Eric Fearnside, *The Joy of Freedom* (Burton-in-Kendal, 1996), 80. On later regret at allowing vengeful feelings to dictate actions at this point see IWM, H. E. Trinder, 27.

38. A. J. Evans, *Escape and Liberation, 1940–1945* (London, 1945), 161. On the SHAEF plan see W. Wynne Mason, *Prisoners of War* (Wellington, 1954), 471.

39. Gale, op. cit., 180. On defence planning, see e.g. in reference to Oflag IVC, Jim Rogers, *Tunnelling Into Colditz* (London, 1986), 183–4; in reference to Oflag 79, Leslie Le Souef, *To War Without a Gun* (Perth, WA, 1980), 332–3. On the transfer of power see e.g. C. Wilmot in Hawkins, op. cit., 371 (Stalag 357); Fancy, op. cit., 191 (Fallingbostel); IWM (Rolf), W. J. Sudworth, 18 (Moosburg); Roland Gant, *How Like a Wilderness* (London, 1946), 117–18 (Mühlberg); G. Taylor, op. cit., 293 (Mühlberg); Edward Lanchbery, *Against the Sun* (London, 1955), 198–9 (Luckenwalde); Cox, op. cit., 116; Keyter, op. cit., 287, 289 (Barth).

40. Rogers, op. cit., 192; IWMSA 9893/6, M. Champion Jones; Bishop, op. cit., 123; Spenser, op. cit., 295.

41. Buckman, op. cit., 93; IWM, G. B. Wright, diary 2 May 1945; Philip Kindersley, *For You the War Is Over* (Tunbridge Wells, 1983), 182; Graham Palmer, *Prisoner of Death* (Wellingborough, 1990), 195; John A. Vietor, *Time Out* (New York, 1951), 163.

42. Gant, op. cit., 124–5, 121; IWMSA 4767/6, J. Greenwood. On authorized foraging see e.g. Le Souef, op. cit., 353; Margarison, op. cit., 183–4; St Clair, op. cit., 250.

43. Kindersley, op. cit., 182; Robert Garioch, *Two Men and a Blanket* (Edinburgh, 1975), 179; IWM, H. E. Trinder, 27; Evans, op. cit., 178.

44. BBC, T60/9/1, transcript of F. Gilland interview with D. Bruce, 17 Apr. 1973.

45. Foot and langly, op. cit., 294; IWM, A. T. Casdagli diary, 29 Mar. 1945. On road accidents see e.g. Francis S. Jones, *Escape to Nowhere* (London, 1952), 193.

46. Rogers, op. cit., 194–6. Conversely, an ex-orderly at Colditz recalled that 'There was no fuss . . . there was no ordering about . . . You were on your own to do as you pleased'. Edwin L. Robinson, *We Fell On Stony Ground* (Lewes,

1998), 113. On bad orders issued by senior men elsewhere see e.g. Rolf, op. cit., 172.

47. Strachen, op. cit., 78; Rosmarin, op. cit., 96; Woolley, op. cit., 179–80.

48. Michael Burn, *Yes, Farewell* (London, 1946), 365–6, 368; LC, POW item 12, Hugh Bruce, 'Lingering Thoughts', 5; see John Chrisp, *The Tunnellers of Sandborstal* (London, 1959), 171–2; IWMSA 4816/9, J. M. Moran.

12 Repatriation and Adjustment

> [T]he repatriation of prisoners shall be effected as soon as possible after the conclusion of peace.
>
> (from Article 75, Geneva Convention, 1929)

> No repatriated person shall be employed on active military service.
>
> (from Article 74, Geneva Convention, 1929)

Whatever private doubts some ex-prisoners may have had about adjusting to life beyond the wire, and however satisfying others might find the chance to roam about and lord it over the locals, just about everyone—even collaborators who hoped they could avoid detection—wanted to go home in the aftermath of liberation. Having made extensive preparations for the processing of former Kriegies, the PWX organization and MI9 were also keen to set the repatriation plan in motion as the war in Europe came to an end. Both the repatriates and the authorities in general emerged reasonably satisfied with the resultant flurry of activity. As with any complex military operation, though, not everything went entirely according to plan, for either the organizers or the organized. Unexpected bumps and detours were encountered along what was supposed to be a smooth and straight path from initial liberation to complete freedom, causing delay and not a little friction. The experience of being a Kriegie, furthermore, often left an imprint strong enough to influence thoughts and behaviour after ex-prisoners returned home.

British and Commonwealth POWs were supposed to be repatriated and processed in the following manner. Until the western and eastern fronts met—something that occurred on 25 April 1945 near Torgau—those Allied Kriegies overrun by the Red Army would be sent east and shipped home through the port of Odessa. Meanwhile to the west, teams of PWX officers attached to formation headquarters would make contact with concentrations of ex-prisoners in camps and on the road as soon as they were located, and make arrangements for their transfer to one of the RAMP (Recovered Allied Military Personnel) transit centres set up by SHAEF. Here immediate medical and other needs would be attended to in preparation for a journey by air to south-east England. On arrival ex-prisoners would be welcomed into one of more than a score of ex-POW reception centres. Here they would receive anything they still needed—everything from identity cards and travel warrants to service-medal ribbons—before being sent off on a lengthy period of leave or, in the case of Commonwealth and Empire men, being shipped home. Speed and tact were to be the watchwords throughout. In practice, however, evolving world events, plus a strong desire among many Kriegies to prove that they, rather than the authorities, knew what was best for them, made the first phases of repatriation rather slower in execution, more varied in form, and sometimes more fractious than anticipated.[1]

Keeping track of the POW population in the last weeks of the war, with tens of thousands of men still on the move and camp nominal rolls increasingly out of date, was problematic to begin with. Adding to the extra time needed to collect and identify ex-Kriegies was their common inability to resist wanderlust in the wake of liberation. After a few days the intoxicating sense of freedom and power associated with touring and looting might begin to wear off, the men involved sobering up sufficiently to see that an impulse-driven gypsy existence could not continue forever, and returning to the fold. This meant delays, however, and some men still enjoying the initial fruits of freedom missed the initial round of PWX-directed withdrawals. 'We were told by an officer that at practically every Ex POW Camp that had been evacuated', Signaller G. F. Warsop later wrote, 'numbers had been left behind owing to the fact that they were either out of camp or drunk.'[2]

Hundreds of other ex-prisoners, meanwhile, had decided that they would make their own way home rather than sit passively waiting for the authorities to begin repatriation. 'Even a few days' delay was intolerable', one such evader from the RAF later explained, '—we did not want to be washed, kitted out, medically inspected and registered. We wanted only to get to England . . . ' Plenty of liberated vehicles were at hand, and with many front-line troops willing to provide petrol, the more independent types simply drove off. 'Soon scores of prisoners in car-loads of three and four were speeding west,' former Fallingbostel inmate John Dominy recorded, 'all bound for the Channel ports, the sea and home.' Such free spirits were determined not to endure incarceration of whatever sort for any length of time, if they could possibly avoid it. 'The feeling of relief as we drove away from the camp—never to see that infernal wire again—was overwhelming', Philip Kindersley remembered of the moment he and friends sped away from Oflag 79 in a looted Mercedes. Picking up abandoned German arms en route only added to the sense of empowerment. Richard Passmore, himself trying to evade the clutches of officialdom, remembered coming across another piratical-looking party that included Larry Slattery, one of the two first RAF aircrew to be shot down and taken prisoner:

He was an odd sight. In one hand he held the by now obligatory Schmeisser [sub-machine gun]. His belt supported several spare magazines, together with a pistol and two stick-grenades. He was a most martial sight. I looked at him open-mouthed.

'In the name of God, Larry,' I asked him, whatever do you plan to do with that lot?'

He smiled, and in his soft brogue he said, 'Sure, I don't know but it's nice to have them.'

We grinned at each other: I understood his feelings completely.[3]

Most such migratory types were eventually intercepted, divested of their vehicles and weapons, and directed to the nearest transit centre. Several made it as far as Paris, though, and those who were taken under the wing of the authorities were known to try to get away again when the opportunity arose. MI9 official A. J. Evans, visiting a staging area at Celle, discovered just how far some freed men were willing to go in order to make their own way home. 'I was warned to immobilize my car in the most thorough manner,' he reported, 'and when I asked "why?" the ex-prisoners of war (PWX) officials rather shamefacedly confessed that the ex-prisoners of war had stolen most of the PWX transport and in it continued their journey westwards.'[4]

Another spanner thrown into the works appeared in the form of hundreds of ex-Kriegies in the Soviet zone of control crossing the Elbe and Mulde rivers into American hands independently, rather than waiting around for negotiations for transfers en masse to be concluded. Initial exposure to the rather wild behaviour of the Red Army had not inspired confidence, men were naturally impatient to get home, and in places such as Mühlberg there were growing fears that one set of captors had simply been exchanged for another. Even when it was known via the radio that SHAEF had ordered them to stay where they were, and at the risk of being shot by trigger-happy Soviet sentries, Kriegies might conclude that they had no alternative but to strike out on their own. Such fears were not entirely unfounded: at Luckenwalde the first US attempt to ferry ex-POWs westward in a truck convoy was blocked by the new camp authorities, and it was only after several more weeks of negotiation and delay that Red Army trucks were provided to ship Allied prisoners to the American zone from Luckenwalde and Mühlberg. Yet however rational the decision to head west independently, the net effect was to add further unexpected variables to a repatriation situation that only resembled the original PWX conception in outline. What was more, even after they had escaped the Soviet zone of occupation some independent souls continued to try to evade officialdom. Squadron Leader Tommy Calnan and another RAF officer got as far as Croydon airport through cadging lifts from sympathetic American personnel before being recognized as ex-prisoners.[5]

To their credit, the Allied authorities seem to have adapted to a potentially chaotic situation with commendable speed. Staging points were rapidly set up in locations from which concentrations of recovered personnel could most easily be passed back to the nearest main transit camp—usually either Brussels or Rheims—and small parties of liberated prisoners heading west in confiscated vehicles were now simply told to make their way to one of these camps to ease the strain on Allied transport facilities. Every effort seems to have been made to send men home by air, but when necessary, arrangements were made to ship them by sea from the Channel ports or Naples (in the case of Kriegies liberated in southern Austria). Seemingly everything was done to speed men through to England, though even in the western zones it might take up to about two weeks between the day of liberation and the date of arrival. Perhaps because it was not understood that the Prominente were no longer among them, the men of Colditz made it home in the record time of sixty hours.[6]

By the time the last stragglers were arriving at reception centres in late May, the authorities had cause to be satisfied with the way in which repatriation had been conducted. Organizing the orderly transfer by air of 40,000 men from Belgium to England in the space of twenty-one days, for example, had been nothing short of a logistical triumph, and overall the air shuttle service (using bombers and transport planes) had worked rather more efficiently overall than SHAEF had anticipated. Problems were swiftly sorted out on the spot, on at least one occasion by no less a person than Air Chief Marshal Sir Arthur Tedder. The deputy supreme commander at SHAEF heard first-hand from a party of Moosburg men waiting at Rheims that they had been told there would be a delay in getting home due to a shortage of planes. He thought for a moment and then announced: 'Gentlemen, you will all be back in England by 11 o'clock tomorrow.' And so indeed they were. As RAAF pilot Geoff Taylor related with reference to his smooth transfer from US hands at Leipzig to British hands at Brussels, every effort really was made to do things 'with a minimum of documentation and a maximum of speed'.[7]

Nevertheless, ex-Kriegies, though they were on balance positively inclined toward what was being done for them, were by no means uniformly uncritical of the way in which they were being treated. There was much to be thankful for, as former prisoners were quick to point out later in memoirs and interviews. Yet even though repatriation was carried out as expeditiously as possible, and the War Office and other departments went to great lengths to make men feel they were valued rather than merely cogs in an impersonal machine, after years of incarceration impatient recovered personnel did not always take kindly to renewed exposure to service bureaucracy, even of a comparatively benign variety.

Some ex-prisoners were aghast at the speed and apparent recklessness with which they were driven from one location to another by US Army truck drivers, but otherwise the British experience in American hands was almost uniformly positive. 'The Americans', Captain Derek Bond commented with reference to the efficient manner in which former POWs were transported away from Moosburg, 'had organised everything splendidly.' This was also a view held by the men of Colditz as they were lorried rearward. 'You couldn't have had a better organisation', Lieutenant Hugh Bruce concluded. Those who passed through the RAMP transit camps under US Army control were even more impressed. Gunner Bernard Piddleston remembered receiving what he called 'VIP treatment' in the way of food and kit while being processed through Namur. 'This was luxury!', RAF Sergeant George Moreton reflected on the mountains of white bread and peanut butter presented to ex-prisoners at Rheims. Rations, delousing, debriefing, new clothing, and transportation were all handled efficiently and speedily. Gunner Albert Paice summed up majority opinion with the comment: 'This was a well-organised set-up.'[8]

The only possible drawback to being processed by the Yanks (usually as a prelude to being sent on to Brussels) was finding oneself subject to foreign authority and procedures that occasionally might offend a Briton's sense of honour. In an effort to make sure that ex-prisoners did not carry parasites further back, American transit centres often issued men with new US Army clothing and destroyed what they had come in wearing. 'This shook me considerably,' Captain John Mansel confided to his diary, on hearing 'that *all* our clothes are to be taken away from us . . . and that we will be issued with American Army issue uniform for use till we reach our reception camp in England.' He went on to explain that: 'as much as I admire the American Army and am su-premely grateful to them for releasing me and proud that my freedom should have come through them, nevertheless I don't want to return home in anything else but British uniform, however dirty or tattered it may be.' Eventually he was able to persuade the camp authorities to spray his battledress liberally with DDT instead. Private John Lawrence, meanwhile, along with some other British Army ex-prisoners being cycled through Rheims, took umbrage at being marched and ordered about by US Army non-coms, and expressed their displeasure by obeying orders only when relayed through a British NCO.[9]

The more cynical among the ex-Kriegies being repatriated through British hands half-anticipated that the 'all bull' world of the parade ground would be *de rigueur* at staging points and the main transit camp in Brussels. And former prisoners were indeed sometimes left with the feeling that they were being mucked about. Though some enterprising chaps managed to smuggle home items ranging from machine-guns and pistols to girlfriends and motorbikes, the authorities did not take kindly to such surreptitious transfers. Vehicles were often confiscated before they could be sold or shipped by those who considered themselves owners of valuable 'liberated' property by right of salvage, and the shipment of German small arms was—quite understandably—heavily frowned upon. The desire of committed men to take foreign women home with them was sometimes accommodated, as when a British chaplain legalized the relationship between Gordon Wilson, a South African gunner, and the Lithuanian woman worker he had befriended, through a quick, on-the-spot marriage ceremony. But other couples were told that the distaff side would have to remain on the Continent pending investigation of background and nationality—an attitude that did not go down well with the parties involved.[10]

Moreover, being deloused and interrogated was not always popular with men naturally anxious to get home. 'We had to undergo several days of red-tape interviews,' Lieutenant R. G. M. Quarrie remembered, 'from which we received the impression . . . that everyone seemed to be obsessed with tracking down the perpetrators of countless atrocities.' Not everyone was happy to be given MI9 questionnaires concerning possible war crimes and traitors to fill in—written replies often ranged from the sullen to the obscene—and it was noted that a large number of pencils went missing. To some men it was all too reminiscent of being processed in the other direction. 'The whole experience was like becoming a prisoner of war all over again', complained Seaman Harold Siddall.[11]

Most of those being processed through Brussels, however, were struck by how every effort seemed to be made to avoid making them feel like they were still Kriegies. Many men were placed in a requisitioned hotel, complete with sheets on the beds, a morning newspaper, thirty free cigarettes, a full-service dining room, and access to both the city and a special Red Cross canteen that stocked everything from toothpaste to writing paper. 'It was like being let loose in Aladdin's cave', a signaller from the Green Howards remembered. The voices of the female Red Cross volunteers helping run the show turned out to be oddly mesmerizing. 'They were the first English speaking persons of the opposite sex we had seen for several years', Squadron Leader C. N. S. Campbell recalled. 'We were fascinated by them, listening to them talking, almost to the point of rudeness, I am afraid to say.' Some men had to sleep in requisitioned Belgian army barracks, but most were conscious of a genuinely positive reception. Even the RSM, according to Rifleman Adrian Vincent, was 'very sympathetic'.[12]

For the thousands of men who had passed into the hands of the Red Army before it met up with Allied forces in April 1945 and were sent home via Odessa, transit eastward often proved something of a trial. Arrangements for the movement of ex-prisoners by the Soviet authorities were, to say the least, rather rough and ready. Though no longer under lock and key, ex-Kriegies were escorted by soldiers who more often than not seemed drunk, intent on looting, or both. They were usually transported without enough food and in some discomfort aboard cattle trucks that seemed to spend as much time in sidings as they did being pulled by clapped-out steam engines. There were at least two major rail accidents: one in Poland, in which nine men were killed and twenty-nine others badly injured, and another in Hungary—a head-on collision—in which twenty-six men died and twelve others were seriously hurt.[13]

After weeks in transit it was a relief for former prisoners to find a more organized set-up waiting for them in Odessa. 'Eventually we arrived at a very large house,' Jim Roberts remembered, 'to be greeted by the marvellous sight of British Red Cross ladies who were dispensing cups of tea, bars of Cadbury chocolate, English newspapers . . . new underwear and cigarettes.' Replacement uniforms were issued in the following days and the correct medal ribbons sewn on. Under such conditions, going through the interviews and paperwork associated with registration as bona fide ex-POWs could be more easily put up with.[14]

What might seem rather less tolerable to some ex-Kriegies who had spent years in the bag and were now savouring their freedom were efforts, real or imagined, at re-instilling service discipline. Sam Kydd recalled the reaction to a short speech made by a visiting military member of the Moscow military mission staff while he and his party were waiting to be shipped home from Odessa:

> 'Now listen carefully, you chaps, you've got to put on a good show for these damned Russkys, so heads up, chests out, and stomachs in. And let's all be on our Best Behaviour, what?'
>
> And from the ranks of the suffering emaciated lot who had seen more action in a week than this 'chap' had seen in a lifetime, a fruity cockney voice enquired 'who's this big prick?'

Annoyed at being confined to their house behind a cordon of Soviet guards, nine prisoners staged an escape one night and proceeded to get drunk on vodka in a dive bar, before staggering back from whence they had come and being arrested by the guards. A verbal reprimand by a British liaison officer dragged from his bed in order to confirm the miscreants' identity had little effect: 'Why don't you put us all in the cooler then', one inebriated soldier replied, '—it will be just like old times!'[15]

Here as elsewhere, ex-prisoners were keen to resume the journey homeward, though those who had brought along girlfriends of Eastern or Central European origin were decidedly unhappy that the Soviet authorities would not allow them to go with their men (though at least two were smuggled on board ship). The sea voyage from Odessa aboard vessels such as the *Duchess of Richmond* and *Highland Monarch* took about three weeks. Once again everything was done to make returning POWs feel that they were not on a troopship—extra food was provided in addition to welcome-aboard issues of Red Cross chocolate and cigarettes, there was plenty of room, concerts were encouraged, and feature films laid on—yet the touchier ex-Kriegies could still take offence when confronted with crass individuals or baffling situations. There was an unfortunate incident aboard the *Nieuw Amsterdam* when a warrant officer (picked up at Naples along with other troops returning home) berated a young Scottish ex-prisoner who, ill to begin with and suffering from seasickness, had had the temerity to use the heads reserved for NCOs. 'Oh, I recognise you now', the warrant officer is supposed to have said, '—you're one of those undisciplined bastards who have been sitting on your arses in Germany enjoying yourselves whilst we've been fighting the war for you.' The result was a near-mutiny on the ex-Kriegie mess-deck, and bloodshed was only narrowly averted through a timely apology broadcast over the tannoy by the offender's CO. Rather than await a further round of processing, several men slipped ashore without leave as soon as their ship reached a British port.[16]

Men waiting to get home from Brussels could look forward to a journey by air that would last only a couple of hours at most. Nevertheless, the idea of flying home in a cargo plane or being crammed into a big bomber did not always appeal. Most soldiers and sailors had never been off the ground in their lives, and even aircrew ex-prisoners were sometimes assaulted by memories of their own aircraft on fire and crashing to earth as they lined up on the tarmac. Inevitably, accidents occurred. Beaufighter pilot Martin Smith eagerly climbed aboard a Lancaster that, during its takeoff roll, lost power on both its port engines, swung off the runway into a crater, and then caught fire: 'We could have been Olympic athletes, the speed we evacuated the aircraft when it finally slid to a halt.' Smith and his fellow RAF ex-Kriegies walked away determined to reserve places aboard the next departing aircraft. Others, however, simply refused to fly at all, and there were in fact several crashes in which everyone aboard was killed.[17]

For those lucky enough to be near a point on their aircraft where they could look out, the first sight of the English coast generated a different but equally strong emotional response. 'Suddenly we came in sight of the Cliffs of Dover,' wrote Major Peter Harwood of his flight from Brussels aboard a Stirling, 'an unforgettable sight after five years, to have seen them so near and yet so far [from Calais] in 1940, and never imagined that you would see them again, and they suddenly hove in sight, and the whole cabin broke into a cheer.' Men aboard other planes were sometimes so overcome they had tears in their eyes that they sometimes could not hold back.[18]

The really big moment, though, was when the aircraft touched down and taxied to a stop at one of more than a dozen airfields in southern England. 'When we landed and got off the plane,' recalled BEF veteran James Stedman, 'I fell to the ground and kissed the earth of good old England.' He was not alone; and then, to the intense surprise of the cynics, it emerged that the authorities intended to greet returning ex-prisoners in a style befitting brave men coming home from the wars.[19]

Waiting on the apron were smiling members of the Women's Auxiliary Air Force who said hello, shook hands, hugged, and sometimes kissed each returning prisoner, and then insisted on carrying any luggage to nearby hangers or tents. Here there were 'welcome home' banners, free newspapers, cigarettes, friendly chatter, and, under the kindly care of motherly types from the Women's Voluntary Service, a sit-down high tea of a richness that nobody had seen since before the war. Speeches by senior officers were warm and mercifully short, and the compulsory squirt of DDT down the inside of one's clothing—a preliminary most returnees had to undergo, whether or not they had been sprayed already—could not detract from the warmness of a welcome that took no account of rank. To some it all had a dreamlike quality; others were so overwhelmed by the expressions of goodwill and the strangeness of it all that they were rendered mute or found themselves on the verge of tears. Newly arrived ex-prisoners might find themselves unaccountably bashful in front of the first Englishwomen they had encountered in years, their chattering voices sounding oddly 'queer and high-pitched', and any perfume they might be wearing heady beyond belief. Even those in a state of mild shock after the sudden assaults on their senses—Roger Mortimer found he could not eat a thing, and beat a retreat to the gents to quietly read through *The Times*—could not gainsay the way in which the RAF, in collaboration with other organizations, was trying very hard to please. Eric Fearnside, a driver in the Royal Engineers captured on Crete, neatly summed up what had happened: 'We were treated like heroes.'[20]

Returning men were next sent to one of the special reception centres set up by the services. Here they could be officially debriefed, given a thorough medical examination, and issued with everything they might still need—clothing, medal ribbons, a free telegram, ration books, identity cards, and some pay—before being sent off on lengthy periods of leave. Drawing on what had been learned from observing earlier repatriates, RAMC psychiatrists expected that former prisoners, still adjusting to being free men, would show signs of 'restlessness' and 'irritability', as well as 'disrespect for discipline and authority.' Steps were therefore taken to make sure that the staff of reception centres did their job as quickly and as sympathetically as possible. 'Now listen to me,' Gunner J. H. Witte recalled the RSM announcing at his reception centre, 'I'm not going to give you any orders, just do what I say and you will get home all the quicker.' For the most part things went smoothly and swiftly. G. F. Warsop of the Sherwood Foresters recalled that 'everything ran on oiled wheels' at the centre near Guilford to which he was sent, whilst former air gunner Russell Margerison found the processing experience at Cosford 'pleasantly satisfying and incredibly easy'. For the most part repatriates were on their way home well inside forty-eight hours.[21]

There were, however, occasional glitches. In transit the often rather motley appearance and prickliness of returnees could lead to misunderstandings and friction. A party of returning RAF officers en route from Oakley were refused admittance to the officers' mess at Bicester on the grounds that they were improperly dressed. Another party of NCO aircrew repatriates, also on their way to Cosford, nearly started a riot when a railway official attempted to eject them from a first-class compartment they had occupied when the rest of the train turned out to be full. They were partially mollified on arrival through discovering that even service policemen were trying hard to be respectful and even friendly, but at some of the reception centres themselves there were intermittent problems. Former prisoners were sometimes sent to the wrong location, occasionally arrived without any warning, and at times encountered bureaucratic snarl-ups of one sort or another. Delays, real or imagined, could try the patience of men desperate to get home. 'I think if they had kept us there for long we would have started an Escape Committee', BEF veteran Len Williamson wrote with reference to the reception centre he passed through at Worthing. News that their paperwork would not be completed before the weekend was up drove a group of ex-Kriegies at another centre to threaten to decamp en masse without leave unless they had their tickets stamped that day, and a number of former Colditz inmates simply did a bunk when told they would have to remain in camp overnight.[22]

Despite the restiveness of ex-prisoners, MI9 persisted in trying to identify and detain any turncoats among them before they could slip away. Some prisoners fingered anyone disliked for any reason when filling in 'En-Dor' questionnaires, which caused all sorts of problems, and a certain amount of bureaucratic miscommunication led to the temporary arrest of BQMS John Brown, widely thought to be a traitor but in fact a double agent. Nevertheless, the authorities eventually managed to catch just about every member of the British Free Corps and most other known traitors, including Sub-Lieutenant Walter Purdy.[23]

Dominion prisoners, meanwhile, were waiting for sea transport to take them home from various concentration points. Like their UK counterparts, they did not always take kindly to anything that might smack of caricature service callousness. Several hundred Australian servicemen waiting at Eastbourne threatened to riot in response to a plan—hastily withdrawn—to begin regular marching drills. Confronted by a blanket order to return home aboard a dilapidated steamer, an even larger number of Canadian aircrew ex-prisoners walked back down the gangplank and staged a sit-down strike on the quayside that only ended after the intervention of a senior RCAF officer induced the Air Ministry to allow anyone who wanted to stay on in England to do so.[24]

Having been cycled through the repatriation centres and promptly sent on leave, British ex-Kriegies next had to confront families and civil life after years of being away. Sometimes this was not a problem, those concerned picking up where they had left off without any apparent difficulty. Corran Purdon, for instance, remembered the reunion with his fiancée on coming home from Colditz as an entirely joyful occasion: 'it was as if we had never been apart.' For many returning men, however, there was a lot to adjust to.[25]

Not every spouse turned out to have been faithful, and men who had been away for a long time could find themselves estranged from their families. Even if this were not the case, ordinary life in the first few weeks could prove disorienting and hard to cope with. Awkwardness in conversation, difficulty in making decisions, avoidance of crowds, extreme irritability, restlessness, and in general a somewhat fragile emotional state were initially quite common behavioural complaints among prisoners returning home. Even among the former inmates of Oflag IVC there were those who found the sudden re-entry into the real world rather daunting.[26]

Observation of those who had made home runs or been repatriated on medical grounds in the middle war years had led psychiatrists in the Royal Army Medical Corps to push for further official intervention. Wives and families were apparently warned about what they could expect when their menfolk returned from Germany and given guidance on how to treat them, and special post-leave resettlement units were set up in order to ease the problems of transition. The results were not always positive from the ex-POW perspective.

Men might be far from pleased to learn that the authorities had been giving their loved ones advice on how to handle them. 'When I first heard this I was so furious I thought I was going to have a stroke', journalist René Cutforth later related:

'Do you mean to say', I yelled, 'that the bloody army gave you lessons on how to be married to me?'

'Well, they told us what we might expect.'

'To hell with that,' I roared, and went off to the pub and stayed away for three days.

When I got back I said: 'I took off because I will not have my life interfered with.' 'Oh yes,' my wife said, 'they told us about that too.'

Others, in addition to being annoyed by an intrusion into the private sphere, were affronted by the underlying assumption that their mental state was less than perfect. 'What a load of bullshit!' an RAF ex-prisoner was overheard to remark, on being told that wives and families were being warned to shield their menfolk from premature exposure to every-day life.[27]

There was also some suspicion concerning post-leave arrangements back at the reception centres. Men had to attend a medical board to determine the state of their health. The older and less fit among them would be given the option of attending a civil resettlement unit or being sent on indefinite leave again pending discharge. The fitter men who had been called up later would be posted directly to refresher courses or sent to rehabilitation units in anticipation of further service in the war against Japan. This was a prospect that was not always welcome to those who thought they had already done their bit, but was rendered moot by the Japanese surrender in August 1945.[28]

Rehabilitation units garnered mixed reviews. Much emphasis was again put on avoiding onerous restrictions, so that attending personnel were (within limits) allowed to do whatever they wanted to do. This was usually much appreciated, but the psychological interviews that accompanied the physical testing did not always sit well with ex-Kriegies. Army corporal Christopher Portway, while finding the absence of normal military restrictions 'a most pleasant surprise', added in his memoirs that it was nevertheless difficult to tolerate 'the numerous interviews with keen young officer psychologists, who asked the most ridiculous questions and quite seriously expected sensible replies'. RAF officer and former Colditz inmate Patrick Welch described the staff at his centre as 'incredibly kind, incredibly nice, and incredibly stupid'. Men still disliked any sign that they were not fully cognizant of their own mental state and capabilities.[29]

Those sent on refresher courses and back into active units sometimes found it difficult to adjust to the routine of regular service life. Aside from those pursuing a career in the forces, they often ended up serving out their time in backwaters until final demobilization. Though a majority of ex-prisoners chose to go back into civilian life directly, 19,000 did attend civil resettlement units on a voluntary basis. Again, opinion was mixed. RAMC psychologists considered the courses at these units, in which discipline was once again very relaxed and men were taught necessary social as well as some vocational skills, to have been a success. A survey carried out in 1946 seemed to indicate that this was indeed the case (only 26 per cent of those who had attended were apparently still experiencing adjustment problems, as against 64 per cent of those who had not), and there were certainly some ex-Kriegies who later described the CRU experience as helpful. Even the psychiatrists had to admit, though, that certain attendees were disruptive and unwilling to accept the group discussions and other communal forms of therapy that had been laid out for them.[30]

Kriegies known to have aided the enemy languished in custody pending trial in Britain and the Dominions. Depending on the severity of their crime, the strength of the evidence, and the country in which they were tried—Canada was the harshest and South Africa the most lenient in terms of sentencing—such men might be set free, fined, given varying prison terms, or sentenced to death. The only prisoner of war actually convicted of treason and due to hang was Walter Purdy, but his death sentence was commuted to life imprisonment on the grounds that he was a follower rather than a leader. Most of those goaled were released back into society within a few years.[31]

Readjustment to normal life continued to be difficult into the post-war decades for some of the more run-of-the-mill ex-POWs. Sometimes there were long-term physical consequences of the rigours of captivity—notably lung and stomach problems—that eventually forced those concerned to apply for war-related disability pensions. In other cases there remained psychological problems with which to grapple. Even men from Colditz might suffer from claustrophobia, nightmares, and depression, and while many worked through their psychological difficulties in the months after the war ended, others were unable to do so and suffered as a result.[32]

Among those with less strain to bear there might still be a fair degree of lingering bitterness. Older BEF officers in particular sometimes felt that spending five years behind the wire had blighted their chances of promotion. Others felt strongly that the process of reimbursement of pay withheld while in captivity was bungled by the authorities, and remained frustrated by the unsatisfactory answers given to queries on the subject

in the decades to come. Not surprisingly, there were also former Kriegies, including some who had spent time inside Oflag IVC, who never
quite came to terms with their erstwhile captors and current allies. 'I
could never like a German', was a comment that continued to be made
by some ex-prisoners decades after the war.[33]

Human beings are remarkably resilient creatures, however. An increase in caloric and vitamin intake did wonders for the health and
stamina of those suffering from malnutrition, while the milder forms of
mental disturbance often disappeared after several months at home.
Some ex-POWs who left the services eventually became major professional figures. Derek Bond, Clive Dunn, Denholm Elliot, Michael
Goodliffe, Sam Kydd, Desmond Llewelyn, and Donald Pleasance, for
instance, all went on to become popular actors on stage, screen, and
television. At least eleven former Kriegies were elected to parliament in
the post-war decades, among them Colditz escaper Airey Neave. Several
eventually rose to ministerial and even cabinet rank. The most successful
was Tony Barber, who was appointed Chancellor of the Exchequer
under Edward Heath twenty-five years after leaving Stalag Luft III.
Among the men who stayed in uniform there were those who found
that captivity did not seem to adversely affect their career in the slightest.
Corran Purdon moved on from Oflag IVC to command successively
larger and more important army formations, eventually retiring as a
major-general. As for the Germans, many of those prisoners who heartily
detested them at the end of the war found their animosity faded with
time. For many men, as the time they had spent behind the wire receded
into the past, only the occasional mark or trace was left: more patience
or a heightened degree of toleration, perhaps, or using the odd bit of
Kriegie slang and expressing a stronger than usual dislike of waste. On
the pay question, some of those involved eventually turned their attention to other things. 'In the end I wrote it off as an act of robbery by the
Treasury', former Colditz escape officer Dick Howe explained. 'You
can't fight a government department. It's like a plastic bag—no recoil.'[34]

Whether finding it difficult or easy to adjust in the post-war world, the
central fact remained that over 160,000 British Empire servicemen who
had been POWs in Nazi Germany for up to five years were free agents
once more. Though some former Kriegies initially felt a little nostalgic
for the comradeship of the camps, and later on might tend to recall only
the funnier moments—especially if they attended reunions—nobody
actually wanted to relive the actual experience of being a prisoner of

war in Nazi Germany. On the other hand, almost everyone would have understood Private N. L. Francis of the Dorset Regiment when, on returning home, he shouted out: 'Bloody hell, I've made it!'[35]

Notes

1. On the repatriation plan see PRO, WO 32/11125, Repatriation and Resettlement of British Prisoners of War, radio broadcast by Adjutant-General, 25 Apr. 1945; W. Wynne Mason, *Prisoners of War* (Wellington, 1954), 471; David Rolf, *Prisoners of the Reich* (London, 1988), 174–5.
2. IWM, G. F. Warsop, 237; see Rolf, op. cit., 184–5.
3. Richard Passmore, *Moving Tent* (London, 1982), 233–4; Philip Kindersley, *For You the War Is Over* (Tunbridge Wells, 1983), 185; John Dominy, *The Sergeant Escapers* (London, 1974), 130. On heading west under one's own steam see e.g. IWMSA 5131/3, R. Buckingham.
4. A. J. Evans, *Escape and Liberation, 1940–1945* (London, 1945), 142. On trying to evade or escape from official clutches see e.g. IWM, F. W. Telfer, 40. On getting as far as Paris see e.g. Ian Ramsay, *P.O.W.* (Melbourne, 1985), 196 ff.
5. T. D. Calnan, *Free As a Running Fox* (London, 1970), 282–322. On deciding to strike out for American or British lines see e.g. IWMSA 15587/3, E. Boyd; David M. S. Ross, *Stapme* (London, 2002), 172–3. On the delays at Luckenwalde see e.g. IWMSA 4933/2, W. Reid. On the growing friction between the British camp authorities still advocating a 'stay put' policy and those increasingly unwilling to listen see e.g. Edward Lanchbery, *Against the Sun* (London, 1955), 202–13.
6. Henry Chancellor, *Colditz* (London, 2001), ch. 19. About one week was the average time-lag elsewhere in the US and British liberation zones. On going home via e.g. Ostend, see IWM (Rolf), R. Maggs, 6. On going home via e.g. Naples see IWM (Rolf), R. R. Dexter, 23. On being directed to make one's way independently to transit centres see e.g. IWM, W. A. Norris diary, 2–5 May 1945.
7. Geoff Taylor, *Piece of Cake* (London, 1980 edn.), 313. On the Tedder encounter see IWMSA 4827/5, R. Loder. In all about 120,000 men were flown to the UK. See *The Times*, 25 May 1945. On repatriation-as-successful-operation from the official perspective see Jonathan F. Vance, *Objects of Concern* (Vancouver BC, 1994), 178, 180; Mason, op. cit., 472.
8. Albert Paice and Alwyn Ward, *For the Love of Elizabeth* (privately printed, 1984), 63; George Moreton, *Doctor in Chains* (London, 1980 edn.), 251; IWMSA 4661/3, G. Piddleston; ibid. 16797/5, H. Bruce; Derek Bond, *Steady, Old Man!* (London, 1990), 170–1. On US trucking see e.g. IWM, T. Tateson, 64.
9. IWM, J. W. M. Mansel diary, 2 May 1945; see John Lawrence, *2.2.9.7.* (Fontwell, 1991), 84–6.
10. See e.g. Stuart Brown, *Forbidden Paths* (Edinburgh, 1978), 158–61; IWM, J. Glass, 76–9. On the Wilson case see Maxwell Leigh, *Captives Courageous*

(Johannesburg, 1992), 286–92. On an understanding attitude see Rolf, op. cit., 185. The more committed types went back to the Continent after the war to try to find their partners. See e.g. James B. Chutter, *Captivity Captive* (London, 1954), 205; Christopher Portway, *Journey to Dana* (London, 1955), 204. On confiscating 'liberated' vehicles see e.g. IWM, F. W. Telfer, 40. On successfully smuggling smaller items home see e.g. Andrew B. Cox, *Our Spirit Unbroken* (Port Elgin, Ont., 1999), 120.

11. http://www.naval-history.net/WW2MemoirAndS012.htm, J. Siddall, 1; R. G. M. Quarrie, *Oflag* (Durham, 1995), 118. On the paperwork problem see Foot and Langley, *MI9* (London, 1979), 295. On the indignities associated with delousing see also e.g. James Spenser, *The Awkward Marine* (London, 1948), 303. On low expectations see e.g. Bond, op. cit., 172.

12. Adrian Vincent, *The Long Road Home* (London, 1956), 207; IWM, C. N. S. Campbell, 37; IWM, T. Tateson (Green Howards), 65.

13. CMAC, RAMC 1787, A. V. Tennuci, 49–54; Barney Roberts, *A Kind of Cattle* (Sydney, 1985), 173–4; see Eric Williams, *On Parade for Himmler* (Hull, 1994), 74; John Nichol and Tony Rennell, *The Last Escape* (London, 2002), 212. On ex-POWs being robbed by Soviet troops see e.g. PRO, FO 916/1195, f. 517, Military Mission Moscow to War Office, 17 Apr. 1945; WO 32/77739, Summary of Information regarding the Treatment of British Prisoners of War released by the Soviet Forces, 3. To be fair, conditions in transit for British ex-POWs were not very different from those deemed acceptable for Red Army troops. See ibid. 1.

14. J. Roberts, *A Terrier Goes to War* (London, 1998), 139–40; see CMAC, RAMC 1787, A. V. Tennuci, 55; Williams, op. cit., 74–77.

15. J. Roberts, op. cit., 141–3; Sam Kydd, *For You the War Is Over...* (London, 1973), 311. In the early 1990s it was alleged that tens of thousands of British and American POWs liberated by the Red Army were never repatriated (Nigel Cawthorne, *The Iron Cage* (London, 1993)). Though some ex-Kriegies, especially those who wandered off on their own, were probably killed by Soviet forces in cases of mistaken identity (see e.g. Nichol and Rennell, op. cit., 166), and those who were on their own or with partisan and resistance groups might be arrested as likely spies (see e.g. Frank Kelly, *Private Kelly* (London, 1954); PRO, WO 208/3327, MI9/S/PG(G)3098; FO 916/2427), no evidence has thus far come to light to suggest a Katyn-style massacre or large numbers of British or American former Kriegies finding themselves in the Gulag. See Timothy K. Nenninger, 'United States Prisoners of War and the Red Army, 1944–45: Myths and Realities', *Journal of Military History*, 66 (2002), 761–82.

16. On the *Nieuw Amsterdam* incident see J. Roberts, op. cit., 151–2. On men jumping ship see e.g. Kydd, op. cit., 314. On conditions aboard the ships see also CMAC, RAMC 1787, A. V. Tennuci, 55–60. On attempts to get women home via Odessa see e.g. IWM, J. Glass, 76–7.

17. Martin Smith, *What a Bloody Arrival* (Lewes, 1997), 141. On fatal crashes see e.g. *The Times*, 18 May 1945.

18. IWM, H. C. F. Harwood, 129; see e.g. IWM, J. H. Sewell diary, 10 Apr. 1945.

19. James Stedman, *Life of a British POW in Poland, 31 May 1940 to 30 April 1945* (Braunton, 1992), 32.

20. Eric Fearnside, *The Joy of Freedom* (Burton-in-Kendal, 1996), 81 (almost exactly the same words—'as though we were conquering heroes'—were used by John D. Harvie in his memoir, *Missing in Action* (Montreal, 1995), 227); Imelda Ryan (comp.), *POWs Fraternal* (Perth, WA, 1990), 141 ('queer and high pitched'). On Roger Mortimer's reaction see Jane Torday (ed.), *The Coldstreamer and the Canary* (Langley, 1995), 164.

21. Russell Margerison, *Boys at War* (Bolton, 1986), 206; IWM, G. F. Warsop, 247; IWM, J. H. Witte, 219; Robert H. Ahrenfeldt, *Psychiatry in the British Army in the Second World War* (London, 1958), 232.

22. Len Williamson, *Six Wasted Years* (Braunton, 1985), 47. On ex-prisoners from Colditz heading off without leave see Corran Purdon, *List the Bugle* (Antrim, 1993), 61. On threatening to decamp at the prospect of waiting out the weekend see Stanley Rayner, *I Remember* (Lincoln, 1995), 193. On the first-class compartment incident see John McMahon, *Almost a Lifetime* (Lantzville, BC, 1995), 238–40. On the Bicester officers' mess incident see IWM (Rolf), F. East, 6.

23. Adrian Weale, *Renegades* (London, 1995 edn.), 190–1; Foot and Langley, op. cit., 295; J. Brown, op. cit., 142–3. On impatience with the level of detail required on MI9 forms see e.g. Robert W. Calvey, *Name, Rank and Number* (Lewes, 1998), 107.

24. J. St Arnaud, in George Dancocks, *In Enemy Hands* (Toronto, 1990 edn.), 218; Donald Watt, *Stoker* (East Roseville, NSW, 1995), 131. A pair of Canadian pilots who—while under the influence—tried to steal a BOAC Sunderland flying boat and fly home were treated leniently once it was ascertained that they intended to leave the service. L. Ray Silver, *Last of the Gladiators* (Shrewsbury, 1995), 181–2.

25. Purdon, op. cit., 62. On having no difficulty adjusting see e.g. IWMSA 11277/3, T. H. Wilson.

26. See Earl Haig, *My Father's Son* (London, 2000), 156 ff.; Alexander Walker, *Lean, Wind Lean* (London, 1984), 183. On general problems see A. J. Barker, *Behind Barbed Wire* (London, 1974), 191. On alienation re civilians and their attitudes see e.g. IWMSA 4787/7, E. Mine. On irritability with families see e.g. IWM (Rolf), A. T. M. Gant, 10; Willatt, op. cit., 128. On initial shyness with wives see e.g. F. A. B. Tams, *A Trenchard 'Brat'* (Edinburgh, 2000), 140. On finding it difficult to converse, not least about being a POW, see e.g. IWMSA 4661/3, G. Piddleston. On family estrangement problems see e.g. Jack Poole, *Undiscovered Ends* (London, 1957), 190. It should be noted that many of these problems were common to returning servicemen who had not been POWs. See Barry Turner and Tony Rennell, *When Daddy Came Home* (London, 1995).

27. René Cutforth, *The Listener*, 19 Dec. 1968, p.810; McMahon, op. cit., 249. On families and the authorities see B. Hatley-Broad, 'Prisoner of War Families and the British Government during the Second World War', Ph.D. thesis, University of Sheffield (2002).

28. On being told that there was still a war to be won against Japan see e.g. IWMSA 15113/2, W. Hart. On post-leave processing see e.g. IWM (Rolf), R. Fermor, 'Information for Ex Leave Personnel' leaflet; IWMSA 4827/5, R. Loder.
29. IWMSA 10643/3, P. Welch; Portway, op. cit., 194–5.
30. See Ahrenfeldt, op. cit., 240–8.
31. Weale, op. cit., 195–7.
32. On long-term mental disability see Rolf, op. cit., 194–5.
33. IWMSA 4661/4, B. Piddleston. On strong anti-German sentiment in the aftermath of war see e.g. IWMSA 16797/5, H. Bruce. On the pay question see e.g. IWMSA 11337/6, H. Bracken. On blighted army careers see e.g. IWMSA 4847/4, C. L. Irwin.
34. Rolf, op. cit., 198. On disliking waste see e.g. IWMSA 4747/7, E. Mine. On the use of Kriegie slang see e.g. Torday, op. cit., 39–40. On greater toleration and understanding see e.g. IWMSA 4827/5, R. Loder. On patience see e.g. IWM (Rolf), T. M. Gant, 10. On fading dislike for the Germans see e.g. IWMSA 48960/3, G. Soane. On service careers that turned out fine see e.g. Purdon, op. cit., *passim*. Ex-Kriegie MPs from the 1950s through the 1970s included Tony Barber, Richard Collard, Frederick Corfield, Stafford Crawley, David James, Angus Maude, Fred Mulley, Airey Neave, John Peyton, Peter Thomas, and Peter Walker. On improving physical health see e.g. IWMSA 4767/7, J. Greenwood. On fading psychological symptoms see e.g. IWMSA 12093/4, A. Topliss.
35. IWM, N. L. Francis, 37. On remembering the better times see e.g. UNB, MS L35, David H. Walker Papers, box 1, series 1, subseries 1, file 12, Biggar to Walker, 4 July 1986. On nostalgic reunions see Rolf, op. cit., 202. Not all former POWs, even decades on, were keen to relive their youth through association meetings or organized visits to the sites of former camps. See e.g. UNB, MS L35, David H. Walker Papers, box 1, series 1, subseries 1, file 8, Gilliat to Walker, 26 Oct. 1982; Willatt, op. cit., 128; Rolf, op. cit., 201–2.

Conclusion
Farewell to Colditz?

Let us file [Colditz] away with all the other camps of a generation ago, before it smothers us all.

(Jerome Caminada, 1974)[1]

Let's accept that we have the good fortune to be part of a legend. Or, if you prefer it, a myth. What does it matter? Much of history is myth. Why scoff at others' esteem?

(Mike Moran, 1982)[2]

The story of Colditz, or more accurately the P. R. Reid version thereof, has for decades directly or indirectly influenced popular perceptions of what it was like to be a prisoner of war in the Third Reich. In marked contrast to the stark images of death or survival against the odds associated with captivity in Japanese hands, a picture developed of German captivity in which optimism prevailed and escape was always uppermost in the mind. From the foregoing chapters it should be clear that the realities of life as a British POW in German hands during the Second World War were rather more complex and often less upbeat than is still commonly imagined. Colditz itself was a mixture of the typical and atypical in ways that do not always accord with its mythic status. It is no slur on those who were held there to suggest that the POW experience in general, and even the Colditz experience in particular, were not always suitable subject-matter for the likes of the *Magnet* or the *Gem*.

Surrendering, interrogation, and both the inward and outward transit experience could be and often were traumatic. Once inside the wire, neither physical nor mental health could ever be taken for granted. Both labour and recreation involved potential hazards. Despite the Geneva Convention, captives were always essentially at the mercy of their captors until the final days of the war. Relations with friends and foes were often not clear-cut. Outright traitors were few in number, and most working Kriegies did not, to say the least, give their all in labouring for the Reich. But only a minority of prisoners of war were ever keen to jeopardize their own lives or the precariously stable lifestyle of their fellows by making or supporting escape attempts. Being a British or Commonwealth POW in Nazi Germany, in short, was more of an endurance test than an adventure. Colditz, and more especially what it has come to symbolize, therefore need to be kept in perspective.

But is this really possible? The BBC television drama series *Colditz* was supposed to mark a break with the version of the story created two decades previously, yet was soon being portrayed as being more of the same. Pat Reid himself, who had not set out to create a legend, found that the effect of his early work was such that not even he could do much later to modify the image he had helped create. Over the past half-century Colditz has become part of the national folk memory, and the escaping exploits of its inhabitants quite understandably continue to inspire admiration. Academic historians have found to their chagrin, in other instances, that once a popular image of a major event has developed it often seems impervious to revision, however strong the supporting evidence may be. 'Audiences know what to expect,' as Tom Stoppard once put it, 'and that is all that they are prepared to believe in.'[3]

Suffused as it is with a mythical boarding-school ethos, and upholding as it does the comforting belief that native pluck and inventiveness are ultimately bound to triumph over greater foreign power and might, the authorized story of Colditz is also a very British tale. Indeed, the true extent to which people did not expect or wish to see this piece of the popular wartime legacy modified or tampered with only became fully apparent when controversy arose over plans for a new, big-screen version of the story at the turn of the century.

In the spring of 2000 Miramax Films had purchased the screen rights to the Pat Reid trilogy, the hope being that the story could be rewritten to allow major American actors such as Tom Cruise, Matt Damon, and Ben Affleck to star in a Hollywood production. The insertion of fictional Americans into non-fictional British escape stories was not new. Both the film version of *The Great Escape* and, to a much lesser degree, the *Colditz* television drama series had been 'Americanized' for the US market, something that had been accepted—albeit somewhat grudgingly—at the time. But in the wake of a series of Hollywood blockbusters that seemed to misrepresent history, and more specifically to underplay or ignore Britain's role in the Second World War—notably *U-571* and, to a lesser extent, *Saving Private Ryan*—a patriotic backlash developed concerning the incipient Americanization of this cherished piece of (specifically British) wartime mythology. 'Colditz is like Dunkirk,' commented film critic Barry Norman angrily, 'one of the great backs-to-the-wall British stories about snatching victory from the jaws of defeat. It's extremely irritating when the Americans muscle in on everybody else's glory. Where's it going to end? Did the Americans win everything in the war?'[4]

Hitherto the story in its original form had not struck much of a chord within the United States. There the books had not sold nearly as well, the original film had made little impression, and the glider story had been given a complete makeover for TV. Despite the presence of Robert Wagner, only the last two episodes of the first series of the BBC's *Colditz* had been broadcast on US television, cobbled together as a single movie. American stars as central characters were therefore going to be vital. Without them, as a Miramax representative explained to a *Daily Telegraph* reporter, 'American audiences would regard the film as foreign, so damaging box office takings'. And to accommodate those stars, whose ability to carry off a non-US accent was questionable, the original script did indeed, as studio chief Harvey Weinstein later admitted, make it seem 'that the Americans won the war and that the British, the French and the Poles didn't get a look in'.[5]

The reaction was negative enough to put Miramax on the defensive. 'We have great respect for the British, Polish and French heroes of Colditz,' a representative was quoted as saying in early May 2000, 'and I can assure everybody that we have no intention of making an American version of events that ignores those who suffered in Colditz and glorifies America.' In March of the following year Weinstein indicated that the original script would be scrapped: 'I do not want history distorted in what will be an important film.' Miramax announced in May 2002 that *Television Française 1* would be co-producing a Colditz film which would be shot in Europe with a European cast, but (as of December 2003) nothing more has been heard about the project. The message was clear: those who tinkered heavily with the established version of the story—and its mythical associations—did so at their peril.[6]

Yet it should not be thought that public interest in the Colditz story is merely a matter of national pride. The numerous and varied escape schemes associated with the story (everything from dressing as Germans to building a glider) were drawn from fact, not fantasy. And it is the appeal of escape stories in general—empathy for those willing to risk their lives to achieve freedom, and admiration for the ingenuity and teamwork involved—that lies at the very heart of the Colditz phenomenon.[7]

It is a phenomenon, furthermore, that seems set to outlast the inevitable demise of the last of those who were held prisoner in the castle. 'A legend has been thrust upon us', Mike Moran wrote to some of those who had shared his experiences at Oflag IVC more than thirty-five years after they had all left the place. 'We are part of it. Whether or not you,—or I,—have deserved our places in that legend is for each of us to decide. Whether or not that legend is to continue is also in our hands. I would not like to think that when "the barge sails over the brink" for the last time, with the ultimate survivor on board,—Colditz, and we who were in Colditz, would sink into oblivion.' Ongoing interest in everything connected with the castle in the following two decades suggest that Moran need not have worried. 'When I suggested that Colditz would be forgotten when we're all gone,' Hugh Bruce recalled of a conversation with Christopher Dowling in the mid-1990s, the current director of public services at the Imperial War Museum replied: 'Not a bit of it. The stories are there for keeps. British interest, at least, will be just as strong in the future as it has been in the past, maybe more so.' As the twenty-first century advances there are few signs that Dowling was wrong.[8]

Nevertheless, the effort at achieving perspective needs to be made, if only in order to lessen the shadow Colditz has cast over events elsewhere. That the public should be attracted to the romance of escape rather than the sordid details of everyday camp life is to be expected. Colditz and the camp from which the Wooden Horse and Great Escape schemes were launched—its name far less familiar than that of the famed Schloss—were not the only places from which daring breaks were made. But who now, for instance, beyond a few scholars and aficionados, remembers the great Warburg Wire Job? Moreover, and perhaps more importantly, the experiences of the majority of prisoners who were more interested in survival than escape are worthy of record. Being a prisoner of the Germans was not generally comparable, say, to being a captive of the Japanese, but it was certainly no picnic. Long ignored by military historians more interested in operational matters and social historians unable to disassociate an interest in military affairs from militarism, POWs have only recently begun to become the subject of serious scholarly investigation. Those servicemen who lived or died in Nazi Germany, along with those lucky and resourceful few who made successful home runs—and not just those from Oflag IVC—deserve a place in the historical record. Better, surely, to try to remember the human drama taking place in all camps than to forget them all in order to help tear down the cult surrounding one particular Schloss, as Jerome Caminada seemed to want. Colditz, and those who escaped from it, are unlikely to be forgotten any time soon; but perhaps other places and other people, individually and collectively, can also have the occasional day or two in the sun.

Notes

1. *The Times*, 8 Jan. 1974.
2. UNB, MS L35, David H. Walker Papers, box 1, series 2, file 3, *Colditz Newsletter*, 5 (Aug. 1982), 3.
3. Tom Stoppard, *Rosencrantz and Guildenstern Are Dead* (New York, 1967), Act II, the Player, p. 84. On the way in which attempts at mild revisionism re the Colditz story have been viewed as the mixture as before see e.g. *The Listener*, 14 Dec. 1972; *The Times*, 8 Jan. 1974; also Tony Barter, 'Film Nazis: The Great Escape', in id. (ed.), *Screening the Past* (Westport, Conn., 1998), 135; Peter Graham Scott, *British Television* (Jefferson, NC, 2000), 208 (with reference to the BBC's *Colditz* drama series; see also Richard Weight, *Patriots* (London, 2002), 492) and *Times Literary Supplement*, 22 Mar. 1985, pp. 330–1 (with reference to the third, much more sober book in the Pat Reid trilogy). On the 1955 film as possessing darker elements which have been ignored in favour of the schoolboy-comedy aspects see Robert Murphy, *British Cinema and the Second World War* (London, 2000), 214–15. On the mythology of the Second World War being resistant to scholarly subversion see Graham Dawson, 'History-Writing on World War II', in Geoff Hurd (ed), *National Fictions* (London, 1984), 2. The resilience of the 'bloody waste' image of Britain's participation in the First World War in the face of evidence presented by military historians is a case in point with reference to the hardiness of popular historical myths. See Brian Bond, *The Unquiet Western Front* (Cambridge, 2002).
4. David Smith, 'Hollywood Travesty as Courage of Colditz is Rewritten', *Daily Express*, 2 May 2000; see http://news.bbc.co.uk/1/hi/uk/733383.stm (accessed 19 Sept. 2002), 'Hollywood Fights the Facts', BBC News, 2 May 2000; http://www.netlondon.com/news/2000-18/2CEAAE5D732529AD802.html (accessed 17 Sept. 2002), 'Controversy over Hollywood Makeover of Colditz Story', 3 May 2000; Simon Jenkins, 'Lights, Camera, Action . . . and Damned Lies', *The Times*, 3 May 2000; Thomas Quinn, 'Sunk by the Yanks Again', *Daily Mirror*, 1 June 2000; http://britsversusyanks.tripod.com (accessed 25 Nov. 2000), 'Are the Yanks stealing our History?', 2000; Will Hutton, *The World We're In* (London, 2002), 40; see also http://www.aiipowmia.com/inter1/in051300.html (accessed 19 Sept. 2002), 'Colditz Castle Movie Bru-haha'. On the mythology of wartime see e.g. Angus Calder, *The Myth of the Blitz* (London, 1991); Malcolm Smith, *Britain and 1940* (London, 2000).

5. http://www.empireonline.co.uk/news/news.asp?3044 (accessed 19 Sept. 2002), 'Hollywood Film in Accuracy Shocker!', 30 Mar. 2001; *Daily Telegraph*, 5 May 2000. On the lack of American interest in the classic British escape stores of the 1950s see Alan J. Levine, *Captivity, Flight, and Survival in World War II* (Westport, Conn., 2000), p. ix. Presumably because Colditz was not a name to conjure with in the USA in the way it was in the UK, the Channel 4 documentary *Escape From Colditz* was retitled *Nazi Prison Escape* and given an American voiceover narration by PBS. The producers were not, however, able to fulfil a request from PBS that one of the handful of American prisoners held at Oflag IVC be contacted and interviewed so as to insert an American angle into the programme. See http://www.main.wgbh.org/wgbh/shop/products/wg2803.html (accessed 19 Sept. 2002); http://members.lycos.co.uk/mkemble/colditz.html (accessed 2 Sept. 2002), 8–9. Another indication of lack of name recognition was the change in subtitle to Henry Chancellor's 2001 book when it was published by William Morrow in the USA: *Colditz: The Definitive History* became *Colditz: The Untold Story of World War II's Greatest Escapes*. It should be noted that two British actors known in the USA, Ewan McGregor and Jude Law, were also considered for the Miramax remake, along with Russell Crowe.

6. http://www.empireonline.co.uk/news/news.asp?3044 (accessed 19 Sept. 2002), 'Hollywood Film in Accuracy Shocker!'; *Daily Telegraph*, 5 May 2000. On the TF-1 deal see e.g. http://www.indiewire.com/film/biz/biz_020520_briefs.html (accessed 8 Feb. 2002). Listed as 'in development' in 2000 on http://upcomingmovies.com, by the summer of 2002 'The Colditz Story' had disappeared. The view from Hollywood was that the British press was being unnecessarily defensive, given that Miramax had indicated that British actors would still be involved in the project. See Matt Wolf, 'Brits lack stiff upper lip in cast flap', *Variety*, 29 May 2000. It is worth noting that even British companies could draw fire for apparently tinkering with the Colditz story. After ITV announced in early 1993 that it was making a two-part drama based on the exploits of Airey Neave in which the Germans would be portrayed more sympathetically than in the BBC series, Kenneth Lockwood took exception to a pro-German approach. 'I certainly wouldn't describe the Germans as likeable,' he told the *Daily Telegraph*, 'and I don't know any other prisoner at Colditz who would.' *Daily Telegraph*, 31 Mar. 2003.

7. Escape stories can appeal to both the right in terms of personal ingenuity and freedom of the individual—see Ken Worpole, *Dockers and Detectives* (London, 1983), 54—and, I would argue, to the left in terms of collective effort toward a common goal. More generally, of course, escape stories appeal to anyone, not least the youthful—which perhaps helps explain the large number of children's editions of books such as *The Great Escape*, *The Wooden Horse*, and of course *The Colditz Story* itself. See *Whittaker's Books in Print* (1949–present). On the generic appeal of the escape story as against specifically national elements, it is worth noting that, despite some resistance at the time the project was first announced, the public flocked to see *The One*

That Got Away (1957), a film that chronicled the true escape efforts of a German officer in British custody. See R. Baker, in B. McFarlane, *An Autobiography of British Cinema* (London, 1997), 51; *Kinematograph Weekly*, 12 Dec. 1957, p. 6.

8. H. Bruce in CSVA 8; UNB, David H. Walker Papers, box 1, series 2, file 3, M. Moran circular, 15 July 1981, attached to *Colditz Newsletter*, 3 (July 1981).

Note on Sources

Though a large number of popular accounts have been published over the years, of varying quality and depth, scholarly investigation of the POW experience in the Second World War has as yet been confined to a rather narrow circle of academics in the English-speaking world. Why this should be the case is open to debate. Liberal distaste for anything even indirectly smacking of militarism, along with unease within the services about exploring a state of affairs sometimes regarded as the antithesis of real soldiering, may well have played roles. The common belief that much of the relevant enemy documentation with regard to British prisoners did not survive the war could also have acted as a deterrent. Yet, as recent work by historians such as Bob Moore, Kent Fedorowich, and Jonathan Vance (among others) has begun to illustrate, much material remains with which to explore not only policy decisions with respect to everything from national labour policy to international relations, but also the collective prisoner experience.[1]

A fair amount of relevant German documentation does in fact still exist. Of greater importance to this particular book, however, focusing as it does on the prisoners' perspective, are the extensive official records on the British side. These include such items as reports on camps made by neutral visitors, debriefing statements of escapees and other freed captives, summary accounts by senior men of the camps they presided over, files on matters of policy, and war-crimes investigation briefs. Even more significant for this project has been the huge amount of personal experience material generated in the past sixty or so years. A good number of censored letters and diaries written up at the time have been preserved. There are also many interviews and questionnaires dating from subsequent decades, in which ex-prisoners were asked by a variety of historians (notably the industrious and philanthropic David Rolf) and museum staffers to recall what had happened to them while guests of the Reich. And, of course, there are the hundreds of memoirs, published and otherwise, in which former captives set down on paper what they remembered about their time in Nazi Germany.[2]

Personal recollection, of course, is by no means an infallible guide to the past. Individual experiences may or may not be representative, attitudes may have changed over the years, recollection of dates, places, and people may be hazy at best, events may have been forgotten or suppressed, and even the most vivid of memories can turn out to be false. Yet, as the men concerned are sometimes at pains to point out when faced with views by younger generations that run counter to their recollection, they were the people on the spot at the time. If cross-checked with contemporary documents as well as the memories of others, such sources provide vital insights into what it was like to be a prisoner of war.[3]

Notes

1. See the Select Bibliography (Secondary Source books and articles). It is noteworthy that among the large number of official histories produced on various aspects of the war in Commonwealth countries there is only one—W. Wynne Mason, *Prisoners of War* (Wellington, 1954)—devoted to POWs. David Walker, a former Colditz prisoner, was initially reluctant to write about the collective experience of captives for a regimental history of the wartime Black Watch, for 'fear of seeming to convey that being taken prisoner is a normal fate for a soldier to accept as all in a day's work'. See UNB, David H. Walker Papers, Box 1, set 1, subseries 1, file 6, Fergusson to Walker, 7 Feb. 1948.
2. The Select Bibliography (Primary Sources), a representative but by no means exhaustive selection. On German records see Vasilis Vourkoutiotis, 'The German Armed Forces Supreme Command and British and American Prisoners of War', Ph.D. thesis, McGill University (2000).
3. A mythical incident cited as fact in more than one memoir illustrates the pitfalls of supposedly twenty-twenty recollection. Men from different camps all remembered a German losing his temper and uttering a phrase that ran something like: 'You think I know fuck nothing—I tell you I know fuck all!' See Patrick Barthropp, *Paddy* (Hailsham, 2001), 46; John Borrie, *Despite Captivity* (London, 1975), 73; Colin Hodgkinson, *Best Foot Forward* (London, 1957), 236; J. M. Green, *From Colditz in Code* (London, 1971), 77; Sam Kydd, *For You the War is Over* (London, 1973), 222. These were words employed before the war to illustrate the Anglophone belief that Central Europeans were excitable types, unable to master the English language; see e.g. David Niven, *Bring On the Empty Horses* (New York, 1975), 119–20. Former POWs also might disagree, sometimes heatedly, about the veracity of each other's recollections; see e.g. Green, *From Colditz* (Hull,

1989 edn.), 221 ff.; Richard Pape, *Sequel to Boldness* (London, 1959), 199 ff. There is even at least one case of someone who was never a POW writing a memoir about his experiences at Stalag Luft III and elsewhere. See Nigel West, *Counterfeit Spies* (London, 1998), 13. On the problems of memory more generally, see e.g. Paul Thompson, *The Voice of the Past* (Oxford, 1988 edn.), 110 ff.; Trevor Lummis, *Listening to History* (London, 1987), 12–13, 27, 83–4, 118, 155. On problems with narrative in general see, e.g., H. White, *The Content of Form* (Baltimore, 1987), 27.

Select Bibliography

Primary Sources

UNPUBLISHED OFFICIAL DOCUMENTS

Public Record Office, London
ADM 1; AIR 40; CAB 65; CRIM 1; FO 370, 371, 916; INF 1; KV 2; WO 32, 208, 224, 309–12

BBC Written Archive Centre
R9/7/115–28; 4/06869A; R19/1252; T5/9/1; T60/9/1; press cuttings, *Colditz* series

India Office Records, British Library, London
L/WS/1/1363

National Archives and Record Service, Washington, DC
T-120

RECORDED INTERVIEWS/TALKS

Abbott, G. W. (IWMSA); Allan, P. (CSVA); Arthur, S. (IWMSA); Atkinson, G. (IWMSA); Ayling, E. (IWMSA); Best, J. (CSVA); Beveridge, W. (IWMSA); Boyd, E. (IWMSA); Bracken, H. (IWMSA); Bristow, J. (IWMSA); Bruce, H. (IWMSA); Buckingham, R. (IWMSA); Buckley, P. (IWMSA); Burn, M. C. (IWMSA); Catlow, T. N. (CSVA); Champion Jones, M. (IWMSA); Chrisp, J. (IWMSA); Churchill, R. (IWMSA); Cole, A. (IWMSA); Cooksey, T. (IWMSA); Courtnay, J. J. (IWMSA); Crawford, A. D. (http://www.awm. gov.au (accessed Sept. 2003)); Davies Scourfield, E. G. B. (IWMSA); Deans, J. (IWMSA); Dhillon, C. (*Guardian*, 6 Nov. 2002); Eggers, R. (IWMSA); Esders, H. (IWMSA); Fergusson, P. (CSVA); Gee, H. (IWMSA); Greenwood, J. (IWMSA); Haig, G. A. D. [2nd Earl] (LC); Hamilton-Ballie, J. (IWMSA); Harewood, G. H. H. L. [7th Earl] (LC); Hart, W. (IWMSA); Hawkins, D. (IWMSA); Hoggard, J. (IWMSA; CSVA); Holmes, R. (IWMSA); Ironside, H. (CSVA); Irwin, C. L. (IWMSA); Jones, A. (IWMSA); Laurie, J. (IWMSA); Lockwood, K. (CSVA); Loder, R. (IWMSA); Marshall, B. (IWMSA); Mine, E.

(IWMSA); Moran, J. M. (IWMSA); Mazumdar, B. N. (IWMSA); Newborough, Lord [M. V. Wynn] (IWMSA); Pannett, F. (IWMSA); Phillips, J. (IWMSA); Piddlestone, B. (IWMSA); Pringle, J. C. (IWMSA); Purdon, W. C. (IWMSA); Reid, W. (IWMSA); Scarborough, C. (IWMSA); Shipp, H. F. (IWMSA); Siska, A. (LC); Smith, S. (IWMSA); Soane, G. (IWMSA); Stein, J. (IWMSA); Steinwitz, F. (CSVA; IWMSA); Stevens, W. (IWMSA); Topliss, A. (IWMSA); Tucki, J.; (IWMSA); Watson, S. (SPM); Welch, P. L. E. (IWMSA); Wilson, J. C. (IWMSA); Wilson, T. H. (IWMSA); Yule, J. D. (CSVA).

UNPUBLISHED DIARIES, LETTERS, NARRATIVES, PAPERS, ETC.

Adkins, G. (IWM [Rolf]); Aleera, H. (IWM); Allan, L. (http://news.bbc.co.uk/hi/english/uk/newsid_523000/523004.stm, accessed 6 Oct. 2001); Allwood, C. (IWM [Rolf]); Askew, G. (IWM [Rolf]); Asquith, W. (IWM); Atkinson, G. A. (IWM); Ayers, F. (IWM [Rolf]; IWM); Bader, D. (RAFM); Bailey, D. S. (IWM [Rolf]); Baker, C. (IWM); Bardford, A. (IWM [Rolf]); Barrington, E. (IWM); Bauress, G. W. (IWM); Bell, A. (IWM [Rolf]); Beard, L. (IWM [Rolf]); Behrman, D. (http://www.binternet.com/~stalag18a/dannybehrman.html, accessed 19 Sept. 2002); Bennett, J. (http://www.binternet.com/~stalag18a/jimbennett.html, accessed 19 Sept. 2002); Berry, T. (IWM [Rolf]); Betts, G. (IWM); Bird, J. (http://www.pegasus-one.org/pow/jack_bird.htm, accessed 19 Sept. 2002); Blaza, M. (IWM [Rolf]); Booth, E. (IWM); Booth, J. (IWM [Rolf]); Bowden, K. J. (IWM); Bowers, H. S. (IWM [Rolf]); Brown, T. J. (http://web.ukonline.co.uk/stephen.clarke/tom1.html, accessed 25 Apr. 2003); Brokensha, D. (IWM); Brooke, B. A. (IWM); Brooker, J. A. (IWM); Brown, J. V. (IWM); Bruce, D. (IWM [Rolf]); Bruce, H. (LC); Buckley, P. N. (IWM); Bull, R. R. (IWM); Campbell, C. N. S. (IWM); Catlow, T. N. (LC); Clark, R. (IWM [Rolf]); Collings, W. (http://www.pegasus-one.org/pow/walter_collings.htm, accessed 19 Sept. 2002); Copeland, J. (IWM); Cocker, J. (IWM [Rolf]); Corfield, F. (SWWEC); Dabner, E. C. (IWM); Darbyshire, W. (IWM); Davies, H. V. (IWM [Rolf]); Davis, E. B. (IWM [Rolf]); Denton, I. P. B. (IWM); Dexter, R. R. (IWM [Rolf]); Dibble, J. (IWM); Dickinson, J. (IWM [Rolf]; http://www.wartime-memories.fsnet.co.uk/pow/stalagixc.html, accessed 5 Oct. 2001); Ding, D. F. (IWM); Dobbins, F. T. (IWM [Rolf]); Dollar, P. W. (IWM); Doughty, S. J. (IWM); Dover, O. (IWM); Drysdale, E. H. (IWM [Rolf]); Dunne, D. T. (IWM [Rolf]); Durnford, R. C. (IWM); Dyson, K. (IWM [Rolf]); East, K. F. (IWM [Rolf]); Edmunds, F. (IWM [Rolf]); Eeles, R. H. (IWM [Rolf]); Eggers, R. (IWM); Eldred, W. S. (IWM [Rolf]); Elliott, H. E. C. (IWM); Ellis, E. C. (IWM); Evans, R. P. (IWM); Farley, A. E. (IWM); Fennel, A. (IWM [Rolf]); Fermor, R. (IWM [Rolf]); Fesel, A. (IWM [Rolf]); Firmage, R. (IWM [Rolf]); Francis, N. L. (IWM); Freeman, J. (IWM); Gant, A. T. M. (IWM [Rolf]); Geary, E. (IWM [Rolf]); Gerner, G. (IWM [Rolf]); Gibbs, A. F.

(IWM); Glass, J. (IWM); Goodliffe, M. (http://dspace.dial.pipex.com/jgoodliffe/mgpow/, accessed 19 Sept. 2002); Griffin, G. (IWM); Grover, A. E. (IWM); Hall, A. (IWM [Rolf]); Hall, G. (IWM); Harcus, L. H. (IWM); Harling, E. A. (IWM [Rolf]); Handley, G. W. (IWM [Rolf]); Harding, W. A. (IWM); Harris, H. G. (IWM); Harvey, K. (IWM [Rolf]); Harwood, H. C. F. (IWM); Hawkins, H. R. (IWM [Rolf]); Haydon, S. (IWM [Rolf]); Haynes, A. J. (IWM [Rolf]); Hemmings, G. (IWM); Hesrer, J. (IWM [Rolf]); Hill, F. J. (IWM [Rolf]); Hilton, A. D. M. (IWM); Hoare, W. (IWM [Rolf]); Hobbs, G. H. (IWM); Hockey, H. (http://www.binternet.com/~stalag18a/harryhockey. html, accessed 19 Sept. 2002); Hopper, G. (IWM); Howarth, W. (IWM [Rolf]); Howe, E. (IWM [Rolf]); Howell, P. E. (IWM [Rolf]); Hoy, D. L. (IWM); Hughes, T. (IWM [Rolf]); Irwin, C. L. (IWM [Rolf]); Jackson, B. (http://www.binternet.com/~stalag18a/bertjackson.html, accessed 19 Sept. 2002); Jackson, F. E. (IWM [Rolf]); Jackson, G. (IWM); James, R. R. (IWM); Jameson, J. (IWM [Rolf]); Jarrett, P. (IWM [Rolf]); Jebbit, D. O. (http://www.pegasus-one.org/pow/david_jebbit.htm, accessed 19 Sept. 2002); Jeffrey, B. C. (http://www.pegasus-one.org/pow/bruce_jeffrey.htm, accessed 19 Sept. 2002); Johnston, G. (PRO); Johnston, J. A. (IWM); Jones, J. G. (http://users.whsmithnet.co.uk/gordonjones/, accessed 24 Apr. 2003); Jones, V. E. (IWM); Kerridge, R. S. (IWM [Rolf]); King, C. G. (IWM); Kirk, E. (IWM); Kite, W. (IWM); Laing, W. K. (IWM); Laker, E. G. (IWM); Law, W. C. (http://www.pegasus-one.org/pow/william_law.htm, accessed 19 Sept. 2002); Lawrence, F. (IWM [Rolf]); Lewis, I. J. L. (IWM [Rolf]); Loder, R. E. (IWM [Rolf]); Long, J. (CMAC); Longmore, C. (IWM [Rolf]); Low, R. (IWM [Rolf]); Luckett, D. W. (IWM); Lyon, A. (IWM [Rolf]); Maggs, R. L. (IWM [Rolf]); Manners, G. R. (IWM); Mansel, J. W. M. (IWM); Martin, H. L. (IWM); Masters, S. C. (IWM); McGee, J. M. (IWM [Rolf]); McGill, E. T. (IWM [Rolf]); McKechnie, A. (IWM [Rolf]); Mercer, R. (IWM [Rolf]); Merryweather, H. H. (IWM [Rolf]); Miller, E. (IWM); Millington, K. (http://www.binternet.com/~stalag18a/kenmillington.html, accessed 19 Sept. 2002); Mooney, R. (PRO); Moore, F. (http://www.pegasus-one.org/pow/fred_moore. htm, accessed 19 Sept. 2002); Morley, R. M. (IWM [Rolf]); Munby, A. N. L. (IWM); Munn, H. T. (wysiwyg://397/http://www.mgb-stuff.org.uk/harrytext, accessed 6 Oct. 2001); Murray, J. (wysigwyg://282/http://www.angelfire.com/nd/domneal/powar.html, accessed 6 Oct. 2001); Neave, A. (HLRO; GL); Nell, D. (IWM [Rolf]); Newey, M. (IWM); Nichols, A. L. (IWM [Rolf]); Norris, W. A. (IWM); Osborne, M. E. (IWM); Palmer, D. B. (IWM [Rolf]); Parker, D. E. (http://www.pegasus-one.org/pow/david_parker.htm, accessed 19 Sept. 2002); Parslow, W. (IWM [Rolf]); Peacock, F. (IWM [Rolf]); Pickering, A. D. (IWM [Rolf]); Pickering, E. (IWM [Rolf]); Platt, J. E. (IWM); Porter, W. J. (IWM [Rolf]); Powell, A. F. (IWM); Prebendary, A. R. (IWM); Purner, D. (http://www.angelfire.com/nd/domneal/powar.html, accessed 6 Oct. 2001); Quinney, W. A. (IWM); Ransom, G. (NRO); Rees, H. K. (http://www.ateal.co.uk/greatescape/, accessed 7 Feb. 2003); Reid, P. R. (GL); Riviere, M. (LC); Roberts, P. (IWM [Rolf]); Robertson, F. A. (IWM [Rolf]); Rowley, T. W. (IWM [Rolf]); Rowleym, R. (IWM [Rolf]); Sadler, W. H. (IWM [Rolf]); Scales, A. (IWM); Seed, J. (IWM); Sewell, J. H. (IWM); Sharpe, J. S. (IWM [Rolf]); Shipp, H. F. (IWM [Rolf]); Shorrock, L. B. (IWM); Siddall, H. J. (http://www.naval-history. net/WW2MemoirAndSo, accessed 6 Oct. 2001); Singer, H. G. (PRO); Smith, G. W. (IWM); Sollars, J. C. (IWM); Southern, W. (IWM [Rolf]); Spanner, L. H. (IWM); Spencer, E. (IWM [Rolf]); Stephens, W. L. (IWM); Stokes, D. D. (http://web.mala.bc.ca/davies/letters.images/collections.index.htm, accessed 15 Dec. 2003); Stonard, E. W. (IWM [Rolf]); Southern, W. (IWM [Rolf]); Suckling, F. A. (IWM [Rolf]); Sudworth, W. J. (IWM [Rolf]); Swift, D. (IWM); Swinney, D. (SWWEC); Tateson, T. (IWM); Taylor, H. (IWM [Rolf]); Telfer, F. W. (IWM); Town, H. R. (http://homepage.ntlworld.com/longley/wardiary. htm, accessed 24 Apr. 2004); Trinder, H. E. (IWM); Tuck, H. W. (IWM [Rolf]); Upton, G. (IWM [Rolf]); Walker, D. H. (UNB); Walker, S. R. (IWM [Rolf]); Ward, S. C. (IWM [Rolf]); Warsop, G. F. (IWM); Watchorn, R. (IWM); Watson, R. (IWM [Rolf]); West, V. (IWM); Whelan, C. J. (IWM [Rolf]); Willatt, G. (IWM); Wilson, C. T. (IWM [Rolf]); Wilson, G. F. W. (IWM); Wilson, P. A. (IWM [Rolf]); Wilson, R. A. (IWM); Witte, J. H. (IWM); Wooler, J. (IWM); Wright, G. B. (IWM); Wylie, N. R. (IWM).

NEWSPAPERS, MAGAZINES, JOURNALS, ETC.

After the Battle; *Broadcast*; *Colditz Society Newsletter*; *Collier's*; *Daily Express*; *Daily Herald*; *Daily Mail*; *Daily Mirror*; *Daily Telegraph*; *[Manchester] Guardian*; *Illustrated London News*; *Independent*; *Lancashire Evening News*; *The Listener*; *New Statesman*; *News of the World*; *Observer*; *Observer Colour Supplement*; *Our Prisoners of War: The Official Magazine of the South African Prisoners of War Relatives Association*; *Prisoner of War: The Official Journal of the Prisoners of War Department of the Red Cross and St. John War Organisation*; *Radio Times*; *Sight and Sound*; *Spectator*; *Sunday Mirror*; *Sunday Telegraph*; *Sunday Times*; *Television Mail*; *The Times*; *Touchstone*; *TV Times*; *Weekend Scotsman*; *Yorkshire Evening Post*.

PUBLISHED MEMOIRS, DIARIES, LETTERS, DOCUMENTS, ETC.

ADAIR, L., *Glass Houses: Paper Men* (Brisbane, 1992).

ADAMS, D. G. (ed.), *Backwater: Oflag IX A/H Lower Camp* (London, 1944).

ALLAN, J., *No Citation* (London, 1955).

ANNETTS, E., *Campaign Without Medals* (Lewes, 1990).

ARKWRIGHT, A. S. B., *Return Journey: Escape from Oflag VIB* (London, 1948).

ARCT, B., *Prisoner of War: My Secret Journal* (Exeter, 1988).

ASTON, W. H., *Nor Iron Bars a Cage: The Adventures of Three British Prisoners of War 1940–1942* (London, 1946).

BARKER, R., *It's Goodnight From Him: The Best of the Two Ronnies* (London, 1976).

BARTHROPP, P., *Paddy: The Life and Times of Paddy Barthropp, D.F.C., A.F.C.* (Hailsham, 2001).

BATES, M., *A Wilderness of Days: An Artist's Experiences as a Prisoner of War in Germany* (Victoria, BC, 1978).

BEATTIE, E. W. Jr., *Diary of a Kriegie* (New York, 1976).

BEAUMONT, J., *Mr Wu's Log: A Canoe, Captivity and the Cloth* (privately printed, 1995).

BECKWITH, E. G. C., *The Wind in the Wire* (privately printed, 1965).

BECKWITH, T. D. (ed.), *The Mansel Diaries: The Diaries of Captain John Mansel* (London, 1977).

BELGION, M., *Reading For Profit: Lectures on English Literature Delivered in 1941, 1942, and 1943 to British Officers, Prisoners of War in Germany* (Harmondsworth, 1945).

BENNETT, A., *Writing Home* (London, 1994).

BENNETT, L. *Parachute to Berlin* (New York, 1945).

BEESON, G., *Five Roads to Freedom* (London, 1977).

BERNADOTTE, Count, *Instead of Arms* (London, 1949).

BISHOP, J., *In Pursuit of Freedom* (London, 1977).

BOND, D., *Steady, Old Man! Don't You Know There's a War On?* (London, 1990).

BORRIE, J., *Despite Captivity: A Doctor's Life as Prisoner of War* (London, 1975).

BRADING, A. C. P., *And So To Germany* (Ilfracombe, 1966).

BRIGHT, B., 'Blinded and a Prisoner of War', *Blackwood's Magazine*, 257 (1945), 242–50.

BROOM, B. (comp.), *Geoffrey Broom's War: Letters and Diaries* (Edinburgh, 1993).

BROOMHEAD, E. N., *Barbed Wire in the Sunset* (Melbourne, 1945).

BROWN, J., *In Durance Vile*, ed. J. Borrie (London, 1981).

BROWN, K., *Bonds of Wire: A Memoir* (Toronto, 1989).

BROWN, S., *Forbidden Paths* (Edinburgh, 1978).

BUCKLEDEE, H., *For You the War is Over: A Suffolk Man Recounts his Prisoner of War Experiences* (Sudbury, 1994).

BUCKMAN, R., *Forced March to Freedom: An Illustrated Diary of the Forced Marches and the Interval Between January to March 1945* (Stittsville, Ont., 1984).

—— *Turned Towards the Sun: An Autobiography* (Norwich, 2003).

BURN, M., *Farewell to Colditz* (London, 1974).

—— *Yes, Farewell* (London, 1946).

BURTON, J., *Mirador: My Term as Hitler's Guest* (London, 1986).

BURTT-SMITH, J., *One of the Many on the Move* (Braunton, 1992).

CALNAN T. D., *Free As a Running Fox* (London, 1970).

CALVEY, R. W., *Name, Rank and Number* (Lewes, 1998).

CAMINADA, J., *My Purpose Holds* (London, 1952).

CAMPBELL, A., *Colditz Cameo: Being a Collection of Verse Written by a Prisoner of War in Germany, 1940–1945* (Ditchling, 1954).

CARDIGAN, Earl, *I Walked Alone* (London, 1950).

CARRUTHERS, P. W., *Of Ploughs, Planes and Palliasses* (Arundel, 1992).

CASTLE, J., *The Password Is Courage* (London, 1954).

CHAMP, J. and C. BURGESS, *The Diggers of Colditz* (Sydney, 1985).

CHARTERS, D. L., *Medical Experiences as a Prisoner of War in Germany* (Liverpool, 1946).

CHESTERTON, N., *Crete Was My Waterloo: A True Account of the Sinking of the Lancastria, the Battle of Crete and P.O.W. Experiences 1940–45* (London, 1995).

CHRISP, J., *The Tunnellers of Sandborstal* (London, 1959).

CHRISTIANSEN, C., *Seven Years Among Prisoners of War*, trans. I. E. Winter (Athens, Ohio, 1994).

CHURCHILL, P., *The Spirit in the Cage* (London, 1954).

CHUTTER, J. B., *Captivity Captive* (London, 1954).

CLIFTON, G., *The Happy Hunted* (London, 1954).

COLLINS, D., *P.O.W.* (London, 1970).

COWARD, R. V., *Sailors in Cages* (London, 1967).

COX, A. B., *Our Spirit Unbroken: Memoirs of a Prisoner of War* (Port Elgin, Ont., 1999).

CREW, F. J., 'Prisoner of War', in *Through Eyes of Blue: Personal Memories of the RAF from 1918* (Shrewsbury, 2002), 147–9.

CUDDON, E. (ed.), *Trial of Erich Killinger, Heinz Junge, Otto Bohringer, Heinrich Oberhardt, Gustav Bauer-Schlichtegroll (The Dulag Luft Trial)*, War Crimes Trials Series, Vol. 9 (London, 1952).

DANCOCKS, D. G., *In Enemy Hands: Canadian Prisoners of War, 1939–45* (Toronto, 1990 edn.).

DARLOW, S., *Lancaster Down! The Extraordinary Tale of Seven Young Bomber Command Aircrew at War* (London, 2000).

DAVIES, J. A., *A Leap in the Dark: A Welsh Airman's Adventures in Occupied Europe* (London, 1994).

DEAN-DRUMMOND, A., *Arrows of Fortune* (London, 1992).

DICK, C., *The Poems of a Prisoner of War* (Morpeth, 1946).

DOENITZ, K., *Memoirs: Ten Years and Twenty Days*, trans. R. H. Stevens (Annapolis, Md., 1990 edn.).

DOMINY, J., *The Sergeant Escapers* (London, 1974).

DOTHIE, W. H., *Operation Disembroil: Deception and Escape, Normandy 1940* (London, 1985).

DUGGAN, M. (ed.), *Padre in Colditz: The Diary of J. Ellison Platt* (London, 1978).

DUKE, F., *Name, Rank and Serial Number* (New York, 1969).

DUNCAN, M., *Underground From Posen* (London, 1954).

DUNN, C., *Permission to Speak: An Autobiography* (London, 1986).

DUNNING, G., *Where Bleed the Many* (London, 1955).

EDGAR, D., *The Stalag Men* (London, 1982).

EGGERS, R., *Colditz: The German Story*, ed. H. Gee (London, 1961).

—— (comp.), *Colditz Recaptured* (London, 1973).

—— *Escape From Colditz*, ed. J. Watton (London, 1973).

ELWYN, J., *At the Fifth Attempt* (London, 1987).

EVANS, A., *Sojourn in Silesia, 1940–1945* (Ashford, 1995).

EVANS, A. J., *Escape and Liberation, 1940–1945* (London, 1945).

FALLON, L., *La Ferveur et l'épreuve: de Saint-Cyr à Verdun via Colditz, Saigon et autres lieux: premiere partie: touristes en Germanie* (Paris, 1985).

FANCY, J., *Tunnelling to Freedom* (London, 1957).

FARR, M., *Vanishing Borders: The Rediscovery of Eastern Germany, Poland and Bohemia* (London, 1991).

FEARNSIDE, E., *The Joy of Freedom: A Graphic Account of Life in a Prisoner of War Camp during the Second World War* (Burton-in-Kendel, 1996).

FERGUSON, I., *Doctor at War* (London, 1955).

FOLKARD, L., *The Sky and the Desert* (Penzance, 1985).

FORBES, B., *A Divided Life* (London, 1992).

FRASER-SMITH, C., with S. LESBERG and G. MCKNIGHT, *The Secret War of Charles Fraser-Smith* (London, 1981).

FRY, S., *Moab Is My Washpot* (London, 1997).

FURMAN, J., *Be Not Fearful* (London, 1959).

GALE, R., *Private Prisoner* (Wellingborough, 1984).

GALLAND, A., *The First and the Last*, M. Savill, trans. (London, 1955 abridged edn.).

GANPULEY, N. G., *Netaji in Germany: A Little-Known Chapter* (Bombay, 1959).

GANT, R., *How Like a Wilderness* (London, 1946).

GARDNER, B., *The Terrible Rain: The War Poets 1939–1945* (London, 1966).

GARIOCH, R., *Two Men and a Blanket: Memoirs of Captivity* (Edinburgh, 1975).

GAYLER, R., *Private Prisoner* (Wellingborough, 1984).

GREEN, J. M., *From Colditz in Code* (London, 1971; Hull, 1989).

GREVILLE, H., *Prison Camp Spies: Espionage Behind the Wire* (Loftus, NSW, 1998).

GROGAN, J. P., *Dieppe and Beyond* (Renfrew, Ont., 1982).

GUENET, M., *Le Secret de Colditz* (Paris, 1979).

HAIG, Earl, *My Father's Son: The Memoirs of Major the Earl Haig* (London, 2000).

HALL, W. V., *Flyer's Tale* (Braunton, 1989).

HAMSON, C. J., *Liber in Vinculus* (Cambridge, 1989).

HANNACK, E., *Stalag VIIIB/344: Erlebnisbericht* (London, 1994).

HARDING, R., *Copper Wire* (Dublin, 2001).

HARDING, W., *A Cockney Soldier, 'Duty Before Pleasure': An Autobiography 1918–46* (Braunton, 1989).

HARRIS, G. H., *Prisoner of War and Fugitive* (Aldershot, 1947).

HARRISON, M. C. C. and H. A. CARTWRIGHT, *Within Four Walls* (London, 1930).

HAREWOOD, Earl, *The Tongs and Old Bones: The Memoirs of Lord Harewood* (London, 1981).

HARSH, G., *Lonesome Road* (New York, 1971).

HARTNELL-BEAVIS, J., *Final Flight* (Braunton, 1985).

HARVIE, J. D., *Missing in Action: An RCAF Navigator's Story* (Montreal and Kingston, 1995).

HASTINGS, M., *Going To the Wars* (London, 2000).

HAWKINS, D. (ed.), *War Report: A Record of Dispatches Broadcast by the BBC's War Correspondents with the Allied Expeditionary Force 6 June 1944–5 May 1945* (London, 1946).

HILL, F., *Prisoner of War* (London, 1994).

HIRST, F., *A Green Hill Far Away* (Stockport, 1998).

HODGKINSON, B. G., *Spitfire Down: The POW Story*, ed. G. E. Condon (Toronto, 2000).

HODGKINSON, C., *Best Foot Forward* (London, 1957).

HOLLIDAY, J. E. (ed.), *Stories of the RAAF POWs at Lamsdorf: Including 500 Mile Trek* (Holland Park, Queensland, 1992).

HORSAM, J., *A Thousand Miles to Freedom* (London, 1942).

HOWELL, E., *Escape to Live* (London, 1947).

HUNT, L. C., *The Prisoners' Progress: An Illustrated Diary of the March into Captivity of the Last of the British Army in France—June 1940* (London, 1941).

HUNTER, J. W., *From Coastal Command to Captivity* (Barnsley, 2003).

HUSSEY, M., *Chance Governs All* (London, 2001).

HUTTON, C., *Official Secret* (London, 1960).

International Military Tribunal, *The Trial of German Major War Criminals*, 23 vols. (HMSO, 1946–51).

INSTONE, G., *Freedom the Spur* (London, 1953).

JACKSON, B., *The Lone Survivor* (North Battleford, Sask., 1993).

JACKSON, R. (comp.), *When Freedom Calls: Great Escapes of the Second World War* (London, 1973).

JAMES, B. A., *Moonless Night* (London, 1983).

JAMES, D., *A Prisoner's Progress* (Edinburgh, 1947).

JERVIS, C. W., *The Long Trek* (Elms Court, 1993).

JOHNSON, S. P. L., *A Kriegie's Log: The Lighter Side of Prison Life* (Tunbridge Wells, 1995).

JOHNSON, T., *Escape to Freedom* (Barnsley, 2002).

JONES, E. C., *Germans Under My Bed* (London, 1957).

JONES, E. H., *The Road to En-Dor* (London, 1973 edn.).

JONES, F. S., *Escape To Nowhere* (London, 1952).

JORDAN, F., *Escape*, trans. N. Indursky, (Cranbury, NJ, 1970).

KEE, R., *A Crowd Is Not Company* (London, 1982 edn.).

KELLY, F., *Private Kelly* (London, 1954).

KEYDER, B., *From Wings to Jackboots: From Diaries Kept as a Wartime Pilot in North Africa, Italy and as a P.O.W. in Stalag Luft I, North Germany* (London, 1995).

KIDD, D., *POW!* (Pontefract, 1986).

KINDERSLEY, P., *For You the War Is Over* (Tunbridge Wells, 1983).

KINGSFORD, P., *After Alamein: Prisoner of War Diaries 1942–45* (East Grinstead, 1992).

KYDD, S., *For You the War Is Over . . .* (London, 1973).

LANG, D., *Return to St. Valéry* (Luneray, 1989).

LANGLEY, J. M., *Fight Another Day* (London, 1974).

LARIVE, E. H., *The Man Who Came in From Colditz* (London, 1975).

LAWRENCE, J., *2.2.9.7.: A POW's Story* (Fontwell, 1991).

LE RAY, A., *Première a Colditz* (Paris, 1976).

LE SOUEF, L., *To War Without a Gun* (Perth, WA, 1980).

LEVY, H., *The Dark Side of the Sky: The Story of a Young Jewish Airman in Nazi Germany* (London, 1996).

LIND, L., *Flowers of Rethymnon: Escape from Crete* (Kenthurst, NSW, 1991).

LONGSON, J. and C. TAYLOR, *An Arnhem Odyssey* (London, 1991).

McFARLANE, B., *An Autobiography of British Cinema* (London, 1997).

MACKAY, A., *313 Days to Christmas: A Human Record of War and Imprisonment* (Glendaruel, 1998).

MACKENZIE, K. W. *Hurricane Combat: The Nine Lives of a Fighter Pilot* (London, 1990 edn.).

MACKENZIE, R., *An Ordinary War, 1940–1945* (Wangaratta, Victoria, 1995).

McKIBBIN, M. N., *Barbed Wire: Memories of Stalag 383* (London, 1947).

McMAHON, J., *Almost a Lifetime* (Lantzville, BC, 1995).

MARGARISON, R., *Boys at War* (Bolton, 1986).

MICHELL, S., *They Were Invincible: Dieppe and After* (Bracebridge, Alberta, 1979).

MILLAR, G., *Horned Pigeon* (London, 1946).

MILLS, J., *Up In the Clouds, Gentlemen Please* (London, 1981).

MOORE, L. S. G., *30 Days—A Lifetime* (Sidney, BC, 1989).

MORETON, G., *Doctor in Chains* (London, 1980 edn.).

MORGAN, G., *Only Ghosts Can Live* (London, 1945).

MORRISON, W., *Flak and Ferrets: One Way to Colditz* (London, 1995).

NABARRO, D., *Wait For the Dawn* (London, 1952).

NEAVE, A., *They Have Their Exits* (London, 1953).

NEAVE, A., *Saturday at M.I.9: A History of Underground Escape Routes in North-West Europe in 1940–5 By a Leading Organiser at M.I. 9* (London, 1969).

NEWMAN, P., *Safer Than a Known Way: An Escape Story of World War II* (London, 1983).

NICHOLS, C., *The Man England Forgot: Diary, Words and Poetry* (Ilfracombe, 1998).

NIVEN, D., *Bring On the Empty Horses* (New York, 1975).

Nuernberg Military Tribunal, *Trials of War Criminals before the Nuernberg Military Tribunals*, 15 vols. (Washington, DC, 1950).

Office of the US Chief Consul for the Prosecution of Axis Criminality, *Nazi Conspiracy and Aggression*, 10 vols. (Washington, DC, 1946–7).

OGILVIE, P. and N. ROBINSON, *In the Bag* (Johannesburg, 1975).

PAICE, A. and A. WARD, *For the Love of Elizabeth: The Memoir of Albert Paice, Prisoner of War, 1940–1945* (London, 1984).

PALMER, G., *Prisoner of Death* (Wellingborough, 1990).

PAPE, R., *Boldness Be My Friend* (London, 1953).

—— *Sequel to Boldness* (London, 1959).

PARTRIDGE, A., *That Split Eternal Second* (London, 1995).

PASSFIELD, A., *The Escape Artist* (Perth, WA, 1988).

PASSMORE, R., *Moving Tent* (London, 1982).

PAUL, D. with J. ST JOHN, *Surgeon at Arms* (London, 1958).

PERRIN, A., *Évadé de guerre via Colditz* (Paris, 1975).

PETITCOLIN, L., *Les Fortes Têtes, 1940–1944: La Fortresse de Colditz* (Paris, 1985).

PHILPOT, O., *Stolen Journey* (London, 1950).

POCOCK, J. W., *The Diary of a Prisoner of War, 1940–1945* (Southampton, 1985).

POOLE, J., *Undiscovered Ends* (London, 1957).

PORTUGAL, J. E. (ed.), *We Were There*, Vol. 7: *R.C.A.F. & Others* (Toronto, 1998).

PORTWAY, C., *Journey To Dana* (London, 1955).

PRINGLE, J., *Colditz Last Stop* (London, 1988).

PRITTIE, T. C. F. and W. E. EDWARDS, *Escape to Freedom* (London, 1953 edn.); formerly *South to Freedom* (1946).

PROUSE, A. R., *Ticket To Hell Via Dieppe* (Toronto, 1982).

PRYCE, T. E., *Heels in Line* (London, 1958).

PURDON, C., *List the Bugle: Reminiscences of an Irish Soldier* (Antrim, 1993).

QUARRIE, R. G. M., *Oflag* (Durham, 1995).

RAE, J. D., *Kiwi Spitfire Ace: A Gripping World War II Story of Action, Captivity and Freedom* (London, 2001).

RAMSAY, I., *P.O.W.: A Digger in Hitler's Prison Camps 1941–45* (Melbourne, 1985).

RAYNER, S., *I Remember* (Lincoln, 1995).

READ, D. H. C., *Prisoners' Quest: A Presentation of the Christian Faith in a Prisoners of War Camp* (London, 1944).

—— *This Grace Given* (Grand Rapids, Mich., 1984).

REID, I., *Prisoner at Large: The Story of Five Escapes* (London, 1947).

REID, M., *Last On the List* (London, 1974).

—— *Into Colditz* (Salisbury, 1983).

REID, P. R., *The Colditz Story* (London, 1952).

RICHARD, O. G., *Kriegie: An American POW in Germany* (Baton Rouge, 2000).

ROBERTS, B., *A Kind of Cattle* (Sydney, 1985).

ROBERTS, J., *A Terrier Goes To War* (London, 1998).

ROBINSON, C., *Journey to Captivity* (Canberra, 1991).

ROBINSON, E. L., *We Fell On Stony Ground* (Lewes, 1998).

ROFE, C., *Against the Wind* (London, 1956).

ROGERS, J., *Tunnelling into Colditz: A Mining Engineer in Captivity* (London, 1986).

ROMILLY, G. and M. ALEXANDER, *The Privileged Nightmare* (London, 1954).

ROSMARIN, I., *Inside Story* (Cape Town, 1990).

RUBINSTEIN, N., *The Invisibly Wounded* (Hull, 1989).

RUSHTON, C., *Spectator in Hell* (Springhill, 1998).

RYAN, IMELDA (comp.), *POWs Fraternal: Diaries of S/Sgt Raymond Ryan, Poems of Pte Lawrence (Bouff) Ryan* (Perth, WA, 1990).

SABEY, I., *Stalag Scrapbook* (Melbourne, 1947).

SAFRANI, A. H., 'A Soldier Remembers', *The Oracle*, 6 (1984), 24–65.

ST CLAIR, S., *The Endless War: Or 1000 Days 'In the Bag'* (North Battleford, Sask., 1987).

SCHRIRE, I., *Stalag Doctor* (London, 1956).

SCOTLAND, A. P., *The London Cage* (London, 1957).

'Sentry', 'Shadow Life in Captivity', *Blackwood's Magazine*, 259 (1946), 286–96.

SILVER, L. R., *Last of the Gladiators: A World War II Bomber Navigator's Story* (Shrewsbury, 1995).

SIMMONS, K. W., *Kriegie* (New York, 1960).

SLACK, T., *Happy is the Day: A Spitfire Pilot's Story* (Penzance, 1987).

SMITH, A. S. (ed.), *The Boys Write Home* (Sydney, 1944).

SMITH, M., *What a Bloody Arrival: A Wartime Story of Survival* (Lewes, 1997).

SNIDERS, E., *Flying In, Walking Out: Memories of War and Escape, 1939–1945* (Barnsley, 1999).

SPENSER, J. [F. H. Guest], *The Awkward Marine* (London, 1948).

SPILLER, H. (ed.), *Prisoners of Nazis: Accounts by American POWs in World War II* (Jefferson, NC, 1998).

STEDMAN, J., *Life of a British POW in Poland* (Braunton, 1992).

STRACHEN, T. (ed.), *In the Clutch of Circumstance: Reminiscences of Members of the Canadian National Prisoners of War Association* (Victoria, BC, 1995).

STRONG, T. (ed.), *We Prisoners of War: Sixteen British Officers and Soldiers Speak from a German Prison Camp* (New York, 1942).

SUGGITT, H. V., *Reluctant Guest of the Reich* (London, 1992).

SWALLOW, T. and A. H. PILL et al., *Flywheel: Memories of the Open Road* (Exeter, 1987).

TAMS, F. A. B., *A Trenchard 'Brat'* (Edinburgh, 2000).

TAYLOR, F., *Barbed Wire and Footlights: Seven Stalags To Freedom* (Braunton, 1988).

TAYLOR, G., *Return Ticket* (London, 1972).

——*Piece of Cake* (London, 1980 edn.).

THOMAS, G., *Milag: Captives of the Kriegsmarine* (Cowbridge, 1995).

THOMAS, R. P., *Student To Stalag* (Wimborne, 1999).

THOMAS, W. B., *Dare To Be Free* (London, 1955 edn.).

THOMPSON, D. W., *Captives To Freedom* (London, 1955).

THROWER, D., *The Lonely Path to Freedom* (London, 1980).

TORDAY, J. (ed.), *The Coldstreamer and the Canary: Letters, Memories and Friends of Roger Mortimer, Prisoner of War No. 481, 1940–1945* (Langley, 1995).

TUCKI, J., *My War, Captivity and Freedom* (London, 1998).

TURNER, J. F., *Prisoner At Large* (London, 1957).

TUTE, W., *Escape Route Green: Flight from Stalag XXA* (London, 1971).

UNWCC, *Law Reports of Trials of War Criminals*, 15 vols. (HMSO, 1947–8).

URQUART, F. (ed.), *Great True War Adventures* (London, 1957).

VAUGHAN, G. D., *The Way It Really Was* (Budleigh Salterton, 1985).

VIETOR, J. A., *Time Out: American Airmen at Stalag Luft I* (New York, 1951).

VINCENT, A., *The Long Road Home* (London, 1956).

WALKER, D., *Lean, Wind Lean: A Few Times Remembered* (London, 1984).

WALKER, E., *The Price of Surrender, 1941: The War in Crete* (London, 1992).

War Office, *A Handbook for the Information of Relatives and Friends of Prisoners of War* (HMSO, 1943).

War Organisation of the British Red Cross Society and the Order of St John of Jerusalem, *Prisoner of War: The First Authentic Account of the Lives of British Prisoners of War in Enemy Hands* (London, 1942).

——Educational Books Section, *The Royal Air Force School for Prisoners of War, Stalag Luft VI* (Oxford, 1943).

WARD, A. (ed.), *Rough Ride from Trier: The Experiences of British Prisoners of War Who Were in German Hands, 1940–1945*, 2 vols. (Sheffield, 1987).

WARD, E., *Give Me Air* (London, 1946).

WARNER, J., *Jack of All Trades: An Autobiography* (London, 1975).

WARRACK, G., *Travel By Dark: After Arnhem* (London, 1963).

WATT, D., *Stoker: The Story of an Australian Soldier Who Survived Auschwitz-Birkenau* (East Roseville, NSW, 1995).

WHITING, D., *Prisoners, People, Places, Partisans and Patriots* (Bognor Regis, 1980).

WILD, D., *Prisoner of Hope* (Lewes, 1992).

WILLAT, G., *Bombs and Barbed Wire: My War in the RAF and in Stalag Luft III* (Tunbridge Wells, 1995).

WILLIAMS, E., *On Parade for Himmler* (Hull, 1994).

WILLIAMS, E., *Arbeitskommando* (London, 1975).

WILLIAMS, E., *The Wooden Horse* (London, 1949).

—— *The Tunnel* (London, 1951).

WILLIAMSON, L., *Six Wasted Years* (Braunton, 1985).

WILLOUGHBY, C. R., *I Was There*, trans. E. Thompson (Brewarrina, NSW, 1994).

WINTER, P., *Free Lodgings* (Auckland, 1993).

WOOD, J. E. R. (ed.), *Detour: The Story of Oflag IV C* (London, 1946).

WOODS, J., *Peace in My Time?!* (Preston, 1995).

WOOLLEY, H. E., *No Time Off for Good Behaviour* (Burnstown, Ont., 1990).

YOUNG, S., *Descent into Danger* (London, 1954).

YOUNGER, C., *No Flight from the Cage* (London, 1981 edn.).

ZEMKE, H. and R. A. FREEMAN, *Zemke's Stalag* (Washington, DC, 1991).

Secondary Sources

THESES

HATLEY-BROAD, B., 'Prisoner of War Families and the British Government During the Second World War,' Ph.D., University of Sheffield (2002).

VOURKOUTIOTIS, V., 'The German Armed Forces Supreme Command and British and American Prisoners-of-War, 1939–1945: Policy and Practice' Ph.D., McGill University (2000).

BOOKS

ADAM-SMITH, P., *Prisoners of War: From Gallipoli to Korea* (Ringwood, Victoria, 1992).

ADDISON, P. and A. CALDER (eds.), *Time to Kill: The Soldier's Experience of War in the West, 1939–1945* (London, 1997).

AITKIN, L., *Massacre on the Road to Dunkirk: Wormhout 1940* (London, 1977).

ANDREWS, A., *Exemplary Justice* (London, 1976).

ANON., *From Colditz to Bangladesh* (Manchester, 1996).

ARMES, R., *A Critical History of the British Cinema* (London, 1978).

BAILEY, R. H., *Prisoners of War* (Alexandria, Va., 1981).

BARBER, N., *Prisoner of War: The Story of British Prisoners Held By the Enemy* (London, 1944).

BARD, M. G., *Forgotten Victims: The Abandonment of Americans in Hitler's Camps* (Boulder, Col., 1994).

BARKER, A. J., *Behind Barbed Wire* (London, 1974).

BARR, C., *Ealing Studios* (London, 1989).

BARRETT, J., *We Were There: Australian Soldiers of World War II Tell Their Stories* (Sydney, 1987).

BARTHES, R., *Mythologies*, trans. A. Lavers (London, 1972).

BAYBUTT, R., *Camera In Colditz* (London, 1982).

BEAUMAN, K. S., *Green Sleeves: The Story of the WVS/WRVS* (London, 1977).

BEEVOR, A., *Crete: The Battle and the Resistance* (London, 1992).

BEST, G., *Humanity in Warfare: The Modern History of the International Law of Armed Conflicts* (London, 1980).

BICKERS, R. T., *Home Run: Great RAF Escapes of the Second World War* (London, 1992).

BISCHOF, G. and R. OVERMANS (eds.), *Kriegsgefangenschaft im Zweiten Weltkrieg: Eine Vergleichhende Perspektive* (Terriatz-Pottschach, 1999).

BLAIR, C., *Hitler's U-Boat War: The Hunted, 1942–1945* (New York, 1998).

BOND. B., *The Unquiet Western Front: Britain's Role in Literature and History* (Cambridge, 2002).

BOWER, T., *Heroes of World War II* (London, 1995).

BRICKHILL, P. and C. NORTON, *Escape to Danger* (London, 1946).

—— *Escape—Or Die: Authentic Stories of the R.A.F. Escaping Society* (London, 1952).

—— *Reach for the Sky: The Story of Douglas Bader* (London, 1954).

BROOME, V., *The Way Back* (New York, 1958).

BURGESS, A., *The Longest Tunnel: The True Story of World War II's Great Escape* (New York, 1990).

BURGESS, C., *Freedom or Death: Australia's Greatest Escape Stories from Two World Wars* (St Leonards, NSW, 1994).

—— *Destination Buchenwald* (Kenthurst, NSW, 1995).

CAINE, P. D., *Eagles of the RAF* (Washington, DC, 1991).

CALDER, A., *The Myth of the Blitz* (London, 1991).

CAMPBELL, I. J., *Murder at the Abbaye: The Story of Twenty Canadian Soldiers Murdered at the Abbaye d'Ardenne* (Ottawa, 1996).

CARTER, C. J., *The Shamrock and the Swastika: German Espionage in Ireland in World War II* (Palo Alto, Cal., 1977).

CAWTHORNE, N., *The Iron Cage* (London, 1993).

Central Statistical Office, *Fighting With Figures: A Statistical Digest of the Second World War* (London, 1995).

CHANCELLOR, H., *Colditz: The Definitive History* (London, 2001).

CONNELL, C., *The Hidden Catch* (London, 1955).

COOPER, A. W., *Free to Fight Again: RAF Escapes and Evasions, 1940–45* (London, 1988).

CRAWLEY, A., *Escape From Germany* (London, 1956).

CREW, F. A. E., *The Army Medical Services: Administration, Vol. I* (HMSO, 1953).

DEAR, I., *Escape and Evasion: Prisoner of War Breakouts and the Routes to Safety in World War Two* (London, 1997).

DERRY, S., *The Rome Escape Line: The Story of the British Organisation in Rome For Assisting Escaped Prisoners of War* (London, 1960).

DOHERTY, M. A., *Nazi Wireless Propaganda: Lord Haw-Haw and British Public Opinion in the Second World War* (Edinburgh, 2000).

DOUW VAN DER KRAP, C. L. J. F., *Contra de Swastika: De strijd van een onverzettelijke Nederlandse marineofficier in Bezet Europa, 1940–1945* (Antwerp, 1981).

DURAND, A., *From Sarajevo to Hiroshima: History of the International Committee of the Red Cross* (Geneva, 1984).

DURAND, A. A., *Stalag Luft III: The Secret Story* (Baton Rouge, 1988).

ELLIOTT, S. and B. TURNER, *Denholm Elliott: Quest for Love* (London, 1994).

ELLIS, J., *The Sharp End: The Fighting Men in World War II* (New York, 1980).

FERGUSSON, B., *The Black Watch and the King's Enemies* (London, 1950).

FOOT, M. R. D. and J. M. LANGLEY, *MI9: Escape and Evasion, 1939–1945* (London, 1979).

FORRESTER, L., *Fly for Your Life: The Story of Wing Commander R. R. Stanford Tuck* (London, 1960 edn.).

FOSTER, J. L., *Catapulting From Colditz: And Other Incredible Escapes* (London, 1982).

GAMMON, V. F., *No Time For Fear: True Accounts of RAF Airmen Taken Prisoner, 1939–1945* (London, 1998).

—— *Not All Glory! Accounts of RAF Airmen Taken Prisoner in Europe, 1939–1945* (London, 1996).

GARRETT, R., *P.O.W.* (Newton Abbot, 1981).

GARRETT, R., *Great Escapes of World War II: And Some That Failed To Make It* (London, 1989).

GENSICKE, K., *Der Mufti von Jerusalem Amin el-Husseini, und der Nationalsozialisten* (Frankfurt-am-Main, 1988).

GILBERT, M., *The Day the War Ended: May 8, 1945—Victory in Europe* (New York, 1995).

GILL, A., *The Great Escape: The Full Dramatic Story with Contributions From Survivors and Their Families* (London, 2002).

GORDON, L. A., *Brothers Against the Raj: A Biography of Indian Nationalists Sarat and Subhas Chandra Bose* (New York, 1990).

GRAHAM, B., *Escape From the Swastika* (London, 1975).

GRAHAM, V., *The Story of WVS* (HMSO, 1959).

HALL, D. O. W., *Prisoners of Germany* (Wellington, 1949).

—— *Escapes* (Wellington, 1954).

HARRIS, W. G., *Natalie & R. J.: Hollywood's Star-Crossed Lovers* (New York, 1988).

HAUNER, M., *India in Axis Strategy: Germany, Japan, and Indian Nationalists in the Second World War* (Stuttgart, 1981).

HEER, H. and K. NAUMANN (eds.), *War of Extermination: The German Military in World War II, 1941–1944* (New York, 2000).

HERNU, S., *Q: The Biography of Desmond Llewelyn* (Seaford, 1999).

HINDSLEY, F. H. et al., *British Intelligence in the Second World War: Its Influence on Strategy and Operations*, Vol. *3*, Pt. *1* (HMSO, 1984).

HOE, A., *David Stirling: The Authorised Biography of the Founder of the SAS* (London, 1992).

HOLLAND, R. W. (comp.), *Adversis Major: A Short History of the Educational Books Scheme of the Prisoners of War Department of the British Red Cross Society and Order of St. John of Jerusalem* (London, 1949).

HOLMES, R., *Firing Line* (London, 1994 edn.).

HOWARD, M., G. J. ANDREOPOULOS, and M. R. SCHULMAN (eds.), *The Laws of War: Constraints on Warfare in the Western World* (New Haven, 1994).

HURD, G. (ed.), *National Fictions: World War Two in British Films and Television* (London, 1984).

HUTCHINSON, J. F., *Champions of Charity: War and the Rise of the Red Cross* (Boulder, Col., 1996).

HUTTON, W., *The World We're In* (London, 2002).

HYNES, S., *The Soldier's Tale: Bearing Witness to Modern War* (New York, 1997).

ICRC, *The International Red Cross Committee in Geneva 1863–1943* (Zurich, 1943).

—— *Inter Arma Caritas: The Work of the International Committee of the Red Cross During the Second World War* (Geneva, 1947).

—— *Report of the International Committee of the Red Cross On Its Activities During the Second World War (September 1, 1939–June 30, 1947)*, 3 vols. (Geneva, 1948).

IVELAW-CHAPMAN, J., *High Endeavour: The Life of Air Chief Marshal Sir Ronald Ivelaw-Chapman* (London, 1993).

JACKSON, R. (comp.), *When Freedom Calls: Great Escapes of the Second World War* (London, 1973).

JOHNSON, M., *Fighting the Enemy: Australian Soldiers and their Adversaries in World War II* (Cambridge, 2000).

JOLLY, C., *The Vengeance of Private Pooley* (London, 1956).

JONES, F. S., *Hit or Miss: Being the Adventures of Driver Randle Barlow* (London, 1954).

KLEIN, H. (ed.), *The Second World War in Fiction* (London, 1984).

KÜBLER, R. (comp.), *Chef KGW: Das Kriegsgefangenenwesen und Gottlob Berger* (Lindhorst, 1984).

LANCHBERY, E., *Against the Sun: The Story of Wing Commander Roland Beamont* (London, 1955).

LAUCK, J. H., *Katyn Killings: In the Record* (Clifton, NJ, 1988).

LEIGH, M., *Captives Courageous: South African Prisoners of War, World War II* (Johannesburg, 1992).

LEVINE, A. J., *Captivity, Flight and Survival in World War II* (Westport, Conn., 2000).

LONG, G., *Greece, Crete and Syria: Australia in the War of 1939–1945*, Series 1 (Army), Vol. II (Canberra, 1953).

LUMMIS, T., *Listening to History: The Authenticity of Oral Evidence* (London, 1987).

MCCORMICK, D., *The Master Book of Escapes: The World of Escapes from Houdini to Colditz* (London, 1974).

MACDONALD, C., *The Lost Battle: Crete 1941* (New York, 1993).

MCGILL, D., *P.O.W.: The Untold Stories of New Zealanders as Prisoners of War* (Naenae, NZ, 1987).

MCKNIGHT, G. and S. LESBERG, *The Secret War of Charles Fraser-Smith* (London, 1981).

MACNALTY, A. S. and V. F. MELLOR (eds.), *Medical Services in War* (HMSO, 1968).

MADSEN, C., *Another Kind of Justice: Canadian Military Law from Confederation to Somalia* (Vancouver, 1999).

MAI, U., *Kriegsgefangen in Brandenburg: Stalag III A in Luckenwalde 1939–1945* (Berlin, 1999).

MALOIRE, A., *Colditz: le grand refus* (Vincennes, 1982).

MARGOLIN, H., *Conduct Unbecoming: The Story of the Murder of Canadian Prisoners of War in Normandy* (Toronto, 1998).

MARTIN, C., *Escape from Colditz* (London, 2001).

MASON, W. W., *Prisoners of War* (Wellington, 1954).

MATTIELO, G. and W. VOGT, *Deutsche Kriegsgefangenen- und Internierteneinrichtungen 1939–1945: Handbuch und Katalog Lagergeschichte und Lagerzensurstemel*, 2 vols. (Coblenz, 1986).

MAYCHICK, D. and L. A. BORGO, *Heart to Heart With Robert Wagner* (New York, 1986).

MOORE, B. and K. FEDOROWICH (eds.), *Prisoners of War and Their Captors in World War II* (Oxford, 1996).

MURPHY, R., *British Cinema and the Second World War* (London, 2000).

NICHOL, J. and T. RENNELL, *The Last Escape: The Untold Story of Allied Prisoners of War in Germany 1944–45* (London, 2002).

O'DRISCOLL, B., *Just Say a Hail Mary: The Story of Maria and Jedrzej Giertych* (London, 1999).

PAPELEUX, L., *L'Action caritiative di Saint-Siege en faveur des prisonniers de geurre (1939–1945)* (Brussels, 1991).

PARIS, M., *Warrior Nation: Images of War in British Popular Culture, 1850–2000* (London, 2000).

PERKS, R., *Oral History: Talking About the Past* (London, 1992).

PHILIPPS, J. A., *The Valley of the Shadow of Death* (New Malden, 1992).

PONTZEELE, D., *Krijgsgevangen! Belgische officieren in het kasteel van Colditz 1940–1943* (Erpe, 2000).

RAY, D., *Colditz: A Pictorial History* (London, 2001).

REID, P. R., *Colditz: The Full Story* (London, 1984).

——*My Favourite Escape Stories* (Guilford, 1975).

——*The Latter Days* (London, 1953).

REID, P. R. and M. MICHAEL, *Prisoners of War* (London, 1984).

ROLF, D., *Prisoners of the Reich: Germany's Captives, 1939–1945* (London, 1988).

ROLLINGS, C., *Wire and Walls: RAF PoWs in Itzehoe, Spangenberg and Thorn 1939–1942* (Hersham, 2003).

ROSS, D. M., *Stapme: The Biography of Squadron Leader B. G. Stapleton* (London, 2000).

ROUTLEDGE, P., *Public Servant, Secret Agent: The Elusive Life and Violent Death of Airey Neave* (London, 2002).

ST GEORGE SAUNDERS, H., *The Red Cross and the White: A Short History of the Joint War Organisation of the British Red Cross Society and the Order of St. John of Jerusalem During the War, 1939–1945* (London, 1949).

SATOW, H., *The Work of the Prisoners of War Department During the Second World War* (Foreign Office, 1950)

SHOEMAKER, L. R., *The Escape Factory: The Story of MIS-X* (New York, 1990).

SMITH, G., *Forty Nights to Freedom* (Winnipeg, 1984).

SMITH, MALCOLM, *Britain and 1940: History, Myth and Popular Memory* (London, 2000).

SMITH, S., *Wings Day: The Man Who Led the RAF's Epic Battle in German Captivity* (London, 1969).

SPEED, R. B., *Prisoners, Diplomats, and the Great War: A Study in the Diplomacy of Captivity* (New York, 1990).

STELZL-MARX, B., *Zwischen Fiktion und Zeitzeugenschaft: Americanische und Sowjetische Kriegsgefangene im Stalag XVII B Krems-Gneixendorf* (Tübingen, 2000).

STEWART, I. and S. L. CARRUTHERS (eds.), *War, Culture and the Media: Representations of the Military in 20th Century Britain* (Madison, Wisc., 1996).

STREIT, C., *Keine Kameraden: Die Wehrmacht und die Sowjetischen Kriegsgefangenen, 1941–1945* (Stuttgart, 1978).

THOMPSON, P., *The Voice of the Past: Oral History*, 2nd edn. (Oxford, 1988).

TOLIVER, R. F., in collaboration with H. J. SCHARFF, *The Interrogator: The Story of Hanns Scharff, Luftwaffe's Master Interrogator* (Fallbrook, Cal., 1978).

TURNER, J. F., *The Bader Tapes* (Bourne End, 1986).

——*Douglas Bader: A Biography of the Legendary World War II Fighter Pilot* (Shrewsbury, 1995).

VANCE, J. F., *Objects of Concern: Canadian Prisoners of War through the Twentieth Century* (Vancouver, 1994).

——*A Gallant Company: The Men of the Great Escape* (Pacifica, Cal., 2000).

——*Encyclopedia of Prisoners of War and Internment* (Santa Barbara, Cal., 2001).

WATT, M., *The Stunned and the Stymied: The POW Experience in the History of the 2/11th Battalion, 1939–1945* (North Perth, WA, 1997).

WEALE, A., *Renegades: Hitler's Englishmen* (London, 1995 edn.).

WEIGHT, R., *Patriots: National Identity in Britain, 1940–2000* (London, 2002).

WILSON, P., *The War Behind the Wire: Experiences in Captivity During the Second World War* (Barnsley, 2000).

WOODS, R., *Night Train to Innsbruck: A Commando's Escape to Freedom* (London, 1983).

WORPOLE, K., *Dockers and Detectives: Popular Reading, Popular Writing* (London, 1983).

WYLIE, N. (ed.), *European Neutrals and Non-Belligerents During the Second World War* (Cambridge, 2002).

ZAYAS, A. M. DE, *The Wehrmacht War Crimes Bureau, 1939–1945*, with W. Rabus (collab.) (Lincoln, Nebr., 1989).

ARTICLES

BARTA, T., 'Film Nazis: The Great Escape', in T. Barta (ed.), *Screening the Past: Film and the Representation of History* (Westport, Conn., 1998), 127–48.

BEAUMONT, J., 'Rank, Privilege and Prisoners of War', *War & Society*, 1 (1983), 67–94.

BHARATI, A., 'Bose and the German INA', *New Quest*, 26 (1981), 73–85.

DAWSON, G., 'History-Writing on World War II', in G. Hurd (ed.), *National Fictions: World War Two in British Films and Television* (London, 1984), 1–7.

DE LEE, N., 'Oral History and British Soldiers' Experience of Battle in the Second World War', in P. Addison and A. Calder (eds.), *Time to Kill: The Soldier's Experience of War in the West, 1939–1945* (London, 1997), 359–68.

GELBER, Y., 'Palestinian POWs in German Captivity', *Yad Vashem Studies*, 14 (1981), 89–137.

HUSEMANN, H., 'The Colditz Industry', in C. Cullingford and H. Husemann (eds.), *Anglo-German Attitudes* (Aldershot, 1995).

LIDDLE, P. and S. P. MACKENZIE 'The Experience of Captivity: British and Commonwealth Prisoners of War in Germany', in J. Bowne, P. Liddle, and J. Whitehead (eds.), *The Great World War 1914–45: Lightning Strikes Twice* (London, 2000), 310–28.

—— and I. WHITEHEAD, 'Not the Image but Reality: British POW Experience in Italian and German Camps', *Everybody's War: The Journal of the Second World War Experience Centre*, 8 (2003), 14–25.

MEDHURST, A., '1950s War Films', in G. Hurd (ed.), *National Fictions: World War Two in British Films and Television* (London, 1984), 35–8.

MOORE, B., 'The Last Phase of the Gentleman's War: British Handling of German Prisoners of War on Board HMT *Pasteur*, March 1942', *War & Society*, 17 (1999), 41–55.

MOORE, B. and B. HATLEY-BROAD, 'Living on Hope and Onions: The Everyday Life of British Servicemen in Axis Captivity', *Everybody's War*, 8 (2003), 39–45.

MÜLLER, R. D., 'Die Behandlung sowjetischer Kriegsgefangener durch das Deutsche Reich 1941–1945', in G. Bischof and R. Overmans (eds.), *Kriegsgefangenschaft im Zweiten Weltkrieg* (Ternitz-Pottschach, 1999), 283–302.

NENNINGER, T. K., 'United States Prisoners of War and the Red Army, 1944–45: Myths and Realities', *Journal of Military History*, 66 (2002), 761–82.

OTLEY, C. B., 'The Social Origins of British Army Officers', *Sociological Review*, 18 (1970), 213–39.

RAMSDEN, J., 'Refocusing "The People's War": British War Films of the 1950s', *Journal of Contemporary History*, 33 (1998), 35–63.

ROLF, D., ' "Blind Bureaucracy": The British Government and POWs in German Captivity, 1939–45', in B. Moore and K. Fedorowich (eds.), *Prisoners of War and their Captors in World War II* (Oxford, 1996), 47–67.

—— 'The Education of British Prisoners of War in German Captivity, 1939–1945', *History of Education*, 18 (1989), 257–65.

ROLLINGS, C., 'Dulag Luft', *After the Battle*, 106 (1999), 3–27.

STEWART, I., 'Presenting Arms: Portrayals of War and the Military in British Cinema', in I. Stewart and S. L. Carruthers (eds.), *War, Culture and the Media* (Madison, Wisc., 1996), 75–90.

TAYLOR, G., 'Corporal Bob Adams', *Blackwood's Magazine*, 259 (1946), 126–34.

THORNDYCRAFT, B., 'The Colditz Syndrome: The Need to Escape from Group Therapy', *Group Analysis*, 34 (2001), 273–86.

VANCE, J. F., 'The Politics of Camp Life: The Bargaining Process in Two German Prison Camps', *War & Society*, 10 (1992), 109–26.

—— 'The War Behind the Wire: The Battle to Escape from a German Prison Camp', *Journal of Contemporary History*, 28 (1993), 675–93.

—— 'Men in Manacles: The Shackling of Prisoners of War, 1942–1943', *Journal of Military History*, 59 (1995), 483–504.

—— 'The Trouble With Allies: Canada and the Negotiation of Prisoner of War Exchanges', in B. Moore and K. Fedorowich (eds.), *Prisoners of War and their Captors in World War II* (Oxford, 1996), 69–85.

FILM, TELEVISION, VIDEO, AND AUDIO SOURCES

Behind the Wire, video documentary (DD Video, 1997).

The Birdmen, made-for-TV film (Universal Television, 1971).

Colditz, TV drama series (BBC TV, 1972–4).

The Colditz Story, feature film (Ivan Foxwell, 1955).

The Colditz Story, 1-part TV documentary (Classic Pictures, 1993).

Doctor Who: Colditz, audio series episode (Big Finish Productions, 2001)

Escape From Colditz, 3-part TV documentary (Windfall Films, 2000).

The Lucky Ones: Allied Airmen and Buchenwald, TV documentary (National Film Board of Canada, 1994).

The Price of Victory, radio documentary (BBC Radio 2, 1995).

The Road to Colditz, videotaped talk by J. Hamilton-Baillie (Applecart TV, 1997).

Secret Lives: Douglas Bader, TV documentary (Twenty Twenty Productions, 1996).

The War Behind the Wire, 2-part TV documentary (Hartswood Films, 2000).

Index